SharePoint 2007
The Definitive Guide

Other Microsoft Windows resources from O'Reilly

Related titles
Essential SharePoint 2007
Programming ASP.NET AJAX
Programming WPF
SharePoint Office
   Pocket Guide

Windows Vista:
   The Definitive Guide
Windows Vista in a Nutshell
Windows Vista Pocket
   Reference

Windows Books Resource Center
windows.oreilly.com is a complete catalog of O'Reilly's Windows and Office books, including sample chapters and code examples.

oreillynet.com is the essential portal for developers interested in open and emerging technologies, including new platforms, programming languages, and operating systems.

Conferences
O'Reilly brings diverse innovators together to nurture the ideas that spark revolutionary industries. We specialize in documenting the latest tools and systems, translating the innovator's knowledge into useful skills for those in the trenches. Visit *conferences.oreilly.com* for our upcoming events.

Safari Bookshelf (*safari.oreilly.com*) is the premier online reference library for programmers and IT professionals. Conduct searches across more than 1,000 books. Subscribers can zero in on answers to time-critical questions in a matter of seconds. Read the books on your Bookshelf from cover to cover or simply flip to the page you need. Try it today for free.

SharePoint 2007

The Definitive Guide

James Pyles, Christopher M. Buechler, Bob Fox,
Murray Gordon, Michael Lotter, Jason Medero,
Nilesh Mehta, Joris Poelmans, Christopher Pragash,
Piotr Prussak, and Christopher J. Regan

O'REILLY®

Beijing · Cambridge · Farnham · Köln · Paris · Sebastopol · Taipei · Tokyo

SharePoint 2007: The Definitive Guide

by James Pyles, Christopher M. Buechler, Bob Fox, Murray Gordon, Michael Lotter, Jason Medero, Nilesh Mehta, Joris Poelmans, Christopher Pragash, Piotr Prussak, and Christopher J. Regan

Copyright © 2007 O'Reilly Media, Inc. All rights reserved.
Printed in the United States of America.

Published by O'Reilly Media, Inc., 1005 Gravenstein Highway North, Sebastopol, CA 95472.

O'Reilly books may be purchased for educational, business, or sales promotional use. Online editions are also available for most titles (*safari.oreilly.com*). For more information, contact our corporate/institutional sales department: (800) 998-9938 or *corporate@oreilly.com*.

Editors: John Osborn and Laurel R.T. Ruma
Production Editor: Rachel Monaghan
Copyeditor: Genevieve d'Entremont
Proofreader: Reba Libby

Indexer: Ellen Troutman Zaig
Cover Designer: Karen Montgomery
Interior Designer: David Futato
Illustrators: Robert Romano and Jessamyn Read

Printing History:

> September 2007: First Edition.

 This book uses RepKover™, a durable and flexible lay-flat binding.

ISBN-13: 978-0-596-52958-1
[M]   [5/08]

Table of Contents

Credits

James Pyles, currently a technical writer for Aquent Studios in Boise, Idaho, is the author of *PC Technician Street Smarts: A Real World Guide to CompTIA A+ Skills* (Sybex) and numerous other technical works. He has also been a SharePoint site administrator for a software group at Micron Technologies. He regularly reviews books on operating systems, web design, and programming for various web and print publications, including *Linux Pro Magazine*. James can be reached at *http://www.wiredwriter.net*.

Christopher M. Buechler, CISSP, SSCP, MCSE, MCSA, MCDBA, is a cofounder and Chief Technology Officer of BSD Perimeter, a company providing IT security services, including firewall support, vulnerability assessment, and penetration testing. He also serves as Network Manager for a regional bank, handling its network security and infrastructure. As an independent consultant, and in past positions in his decade-long career, he has provided security, network, and other services for organizations in the public and private sector, ranging from small organizations to Fortune 500 companies and large public sector organizations. He can be reached at *http://ChrisBuechler.com*.

Bob Fox, MCP, MCTS, is currently Technical Lead, SharePoint Technologies, at B&R Business Solutions, LLC. He is a Microsoft Windows SharePoint Services MVP, and his MVP blog can be viewed at *http://bobfox.net/splog*. Bob writes: "I have been working as an IT Professional since the mid 90s…I have spent a great deal of time working as a Systems Administrator dealing mainly with Microsoft Technologies. For the past five years my primary focus/passion has been Microsoft SharePoint Services. I specialize in Deployment, Portal and Site Customization, Administration, and Collaboration Solutions. I have in the past worked for such companies as Merrill Lynch, BISYS Retirement Services, Educational Testing Service, and Pfizer, to name a few. I am based out of Lawrenceville, NJ, where I live with my wife, Barbara, and our children, Zachary and Sarah."

Murray Gordon is the Director of Technology at Cambar Solutions (*www.cambarsolutions.com*), a premier consulting company committed to value chain improvement through best practice consulting and technology innovation. He brings more than 10 years of technology consulting and solutions architecture experience to bear. In addition to his other duties, it is his charge to guide Cambar Solutions' primary focus of providing strategic business-driven technology solutions. Murray is also a coauthor of *MCPD Self-Paced Training Kit (Exam 70-547): Designing and Developing Web-Based Applications Using the Microsoft .NET Framework* and *MCTS Self-Paced Training Kit (Exam 70-529): Microsoft .NET Framework 2.0 Distributed Application Development* (both by Microsoft Press).

Michael Lotter is a SharePoint Solution Architect and Microsoft Certified Technology Specialist, currently working for B&R Business Solutions (*www.bandrsolutions.com*). He travels throughout the country doing SharePoint and InfoPath solution-based contract work. You can reach Michael at *Michael.Lotter@bandrsolutions.com*.

Jason Medero, MCP, MCT, MCTS, MVP (WSS), is a systems architect with a concentration in Microsoft Office SharePoint Server (MOSS) and its related Microsoft technologies. He is a managing partner of B&R Business Solutions, a central New Jersey–based firm specializing in SharePoint and surrounding technologies, infrastructure, real-time communications (OCS), and application development. Jason is an active member of the SharePoint User Group in New York City, where he sits on the speaker selection committee. He also contributes his SharePoint knowledge as a mentor for some of the popular forums (MSD2D, MSDN). You can visit his blog at *www.sharepointblogs.com/JasonMedero* or his company's page at *www.bandrsolutions.com*.

Nilesh Mehta, current President of NGenious Solutions, Inc., is a recognized senior architect in Microsoft solutions, specializing in Microsoft's Office, SharePoint Server, Project Server, Exchange Server, and Active Directory technologies. He can be reached at *http://www.ngenioussolutions.com*.

Joris Poelmans is currently Application Group Manager at Dolmen (*www.dolmen.be*), a leading Belgian IT services company and Microsoft Gold Partner. His main competence area is Information Worker solutions, where he currently focuses on the SharePoint Products and Technologies platform. In October 2005, he was given the Microsoft MVP award for Windows SharePoint Services. He can be contacted through his blog at *http://jopx.blogspot.com*.

Christopher Pragash has more than 11 years of IT experience and has been predominently focused on Microsoft solutions. Under his current capacity as a Senior SharePoint Architect, Christopher has implemented portals based on Microsoft SharePoint technologies. His expertiese in Microsoft SharePoint Technologies ranges from helping organizations translate business requirements into SharePoint solutions, building the solution, and training SharePoint administrators and developers.

Piotr Prussak, usually a journeyman consultant, is currently serving as Enterprise Architect for a manufacturing company in New Jersey. When not involved in architecture, he works with SharePoint technologies, which he's been working with since 2000. He's been involved with the SharePoint developer community for the last five years, worked with early betas of all releases of SharePoint, and uses SharePoint for fun wherever he goes. He can be reached at *http://spsdreamjob.spaces.live.com/*.

Christopher J. Regan, MCP, MCTS, MCT, currently serves as a Managing Partner of B&R Business Solutions, a central New Jersey–based Microsoft Partner that specializes in Microsoft SharePoint Server–centric solutions and custom development. Prior to his founding of B&R, Chris worked as the Director of Information Systems for a private pharmaceutical marketing company, where he managed a global staff of IT professionals. Chris received his Bachelors of Science from The College of New Jersey in Ewing, New Jersey, and is a Microsoft Certified Technical Specialist. Chris can be reached at *cregan@bandrsolutions.com*.

Preface

Why did I write this book? Actually, it took an army to write this book (read all of the names on the front cover if you don't believe me). While I'm credited as the "lead author," the experience and expertise of everyone who authored content for *SharePoint 2007: The Definitive Guide* is what is at the center of this work. Without all the combined talent represented by all of these writers, this book would be a shadow of what it is.

The fact that so many people have been involved in this project is what makes it "definitive." One or two authors can contain a fair amount of experience and background in a particular area or topic, but 11 subject-matter experts can cover a huge cross-section of understanding.

In this case, that "cross-section of understanding" is about Microsoft Office Share-Point Server (MOSS) 2007, which in many ways is a completely different breed of cat from its predecessor. For example, MOSS is fully integrated with a number of other Microsoft products including the rest of the Office 2007 suite. If you've taken a look at the interface for Office 2007 ("the ribbon," for instance), you know that it's not just Office 2003 with a couple of extra widgets added.

The same is true of SharePoint 2007. A few of the features are relatively unchanged, such as SharePoint's discussion boards (unfortunately), but there are a great many additions, improvements, and just plain differences. If your company has migrated to or is thinking of adopting SharePoint 2007, you need to be ready for this change. MOSS 2007 isn't just SharePoint Portal Server 2003 with a few widgets added. It's a very different thing.

SharePoint 2007: The Definitive Guide gives you the theory and practice you need to either leverage your current SharePoint skills for this product or to ramp up to using MOSS 2007 as your first SharePoint experience. If you want to tap into the background and knowledge of almost a dozen SharePoint subject-matter experts and Microsoft MVPs, this is the book you'll need.

Who This Book Is For

Who is the book written for?

- If you administrate SharePoint Portal Server 2003 and are considering upgrading to MOSS 2007, this book is for you.

- If you administrate MOSS 2007 and need to learn more about how to manage the application and its features, this book is for you.

- If your company is considering purchasing MOSS 2007 to use for business collaboration, and you are either part of the evaluation team or are targeted to administer SharePoint 2007, this book is for you.

- If you have a background in site or server administration or supporting Microsoft Office products, and you'd like to expand your knowledge to SharePoint 2007, this book is for you.

If you're a .NET or Microsoft Office developer and would like to learn what tools you'll need to build a SharePoint development platform, this book *isn't* for you. Although some portions of the book touch on this area, it isn't written specifically for programmers.

How This Book Is Organized

What can I say? SharePoint is vast. In many ways, this makes it a challenge to properly organize content written for this product. Nevertheless, the authors made a valiant effort to put the information together in a way that would make the most sense. The first four chapters cover what you will need to know in terms of changes to the WSS architecture, installation procedures, and issues related to MOSS 2007 in a server farm. The bulk of the text covers the services and features offered by SharePoint, including interoperability with other Microsoft Office applications. The final part of the book includes upgrading, web content management, web services, and the SharePoint object model.

Chapter 1, *Introducing Microsoft Office SharePoint Server 2007*
> This chapter formally introduces MOSS 2007 including its two-pronged purpose: facilitating collaboration between geographically dispersed team members and managing business content in an effective and secure manner. SharePoint's six key components are presented: Collaboration, Portal, Enterprise Search, Enterprise Content Management, Business Process and Forms, and Business Intelligence.

Chapter 2, *Changes in the WSS Architecture*
> MOSS 2007 is built on Windows SharePoint Services 3.0 (WSS) and all of the updates to WSS 3.0 are contained in this chapter including ASP.NET 2.0, master pages, page templates, event handlers, and many others.

Chapter 3, *Installing SharePoint 2007*

What book on a technology would be complete without a chapter providing an in-depth look at how to install it? This chapter focuses on the pre-installation and installation tasks of installing MOSS 2007 on a standalone server, and gets you on your way to using SharePoint quickly.

Chapter 4, *Configuring a Multiserver Farm*

Whereas Chapter 3 described all of the tasks necessary for installing MOSS 2007 on a standalone server, this chapter will show you the installation procedure for installing SharePoint in a multiserver farm. Topics include availability, scalability, and Multiple Web Front Ends (WFE).

Chapter 5, *Designing SharePoint Sites*

The primary interface for working with SharePoint is the web site, and this chapter goes into constructing sites and site collections in MOSS. Concepts introduced are the portal site, top-level sites, and subsite collections.

Chapter 6, *Understanding the Datasheet and Explorer Views*

While sites and site collections are the framework of SharePoint, some of the basic building blocks within that framework are lists and libraries. This chapter introduces two views that create an alternate interface for examining that structured data—the Datasheet and Explorer views—and demonstrates some of the powerful features associated with each.

Chapter 7, *Applying Templates, Page Layouts, and Themes*

This chapter builds on the basic site and site collection structure in SharePoint and describes how to use site templates, page layouts, and themes to apply the "look and feel" you want your SharePoint sites to have. This is especially important when businesses want to brand their sites and give them their own unique corporate identity.

Chapter 8, *Creating Web Parts*

A large part of SharePoint functionality comes in the form of Web Parts and Web Part pages. This chapter presents the various Web Parts that come out of the box with MOSS and that allow you to manage forms, images, lists, and content types such as HTML and XML.

Chapter 9, *Creating and Managing Document Workspaces and Libraries*

In SharePoint, documents can be contained and manipulated in document libraries. Major collaboration efforts on shared documents can also be handled by using Document Workspaces, which act as specialized sites within SharePoint. This chapter focuses on these technologies and their significance within the corporate environment.

Chapter 10, *Creating and Managing Meeting Workspaces*

While it may seem obvious that business meetings have an inherent collaborative nature, SharePoint Meeting Workspaces provide the platform to truly organize collaborative business efforts. This set of specialized sites allows you to control all aspects of single and recurring meetings from invitation to tracking and follow-up of assignments.

Chapter 11, *Creating and Managing Discussions*
Internet Relay Chat (IRC) and discussion forums have long been traditional methods of creating and managing interactive communications among large numbers of people on the Web. SharePoint comes with its own built-in discussion group site that allows you to create and moderate discussions among SharePoint users.

Chapter 12, *Creating and Managing SharePoint Groups and Users*
SharePoint 2007 wouldn't be much good without a collection of users to access and utilize its many services. This chapter goes into adding authenticated users to SharePoint site access groups, how to assign user permissions using groups, and performing routine user and group management.

Chapter 13, *Creating and Managing Picture Libraries*
Like documents, graphics and images are managed using specialized libraries within SharePoint. You can collect all of your business-relevant graphics and figures in one location and then use Image Web Parts to display them on sites and web pages in your corporate site collection. Any graphic image can be stored in and accessed from a library, including PowerPoint slides.

Chapter 14, *Creating and Managing Lists*
From SharePoint's perspective, all information consists of lists. You are provided with a number of default lists that allow you to store and manipulate information including announcements, contacts, discussion boards, links, and calendars. This chapter describes the full complement of lists in SharePoint, their capacities, and how they are managed.

Chapter 15, *Business Intelligence and SharePoint*
Business Intelligence, or BI, is one of the major new features in SharePoint 2007. This chapter describes the Report Center, Dashboards, Excel Services, external data sources, Filter Web Parts, and Key Performance Indicators (KPIs), and how each of these elements works together to provide a unified method of viewing and manipulating corporate information in new and meaningful ways.

Chapter 16, *Sharing Contacts and Meetings with Outlook*
While Chapter 10 introduced the default set of meeting workspaces in SharePoint and how they help teams collaborate, this chapter expands on this concept by introducing the interoperability between SharePoint and Outlook messaging and calendaring features.

Chapter 17, *Creating, Editing, and Managing Word Documents with SharePoint*
The previous chapter showed you how Outlook and SharePoint interoperate. This chapter continues with that theme by showing you how other applications within the Microsoft Office 2007 suite work with SharePoint. Here, you'll learn

the different ways in which Word and SharePoint interact, including document versioning, workflow, and content type management.

Chapter 18, *Creating, Editing, and Managing Excel Documents with SharePoint*
Excel Services was introduced in Chapter 15 as part of SharePoint's Business Intelligence capacities. This chapter puts the spotlight on Excel and SharePoint interoperations, including such features as Excel Calculation Services (ECS), Excel Web Access (EWA), and Excel Web Services (EWS).

Chapter 19, *Creating in SharePoint Designer 2007*
While previous versions of SharePoint used Microsoft FrontPage as the designer tool of choice, MOSS 2007 utilizes SharePoint Designer to take the basic web design of SharePoint to the next level, including working with Master Pages, customizing sites, and building applications.

Chapter 20, *InfoPath and SharePoint*
While prior chapters have shown you how SharePoint works with other Microsoft Office 2007 suite software, this chapter introduces the interoperability between SharePoint and Microsoft InfoPath 2007. Learn how to create XML-based forms directly within SharePoint using InfoPath Forms Services.

Chapter 21, *Designing SharePoint My Sites*
SharePoint My Sites are like giving each SharePoint user his own small site collection. My Sites utilizes personalization and audience features to allow users to create an environment where they can access and work with their own documents, lists, and other data, regardless of where that data might be located in the site collection. Utilizing the audiences feature, administrators are able to target user-specific information directly to the appropriate groups using their My Sites.

Chapter 22, *Applying Security to Your SharePoint Site*
Security is a fact of life in any computerized system. SharePoint is designed to contain and manipulate a wide variety of enterprise-level data, including mission-critical information. This chapter shows you the features in MOSS that allow you to ensure the safe storage and presentation of information, allowing only the correct audiences to view and act upon documents and data.

Chapter 23, *SharePoint Administration*
You may think by now that you have been getting a lot of information about administering SharePoint, but this chapter presents the various backend tools used by MOSS administrators to manage the application as a whole—including the SharePoint products and technologies configuration wizard, Central Administration web site, and command-line utilities.

Chapter 24, *Upgrading from SharePoint Portal Server 2003*
Previously you learned how to install MOSS as a fresh installation in either a standalone server or multiserver farm environment. This chapter will show you how to take SharePoint Portal Server 2003 and upgrade it to SharePoint 2007, including upgrade prerequisites and different upgrade procedures.

Chapter 25, *Using Server-Side and Client-Side Web Parts*
> Chapter 8 introduced the different default Web Parts that you can use in Share-Point 2007. This chapter will take you behind the scenes and explore the nature of Web Part design and utilization, including specialized ASP.NET Server Control, Web Part customization, and personalization.

Chapter 26, *Using SharePoint Web Services*
> This chapter takes the lid off of SharePoint web services, showing you how MOSS utilizes this set of standards and protocols to enable the exchange of information with dissimilar systems using XML. Included is relevant information on the Business Data Catalog (BDC) and XML and Web Services for Remote Portlets (WSRP) Web Parts.

Chapter 27, *Using SharePoint Server for Search*
> Search in MOSS 2007 offers many significant improvements over SharePoint Portal 2003, and starting with the Office 2007 release, it is also available as a standalone product. Search is an increasingly important tool for the end users, as more and more data is stored in repositories that are indexed by MOSS Search. This chapter shows you the improved capacities in MOSS 2007 Search and why they are important to you.

Chapter 28, *Using the SharePoint Object Model*
> MOSS 2007 is an extension of WSS and provides extended features, such as enhanced portal capabilities, improved search, and the Business Data Catalog (BDC). Because both WSS and MOSS are based on ASP.NET, you can tweak, tune, customize, enhance, and extend the core SharePoint platform to meet your organization's needs. In this chapter, you will learn about the SharePoint Object Model, which defines how SharePoint works and provides you with the core API for modifying SharePoint for your needs.

Chapter 29, *Web Content Management*
> Web Content Management (WCM) is a set of features integrated into Share-Point 2007 that allows nontechnical users to create and manage content-centric web sites, providing the ability to author, review, and publish content over the Web. These features were part of Microsoft Content Management Server 2002 (MCMS), which has been incorporated into Office SharePoint Server 2007. This chapter shows you how to use the rich set of features for web-based content management in SharePoint.

What You Need to Use this Book

You'll need access to a computer or server running Windows Server 2003 with Microsoft Office SharePoint Server 2007 installed. For many of you that will mean working in an environment running MOSS 2007 on either a single server or in a server farm. You can also acquire evaluation copies of Windows Server 2003 and MOSS 2007 from Microsoft and install them on a computer that meets the hardware requirements for this software. You can find the instructions for installing SharePoint Server 2007 on a standalone computer at *http://technet2.microsoft.com/Office/en-us/library/bd99c3a9-0333-4c1c-9793-a145769e48e61033.mspx?mfr=true*, or you can check out Chapter 3 for a detailed walkthrough.

Conventions Used in This Book

The following typographical conventions are used in this book:

Plain text
> Indicates menu titles, menu options, menu buttons, and keyboard accelerators (such as Alt and Ctrl).

Italic
> Indicates new terms, URLs, email addresses, filenames, file extensions, pathnames, directories, controls, and Unix utilities.

`Constant width`
> Indicates commands, options, switches, variables, attributes, keys, functions, types, classes, namespaces, methods, modules, properties, parameters, values, objects, events, event handlers, interfaces, XML tags, HTML tags, macros, the contents of files, or the output from commands.

`Constant width bold`
> Shows commands or other text that should be typed literally by the user.

`Constant width italic`
> Shows text that should be replaced with user-supplied values.

 This icon signifies a tip, suggestion, or general note.

 This icon indicates a warning or caution.

Using Code Examples

This book is here to help you get your job done. In general, you may use the code in this book in your programs and documentation. You do not need to contact us for permission unless you're reproducing a significant portion of the code. For example, writing a program that uses several chunks of code from this book does not require permission. Selling or distributing a CD-ROM of examples from O'Reilly books does require permission. Answering a question by citing this book and quoting example code does not require permission. Incorporating a significant amount of example code from this book into your product's documentation does require permission.

We appreciate, but do not require, attribution. An attribution usually includes the title, author, publisher, and ISBN. For example: "*SharePoint 2007: The Definitive Guide*, by James Pyles et al. Copyright 2007 O'Reilly Media, Inc., 978-0-596-52958-1."

If you feel your use of code examples falls outside fair use or the permission given above, feel free to contact us at *permissions@oreilly.com*.

We'd Like to Hear from You

Please address comments and questions concerning this book to the publisher:

O'Reilly Media, Inc.
1005 Gravenstein Highway North
Sebastopol, CA 95472
800-998-9938 (in the United States or Canada)
707-829-0515 (international or local)
707-829-0104 (fax)

We have a web page for this book, where we list errata, examples, and any additional information. You can access this page at:

http://www.oreilly.com/catalog/9780596529581

To comment or ask technical questions about this book, send email to:

bookquestions@oreilly.com

For more information about our books, conferences, Resource Centers, and the O'Reilly Network, see our web site at:

http://www.oreilly.com

For more information about James Pyles, please visit:

http://www.wiredwriter.net

Safari® Books Online

 When you see a Safari® Books Online icon on the cover of your favorite technology book, that means the book is available online through the O'Reilly Network Safari Bookshelf.

Safari offers a solution that's better than e-books. It's a virtual library that lets you easily search thousands of top tech books, cut and paste code samples, download chapters, and find quick answers when you need the most accurate, current information. Try it for free at *http://safari.oreilly.com*.

Acknowledgments

I'd like to thank Colleen Gorman, with whom I spent a great deal of time working through this book, and Jeff Pepper, who got me into this in the first place. They were both great to work with, and I hope I get the opportunity to do more books with them in the future. I also want to thank Adam Witwer (who I've interacted with just once) and John Osborn, who have both been the driving force behind getting the book through its final stages. John's done a great job getting 11 different authors who all live and work who-knows-where to get together and put the final touches on their words. The same goes for Rachel Monaghan, Laurel Ruma, and Jessamyn Read, who have had the same task related to our graphics and screen captures.

There's just a tremendous amount of work to be done by the editorial staff when a book is about to go to print, and I admire the efforts of those mentioned and everyone at O'Reilly for all they do. Lest I forget, thank yous go out to Jawahar Puvvala and Rob McGovern as the technical editors who kept us on our toes, and to Caitrin McCullough for all the hard work she's done as Editorial Assistant for this text. You've all been a pleasure to work with. Cheers.

— James Pyles

Murray Gordon wishes to acknowledge his family—Tim, Jerri, and Mary Greta—who have always been there for him. Also huge thanks to Cecil Duffie, CEO, and Robert Moore, CFO, of Cambar Solutions for bringing him to Charleston to work in such a great city with such a great team of industry and technology experts.

Michael Lotter wishes to acknowledge his wife, Heather, for her patience with the tremendous amount of travel and the long weekend hours while at home. Without her he wouldn't be where he is today. He would also like to thank his parents for teaching him that nothing is impossible if you work hard enough and never give up, and in addition, O'Reilly Media, Inc. and Bob Fox for providing him the chance to write a chapter for this book.

Christopher Pragash would like to thank his wife, Pushpa Babitha, for her patience and help in writing the chapters for this book.

Christopher Regan would like to thank his family and fiancée, Ashley, for their unwavering support during these incredible times. Without them, he would have given up a long time ago. In addition, he would also like to thank Jason Medero for convincing him of the power of SharePoint years ago and risking it all to build something terrific. Finally, he would like to recognize the entire B&R Business Solutions team, for their dedication and passion toward all of the work they perform—they are an incredible group and are capable of amazing things.

CHAPTER 1

Introducing Microsoft Office SharePoint Server 2007

Microsoft Office SharePoint Server 2007, or MOSS, is a product of two factors. Both are changing the way businesses operate, in what Microsoft commonly refers to as the "new world of work."

The first factor is that teams working together are typically located in different locations throughout the country, or even the world. This presents some interesting challenges to collaboration between teams both within and outside of an organization.

The second is that there is an explosion of content created within these organizations. Documents and content of all shapes, sizes, and types are being created every day, and companies are struggling to keep up with this content explosion and increasingly complex compliance requirements, while enabling users to collaborate and share information. Organizations must allow effective collaboration in order to stay competitive, but they also must satisfy the security and privacy issues associated with collaboration in order to keep their competitive advantage and remain compliant with corporate regulations.

Microsoft has developed SharePoint to provide organizations with a solution to these complex business problems. MOSS brings together six key functional areas of features and benefits that allow organizations to more effectively address these industry phenomena and stay competitive. These areas are *Collaboration, Portal, Enterprise Search, Enterprise Content Management, Business Process and Forms,* and *Business Intelligence* (Figure 1-1). This chapter introduces these functional areas and explains their respective features.

Collaboration

The bottom line with Microsoft Office SharePoint Server 2007 (MOSS 2007) is that it helps organizations get more done. The Collaboration area of MOSS allows users to share information and work together.

MOSS is a critical piece to Microsoft's collaboration vision, and provides a hub where all Microsoft Office products can integrate effectively.

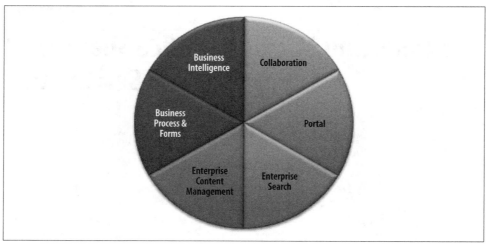

Figure 1-1. Six functional areas of Microsoft Office SharePoint Server 2007

Features

The "Collaboration" functional area can be summed up with the following feature list:

- Document collaboration
- Wikis
- Discussions
- Blogs
- Contacts
- Calendars
- Tasks
- Email integration
- Outlook integration
- Project management "lite"
- Offline lists and documents

Document collaboration

The document collaboration feature includes the following elements:

- The ability to check out documents locally.
- Direct support within Microsoft Office Outlook 2007 for an offline document library. This allows users to work on documents when they do not have access to the MOSS server.

- The ability to use major and minor version numbering and tracking in document management. This is a valuable feature, particularly if you have ever worked on a team where documents are being updated by multiple users simultaneously.

- Direct support for multiple content types. These content types include Microsoft Word, Excel, PowerPoint, Access, and others. Other types are recognized if the corresponding application type is installed on the MOSS server. Vendors also can create add-ins to MOSS that allow native MOSS support for that content type. This makes MOSS very extensible for vendors.

- Policies, auditing, and workflow are also included. This is great for managing the flow of a document's usage throughout an organization.

- Tree-view support allows users to structure an organization of documents and content that is easier to interpret and act on. Similar to Windows Explorer, MOSS enables this same type of document and content organization within MOSS.

Wikis

The "wiki" template is a new site template in Windows SharePoint Services 3.0. Similar to the wikis throughout the Internet, and best demonstrated on *www.wikipedia.com*, wikis allow users to easily create, edit, link, and restore individual web pages. Wikis are typically used as creative forums to brainstorm ideas, manage knowledge bases, create designs and instruction guides, or simply gather information in an easy-to-edit format. Wikis are easy to create, modify, and annotate. These features, along with the ability to track contributions and changes, make wikis a perfect addition to MOSS. Wikis also leverage the existing MOSS functionality included in search, navigation, alerts, and custom fields (see Figure 1-2).

The following are key features included in MOSS wikis:

- Quick and easy page creation
- Quick and automatic linking
- Versioning
- What you see is what you get (WYSIWYG) content editing

Discussions

The discussions (real-time presence and communication) feature existed in Share-Point Portal Server 2003 (SPS 2003), but it is improved upon with the release of MOSS 2007. The enhanced real-time presence smart tag icon is now displayed virtually everywhere a person's name appears within a site. This feature indicates whether a user is online, similar to how MSN Messenger functions when one of your chat buddies is online. Additionally, you can see whether the user is available to chat by telephone or audio conference call, instant messenger, or a two-way video conference.

Figure 1-2. Wiki site in MOSS 2007

There is also a new "Social Networking Web Part," which provides information about your organization, communities, and communications in your Public My Site pages to help establish connections between users with common interests.

Surveys are also included. These existed in SPS 2003, but they have been improved with MOSS 2007. Surveys now include conditional branching, and users can insert page breaks in long surveys—a huge help when filling out long surveys.

Discussions are essentially like the forums that you might find on Internet support pages for your favorite pieces of software (see Figures 1-3 and 1-4).

Blogs

Blogs provide a function that has been popular on the Web for the past few years on sites such as Blogger, Wordpress, Movable Type, and MySpace. This feature provides a publishing-oriented experience for a single user or a team. Users can publish content and receive feedback on that content. Windows SharePoint Services 3.0 includes a Blogs site template that supports the following (see Figure 1-5):

- Article posting
- Reader comments
- Archive views
- RSS feed generation

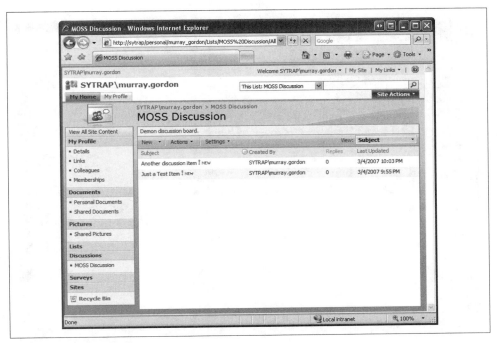

Figure 1-3. List of two discussions

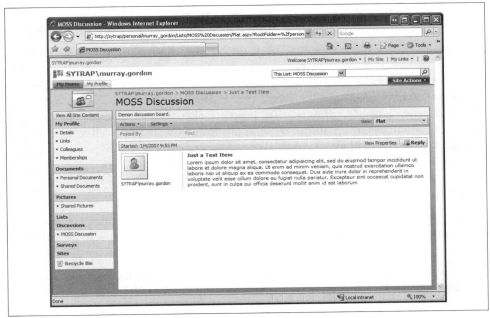

Figure 1-4. Discussion Item details

Figure 1-5. Blog site MOSS 2007

Contacts

The contacts ("People and Groups") lists offer a unified place to find and communicate with people. It also allows easy management of users' permissions. There is support for custom fields, such as Department, Office #, and Area of Focus. There is also a new Person field type. This field type enables the creation of rich displays of lists of people, as well as the use of a People Picker control for browsing a list of users. The Member Group allows reuse of groups across sites as well as distribution lists for the members of a site. All of these elements make it much easier to manage users and bring team members together.

Calendars

The Calendars have been enhanced in MOSS 2007 with richer calendar views and expanded support for recurring and all-day events. This more closely mirrors how calendars behave in Outlook 2007.

You can easily synchronize your MOSS calendars with your Exchange or Outlook calendar (see Figure 1-6).

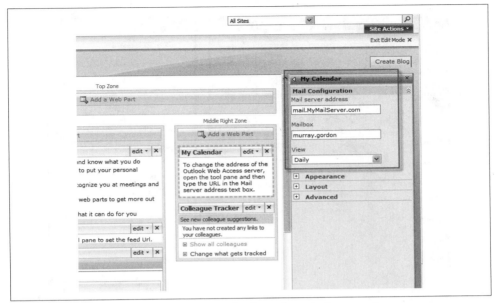

Figure 1-6. Synchronizing a MOSS My Site calendar with an Exchange mail server

Tasks

Task lists have been a staple of SharePoint since its creation. The Tasks template provides lightweight task management functionality (Figure 1-7). The new Project Tasks template includes Gantt charts for visualization of task relationships and status.

Email Integration

The Email Integration feature allows for document libraries, discussion boards, calendars, and announcements that can receive new postings via email. This makes it very easy to post items without logging into MOSS directly to make additions, which is a great time-saver. In addition, extensible support is provided for custom email handlers in Windows SharePoint Services 3.0.

Features that are similar to that of public folders in Microsoft Exchange Server are also available. These email-enabled discussion boards support:

- A scalable topic-based architecture
- "Super rich-text" field types
- Unified experience for both email- and web-based discussions
- One-step creation of Active Directory distribution lists as a part of site creation
- Unified MOSS group and Active Directory service management functions

Figure 1-7. Task list

Outlook integration

Outlook integration is very seamless, and you can integrate nearly everything you use in Outlook into your My Site in MOSS 2007.

From within MOSS 2007, you can easily sync content to Outlook (Figure 1-8).

With Office Outlook 2007, users can view calendars and contact lists stored on SharePoint sites, and can create and manage sites for editing documents and organizing meetings. Microsoft Office Outlook 2007 and Windows SharePoint Services 3.0 support a new set of significantly enhanced features, including:

- Check out and edit documents offline with true Smart Client capabilities
- Roll-up views of calendars and tasks across multiple lists and sites
- Synchronization of offline document libraries and lists
- View of personal and MOSS tasks in Outlook 2007
- Read and write access to MOSS calendars, tasks, contacts, discussions, and documents from Outlook 2007 (Figure 1-9)

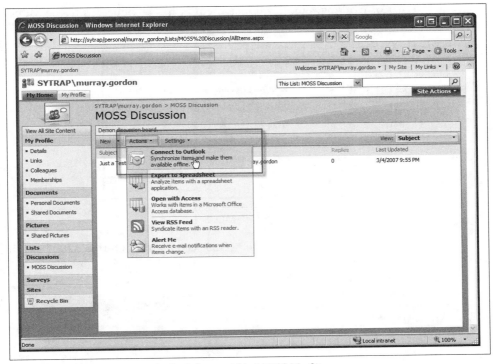

Figure 1-8. Easily connect to Outlook from within MOSS My Site

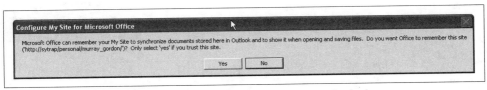

Figure 1-9. Creating your My Site prompts you for integration into Outlook

Project management "lite"

As mentioned previously in the Tasks feature, the new Project Tasks list template provides lightweight task management functionality. This template also includes Gantt charts for visualization of task relationships and status. This is great for coordinating teams of users while executing a specific task list. This is more of an ad-hoc project management tool, which is all many users and small teams need to get the job done.

Offline lists and documents

Tight integration into Outlook 2007 gives users the ability to work on lists that are available online in MOSS as offline content when the user is either disconnected from the Internet or working remotely. Once the user has reconnected to the MOSS server, the content synchronizes with the MOSS server (Figure 1-10).

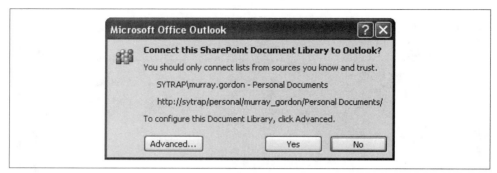

Figure 1-10. Users can synchronize documents with MOSS

You can easily look at documents from the MOSS server within Outlook 2007 as if it were any other type of email document (Figures 1-11 and 1-12).

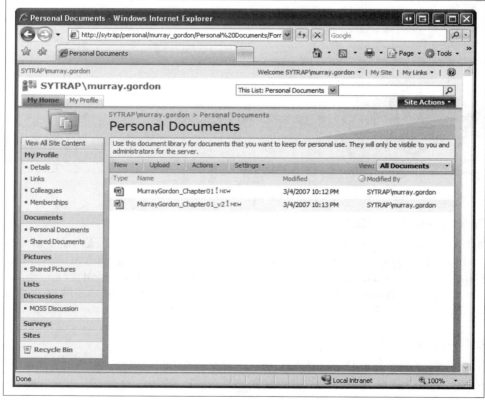

Figure 1-11. Personal Documents in MOSS My Site

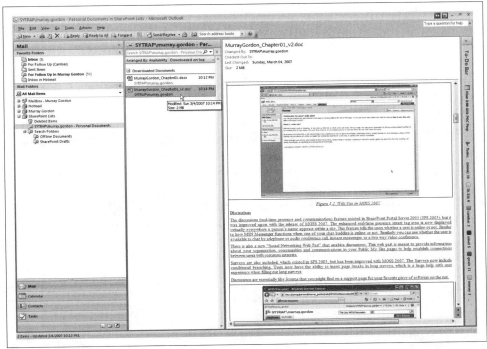

Figure 1-12. The same MOSS Personal Documents viewable in Outlook 2007

Portals

Portal sites connect users to information, expertise, and applications, and MOSS has some very compelling portal features. It has truly become a world-class Enterprise Portal platform. MOSS provides organizations with a foundation on which they can build solutions for every aspect of their business.

Features

The "Portals" functional area can be summed up with the following feature list:

- Intranet template
- News
- Site directories
- My Sites
- People finding
- Social networking
- Privacy

Intranet template

Preconfigured portal site templates streamline the creation, customization, and deployment of divisional portals, organization-wide intranet portal sites, and corporate web sites.

You can easily pick the type of template you would like to use for each site you create (see Figure 1-13).

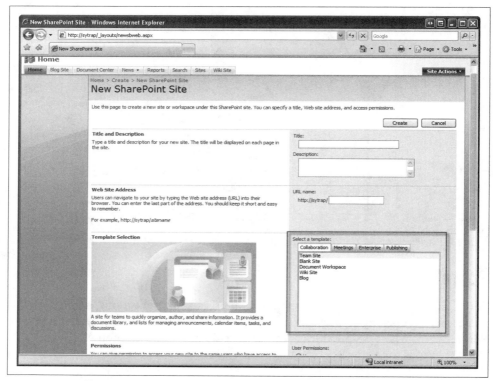

Figure 1-13. Different site templates

News

Creating news items has always been available with SharePoint (Figure 1-14), but the new content syndication features take "News" to a new level. The ease with which MOSS can subscribe to content makes it that much easier to keep content relevant and up-to-date for users.

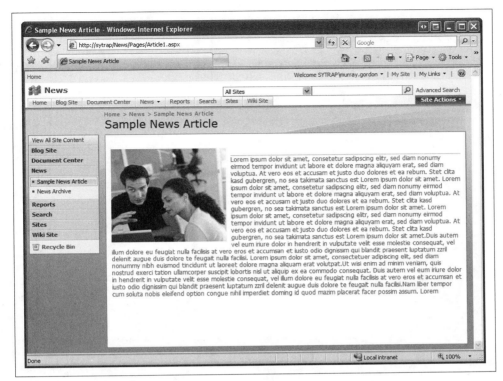

Figure 1-14. News article

The new content syndication feature allows the use of Really Simple Syndication (RSS) feeds to syndicate content managed in a portal site (Figure 1-15). You can easily post and publish internal company news or subscribe to remote RSS feeds with this feature.

Site directories

The Site Manager manages a SharePoint site's navigation, security access, and general look and feel using an easy drag-and-drop tool. Site Manager unifies site management tasks for portals and web sites, including management of areas, pages, listings, SharePoint site lists, and associated component parts (see Figures 1-16, 1-17, and 1-18).

Figure 1-15. Easily syndicate content

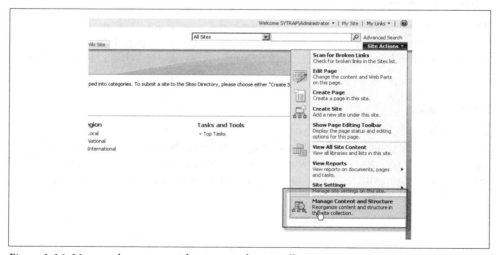

Figure 1-16. Manage the content and structure of a site collection

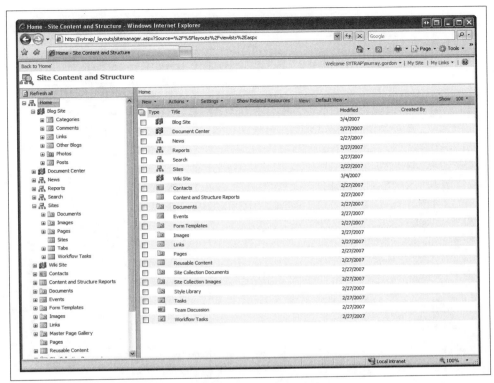

Figure 1-17. Easily change the settings and structure of your site content

My Sites

The My Site personal site gives each user an opportunity to aggregate information "for me," "by me," and "about me" (Figure 1-19). The significant enhancements to this feature in MOSS 2007 include social networking, privacy controls, SharePoint Sites and Documents Aggregation Web Parts, and Colleagues and Memberships Web Parts.

People-finding

The new focus on collaboration has brought people-finding to the forefront and made it a primary feature of MOSS 2007. Nearly every screen contains the ability to search out users by the content they create or their user-specific details (see Figure 1-20). This feature makes it that much easier to connect with a particular person or a specific user's content.

Figure 1-18. Site Directories allow for easy navigation

Social networking

It's very easy to search for users in your organization and quickly connect to them for the purposes of collaboration. Additionally, you can use the Colleagues and Memberships Web Parts feature to easily track your colleagues and others with whom you are interested in staying connected (Figure 1-21). This tool lists people the user knows and people who belong to common distribution groups.

Audience targeting is another powerful feature that adds to MOSS 2007's social networking capabilities. This function uses Web Part pages, Web Parts, and content to target distribution lists and groups in addition to SharePoint audiences (Figure 1-22).

Privacy

The privacy and security features allow the user to control, in detail, the authorizations and visibility of information in a My Site public view. Figure 1-23 shows how you can see and edit permissions on the targeted content.

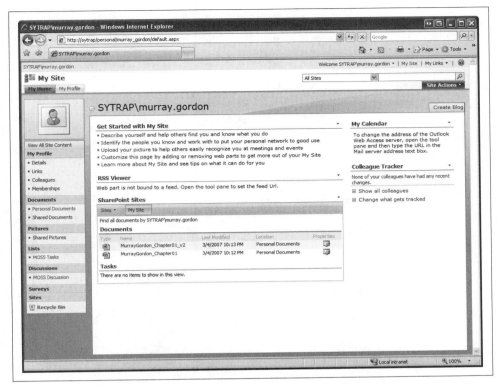

Figure 1-19. My Site

Enterprise Search

Microsoft Office SharePoint Server 2007 is the new Microsoft enterprise search solution for organizations. It increases productivity and reduces information overload by providing users with the ability to find relevant content in many different locations and formats. The key is actionable search results that respect security permissions.

Features

The "Enterprise Search" functional area can be summed up with the following feature list:

- Relevance
- Business data search
- Metadata
- Customizable user experience
- Extensibility

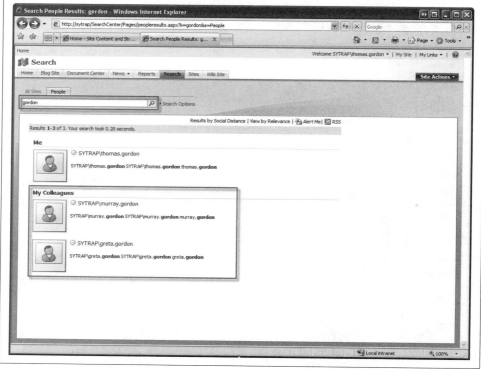

Figure 1-20. People-finding search capabilities

Relevance

Relevance is very important when searching for data. If you have ever searched on Google, you have probably realized that the relevance of your search is the key to getting usable results. The new and improved search algorithms within MOSS 2007 are tuned for enterprise content. The use of relevance and ranking factors—such as click distance, hyperlink anchor text, URL depth, and metadata extraction—provide effective algorithms for yielding the best results for enterprise content. Microsoft has invested a great deal in fine-tuning this solution.

Another aspect of relevance is the search results are rendered more clearly. Search results are security trimmed, which keeps users from seeing content to which they do not have access. The results also include user-friendly features such as hit highlighting, duplicate collapsing, and synonym suggestion. Another cool feature allows integration with real-time communications tools, so users can easily contact content authors and experts. You can execute a search, view the results, see whether the creator is online, and then open a chat with the content developer. That kind of ease of use will be invaluable within a large enterprise.

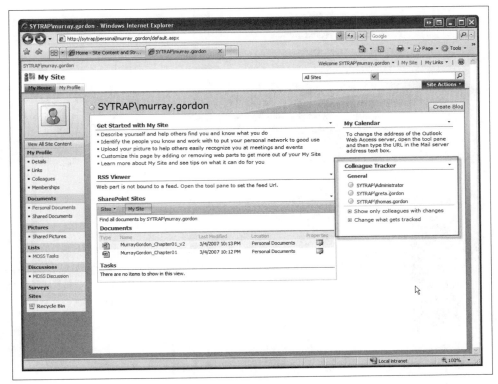

Figure 1-21. Colleagues Web Part

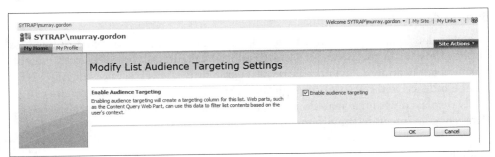

Figure 1-22. Audience-targeting feature of MOSS 2007

The people search capabilities bring even more relevance. Users can now find people not only by department or job title, but also by expertise, social distance, and common interests.

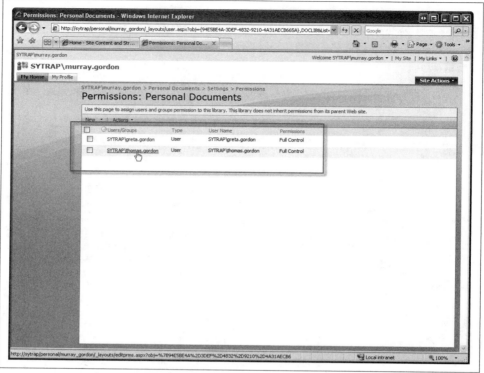

Figure 1-23. Screen for editing public permissions on content in "Personal Documents"

Business data search

Business data search allows you to search the data residing in your line-of-business applications using the Business Data Catalog. Structured content sources, line-of-business application data, and reports accessible through web services or ADO.NET can be indexed and retrieved through the Business Data Catalog. The results can be easily displayed within a SharePoint list, allowing users to make relevant decisions on data using an integrated environment.

Metadata

Content types help users organize their SharePoint content in a more meaningful way. A content type is a reusable collection of settings that you can apply to a certain category of content. Content types enable you to manage the metadata and behaviors of a document or item type in a centralized, reusable way. You can store multiple types of content in the same SharePoint library or list. Using content types, MOSS 2007 allows users to create and manage metadata, which helps generate content search results that are more relevant to the user.

Customizable user experience

MOSS 2007's new user experience is simple and clean, but also very powerful. The user interface has industry-standard query syntax as well. The fact that scopes are decoupled from content sources allows users to easily broaden or narrow the scope of a content search. Searches can be based on content properties such as type, URL, and author. Actionable search results can be sorted and filtered. The search results can be shared with other users, and users can also create alerts and RSS feeds to provide updated results for common queries.

Extensibility

Enterprise content sources can be searched for more than 200 file types in nearly every possible content location. The enterprise search capabilities allow data to be searched in files shares, SharePoint sites, web sites, Exchange Public Folders, and Lotus Notes databases out of the box, with the ability to extend to additional third-party repositories and file types through the use of Protocol Handlers and iFilters.

The administration and management features have also been improved. The user interfaces and admin application programming interface (API) provides broad support for various search and indexing scenarios. There is also extensive support for central controls for resource-intensive operations to allow for more granular control over processes that might otherwise bring a server to its knees. Users also have new, robust tools for management and reporting.

The security features have also improved. The administrator permissions are no longer required by the content crawler. This is a very important security feature that essentially allows the organization to have a higher security level that limits a search engine from crawling all the data within an organization. The access control list (ACL) and ACL-only crawl index content based on permissions set up by the organization to follow organization-specific compliance, privacy, and protection of intellectual property (IP). As a result, security-trimmed search results allow users to see only the content they are allowed to access.

Organizations create huge volumes of unstructured content. This content includes every flavor of document: Microsoft Word documents and Excel spreadsheets, videos, web pages, XML, instant messages, and much more. Many companies still have public shares on a corporate server where users drop content on a daily basis. Unfortunately, the content typically goes unread because the data is either hard to find or users just do not know that it exists. Much of this problem is addressed with the Enterprise Search features in MOSS 2007, but the main task of organizing that content and sharing it with the organization is accomplished with the new Enterprise Content Management (ECM) feature.

Enterprise Content Management

Web content management was previously covered by Microsoft's Content Management Server 2002. With the release of MOSS 2007, the realm of web content management is now rolled into SharePoint. Organizations now have a cost-effective, enterprise-ready web content management system rolled into their corporate portal. This allows companies to cut their total cost of ownership down to supporting one technology for both their portal and their web content management. That fact alone should excite small- to medium-size businesses that maintain a web presence.

Features

The "Enterprise Content Management" (ECM) functional area can be summed up with the following feature list:

- Authoring
- Workflow
- Web publishing
- Document management
- Records management
- Policies
- Multiple languages

Authoring

The content authoring features of ECM allow users to create rich content for their corporate web site using a web browser. This has been a feature in web content management solutions since their inception, but it has been limited in SharePoint until now.

The "what you see is what you get" (or WYSIWYG) web content editor truly empowers users to create very compelling content without leaving their browsers (Figure 1-24). The SharePoint user interface has also been extended with additional commands and status indicators for in-context web page authoring.

The page layouts function is another feature that allows users to quickly and easily author and publish content. The defined structures guide authors through the publishing process, which allows users to concentrate on the content and spend less time worrying about the publish-and-deploy process. The flexible page layouts also allow users to employ different Web Parts, ASP.NET applications, and authoring templates in any configuration to create compelling sites that meet the needs of the business.

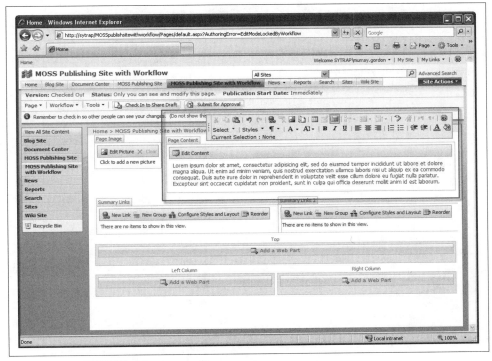

Figure 1-24. WYSIWYG rich-content editor

Workflow

The business document workflow support, which did not exist in SPS 2003, allows users to automate document review, approval, signature collection, and issue tracking using workflow applications (Figure 1-25). This feature includes the ability to perform the following basic workflow tasks:

- Collect feedback
- Collect signatures
- Request and get approval
- Disposition approval

Web publishing

The new content publishing and deployment features include built-in approval workflow. This workflow provides MOSS users with the ability to control when content is published live to the Internet. Users can set up jobs and a "live" time period for each page. This allows users to specify how long the content will be active and viewable.

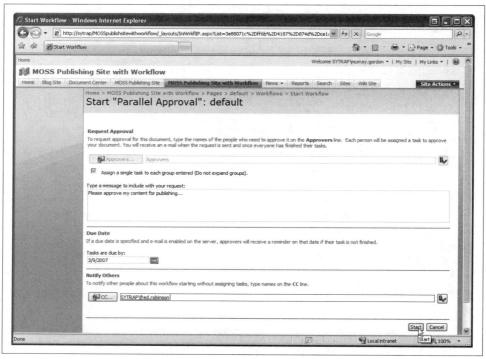

Figure 1-25. Parallel Approval workflow for a new content page

The new web-publishing features take MOSS to the next level of content publishing, allowing finite control over access and lifetime of content.

Document management

Templates help organizations define large-scale document management sites. The Divisional Library site template includes managed document libraries, dashboards, key performance indicators (KPIs), and other reporting tools. The Translation Library site template helps organizations manage multiple translations of a document.

MOSS 2007 also includes integration with Microsoft Information Rights Management (IRM). This feature helps organizations ensure that access rights applied to different types of Microsoft Office documents stay with the document. Even if the document is downloaded to a user's machine, rights and access constraints travel with that document. This is great for controlling intellectual property of an organization and ensuring that the document does not fall into the wrong hands, at least as long as it is in a digital format.

Records Management

The Records Management feature includes what is referred to as the *records repository*. The records repository helps ensure the integrity of the files stored there. It also supports information management policies so that access on documents is enforced, essentially controlling the auditing and expiration of records.

Policies

The policies, auditing, and compliance features of MOSS 2007 are implemented with Windows SharePoint Services 3.0, which serves as the foundation to MOSS 2007. The following policies and auditing and compliance features are included in MOSS 2007:

- Document retention and expiration policies
- Official document-of-record repositories
- Logging of all actions on sites, content, and workflows
- Customizable policies
- Workflow process to define expiration
- Access control and security
- IRM policies applied to documents
- Tracking and auditing
- Site for storing or archiving enterprise-approved content types

Multiple languages

MOSS 2007 includes a new feature for multiple languages. Essentially, the multiple language support is enabled with MOSS Language Packs. Language packs enable site owners and site collection administrators to create SharePoint sites and site collections in multiple languages without requiring separate installations of MOSS 2007.

You also can purchase and install a language pack that includes language-specific site templates. This enables your users to author and interact with content on your MOSS server in another language. This is a very powerful feature, and it is typically used within an organization that has multinational deployments and server farms that support users in multiple languages.

Business Process and Forms

Microsoft Office SharePoint Server 2007 provides built-in workflow templates to automate approval, review, and archiving processes. You can also use MOSS 2007 to create, maintain, and analyze custom workflows, enabling you to streamline your collaborative processes. Electronic forms provided through InfoPath Forms Services are an integral part of such workflows. These InfoPath-designed electronic forms make it easy to collect and validate information that drives your business processes. Additionally, you can collect and validate this information right from the Microsoft Office client applications you use every day.

Features

The "Business Process and Forms" functional area can be summed up with the following feature list:

- Rich web forms
- Self-service forms
- Real-time data validation
- Line-of-business actions
- Pluggable Single Sign-on

Rich web forms

Rich browser-based forms provided in the Microsoft Office InfoPath Forms Service make it possible to design web-capable forms in Microsoft Office InfoPath 2007 and distribute them to users with MOSS 2007. InfoPath has always seemed to be a tough sell to most companies because, even though InfoPath is a great product, it's expensive for what you get. However, by allowing users to interact with InfoPath forms on the Web without an installed copy of InfoPath on the client machine, InfoPath finally is a compelling and usable tool in the enterprise setting. Users can also fill out forms in a browser or HTML-enabled mobile device without having to download InfoPath or install client components.

Self-service forms

The idea of self-service forms encompasses a few different features in MOSS 2007. The most important feature is the integrated deployment model for "no-code" forms. The publish wizard in Microsoft Office InfoPath 2007 makes it easy to publish forms from the Windows SharePoint Services library. As long as your forms do not contain code, they can be made available to users as a browser-based form or accessed using an InfoPath client.

Real-time data validation

Real-time data validation is accomplished with the compatibility checker. This compatibility checker helps forms designers validate the content they are publishing. The compatibility checker makes sure the forms work across the broadest range of web browsers and target environments.

Line-of-business actions

Line-of-business actions, or business data actions, allow users to create web pages that interface line-of-business applications, without custom coding. These actions allow users to launch InfoPath forms and other common tasks within the client environment.

Pluggable Single Sign-On

The pluggable Single Sign-On (SSO) feature of MOSS 2007 allows users to enter one username and password before using a variety of backend applications. This feature significantly reduces the cost to maintain access to multiple data sources and systems. SSO is used for integrating back-office systems and line-of-business applications that require separate credentials databases. Development of single sign-on capabilities has been difficult for many large and small organizations, but the SSO features in MOSS 2007 have helped organizations move toward reaching SSO across their businesses.

Business Intelligence

Business Intelligence with Office SharePoint Server 2007 makes it easy for decision-makers to access and analyze information anytime, anywhere. You can get up-to-date information wherever people work, collaborate, and make decisions, whether it's on the desktop or over the Web. Now, aligning employees' objectives with your corporate goals is as easy as creating a spreadsheet or report.

Features

The "Business Intelligence" functional area can be summed up with the following feature list:

- Excel Services
- Report Center
- Dashboards and Key Performance Indicators (KPIs)
- Business Data Web Parts
- Business data in lists
- SQL Reporting Services/AS Integration

Excel Services

MOSS 2007 has introduced a new feature to SharePoint that enables spreadsheet authors to easily share their work. The web-based Business Intelligence features use Excel Services to provide new Business Intelligence functionality through the browser. These spreadsheets allow users to develop interactive, data-bound spreadsheets that include charts, tables, and PivotTable output. These views can be created and included as part of a portal, dashboard, or business scorecard, without requiring any development.

Report Center

The Report Center feature of MOSS 2007 provides users with an out-of-the-box site optimized for report access and management. The Report Center includes a report library, data connection library, and a Dashboard template, and allows users to consistently manage reports, spreadsheets, and data connections.

Dashboards and KPIs

The new key performance indicators (KPIs) in MOSS 2007 allow users to easily communicate goals and project status to stakeholders and business users. Users can harness the power of the KPI Web Part without writing a single line of code. Specifically, data from Microsoft SQL Server Analysis Services, Excel spreadsheets, and SharePoint lists can be displayed in the KPI Web Part. Users can also manually create content to be displayed in the KPI Web Part. This is a great way to give key stakeholders actionable content that they can easily digest and act upon.

Business Data Web Parts

Business Data Web Parts allow users to view lists, entities, and related information retrieved through the Business Data Catalog. Table 1-1 shows a list of the available Web Parts.

Table 1-1. Business Data Web Parts

Web Part	Usage
Business Data List Web Part	Displays a list of entity instances from a business application registered in the Business Data Catalog
Business Data Items Web Part	Displays the details of an entity instance from a business application
Business Data Related List Web Part	Displays a list of related entity instances from a business application
Business Data Actions Web Part	Displays a list of actions associated with an entity as defined in the Business Data Catalog

Business data in lists

Windows SharePoint Services 3.0 provides custom field types. MOSS 2007 leverages this feature to provide a new field type called Business Data that is available to all lists in SharePoint Server 2007. The Business Data field type enables users to add data from business applications registered in the Business Data Catalog to any SharePoint list. This allows users to view the data and perform actions associated with that data from within the Document Library.

SQL Reporting Services/AS Integration

The seamless integration of MOSS 2007 into SQL Reporting Services and other back-end line-of-business applications allows users to create actionable content and to visualize information that exists in these backend line-of-business applications. These features allow users to create rich, interactive Business Intelligence dashboards based on Business Intelligence data sources.

Conclusion

Though this chapter has been able to cover only a small subset of all the new capabilities in MOSS 2007, there is a wealth of online information to satisfy your search for answers. Additionally, the rest of the chapters in this book go into more detail about the different functions and features introduced here.

CHAPTER 2

Changes in the WSS Architecture

Microsoft Windows SharePoint Services Version 3.0

Windows SharePoint Services (WSS) contains a subset of the capabilities provided in the full Microsoft Office SharePoint Server 2007 product. WSS provides a secure, scalable, enterprise-level portal environment for collaboration, and is comprised of a set of components and services that serve as an add-in to Windows Server 2003. WSS provides the plumbing infrastructure for the SharePoint Products and Technologies, more commonly referred to as SPT. Essentially, this term includes both Windows SharePoint Services (WSS) and Microsoft Office SharePoint Server 2007 (MOSS). Figure 2-1 describes the components included in SPT.

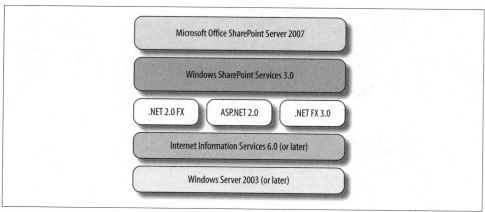

Figure 2-1. SharePoint products and technologies

At its base, WSS is a scalable site-provisioning engine that allows companies to create and manage hundreds, if not thousands, of web sites in a highly scalable web farm environment. WSS is designed to enable an architecture where stateless front-end web servers in a web farm interact with a SQL Server database engine to provide users with the ability to perform basic CRUD (create, update, and delete) operations on the UI components. Best of all, WSS automatically coordinates where and how content is stored in the database.

 WSS 3.0 is the third and latest major version of WSS. This release goes by the name of Windows SharePoint Services 3.0 and is often abbreviated as either WSS 3.0 or WSS v3.

The previous version of WSS, which was released with the Office 2003 system, originally did not carry a version number. However, to avoid confusion, it should now be referred to as Windows SharePoint Services 2.0 or WSS v2. When progressive SharePoint developers talk about WSS without using a version number, they are talking about the latest and coolest version, which today is WSS 3.0.

To developers, WSS is a full-fledged development platform that builds on top of ASP.NET 2.0. Essentially, it provides a solution for building business solutions using the core building blocks of ASP.NET 2.0, such as .aspx pages, ASP.NET controls, Web Parts, custom lists, document libraries, content types, event handlers, custom workflow, site definitions, site features, and site solutions.

WSS also ships with out-of-the-box collaboration features that allow users to create and design web sites with shared elements. These features allow developers and users to quickly create web sites with contacts lists, schedules, document libraries, task lists, and customized page views, without requiring developers to write a single line of code. WSS 3.0 also adds news features, such as Really Simple Syndication (RSS), blogs, and wikis. This is the real power of WSS 3.0: the ease with which developers and users can create usable content for their teams.

This chapter explains the differences between WSS 3.0 and the previous version of Windows SharePoint Services. Specifically, it outlines the differences between SharePoint Portal Server (SPS) 2003 and Microsoft Office SharePoint Server (MOSS) 2007. Figure 2-2 shows the transition in core services from SPS to MOSS.

The following list outlines the changes discussed in this chapter:

- ASP.NET 2.0
- Master pages
- Page templates
- Event handlers
- Site definitions, features, and solutions
- Internet-style security
- Web Parts
- Content storage
- Workflows

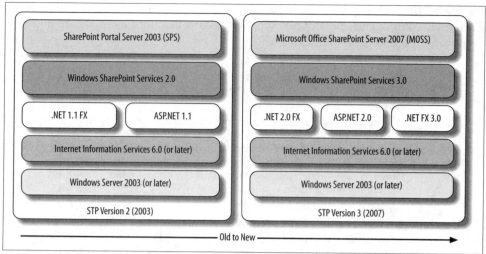

Figure 2-2. Transition from SPS to MOSS

ASP.NET 2.0

In WSS 3.0, if you want to create a WSS site, you must run an administrative tool to extend the WSS functionality to an IIS web site.

This process is similar in WSS 2.0, with the main difference really in the terms used to describe how you extend functionality to one or more IIS web sites. In WSS 2.0, this was referred to as creating a "virtual server," which was essentially an IIS web site that had WSS 2.0 functionality. In WSS 3.0, they are no longer referred to as "virtual servers"; they are now referred to as "web applications." This is a minor difference, but helpful in determining which version of WSS someone is referring to with respect to WSS functionality.

Another key difference between WSS 2.0 and WSS 3.0 is that WSS 3.0 is built on top of ASP.NET 2.0, whereas WSS 2.0 was build on top of ASP.NET 1.1. ASP.NET 2.0 provides significant improvements over ASP.NET 1.1. For example, WSS 2.0 tied into IIS 6.0 and ASP.NET 1.1 using an ISAPI filter DLL. The problem with this was that requests were routed directly to WSS without first being initialized with ASP.NET context. This could be problematic in certain situations where the developer wanted to process and handle requests with custom code before WSS processed a request. WSS 3.0 solved this problem by making all HTTP requests enter the ASP.NET 2.0 runtime environment. As a result, the requests are fully initialized with ASP.NET context before they are forwarded to the WSS 3.0-specific code.

The WSS 3.0 team accomplished this by removing the ISAPI filter and adding an HttpModule and an HttpHandler. HttpModule and HttpHandler are registered with ASP.NET 2.0 using entries in a *web.config* file. As a result, all incoming HTTP requests are mapped to the ASP.NET runtime, regardless of file type. After ASP.NET 2.0 processes the request and adds context, the requests are forwarded to WSS 3.0 to be processed.

Another interesting change is how WSS 3.0 handles the parsing and compiling of *.aspx* pages. ASP.NET 2.0 has the ability to retrieve *.aspx* pages from any location. In the case of WSS 3.0, that is typically a SQL Server database. This offers WSS 3.0 a significant improvement over WSS 2.0 in terms of page parsing. This is accomplished by using a virtual path provider, called SPVirtualPathProvider, which is a pluggable component type. Essentially, an *.aspx* page is retrieved by the virtual path provider and then is passed to ASP.NET 2.0. ASP.NET 2.0 performs the required parsing and compilation and then passes the *.aspx* page off to SharePoint, which controls how the *.aspx* page is parsed and compiled. The SharePoint component used to compile and parse the *.aspx* page is the PageParserFilter. WSS 2.0 handled this much differently. With ASP.NET 1.1, *.aspx* pages could be parsed and compiled only if they resided on the local filesystem. This was a significant limitation when WSS inherently used SQL Server as the location from which it retrieved *.aspx* pages.

Master Pages

In WSS 2.0, WSS and SharePoint developers had a tough time creating a consistent look and feel throughout an entire site due to the limitations in ASP.NET 1.1. As a result, developers would spend many tedious hours cloning and recreating HTML from site to site. With WSS 3.0 and ASP.NET 2.0, this has all changed for the better. ASP.NET 2.0 introduced a new feature called the *master page*. If you have ever worked with products like Dreamweaver (which is now an Adobe product), you know that the concept of a master page is a beloved feature for developers. Developers could create a master page, where they put all the look and feel that drives the site. When that developer wanted to change the look of the site, he needed only to change the master page and save the change, and the tool would recurse through all the associated pages and make the appropriate changes to match that master page. ASP.NET 2.0 introduced master pages to provide developers with this type of functionality, but with a much more elegant solution that did not require a tool to recurse through all the pages of a site. In ASP.NET 2.0, the pages that link to a master page, known as *content pages*, take on the shared layout of the master page and then extend the master page by inserting customized content in the named placeholders.

WSS 3.0 was designed from the ground up to leverage ASP.NET 2.0 master pages. When a WSS 3.0 site is created or provisioned, a Master Page Gallery catalog is created that contains a *default.master* master page. This master page defines to share layout for the home page (*default.aspx*) and the form pages associated with lists and document libraries, such as *AllItems.aspx*. This master page includes navigation controls, menus, and visual aesthetics. Like most master pages, this master page contains placeholders for different custom content, such as PlaceHolderPageTitle and PlaceHolderMain. Making changes to a content page is as easy as changing the content contained within these placeholders:

```
<%@ Page language="VB" MasterPageFile="~masterurl/ default.master" %>
<asp:Content ContentPlaceHolderId="PlaceHolderMain" runat="server">
<h2>Check out my simple customization with WSS 3.0</h2>
<h3>I can't believe how easy this is to do compared to WSS 2.0</asp:Content>
```

The content page definition simply places HTML content inside PlaceHolderMain, but it produces the typical page layout with site icons, menus, and navigation bars. The amount of work associated with changing and branding the look for a site has been drastically reduced. You can also edit the standard set of placeholders defined in *default.master*. This allows the developer to replace WSS elements such as menus and navigation bars with her own ASP.NET controls. You can even use new AJAX-type controls provided in ASP.NET 2.0 for pages both at the scope of a site and at a site collection.

In WSS 3.0, master pages and content pages are stored and loaded in the same way as page templates and page customizations (discussed in the next section, "Page Templates"). Master pages and content pages can be stored both on the filesystem and in SQL Server, depending on whether they are uncustomized or customized. Users can change these master pages and content pages using SharePoint Designer. As a result, the customized master page or content page will be stored in SQL Server. Both WSS and SharePoint Designer provide simple menu commands that allow users to discard customizations and revert to the original master page or content page (Figure 2-3).

Page Templates

A great feature of both WSS 2.0 and 3.0 is the ability to store an *.aspx* page template on the local filesystem of a frontend web server, which can be used across many different web sites. This template then can be used thousands of times by hundreds of web sites, while requiring the *.aspx* template to be loaded only once into memory. The performance benefits here are tremendous.

When a user wanted to customize or modify the *.aspx* template in WSS 2.0, the modifications and customized version of the template would then be stored in SQL Server. In reality, this feature has not changed from WSS 2.0 to WSS 3.0; the only difference is the nomenclature. In WSS 2.0, this was referred to as *ghosting* and *unghosting*. The ghosted *.aspx* page was a template that had not been modified. As soon as the developer made modifications to the template, and the template transformed into a customized template stored in SQL Server, that template or page was then referred to as "unghosted." In WSS 3.0, the "ghosted page" is now referred to as an *uncustomized page*, and the "unghosted page" is now referred to as a *customized page*. This is a simple change, but relevant enough to bring up in this context.

There has also been a change in the tools used to modify pages or templates. Previously, Microsoft Office FrontPage 2003 was used to modify *.aspx* pages for use in

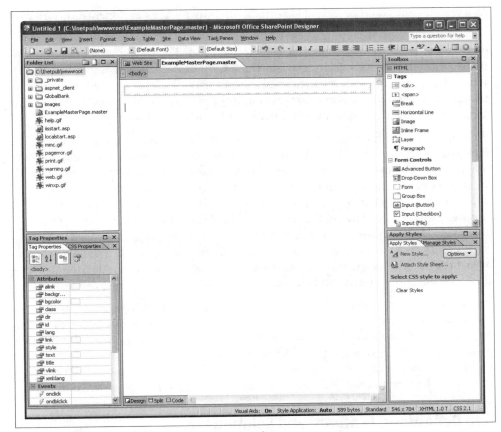

Figure 2-3. Microsoft Office SharePoint designer editing a master page

WSS 2.0. Microsoft has recently released Office SharePoint Designer 2007, which is essentially the most recent release of FrontPage. The target audience for this new tool will still be WSS developers. SharePoint Designer is a great WYSIWYG editing tool with some powerful features for editing HTML and styles, and new features for creating lists and document libraries. Microsoft has also added a wizard for creating custom workflows in a WSS site. The name change from Microsoft Office FrontPage 2003 to Office SharePoint Designer 2007 is significant for a product that has been around for nearly 10 years. FrontPage has been replaced by a new product called Microsoft Expressions Web, which is a tool targeted at pure web developers.

Event Handlers

WSS 2.0 supported event handlers only in document libraries, not in lists. It also supported only asynchronous events, which are events that fire after a user action is committed to the SQL Server Database. The big problem here was that this limitation did not provide a way for developers to cancel a user's action inside the event handler.

As a result, code could be executed without any way for the developer to control execution. These limitations have been resolved with WSS 3.0.

In WSS 3.0, synchronous event support has been added. This feature allows developers to cancel user actions when an event is fired, for example, when a user initiates an action that is not allowed. Asynchronous events are still supported, but synchronous events represent a new feature that gives more control to the developers. Also, event handlers are now supported in both document libraries and lists.

WSS 3.0 provides developers with the ability to write an event handler by creating a class that inherits from a WSS 3.0 receiver class. The developer needs only to override the methods in order to handle events. A developer can also bind an event handler to lists or document libraries, which is done by creating code that extends the object model. They can also define an event receiver in a WSS 3.0 feature. (WSS 3.0 features are discussed later in this chapter.) The WSS 3.0 receiver classes use overridable methods that have different naming conventions for synchronous and asynchronous events. Synchronous events use method names such as PageUpdating, whereas asynchronous events use method names such as PageUpdated. As mentioned previously, synchronous events can be cancelled, but asynchronous events cannot.

As also mentioned previously, events are supported on both lists items and document libraries. There are some new features you should be aware of in this area. Developers now have the ability to fire events when a user changes the definition for a list. For example, this gives the developer the ability to cancel a user's action to rename, move, or delete columns in a custom list. This is a very powerful feature for developers looking to control the look and feel of their custom lists or site collections.

Site Definitions, Features, and Solutions

Site definitions—a feature of both WSS 2.0 and WSS 3.0—provide developers with a great amount of control and reusability. A site definition is a directory on the front-end web server containing XML files and .aspx page templates that define a blueprint for the site. The site definition includes list schemas as well as page layouts. Collaborative Application Markup Language (CAML) is the XML-based language that is used inside site definition files.

If you have ever worked with WSS 2.0 site definitions, you know there are a few issues:

- Site definition XML files are poorly factored, making them tough to work with.
- There is no support for changing a site definition once it has been used to create sites. Essentially, in WSS 2.0 you could not easily add new features to a site definition after the site was created.
- Managing deployment of site definitions and their custom assemblies was an enormous headache.
- There was no way to localize a site definition, which severely limited a company's ability to internationalize its business solutions.

Fortunately, WSS 3.0 has provided solutions to all of these limitations and headaches.

The first a new enhancement to WSS 3.0 is *features*, which are similar to site definitions. They contain CAML-based XML files and page templates. The difference is that features allow a more modular approach to evolving or updating running WSS or MOSS sites. Features allow developers to define something as small as a single site element, such as a new menu, and then easily roll that feature out to any WSS 3.0 or MOSS site. The ease of use is provided through the flexibility of deployment. As a developer, you can deploy a feature using the WSS user interface or the command line, or even using custom code written using the WSS 3.0 object model. Also, features do not have to be defined within the content of a site definition.

The deployment headache also has been removed. With WSS 3.0, a new deployment mechanism called a *solution* was introduced. A solution is similar to a Web Part package because it is an aggregate *.cab* file containing XML instructions and files that must be deployed to frontend web servers. This is much easier to manage. Solutions support the deployments of features and site definitions, as well as event handler and workflow assemblies. Solutions are very easy to deploy. The developer simply needs to copy the solution *.cab* file into the configuration database and then run a command to deploy the solution. The WSS 3.0 timer job handles the push of the solution *.cab* file out to each frontend web server and then installs it.

The last milestone for this group of features is localization support. Localization is a core component to ASP.NET 2.0. WSS 3.0 takes full advantage of this ability and extends it to localize site definitions using *.resx* files. The following example shows how you would use standard ASP.NET 2.0 syntax to localize content for a WSS 3.0 site:

```
<%$Resources:AdventureWorks,MyString%>
```

Internet-Style Security

If you have worked with WSS 2.0, you know only too well that authentication is based on Windows accounts and their associated Security IDs (SIDs). Essentially, Active Directory is the foundation for authenticating users. For companies looking to create WSS 2.0 intranets or SharePoint Portal Server 2003 intranets, this was not a problem. You already have users in Active Directory, so employing it as your authentication tool is not a hassle or an inconvenience.

However, this is not the case when you are looking to deploy your WSS 2.0 site as an extranet to users who are not already maintained in Active Directory. This tight coupling to Active Directory forced organizations to maintain accounts for outside vendors and customers, which can present security risks and maintenance headaches for your IT Support team.

This limitation has been resolved by building WSS 3.0 on top of ASP.NET 2.0. ASP.NET 2.0 introduced a new feature that has greatly eased the maintenance and implementation headache associated with enabling forms authentication in web sites. ASP.NET 2.0 has a forms authentication provider that allows developers to maintain user accounts in a SQL Server database or some other identity repository, such as LDAP (Lightweight Directory Access Protocol) data sources. This feature provides WSS 3.0 with support for the same capabilities that are available in ASP.NET 2.0. The forms authentication provider allows easy support for creating and maintaining user accounts, and it also allows users to change and reset their passwords. Being able to change your password without calling the IT Support team has a huge maintenance and usability benefit.

Web Parts

Custom Web Parts have always been a powerful and compelling feature for WSS developers. However, the amount of effort associated with creating WSS 2.0 Web Part pages was significant. Microsoft recognized this and has provided a new model for developing WSS Web Part pages without losing backward compatibility with WSS 2.0 Web Part pages. It was a very important design goal for Microsoft to support both patterns of Web Part development. This was accomplished by building WSS 3.0 support for Web Parts on top of the ASP.NET Web Part infrastructure. Support for WSS 2.0-type Web Parts was accomplished by changing the *Microsoft.SharePoint.dll* so the older Web Parts would be compatible with the WSS 3.0 environment.

Now you have the ability to create WSS 3.0 Web Parts either based on ASP.NET 2.0 or in the WSS style. In order to create WSS-style Web Parts, you must have a dependency on the *Microsoft.SharePoint.dll* and you must inherit from the WebPart base class in the Microsoft.SharePoint.WebPartPages namespace. This is the same way Web Parts were created in WSS 2.0, so not much has changed in that respect.

The new way of creating WSS 3.0 Web Parts based on ASP.NET 2.0 is different from the WSS-style. In order to create ASP.NET-style Web Parts, you have a dependency on *System.Web.dll* and inherit from a base class named WebPart in the System.Web.UI.WebControls.WebParts namespace.

To create an ASP.NET-style Web Part, you must create an *.aspx* page that contains only one instance of the *WebPartManager* control. Then, you add one or more WebPartZone controls. The *WebPartManager* control is responsible for serializing, storing, and retrieving Web Part-related data from tables in the ASP.NET services database. The resulting *.aspx* page can contain editor and catalog parts that allow the user to customize and personalize content as well as add new Web Parts into zones. Best of all, WSS 3.0 does the heavy lifting associated with adding catalog and editor parts into the page; the developer no longer needs to do this explicitly. This is different from the WWS-style Web Part creation process.

The WSS 3.0 Web Part infrastructure is built on *SPWebPartManager*, which is a control that derives from the ASP.NET 2.0 *WebPartManager* control. In order to create a WSS-style Web Part page, you need to do two things. First, create logic that interacts with the *WebPartManager* control, which will allow the Web Part to manage the display mode. Second, add editor and catalog parts with the HTML layout to handle them. This is different from creating Web Part pages for WSS 3.0 sites. With WSS 3.0 sites, the *.aspx* must inherit from the `WebPartPage` class defined in the `Microsoft.SharePoint.WebPartPages` namespace. This is a huge time-saver because WSS 3.0 handles all the work of dealing with the display mode, adding editor and catalog parts, and adding the HTML layout needed to accommodate the parts. This is another powerful feature for WSS developers.

 When creating WSS 3.0 Web Part pages, you should use the *WebPart-Zone* control defined in the `Microsoft.SharePoint.WebPartPages` namespace. You do not want to use the *WebPartZone* control contained within ASP.NET 2.0.

You will typically use the *WebPartZone* control in content pages, rather than templates. The *.aspx* page would typically link to *default.master*. The difference you should note is that the *.aspx* inherits from the `WebPartPage` base class (Figure 2-4).

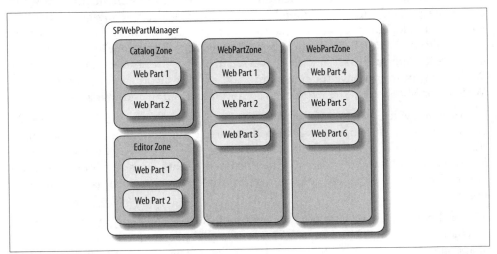

Figure 2-4. Different controls contained in a WSS-style Web Part page

The preferred way to create Web Parts for WSS 3.0 sites is to create the ASP.NET-style Web Parts. As discussed before, this means inheriting from the `WebPart` base class in the `System.Web.UI.WebControls.WebParts` namespace and overriding the `RenderContents` method.

Content Storage

WSS 2.0 introduced some powerful features for document libraries, such as versioning, events, and folders. These features were not extended to lists, but fortunately this long-awaited missing feature has been introduced with WSS 3.0. Now lists support the same features around versioning, events, and folders. WSS 3.0 went one step further and introduced an exciting new feature that bloggers and blog readers have been familiar with for some time: automatic RSS feeds. Automatic RSS feeds allow users who are interested in data in lists and document libraries to subscribe to automatic feeds from those sources.

Another interesting feature that was overlooked in WSS 2.0 but is now provided in WSS 3.0 is column indexing. Column indexing alleviates some of the performance issues related to document libraries and lists in WSS 2.0. In WSS 3.0, you now can add an index to a column in a list or document library. This is not a physical index in SQL server; this index is created in WSS 3.0 with a table that holds the integer ID of the document or list item and the value of the indexed column. This improves performance because WSS 3.0 uses the table to more quickly return data from views. The speed increase is even more apparent when you are accessing data in a view that is based on a filter driven by the indexed column.

Yet another new content storage feature of WSS 3.0 is extensible field types, which create the potential for more granular control over field rendering and validation. Now the developer can create an extensible field type in C# or Visual Basic, just like you would in ASP.NET 2.0 applications. The caveat is that you need to inherit from one of the built-in SharePoint field types, such as `SPFieldNumber` or `SPFieldText`. With this feature you have the freedom to add all your favorite web controls to your WSS 3.0 or MOSS 2007 site in order to control initialization and validation.

Another innovative new feature of WSS 3.0 is custom site columns. The custom site column allows a developer to create a definition for a site column and then apply that site column to many lists within a SharePoint site. In WSS 2.0, you could define a custom site column only for a specific document library. This was limiting because you had to recreate the site column over and over again in each list or document library.

The backbone of the new custom site column feature is *content types*, a new storage mechanism. A content type is a WSS 3.0 type that allows developers to define the shape and behavior for an item in a list or document that resides in a document library. Essentially, developers can define multiple content types that apply to a specific list. For example, say you created a content type that had specific columns and its own document template, and then you create a second content type that has a completely different set of columns and events, as well as a new document template. You would be able to have both those content types in the same list or document library. This feature allows developers to deal with very complex heterogeneous types of content in lists and document libraries.

Workflows

The workflow features in the WinFX runtime components are very exciting. These were released recently as the .NET Framework 3.0, in concert with the launch of Windows Vista. The renaming of WinFX to the .NET Framework 3.0 has been a bit confusing for most developers who are used to the .NET Framework 1.1 and 2.0, which each contained new compilers, libraries, and common language runtimes. Essentially, the .NET Framework 3.0 is an add-in set of new libraries that support the Windows Workflow Foundation (WWF), Windows Presentation Foundation (WPF), and Windows Communications Foundation (WCF). The WWF within the .NET Framework 3.0 includes an engine, pluggable components for persisting workflow state, and a Visual Studio 2005 designer. The designer makes it easy to create custom workflows by dragging and dropping components onto a workflow design surface.

Similar to WSS 3.0 building on ASP.NET 2.0, it also builds on top of the WWF. WWF gives WSS 3.0 the structure for attaching business logic to list items and documents. WSS 3.0 extends the basic workflow model in WWF by associating a task list and a history list with each workflow. This adds accountability to workflows that are human-oriented. A perfect example of this is a content management web site. In most enterprise content management systems, you have a workflow of approval for content that is to be published live to the Internet. Approval procedures limit a company's exposure to erroneous content and malicious behavior. The same approach to workflow can be applied within WSS 3.0.

WSS 3.0 and MOSS 2007 both have basic workflows installed and ready to use. WSS 3.0 has some basic routing workflows, and MOSS 2007 has some more complex workflows similar to what is described in the content management example. However, the real power lies in the developers' abilities to create custom workflows.

CHAPTER 3

Installing SharePoint 2007

Introduction

In the previous chapters, you had the opportunity to read about some of the new features available in Microsoft Office SharePoint Server (MOSS) 2007, as well as how it has changed from SharePoint Portal Server 2003. At this point, you are probably eager to jump right in and get started with this exciting new product. This chapter provides an in-depth look at the installation process, ensuring that you are able to get MOSS up and running quickly and easily. It defines preinstallation tasks and prerequisites and then walks you through a single-server installation. If you are interested or ready to expand your deployment to more than one server, make sure to read Chapter 4.

Setting up a single MOSS server is a great way to expose yourself and your organization to this powerful application, and can provide many benefits:

- If you are a developer creating Web Parts or applications that you want to integrate into MOSS, a single server acts as an excellent test environment.

- If you are an IT professional looking to become acquainted with MOSS, you can bring up the single server to "play around with" without the fear of blowing anything up.

- If you are an executive who needs to be convinced of MOSS's value, then your IT staff can deploy a single server as a proof of concept. A representative subset of your user population can work with this proof of concept and provide feedback to you on whether MOSS brings enough value to the organization to warrant a full-blown implementation.

- If you are a trainer and need to establish individual work environments for the students in your class, a single server is a great way to provide students with a hands-on experience.

- If you have a limited IT budget but a strong need for MOSS, start with a single server and then expand as your budget allows.

Preinstallation

Before you grab your MOSS 2007 CD or download and run the installer, there are a number of items you must consider:

1. Licensing
2. Standard versus Enterprise Editions
3. Hardware requirements
4. Software prerequisites

The following sections discuss each of these points in more detail, ensuring that you have the necessary knowledge to move forward and enjoy a successful installation.

Licensing

 The following licensing information is for guidance only. You should consult with your local Microsoft licensing specialist to obtain the latest and most appropriate licensing information for your individual situation.

Unlike its predecessor, MOSS 2007 comes in two versions, Standard and Enterprise, which vary significantly in the feature sets offered. When you install MOSS, the only difference between the two versions during the process is the product key that you specify. You can always install the Standard version and upgrade at a later date by entering an Enterprise Edition product key (once you purchase Enterprise Edition client access licenses for all of your users), but you cannot downgrade from Enterprise Edition to Standard Edition.

It can sometimes be difficult to determine exactly which licenses you need. Currently, in order to properly license MOSS 2007 from Microsoft, you must purchase both the server licenses and the individual client access licenses, or CALs. This means that for every MOSS 2007 server you bring online, you must have a valid server license, and for each client accessing MOSS, a client access license must be purchased.

There is only one license type for each MOSS server, whereas the client access licenses come in both Standard and Enterprise Editions, and are additive. This means that you must purchase a Standard Edition license for each client utilizing MOSS, and if you would like to utilize the features included in the Enterprise Edition, you must then purchase an Enterprise CAL for each of those users as well. In the end, this means that each of your users must be licensed for both a Standard CAL and an Enterprise CAL; you cannot have a mix of users, some with just Standard CALs and others with both CALs—all users must have either Standard or Standard plus Enterprise.

When purchasing the individual CALs (no matter which version you are purchasing at the time), you should note that they are offered as both User CALs and Device CALs.

User CALs are assigned to individual users accessing MOSS and license all of the user's connections to MOSS (laptop, desktop, PDA, etc.). Device CALs are assigned to the individual devices that connect to MOSS, and do not have any regard for the number of users accessing that particular licensed device. An example of an organization that would purchase Device CALs instead of User CALs is one that has a set number of computers that multiple shifts of employees utilize. For example, if an organization has 300 employees but only 100 desktop computers that can be used to access MOSS at any given time, the Device CAL would be more cost-effective, since 100 Device CALs need to be purchased instead of 300 User CALs.

MOSS 2007 has become much more extranet- and intranet-friendly, and is easier than ever to expose to the Internet and external users who may or may not be employees. Because of this, Microsoft offers a MOSS 2007 for Internet Sites server license, which allows you to have an unlimited number of external (non-employee) users connected to a MOSS server and utilizing the Enterprise Edition features. This license is purchased for each MOSS server, and is only to be used to collaborate on information that is not exclusively for internal use. For example, this license is useful for allowing clients access to an extranet site where they can monitor the progress of projects within your organization and communicate with the team. However, this license cannot be used for allowing your employees access to intranet-based resources.

A common point of confusion with SharePoint licensing is with SQL Server. If your deployment utilizes any version of SQL Server (other than SQL Express) as the back-end database system, then for each user accessing SharePoint, you must also have an appropriate SQL Server client access license. If you have a large number of MOSS users, you should look at licensing SQL on a per-processor basis. This type of license allows you to host an unlimited number of SQL users on a server. The only difference is that you must own one of these SQL licenses per physical processor on your server.

Finally, you must also keep in mind that you need to properly license Windows Server 2003, including licenses for clients. Windows Server clients can be licensed via individual CALs or an External Connector. This licensing is outside the scope of this chapter, so please check with your licensing specialist for additional details.

 You will probably hear about Microsoft Office SharePoint Server 2007 for Search and Microsoft Forms Server 2007. These are two separate licenses offered by Microsoft to organizations that would like to utilize the power of SharePoint's search engine and/or InfoPath forms that are web-enabled, without actually implementing the entire MOSS 2007 product.

Standard Versus Enterprise Edition

As mentioned in the previous section, MOSS 2007 comes in both Standard and Enterprise Editions. Based on the needs of your organization, you can choose to implement Standard Edition and upgrade to Enterprise Edition at a later time, or immediately implement Enterprise Edition with all of its additional features. Although there are many small differences between the two editions, the following are the significant features included in Enterprise Edition but not in Standard Edition:

Excel Services
> This feature provides access to Excel spreadsheets through a web browser and offloads the calculations to the server. It makes only specific areas of the spreadsheet visible to users, and ensures that there is "one version of the truth," since only specified users can modify the underlying data. For more information, see Chapter 15.

Report Center
> This is a site provided out of the box that has been designed to simplify the management of reports and data connections. For more information, see Chapter 15.

Business Data Catalog
> This feature is a simplified way to bring data from external sources into SharePoint without costly custom development. With it, users do not need to access multiple systems to view the data they need—it is all available from one common interface provided by MOSS. For more information, see Chapter 28.

Business Data Search
> This feature allows users to search data that has been stored in separate systems exposed through MOSS (such as those connected via the Business Data Catalog). For more information, see Chapter 27.

Forms Services
> You can create forms within Microsoft Office InfoPath 2007 and publish them to SharePoint using Forms Services, allowing users without the InfoPath client to complete forms entirely through their web browsers. For more information, see Chapter 20.

It is recommended that you take some time to familiarize yourself with each of these features in-depth. If you are in the process of preparing your budget for a MOSS project, and you think you might need one or more of the Enterprise Edition features, it would be wise to include the necessary CALs in your budget calculations. You do not want to be caught in a situation where you have implemented Standard Edition and management requests a feature available only in the Enterprise Edition, but you have no budget left for the appropriate licensing.

Hardware Requirements

It is often difficult to determine exactly which hardware is needed to perform the task at hand, especially with a product such as MOSS. Take a moment to consider some of the different functions a user could perform:

- Browsing the site and downloading documents
- Uploading documents and starting workflow processes
- Completing online forms
- Publishing or reviewing Excel spreadsheets
- Retrieving data in separate systems using the Business Data Catalog
- Searching across the entire enterprise for specific data
- Running reports and aggregating data

In addition, you need a solid idea of the number of users who will be performing the different functions, along with the amount of data that is going to be stored within MOSS. From a simplified single-server, "get up and running quick" perspective, Microsoft specifies the hardware requirements listed in Table 3-1.

Table 3-1. Minimum requirements for installing a single-server instance of MOSS

Component	Minimum Requirement
Processor	Single processor, 2.5GHz
Memory	1 GB
Hard drive	3 GB of free space
Display	1,024 × 768 resolution
Operating system	Windows Server 2003
Network	56 Kbps between clients and server

It is recommended that you review Microsoft's "Plan for performance and capacity" article on TechNet, available at *http://technet2.microsoft.com/Office/en-us/library/ 8dd52916-f77d-4444-b593-1f7d6f330e5f1033.mspx?mfr=true*. This site will provide you with all of the information you need to purchase the appropriate hardware and scale as necessary for the additional MOSS components.

For the purpose of this chapter, we only concern ourselves only with the minimum requirements as specified in Table 3-1. In addition, it should be noted that MOSS 2007 can run in a virtualized environment: specifically, on a Windows Server 2003 that is virtualized using an application such as Microsoft's Virtual PC.

Software Prerequisites

This section explains the software prerequisites.

Client-side

MOSS 2007 has made significant advances over SharePoint Portal Server 2003 in supporting a larger number of web browsers. Microsoft now supports two "levels" of browsers, with level 1 browsers providing users with full functionality, and level 2 browsers providing limited functionality. Microsoft states:

> Level 2 Web browsers provide basic functionality, so that users can both read and write in SharePoint sites and perform site administration. However, because ActiveX controls are supported only in level 1 browsers and due to the functionality differences within different browsers, a different user experience might be provided and there could be some variances from the user experience from the level 1 browsers.

Level 1 browsers include:

- Internet Explorer version 6.0 or 7.0 running on:
  - Windows 2000
  - Windows XP
  - Windows Server 2003
  - Windows Vista

Level 2 browsers include:

- Firefox 1.5, Mozilla 1.7, or Netscape 8.1 running on:
  - Windows 2000
  - Windows XP
  - Windows Server 2003
  - Windows Vista
- Firefox 1.5 or Netscape 7.2 running on:
  - Unix
  - Linux
- Firefox 1.5 or Safari 2.0 running on:
  - Mac OS X

Any browsers not listed are not officially supported. However, many members of the SharePoint community have created workarounds that support other browser versions and types. Also, Microsoft occasionally releases updates that support new browser versions.

In addition to browser support, clients should have access to an email address and Microsoft Office 2007. Microsoft Office 2007 provides additional features over Office 2003 with MOSS, such as:

- The ability to publish spreadsheets to Excel Services
- The ability to publish forms to Forms Services

- Integration of PowerPoint presentations with the slide library
- Two-way synchronization of lists and libraries in SharePoint with Outlook 2007
- Integration with Microsoft Office Groove for decentralized and offline collaboration

Although the latest version of Office is not required for using MOSS, if the features just listed are desired, Office 2007 is required.

Finally, if you are interested in the ability to modify your MOSS sites through a WYSIWYG editor such as FrontPage, you will need to purchase SharePoint Designer. SharePoint Designer is a new Microsoft product offering that replaces Microsoft FrontPage, specifically for editing MOSS sites and pages. Designer allows you to build custom workflows, modify master pages, and build ASP.NET pages, all from a simplified user interface.

Server-side

Once you have ensured that your clients can utilize MOSS, you need to make sure that the server on which you want to install MOSS can support it. The following outlines the server-side software requirements, some of which will be discussed in detail in the step-by-step installation instructions.

MOSS 2007 can be installed on the following operating systems:

- Windows Server 2003, Standard Edition
- Windows Server 2003, Enterprise Edition
- Windows Server 2003, Datacenter Edition
- Windows Server 2003, Web Edition

 If you are installing MOSS as a single-server deployment on Windows Server 2003, Web Edition, then you can utilize only SQL Server 2005 Express Edition or SQL Server 2000 Desktop Engine (MSDE).

Once the operating system is installed, Internet Information Services (IIS 6.0) must be installed, including the following components:

- WWW
- SMTP
- Common Files

Finally, you must make sure that Microsoft .NET Framework version 3.0 is installed as well, with ASP.NET 2.0 enabled.

MOSS does not require any database engine to be preinstalled. If SQL is not installed within your environment for use by MOSS, then MOSS will install an instance of SQL Server Express Edition, where all of its data will then be stored. However, if you prefer to use a licensed version of SQL, MOSS supports the following:

- SQL Server 2000 with SP3a or later
- SQL Server 2005 with SP1 or later

Installation

The following steps and associated screenshots will walk you through the process of getting Microsoft Office SharePoint Server 2007 up and running within your environment, using SQL Server 2005 Express Edition as the database engine. By following these instructions, you will be able to quickly begin working with the powerful features of MOSS. While following along, you should be logged into the server as a user with local administrator privileges.

The first thing you must do is install IIS 6.0:

1. Click on the Start menu, select Control Panel, and then select "Add or Remove Programs."
2. On the lefthand side of the window, select Add/Remove Windows Components.
3. Click to add a checkmark next to Application Server.
4. Then, double-click Application Server and ensure that the following components are checked:
   - Application Server Console
   - Enable Network COM+ Access
   - SMTP Service
   - Internet Information Services (IIS)
5. Next, double-click Internet Information Services and make sure the following components are checked:
   - Common Files
   - Internet Information Services Manager
   - World Wide Web Service

   Make sure that FrontPage 2002 Server Extensions are *not* checked!
6. Double-click World Wide Web Service and make sure that the World Wide Web Service is checked.
7. Click OK three times and then click Next. The IIS components will then install. Note that you may be prompted to provide the Windows Server installation CD, so be prepared.

Next, you must install the .NET Framework 3.0:

1. Download the Microsoft .NET Framework 3.0 Redistributable Package from the Microsoft web site at *http://go.microsoft.com/fwlink/?LinkID=72322&clcid=0x409*.
2. Run *dotnetfx3setup.exe* to start the installer.

3. Once you have reviewed and accepted the license agreement, click Install.

4. The installer will then need to connect to the Internet and download a number of files totaling approximately 54 megabytes. The installer will run in your task-bar and stay hidden until it is done; however, you can click on the icon at any point to check the status.

5. Once the necessary files have been downloaded, the installation will commence. Upon completion, you should be presented with the screen shown in Figure 3-1.

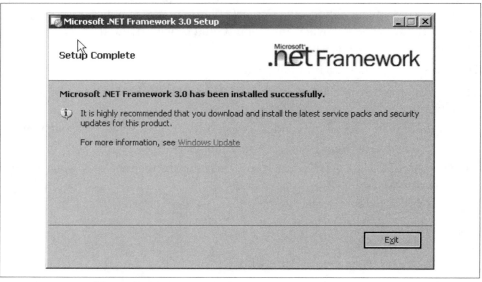

Figure 3-1. Successful install of the .NET Framework 3.0

Once the .NET Framework 3.0 has been successfully installed, you need to enable ASP.NET 2.0 within IIS:

1. Click Start, select All Programs, and then select Administrative Tools and Internet Information Services Manager.

2. Click the plus sign next to the server name to expand the view.

3. Select Web Server Extensions.

4. In the righthand window pane shown in Figure 3-2, highlight ASP.NET v2.0. 50727 (or the latest 2.0 build of ASP.NET) and then click the Allow button. The status will change from Prohibited to Allowed.

5. Exit from IIS.

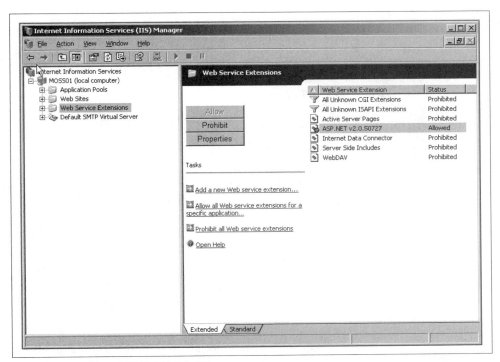

Figure 3-2. Enabling ASP.NET 2.0 in IIS

It is now time to install Microsoft Office SharePoint Server 2007:

1. If you are installing from a CD, insert the CD and then select *setup.exe*. If you have downloaded MOSS, run the *OfficeServer.exe* executable by double-clicking it.

2. The installer will begin, and you will be immediately prompted to enter your license key (Figure 3-3). Depending on the version you purchased, input either the Enterprise or Standard Edition license key in the space provided. If you have entered the proper key, a green checkmark will appear next to the key. Click Continue.

3. On the next screen, you must review and accept the Microsoft Software License Terms. Do so by checking the box next to "I accept the terms of this agreement" and then click Continue.

4. You are now provided with the opportunity to choose the type of installation you want (Figure 3-4). Choose Advanced. Although you can choose Basic, choosing Advanced allows you to specify an alternate installation location and decide whether you wish to participate in the customer experience program.

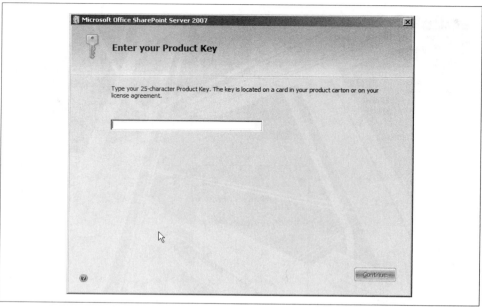

Figure 3-3. Product key input screen

If you were to choose Basic, the install would immediately start and MOSS would be installed in the following default locations:

- Application files: *C:\Program Files\Microsoft Office Servers*
- Search indexes: *C:\Program Files\Microsoft Office Servers\12.0\Data*

5. On the Server Type tab of the Advanced installation screen, choose "Stand-alone" (Figure 3-5). This will install SQL Server 2005 Express Edition along with MOSS 2007.

6. Next, click on the File Location tab (Figure 3-6). Browse to the folders in which you would like to install the MOSS application files and the search indexes. Note that if you plan to index a large amount of content, you should have a large amount of space available on the chosen hard disk.

7. Select the Feedback tab (Figure 3-7). Based on your organization's privacy preferences, you can choose whether or not to send anonymous feedback to Microsoft.

8. You are now set to install MOSS. Click the Install Now button to begin.

9. Once the initial installation is successful, you will then be presented with the screen shown in Figure 3-8. Run the SharePoint Products and Technologies Configuration Wizard by checking the box next to "Run the SharePoint Products and Technologies Configuration Wizard now," and then click Close.

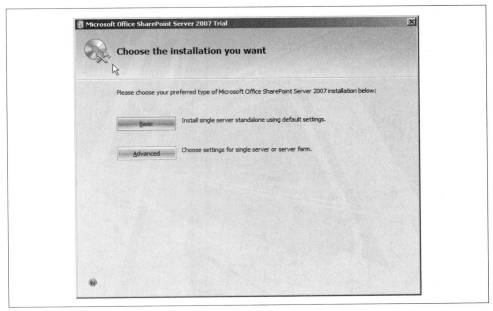

Figure 3-4. Choosing your installation type

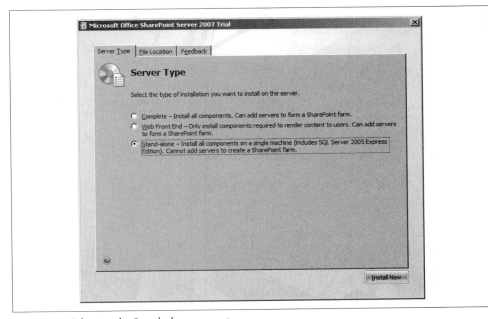

Figure 3-5. Selecting the Stand-alone server type

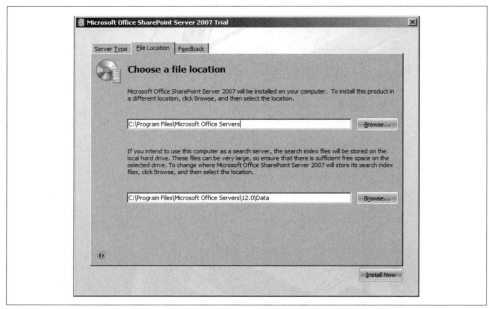

Figure 3-6. File location options

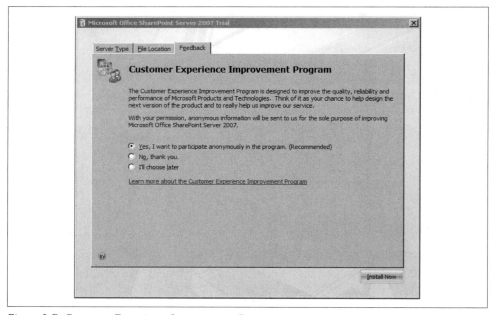

Figure 3-7. Customer Experience Improvement Program options

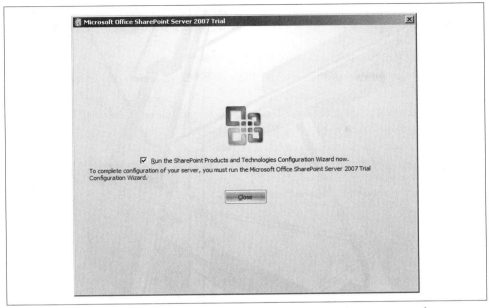

Figure 3-8. Initial install is successful and you can move on to the configuration wizard

10. On the wizard's welcome screen, click Next.

11. You will then be presented with a window asking whether IIS, the SharePoint Administration Service, and the SharePoint Timer Service can be started or reset during configuration (Figure 3-9). Click Yes.

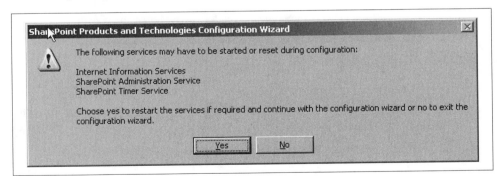

Figure 3-9. Confirm that the services can be started or reset

12. The configuration wizard will then take some time to run. As it runs, you will be presented with a status indicator, showing where the process is within the 10 configuration steps. If at any time the wizard encounters a problem and stops functioning, you can check the configuration log located at:

> C:\Program Files\Common Files\Microsoft Shared\web server extensions\12\LOGS

Once the wizard has completed successfully, you will be presented with the success screen shown in Figure 3-10. Click Finish.

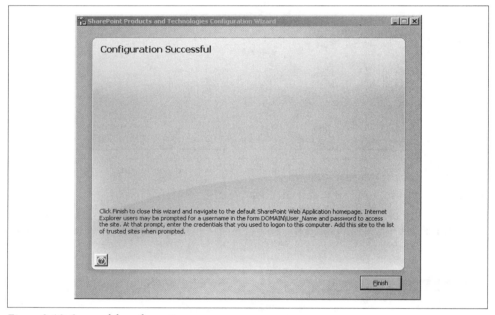

Figure 3-10. Successful configuration screen

13. After clicking Finish, a browser window will open and you will be taken to your first MOSS Site, which should look like Figure 3-11. You can explore the site, but then close your browser window. Congratulations—MOSS has been successfully installed!

Post-Installation Tasks

Now that your site is up and running, you are probably eager to start working with MOSS. However, you must now go through the process of starting and configuring some of the additional MOSS services and features. Luckily, Microsoft has streamlined and simplified this process through an Administrator's task list.

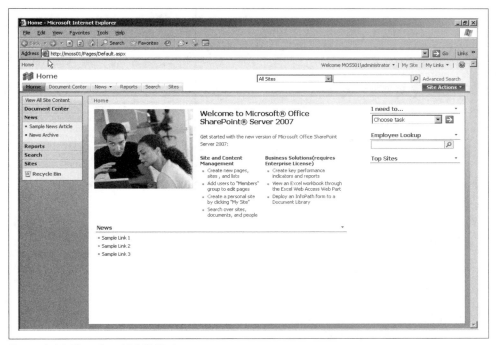

Figure 3-11. Your first MOSS Site!

1. Click Start, then All Programs, then Microsoft Office Server and SharePoint 3.0 Central Administration.

2. Your browser will load, and you will be presented with the Central Administration home page, which contains the following areas:

   Administrator Tasks

   These tasks have been provided by Microsoft to ensure that you complete the setup of MOSS successfully. It is recommended that you follow these tasks in order. As you complete each task, you will want to delete it from the list. You can do this by clicking on the task name, and then clicking the Delete link in the task detail screen.

   Farm Topology

   This area shows all of the servers in your MOSS farm and what services are running on each. Since you have just completed a single server installation, you will see only one server listed, along with all of the services associated to it.

   Resources

   This is an area where you can add links to useful resources that assist you with the management of MOSS 2007.

   Your screen should appear similar to Figure 3-12.

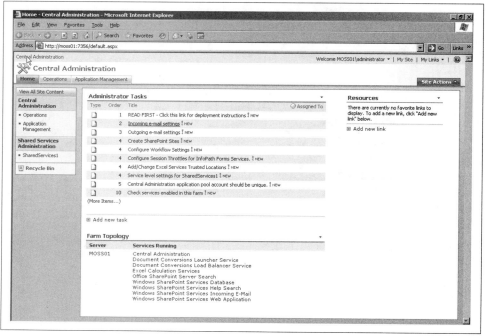

Figure 3-12. Central Administration after a single-server installation

3. To get started with your additional MOSS configuration steps, click the first task in the Administrator Task list, entitled "READ FIRST – Click this link for deployment information."

4. By clicking on the title of the task, you are taken to a details page that contains additional information about the task (Figure 3-13). Once you have read the details and the task has been completed, click the Delete button at the top of the window to remove the task from your list. For each task, you will notice an Actions field. Within this field there will typically be an associated link, which will take you to important instructions or a page associated with completing the action.

5. For Task 1, click the link under the Action field to "Read the Quick Start Guide." The guide will load, and it will provide you with a wealth of additional information on how to complete the setup of additional settings. You should read the section entitled "Learn how to deploy Office SharePoint Server 2007 on a single server." This section details the information you need to configure the following:

   • Incoming Mail Settings

   • Outgoing Mail Settings

   • Diagnostic Logging Settings

   • Antivirus Protection Settings

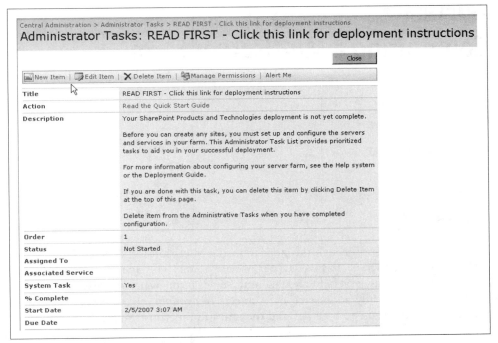

Administrator Tasks: READ FIRST - Click this link for deployment instructions

Close

New Item | Edit Item | ✖ Delete Item | Manage Permissions | Alert Me

Title	READ FIRST - Click this link for deployment instructions
Action	Read the Quick Start Guide
Description	Your SharePoint Products and Technologies deployment is not yet complete. Before you can create any sites, you must set up and configure the servers and services in your farm. This Administrator Task List provides prioritized tasks to aid you in your successful deployment. For more information about configuring your server farm, see the Help system or the Deployment Guide. If you are done with this task, you can delete this item by clicking Delete Item at the top of this page. Delete item from the Administrative Tasks when you have completed configuration.
Order	1
Status	Not Started
Assigned To	
Associated Service	
System Task	Yes
% Complete	
Start Date	2/5/2007 3:07 AM
Due Date	

Figure 3-13. Example of the task detail screen

6. Once you have reviewed this information, you should move forward in the list of Administrator Tasks, completing each one until all of them have been completed.

 If you accidently delete an item from the list, you can click on the Recycle Bin in the lefthand column. From within the Recycle Bin, you can restore individual items to their original location within SharePoint.

7. Congratulations! You have now installed and configured Microsoft Office Share-Point Server 2007! You are now ready to begin to build out your site.

CHAPTER 4

Configuring a Multiserver Farm

Introduction

In Chapter 3, we went through the steps to install Microsoft Office SharePoint Server 2007 onto a single server. In this chapter, we are going to broaden this basic installation out to numerous servers to create a multiserver farm. When we discuss multiserver farms, we are really addressing the subjects of *availability* and *scalability*. These topics are often discussed together and they mean numerous things. They can mean having a fast-responding environment (Multiple Web Front Ends [WFE] handling user requests) or it can mean having a redundant environment to provide increased uptime. In either case, we are looking at moving from a single server implementation to a multiple server environment. This chapter details the trade-offs, decisions, and processes in creating a multiserver MOSS implementation.

One of the challenges in scaling out a MOSS site is deciding which services need their own server(s). In this chapter, we will specifically look at Search, Index, Excel Services, and Shared Services. There are valid reasons why we place Excel Services on its own dedicated server or servers if it is being heavily used. Excel Services is a huge resource hog. Similarly, Index, Query, and Search are often best installed on their own server(s) for performance reasons. We want to isolate all of these services if possible, and using a multiserver farm allows for this type of architecture.

A small company may do very well with a server environment where the entire SharePoint environment resides on a single server. This is perfectly acceptable, but you should be aware that when running on a single server, you will have no redundancy. As your needs grow, you can always scale out by adding additional WFEs and Application servers, but if your core server goes down, your MOSS environment is dead until you recover.

You can also run your SQL environment from the core server. However, we are again looking at a failure point, and the performance degradation you will see may warrant the need to separate the WFE from the Database Server. Medium to large companies will, however, benefit from multiple servers in their farm, as it will allow more users to work without interruption in their portal environments.

 Microsoft has put together some worksheets that the implementer or decision maker can use to decide whether availability is crucial to your company and how to provide for it. The link is available in the "Conclusion" section at the end of this chapter.

At the end of this chapter, you will:

- Understand the different Sharepoint Farm Topologies
- Be able to decide where to place the different resources, such as Search, Index, and Excel Services
- Be able to install a medium to large MOSS 2007 farm

Planning for Scalability

In order to scale MOSS, you have to think about which parts you can scale and also the costs you incur and benefits you gain in each scaling approach. In MOSS, you can scale in several different ways:

- Adding Web Front Ends (WFEs)
- Adding application servers
- Scaling and clustering the database

In Figure 4-1, I have broken our environment into three tiers: Web Front Ends, Application Servers, and Database Servers. Again, as discussed earlier, this entire picture can fit onto one single server. MOSS 2007 does make it easy to scale out. Later in the chapter, we will walk through the process of adding an additional server to our farm, but first I want to explain the different tiers and help you to understand the picture in Figure 4-1 more clearly.

The Web Front End's primary role is to render web content to the end user. Optionally, when you set up your search environment, a single WFE or multiple WFEs can also be used to query the Index server. Users interact directly with the Query server, and you can run it either on a dedicated server or on all WFEs.

Application Servers are where you set your various roles, such as Central Administration, Excel Services, Search/Index and Shared Service Providers.

Database Servers are your repositories for all that is SharePoint. What I mean is that SharePoint stores everything in SQL Server. A common question that comes up from time to time is "Where are the documents stored?" Plan your database implementation properly, and you will ensure a healthy and reliable SharePoint environment.

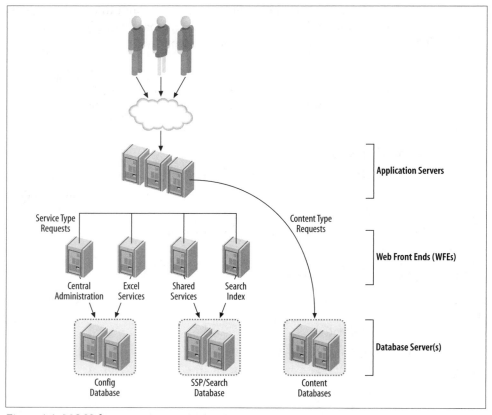

Figure 4-1. MOSS farm components

Roles That Can Be Redundant

Before we begin our installation, it is important to plan where you want to place the various roles, such as Excel Services, Shared Service Provider, Search, Index, and so on. This is critical in ensuring a successful implementation.

These application server roles can be deployed to multiple servers. The code that is deployed to each server is identical, and the application server roles do not store any data. In other words, each instance of these server roles remains identical, so if one of the server computers fails, no saved data is lost. The web servers automatically load balance all requests to these server roles across the available application server computers.

The following application server roles can be deployed redundantly:

Query

The query role can be deployed to any number of application server computers, or it can be deployed across web servers. There is one limitation, however: if the query role is deployed to the same server that hosts the index role, the query role cannot be deployed to any other server computers. This is because the index role recognizes that the query role is on the same server and, consequently, does not attempt to propagate the index. In some scenarios, you can optimize the throughput of your server farm by deploying the query role across your web servers. For example, if more than half of the content requests coming into the server farm are requests for static content, performance can be optimized by hosting the query role on the web servers. This is because the query role caches the content that it serves, making it available for subsequent requests during the search process.

Excel Calculation Services

The Excel Calculation Services role performs Excel calculations on the Excel workbooks that are stored in the content databases. This application server role is unique in that it stores session-state information throughout the duration of a user session. When a workbook is opened, the web server role continues to route the user requests to the same Excel Calculation Services server until the workbook is closed and the user finishes the session. The Excel Calculation Services role can be a resource-intensive role. You can optimize the performance of your farm by deploying this role across multiple servers.

Roles That Cannot Be Redundant

The following table indicates which application server roles can be deployed redundantly and which roles can be deployed to multiple servers but are not redundant.

Application server role	Multiple servers hosting this role are redundant?
Query	Yes
Excel Calculation Services	Yes
Office Project Server 2007	Yes
Index	No
Windows SharePoint Services 3.0 search	No

Application server roles that cannot be redundant include Windows SharePoint Services 3.0 and Index search:

Windows SharePoint Services 3.0
> The Windows SharePoint Services 3.0 search application role is an option if you are not using Office SharePoint Server 2007 query and indexing. These components cannot be split. Additionally, Windows SharePoint Services 3.0 search is required to provide full-text search of Help.

Office SharePoint Server 2007 Index
> The index role is associated with a Shared Services Provider (SSP) and builds one index per SSP. One index server can be associated with multiple SSPs. You can deploy multiple index servers to improve capacity. In this case, each index server is associated with a different SSP. Content indexes produced by the MOSS 2007 index role are continuously pushed to all servers that host the query role in a farm.

These application server roles can be deployed to multiple servers; however, the multiple servers are not redundant. These server roles are configured to crawl content and generate content indexes. If you deploy these roles to multiple servers, each server will need to crawl different content.

Evaluating the Risks of Application Server Failures

The following list explains the risks associated with an application server failure. A better understanding of this will help with the planning and design of your implementation.

Query
> In the case of failure, users will not be able to issue full-text queries. Users can still browse through sites and access content exposed through the sites, however. If your application depends on users or customers being able to find content by searching, plan to deploy the query server role to multiple servers. In a five-server farm, this can easily be accomplished by deploying the query role to the two web server computers.

Excel Calculation Services
> Server-side rendering of Excel and business intelligence data will not be available. Spreadsheets cannot be loaded, recalculated, refreshed, or retrieved by Excel Calculation Services. Scorecards and features that use the Excel Web Renderer also are not available. Users will still be able to open spreadsheets from SharePoint libraries by using the Excel client application. However, if users don't have permission to open files in the client, they will not be able to view those files until the Excel Calculation Services role is back online.

Index

Query servers will continue to use existing content indexes until the index service is restored and new or updated indexes are generated. Consequently, search results will not include new or changed content while the index role is unavailable.

Windows SharePoint Services 3.0 search

Search is unavailable. The amount of time required to restore the search capability depends on whether existing content indexes can be restored or if new indexes must be generated by recrawling the content.

The general redundancy recommendation is to plan to install an application server role to at least two application server computers if:

- Your solution is primarily based on the features provided by the application server.
- Your availability requirement for the features provided by the server role is 99 percent or greater.

If your organization can tolerate temporary loss of this functionality for the amount of time it takes your IT team to deploy an application server role to a different server or to restore service to the existing server, consider deploying the role to a single application server.

Topologies

In previous versions of SharePoint, we were provided with different size farms. *Small farms* (Figure 4-2) could consist of one WFE, the Application Server Role, and Database server all residing on the same box. Alternatively, it could be branched out to two servers. The frontend servers are designated as web servers and provide web content to clients, and the Application Server Role provides services such as Excel Services, Business Data Catalog, search queries, crawling, and indexing content. This model typically is fine for a small organization, but its suitability will really suffer when we start to look at fault tolerance and recoverability. This is where the medium to large farms come into play. Not only do the larger farms assist in spreading some of the load, but you can also gain some fault tolerance benefits with these models.

Figure 4-2. Small farm topology

A *medium server farm* (Figure 4-3) typically consists of a database server, an application server running Office SharePoint Server 2007, and one or two frontend web servers running Office SharePoint Server 2007 and IIS. In this configuration, the application server provides indexing services and Excel Calculation Services, and the frontend web servers service search queries and provide web content.

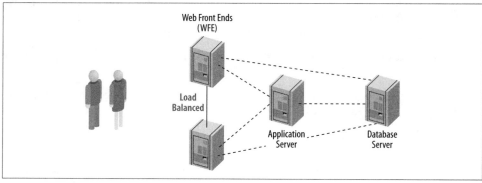

Figure 4-3. Medium farm topology

A *large server farm* (Figure 4-4) typically consists of two or more clustered database servers, several load-balanced frontend web servers running IIS and Office SharePoint Server 2007, and two or more application servers running Office SharePoint Server 2007. In this configuration, each of the application servers provides specific Office SharePoint Server 2007 services, such as indexing or Excel Calculation Services, and the frontend servers provide web content.

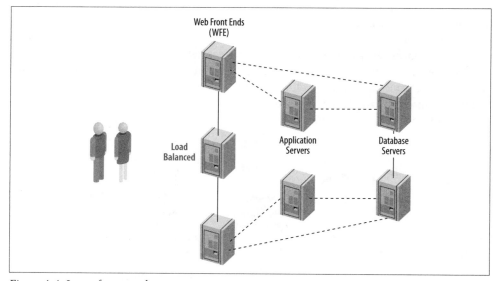

Figure 4-4. Large farm topology

All of the web servers in your server farm must have the same Share-Point Products and Technologies installed. For example, if all of the servers in your server farm are running Microsoft Office SharePoint Server 2007, you cannot add to your farm a server that is running only Microsoft Office Project Server 2007. To run Office Project Server 2007 and Office SharePoint Server 2007 in your server farm, you must install Office Project Server 2007 and Office SharePoint Server 2007 on each of your web servers. This also would be the case for other products, such as Knowledge Networks. To enhance the security of your farm and reduce the surface area that is exposed to a potential attack, you can turn off services on particular servers after you install SharePoint Products and Technologies.

Implementing a Multiserver Farm

The following sections go through the process of implementing a multiserver farm.

Before You Begin

Before you begin, it's important to remember the following:

- The account that you select for installing Office SharePoint Server 2007 must be a member of the Administrators group on every server on which you install Office SharePoint Server 2007, and this account is automatically assigned as the SSP administrator. Therefore, by default the SSP administrator is also the local administrator on all of the farm servers. You can, however, remove this account from the Administrators group on the servers after installation.

- To deploy Office SharePoint Server 2007 in a server farm environment, you must provide credentials for several different accounts.

- You must install Office SharePoint Server 2007 on the same drive on all load-balanced frontend web server computers.

- You must install Office SharePoint Server 2007 on a clean installation of the Microsoft Windows Server 2003 operating system with Service Pack 1 (SP1) or later. If you uninstall a previous version of Office SharePoint Server 2007 and then install Office SharePoint Server 2007, Setup might fail to create the configuration database, and the installation will fail.

- You must install the same language packs on all servers.

- All the instances of Office SharePoint Server 2007 in the farm must be in the same language.

- You must use the *Complete* installation option on all computers you want to be index servers, query servers, or servers that run Excel Calculation Services.

- If you want to have more than one index server in a farm, you must use a different Shared Services Provider (SSP) for each index server.

Run Setup on the First Server

1. Install the role of Application server onto each farm server. (For detailed instructions, refer to Chapter 3.)

2. Install .NET 3.0. (For detailed instructions, refer to Chapter 3.)

3. From the product disc, run *Setup.exe* on one of your web server computers. Alternatively, from the product download, run *Officeserver.exe*.

4. On the "Enter your Product Key" page, enter your product key, and then click Continue.

5. On the "Read the Microsoft Software License Terms" page, review the terms, select the "I accept the terms of this agreement" checkbox, and then click Continue.

6. On the "Choose the installation you want" page, click Advanced. (The Basic option is for standalone installations.)

7. On the Server Type tab, select Complete.

8. Optionally, to install Office SharePoint Server 2007 at a custom location, select the File Location tab, and then type the location or Browse to the location.

9. When you have chosen the correct options, click Install Now.

10. When Setup finishes, a dialog box appears that prompts you to complete the configuration of your server. Be sure that the "Run the SharePoint Products and Technologies Configuration Wizard now" checkbox is *not* selected.

11. Click Close to start the configuration wizard. Instructions for completing the wizard are provided in the next set of steps.

12. Follow steps 1 through 11 on all additional servers in this farm.

In step 10, we unchecked the box for running the configuration wizard. If you recall from the last chapter, the configuration wizard gives you a task list of configuration items to complete after installation. On larger farms, you will generally want to finish installing your entire farm before going back through and performing configuration. After we have installed the bits to all of our servers, it's time to run the SharePoint Configuration Wizard on our first server. Microsoft also recommends a certain order when installing.

Recommended order of install

1. Microsoft recommends that the Central Administration web application be installed on an application server, such as a query server or a server that runs Excel Calculation Services, but not on an index server (for performance reasons). If your farm will have an application server, install Office SharePoint Server 2007 on that server first. This also installs the Central Administration site.

2. All your frontend web servers.

3. The index server (if using a separate server for search queries and indexing).

4. The query servers, if separate from the index server.

 To configure more than one query server in your farm, you cannot configure your index server as a query server.

5. Other application servers (optional).

In Chapter 3, we went through the steps of running the Configuration Wizard on our first server. In Figure 4-5, we see the results after installing this first server. Notice that, at this point, simply the Database Instance and the first server are showing. We are going to change that with the next series of steps.

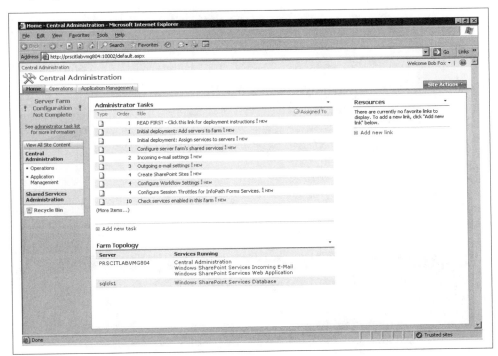

Figure 4-5. Central Administration console (first server)

At this point, the first server has been configured, and now we want to run the Configuration Wizard on the rest of the boxes in our farm. If you refer to the Recommended Order of Install, you can run the Configuration Wizard on every box in your farm in any order, but it must be done one server at a time. The recommended order applies when you actually start to place the services on the respective boxes in your farm, and this can be completed after you have joined the servers to the farm, which happens during the next series of steps.

Steps

1. When the Initial Configuration Screen (Figure 4-6) opens, click Next.

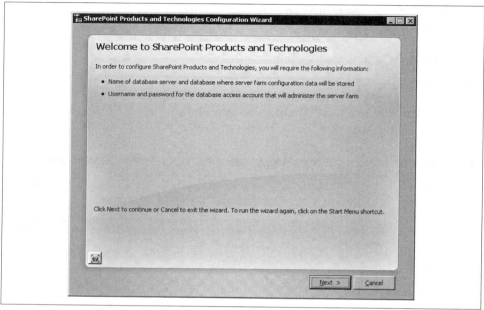

Figure 4-6. Initial configuration screen

2. You will be greeted with a notification that services will be restarted automatically (Figure 4-7). This is normal. Click Yes.

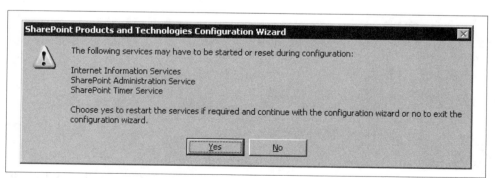

Figure 4-7. Notification of service resets

3. Since we're joining servers to an existing farm, we will select the radio button as shown in Figure 4-8 ("Yes, I want to connect to an existing server farm").

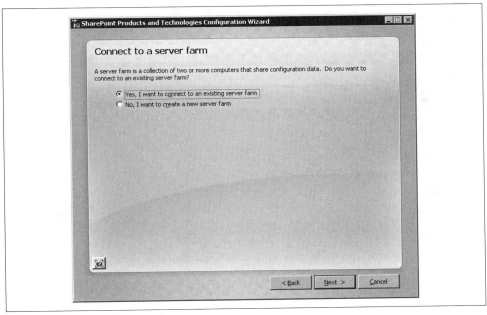

Figure 4-8. Connect to existing farm

4. In the next screen (Figure 4-9), enter the name of your database server. Once you do this, the button Retrieve Database Names will become active (see Figure 4-10). Click it.

5. After clicking Retrieve Database Names, the configuration wizard finds the correct configuration database (Sharepoint_Config) and fills in the username. Next, enter the database account password (Figure 4-11).

6. Click Next after entering the SQL Account Password, and then click the Advanced Settings button, as shown in Figure 4-12.

7. After clicking Next, you will have two choices (Figure 4-13). This screen simply asks whether you want to allow this server to host an instance of the Central Administration Web Application. Generally you should have two servers in a farm with this role, so you can fall back on one if the other is down. In this case, select the top radio button: "Do not use this machine to host the web site." If you want to add this role to another box at a later time, you can do so via the Central Administration Web Console.

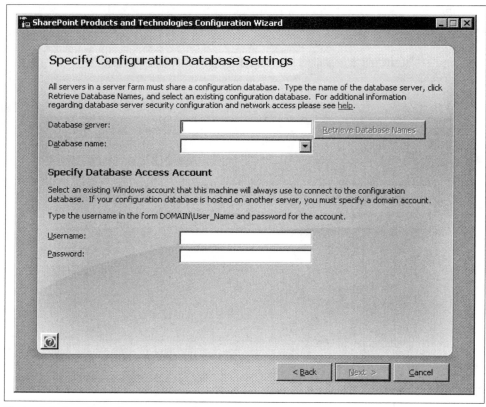

Figure 4-9. Specify Configuration Database Settings

8. At this point (Figure 4-14), we are ready to begin the configuration; the wizard has all the information it needs. Click Next.

9. After selecting Next, the wizard will go through a series of nine steps (Figure 4-15). You do not need to do anything, and generally this completes within five minutes.

After the configuration part of the installation is complete (Figure 4-16), click Finish. You can go back to your Central Administration Console (Figure 4-17) and see that this server has been added to the farm.

Continue to run the installation procedure on every server that belongs in the farm. The end result should resemble Figure 4-18.

Conclusion

This chapter provides a step-by-step guide for building a Microsoft Office Share-Point Server 2007 multiserver farm implementation. Essentially, the build process is

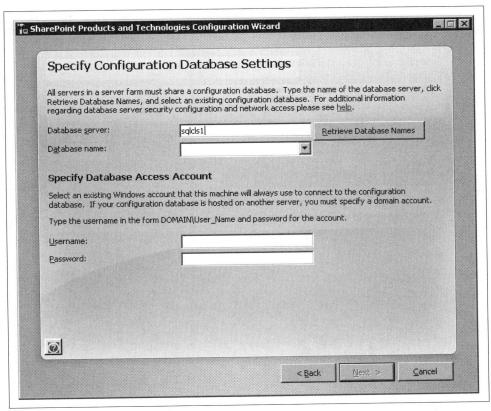

Figure 4-10. Click Retrieve Database Names

very simple and straightforward, but what happens after the build can make or break your implementation. Placement of services is critical, and there are many details that must be taken into consideration. As stated earlier in this chapter, there are times when a small farm will make more sense than a medium or large farm, and visa versa. Consider the following areas to start with your planning:

- Number of users (multiple WFEs)
- Number of documents (SQL storage)
- Fault tolerance/allowable downtime (multiple WFEs, application servers, clusters)

As mentioned earlier in this chapter, there are a number of worksheets that Microsoft has placed on TechNet that will assist with planning your environment. Without proper planning, your implementation will fail or at the very least cause unnecessary headaches down the line. Using Microsoft's planning worksheets can alleviate some future stress and allow you to provide for your customers with a well-thought-out implementation. This link will take you to the appropriate TechNet page:

http://technet2.microsoft.com/Office/en-us/library/b28ba53d-a3e8-440f-9fcb-f592d858894a1033.mspx?mfr=true

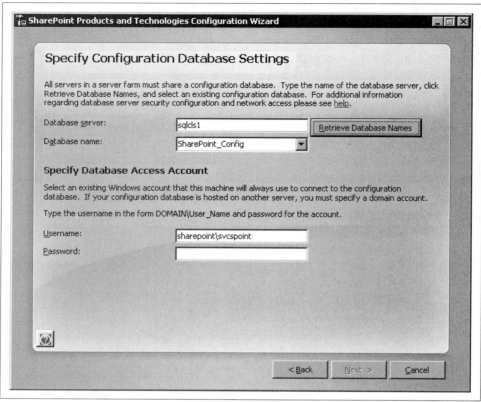

Figure 4-11. Configuration Database Settings, continued

 I suggest making these forms reusable and, in some ways, "smart documents." With Infopath 2007, you can simply convert these forms and place them into a "Site Planning Page" on your MOSS environment. This page can then be used as a template for planning other sites in your environment. Just imagine walking into a kickoff planning meeting and having this type of a form already in place. You will be an instant hero!

Some of the information regarding roles and redundancy were taken from Microsoft's Planning and Architecture for Microsoft Office Sharepoint Server 2007 document:

http://technet2.microsoft.com/Office/en-us/library/d3e0e0fc-77b6-4109-87d6-53ad088db01d1033.mspx?mfr=true

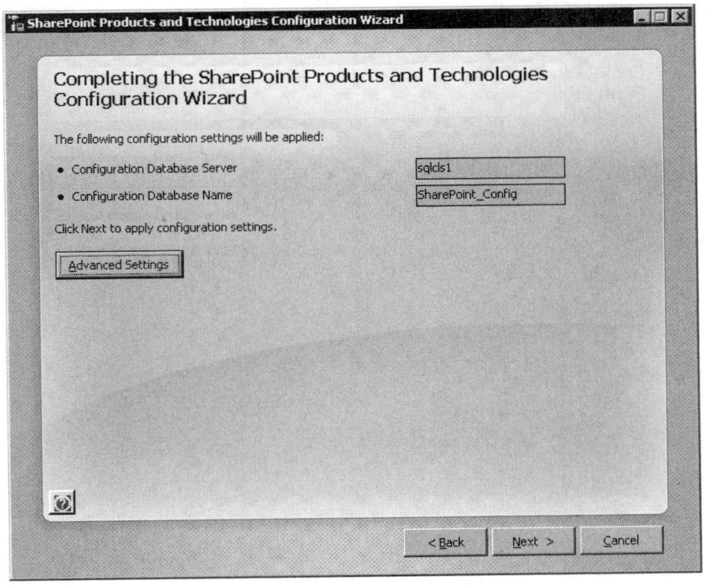

Figure 4-12. Installation summary

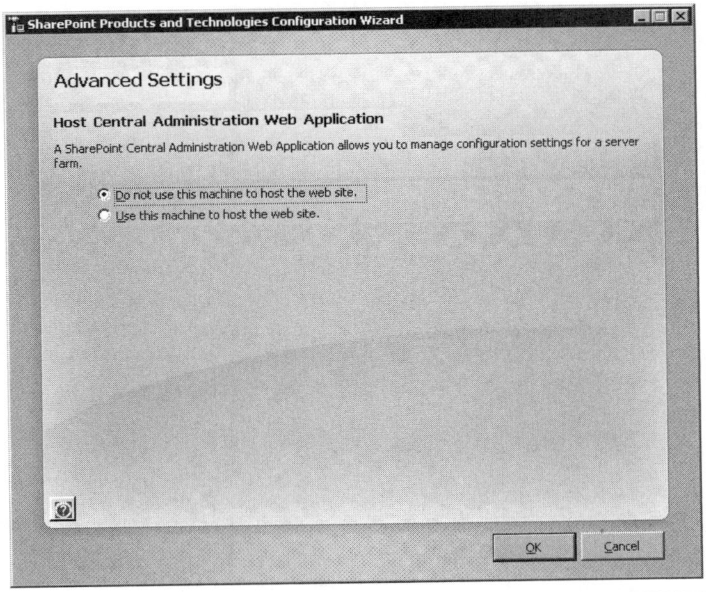

Figure 4-13. Advanced Settings

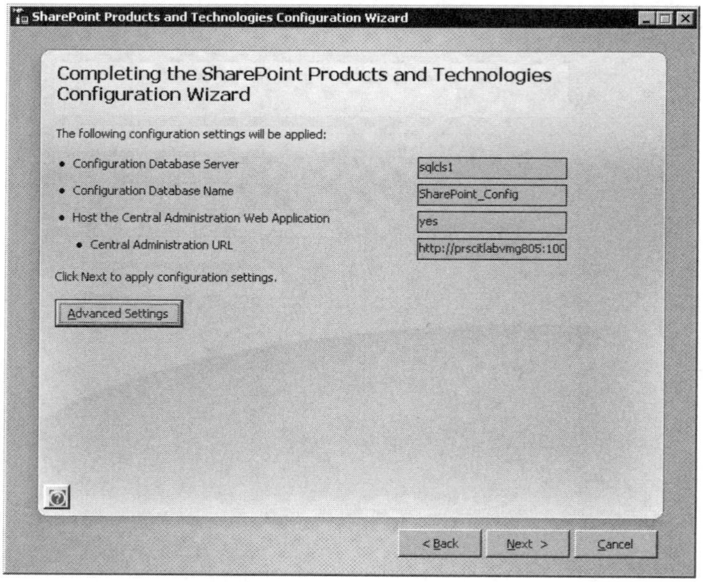

Figure 4-14. Final summary window

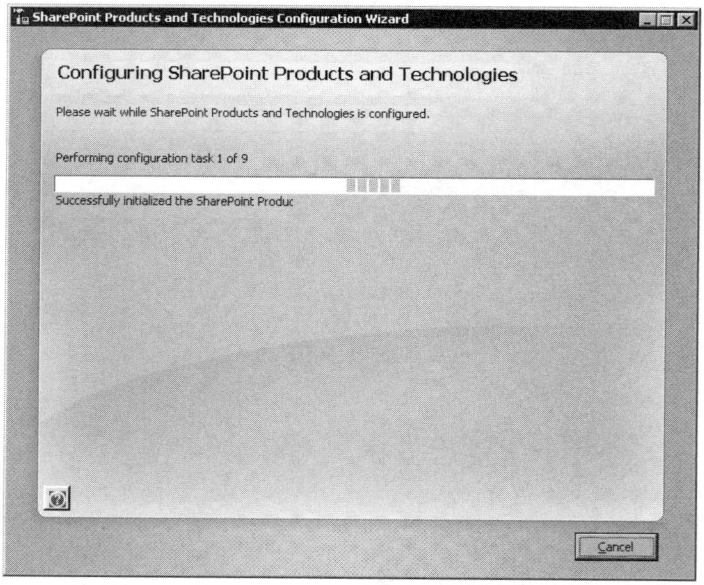

Figure 4-15. Configuration progress window

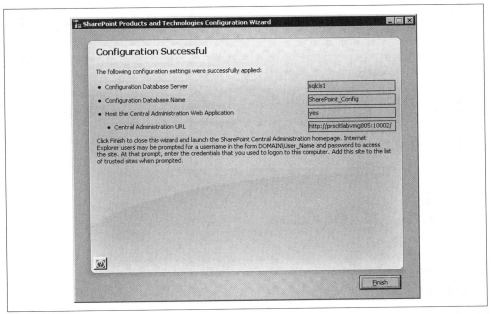

Figure 4-16. Configuration complete

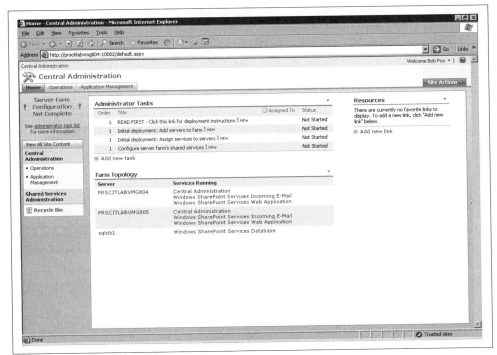

Figure 4-17. Second server in farm complete

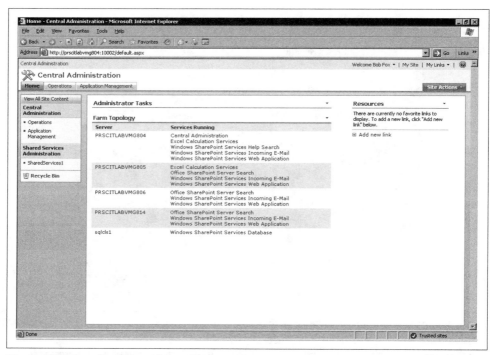

Figure 4-18. Completed view of server farm

CHAPTER 5

Designing SharePoint Sites

Introduction

As with previous versions of SharePoint, MOSS 2007 organizes information as web sites. These sites can be accessed either through your company's intranet or from the Internet. After installing and configuring MOSS 2007, a default top-level site will automatically be created. Your next job is to modify the top-level site and begin constructing your site collection. A site in SharePoint is the same as any web site you have ever accessed: a collection of web pages interrelated to allow a group or organization to share information, organize data, and conduct collaborative meetings and discussions.

A *top-level site* is the main web interface into your organization. Think of it as *http://www.microsoft.com* or *http://intranet.microsoft.com*. This site is the access point that allows your company and any partners entry into your information and communication channels in MOSS 2007.

Subsites are subsidiary web sites or child sites that are referenced through the top-level site. Often, subsites are created for specific teams or projects within your company. If your company designs and supports various software suites, a subsite could be created for a specialized group to develop a new application within a suite. Any subsite can have numerous subsites underneath it. A top-level site with an underlying tree structure of subsites is called a *site collection*. The top-level site and subsites are all organized under portal hierarchy, meaning that there can be numerous site collections per portal site.

It is also possible to create a site collection as a single action, rather than creating sites individually. The portal site administrator can create site collections that are not part of the portal site's main navigation. Creating site collections from the Site Directory lets you organize your sites based on your company's business structure or by working group, rather than the default portal hierarchy.

Each user on a site can also configure a personal site called My Site. My Site provides the individual with a private workspace that is not accessible by anyone else. The user can allow access by others if desired. Before moving on, let's take a look at the different ways sites can be created.

My Site collections are discussed in Chapter 21.

Sites can be created in a number of ways:

- Using administrative privileges
- Using self-service site creation
- Using the command line
- Using a program
- With a compatible web design application

On a broader scale, site creation can be differentiated by:

- Creating top-level site and subsites
- Creating separate site collections

Sites Versus Site Collections

Before you begin creating sites, it's important to know which features you need to meet your goals. Your first choice is to create either one top-level site and several subsites as a single site collection or several independent top-level sites and subsites under each top-level site in multiple site collections. Figures 5-1 and 5-2 illustrate the differences.

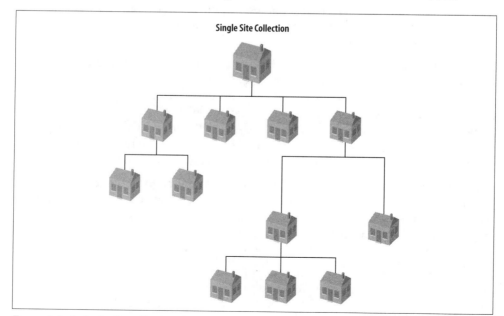

Figure 5-1. A single site collection showing one top-level site and several subsites

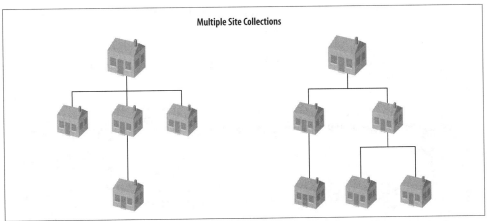

Figure 5-2. *Two separate site collections, each one containing a top-level site and several subsites*

Security is the primary driver of your choice of site structure. Separate site collections don't share the same navigation structure, elements, or parent permissions and must be administered separately. Table 5-1 demonstrates the differences.

Table 5-1. *Single and multiple site collection features*

Single site collection	Multiple site collections
Shares navigation.	Do not share navigation.
Subsites inherit permissions from parent site.	Permissions are not inherited among site collections.
Lists are shared within the site collection.	Lists are not shared among site collections.
Design elements are shared within the site collection.	Design elements are not shared among site collections.
The site collection resides in the same database.	Site collections can reside in separate databases.
The entire site collection must be backed up and restored.	An individual site collection can be backed up and restored without affecting other site collections.
The scope of workflow spans the site collection.	The scope of workflow is limited to within individual site collections.
The search scope spans the site collection.	The search scope is limited to within individual site collections.

Creating multiple site collections under your portal isn't absolutely necessary for the sake of security, and each subsite can have a different set of permissions from the parent site. However, if you want to make sure that no user in a group shares any access whatsoever to the data of another group, create a site collection for each group.

Site Creation and Management

Once SharePoint 2007 is installed on Windows Server 2003, the default site is created and located at *http://server_name/Pages/Default.aspx* (Figure 5-3). This is your top-level site. You can modify the content and presentation of this site to make it consistent with your business type and image. All sites you create under this site will be part of your organization's site collection.

 See Chapter 7 for more information about customizing the appearance of your site collection.

Figure 5-3. Default SharePoint site

All Site Content

Before creating new sites or modifying the default site, take a few minutes and tour the features of this site. Start with the lefthand Quick Launch menu and click the first link, View All Site Content.

As you can see in Figure 5-4, all of the standard Libraries, Lists, Discussion Boards, Surveys, and Sites and Workspaces already exist and are ready for you to use. For example, if you click on the Documents library, you are taken to an empty repository (Figure 5-5). No documents are created there by default, but you can easily upload documents from any source accessible on the server or the network. The Sites and Workspaces listed in the following sections are available to use with the default portal site.

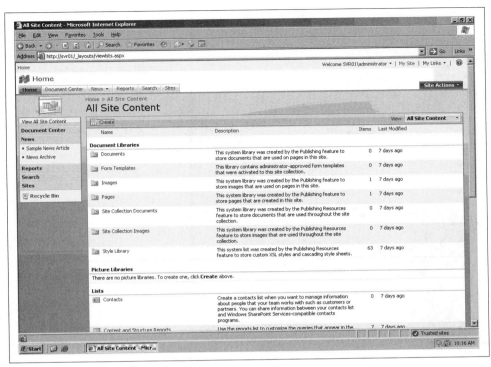

Figure 5-4. SharePoint All Site Content page

Document Center Site

Whereas the Documents Library in All Site Content acts as a collection point for all documents relevant to your site collection, the Document Center Site (Figure 5-6) exists as a management interface, allowing you to organize work related to site documents, announce upcoming tasks involving documentation, and assign work teams to these tasks.

News Site

You have a full-featured News site available to you. Included on this site is a sample news article, a news archive, and an RSS Viewer Web Part already added to the page (Figure 5-7).

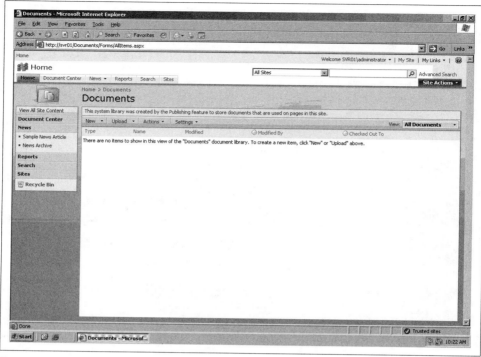

Figure 5-5. Empty Documents library

The Report Center

The Report Center (Figure 5-8) is at the heart of the MOSS 2007 Business Intelligence solution.

Learn more about Business Intelligence in Chapter 15.

The Report Center provides a single interface to organize a variety of business information types from sources scattered across the local network and the Internet.

Search

A built-in search engine is available, allowing you to look for and locate resources on your site (Figure 5-9).

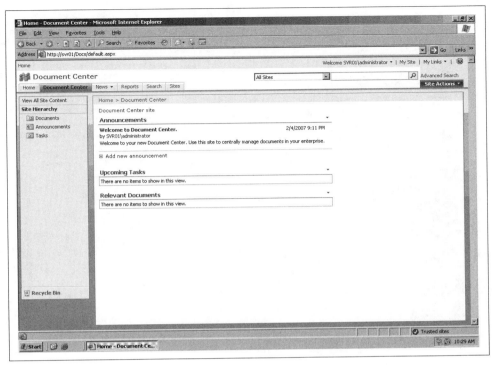

Figure 5-6. Document Center site

The Site Directory

The Site Directory (Figure 5-10) is the organizational interface to the site collection. From this page, you can manage all of the sites in the site collection and create new sites.

Determining Which Type of Site to Create

SharePoint provides a variety of site templates for different purposes. Before you create a site, you should plan out the structure by mapping your business needs to your site and subsite definitions. A good place to start is to revisit your organization's business goals. Determine which subset of your goals you want to address in the creation of this site or site collection.

Who Is the Target Audience?

Determining who will be using this site will help you decide what kind of security to establish, as well as the type and presentation of content material, which could include news, reports, and galleries. The target audience will also drive the level of

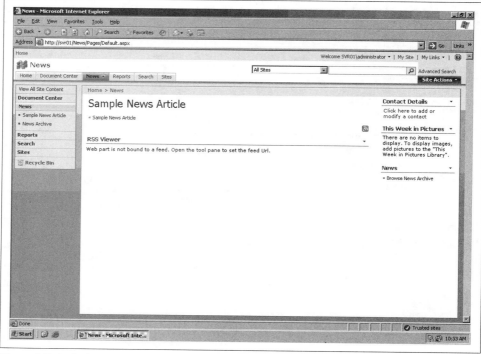

Figure 5-7. Default News site

site or sites you will create. For example, you will most likely create a top-level site for your entire organization and then subsites and My Sites for customers, the general public, teams, and individuals.

My Sites are addressed in Chapter 21.

What Site Content Will You Include?

The content for your top- and lower-level sites will vary depending on the intended audience of each site. You can create several types of Workspace sites to manage the content for each type of user. Workspace sites include:

- Document Workspace
- Basic Meeting Workspace
- Blank Workspace
- Decision Workspace
- Social Workspace
- Multipage Meeting Workspace

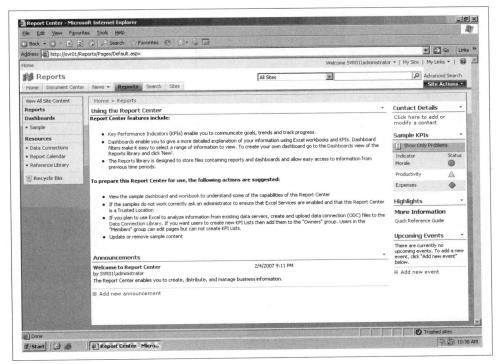

Figure 5-8. The Report Center

Workspace sites are presented in detail in Chapters 9 and 10.

Site Templates

You can also use site templates to control content on your sites. When creating a new site, SharePoint provides the following default site template categories:

- Collaboration
- Meetings
- Enterprise
- Publishing

Each template category contains several different site template types.

Find out more about site templates in Chapter 7.

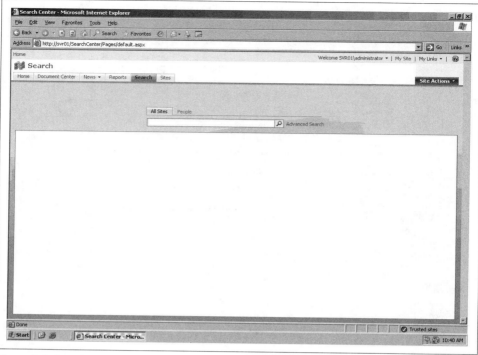

Figure 5-9. Search page

Site Navigation

Site navigation types are yet another way you can organize access to site content. Types of site navigation tools include:

- View All Site Content
- Quick Launch
- Tree View
- Top link bar
- Content breadcrumb bar
- Global breadcrumb bar

Establishing Site and Site Collection Access

If you are going to create a site for your company's management team, obviously you want only the management team to have access. There are a number of tools available in MOSS 2007 that you can use to create security groups and permissions. You can use them to limit access to any site based on the target audience.

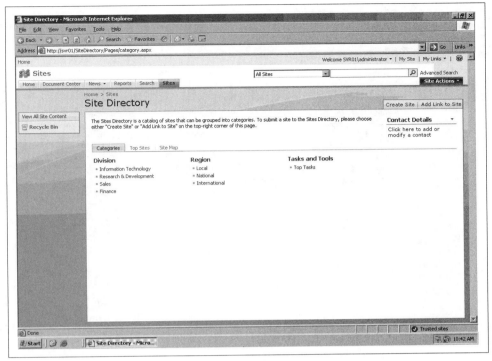

Figure 5-10. The Site Directory

 Discover more information about creating and managing groups and site security in Chapter 22.

Create a New Site Using Site Actions

There are several ways you can initiate site creation. One way is to use the Site Actions link (Figure 5-11), which is available from any page on your top-level site. The link is located near the upper-righthand corner of the page. Follow these steps:

1. Click Site Actions.
2. Click Create Site from the menu selections. This will open up the New SharePoint Site page (Figure 5-12).
3. In the Title field on the New SharePoint Site page, type the name of the site.
4. In the Description field, type a brief description of the site's purpose.
5. In the Web Site Address section, complete the URL for the site.
6. In the Template Selection section, choose a template, such as Collaboration.

Figure 5-11. Using Site Actions to create a site

7. In the template, select the type of site.

8. In the Permissions section (Figure 5-13), select the type of user permissions you want.

9. In the Navigation Inheritance section, determine which type of site navigation to use.

10. In the Site Categories section, decide whether to show this site in the site directory and whether to assign this site to one or more category types, and then click the appropriate checkboxes.

11. Scroll to the bottom of the page and click Create.

You will be taken to the "Operation in Progress" page while the new site is being created.

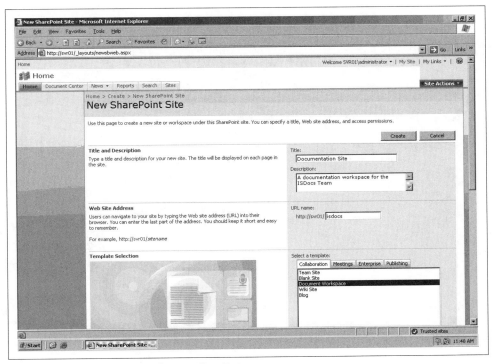

Figure 5-12. Creating a new subsite in SharePoint

Your first subsite of the top-level site has now been created (Figure 5-14) and is ready to be modified and receive content. This is the first site you've added to your site collection. Links to this site are now displayed on the top and sidebar menus on the top-level site.

Enabling Self-Service Site Creation

Self-Service Site Creation allows you to delegate the creation of SharePoint sites to users other than the administrator. This service also lets you create sites and site collections from inside the Site Directory, rather than from the top-level site home page or from Site Actions. You can enable Self-Service Site Creation only from the Central Administration page (Figure 5-15) at the top-level site.

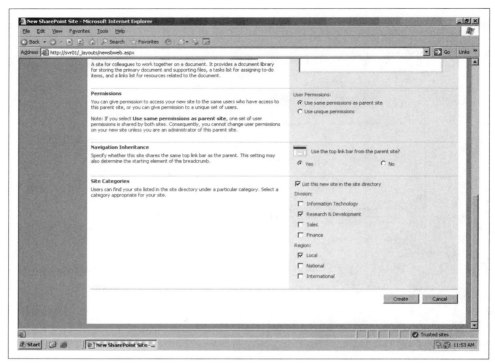

Figure 5-13. Selecting the type of user permissions you want

The default URL for the Central Administration site is *http://server_name: 47216/default.aspx*. There is no direct link from the top-level SharePoint site. The port number referenced in the URL can actually be any port number between 1 and 65535.

Also note, when you attempt to access the Central Administration page, you may be required to authenticate using the username and password of your administrator account.

1. Click Application Management.

2. On the Application Management page (Figure 5-16) under Application Security, click "Self-service site management."

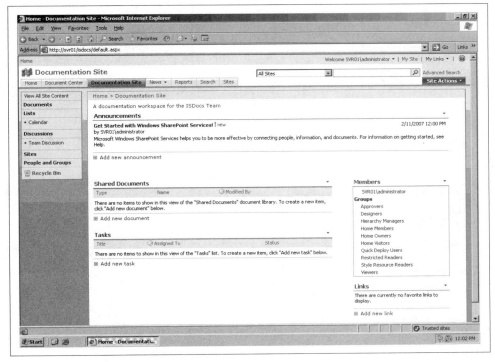

Figure 5-14. New SharePoint site

3. On the Self-Service Site Management page, click Web Application to change it.

4. On the Select Web Application page, choose the web application you want enabled for Self-Service Site Creation (Figure 5-17).

You can also require that users of Self-Service Site Creation supply the name of a secondary contact when creating a new site.

5. Click OK.

A link should be posted in the Announcement section of the top-level home page that users can click to create a new site.

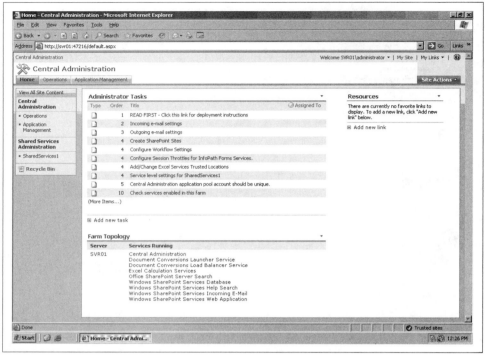

Figure 5-15. Central Administration page

Create Sites and Site Collections from the Site Directory

Creating sites and site collections from the Site Directory has several advantages. Creating a site, as we saw in the previous example, forces you to organize sites by site hierarchy rather than by some other structure. Although most Internet and intranet sites are organized this way, it may not be the optimal structure for your company. Using the Site Directory allows you to organize your sites by department or product type.

1. In the top navigation bar, click Sites.
2. On the Site Directory page, click Create Site, which is located in the upper-lefthand corner of the pane.
3. On the New SharePoint Site page, to create a Site Collection, replace the URL:

   http://server_name/SiteDirectory/_layouts/newsbweb.aspx

   with:

   http://server_name/SiteDirectory/_layouts/scsignup.aspx

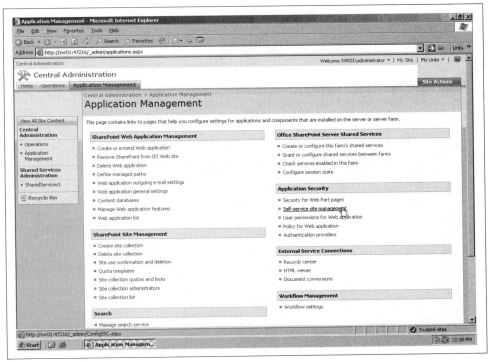

Figure 5-16. Application Management page

4. Continue configuring the page using the steps in the previous section, "Create a New Site Using Site Actions."

After you click Create, your new Site Collection is created (Figure 5-18).

Managing Sites from the Site Directory

Once you've created sites and site collections from the Site Directory, you can use the Directory to manage those sites. As a SharePoint administrator, you can use the Directory as your central interface to view the site collection structure, edit sites and site content, approve or reject new site creations, and delete sites.

View Site Collection Structure

There are two ways you can view the site collection structure from the Site Directory.

The first way is to click Site Map in the Site Directory. (See Figure 5-19.)

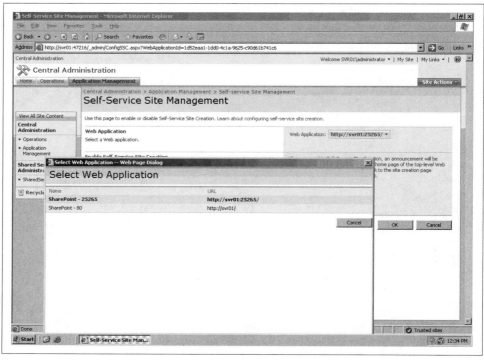

Figure 5-17. Select Web Application for Self-Service Site Creation

Notice that in Figure 5-19, you can see all of the default sites created when Share-Point was installed, as well as the Documentation Site and Software Development Site Collection created earlier in this chapter.

The second method of viewing the site collection structure from the Directory requires following these steps:

1. Click View All Site Content.

2. On the All Site Content page under Lists, click Sites.

 There is also a Sites link under "Sites and Workplaces" on the View All Site Contents page. However, it leads to the same Sites page you viewed when you clicked Sites directly from the Site Directory. Do not confuse these two links.

Notice that in this view (Figure 5-20), you can only see the sites and site collections that were created, not the default sites. You can also see the My Site setup, which is discussed in more detail in Chapter 21.

You can edit some of the features of these sites from this page by clicking to the right of a site title and then choosing an option from the menu (Figure 5-21).

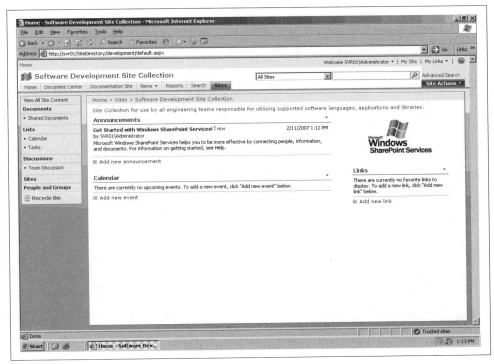

Figure 5-18. New Site Collection

Approving or Rejecting Sites

As you've just seen, one of the actions you can perform on the Sites page is to either approve or reject a pending site. With Self-Service Site Creation enabled, users other than the administrator can create a new site. However, once a site is created, its status is not final until an administrator either approves or rejects it. The approval process allows the administrator control of which sites will remain as part of the site collection.

To approve or reject a site:

1. On the Sites page (Figure 5-22), click to the right of the site you want to approve or reject.
2. Select Approve/Reject.
3. Select either Approve or Reject (the default selection is Pending).
4. Click OK to finalize your choice.

While still pending, the site was visible only to users with Manage Lists permissions or higher. Once approved, the site is visible to all users. If a site is rejected, it is not visible to any users and is returned to its creator.

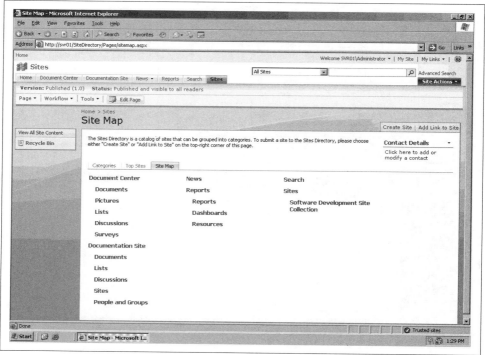

Figure 5-19. Site Map

Deleting Sites

Sites aren't always meant to be permanent. Some sites are created for the lifespan of a particular project, and once that project is over, the site can be terminated. Deleting a site is a fairly simple process:

1. On the Sites page, click to the right of the title to open the menu.
2. Select Delete Item.
3. Click OK when the confirmation dialog box appears.

The site is deleted and removed from the Sites list.

 The deleted site is sent to the Recycle Bin and can be restored from there as long as it remains in the bin. Once it's deleted from the Recycle Bin, it's gone forever.

Editing Sites

You can edit the properties of any site in the site collection:

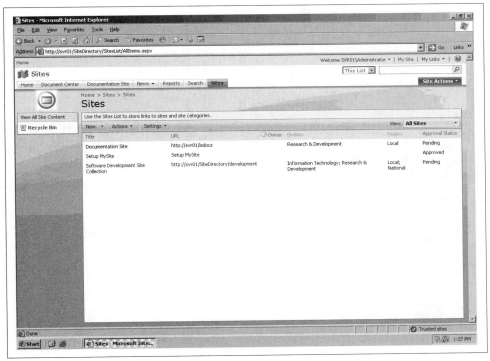

Figure 5-20. All Sites page

1. On the Sites page, click to the right of the title of the site you want to edit.

2. Select Edit Item.

   On this page, you can modify or delete the following properties of the site:

   - Title
   - Division
   - Description
   - Region
   - URL
   - Top Site
   - Tasks and Tools
   - Owner
   - Link Status

3. Click OK to save your changes.

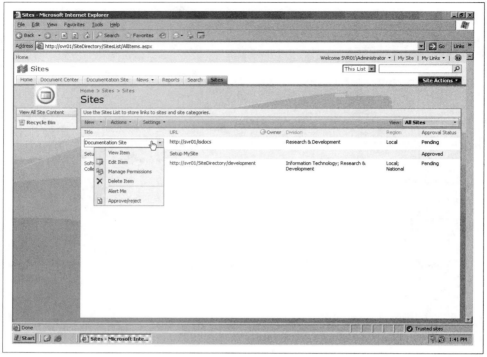

Figure 5-21. Editing Sites on the Sites page

After you modify the site's properties, you will have to approve it again on the Sites page.

Promoting a Top Site

Of all the sites you'll create in your Enterprise environment, there are sure to be certain key sites you'll want users to know about and be able to find easily. You can promote a site to Top Site on the Sites page found under Lists:

1. On the Sites page, click to the right of the title of the site you want to promote.
2. Select Edit Item.
3. Scroll down the page until you see the Top Site category.
4. Click the checkbox.
5. Click OK.

When you return to the Site Directory, click on Top Sites. The site you promoted will be on the list.

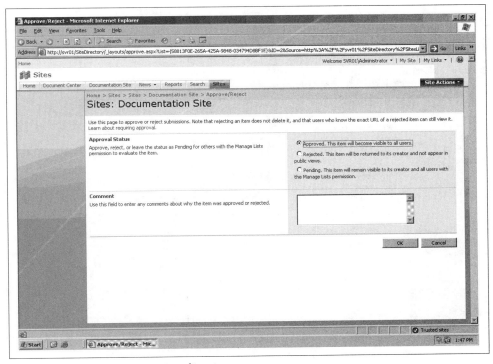

Figure 5-22. Approve or reject a pending site

Editing a Site Directly from the Site

You can modify a wide variety of settings directly from within the site:

1. From the top-level site, click the link to the site you want to edit.
2. Click Site Actions, and select Site Settings from the menu (Figure 5-23).

You can select the links under any of the categories to edit the site.

Show New Categories on the Create Site Page

As you may have noticed, the default categories available on the site creation page are pretty limited. Fortunately, SharePoint gives you the option to show additional categories.

1. In the Site Directory, click Site Actions.
2. On the Menu, select Site Settings, and then select Modify All Site Settings (Figure 5-24). This takes you to the same page you visited in the previous section of this chapter, "Editing a Site Directly from the Site."

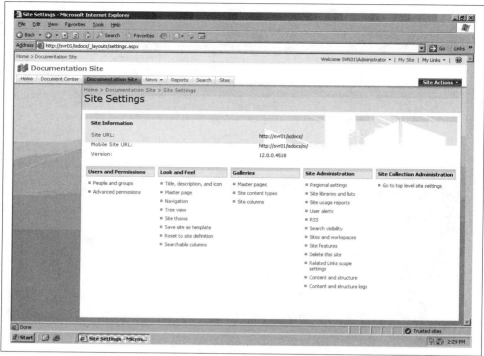

Figure 5-23. Site Settings page

3. In the Site Administration column, click "Site Libraries and Lists."

4. On the "Site Libraries and Lists" page, click Customize Sites.

5. On the Customize Sites page, in the Views section, click Site Creation Categories. (It's near the bottom of the page, so depending on your screen resolution, you may have to scroll down to see it.)

6. In the Columns section (Figure 5-25), select the checkboxes for any category you want to appear on the Create Site page. (Notice that the default selections Division and Region are already checked.)

7. In the Position from Left column, you can use the drop-down arrows to choose the order in which each category will appear from left to right.

8. When you are finished, click OK.

 Remember that once you make these changes, the site will need to be approved again.

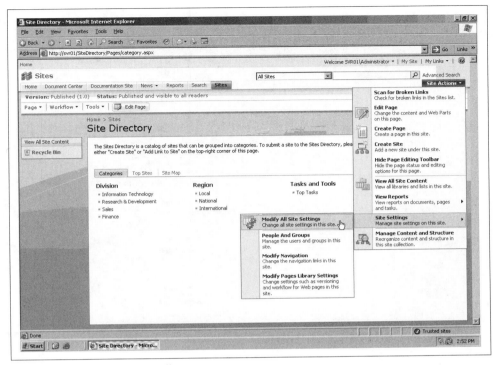

Figure 5-24. Selecting Modify All Site Settings

Add or Edit Site Directory Categories

Just as the default categories on the Create Site page are limited, so are those available on the Site Directory page. SharePoint allows you to add or edit the categories on this page to suit your needs.

Add a New Category

1. On the Site Category page, click Site Actions.

2. Select Edit Page from the menu.

3. In the Categories box (Figure 5-26), click Create New Category. Figure 5-27 demonstrates the options for a new category.

4. Type the name of the new category in the "Column name" field.

5. Under the Title field, select the Choice radio button.

6. Add a description in the Description field.

7. Select Yes under "Require that this column contains information."

Figure 5-25. Edit View: Sites page

8. In the "Type each choice on a separate line" field, replace the text "Enter Choice #1," "Enter Choice #2," and "Enter Choice #3" with your selections. Type each selection on a separate line in the box.

9. Under "Display choices using," click "Checkboxes (allow multiple selections)."

10. Select the "Add to default view" checkbox.

11. Click OK.

When you return to the Site Directory page, you will see the new category added, along with the selections under it.

Edit or Delete Categories in Site Directory

1. On the Site Directory page, click Site Actions.

2. Select Edit Page from the menu.

3. In the Categories box, click Edit Sites and Categories.

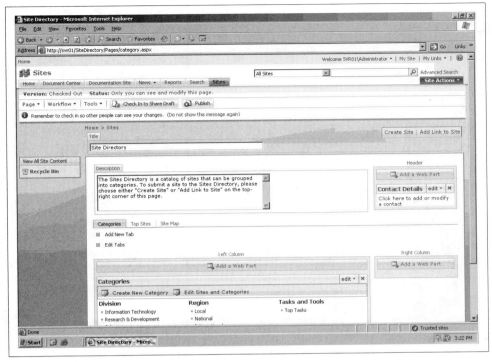

Figure 5-26. Creating a new category

4. On the Sites page, click Settings and then select List Settings from the menu (Figure 5-28).

5. On the Customize Sites page, under Columns, click the name of the category you want to edit.

6. On the Change Columns page, modify the available settings and options.

You are editing the same page that you originally configured, as shown in Figure 5-27.

7. Click OK to save your changes.

There is a Delete button available if you want to delete this category.

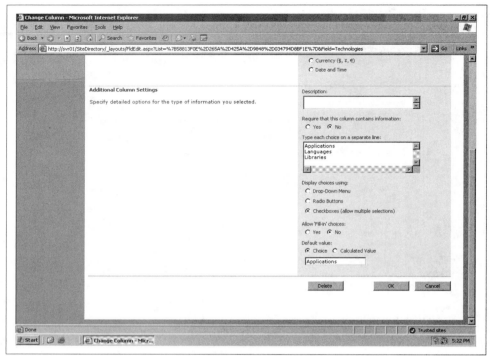

Figure 5-27. Selecting options for a new category

Scan for Broken Links in Site Directory

When you create a site under your top-level site, links are automatically generated to the new sites. If sites are moved in the hierarchy and the links aren't modified to reflect the move, those links will be broken and will not lead you to the site. SharePoint offers you the option of scanning for broken links in the Site Directory:

1. In the Site Directory, click Site Actions and then select "Scan for Broken Links."

2. On the Broken Site Directory Links page, click the menu arrow under View and choose an option. The available options are:

   - All Sites
   - Broken Sites
   - Categories
   - Rejected Sites
   - Site Creation Categories
   - Submitted Sites

3. Click OK to start the scan. The scan will return the number of broken site links, nonbroken site links, and unknown links.

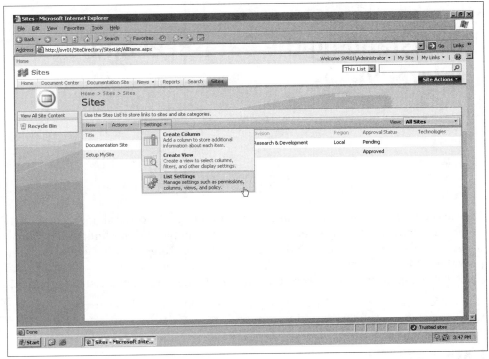

Figure 5-28. Changing site settings

4. When the scan is finished, click OK.

You will be taken to the Sites page using the Broken Links view. If there are no broken links, this view will be empty.

 You'll learn more about views and filters in Chapter 13.

Conclusion

As you can see, you have a great deal of latitude in how you create and organize your main site and site collections. All the sites in your collection can have a common purpose, or they can be separately configured to serve the needs of different departments or different companies. You can even create public and private site collections so that SharePoint can serve as your organization's Internet portal for customers and you can simultaneously reserve a separate collection to service the internal needs of your business. SharePoint sites are as dynamic as your business: when your needs change, so can your site. MOSS 2007 leaves you in full control of how your sites provide for your requirements and goals.

CHAPTER 6

Understanding the Datasheet and Explorer Views

Lists and document libraries are fundamental building blocks for almost every Share-Point site. Unfortunately, the default view is fairly simple and has limited functionality with regards to adding, updating, deleting, or organizing data. SharePoint provides two views that create an alternate interface for examining your structured data. This chapter demonstrates some of the powerful features associated with each.

If you aren't familiar with lists, you might want to skip ahead to Chapter 14 to read more about the various types and features of lists.

Datasheet View

The Datasheet view (Figure 6-1) displays data from a list or document library in grid format, similar to that of Microsoft Excel. The advantage of a datasheet is that the Excel-like interface provides the same easy methods of inserting, editing, and deleting data but still uses the data validation that is part of a list or document library.

The features of the Datasheet view depend on which version of Microsoft Office is currently installed on the machine accessing the SharePoint site.

A Datasheet view is automatically created with each new list or document library. Additional Datasheet views can be created in compatible lists or document libraries by using the Create View menu option available from the Settings toolbar menu option.

In this chapter, we focus on the following aspects of the Datasheet view:

- What's new for the Datasheet view
- System requirements and browser compatibility
- How to work with the data
- Toolbar
- Task Pane

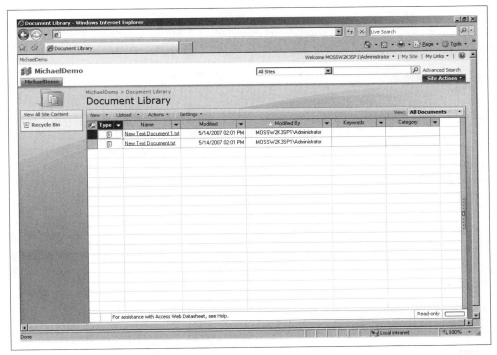

Figure 6-1. Datasheet view

System Requirements and Browser Compatibility

The Datasheet view relies on several client applications, and you must allow the browser to run Microsoft ActiveX controls. If all the requirements are not met, then the option will not be available in the Actions menu from the Standard view. Microsoft Office and Internet Explorer applications are required, as well as Microsoft Office List Datasheet Component or Microsoft Office Access Web Datasheet Component, depending on which version of Microsoft Office is running. The following sections detail the requirements.

Microsoft Office 2007

- Microsoft Office 2007 installed
- Microsoft Office Access Web Datasheet Component installed
- Internet Explorer 5.01 with Service Pack 2 or higher installed
- Browser support for ActiveX controls

Microsoft Office 2003

- Microsoft Office 2003 Professional installed
- Microsoft Office List Datasheet Component installed
- Internet Explorer 5.01 with Service Pack 2 or higher installed
- Browser support for ActiveX controls

The Microsoft Internet Explorer browser 5.01 with Service Pack 2 or higher is the only browser able to support the Datasheet view because it is still an ActiveX control. The "Edit in Datasheet" menu option under the Actions menu will appear only if the browser supports the requirements. This extra feature is very helpful because the user no longer sees the menu option and therefore gets no error message when the system doesn't meet the requirements.

Datasheet view availability in List Templates

The Datasheet view is not available in all of Microsoft's prebuilt list templates. Table 6-1 indicates the list templates that have and don't have the Datasheet view capability.

Table 6-1. Microsoft's prebuilt list template

Datasheet view capable		Datasheet view noncapable
Agenda	Objectives	Calendar
Announcements	Project Tasks	Discussion Board
Contacts	Report Library	KPI List
Custom List	Sites List	Picture Library
Data Connection Library	Slide Library	Survey
Decisions	Tabs List	Text Box
Document Library	Tasks	
Form Library	Things to Bring	
Issue Tracking	Translation Management Library	
Languages and Translators	Wiki Page Library	
Links		

Working with the Datasheet Table and Data

This section covers some of the details on how to work with the data in the datasheet table and the features that it uses to validate and populate new data that has been inserted. The datasheet table is similar to an Excel worksheet. Only the first 100 rows of data are retrieved, and the rest of the data is retrieved asynchronously when first opened. When retrieving for sorting or filtering, then all data is retrieved and displayed in the requested way. The status bar gives visual notification when it is working (the connection box will have a moving green line in it), and there is a status bar located at the bottom of the datasheet table.

A data conflict or error could occur when adding data using the Datasheet view (Figures 6-2 and 6-3).

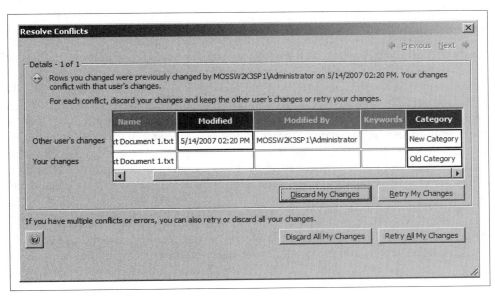

Figure 6-2. Resolve conflicts

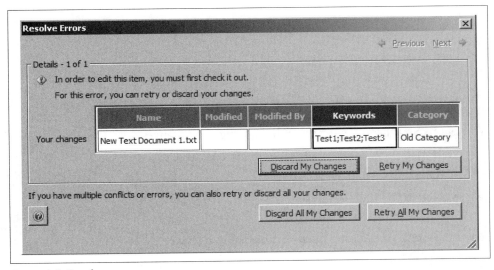

Figure 6-3. Resolve errors

For example, data conflicts can occur when two people are editing the same column, row, or cell at the same time. When this happens, the data conflict icon appears on the row or rows that contain the conflict and in the first column on the status bar. The third column text also changes to "You have data conflicts with another user. Resolve." When an error occurs, the error icon appears on the row or rows that have the data conflict and in the second column on the status bar. The third column text also changes to "You have errors. Resolve."

The word "Resolve" and any of the icons are links to launch the Resolve Conflicts or Resolve Errors pop-up windows. The pop-up windows give details of the conflicts or errors, and contain the Discard My Changes, Retry My Changes, Discard All My Changes, and Retry All My Changes options, along with the help option. When there are multiple conflicts or errors, each item can be seen by using the Previous or Next options in the upper-right corner of the pop-up window. If there is only one conflict or error, then these options are grayed out. You can magnify any cell inside the table that displays the row or rows by hovering over the cell and then clicking it when the magnifying glass appears. The item in question will have a dark black box around it.

The Discard My Changes and Retry My Changes options are for the current conflict or error being displayed in the details section of the pop-up window, and the Discard All My Changes and Retry All My Changes options are for all the conflicts or errors that have been identified. The Help button launches the Access Web Datasheet Help application.

Errors can occur when you:

- Open a Datasheet view
- View or edit data in the view
- View or edit the list structure
- View or edit the view definition

Types of errors

You can resolve the following errors by retrying your changes:

- No response from the server. This could be because of a timeout.
- Server is busy or cannot be found.
- Server response is not legible.
- Any other unexpected error.

You can resolve these errors by discarding your changes:

- You do not have the necessary permissions to make the change.
- You have been blocked from adding content to the site.
- You have exceeded your storage limits for the site.

Additional detailed information on resolving data conflicts or errors can be found by clicking any of the help links.

Another detail worth mentioning is the ability to move columns by left-clicking and dragging them to a different location. This option prevents you from having to go to the View Properties screen to make the changes. To move the columns, navigate to a list or document library Datasheet view. Hover over a column name until the "Move" pointer (a four-prong icon) appears. Click and drag the column to the desired location and then release the mouse button—the column has been moved. Something to keep in mind when moving columns from the Datasheet view is that it changes the properties of the current view permanently. When you switch back to "Show in Standard View," the column will appear in the new position.

If you fall into a repetitive error cycle when working on a task with the table, column, row, or cell, click to display the task pane, then click the Undo button to back out to the original state. Undo is an option until the change has been successfully committed.

Table

If you highlight the whole table by clicking on the Access icon in the upper-left corner of the table, the following menu options are present:

Cut
> The Cut menu is unavailable when the table is highlighted.

Copy
> The Copy menu acts just like any other Microsoft Office application Copy function. In all the different scenarios I tried, it was available and allowed for the highlighted data to be copied.

Paste
> The Paste menu acts just like any other Microsoft Office application Paste function, but when you're pasting into any datasheet table, all validation rules will be enforced. For example, if you copy data from a table and paste it into another that uses Check-in and Check-out, the warning message "The selected cells are read-only" will be displayed.

Add Column
> The Add Column menu takes you to the Create Column screen and allows for a new column to be created. Fill in the desired information and click OK to create the column. If the default view is being used, leave the "Add to default view" checkbox checked, and the column will appear in the datasheet table. If the default view is not being used, you will have to manually update the view to make the new column show up.

Unhide
> The Unhide menu is available only when one or more columns are hidden on the datasheet table. If multiple columns are hidden, all of them will appear if you click this option.

Column Width

The Column Width menu will adjust all highlighted columns to the specified width. Once this option is used, there is no automatic way to convert the columns back to the original width without doing so manually; even switching back to the Standard view or closing the browser doesn't reset the columns to the original width.

Turn Wrap Text Off

The Turn Wrap Text Off menu does exactly what it implies—it doesn't wrap the text if it is longer than the column width. For example, if you turn wrap text off and the column has been modified to a length of 10, but data in the column is typically longer than 20 characters, nothing after 10 is visible unless the field is in Edit Mode.

Fill

The Fill menu has two submenu options, AutoFill and Fill Down, neither of which are available when the full datasheet table is highlighted. These options are available only when a column or cell is highlighted.

Alert Me

The Alert Me menu opens the New Alert page, allowing for configuration. The New Alert page in this instance allows for the Alert Title, Send Alerts To, Change Type, Send Alerts for These Changes, and When to Send Alerts sections to be adjusted. When everything is correct, click OK to create the alert.

Help

The Help menu launches the Access Web Datasheet Help application.

About

The About menu launches the About Access Web Datasheet pop-up window. This pop-up window is similar to all the other Microsoft application About pop-up windows.

Column

By hovering over the column title and clicking it when the down arrow pointer appears, the whole column is highlighted and the following menu options are available. A brief description is listed for each:

Cut

The Cut menu is not available when the full column is highlighted.

Copy

The Copy menu acts just like any other Microsoft Office application Copy function. In all the different scenarios I tried, it was available and allowed for the highlighted data to be copied.

Paste

The Paste menu acts just like any other Microsoft Office application Paste function, but when you're pasting into any datasheet column, all validation rules will be enforced. For example, if pasting a string column into a URL column, you're given the warning message "Field 'URL' contains invalid data. Enter a valid URL."

Add Column

The Add Column menu takes you to the Create Column screen and allows for a new column to be created. Fill in the desired information and click OK to create the column. If the default view is being used, leave the "Add to default view" checkbox checked, and the column will appear in the datasheet table. If the default view is not being used, you will have to manually update the view to make the new column show up.

Edit/Delete Column

The Edit/Delete Column menu opens the Change Column page and allows for editing of column properties. The properties can be different for each data type. At the bottom of this screen, the Delete button will be available if the column can be deleted. Columns required by the list or document library will not have this option.

Column Width

The Column Width menu will adjust all highlighted columns to the specified width. Once this option is used, there is no automatic way to convert the columns back to the original width without doing so manually; even switching back to the Standard view or closing the browser doesn't reset the columns to the original width.

Hide

The Hide menu hides the column from the Datasheet view. The column is still really there, but the width has been set to zero to make it appear hidden. You can restore the column to its original width by hovering over it and clicking the Unhide menu option, by navigating to the Standard view and then back to Datasheet view, or just by refreshing the page by clicking the browser's refresh button.

Unhide

The Unhide menu makes the hidden column reappear. This option is only available when a hidden column is highlighted.

Turn Wrap Text Off

The Turn Wrap Text Off menu option does exactly what it implies—it doesn't wrap the text if it is longer than the column width. Once this option has been applied, it will not convert back unless it is executed again. This option is useful when a column spans multiple lines but allows only, say, 10 rows to appear on screen. By using this menu for that column, you can turn the multiple lines of text into a single line, allowing for more rows to appear on the screen at once.

Fill

The Fill menu has two submenu options, AutoFill and Fill Down:

AutoFill

AutoFill fills in the blank cells after the last populated cell by using all populated cells above the first blank cell. For example, say you have a datasheet view with 10 rows and one column that has values only for the first two cells, m and n. If you highlight that column and use the option AutoFill, the remaining eight columns will be autopopulated with the pattern of m and n values.

Fill Down

Fill Down fills in all cells in the column with the value from the first cell.

Help

The Help menu launches the Access Web Datasheet Help application.

Row

If you hover over the first (gray) cell in a row and click when the right arrow pointer appears, the whole row is highlighted, and the following menu options are available (some of these menu options are specific to a list or document library and its configuration settings):

Cut

The Cut menu removes the highlighted row from the datasheet table.

Copy

The Copy menu copies the highlighted row of data.

Paste

The Paste menu pastes a row or rows into the current datasheet, unless validation rules are not met.

Open Folder

The Open Folder menu opens the selected folder.

Delete Folder

The Delete Folder menu deletes the selected folder. A message is given advising that all subfolders and documents will be deleted and moved to the Recycle Bin before the command is completed.

Add Row

The Add Row menu adds a new row into the datasheet table. This option is handy when the new blank row is not visible on the screen—using this option will move the screen down to that row.

Delete Rows

The Delete Rows menu deletes all highlighted rows and moves them into the Recycle Bin. It will ask for a confirmation before deleting the selected rows. The Delete Rows menu option is available only for list types.

Delete Document

The Delete Document menu deletes the highlighted documents and moves them into the Recycle Bin. It will ask for a confirmation before deleting the selected documents. The Delete Document menu option is available only for document library types.

Row Height

The Row Height menu resets the row height for all rows in the datasheet table. This option will not work for a single row.

Fill

The Fill menu has two submenu options, AutoFill and Fill Down:

AutoFill

The AutoFill option fills in the blank cells after the last populated cell by using all populated cells above the first blank cell. For example, say you have a datasheet view with 10 rows and one column that has values only for the first two cells, m and n. If you highlight that column and use the option AutoFill, the remaining eight columns will be autopopulated with the pattern of m and n values.

Fill Down

The Fill Down option fills in all cells in the column with the value from the first cell.

Export Contact

The Export Contact menu is available when working with the Contact List type. The contact is exported out in vCard format.

Item

The Item menu has a single option, Versions, which appears on the menu only when versioning has been turned on. The Item menu option is specific to list types and will not appear on document library types.

Document

The Document menu has the following submenu options:

Open Document (Read-Only)

The Open Document (Read-only) menu allows for the document to be opened in read-only mode and will not allow for editing. If you are using Microsoft Word 2007, the document will open but will not allow you to type any new text into it. If you need to edit the text, you can click the Edit Document button in the message bar.

Edit Document

The Edit Document menu option opens the document in Edit Mode.

Check Out Document

The Check Out Document menu checks the document out to you. If the document is opened by someone else, it will be in read-only mode and is not editable by anyone else until it's checked back in.

Check In Document

The Check In Document menu checks back in a checked-out document. This option is not available if the document is not checked out.

Document Versions

The Document Versions menu opens the "Versions saved for" page that displays all the versions for that document. This menu option is not available if the document library does not have versioning turned on.

Discuss

The Discuss menu uses the browser base discussion feature that is available only from the Datasheet view. This feature may not work depending on how the document type is being opened. This option is available only in document library types.

Alert Me

The Alert Me menu opens the New Alert page, allowing for configuration. The New Alert page in this instance allows for the Alert Title, Send Alerts To, Change Type, Send Alerts for These Changes, and When to Send Alerts sections to be modified. When everything is correct, click OK to create the alert.

Help

The Help menu launches the Access Web Datasheet Help application.

Cell

When you make a cell active, the following menus are available (some of these menu options are specific to a list or document library and its configuration settings):

Cut

The Cut menu cuts the content out of a regular cell and makes it available for pasting. There are many field types—for example, Boolean and Calculation fields—that will not allow the content of the cell to be cut but still allow for it to be copied and available for pasting.

Copy

The Copy menu copies the content of an active cell and makes it available for pasting.

Paste

The Paste menu pastes a cell's content into another cell with the same column type if validation rules allow it. If the pasting of the data is not allowed, then a

"You cannot perform this operation on a…" warning pop-up box will appear. Almost any field type that is copied or cut can be pasted into a string data type. For example, if you copy a checkbox cell and paste the value into a string cell, then the value will be either 0 or 1.

Open Folder

The Open Folder menu opens the selected folder.

Delete Folder

The Delete Folder menu deletes the selected folder. A message is given advising that all subfolders and documents will be deleted and moved to the Recycle Bin before executing the command.

Add Row

The Add Row menu adds a new row into the datasheet table. The ideal situation to use this option is when the new blank row is not visible on the screen and using this option moves the screen down to that row.

Delete Rows

The Delete Rows menu deletes all selected rows and moves them into the Recycle Bin. The Delete Rows menu option is available only for list types.

Delete Document

The Delete Document menu deletes the document associated with the active cell and moves it into the Recycle Bin. The Delete Document menu option is available only for document library types.

Add Column

The Add Column menu takes you to the Create Column page and allows for a new column to be created. Fill in the desired information and click OK to create the column. Leave the "Add to default view" checkbox checked to add the column to the default view automatically. The new column will be inserted to the right of the active cell.

Edit/Delete Column

The Edit/Delete Column menu opens the Change Column screen and allows for editing of column properties. The properties can be different for each data type. At the bottom of this screen, the Delete button will be available if the column can be deleted. Required columns can't be deleted, so the button will not appear.

Fill

The Fill menu has two submenu options, AutoFill and Fill Down:

AutoFill

The AutoFill option fills in the blank cells after the last populated cell by using all populated cells above the first blank cell. For example, say you have a datasheet view with 10 rows and one column that has values only for the first two cells, m and n. If you highlight that column and use the option AutoFill, the remaining eight columns will be autopopulated with the pattern of m and n values.

Fill Down

The Fill Down option fills in all cells in the column with the value from the first cell.

Pick From List

The Pick From List menu makes available existing values that have been entered into that column. This option is not available for data types.

Export Contact

The Export Contact menu is available when working with the Contact List type. The contact is exported out in vCard format.

Item

The Item menu has a single submenu option, Versions, which appears on the menu only when versioning has been turned on for the list. The Item menu option is specific to list types and will not appear on document library types.

Document

The Document menu has the following submenu options:

Open Document (Read-Only)

The Open Document (Read-only) menu opens the document in read-only mode and will not allow for editing. If you need to edit, click Edit Document in the message bar.

Edit Document

The Edit Document menu opens the document for editing.

Check Out Document

The Check Out Document menu option checks the document out to you. If the document is opened by someone else, it will be in read-only mode and is not editable by anyone else until it's checked back in.

Check In Document

The Check In Document menu checks back in a checked-out document. This option is not available if the document is not checked out.

Document Versions

The Document Versions menu opens the "Versions saved for" page and displays all the versions for that document. This menu option is not available if the document library does not have versioning turned on.

Discuss

The Discuss menu uses the browser base discussion feature that is available only from the Datasheet view. This feature may not work depending on how the document type is being opened. This option is available only in document library types.

Alert Me

The Alert Me menu operates the same way as the row Alert Me menu and does not allow for single cell alerts.

Help

The Help menu launches the Access Web Datasheet Help application.

Status bar

As mentioned earlier, the Status bar displays:

- A data conflict icon and message text with a link to the data conflict resolve pop-up window
- An error icon and message text with a link to the data conflict resolve pop-up window
- A Help link supplied by Microsoft
- A message if data is read-only
- The connection status

The status bar will display a calculation formula when either the column or a cell in that column is selected. This feature is very helpful in identifying whether the column is built from a calculation.

All the options are pretty self-explanatory, and determining whether the data is editable or not is pretty simple. If the data can't be edited, the text "Read-only" will appear next to the connection box on the far righthand side of the status bar. For example, system columns in the datasheet table can't be edited, so "Read-only" should appear if you click them.

Toolbar

The menu toolbar for SharePoint 2007 has been changed to use a category-style menu that groups all menu options and expands to display the available ones. A drop-down list has been added for displaying the available views. Unlike the previous version, the menu toolbar now filters out menu options that aren't compatible with a user's browser or machine.

The menu toolbar now displays three or four different menu categories, depending on the level of security assigned and the type of list or document library being viewed.

List

New

The New menu allows you to create a new item. When the Content Types option is used, multiple items will appear under the menu. New Item usually appears as the default item, but there are exceptions—for example, Discussion Board list types use Discussion instead.

Actions

The Actions menu lists all the options available for that type of list. For example, when the Announcement template is used to create a list, the Actions menu items from the Datasheet view are: Show in Standard View, New Row, Task Pane, Totals, Refresh Data, Export to Spreadsheet, Open in Access, View RSS

Feed, and Alert Me. When you're using a Contacts list, the Connect to Outlook item is also available.

Settings

The Settings menu has Create Column, Create View, and List Settings menu items.

Document Library

New

The New menu creates a new document or folder. The type of document is determined when the library is created. Additional document types can be added by creating and adding new Content Types to the library.

Upload

The Upload menu has Upload Document and Upload Multiple Documents menu items.

Actions

The Actions menu lists all the available options for that type of document library. For example, when the Document Library template is used, the Open with Windows Explorer, Show in Standard View, New Row, Task Pane, Totals, Refresh Data, Connect to Outlook, Export to Spreadsheet, View RSS Feed, and Alert Me options are available. If the Wiki Page Library template was used, the Open with Windows Explorer option is not available.

Settings

The Settings menu has Create Column, Create View, and Document Library Settings menu items.

A couple of options from the menu toolbar worth mentioning are Totals and Connect to Outlook:

Totals

The Totals menu makes the total row appear, and it will stay visible until the menu option is used again. The total row gives basic totaling functionality to all columns. The available options for each column can be displayed by clicking the "total now" row cell for that column. For most data types, two options will be available: None and Count. For data types of Number and Currency, eight options are available: None, Average, Count, Maximum, Minimum, Sum, Standard Deviation, and Variance.

Connect to Outlook

The "Connect to Outlook" menu is not available for all list and document library types. When it is available, it gives the capability to synchronize items and make them available offline. Calendar, Contacts, Tasks, and Document Library are a few types that have this capability. This option provides a taste of offline synchronization.

There will be occasions when other menus will appear on the toolbar. An example of this is the Slide Library, which has the Copy Slide to Presentation menu.

A good example of security-sensitive menus is when a user assigned to the reader roll of a list is able to see only the Actions menu and not any other Toolbar menu. The reverse is also true; if you are the site collection administrator, you would be able to see New, Actions, and Settings menus for that list.

In my opinion, the reason for the new style of menus is because the lists and document libraries of SharePoint 2007 now have more menu options available, depending on security level, browser compatibility, and type of list or document library.

The menu option differences in the Actions menu are very evident when looking at a library created from the Document Library template versus a library created from the Slide Library template (see Figures 6-4 and 6-5).

Figure 6-4. Document Library Actions menu options

The navigation of the current list or document library links has been moved from the lefthand side of the screen to the righthand side of the menu toolbar in a drop-down list. The drop-down list also gives the capability to modify the current view and create a new view. The Modify and Create options are also available from the Settings menu.

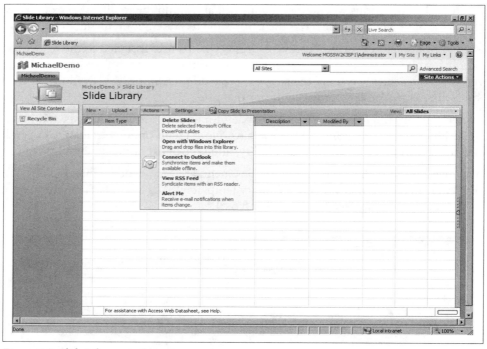

Figure 6-5. Slide Library Actions menu options

If a user accesses the Datasheet view for a document library and doesn't have Microsoft Outlook 2007 installed on his machine, he won't see the menu option Connect to Outlook under the Actions menu. In the previous version of SharePoint, all toolbar menus would be visible but would display a warning message if used without the proper software or browser. This improved feature should make life a lot easier on IT teams because they will no longer have to explain why the menu option is available to click on but doesn't work.

Task Pane

The Task Pane (Figure 6-6) is one of the most powerful tools of the Datasheet view because of its capacity for doing quick reporting and charting with Microsoft Office Access and Excel. These features are often underutilized by many organizations simply because they are hidden until the Task Pane menu link is clicked from the Actions menu or the Show Task Pane menu bar is expanded.

The Task Pane consists of two categories of options that can be used with the data displayed in the Datasheet view: common options and Office Links.

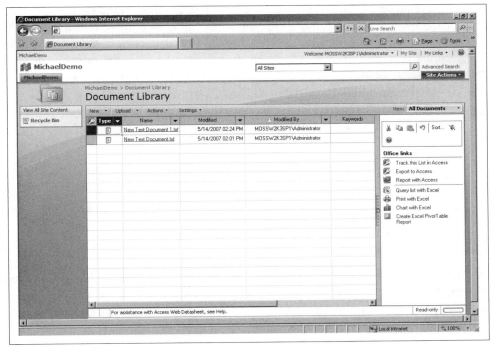

Figure 6-6. Document Library Actions menu options

Common options are:

- Cut
- Copy
- Paste
- Undo
- Sort
- Filter
- Help

All these options are also available from a Column menu in Datasheet view, the right-click menu within the Datasheet view, or through keyboard shortcuts.

 For a list of all the keyboard shortcuts, open Help from the Datasheet view and navigate to "Keyboard shortcuts" under Office List Datasheet View 2007, "Startup and settings," and Accessibility.

The Task Pane grays out the options when they are not available for use. For instance, the Undo option is available only when changing content on the datasheet table and is unavailable once the changes have been committed. If you are changing the formula of a column and you want to convert it back to the original formula before the changes are committed, click the Undo button. Then tab off the cell to have the changes commit.

Office Links consist of:

- Track this List in Access
- Export to Access
- Report with Access
- Query list with Excel
- Print with Excel
- Chart with Excel
- Create Excel Pivot Table Report

All the Office Links options are available only from the Task Pane. The options are always available to click even if the corresponding Microsoft Office application is not installed. The messages:

> This operation cannot be performed because a compatible version of Microsoft Office Access either is not installed on this computer, or it is not the default version.

and

> This operation cannot be performed because a compatible version of Microsoft Office Excel either is not installed on this computer, or it is not the default version.

are displayed if the respective Microsoft application is not installed or compatible.

If you're a previous user of SharePoint 2003 and Microsoft Office 2003, you're well aware of integration with Microsoft Excel 2003. When going through the details of each of the following options, you will notice that some of the two-way integration switched to Microsoft Access 2007 and was removed from Microsoft Excel 2007. (When I discovered this during my initial testing last year, I was not too enthused but quickly changed my mind because of all the great improvements in Microsoft Access 2007 and SharePoint 2007.)

The sections that follow give additional information about each option available under Office Links.

Track this List in Access

"Track this List in Access" provides a richer environment for working with Share-Point list data because of the new and improved features of Microsoft Access 2007, which make it a lot more enjoyable then the previous version.

This feature takes the current SharePoint List and the User Information List and creates or uses an existing Microsoft Access 2007 Database and adds the SharePoint lists as linked tables. Double-clicking one of the linked tables in Navigation Pane brings the datasheet into the righthand side of the window, and the Datasheet menu also appears. If you click the "Datasheet" menu, the menu ribbon appears. More menus can be found by right-clicking the SharePoint list name in the Navigation Pane and choosing SharePoint List Options.

Another big push with this version of SharePoint and Office is offline capabilities. This feature allows users to work offline once the SharePoint list tables have been linked to a Microsoft Access database by clicking the "Online with SharePoint" menu option and then clicking the Work Offline menu option. The "Online with SharePoint" menu option can be found on the righthand corner of the status bar. The Work Offline and Work Online menu buttons can also be found on the External Data menu ribbon on the far right side. There are several other menu options on the ribbon to help with synchronization, caching, and relinking to the SharePoint list.

While working with this capability, the one shortcoming I found was not being able to check out a list item under version control. The new and improved Microsoft Access 2007 could be very helpful to anyone who wants to do a little more with her list data.

For example, say you created an Issue Tracking SharePoint List, and you want to create custom reports to help track metrics. By using this capability, you are able to link the Issue Tracking SharePoint List and create custom reports to be used any time they are needed—e.g., by your boss or for a meeting—and still have the flexibility to add a new SharePoint list. This super tracking capability could become your new best friend when you need results quickly or over a long period of time. Think of it as your personal report center.

By following these steps, you'll be able to successfully link SharePoint list data to a new or existing Microsoft Access 2007 database. In this example, we will use a new Microsoft Access 2007 database called SPListAccessLinked:

1. Navigate to the SharePoint list or document library you want to use and click "Edit in Datasheet" under the Actions menu on the toolbar.

2. Click the Task Pane menu option under the Actions menu located on the toolbar, or by clicking the Show Task Pane bar on the far righthand of the screen.

3. Click "Track this List in Access" to launch Microsoft Access 2007.

4. Click New Database and then OK to create the Microsoft Access 2007 database.

5. From the File New Database pop-up screen, navigate to the location where you want the database to be stored and then change the filename to *SPListAccessLinked*. Click Create to create the database.

6. The database should launch and show the linked SharePoint list data.

Export to Access

"Export to Access" is very similar to the "Track this List in Access" feature because it exports the current SharePoint list data to an existing or new Microsoft Access 2007 database and adds it to a new table that is not linked to the SharePoint list data.

This feature gives a lot more flexibility when you want to remove data or add new data to the table without it affecting the SharePoint list structure or data. It could also be used for static reporting.

For example, let's say that your boss wants a monthly report, but not all the data is in the SharePoint list, so you have to import it from other data sources. The last thing that you want to worry about is the data changing and messing up your reporting numbers. By using this feature, you are able to take a snapshot of the data each month and import it into a Microsoft Access 2007 database table that is static and is updated only from Microsoft Access 2007. This would give you the flexibility to import all the other data sources necessary for creating monthly reports. It would also give you the flexibility to always go back and review the data without wondering whether something had changed.

By following these steps, you'll be able to successfully export the current SharePoint list data to a new or existing Microsoft Access 2007 database. In this example, we will use a new Microsoft Access 2007 database called SPListAccessExport:

1. Navigate to the SharePoint list or document library you want to use and click "Edit in Datasheet" under the Actions menu on the toolbar.

2. Expand the Datasheet View task pane by clicking Task Pane under the Actions menu located on the toolbar or by clicking the Show Task Pane bar on the right-hand side of the screen.

3. Click "Export to Access" to launch Microsoft Access 2007.

4. Click New Database and then click OK to create the Microsoft Access 2007 database.

5. From the File New Database pop-up screen, navigate to the location where you want the database to be stored, and then change the filename to *SPListAccessExport*. Click Create to create the database.

6. The database should launch and show the imported SharePoint list data.

Report with Access

"Report with Access" is very useful when you want to create quick reports from SharePoint list data through Microsoft Access 2007. It automatically creates a default report when it is first used.

"Report with Access" is very similar to "Track this List in Access" because it links to the current SharePoint list and the User Information List to allow for easy access to new data that is being entered into the SharePoint lists.

When Microsoft Access 2007 first opens, there will be two tabs. The first tab is the current SharePoint list data in the standard Datasheet view and the second tab (the active tab) is a prebuilt report. When changing between the tabs, the menus above will change.

Once again, Microsoft Access 2007 has an improved reporting model and interface that makes it a lot easier for creating more professional-looking reports quickly.

By following these steps, you'll be able to successfully link the current SharePoint list data to a new or existing Microsoft Access 2007 database for reporting. In this example, we are going to use a new Microsoft Access 2007 database called SPListAccessReport:

1. Navigate to the SharePoint list or document library you want to use and click the "Edit in Datasheet" menu option under the Actions menu on the toolbar.
2. Expand the Datasheet View task pane by clicking the Task Pane menu under the Actions menu located on the toolbar, or by clicking the Show Task Pane bar on the righthand side of the screen.
3. Click "Report with Access" to start the process.
4. Click New Database and then click OK to create the Microsoft Access 2007 database.
5. From the File New Database pop-up screen, navigate to the location where you want the database to be stored and then change the filename to *SPListAccessReport*. Click Create to create the database.
6. The database should launch and show the imported SharePoint list data.

Query list with Excel

"Query list with Excel" exports the data out of the SharePoint list and imports it into a Microsoft Excel 2007 spreadsheet. The connection that was created stays connected unless you terminate it by clicking the Unlink option located in the External Table Data ribbon section. The connection created is a one-way connection; data you add to the spreadsheet will not be synced to the SharePoint list. Many users will be surprised by this limitation because the functionality was there in the previous version of Microsoft Excel 2003 and SharePoint 2003.

Excel may display an error message that says, "Microsoft Office has identified a potential security concern." Click Enable to allow the data to be imported from your SharePoint list. This new security feature helps users verify that the data being imported is safe.

"Query list with Excel" gives a friendly environment in which to manipulate Share-Point list data with all the trustworthy and new features of Microsoft Excel 2007.

By following these steps, you'll be able to successfully link the current SharePoint list data to a new Microsoft Excel 2007 workbook:

1. Navigate to the SharePoint list or document library you want to use and click "Edit in Datasheet" under the Actions menu on the toolbar.

2. Expand the Datasheet View task pane by clicking the Task Pane menu under the Actions menu located on the toolbar, or by clicking the Show Task Pane bar on the righthand side of the screen.

3. Click "Query list with Excel" to start the process.

4. Click Enable when the "Microsoft Office has identified a potential security concern" security message appears.

5. Microsoft Excel 2007 should launch and show the imported data from the SharePoint list.

Print with Excel

"Print with Excel" takes the data from the SharePoint list and imports it into a Microsoft Excel 2007 workbook, then automatically launches the Excel print window.

"Print with Excel" is very similar to "Query list with Excel," but it also automatically launches the Excel print window. The data that is imported into the Excel Workbook is linked and can be refreshed by selecting the Refresh All menu option on the Data ribbon.

Excel may display an error message that says, "Microsoft Office has identified a potential security concern." Click Enable to allow the data to be imported from your SharePoint list. This new security feature helps users verify that the data being imported is safe.

By following these steps, you'll be able to successfully link the current SharePoint list data to a new Microsoft Excel 2007 workbook for printing:

1. Navigate to the SharePoint list or document library you want to use and click "Edit in Datasheet" under the Actions menu on the toolbar.

2. Expand the Datasheet View task pane by clicking the Task Pane menu under the Actions menu located on the toolbar or by clicking the Show Task Pane bar on the righthand side of the screen.

3. Click "Print with Excel" to start the process.

4. Click Enable when the "Microsoft Office has identified a potential security concern" security message appears.

5. Microsoft Excel 2007 should launch with the print window being active and show the imported data from the SharePoint list in the background ready to be printed.

6. Click OK to print the worksheet.

Chart with Excel

"Chart with Excel" takes the data from the SharePoint list and imports it into a Microsoft Excel 2007 workbook and then automatically launches the Excel Create Chart window to allow the type of chart to be selected before inserting the chart onto the worksheet. Once the chart has been inserted onto the worksheet, the Design menu ribbon becomes active. The Design menu ribbon is part of the Chart Tools section.

"Chart with Excel" is very similar to "Query list with Excel" but it adds the additional feature of automatically launching the "Excel create chart" window. The data that is imported into the Excel Workbook is linked and can be refreshed by selecting the Refresh All menu option on the Data ribbon.

Excel may display an error message that says, "Microsoft Office has identified a potential security concern." Click Enable to allow the data to be imported from your SharePoint list. This new security feature helps users verify that the data being imported is safe.

By following these steps, you'll be able to successfully link the current SharePoint list data to a new Microsoft Excel 2007 workbook:

1. Navigate to the SharePoint list or document library you want to use and click "Edit in Datasheet" under the Actions menu on the toolbar.

2. Expand the Datasheet View task pane by clicking the Task Pane menu under the Actions menu located on the toolbar or by clicking the Show Task Pane bar on the righthand of the screen.

3. Click "Chart with Excel" to start the process.

4. Click Enable when the "Microsoft Office has identified a potential security concern" security message appears.

5. Microsoft Excel 2007 should launch with the Create Chart window being active and show the imported data from the SharePoint list in the background ready to be charted.

6. Choose the chart and then click OK to insert it.

Create Excel Pivot Table Report

"Create Excel Pivot Table Report" takes the data from the SharePoint list and imports it into a Microsoft Excel 2007 workbook. It then automatically launches a worksheet with the pivot table control located on the top left side of the screen, activating both the Pivot Table Field List task pane and the Options menu ribbon from the PivotTable Tools section. A simple way of adding a column or row is by clicking and dragging the field down into either the Column Labels or Row Labels box.

"Create Excel Pivot Table Report" is a little different from the other Excel options because it doesn't show any of the data until a field has been added to either the Report Filter, Column Labels, Row Labels, or Values box. Data for each field can be seen by hovering over the field and clicking the upside-down triangle on the right end of the bar. The Options menu ribbon gives a lot of additional features. The data is linked and can be refreshed by clicking the Refresh option on the menu ribbon.

Excel may display an error message that says, "Microsoft Office has identified a potential security concern." Click Enable to allow the data to be imported from your SharePoint list. This new security feature helps users verify that the data being imported is safe.

By following these steps, you'll be able to successfully link the current SharePoint list data to a new Microsoft Excel 2007 workbook with a Pivot Table already inserted and ready for designing:

1. Navigate to the SharePoint list or document library that you want to use and click "Edit in Datasheet" under the Actions menu on the toolbar.

2. Expand the Datasheet View task pane by clicking the Task Pane menu under the Actions menu located on the toolbar, or by clicking the Show Task Pane bar on the righthand of the screen.

3. Click "Create Excel Pivot Table Report" to start the process.

4. Click Enable when the "Microsoft Office has identified a potential security concern" security message appears.

5. Microsoft Excel 2007 should launch a new worksheet with a pivot table inserted in the upper-lefthand corner of the worksheet and the Pivot Table Field List task pane present on the righthand side of the screen.

6. Left-click and drag any field from the task pane down into the desired box at the bottom of the task pane, and then the pivot table control will display the changes.

Explorer View

Explorer view in general is a quick way to upload large amounts of documents without manually loading the documents one at a time. This view is available both embedded within the browser and as a regular Windows window. The general menu options for the most part are the same as a regular Windows Explorer view and don't have specific SharePoint menu options. Any SharePoint-specific options will need to be done from the browser or the associated Office application.

This section goes into general detail about the availability and functionality that the view offers, and some of the limitations and possible problem areas that might be encountered in the workplace.

Explorer View Availability

Explorer view is available for the Document Library, Form Library, Picture Library, Report Library, Translation Management Library, Data Connection Library, and Slide Library, but not for the Wiki Page Library.

Microsoft offers support for the "Open with Windows Explorer" option only in Internet Explorer versions 6 and 7. This is not to say that it won't work in older versions, but there's no support for it if problems do occur.

Forms Folder

When you first open Explorer view for a new library, you will notice that there is a folder called *Forms*—this is a system folder that contains all the ASPX pages that make up the library. In older versions of SharePoint, this folder could be deleted, which made the library unusable. It is no longer possible to delete the *Forms* folder, but users may wonder why it's present. If they do try to delete the folder, they will get an error message.

Check-In and Check-Out Capabilities

One of the biggest downsides of using the Explorer view in SharePoint 2003 was the lack of ability to check files in or out. For example, you had the capability to copy and paste large amounts of documents into Explorer view, but each document had to be checked in from the standard Library view. In SharePoint 2007, this is still true, but there has been an improvement. When versioning is turned on and the documents you are copying already exist in the library, a new version will be created for each replaced document.

The new versions of SharePoint and Office are very tightly integrated, and SharePoint relies on Microsoft Office 2007 to perform the tasks that it is unable to handle from Explorer view. For example, the setting requiring documents to be checked out before they can be edited is enforced from the Microsoft Office application, rather than from the Explorer view. If the document is opened from the browser, a pop-up window asks the question before the Microsoft Office application is launched.

If a document is opened from the Explorer view and then checked out from the Microsoft Office application with changes saved, when you check it back in, it returns an error message. If you do not check it back in until you are closing the application and it prompts you to do so, there is no error message, and everything works as expected.

Security Behavior

The security behavior is a little different when using the Explorer view versus the Browser view. In the Browser view, if you don't have access to something, it's not shown, but that's not the case in Explorer view.

Reader privileges

When I tried to add a document library as a reader, I got this warning message: "An error occurred copying some or all of the selected files."

When I tried to delete a document from the document library as a reader, I got this message: "Unable to delete *filename*. You do not have the correct permissions. Please contact the server administrator."

Because the messages may vary, it might be a good idea to inform other users what messages they might receive when using the Explorer view to help reduce confusion.

Workflow

Workflow is a new feature for SharePoint 2007. If a library has a workflow assigned to it, and the workflow is set to start when a document is inserted or updated by adding a document through Explorer view, it will trigger the workflow. A workflow can be set up to start manually by a user, but this capability is not available from Explorer view. Any other type of interaction with the workflow needs to be done from the browser.

Metadata

Any update to metadata will have to be done from the browser or the associated Microsoft Office application. Microsoft Office 2007 has improved the ability of updating the document's metadata by now displaying the fields in the message bar.

If you are using columns in the library that match the document default properties (Title, Subject, Author, Category, Keywords, and Comments), these values will be automatically populated if the columns are text data types (Single, Multi-Line).

When working with the Explorer view and Browser view, I noticed that caching issues occurred. For example, if a document was deleted from the standard Library view and then Explorer view was opened, the document was still there until the Explorer view was refreshed.

Another thing to be careful about is the "Move to" and "Copy to" options. When these options are used from Explorer view, Explorer view doesn't use the new feature Manage Copies but instead uses the regular Windows options. (This should have been assumed but I was hoping for a little more from Explorer view this time around.)

CHAPTER 7

Applying Templates, Page Layouts, and Themes

Introduction

It's said that "appearances can be deceiving," yet so many things in people's lives seem centered on appearances. Even a casual viewing of television commercials or magazine ads reveals a great concern about hairstyles, clothing, makeup, and oral hygiene. Translating that to the World Wide Web, some of the things people look for in a web site are how it displays and how it functions. The discipline of Web Usability exists to test web sites and determine how to make them better and easier to use by their target audience.

You want everything about your business to be professional and attractive to customers. This includes your external web presence, intranet, extranet, and any other HTML-based interface to your company. MOSS 2007 contains various tools that affect the general layout, style, and color of your site collection and its content in order to achieve this goal. In general, the elements you will be modifying to establish the "look and feel" of your site collection are site templates, page layouts, and themes:

Site templates
> These let you provide a consistent and professional appearance for your site collection including the Portal Site. This includes the general layout and structure of sites and eliminates the need to create sites and subsites from scratch.

Page layouts
> This element governs what type of site content is displayed and the location and function of fields on the page.

Themes
> Themes are a collection of colors, fonts, and other decorative elements on your site that can enhance its appearance and reflect your corporate identity, purpose, and goals.

There are a number of other templates available in addition to site templates:

- Form templates
- Libraries templates
- List templates
- Role-based templates for My Sites

 These templates are better addressed in Chapters 13, 14, and 21.

Site Templates

MOSS 2007 comes with four default site templates: Collaboration, Meetings, Enterprise, and Publishing.

You can also create one or many customized site templates yourself. Begin by customizing a site. You can select a theme, choose from a variety of Web Part pages, workspaces, and Web Parts, and then save your customized site as a template. After you've constructed numerous site templates, they are available to apply to any sites you make.

 See Chapter 5 for information on how to create a site or site collection.

Default Site Templates

As just mentioned, when you create a SharePoint site, you can choose from four default templates, each of which will impose a particular structure and function:

- Collaboration
- Meetings
- Enterprise
- Publishing

Within each template, you can select from several types. For example, in the Collaboration site template, you can select from one of six different types. Let's take a more complete look at the choices you have when you are on the New SharePoint Site page.

Collaboration Site Template

The general purpose of the Collaboration template is to provide a platform for teams or groups, in either the same or different departments, to collaborate on tasks, documents, and other efforts (Figure 7-1).

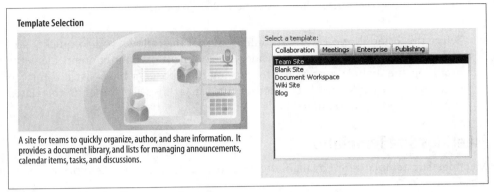

Figure 7-1. Collaboration site template selections

Depending on your exact needs, you can select one of six functional choices for your collaboration site:

Team Site
> This site can be used for any purpose that requires a group to collaborate on any work task or project. Default Web Parts included with this site are a document library, an announcements list, a calendar, a contacts list, and a links list.

Blank Site
> This is a general-purpose site with no default formatting. With a Blank site, you choose whatever Web Parts you want and customize the site for whatever purpose you desire. You also have the option to use Microsoft Office SharePoint Designer 2007 or any other SharePoint-compatible web design program to insert design elements and functional features into the site.

Document Workspace
> You can use this site option when your primary task is to initiate a collaborative team documentation project. This would be ideal for a company's technical writing group or a similar team that needs to have several people create and modify common documentation. Lists and libraries included are a document library, an announcements list, a tasks list, a members list, and a links list.

Wiki Site

Use this site when you want to create an information repository that can be quickly and easily edited by team members. Properties of the Wiki site include pages where users can record information, link data through keywords, and have a recorded history, allowing you to restore deleted content. Content elements included are Wiki pages, a links list, and a Wiki page library.

Blog

Select this option if you want an online journal that allows you to quickly add and edit information and allows readers to comment on your content. Elements in a blog site include a posts list for storing blog posts, a blogs list for links to other blogs, a categories list, a comments list, a links list for links to related resources, and a photo library.

Meetings Site Templates

Meetings site templates are available to help teams manage various types of meetings (Figure 7-2).

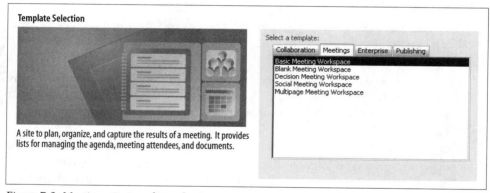

Figure 7-2. Meetings site template selections

Meetings can be recurring (such as weekly staff meetings) for a particular project that will include a limited series of meetings, or single event meetings, such as introducing a company's new health insurance provider. Depending on the nature and scope of your meetings, you can choose from any of the following templates:

Basic Meeting Workspace

This is a general-purpose meeting template and is typically used for most meeting types. Elements that come with this template by default are an objectives list, an attendees list, an agenda, and a document library.

Blank Meeting Workspace

This is a completely unformatted meeting site that you can customize to meet your needs.

Decision Meeting Workspace

Use this site template when the purpose of your meetings is to review documents, lists, and other information sources related to making a particular decision. This site is ideal for a team meeting to make decisions, such as how to design a new data center or what sales objectives to pursue in the coming year. Default elements included in this template are an objectives list, an attendees list, an agenda, a document library, a tasks list, and a decisions list.

Social Meeting Workspace

This site template is used when you want to plan and organize a social event, such as a company picnic, holiday party, or potluck. Elements included in this site are an attendees list, directions, an image log, a "Things to Bring" list, and a photo library.

Multipage Meeting Workspace

This template is similar to the Decision Meeting Workspace template, except that it's designed to accommodate very complex and involved data and decision processes. The site comes with two web pages by default, but you can add up to 10 individual pages per meeting. This site includes an objectives list, an attendees list, and an agenda.

Enterprise Site Template

The Enterprise site template is commonly used for a top-level or high-level site in your organization's site collection. It is designed to accommodate the needs of a national or multinational company in the areas of document management, information management, and records management (Figure 7-3).

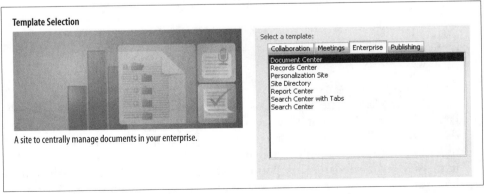

Figure 7-3. Enterprise site template selections

Document Center

Use this site when you need a central interface to manage your enterprise-level documentation. This site template includes a Document Library, Relevant Documents Web Part, Upcoming Tasks Web Part, and Tree View navigation. Several document management features are enabled on this site, including major and minor versioning, required check out, and support for multiple content types.

Records Center

The Records Center template is one of the major templates used in SharePoint 2007's Business Intelligence (BI) solution. It is the central interface for managing all enterprise-level data and data sources for an organization. Elements included in this template are a Records Vault, information management policy enforcement, a Holds list, a Record Routing list, and an Unclassified Records library.

Learn more about Business Intelligence in Chapter 15.

Personalization Site

This site is used for customizing a view of site collection data to fit individual users' needs, which can then be fed to their My Site pages.

Learn more about My Sites in Chapter 21.

Site Directory

This template is used when you want to create a site for organizing and managing your site collection. Features included are categorized sites, top sites, and a site map.

Find out how a Site Directory is used for creating and managing sites in Chapter 5.

Report Center

The Report Center site template is the core of SharePoint's Business Intelligence. It provides the central collection point for all manner of business-related data sources. The Report Center comes with multiple data interface tools in order to present the widest possible mix of information. Web elements included in this site are dashboards, key performance indicators (KPIs), special document libraries, and connections to external data sources. You can further customize the Report Center with additional site templates and Web Parts, depending on your requirements.

Search Center
> This site provides a search engine and includes search results pages and advanced search features.

Search Center with Tabs
> This site is similar to the Search Center template except that it has two tabs: one for general searches and the other for searching for people and information. You have the option of customizing the tabs for other search scopes and results.

Publishing Site Template

The Publishing site template is used to design, create, and publish different types of Web Portal sites for the enterprise. These sites can then be deployed as departmental or corporate intranet sites or as the organization's Internet web presence (Figure 7-4).

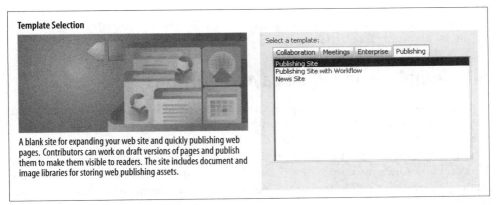

Figure 7-4. Publishing site template selections

Elements included in the template's sites are a page editing toolbar, content editor, and check out.

Publishing Site
> This is another general-purpose site template, but one designed to let you quickly publish WebPages on the SharePoint site. Default Web Parts included are document and image libraries for storing web publishing assets.

Publishing Site with Workflow
> Use this site template when you need a web interface for content that must go through an approval workflow before it is published.

News Site
> This site is used to display a variety of news-related content to your audience. This template includes a sample news page, easy-to-use layouts, an archive for storing older news items, and two news delivery Web Parts: RSS Viewer and This Week in Pictures.

By default, you can only create Publishing web sites beneath this template.

Collaboration Portal

Use this site template if you need a general portal site for a department, division, or other group within your organization. This site includes features from several other Publish site templates, such as a home page, a News site, a Site Directory, and a Search Center with Tabs.

Publishing Portal

This template is similar to the Publishing Site but with a larger scope. Use this site when you want to create a portal site for web content and serve it to the Internet or a large intranet audience. Features include a home page, a sample press releases subsite, a Search Center, a login page, and publishing with workflow.

My Site Host

This template is used for creating a site that will host My Site sites. (You'll learn more about My Sites in Chapter 21.)

Site Template and Page Layout Settings

In addition to the default site templates available in SharePoint 2007, you can create customized site templates. Any user with Owners or Design permissions can enter the Site Template Gallery and modify any site template. Typically, site templates are modified in order to then create sites with the organization's unique branding and look and feel. Once the corporate site template is created, users can create sites in the site collection that all conform to the same styling and format used throughout the company.

One of the most common ways to create a unique site template is to modify your default site so that it reflects the functionality and image you want to project, and then save the site as a site template.

Save a Site As a Site Template

Once you've created a site that fulfills all of your functional and design goals, you can save it as a template and then select the template when you create additional sites.

1. On the customized site, click Site Actions and choose Site Settings from the menu.

2. On the Site Settings page, in the Look and Feel section, click "Save site as template" (Figure 7-5).

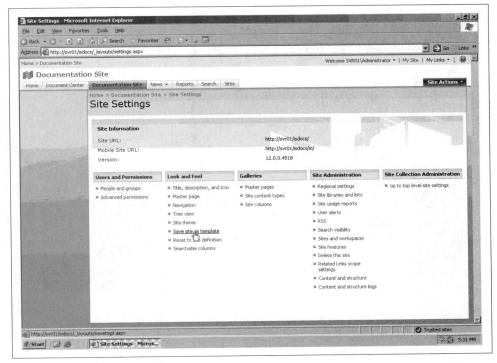

Figure 7-5. Save file as a template

3. On the "Save Site as Template" page, in the File Name section, type the name of the template file in the Name field.

4. Type the name of the template in the Title field.

5. Type a brief description of the template's purpose in the Description field.

6. In the Include Content section, click the Include Content checkbox if you want all of the Web Parts and other elements in this site to be included in subsequent sites created with this template (Figure 7-6).

7. Click OK to save the template.

As you can see in Figure 7-7, you can either go to the Site Template Gallery by clicking the link or click OK to return to the site administration page. When you go to the Site Template Gallery, you can see your new template in the main pane (Figure 7-8).

Notice that none of the default site templates are available in the Site Template Gallery.

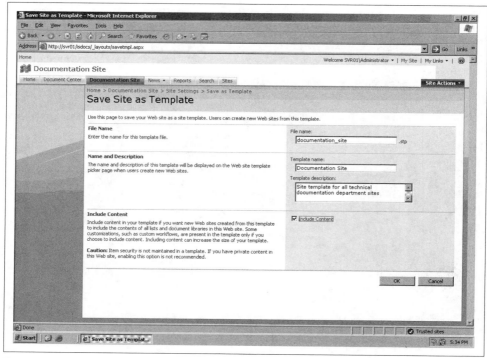

Figure 7-6. Finalizing the creation of a new site template

In addition to creating a site and saving it as a template, site templates can be imported from external sources. You can import a site template created on another SharePoint site or one created by a web site designer using Microsoft Office Share-Point Designer 2007 or another SharePoint-compatible tool.

Upload a Site Template into a Site Template Gallery

Adding a site template to your Site Template Gallery is as easy as uploading a document to a folder on your hard drive:

1. On your site, click Site Actions and choose Site Settings from the menu.

2. On the Site Settings page in the Galleries area, click "Site templates."

3. On the Site Templates Gallery page, click Upload.

4. Click the Browse button and navigate to the location of the desired template.

 You can also type the path to the template in the Name field.

5. Click OK to add the template to the Template Gallery.

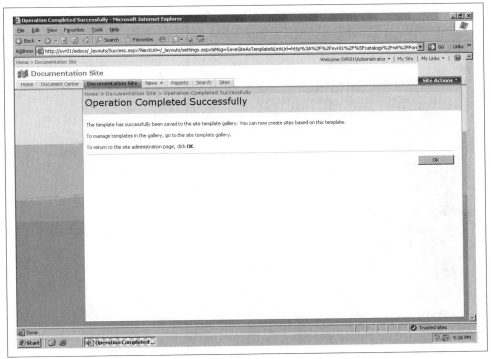

Figure 7-7. Operation successfully completed

Change the Layout and Permissions in a Site Template Gallery

Periodically, you may find it necessary to change the layout or access permissions for your Site Template Gallery. To do this, you must be on the top-level site of your site collection:

1. Click Site Actions, select Site Settings from the menu, and then select Modify All Site Settings (Figure 7-9).

2. On the Site Settings page in the Galleries section, click "Site templates."

3. Click Settings, and then click Gallery Settings (Figure 7-10).

4. On the Customize Site Template Gallery page, locate the name of the property you want to modify under the available sections and click that property's link.

5. Make whatever modifications you require and click Save (Figure 7-11).

You are returned to the Customize page. Notice that the Site Template Gallery title reflects the changes that were just made (Figure 7-12).

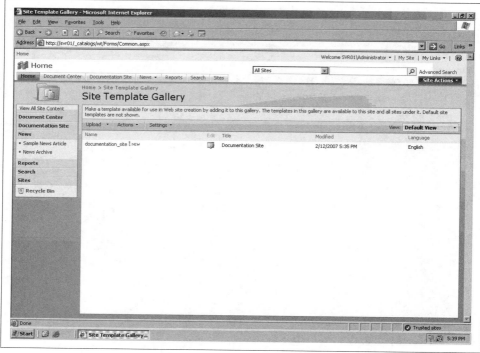

Figure 7-8. Site Template Gallery with newly created site template

Delete a Site Template from a Site Template Gallery

Not all site templates are forever. For example, your organization may completely redesign its logo and entire look and feel. Your corporate Internet and intranet sites will need to reflect these changes, and any site templates that are oriented to the old look and feel will need to be deleted to prevent accidental (and embarrassing) use. You must be on the top-level site of your site collection to do this:

1. Click Site Actions, select Site Settings from the menu, and then select Modify All Site Settings.

2. On the Site Settings page in the Galleries section, click "Site templates."

3. Locate the name of the template you want to delete from the list, and click Edit (Figure 7-13).

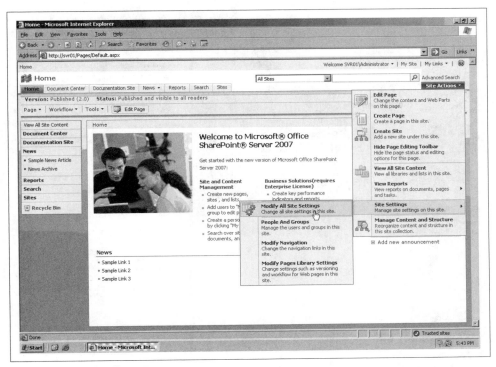

Figure 7-9. Modify All Site Settings

4. On the Edit Item page, click Delete Item (Figure 7-14).

> Notice that you can also check out and edit the Name, Title, and Description of the template.

5. When the confirmation dialog box appears, click OK (Figure 7-15).

You are returned to the Site Template Gallery and can see that the site template has been deleted (Figure 7-16).

Set Preferred Site Templates

You can configure options related to how site templates will act on your site collection. For example, you can either allow a user creating a new site to use any template in the Site Template Gallery or limit the templates that can be used.

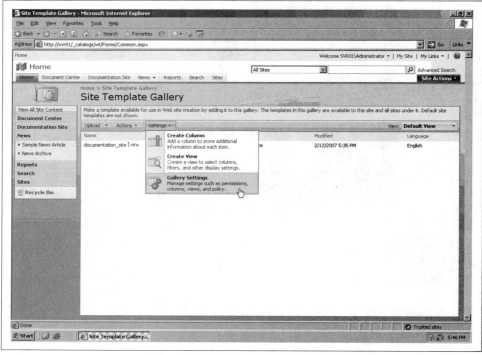

Figure 7-10. Modify Gallery Settings

1. Click Site Actions, select Site Settings from the menu, and then select Modify All Site Settings.

2. On the Site Settings page, in the Look and Feel section, click "Page layouts and site templates." In the Subsite Templates section, you have several options:

   - Select "Subsites can use any site template."

   - Select "Subsites can only use the following templates," choose which templates can be utilized, and then click Add.

   - Select "Reset all subsites" to inherit these preferred subsite template settings.

3. Click OK to save your changes.

What Is a Page Layout?

A *page layout* is the overall structure of a Web Part web page. Web page layouts are controlled by the content type of the web page. For example, when you create a Web Part page, you can select the specific layout of the fields that will be used to contain Web Parts.

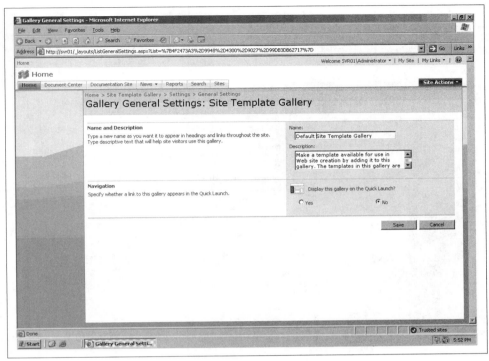

Figure 7-11. Saving Changes to the Site Template Gallery's title

For pages with a designated content type, fields can hold only certain types of content. Each content type has columns that are related to the fields on the page. The columns are controlled by column templates that determine what each field can hold. Examples are a single line of text, a hyperlink, or a calculated value.

When you view or edit a particular page, the page content is displayed in field controls. This is like "Design this page view" in SharePoint 2003, and allows you to see the underlying layout of the page fields as well as the content type.

Page layouts are stored in a Document Library called the Master Page Gallery. The Master Page Gallery is created when you first install MOSS 2007. Each Master Page Gallery contains the master page, which is the default layout for each site. Master pages can be customized to suit your specific needs.

Create or Edit a Master Page

When you create a site, the master page is created by default. To create a new master page, you can modify and save the current master page under a new name. You can also simply edit the master page and save it with its original name.

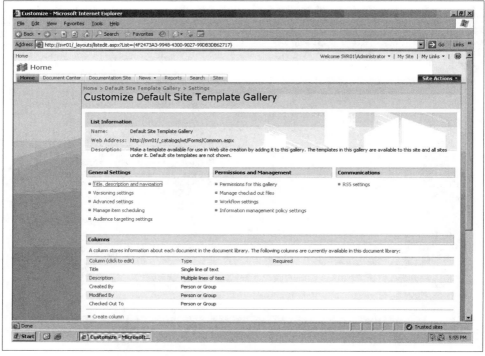

Figure 7-12. Modifications to the Site Template Gallery are confirmed

 To edit a master page, you must use a SharePoint-compatible web design program such as Microsoft Office SharePoint Designer.

1. On your site, click Site Actions and select Site Settings from the menu.

2. On the Site Settings page in the Galleries area, click "Master pages."

3. On the Master Pages page, click the master page you want to modify.

4. Open the master page in your web design program by clicking Edit.

5. Use the features provided by your web design program to modify the master page.

6. Save the master page either with its original name or with a new name if you want to create a new master page.

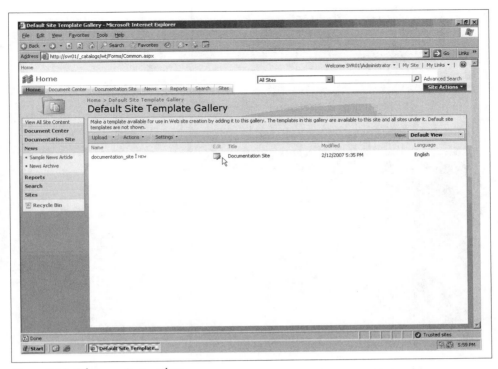

Figure 7-13. Editing a site template

Set Preferred Page Layouts

Setting your Preferred Page Layouts is very similar to setting your Preferred Site Settings:

1. Click Site Actions, select Site Settings from the menu, and then select Modify All Site Settings.

2. On the Site Settings page, in the Look and Feel section, click "Page layouts and site templates." In the Page Layouts section, you have several options:

   • Select "Pages in this site can use any layout."

   • Select "Pages in this site can only use the following layouts," choose which layouts you want to use, and then click Add.

   • Select "Variations" if you have source variations configured, and then select the source variation you want to apply to your page layouts.

   • Select "Reset all subsites" to inherit these preferred page layout settings.

3. Click OK to save your changes.

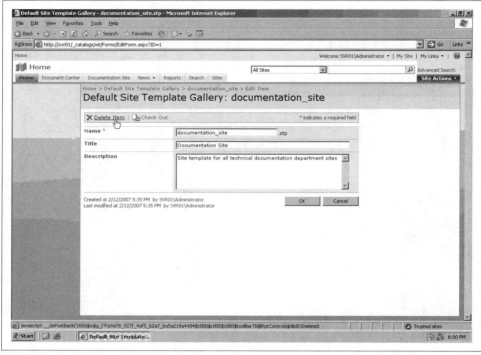

Figure 7-14. Deleting a site template

Managing Site Themes and Images

In addition to site templates and page layouts, you can modify the appearance of your site and site collection using themes. A *theme* is a collection of colors, fonts, and other design elements that lets you control the look and feel of your SharePoint site. You can select from among a series of default themes and apply them to your site. The application of any theme will have no impact on any portion of a site template or page layout.

 You can also create a custom theme for your site with a SharePoint-compatible design program such as Microsoft Office SharePoint Designer.

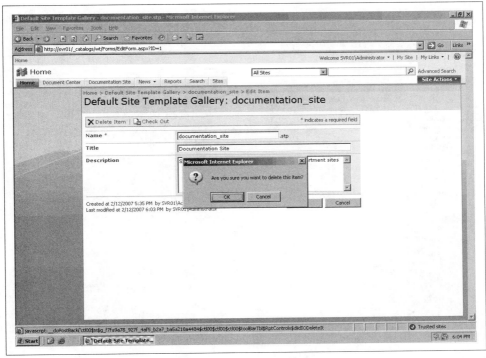

Figure 7-15. Confirm that you want to delete the site template

Changing a Site's Theme

Not everyone appreciates the default theme that's applied when you first create a SharePoint site. Fortunately, changing to another theme is quite easy:

1. On your site, click Site Actions and select Site Settings from the menu.
2. In the Look and Feel column, click "Site theme."
3. On the Site Theme page, select the desired theme (Figure 7-17).

 Notice that you can examine a preview of the selected style before applying it.

4. Click Apply to apply the theme to your site.

As you can see, the new style is now applied to the site (Figure 7-18).

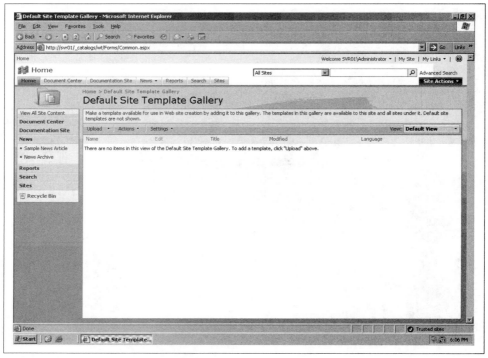

Figure 7-16. Empty Site Template Gallery

Changing Default Images

Yet another visual aspect that affects the presentation of your site collection is images. The most important image that appears on your site is your organization's logo. Also, each department and team within your company may have their own unique logos or other images associated with them.

Although you can edit images in SharePoint, you cannot use SharePoint to create original graphics. Instead, you will need to use a commercially available product to create images for your site collection. Chances are you either have an art department in your organization that handles this area or have hired one to create your company logos, color schemes, and other design elements. Once those images are created, you can upload them into an image library in SharePoint and then place them wherever you want in your site collection.

Chapter 8 shows how to add image Web Parts to pages, and Chapter 13 covers picture libraries in detail.

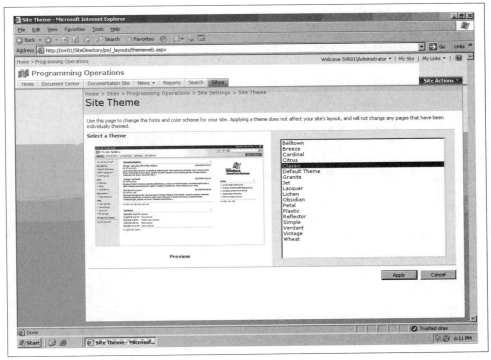

Figure 7-17. Changing from Default Theme to Classic Theme

Add a Company Logo Image

SharePoint site pages contain a default logo image in the upper lefthand corner of the page. You will most likely want to replace that image with your company's logo. You will need the URL that points to where your logo image is stored. Although you don't have to store the logo in a SharePoint picture library, it makes more sense to keep all your site assets organized within SharePoint.

Prerequisites for this action are that the image must already have been created and uploaded into a SharePoint picture library. You will also need to know the URL of the image:

1. On your site, click Site Actions and select Site Settings from the menu.

2. On the Site Settings page in the Look and Feel column, click on "Title, description, and icon."

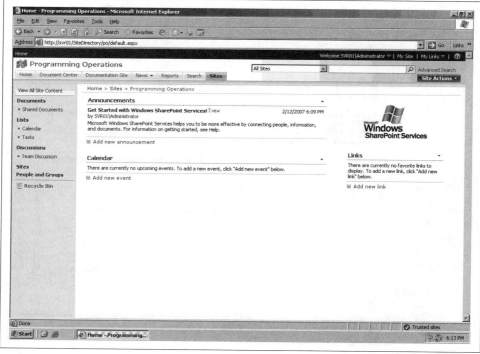

Figure 7-18. New site style is applied

3. In the "Logo URL and Description" section, replace the default URL in the URL field with the URL to your logo image (Figure 7-19). The easiest way to do this is to copy it from the picture library and paste it in the URL field.

4. Type a description of the image in the Description field. The description is the alternate text for your image in the event that the image cannot be viewed.

5. Under the URL field, click "Click here" to test (Figure 7-20).

6. Close the window displaying the image.

7. Click OK to apply your changes.

Change an Image on the Main Site Page

By default, an image is placed in the body of the top-level site's main page. This is basically a temporary placeholder that is meant to be replaced or deleted once you've installed SharePoint and modified the top-level site. To make the process easier, first put the image you want to use in a SharePoint image library and copy the URL to the image:

1. Click Site Actions and select Edit Page from the menu.

2. Locate the Site Image Web Part and click Edit Picture (Figure 7-21).

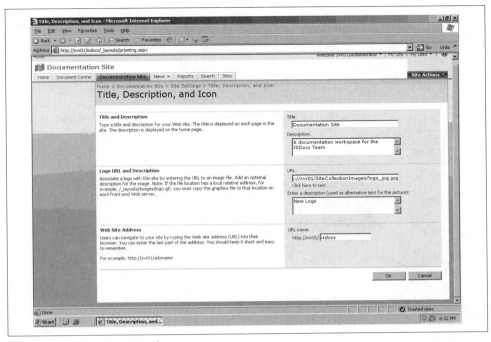

Figure 7-19. Changing a site's logo

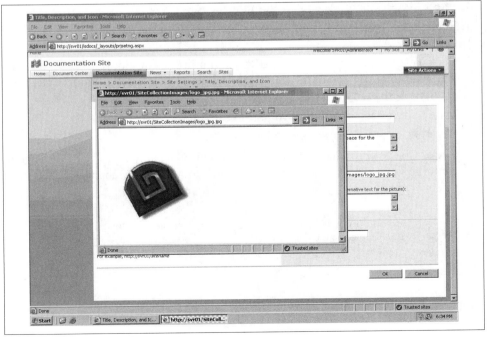

Figure 7-20. Verifying the link to the image

Figure 7-21. Top-level site's home page in Edit Mode

3. Select Modify Shared Web Part from the menu.

4. Replace the URL in the URL field with the URL to the image you want to use (Figure 7-22).

5. Click Test Link to verify that the URL to your image is valid. A separate window will open to notify you of the link's validity. You can close this window after you are done with it.

6. Type a short description of the image in the Alternate Text field.

7. Click OK to save your changes (Figure 7-23).

8. Click "Check In to Share Draft." At this point, you can either click Edit Page to continue your modifications or click Publish to apply your changes to the most recent version.

 If you do not publish your draft, the prior version of this page is the one visible to all users.

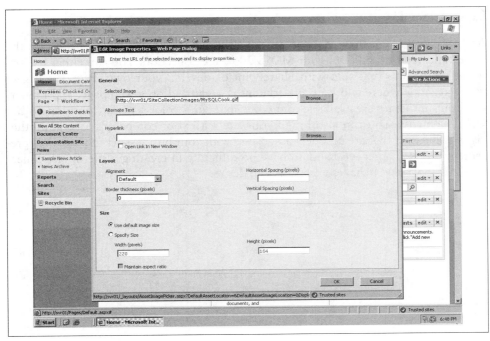

Figure 7-22. Replacing an image URL

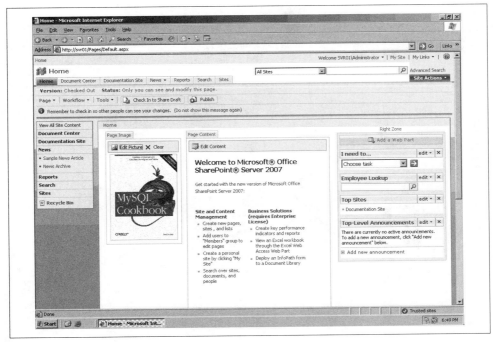

Figure 7-23. The new image is displayed on the page

Conclusion

As you can see, you have a great deal of flexibility in how you can customize the appearance and usability of your MOSS 2007 site collection. You can either use the default templates that ship with SharePoint or develop your own. Page layouts let you determine where and how site content is organized on a web page, and numerous built-in themes are available to modify your site's color scheme, fonts, and other visual elements. You can also brand your site with your company's logo and other visual indicators that are uniquely associated with your business. Using the tools presented in this chapter, you should have no difficulty in creating a site or site collection that looks and behaves exactly as you desire.

Creating Web Parts

Introduction

A *Web Part* is the basic web element used in MOSS 2007 to contain and organize information on a Web Part page. A Web Part page is a specialized web page that contains one or more Web Parts and provides a container for different types of Web Parts. Web Parts are designed for different purposes, such as to contain lists, organize documents, and create forums.

MOSS 2007 comes with a default set of Web Parts:

- Content Editor Web Part
- Form Web Part
- Image Web Part
- List View Web Part
- Page Viewer Web Part
- Site Users Web Part
- XML Web Part

These default Web Parts can be customized to suit your specific needs.

Default Web Parts

Each Web Part serves a particular need within a Web Part page. A Web Part page can contain as few or as many Web Parts as it is formatted to contain, and individual Web Parts can be set up to connect to one another, providing a unique presentation of data.

Content Editor Web Part

This Web Part is used to add formatted text, images, tables, and hyperlinks to a Web Part page. The information can be added in HTML format using the Source Editor, the Rich Text Editor, or a Content Link. The most common use for this Web Part is to add textual and graphic data, similar to how a typical web page presents on the Internet. Hyperlinks can be included, but a remote web page cannot be presented in a frame in this Web Part. Instead, use the Page View Web Part to display web content in frames. Although the Content Editor Web Part can accept most HTML tags, it is not compatible with the FORM element. If you need to create a form page within a Web Part page, you must use the Form Web Part.

 See the "Form Web Part" and "Page Viewer Web Part" sections later in this chapter.

How you enter information in this Web Part depends on how it is formatted, which input method you prefer, and occasionally, where the data is located:

Source Editor

Information is entered into a simple text editor in HTML format. This acts similarly to other text editors, such as Notepad, and requires that the author know basic HTML syntax and construction. Text not using proper HTML formatting will not display correctly. Also, any images, tables, or hyperlinks included with this editor must be written with the relevant HTML tags.

Rich Text Editor

This editor allows you to enter information in plain text without HTML formatting. A set of tools allows you to insert hyperlinks, images, tables, and bullet lists and to format the size and color of text. The Rich Text Editor is limited compared to Microsoft Office Word, so don't expect have all of the options of adding and editing content that are available in a full-featured word processor.

Content Link

You can use this method to link the Web Part to a text file that contains HTML formatting. This method does not support connections to web pages that contain FORM tags and will produce an error if this is attempted. If you try to connect to web content from a web page outside of the site, this may fail if that site does not have anonymous access enabled. Only *http://* or *https://* protocols are supported.

Form Web Part

This Web Part is used to connect simple form controls to other Web Parts. It also can be used to filter lists—for example, presenting a view of a products list that displays only items within a certain price range. This Web Part can be customized to utilize many typical form elements, such as radio buttons, checkboxes, and text boxes.

- Connect the Form Web Part to any other Web Part on the site. An example of this is using the Form Web Part to connect to one or more Web Parts on another Web Part page on the site, to present a filtered view of your selections in the Form Web Part.
- Customize the Form Web Part with either the built-in Source Editor or a web design application such as Microsoft Office SharePoint Designer 2007 to add a text box, text area, checkbox, Option button, or drop-down menu.

Image Web Part

You can use this Web Part to add one or more graphics to a Web Part page. This includes your corporate logo, product images, diagrams, or drawings. The image should exist on the site for faster load times, but you can link to an off-site image. This image will be static unless it is an animated GIF or some other similar graphic.

 You can also add an image directly in a Content Editor Web Part, either by writing the link in HTML in the Source Editor or by using the image tool available in the Rich Text Editor.

You also have the option of connecting the Image Web Part to another Web Part that provides the path or hyperlink to an image. This allows the image to behave dynamically, depending on what is happening on the remote Web Part. Compatible graphics formats include:

- Bitmap (*.bmp*)
- Enhanced Metafile (*.emf*)
- Graphics Interchange Format (*.gif*)
- Joint Photographic Experts Group (*.jpg*)
- Portable Networks Graphics (*.png*)

Custom properties of this Web Part allow you to configure alternate text for the graphic, align the image vertically and horizontally, and modify the default background color of the Web Part.

List View Web Part

Despite the name, there is no distinct Web Part called List View Web Part. This is more of a feature of certain types of Web Parts that include lists. For example, you can create a list called Technologies and categorize the different technologies in the list as either Applications, Languages, or Libraries (APIs). After the list is constructed, if you want to look at just the Languages technologies, you can choose the Languages list view. This option filters the list, displaying only those list items categorized as Languages.

MOSS 2007 contains a variety of specific List Web Parts that you can use, depending on what kind of data you have and how you want it presented. Lists that have the View List View option are as follows:

- Announcements
- Contacts
- Custom Lists
- Document Libraries
- Events
- Form Libraries
- Issues
- Links
- Lists with Data Imported from Spreadsheets
- Tasks

You can create multiple views for a List and specify a variety of properties per view. You can also link different list items, such as Document Name and Edit, so that when the name of a document is selected, an editing window opens, allowing you to modify the item's properties. The custom properties of a List View Web Part are:

- Selected View
- Edit the Current View
- Toolbar Type

When you open a List View Web Part, the default view is Current View, which represents the view that was most recently selected. For example, if you previously chose Languages from the Technologies list and then saved and closed the list, when you access it again, the Current View would be the Languages View. You can change from Current View to any other view you have created, but be careful to save the selection by clicking OK; otherwise, you might lose your changes. Selected View Types are:

- "All *list_name*" or All Documents, which displays the entire list.
- Explorer view shows all files as icons.
- Summary view shows a summary of the list content.
- Additional List Views are the views that you have customized, such as Applications, Languages, and Libraries (APIs).

The "Edit the current view" options let you modify how the list will be displayed, including the columns, sort order, and which filter is used.

The Toolbar Type option lets you choose between Summary Toolbar, Full Toolbar, and No Toolbar. Full Toolbar is the default setting for Custom Lists.

Page Viewer Web Part

This Web Part is essentially a web frame that displays the content of any web page to which it is hotlinked. You can link the Page Viewer Web Part to any web page, folder, or document available over a network connection. This can be handy for viewing information that changes frequently, such as a spreadsheet accessed by members of a team.

You must use a web browser that supports HTML IFRAME to view information in a Page Viewer Web Part. To view files or folders in the Page Viewer, you must use Internet Explorer.

As with any other frame, the information displayed in the Page Viewer Web Part is independent from the rest of the Web Part page. For example, if you click links on the web page in the Page Viewer Web Part, you are navigating only within the linked page, not within the SharePoint site. You remain on the same Web Part page, regardless of where you browse on the remote site.

The Page View Web Part has two custom properties that work in unison to display either a web page, folder, or file:

- The Web Page, Folder, or File Group lets you choose which type of information you want displayed. If you choose the Web Page option, the *http://* notation is automatically included in the Links field (see the next bullet point). If you choose either Folder or File, no change will occur to the Links field until you make it.
- Links lets you enter the hyperlink protocol (*http* or *https*) and URL to the web page, or the relative or absolute URL to the folder or file you desire. The field will not accept file paths such as *C:\documents* and *settings\jpyles\My Documents\ webfile*.

Site Users Web Part

A Site Users Web Part is a specialized list that displays a list of individual users and groups who have access to the MOSS 2007 site. As explained previously in "List View Web Part," most lists can be filters to display more than one view of the information they contain. For example, let's say you have a list containing all of the users in your department. You can filter it by work group so that only a specific team appears on the list. Then you can add that filtered Site Users Web Part to the main page of the team's subsite.

The Site Users Web Part is added by default to the home page of a Document Work-space site but can be added manually to any Web Part page. Clicking on the Smart Tag next to any user's name takes you to a page displaying that person's contact information. Here you'll find the same messaging options available in many other

Office products, allowing you to send an email or instant message, add the user's contact information to your address book in Outlook, or schedule a meeting.

You can configure three custom properties in the Site Users Web Part:

- "Number of items to display" lets you choose the number of user names appearing in the list. The range is from 1 to 1,000.
- Display Type lets you choose which types of users or groups will appear in the list.
- Toolbar Type lets you include or remove the "Add new user" link from the Web Part.

XML Web Part

This Web Part displays Extensible Markup Language (XML)-formatted data and applies Extensible Stylesheet Language Transformations (XSLT) styling to that data prior to it being displayed. As with the Content Editor Web Part, the XML Web Part does not support the use of the HTML FORM element. If you must use FORM tags, you'll be required to choose either the Page Viewer Web Part or the Form Web Part.

The XML Web Part is commonly used to display XML documents or forms as well as structured data from database tables. There are two methods you can use to add data to this Web Part:

XML and XSL Editors
Plain-text editors that allow you to create and modify information within the Web Part. You need to be familiar with XML and XSLT syntax and structure to effectively use this method.

XML and XSL Links
Let you hyperlink to a document containing XML and XSLT source code. This is an ideal method to display information that is frequently updated by an automated process. The two valid hyperlink protocols supported are HTTP and HTTPS. As with the Page Viewer Web Part, you can use either relative or absolute URLs, but file paths—such as *C:\documents* and *settings\jpyles\My Documents\XMLfile*—are not supported.

The two methods of adding information to the XML Web Part are not mutually exclusive. Although it's not supported, this Web Part allows you to combine edited and linked data. As previously stated, one reason to use linked XML documents is to display frequently updated information. You can add edited XML in the same Web Part to display a message to users in case the linked data becomes unavailable (due to a network problem, for example).

Select a Web Part Page

Customizing a Web Part page by adding Web Parts allows you to organize and present text, graphics, lists, links, and other information in the way that makes the most sense for your team, department, or organization. Different Web Part pages contain different field formatting. The fields available on the various Web Part pages are determined by the content type of the master pages in SharePoint's Master Page Gallery.

 See Chapter 7 for more information about master pages.

To select a Web Part page to suit your needs, do the following:

1. On your site, click Site Actions and select Create from the menu.

2. In the Web Pages column, click Web Part Page, as Figure 8-1 illustrates.

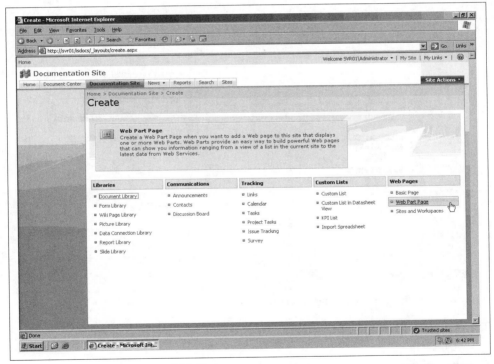

Figure 8-1. Beginning to create a Web Part page

3. On the new Web Part page page, give your new Web Part page a name by typing it in the Name field.

The name will become part of the Web Part page's URL and will have an *.aspx* extension, like all SharePoint pages.

4. In the Layout section, choose the type of page layout you want from the list.

5. Under Save Location, choose the document library where you want to save your new Web Part page.

6. Click Create, as shown in Figure 8-2.

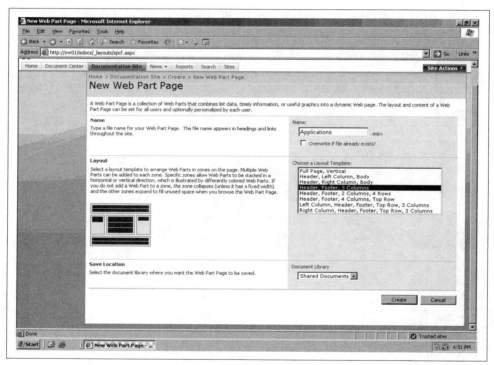

Figure 8-2. Finalizing the creation of a new Web Part page

The new Web Part page opens in Edit Mode and is ready to be customized.

Customize a Web Part Page

Once you have selected the content type for your Web Part page, you can customize it in a variety of ways.

Edit the Web Part Page Title Bar

The title bar of a Web Part page includes a logo image, the name of the page or site, a caption, and a description. The default content for these elements will have to be changed in order for this page to reflect your particular team, department, or site:

1. On the Web Part page, click Site Actions and select Edit Page from the menu.
2. Click on Edit Title Bar Properties.
3. Edit the Title, Caption, and Description fields by typing in the desired text.
4. Replace the default image URL in the URL field with the URL to your corporate or department logo.

 Typically, all of your site's images are stored in a SharePoint image library. You can then use an Image Web Part to hotlink to the location of the image using the image's URL. See Chapter 13 for more information.

5. If you don't want to require authentication for users to access the site, you can enable anonymous access with the Authentication button.
6. Click OK to save your changes, as illustrated in Figure 8-3.

 Clicking Apply instead of OK saves the changes but continues to display the toolbar. Click OK to finish and return to the normal page view.

Add a Web Part

After you've modified the Web Part page title bar, you will want to customize the Web Part page by adding specific Web Parts. When you begin accessing Web Parts, the Web Part page will enter Edit View, which will show the underlying Web Part page fields. Once you access a Web Part, you can choose to drag and drop it in the desired field. You can also click directly in the field to add a Web Part. The first thing you need to do is locate the desired Web Part.

1. On the Web Part page, click Site Actions and select Edit Page from the menu.
2. In the title of the desired Web Part field, click "Add a Web Part."
3. Check the box of the desired Web Part and click Add, as shown in Figure 8-4.

 You may have to scroll down to find the necessary Web Part.

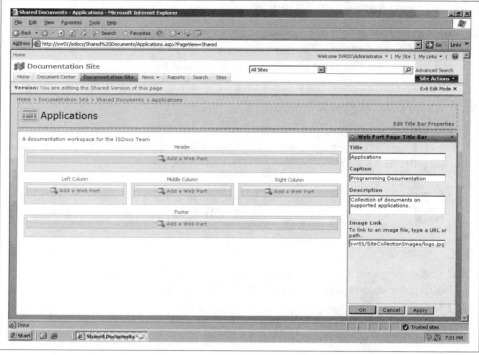

Figure 8-3. Editing the Web Part page title bar

As you saw earlier in this chapter, there are a variety of Web Parts available for use on your site, and your selections depend on what you want to do with that page. Once you have populated a Web Part page with Web Parts, you can move those Web Parts around to different fields on the page if necessary.

Change the Layout of a Web Part Page

Although you can move Web Parts to any Web Part field on the page, usually you cannot alter the structure and placement of the fields. However, these fields can be edited if you use a SharePoint-compatible web design tool, such as Office SharePoint Designer 2007. Otherwise, you are limited to adding, moving, and deleting Web Parts in the existing page structure:

1. On the Web Part page, click Site Actions and select Edit Page from the menu.

2. Once the page is in Edit Mode (Figure 8-5), you can drag and drop the Web Parts wherever you want.

3. Once you are finished editing the Web Part page, as in Figure 8-6, click Exit Edit Mode.

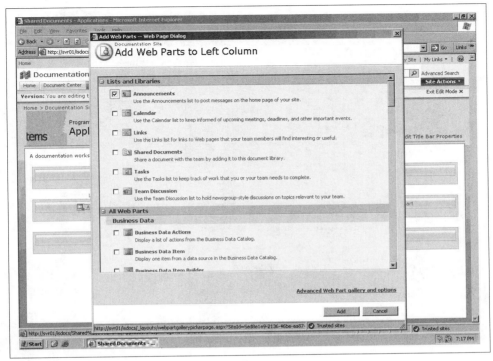

Figure 8-4. Selecting a Web Part for a Web Part page

Connect Data in Web Parts

You have the ability to connect data from two different Web Parts and present it in a customized view. This way, you can make changes to one Web Part that will affect the behavior of the other Web Part. The basic characteristics of this process are as follows:

- Information flows in only one direction, from the source to the recipient Web Part.
- Information can be in the form of lists, rows, cells, or parameter values.
- You can connect only Web Parts that exist on the same Web Part page.

 You can connect Web Parts on two separate Web Part pages by using a SharePoint-compatible web design tool, such as Microsoft Office SharePoint Designer 2007.

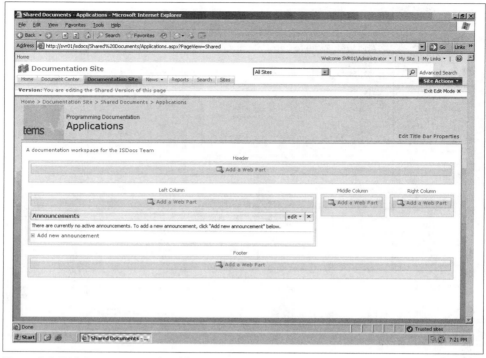

Figure 8-5. Web Part page populated by one Web Part

A practical example of creating a data flow connection between two Web Parts is connecting the Attendees list from a Meeting Workspace to an Image Web Part. If the Attendees list contains photos of the people on the list, every time you select an individual meeting attendee on the list, that person's photo will be passed to the Image Web Part and displayed.

This process requires a certain amount of planning in order to get the result you want. The first thing is to decide the rationale for connecting the two Web Parts and the advantages of this connection. Once you've decided which two types of information you want to connect, select the two Web Parts and add them to the desired Web Part page. Connect the two Web Parts and verify that information is being shown the way you want it.

> Be careful. You can correctly connect two Web Parts and still end up displaying meaningless results. For example, you can pass data from a Web Part that contains employee ID information to a Web Part that displays product ID information. Even though the connection is correct, the displayed data doesn't satisfy your requirements. To see how to avoid this problem, read the "Using the Configure Connection Dialog Box" section, later in this chapter.

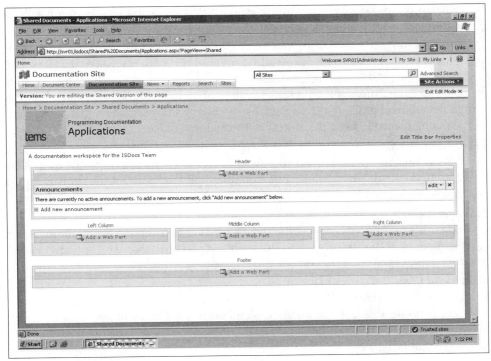

Figure 8-6. Moving a Web Part in a Web Part page

Types of Web Part Connections

There are several different types of Web Part connections you can configure. You can also connect more than one pair of Web Parts on a single Web Part page. The following is a list of the most commonly used Web Part connections:

Alternate Data Views

This connection type allows you to send data from a List View Web Part to a Web Part that provides a different view of the data. Examining data in an alternate view can let you filter the information by relationships or categories not apparent in the sending Web Part. Data types that you can pass from the List View Web Part include cells, fields, lists, or parameters. For example, you can pass list data to an organizational chart to show relationships between departments, pass row data to a chart to display demographic information, or pass cell data to display a percentage of progress toward a goal.

Calculations

SharePoint contains several Web Parts that can perform calculations without a connection to a separate Web Part. The advantage of creating a connection is displaying the calculation in a different view. For example, you can perform a calculation on tax payments in the sending Web Part and pass it to a list Web Part to see what your payments will be on a quarterly basis.

Data Enhancement

This type of connection lets you add different information types to list data. For example, suppose your regional office is having an annual meeting for sales staff coming from different field offices in different states. You can access the address of the regional office in the sending list Web Part and pass it to a map Web Part, showing the route from the airport to the regional office.

Master and Details

This connection type is used to pass general information from a list to a Web Part that can display details. For example, you can pass information from an employee list to a Web Part that can display details about individual employees.

Parent and Child

Use this type of connection if you want to pass data from one list to another. For example, you can pass row data from one list and have that data and any related row data displayed in the receiving list.

Search and Filter

Use this connection type to conduct a search in one Web Part and have all search results displayed in another Web Part filtered by columns, such as name, address, and phone number.

Summary and Details

This connection type is commonly used to pass summary data from a list to a Web Part that can display detailed information from the summary.

Create or Edit Web Part Connections

The following describes the basic action of connecting two Web Parts and editing that connection. You can create the connection from either Web Part:

1. On the Web Part page, click Site Actions and select Edit Page from the menu.
2. Choose one of the two Web Parts, click on Edit in the Web Part menu, and then select Connections, as shown in Figure 8-7.

 If the Connections link is grayed out, it means that the Web Part you've selected does not allow authoring of connections.

3. Select the type of connection you want to create.
4. Click the name of the Web Part.

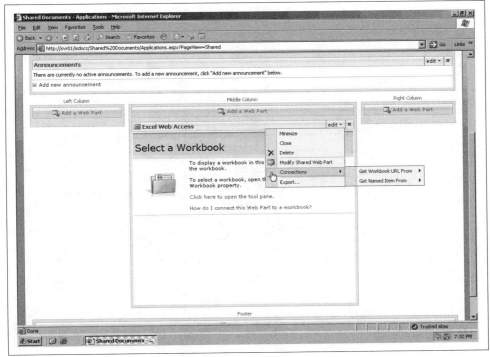

Figure 8-7. Initiating a connection between two Web Parts

5. When the Configure Connection Dialog Box appears, select the desired Field Name and click Finish, as shown in Figure 8-8.

6. Once the connection is made, click on Exit Edit Mode.

 For some connection types, you might have to use the Configure Connection dialog box. See the "Using the Configure Connection Dialog Box" section, later in this chapter.

Verify that you are seeing the desired effect.

Key Connection Submenu Commands

When you are creating or modifying a connection between two Web Parts, after you click on Edit and select Connections, you will see several different command options that you can use. Here's the rundown on the key command selections.

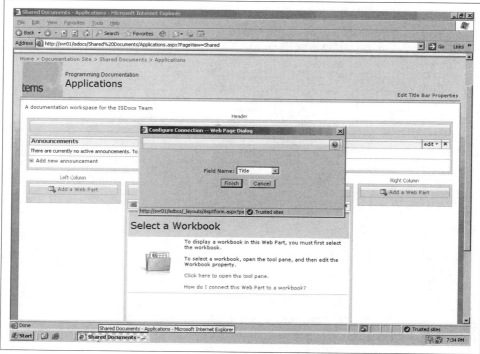

Figure 8-8. Completing the connection between two Web Parts

Provide Row To

If you are using a List View Web Part, you can select a row in the list to pass to the other Web Part.

 How that row data is used by the receiving Web Part depends on which type of Web Part it is. The row data may be simply displayed or it might be treated as a parameter value.

This command option allows you to pass List View Web Part row data to more than one Web Part on the same Web Part page. You cannot pass data from more than one row to the receiving Web Part. You also cannot pass data from the New Row or the Total Row. How you edit the connection depends on the view you are using to access the Connection submenu:

Standard view

Use the options in the Select Item column to choose which row to pass to the receiving Web Part. You can select only one column from this view.

Datasheet view

You can select multiple rows in a List View Web Part in this view, but only the row data with the active cell will be passed on to the receiving Web Part.

Provide Data To

Use this command to send List View Web Part information to another Web Part specifically designed to display list data. This connection type also supports passing row data from the List View Web Part to more than one other Web Part on the same Web Part page. Regardless of whether you are in Standard or Datasheet view, only the row data in the view is passed to the receiving Web Part.

Get Sort/Filter From

The prior two commands are used to set up the connection from the sending Web Part. Use the Get Sort/Filter From commands to configure the connection from the receiving Web Part. This command is used when the sending Web Part is a List View Web Part. This connection type supports only a single connection from one Web Part to another on the same Web Part page. The receiving Web Part must be capable of displaying one of the following types of information:

- A column of data by sorting it either in ascending or descending order in a List View Web Part
- Name and value pairs in one or more columns in a List View Web Part

Using the Configure Connection Dialog Box

Use the Configure Connection dialog box to match a specific data source in one Web Part to another. This avoids having a data type displayed incorrectly in the receiving Web Part. You can use this tool to match row data in the sending Web Part to a cell or field in the receiving Web Part. Another example is matching row data to a column in the receiving Web Part and then filtering the result. The most important issue to remember is that the underlying data types must be the same between sender and receiver, even if the actual Web Part items (rows, cells, and so on) don't have identical names.

Disconnect Web Parts

One of the advantages of working with Sites and Web Part pages is that your environment can remain fluid. As your business and information needs change, so can your site. At some point, a connection between two Web Parts that was once useful will become obsolete. In that case, you can easily break the connection.

1. On the Web Part page, click Site Actions and select Edit Page from the menu.
2. Choose either Web Part, click the menu, select Connections, and then select the connection type and the name of the Web Part on the other end of the connection.
3. When the Remove Connection confirmation dialog box appears, as in Figure 8-9, click Finish.

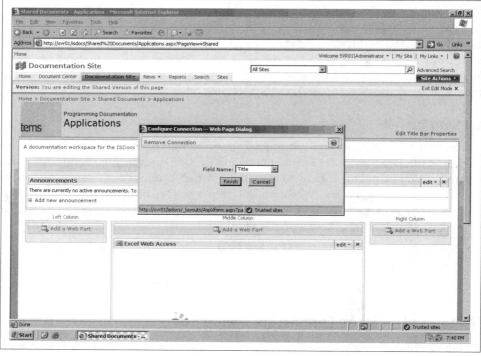

Figure 8-9. Disconnecting a Web Part connection

Using Content Editor Web Parts

You can use a Content Editor Web Part to display text, hyperlinks, tables, and images on a Web Part page. Often this Web Part is used for the majority of the content on a Web Part page because it can be configured to display a variety of content types.

Information can be added and edited on the Content Editor Web Part using either a Rich Text Editor or a Source Editor. The Source Editor will let you enter information in HTML format, so knowledge of HTML is required to use this editor. You can also link to data on another page using the Content Link option. Inserted and linked data can be combined on a Content Editor Web Part to provide a wider range of information sources. The valid hypertext protocol formats for the Content Link option are *http://* and *https://*.

Modifying a Content Editor Web Part

1. In Edit Mode, click the Edit button on the Content Editor Web Part and click Modify Shared Web Part, as shown in Figure 8-10.

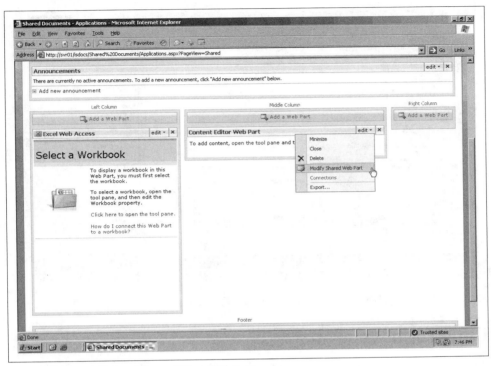

Figure 8-10. Modifying a Content Editor Web Part

2. Open the tool pane, click Source Editor to open the HTML text editor, and then add some HTML content, as shown in Figure 8-11.

3. Click Save to apply the changes in Edit view (Figure 8-12), and then click OK to view the changes in Standard page view.

4. Click the Edit button on the Web Part again, select Modify Shared Web Part, and then click the Rich Text Editor button.

5. When the Rich Text Editor opens (Figure 8-13), you can use the editor to modify the text in the Web Part without having to use HTML

6. When you are done with your editing, click Save, and then click OK.

7. To leave Edit Mode, click Exit Edit Mode, as shown in Figure 8-14.

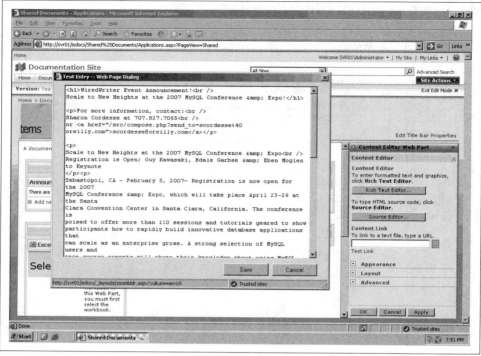

Figure 8-11. Adding HTML content to the Content Editor

Using Form Web Parts

As previously mentioned in this chapter, Form Web Parts are most commonly used to receive List View Web Part data through a data connection and then filter the data. Filtered data can be presented by name, number sequence, or some other value.

Connecting Form Web Parts

As you read in the "Connect Data in Web Parts" section earlier in this chapter, you can connect two compatible Web Parts and use the receiving Web Part to display information from the sending Web Part. The following steps specifically describe how to connect two Form Web Parts:

1. On the desired Web Part page, click Site Actions and select Edit Page from the menu.

2. Click on the Web Part menu, select Connections from the menu, and then select Provide Form Value To.

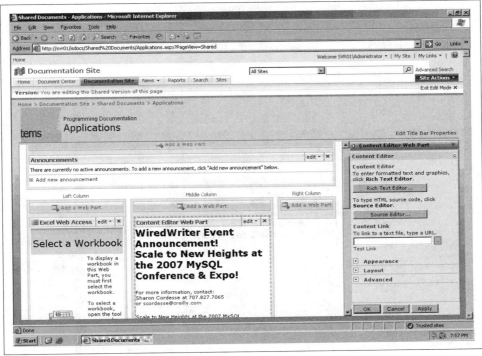

Figure 8-12. Viewing changes made with the Source Editor

3. Click on the name of the Form Web Part to which you want to connect.

4. Type whatever text you want to display in the text field, and then either click GO or press Enter.

Customizing a Form Web Part

You can customize the functionality and appearance of the Form Web Part with the Source Editor. When you open the Source Editor, you can add content or features to this Web Part in HTML; however, there are a number of caveats to consider. You can add only certain types of HTML FORM elements to the Form Web Part. Table 8-1 lists those elements, what they control, and what value is passed.

Table 8-1. HTML FORM element controls

HTML element	Control	Value passed
`<INPUT TYPE="checkbox">`	Checkbox	The VALUE attribute if selected; the string "off" if not selected.
`<SELECT>`	Drop-down list menu	A comma-delimited string of the VALUE attributes of the selected options; the string "off" if no selection. For example, if "cogs" and "sprockets" are selected, the VALUE attribute is "cogs,sprockets."

Table 8-1. HTML FORM element controls (continued)

HTML element	Control	Value passed
`<INPUT TYPE="radio">`	Option button	The VALUE attribute if selected; the string "off" if not selected.
`<TEXTAREA>`	Text area	The VALUE attribute.
`<INPUT TYPE="text">`	Text field	The VALUE attribute.

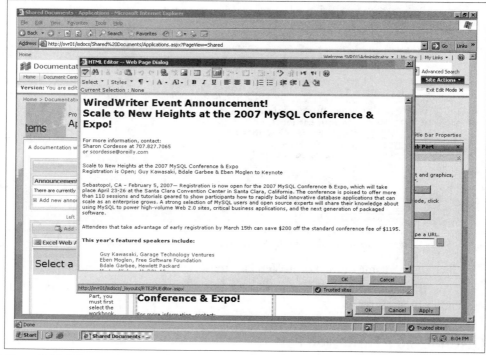

Figure 8-13. Editing a Content Editor Web Part with the Rich Text Editor

Other issues regarding modifying the Form Web Part in the Source Editor include:

- Give all form fields unique names.
- Do not modify the code for the GO button, and do not add a second GO button.
- Do not modify the onkeydown or onclick event code; you may break the Form Web Part.

 These event codes are part of a scripting routine dynamically created by the Form Web Part at runtime to make it possible to connect the Form Web Part to another Web Part.

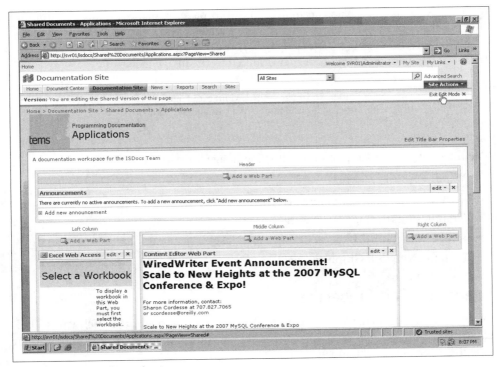

Figure 8-14. Exit Edit Mode

You can customize the Form Web Part only when you are in Shared view. Although this process enables you to customize the Form Web Part and add buttons, checkboxes, and input fields, Microsoft's SharePoint documentation recommends the use of a SharePoint-compatible web design program, such as Office SharePoint Designer 2007, to reduce the amount of effort involved.

Using Image Web Parts

Image Web Parts let you place pictures and graphics on Web Part pages in your SharePoint sites. Image Web Parts display graphics stored in a SharePoint Image Gallery or anywhere else that can be reached over a network connection.

 It is not recommended that you hotlink to an image stored on an Internet host due to bandwidth limitations across a WAN. Also, if you do not own the image, you may be violating copyright laws by displaying it on your site.

Although you can also place an image on a web page by using a Source Editor and creating the link in HTML, the Image Web Part lets you control the image's background color and alignment on the page. You can also use this Web Part to display an image from another Web Part that is linked to the image gallery.

 See the "Change an Image on the Main Site Page" section in Chapter 7 to see how to add a basic image to an Image Web Part.

The Image Web Part supports the following image formats:

- Windows Bitmap (*.bmp*)
- Windows Enhanced Metafile (*.emf*)
- Graphics Interchange Format (*.gif*)
- Joint Photographic Experts Group (*.jpg*, *.jpeg*)
- Portable Network Graphics (*.png*)

Image Web Part Properties

When you add an Image Web Part to a Web Part page and edit the Web Part to link to an image or another Web Part, there are several properties you can modify that will affect the placement and appearance of the image:

Image Link
This is the specific path or URL leading to the image location. The Image Link won't be available if this Web Part is connected to another Web Part.

Alternative Text
This is the text that will appear if the image cannot be displayed for some reason or if you use your cursor to hover over the image.

Image Vertical Alignment
This property controls the vertical position of the Image Web Part. The default value is Middle, but you can specify either Top or Bottom.

Image Horizontal Alignment
This property controls the horizontal position of the image in the Image Web Part. The default value is Center, but you can specify either Left or Right.

Web Part Background Color
You can use this property to determine the color that will appear behind the image. The default background color is determined by the theme set for your site. You can select a color either by using a color grid or by typing in the RGB or Hexadecimal value. You can also set the background to transparent if you want to return to the background color set by the site's theme.

Read more about site themes in Chapter 7.

Connecting Image Web Parts

You can connect one Image Web Part to another Image Web Part or any other Web Part that has a link to a graphic in an Image Gallery.

1. On the Web Part page, click Site Actions and select Edit Page from the menu.
2. Click on the Web Part menu, select Connections, and then select "Get an Image From."
3. Click the name of the Web Part to which you want to connect.

Using List View Web Parts

As stated earlier in this chapter, there really is no such thing as a "List View Web Part." List View Web Parts are what result when a new list or library is created in SharePoint. The Web Part is a full or filtered display of the list you created.

For instance, let's say you create a list of hyperlinks to the corporate web sites of all the companies you purchase from. You may buy only three basic products but use dozens of vendors. A full, unfiltered list shows every link, but you can create filters for the list and then filter those links by product type. From there, it's just a matter of placing the Web Parts where you want them in your site and filtering them for the relevant view. Keep in mind that you can also connect your lists to other Web Parts and further customize how information is displayed.

List View data is always displayed in a tabular format. There are two basic views for this tabular data: Standard and Datasheet. To use Datasheet View, you will need a SharePoint-compatible Office program such as Excel 2007 or Access 2007, as well as support for ActiveX Controls.

Connecting a List View Web Part to Another Web Part

If you connect a List View Web Part to a non-List View Web Part, you can run into some issues. Most tabular data types don't display in a nontabular format when you connect these two Web Parts together. You can only use list and list column data types that are supported for connections to nonlist Web Parts (Table 8-2).

Table 8-2. Supported list and list column data types

Supported list types	Supported list column types
Announcements	Single line of text
Contacts	Choice
Events	Number
Issues	Currency
Links	Date and Time
Tasks	Hyperlink or Picture (for matching columns)
Custom lists	Lookup
Lists that contain data imported from a spreadsheet	Yes/No
Document libraries	Calculated
Form libraries	

You can be in either Standard or Datasheet view when you create a connection between a List View Web Part and another Web Part:

1. On the Web Part page, click Site Actions and select Edit Page from the menu.
2. Click on the Web Part menu, select Connections, and then select either Provide Row To or Get Sort/Filter From, depending on whether you are at the sending or receiving Web Part.
3. Click the name of the Web Part you want to connect to.
4. To filter the list view and display only a subset of the list, click the Selected View property and select a view from the list.

 You can also click "Edit the Current View" to modify that view to present the desired display.

Customizing a List or Library View

As you just learned, it is possible to edit the list view of a list so that only a portion of it appears in the Web Part. There are actually quite a number of properties you can configure that will change the list or library appearance:

1. On the Web Part in Standard view, click the title of a list or library Web Part, such as Announcements.
2. Click Settings, and then select List Settings, as shown in Figure 8-15.
3. Scroll down to the bottom of the page, and under Views, click All Views.
4. When the Customize All Views page opens, you can modify the following properties:

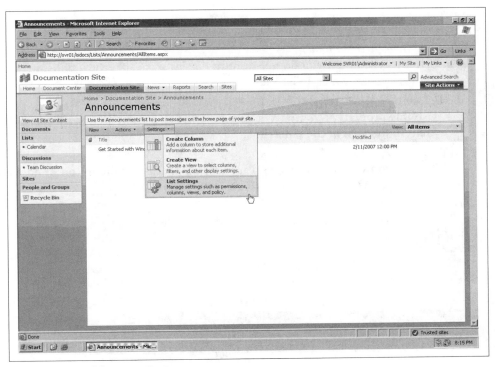

Figure 8-15. Modifying List Settings

Columns

Display columns by checking their checkboxes. Clear the checkboxes by any column names you don't want to display. You can also order columns left to right by choosing a number from the drop-down menu next to the column name. (See Figure 8-16.)

Sort

You can choose any two columns by which to sort. For example, you can sort first by "Created by" and then by "Issue."

Filter

You can filter by any of the criteria available in the Columns section, providing a more restricted view of the entire list. Filter when you want to show only relevant data from the list and not the entire contents.

Group By

Use this to group all list items that have a common value. You can group documents by the author or subject so they appear together in the list view.

Totals

You can display the totals of any item in the Columns area, such as the total number of Issues or the total number of items authored by a particular user.

Style

You can apply a style to your list view, such as Shaded or Bulleted Table.

Show all items without folders

Select this option if you do not want to display a tree-like view of list items. This is also known as a Flat View.

Limit Item

Use this property if you have a very long list and don't want to display all items in the view at the same time.

Mobile

This option is available if you want to view the list or library on a mobile device such as a PDA.

 You can also click on Create View and modify the same options.

5. Click OK to save your changes.

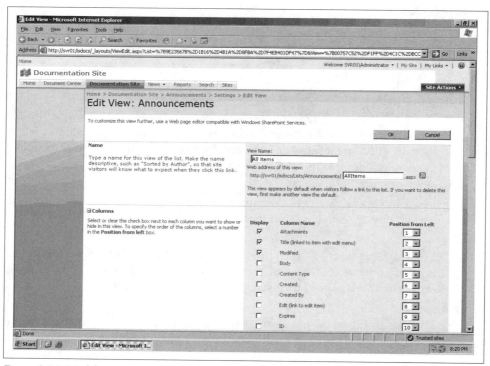

Figure 8-16. Modifying List Properties

Of the property types listed, only "Show all items without folders" and Mobile are new in MOSS 2007. All other properties are present in SharePoint 2003.

Custom Properties of the List View Web Part

Once you've edited the list or library view and placed the List View Web Part on a Web Part page, you can further modify the appearance of the list by editing the Web Part:

1. On the Web Part page, click Site Actions and select Edit Page from the menu.
2. Click the Web Part menu, and then select Modify Shared Web Part.
3. Click the Selected View arrow and select a view from the list. Your options are:
   - All Documents
   - List Name View
   - Explorer View
   - Summary View
   - Additional Views List (custom views created by the user)
4. Click "Edit the Current View" if you want to edit this view rather than change to a different view.
5. Select a toolbar type. Your options are:
   - Summary Toolbar
   - Full Toolbar
   - No Toolbar
6. Click OK to save your changes.

Using Page Viewer Web Parts

As stated earlier in this chapter, the Page Viewer Web Part is used to link to another web page and present that content in a frame, and to display any folder or file, including document and spreadsheet files. In order to display web content in a frame, you must be using a web browser that supports the HTML IFRAME element.

Display Web Content in a Page Viewer Web Part

On the Web Part page, enter Edit Mode. In the Web Page custom properties, do one of the following:

- Choose Folder if you want to display folder data in the Web Part.
- Choose File Group if you want that content to be displayed.
- Choose Webpage if you want content from a remote web page to be displayed.

Using Site Users Web Parts

Use this Web Part to display lists of employees in a team, department, or company. You can also use it to show lists of Domain Groups. This Web Part appears by default whenever you create a Document Workspace.

 See Chapter 9 for more information.

When a list of users or groups is placed on a Web Part page, you can access information about particular users or use the list to contact them. To find detailed information about the user, click the user's name. Depending on what information was entered when the list was created, you can find the user's address, department, email address, phone number, and more.

Click the Smart Tag by the user's name to access available contact information and either email the user, add him to your address book, schedule a meeting, make a phone call, or send an instant message.

There are three properties specific to this Web Part:

Number of Items to Display
> You can limit the number of names you can show in the list in a range between 1 and 1,000.

Display Type
> Use this option when you want to specify which users or groups you want to appear in the list.

Toolbar Type
> This controls the presence or absence of the "Add new user" option.

Adding Members to a Site Users Web Part Group

 See Chapter 14 for more information about creating lists.

When you add a Site Users Web Part to a Web Part page, in addition to the administrator, the following groups are added to the page by default:

- Approvers
- Designers
- Hierarchy Managers
- Home Members

- Home Owners
- Home Visitors
- Quick Deploy Users
- Restricted Readers
- Style Resource Readers
- Viewers

 You'll read more about SharePoint Users and Groups in Chapter 12.

To add a Site Users Web Part to a Web Part page, do the following:

1. On the Web Part page in the Site Users Web Part under Groups, click the group where you want to add a member, as shown in Figure 8-17.

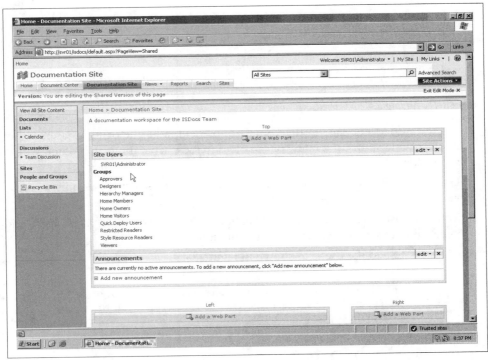

Figure 8-17. Selecting a Group in the Site Users Web Part

2. On the "People and Groups" page, click New and select either Add Users or New Group from the menu, as in Figure 8-18. In this exercise, we will select Add Users.

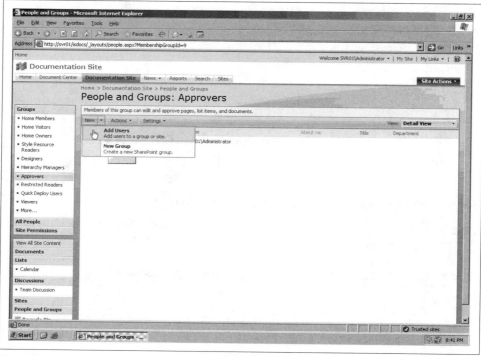

Figure 8-18. Adding a New User to a group

3. On the Add Users page in the User/Groups field, add one or more users either by user names, group names, or email addresses, separating each name with a semicolon.

4. Under Give Permission, use the drop-down menu to select the permission type you want to assign the user or users.

5. You can also click the "View permissions this group has on sites, lists, and items" link to see the details of this permission type.

6. Click OK to add the users, as shown in Figure 8-19.

 The user or group name or email address you enter must be present in SharePoint's database as a registered user; otherwise, you will receive an error message when you try to add them.

Using XML Web Parts

As mentioned at the beginning of this chapter, you can use this Web Part to display XML-formatted data and apply XSLT to style the data prior to showing it.

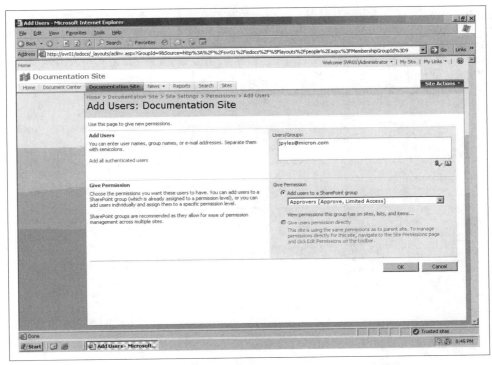

Figure 8-19. Validating the addition of a user to a group

Custom Properties of the XML Web Part

As with the other Web Parts discussed in this chapter, the XML Web Part possesses a set of unique properties:

XML Editor
> This is a plain-text editor that you can use to write XML code. Knowledge of XML is necessary to use this editor.

XML Link
> This property contains a field where you can enter a hyperlink to a file containing XML content. Valid hypertext protocols are *http://* and *https://*.

XSL Editor
> This is a plain-text editor that you can use to enter XSLT source code. Knowledge of XSLT is required to use this editor.

XSL Link
> This property contains a field where you can enter a hyperlink to a file containing XSLT content. Valid hypertext protocols are *http://* and *https://*.

Using the Source Editors in the XML Web Part is almost the same as using the Source Editor in the Content Editor Web Part, as you can see in Figure 8-20. When you click either the XML Editor or XSL Editor buttons, a blank text editor opens, just as in the Content Editor Web Part. You are free to enter the appropriate XML or XSLT content or to use the XML or XSL Links to link to pages containing the relevant content, as shown in Figure 8-20.

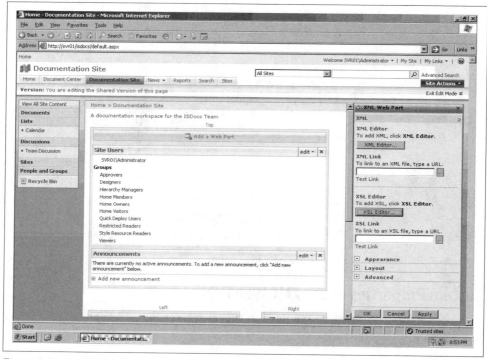

Figure 8-20. XML Web Part

Conclusion

As you've learned, Web Parts and Web Part pages are the key elements in how content is presented on your MOSS 2007 site and site collection. Individual Web Parts can stand alone or connect to other Web Parts to present a different display of the information contained on the "sending" Web Part. Web Parts can present data forms such as text, HTML, XML, various graphics formats, interactive forms, and many other methods. There is virtually no limit to how data presentation can be modified to fit your needs.

CHAPTER 9

Creating and Managing Document Workspaces and Libraries

Introduction

This chapter examines how users can leverage document libraries and more (specifically, Document Workspaces) to better facilitate online document collaboration. This chapter covers MOSS 2007 document library capabilities exclusively. Windows SharePoint Services 3.0 (WSS) may not have some of the document library or Document Workspace capabilities, so keep this in mind if you are operating in a WSS-only environment. When I reference MOSS 2007 or WSS, I am specifically talking about Microsoft Office SharePoint Server 2007 (MOSS) and Windows SharePoint Services Version 3.0 (WSS). Finding ways for the information worker to better share, review, and manage documents in the workplace is always one of the top priorities in any organization. Microsoft Office SharePoint Server 2007 (MOSS 2007) comes with a document repository component that is technically referred to as a *document library*. This chapter covers the ins and outs of creating and managing the document library component. It explains the guidelines that should be used when configuring document libraries and provides step-by-step instructions for doing so. Other topics that will be covered briefly in association with document libraries are: content types, custom metadata, site columns, workflow, and integration with 2007 Microsoft Office System clients.

This chapter also discusses Document Workspace sites, which can help coordinate the development process of one or more related documents with other individuals. I provide some sample scenarios that illustrate how Document Workspaces can be useful in an organization. I also cover the different configuration options that are available when creating and managing these workspaces, providing step-by-step instructions on doing so. Document Workspace sites can be an integral part of any project, in that they provide a tool for facilitating team collaboration. Some of the different lists that you will find when provisioning a Document Workspace are announcements, tasks, relevant links, and shared documents. It is very important to understand the capabilities of document libraries and Document Workspaces—if implemented improperly, they can become a nightmare to deal with on a day-to-day basis.

After reading this chapter, you should understand the following:

- The differences between a document library and network file shares
- The benefits of using document libraries instead of file shares
- Configuring document libraries: custom metadata, site columns, content types, and workflow
- The many different file types within a document library
- Integration points with 2007 Microsoft Office Clients
- How to effectively manage and deploy document libraries in your organization
- When to create Document Workspace sites for collaboration needs, and which options to use

What Is the Significance of Document Libraries?

A *document library* is a SharePoint repository that can store many different types of files. The document library is available for creation in most, if not all, of the site templates that come out of the box with MOSS 2007. For example, if we were to go and provision a team site, when the site is complete, one of the first Web Parts that you will notice is Shared Documents. This is actually a document library that was provisioned on site creation. So, what is a document library? Document libraries provide a place where users can centrally manage, store, and organize documents across their organization. Document libraries are like any other standard list you will find within MOSS, except they are specifically optimized to hold documents as their items. Any other standard SharePoint list item will consider the document as an attachment to that list item. In other words, a document library lists the documents and other file types, whereas a standard list will store a document as an attachment instead of the list item itself. Document libraries are not limited to documents. As you can see in Figure 9-1, document libraries can manage other file types, such as spreadsheets, presentations, forms, and other common file types.

Once users begin using document libraries on a daily basis, they will quickly realize their benefits. The document library is a user-friendly, intuitive tool that can be easily customized to meet the changing needs of the information worker.

Utilizing Document Libraries

Now let's dive into some of the details of working with document libraries on a daily basis. When using document libraries, there are a few basic tasks that we should first understand before going into the configuration options. These are:

- Navigating to a document library in the web browser
- Uploading documents into a document library
- Uploading multiple documents into a library

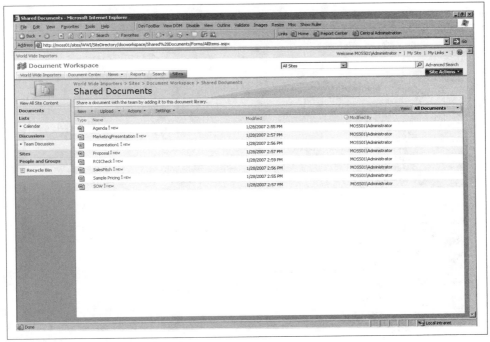

Figure 9-1. Microsoft Office SharePoint Server 2007 document library

- Creating new documents from the library
- Working with the Explorer and Datasheet views
- Exporting a document library to a spreadsheet

Creating a Document Library

If your site does not have a document library or you would like to create your own, you can follow these simple steps:

1. Navigate to your SharePoint site.
2. Click the View All Site Content link on the top of the lefthand side Quick Launch bar, and you should see something like Figure 9-2.
3. Click on the Create button under the All Site Content page title. You should see the Create screen.
4. Select Document Library, which is located underneath the Libraries section header. You should see the New page, shown in Figure 9-3.
5. Add a descriptive title for the document library.
6. Then, select whether you would like to display it on the quick launch bar.

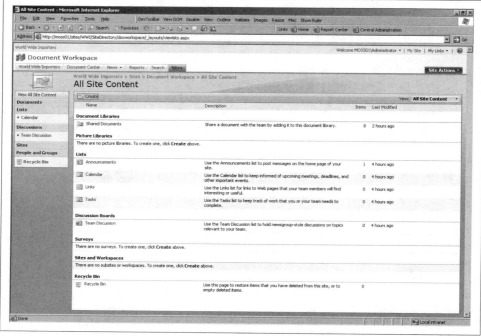

Figure 9-2. The All Site Content page

7. Enable document versioning. (We are going to visit this topic later in the chapter, and this will need to be enabled.)

8. Click Create at the bottom of the page.

Your document library has now been created.

Navigating to a Document Library

Navigating to a document library is a simple task that requires opening your browser and performing the following steps:

1. Open your web browser and log onto your SharePoint site.

2. If you logged into a newly created site, you should see a Shared Documents Web Part.

3. Click this link and you will then be directed to the document library's *Allitems.aspx* page; the URL should look something like this:

    http://servername/sites/sitename/ Shared%20Documents/Forms/AllItems.aspx

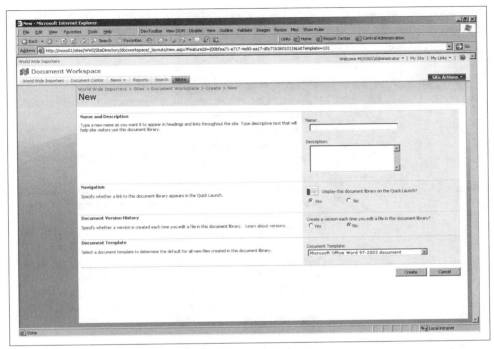

Figure 9-3. The New page for creation of a document library

4. If the Shared Documents Web Part is not on your page, you should have a Documents link in the Quick Launch section; click that link. That page will display all the document libraries for that site.

5. Click the link for the document library that you want to open.

Once you have created and navigated to your document library, there are a number of different actions that can be performed.

Uploading Documents to the Document Library

Now that we have gone through the steps of creating a document library, it's time to explain the options that you have when uploading documents into the library. It is important to understand each of these methods and some of the considerations that should be taken when using them on a daily basis. Users have quite a few options when uploading documents into a library:

- Uploading via the upload action button
- Uploading from a Microsoft Office client
- Using the Explorer view to upload
- Uploading via the Windows Explorer action

Now let's look at each of these methods and the pros and cons that come with each of them in Table 9-1.

Table 9-1. Pros and cons of the different upload methods

Upload method	Pros	Cons
Document library; upload button from toolbar	Uploading single documents; will prompt for required metadata Easy and intuitive to use Ability to browse for documents and check off multiple documents at once for upload	When uploading multiple documents, required metadata will not be prompted for and will remain blank Office client 2003 or 2007 are required when uploading multiple documents
Microsoft Office client	Ability to fill in required metadata easily from client's document information panel	Must have Office 2007 in order to take advantage of document information panel Can be difficult to initially navigate to the document library when saving
Explorer View	Easily upload multiple documents by dragging and dropping into the Explorer View window Ability to move and copy documents between the Windows Explorer folder and document library	Must have Office client 2000 or later installed on machine Required metadata for document library will remain blank
Windows Explorer	Most users are familiar with and understand how to use this method Drag-and-drop functionality when a separate Windows Explorer window pops up with document library contents Upload multiple documents more quickly than uploading each document separately Ability to open up Windows Explorer and save it quickly under *My Network Places* or map a network drive	Required metadata for the document library will remain blank

Now that we have laid out the options for uploading documents into a library, let's run through each of them and provide some step-by-step demonstration instructions.

Uploading Documents from the Document Library

The first option we will look at is uploading documents from the document library's Upload button, located on the toolbar. This method is fairly easy in that the steps are very straightforward. Any user with web browsing experience should be able to grasp this method with ease. So, let's take a look at the steps needed to perform this action.

Uploading a single document using the document library Upload function

1. You must log on to your SharePoint site and navigate to the document library. Follow the steps provided earlier in the chapter under "Creating a document library" or "Navigating to a document library" before proceeding onto the next steps.

2. Once you have navigated to the document library, you will find the Upload button on the toolbar.

3. Click the Upload button, and you should see the options shown in Figure 9-4.

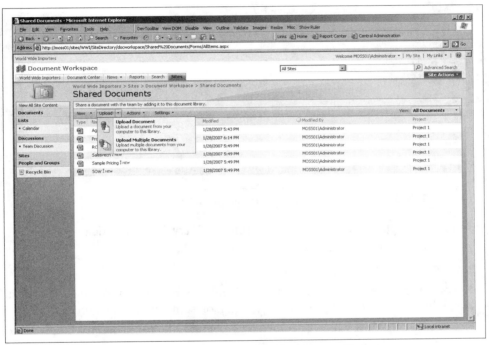

Figure 9-4. Displaying upload document options within the document library

4. First we are going to look at the Upload Documents option, so click that.

5. You will then be taken to a screen where you are asked to browse for your specific document. Browse to your specific document and click OK.

6. If you have specified some required fields (which will be covered in more detail later in this chapter), you will be prompted to enter those required fields (Figure 9-5).

7. Once you have filled out the appropriate required fields, click the OK button, and your document will be successfully downloaded with all the required fields.

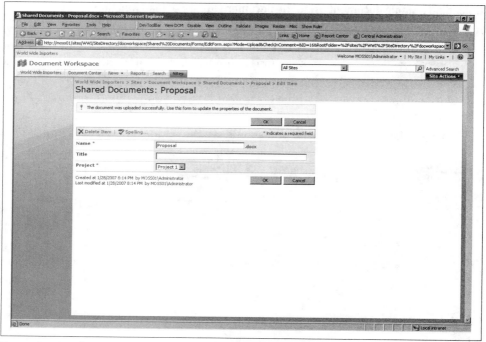

Figure 9-5. Displaying required fields when uploading a document

Uploading multiple documents using the document library Upload function

1. Follow steps 1 and 2 in the previous demonstration.

2. Click Upload Multiple Documents.

3. You should then be presented with a Windows Explorer tree-like view of your machine's filesystem. Your screen should look something like Figure 9-6.

4. You can check off which documents you would like to upload by simply clicking the empty box next to each item.

5. Once satisfied with the amount of items you wish to upload to the document library, click the OK button at the bottom of the screen. Your documents are now uploaded to the document library.

6. Remember that uploading documents to the document library with this method bypasses the required metadata for the library.

Uploading via the Explorer and Windows Explorer

These next two methods provide users with a common Windows Explorer-like look and feel. They both enable users to drag and drop documents into the library with ease. The Windows Explorer method uses the Web Distributed Authoring and Versioning

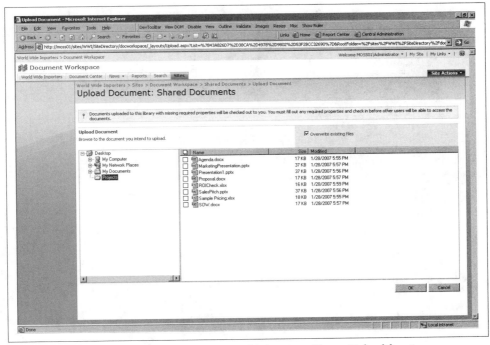

Figure 9-6. Uploading multiple documents using the document library Upload function

(WebDAV) protocol. One important consideration for this method when moving multiple documents from one document library to another is that you lose all version history for that document. So, with that in mind, let's quickly look at the steps for moving documents from one document library to another using each of these methods. Take into consideration that the default upload size limit for MOSS is 50MB. This limit can be changed, but as a general rule, it is dependent upon server and network speeds, and the limit should not be pushed to more than 300MB. After that threshold, performance will vary and some users may begin experiencing server time outs when uploading.

First, the Explorer View:

1. Navigate to the document library (steps shown earlier in this chapter).

2. Click the down arrow on the right side of the screen, underneath View.

3. Click Explorer View. Note that in order for this view to work, your machine must have Microsoft Office 2000 or later.

4. You screen should then look like Figure 9-7.

5. You can now drag and drop these documents as you would in Windows Explorer. You can also copy and paste from here.

Figure 9-7. Displaying your documents in the Explorer View

Using Windows Explorer:

1. Navigate to the document library.

2. Click on the Actions down arrow, and select "Open with Windows Explorer."

3. A Windows Explorer window will pop up with all the documents that are in the library.

4. You can now drag and drop or copy and paste to move files as you wish.

Email-enabled document libraries

Document libraries within MOSS 2007 come with the capability to receive emails and attachments. The library must have an email address associated with it in order for it to receive emails. Once the document library has been configured, you can send attachments directly to this email address from your email client. Please reference this URL for a step-by-step guide to implementing email-enabled document libraries in your environment:

http://office.microsoft.com/en-us/winsharepointadmin/HA011608031033.aspx

Organizing Documents

Now that we have an understanding of how documents are uploaded into a document library, let's take a look at organizing these documents. Even though document libraries are designed to hold a large amount of documents, there are still some considerations to note. Limiting the number of documents in a document library is critical in keeping a friendly user experience. The limit that Microsoft has set is a hard limit of no more than 2,000 files per folder; the same goes for the root of the document library, with a limit of 2,000 files. Having more than 10,000 documents in a library will at best provide an unfriendly user experience, with varied performance depending on the pure size of the documents. Organizing these files in an effective and efficient manner that allows users to find what they are looking for in document libraries of this size can become very challenging.

This brings up another consideration about using folders within a document library. Users who are unfamiliar with document libraries and the search engine in MOSS 2007 will create folders within document libraries. Organizing using folders is what they are used to, since organizing file shares is most likely what they were using before document libraries. Document libraries are not meant to be a *complete* replacement for file shares. File shares should continue to have their place in an organization. Don't get me wrong; live documents that are constantly under revision should live in a document library. However, if you are looking to just copy all of the documents from the file share to a document library in one quick swoop, don't do it. If you are looking to do this so you can have a central place to go and search through these files, then have MOSS go out and crawl and index these file shares.

Utilizing the metadata and views when organizing a large amount of documents is much more powerful than nesting them in a bunch of folders. The metadata that is attached to these documents play a critical role in your ability to quickly and effectively filter out the documents you do not need, and display the documents that you are looking for. Metadata also plays a mission-critical role when using the enterprise search capabilities of MOSS. Managed properties can be set up on the MOSS search side, which enable a user to quickly search for a document when she is aware of a specific property of that document. For example, a user is searching for a document, and she is unsure of the title of the document, but she does know who authored the document. Because the author property is required metadata, the user will return much more relevant search results when querying.

Metadata is also known as *custom columns*. Custom columns can be created in a document library to help users organize and manage document libraries. These custom columns are helpful because they describe some key properties about that document without ever opening the document to see what it is. This in itself saves a huge amount of time when a user is not sure exactly what the document is.

Let's go through the steps of creating a custom column for categorizing the different projects that are associated with each document. When selecting a data type that will be used for your custom column, consider how you are going to organize your library. For example, if you would like to organize and sort your information by data and time, then choose the data and time data type. The single line of text and multiple lines of text data types are free text fields, and therefore are somewhat more difficult to organize methodically. Free text fields make it considerably harder to know what is to be entered into those columns and organized by what one user types to the next.

Creating custom columns

1. Navigate to the document library.
2. Click on the arrow in the Settings menu, and then click on "Create column."
3. Add a name for your column.
4. Select a data type for your column.
5. Add some detailed options for the type of information you selected.
6. Add some additional column information, which depends on what column type you select.
7. Click OK.

Now that we have created some custom columns, I want to briefly cover site columns. *Site columns* are custom columns that can be reused across multiple lists and across many SharePoint sites. Site columns are useful when you have a custom column that you would like to consistently use across your SharePoint sites. By pointing to an existing site column, you do not have to recreate this custom column when you need it. For example, suppose you define a site column as Project. You can then add that site column to any content type (explained later in chapter), list, or library. This insures complete control over the columns properties when it is first created. The following are step-by-step instructions for creating a site column.

Creating a site column

1. Navigate to your SharePoint site.
2. Click on the Site Actions menu.
3. Then click on Site Settings.
4. Under Galleries, click on Site Columns. You should see something similar to Figure 9-8.
5. On the Site Column Gallery page, click Create.
6. Fill out the Name and Data Type you want to store in the Site Column.

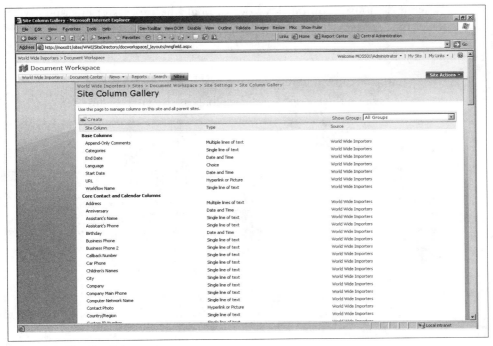

Figure 9-8. The Site Columns page

7. In the Group section, either select an existing group or create a new group in which you would like to store this site column.

8. In the Additional Column Settings section, add the supplementary information, which is dependent on the data type that was previously selected.

Document library views

Creating document library views is a powerful way to enable your users to quickly filter through and group documents within a document library. When looking at files within a document library, you can sort and filter by some of the metadata (columns) across the top of the library. This is great, but what if you want a consistent sort and filter automatically when navigating to that document library? Views can be configured directly through the web interface and include options such as Sort, Group by, Filtering, and Styles. Each option enables you to better organize your document into specific views that can be quickly used when sorting through large document libraries. For example, suppose you're a project manager who is storing multiple project documents inside one document library. You want to be able to quickly group all of your documents by their associated projects, and to have these documents sorted by their project name in alphabetical order. You can create a simple view that groups and sorts these documents by the metadata assigned to these documents when they are uploaded into the document library.

The following demonstration quickly goes through the process of creating a view that satisfies this scenario.

Creating views

1. Navigate to the document library.
2. Views are shown on the far right of the toolbar, as shown in Figure 9-9.

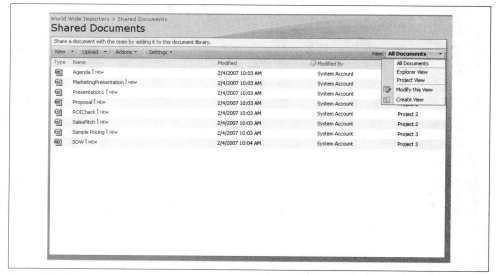

Figure 9-9. View options

3. To create a new view, click the Settings button on the toolbar.
4. Click Create View.
5. You can choose among Standard view, Calendar view, Access view, Datasheet view, and Gantt view. Click Standard view for this demonstration.
6. In the View Name field, type a descriptive name for this view.
7. If you would like to see this view by default when navigating to the document library, then pick this view as the default. This view applies only to public views.
8. In Audience, select whether this view should be personal or public. Personal views can be created and pertain only to you.
9. In the Columns section, pick which columns you would like to show within this custom view.
10. In the Sort section, choose which column you would like to sort by in ascending or descending order. You can sort by multiple columns (e.g., sort by column A then sort by column B).

11. In the Filter section, select options for whether you want to filter files and how you want to filter them. A filtered view displays a smaller section of the files, which is good in document libraries with large amounts of files.

12. In the "Group by" section, you can group items in a document library with the same column values. For example some documents may apply to a specific location. As long as location is a custom column and this column has the same value as others, then these items can be grouped together.

13. The Totals section allows you to count the number of items in a column, such as the total number of tasks.

14. The Styles section lets you select a certain style for a specific view. Applying styles to views can make it more aesthetically pleasing for the user. For example, you could create a library in which every other row is shaded.

15. The Folders section lets you choose a flat view, which will display items without folders.

16. The Items section allows the view creator to limit the amount of items returned to the user.

17. If you are planning on accessing this site using a mobile device, the mobile section allows you to enable the view for the mobile device.

18. Figure 9-10 displays the Create View page and all of its configurable sections.

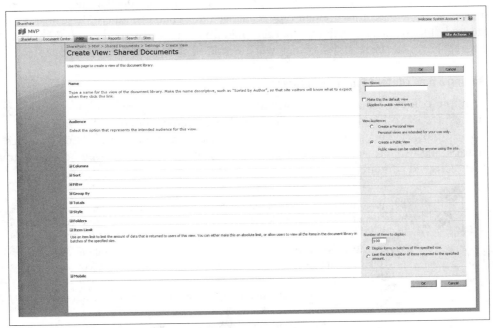

Figure 9-10. The Create View page with configuration sections

Content types

Content types, a new feature in MOSS 2007, enable organizations to more efficiently and effectively organize and centrally manage content across a site collection. You can define content types for specific kinds of documents and informational products. Content types can be defined in a list or library and can consist of multiple item types or document types. This is very useful because document libraries and lists can now contain multiple document and item types. For example, your HR department has multiple documents that they would like to make available so that users can come and create a new document from these document type templates. When users navigate to the document library, they can use the New command within the toolbar of the document library and create a new document from the chosen document type. The major advantage of using document types is that they may contain unique document properties and policies that are specific to this document. Content types such as this can, for example, be associated with a workflow so when a user creates a new document from this content type, a workflow can be initiated.

When a list content type is added to a document library or list, it is considered a child of the content type from which is was created. This child content type will inherit all of the properties of its parent's content type. Some of the properties that can be attached to the parent site and inherited by the child site include its associated workflow(s), document templates, read-only settings, and all metadata. The child list content type can be customized for its specific container (i.e., list or library) without affecting the parent content type. If the parent list content type is changed, the child can inherit these changes if desired. If there are any attributes that the child list content type shares with the parent, these changes can be inherited, which will override all child attributes.

Adding a new content type to a library

Multiple content types can be attached to a document library. Adding this ability makes it easy to build a document library that can store different document types. For example, a document library can contain the documents and related graphics that belong to a project. These different types of files will be organized according to their assigned content type.

Before content types can be added to a document library, the library must be set to allow multiple content types. Follow these steps for checking that the document libraries settings support multiple content types:

1. Navigate to the library in which you would like to enable multiple content types. Note that you cannot enable multiple content types on a Wiki library.
2. Click on the Settings menu, and then click "Document library settings."
3. Under General Settings, click Advanced Settings.
4. In the Content Type section under "Allow management of content types," select "yes" on the radio button.
5. Click OK.

Now that we have enabled this library to allow the management of content types, let's add a content type to the library.

 To add a content type to a library, the user must have at least Design permissions for that document library:

1. Navigate to the document library in which you'd like to add a content type. Make sure content type management has been enabled.

2. Click on Settings, and then Document Library Settings.

3. Under the Content Types section, click "Add from existing site content types."

4. Figure 9-11 shows the Content Type section, which includes the "Add from existing site content types" link.

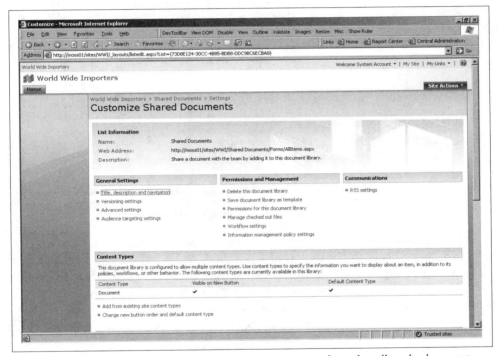

Figure 9-11. The document library with content type settings configured to allow the document library to manage multiple content types

1. Look at the Select Content Types section. In the "Select site content types from" list, click the down arrow to select the group of site content types from which to choose.

2. Click the content type that you would like to use from the "Available site content types" section, and then click Add to move the selected content type to the "Content types to add" list.

3. You can add additional content types by repeating steps 3–6.

In Figure 9-12, I have added a marketing presentation template document as my associated content type to this document library. I have added this so that when users from my marketing team need to create a new presentation, they can come here and use this centrally managed template. They will always know that this is up-to-date because any changes made to the template also will be made here. This document library can now store multiple document types in an organized, efficient manner.

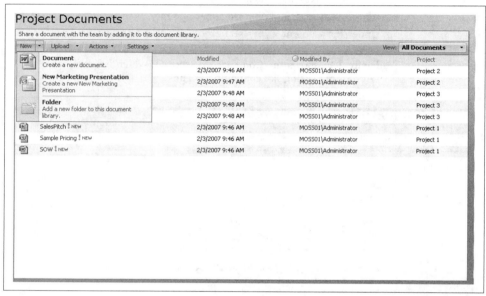

Figure 9-12. A new PowerPoint template as an associated content type

The New Button order can be customized to display in the order that you specify. The first content type that is displayed when the New button is clicked becomes the default content type for the library. You can either change the order or make certain content types are not visible on the New button. To change the default content type or reorder the content types, follow these steps:

1. Navigate to the document library in which you would like to change the order of the content types shown when the New button is clicked.

2. Click on Document Library Settings.

3. Under the Content types section, click "Change new button order and default content."

4. Once you have navigated to the Content Type Order section, you can perform either of the following:

    a. Clear the Visible checkbox if you would like the content type to not be shown when the "New button" is selected.

    b. Change the order in which the content type appears on the "New button" by clicking the arrow next to the corresponding content type in the "Positions from top" column and selecting the order number as desired.

Document Management and Workflow

Document management is a critical focus point in any organization. Building workflows to automate the business process around document management is where companies have really started to focus their energies. One of the many highlights around MOSS 2007 and its out-of-the-box capabilities is in the business process management (BPM) area. MOSS 2007 comes out of the box with some predefined workflows that are specifically designed to support common business processes. This is just the starting point for your company to create custom complex workflows that go above and beyond what is found outside of the box. This next section looks at some of these out-of-the-box workflows and how they can be added to document libraries and content types that may be used within these document libraries. We will also look at some of MOSS's document management features, such as versioning, document approval, document routing, and Information Rights Management (IRM).

Workflow

Workflow is very powerful because it enables organizations to streamline their common business processes, which in turn can save the company from having to go through the time taking manual steps to complete common business processes. MOSS 2007 has some predefined workflow templates that can be used to automate some of these common business processes. The predefined workflows that can be added to a document library in MOSS 2007 are Approval, Collect Signatures, Collect Feedback, and Disposition Approval.

This chapter is not focused on workflow, so I will not discuss each workflow in detail. Instead, this section will simply provide some demonstration steps on how to add workflows to your document library. It is important to note that outside of the predefined workflows that can be attached to a document library, custom workflows also can be developed and added to a document library. For example, SharePoint administrators can design no-code workflows with Microsoft Office SharePoint Designer 2007 that can be used in a specific document library. A custom workflow that is created in SharePoint Designer can only be connected to its associated container. So, for example, you cannot create a custom workflow template in SharePoint designer and then reuse it across different lists and document libraries. On the other hand, developers can create custom workflow solutions with Visual Studio 2005 Extensions for Windows Workflow Foundation. These workflows can then be deployed as a solutions package across multiple sites.

Now let's take a look at adding a predefined workflow to a document library:

1. First, navigate to the document library to which you would like to add a workflow.

2. Click on the Settings button, and then click on Document Library Settings.

3. Under the "Permissions and Management" section, click on Workflow Settings.

4. If there are not any workflows added to this library, you should be taken right to the "Add a Workflow" page.

5. Select the workflow template that you would like to use. In this example, we will select Approval.

6. Type a descriptive name that you can use to identify this workflow later.

7. In the Task List section, specify a task list that the workflow will use. You can choose to use the system default tasks lists, which users can use to view their workflow tasks easily by selecting the My Tasks view, or you can create a new task list that if there is a need to conceal workflow information.

8. Select a history list to use with the workflow. The history lists displays each event that occurs throughout the life of the workflow.

9. Next, select the Start Options to specify how and when this workflow is initiated. Certain start options are available with certain configurations. For example, the start option "Start this workflow to approve publishing a major version" is enabled only when major and minor versioning has been enabled for that document library. Figure 9-13 shows the "Add a Workflow" window and all of the configuration options that come with the Approval workflow.

10. Click Next and configure your workflow customization as desired.

Once you have added workflow capabilities to a document library, you can now manually start your workflow on a document from within the document library. When starting a workflow, you must have at least Edit items permissions, and some workflows may require the Manage Lists permission. Your workflow may be set to automatically begin once the document has been uploaded to the document library. Otherwise, you can begin any workflow manually by following these steps:

1. Navigate to the document library where you have configured your workflow, as shown in previous demonstration steps.

2. Click the drop-down arrow next to the document in which you would like to manually start the workflow.

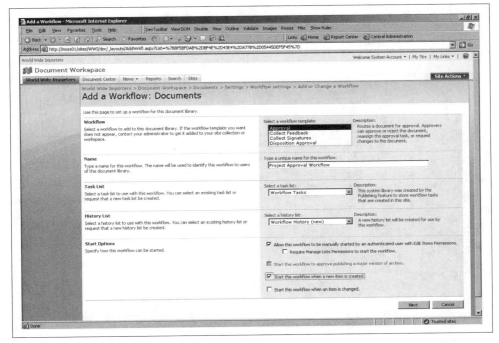

Figure 9-13. Add a workflow page

3. Click Workflows.

4. Figure 9-14 shows the custom workflow that we created in the previous demonstration called Project Approval Workflow.

5. Under the "Start a new workflow" section, select your custom workflow.

6. Add the names of the approvers who you would like to approve the document. You can select the Approvers people-picker button and search through directory services to select different people or groups.

7. Fill out the other sections appropriately.

8. Click Start to initiate the workflow.

9. To view your workflow tasks at any time, you can navigate to that site's task list and click on the My Tasks view, which should display all of the workflow tasks that are assigned to you.

Versioning and document approval

Version control has been improved from its predecessor, SharePoint Portal Server 2003 (SPS 2003). SPS 2003 did not have the ability to capture major versions versus minor versions. This is where MOSS 2007 fills the gap, giving the users the ability to specify major or minor versions when checking in documents. You can even take it a step further and specify how many versions to retain and which types to retain.

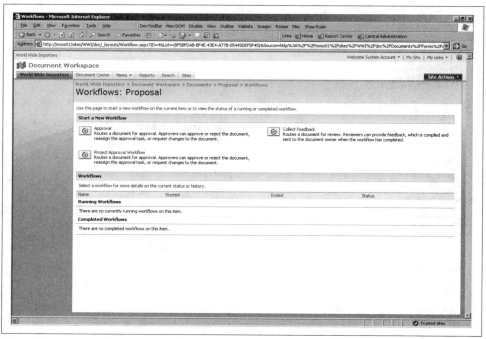

Figure 9-14. A custom project workflow to be started manually

This is critical for an organization that is constantly making changes to a living, breathing document. With major and minor versions, team members can quickly differentiate between a major release of the document and a small grammatical change.

By default, major and minor versioning are not turned on and must be configured in the Document library settings. Under the General section, you will find Versioning settings. Figure 9-15 shows the versioning page in which you can configure the specifics of versioning and related settings that affect versioning.

Content approval is considered an interaction with versioning because if it is required, a file remains a draft until it is approved or rejected. If the file is approved, then it is assigned approved status in the library and is accessible to anyone who has permissions to view it. This is the same when the file is rejected, except it can only be seen by the user who submitted the document. Users can wrap a workflow around this common business process to automate this type of scenario.

Within the versioning configuration page, users can require check out for all documents in the library. Once they are checked out and changed, the documents must be checked back in with their respective version (major or minor) selected, along with any comments that go along with the version change. This ensures that a version is created only when a user checks out a file, makes a change, and then check it

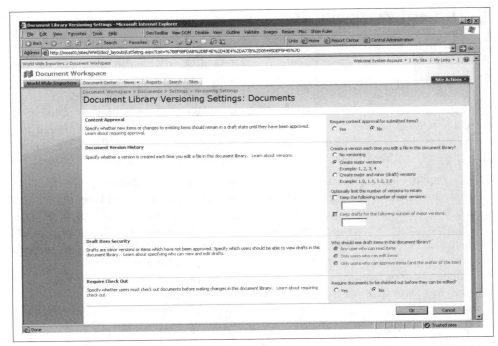

Figure 9-15. The Document Library Versioning Settings page

back in. This option helps to ensure a more effective versioning procedure, and also includes comments for each version.

Document routing

Sometimes it is necessary to keep two copies of the same file within two different places. You can specify a custom Send To destination for a document library so that people can easily copy the necessary files to the specified destination. The Send To menu option appears on the drop-down menu for each file within the library. For example, you may have a drafting document library in which your team drafts important documents that will one day be available to all employees within the organization. Once these documents are ready to be consumed by the rest of the organization, you can place them in a general published document library, where they can be consumed by all people within your organization.

The Send To command does not simply copy the files to a new location; it also keeps tabs on the source file for any changes that might occur. When a user uses the Send To command, they can choose whether to update existing copies within the destination container. The server tracks the relationship between the source file and all of its destination copies. Users can centrally manage all of the copies through the Manage Copies page.

Document Workspaces

Document Workspace sites are specifically designed to help coordinate the development process of one or more documents. These sites provide the tools necessary to facilitate this sometimes complex and hectic process. Document Workspace tools include a document library, a list of members who are currently working in the workspace, a task list, announcements list, and a list of links to important information. These tools ensure that the work is performed directly on a document, and that it will have rich version history along with required check out so that users cannot overwrite each other's work by editing the document at the same time.

Users of a workspace can set up alert subscriptions to be emailed on a weekly, daily, or immediate basis when the document has been changed. This will keep team members constantly in the loop about what changes are being made at any one time in the life of a document. Workspace members can also utilize the tasks list to prioritize a project's tasks. Most of the time, Document Workspaces will be created temporarily and in an ad-hoc format, but they can be retained for as long as might be required. A Document Workspace does not function any differently than any of the other sites you might create within MOSS 2007. The only differences are the lists that are created upon site provision and the features associated with the document when the Document Workspace is created.

A Document Workspace can be created in a few different ways. The first way is to create a Document Workspace from a document within a library. This is probably the better-known method because you are dealing with all of these documents within a document library and while doing so may decide that a document warrants a workspace. To create a Document Workspace from a document within a library, follow these steps:

1. Navigate to the document library where your document is being stored.
2. Point to the name of the document and click the drop-down arrow.
3. Point to the Send To command.
4. Select Create Document Workspace. Figure 9-16 shows the pop-up menu that you will see when creating a Document Workspace from a document within a library.
5. Click OK.

Notice that the URL of the document library is the name of your document. For example, if your original site was *http://moss01/sites/WWI/DOC* and you created a Document Workspace from a document library within the site "DOC," SharePoint takes the name of your document and appends it to the end of the URL from which you created your workspace. So, your newly created Document Workspace will now

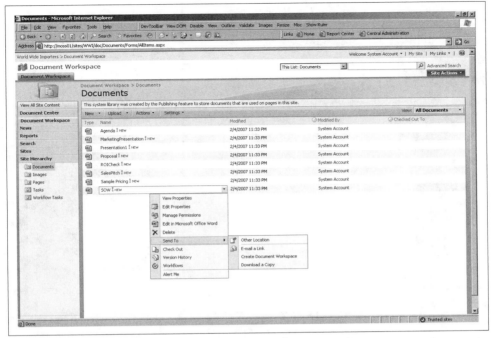

Figure 9-16. The Create Document Workspace command

look like *http://moss01/sites/WWI/DOC/DocumentName*. The document from which you created this workspace will automatically be added to the Shared Documents document library on site creation. When a Document Workspace is created based on that document, you can publish that document back to its source location at any time. Figure 9-17 shows the "Publish to Source Location" command. Once you click this command, it will replace the source document with the most current version of the Document Workspace document.

If you want to create a Document Workspace but do not want to have it associated with a document within a document library, you can always create an empty Document Workspace. To create an empty Document Workspace, create a site like you normally would for a Team site or a Publishing site, but select the Document Workspace option, which is under the Collaboration tab on the Create page.

The Document Workspace can also be created when authoring a document through Microsoft Office Word 2007. This can also be done through Microsoft Office Word 2003, but the following step-by-step demonstration applies to Word 2007. Microsoft Office Word 2007 has many integration points with MOSS 2007, some of which we will briefly cover in the following chapters of this book. Figure 9-18 displays how a Document Workspace can be created from within the Office 2007 application itself.

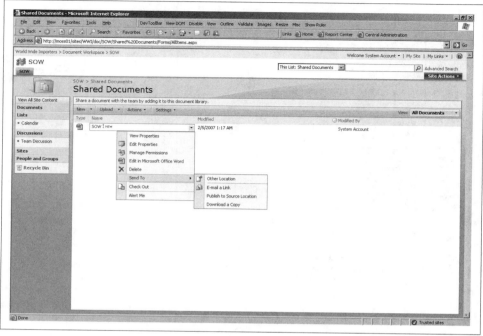

Figure 9-17. The Publish to Source Location command

To create a Document Workspace from within Word 2007, follow these steps:

1. Open Microsoft Office Word 2007 and the document from which you would like to create a Document Workspace.

2. In the right task pane in "Location for new workspace," type in the URL or choose from the options given in the drop-down.

3. Select Create.

4. After the Document Workspace is created, the document you are authoring will be automatically saved to that workspace.

When working on a document through Microsoft Office Word 2007 that is stored inside a Document Workspace, you can access all of the great integration features. For example, there might come a time where the copy that you opened in Word is not the same copy that is in the Document Workspace. Word 2007 is smart enough to recognize this by communicating with the server. In the task pane on the right and in the document information panel, you will see a message stating that there is a conflict. You will then be presented with a screen that looks like Figure 9-19.

As you can see, Word 2007 has recognized this conflict and gives you many options for dealing with it. The task pane on the right also allows you to add members directly from Word to your Document Workspace. It also shows you the task list from the Document Workspace and the document library and all its contents,

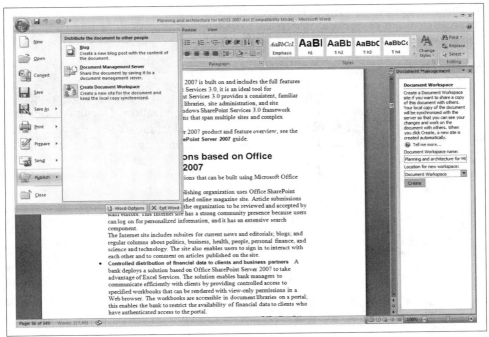

Figure 9-18. The Create Document Workspace option from within Microsoft Office Word 2007

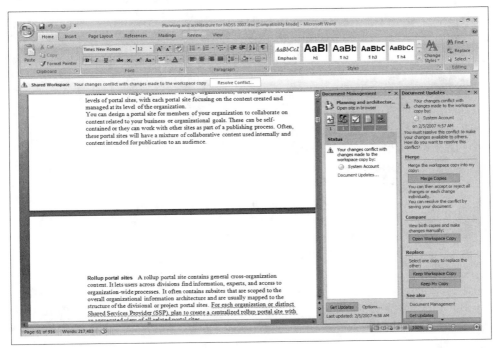

Figure 9-19. Document conflict options

all from within the task pane. This is a key integration piece that enables the user to control just about anything he desires, all from within one application interface.

Conclusion

In conclusion, document libraries can play an integral role when it comes to organizing and utilizing documents and files within an organization. Document libraries have vastly improved from older versions. Utilizing documents libraries and Document Workspaces together empowers users to facilitate team collaboration at its highest level.

CHAPTER 10

Creating and Managing Meeting Workspaces

Introduction

A *Meeting Workspace* is a web site you can use to collect all of the materials related to a project, such as documents, agendas, and reports for a single meeting, a series of reoccurring meetings, or meetings pursuant to a long-term project. As with other elements in MOSS 2007, such as the Enterprise Report Center site template, the Meeting Workspace serves as a single interface for data from many scattered sources.

The Workspace doesn't exist only for the sake of presenting information during the meeting; it also provides a dynamic web site for attendees to check and find out the latest information on meeting topics. Meeting Workspaces are a handy way to communicate with attendees ahead of time so they can be prepared to bring specific materials or so they have the latest updates on the agenda. The workspace could also be the dynamic repository for data related to regularly held meetings, such as staff meetings. A Meeting Workspace can exist for years or be deleted after a single meeting, depending on its purpose.

You can create a Meeting Workspace when you create an event in your calendar. This can be the calendar present in either Microsoft Windows SharePoint Services 3.0 or Microsoft Office Outlook 2007. It's also possible to create a Meeting Workspace without creating a calendar event.

Meeting Workspace Templates

Depending on the nature of your meeting and what information you require, you can choose from among five default templates:

Blank Meeting Workspace
> Comes without any special features and can be completely customized by you. This template is typically used when the other default templates are not quite right for your needs or if you just prefer to design the workspace yourself.

Basic Meeting Workspace

> The "bare bones" workspace template, including only the Objectives, Attendees, Agenda, and Document Library Web Parts.

Decision Meeting Workspace

> Designed for meetings where information and material are reviewed pursuant to making a decision. Web Parts included are Objectives, Attendees, Agenda, Document Library, Tasks, and Decisions.

Social Meeting Workspace

> Available to organize any social occasion, such as a holiday party, birthday, or company picnic. For this purpose, the Web Parts involved are Attendees, Directions, Image/Logo, Things to Bring, Discussions, and Photo Library.

Multipage Meeting Workspace

> Used when a single web page for your Meeting Workspace is insufficient. The Web Parts available by default are Objectives, Attendees, and Agenda. However, you also have two additional web pages that are completely blank and ready for you to customize.

Creating and Designing a Meeting Workspace Site

In Chapter 5, you learned how to create and manage SharePoint sites. This chapter drills down into the details of creating and managing the Meeting Workspace site. Meeting Workspace sites generally follow this format, as seen in Figure 10-1:

- The top of the site's main page contains a description of the meeting.
- Page tabs are located at the top left of the main page.
- The top-right corner of the page contains a menu you can use to customize the site.
- The Agenda, Attendees, Document Library, and Objectives Web Parts are all contained in the body of the main page.

Besides the default elements included in a Meeting Workspace, you can add whatever Web Parts are necessary to fulfill your goals. One basic task in creating the right meeting site for your group is to choose the desired Meeting Workspace template, discussed in the previous section.

Meeting Workspace sites can be used not only during a meeting, but before and afterwards as well. During the meeting, participants can add or modify relevant documents, tasks, decisions, or the agenda for subsequent meetings.

Prior to the meeting, members can check the agenda, review any tasks recently assigned to them, and see any other changes that have been made.

After the meeting, the meeting organizer can publish the meeting's minutes, and members can review any new tasks and add any comments about the meeting.

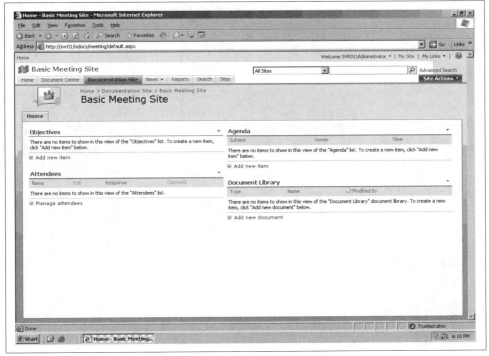

Figure 10-1. Design of a Basic Meeting Workspace site

As with creating any other type of SharePoint site, you must have administrator or site owner privileges. Administrators and site owners can delegate site creation rights to a user or group by giving that user or group site creation rights.

 Although you can assign rights to an individual, administrative best practices usually require that you create a group with those rights and then add the necessary users to that group.

Creating a Meeting Workspace Site

1. On your site, click Site Actions and then select Create from the menu.

2. In the Web Pages column, click "Sites and Workspaces."

3. On the New SharePoint Site page, type the name of the Workspace site in the Title field.

4. Type a brief description of the site in the Description field.

5. Complete the site's URL in the URL Name field.

6. Under Template Selection, click the Meetings tab and select a template from the list (Figure 10-2).

7. Configure Permissions, Site Navigation, and Site Categories as desired.

8. Click Create.

 See Chapter 5 for more on site creation.

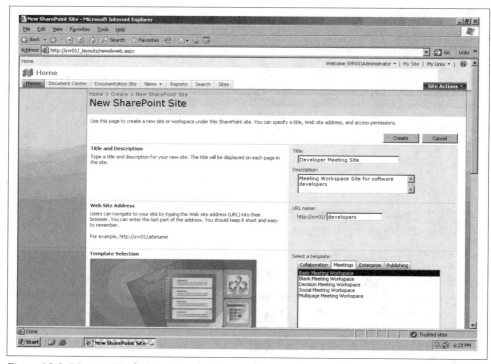

Figure 10-2. Meeting Workspace site creation

Creating a Workspace Site When You Create an Event

You can create a Meeting Workspace site automatically when you enter an event in your calendar. You can also create a workspace site from a SharePoint-compatible calendar and email program such as Microsoft Office Outlook 2007. This exercise will use the SharePoint calendar tool.

 Red asterisks indicate required fields.

1. On your site, open the SharePoint calendar in one of the following ways:
   - Go to Quick Launch and click the calendar name.
   - Click on View All Site Contents and then locate and click the calendar name.
2. Click New to open the menu, and then click on New Item, as shown in Figure 10-3.

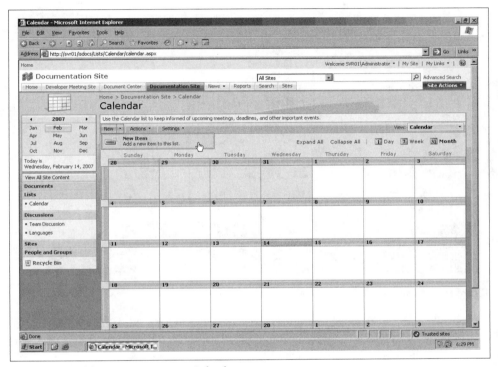

Figure 10-3. Adding a New Item to a Calendar

3. Enter the appropriate information for your event in the following fields:
   - Title
   - Location
   - Start Time
   - End Time
   - Description
4. If you are scheduling a recurring meeting, under Recurrence check the "Make this a repeating event" checkbox.
5. Set the frequency of the recurring meeting: daily, weekly, monthly, or yearly.

6. Set the Start date and the End date if relevant. Refer to Figure 10-4 to see what the page you created should look like.

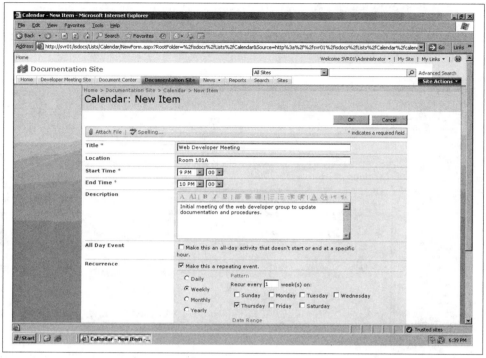

Figure 10-4. Creating an Event and a Meeting Workspace site

7. Scroll to the bottom of the page and check the "Use a Meeting Workspace to organize attendees, agendas, documents, minutes, and other details for this event" checkbox, and then click OK.

8. When the New or Existing Meeting Workspace page appears, if you want to link to the Meeting Workspace, click the "Link to an existing Meeting Workspace" radio button (Figure 10-5).

9. Verify that all of the other information on the page is correct, and then click OK.

Customizing a Meeting Workspace Site

Once you've created your Meeting Workspace site, it's time to customize it and give the site all of the details you require to satisfy your goals. You can change the content and design of the site by adding or moving Web Parts and Web Part content. Features you can include on your site are document libraries, sales contacts, productivity charts, and any other elements relevant to your meetings.

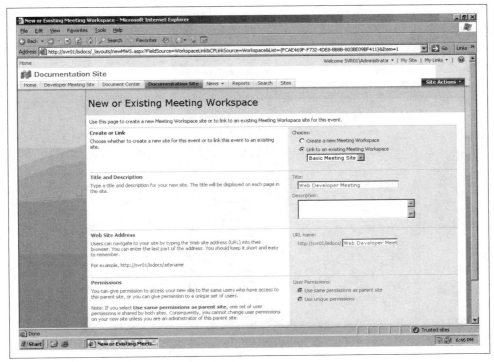

Figure 10-5. New or Existing Meeting Workspace page

Chapters 7 and 8 have more information about customizing Share-Point sites.

Adding a List or Library to Your Workspace Site

In Chapter 8, you saw how to add a List View Web Part to a Web Part page. This type of Web Part can display all or a filtered portion of a list or library, such as a sales contacts list, and can be an asset to your Meeting Workspace site.

You can also see Chapter 14 for more information about lists.

1. On the site, click Site Actions and select Edit Page from the menu.

2. Click Add Web Parts on the desired Web Part field's title bar, as shown in Figure 10-6.

3. On the Add Web Parts page under Lists, check the checkbox next to the list you want to add, and then click Add.

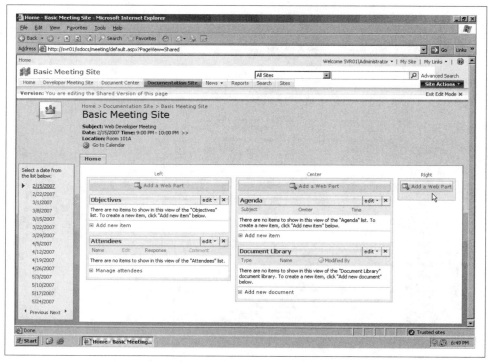

Figure 10-6. Adding a Web Part to a Meeting Workspace site

Alternate Method of Adding a List or Library

You may want to have a wider selection of lists or libraries than those offered by default. You can expand your choices in the following way:

1. On the site, click Site Actions and select Edit Page from the menu.

2. Click Add Web Parts on the desired Web Part field's title bar and in the Add Web Parts window, click the Lists and Libraries title to show all lists and libraries, as illustrated in Figure 10-7.

3. Check the checkbox of the desired Web Part and click Add.

As seen in Figure 10-8, when you have completed this action, if you scroll to the far right, you can use the Add Web Parts box to Browse, Search, Import, or Create Lists. You can also select between different Web Part Galleries.

You may want to remove a list or library that you've added to the workspace. There are two methods available to you, described in the following sections.

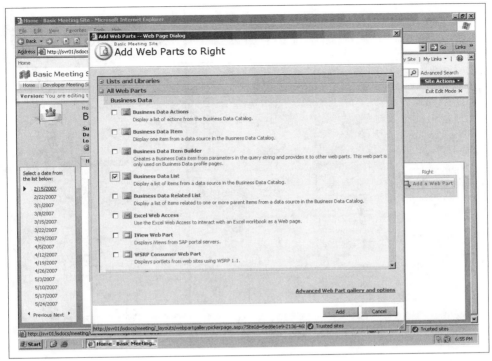

Figure 10-7. Expanded Lists and Libraries

Removing a List or Library View

This method removes the list or library view from the Web Part page; however, the original content will continue to exist in the list or library gallery:

1. On the Web Part page, click Site Actions and select Edit Page from the menu.
2. Click the menu arrow next to the appropriate Web Part title and select Delete, as shown in Figure 10-9.
3. When the confirmation dialog box appears, click OK.

Since you have removed only the view of the list or library, the actual content still exists. To restore it, add the appropriate Web Part to the Web Part page as outlined earlier in this chapter.

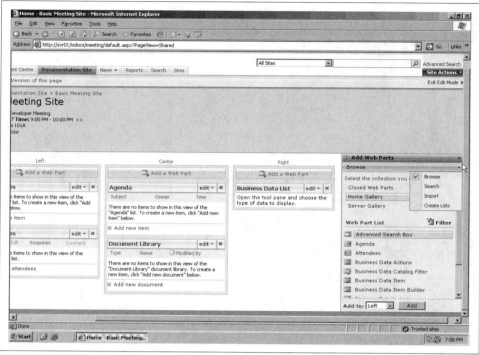

Figure 10-8. Alternate method of adding Web Parts

Deleting a List or Library

When you remove a list or library view from a Web Part page, the information still exists in SharePoint and is available for access by other sites in your site collection. On some occasions, though, you will create a list or library that is specific to your meeting or series of meetings, such as information relevant only to a particular project. Once the project is over, that list or library is no longer useful and can be permanently deleted:

1. On the Web Part page, click the title bar of the list or library you want to permanently delete, and then select Settings.

2. Click either List Settings or Library Settings, depending on the type of Web Part you are working with.

3. Under Permissions and Management, click the Delete selection for the list or library you are working with, as shown in Figure 10-10.

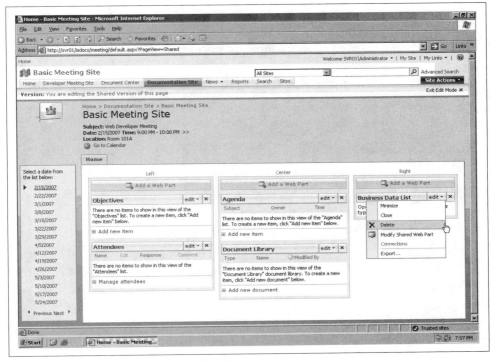

Figure 10-9. Deleting a List or Library Web Part

For example, for a list, you'll click "Delete this List." For a library, your options could be "Delete this Document Library" or "Delete this Picture Library," depending on the type of library you want to eliminate.

This list or library has now been permanently deleted from SharePoint.

Unless you are absolutely sure you will never need any information in the list or library again, it is better simply to remove the view from your workspace site rather than delete all of the data. Also, depending on the type of information you are dealing with, company policy or a legal statute may require that your organization retain that information for a certain period of time, even after it has become obsolete.

Share Meeting Workspace Lists and Libraries

As mentioned earlier in this chapter, one of the advantages of a Meeting Workspace site is that you can share information—not just in the meeting, but at any other time

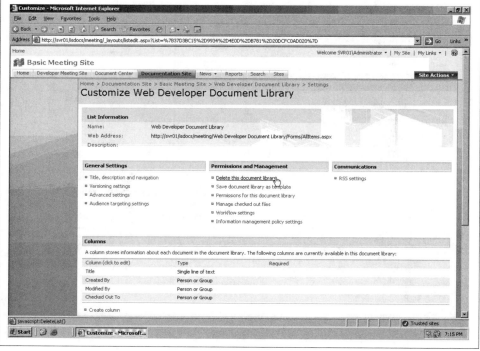

Figure 10-10. Deleting a list or library

as well. Lists and libraries on this workspace are not shared by default. Here is the procedure for sharing them with others:

1. On your workspace site, click Site Actions and select Site Settings from the menu.

2. In the Site Administration column, click "Site libraries and lists," as shown in Figure 10-11.

3. Click the Customize link for the list or library you want to share, as illustrated in Figure 10-12.

The exact title of the link will vary depending on what type of list or library you're trying to share.

4. Under General Settings, click "Advanced settings."

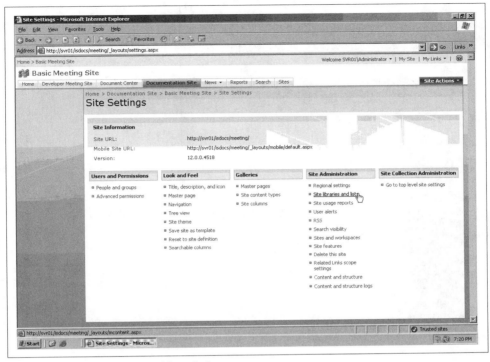

Figure 10-11. "Site libraries and lists" link

5. Scroll down and click the Yes radio button next to Share List Items Across All Meetings (Series Items), as shown in Figure 10-13.

6. Click OK.

 Once this becomes a Series Item, the setting cannot be reversed.

Other Ways to Modify a Meeting Workspace Site

Other ways you can customize this workspace site are methods common to modifying sites and Web Part pages in general. For example, you can move Web Parts around on your Web Part pages, as described in the section "Change the Layout of a Web Part Page" in Chapter 8. You can also change the theme or add or remove pictures, as explained in the section "Managing Site Themes and Images" in Chapter 7.

You may also want to take a look at Chapter 9 to see the similarities and differences between document and Meeting Workspaces, as well as Chapter 16.

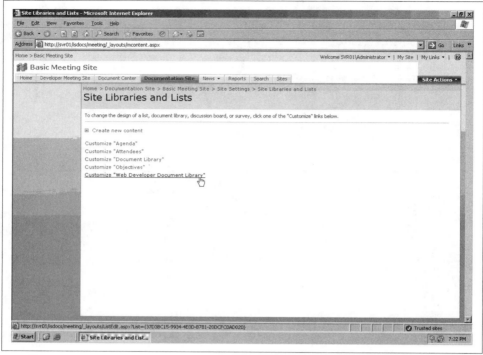

Figure 10-12. Site Libraries and Lists page

Working with Pages in a Meeting Workspace Site

So far, we've been working only with the default home page on a Meeting Workspace site. For many meetings, regardless of whether they are reoccurring, this might be sufficient. However, the content and processes involved in your meetings may be complex and require additional pages to organize and contain.

Fortunately, you can add up to 10 more pages to your workspace site. Rather than combining all of your activities and information on a single Web Part page, you can spread them across several pages, dedicating an entire page to documentation and another to task assignment and tracking.

You can create 10 pages for an individual meeting or for reoccurring meetings, and you can create 10 pages per specific meeting date (that is, 10 pages for the June 7th staff meeting, 10 pages for the June 14th staff meeting, and so on).

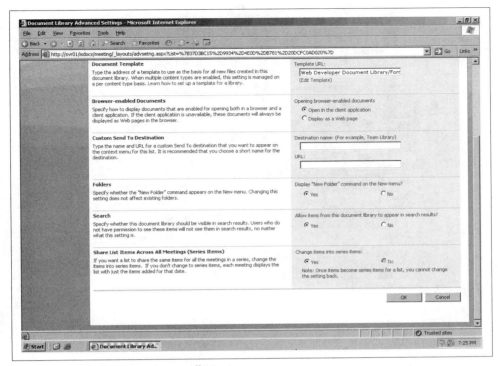

Figure 10-13. Sharing a List Across All Meetings

Adding a Web Page to a Meeting Workspace Site

1. On your workspace site, click Site Actions and select Add Pages from the menu, as seen in Figure 10-14.

2. When the Pages task pane appears, type the name of the web page in the Page Name field.

> You may have to scroll to the right, depending on your screen resolution.

3. Click one of the following options, depending on how you want this page to appear:

   - Click "Appears for this meeting only" if you only want the page to be visible for a single meeting.

   - Click "Appears for all meetings" if you want the page to be continually available (see Figure 10-15 for the results).

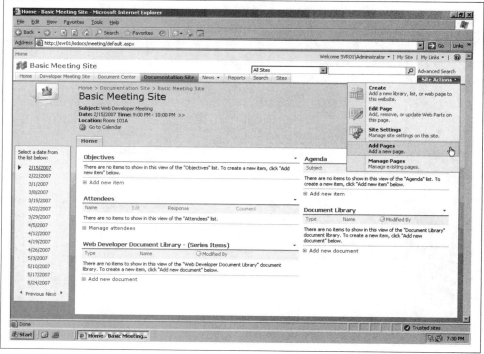

Figure 10-14. Adding a web page to a Meeting Workspace site

Once the page is created, you are free to customize it as described earlier in this chapter. You can also create another web page for your site at this time. When you have created one or more pages, you can access them on the workspace by clicking their tabs. Web page tabs are located at the top-lefthand corner of any page on the workspace.

Changing the Name of a Web Page

1. On the workspace site, click the tab of the desired web page.

2. Click Site Actions and select Manage Pages from the menu, as seen in Figure 10-16.

3. In the Pages task pane, click the arrow next to Order, and select Settings from the list, as in Figure 10-17.

4. Click the current name of the web page to highlight it, and then type the new name for the page.

5. Click OK to save your changes.

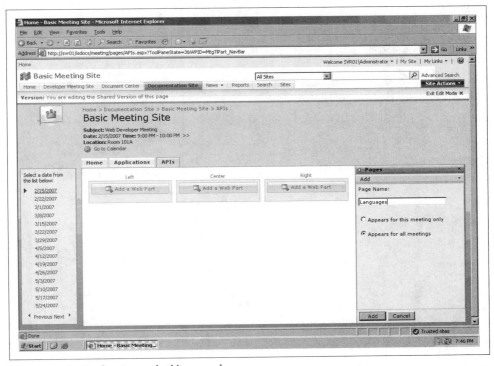

Figure 10-15. Configuring and adding a web page

Changing the Order of Web Pages

Anyone who has ever created a web site with more than one page knows that pages are usually constructed in some sort of directory hierarchy. Some site architectures can be in the form of a complex directory tree, whereas others can have a completely flat structure with all pages and other files stored in a single folder.

By default, web pages in a workspace site are ordered by when they were created. Except for the home page, which will always be the first page, the order in which your pages appear can be changed.

If you are familiar with the Mozilla Firefox Web Browser's tabbing function, you know you can change the order of tabs with a drag-and-drop action. Changing the order of the web page tabs in a SharePoint workspace is a bit more involved:

1. On the workspace, click Site Actions and select Manage Pages from the menu.

2. In the Pages task pane under Order, select the page you want to reorder.

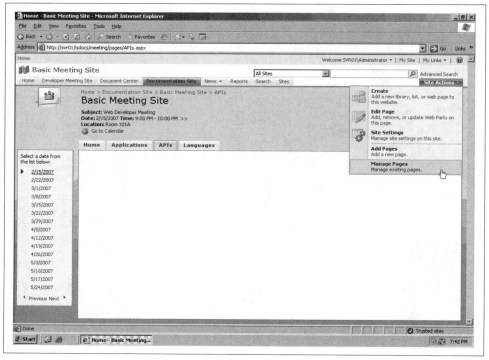

Figure 10-16. Managing a web page

3. Click either the Move Up or Move Down arrows as many times as necessary to place the web page where you want it, as shown in Figure 10-18.

The page's position will move one place either up or down for each click on the appropriate arrow.

4. When you are finished with your changes, click OK.

Deleting a Web Page from a Meeting Workspace Site

While it's said that "diamonds are forever," the dynamic nature of the Web and business-related meetings guarantees that web pages are not. Deleting a web page from your workspace site is a fairly simple process. The only web page you cannot delete is the home page.

The only way you can delete the home page is by deleting the entire workspace site. See the "Delete Sites and Site Collections" section in Chapter 5 for more information.

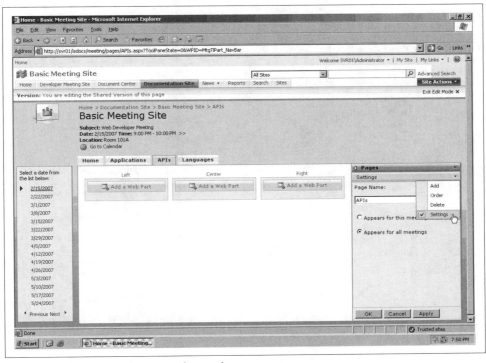

Figure 10-17. Changing the settings for a web page

1. On the workspace, click Site Actions and select Manage Pages from the menu.

2. In the Pages task pane, click the arrow next to Order and select "Delete from the list," as in Figure 10-19.

3. Select the page you want to delete and click Delete.

4. When the confirmation dialog box appears, click OK.

Assigning and Tracking Tasks in a Meeting Workspace Site

Very often as part of a business meeting discussion, issues arise regarding tasks that need to be done in a group or organization. While many attendees take notes either electronically or the old-fashioned way with pen and paper, information about who was supposed to do what seems to disappear sometime after the meeting is over.

One of the ways you can use your Meeting Workspace site is to create a task list, assign tasks to meeting attendees, and track the progress of those tasks to (hopefully) completion.

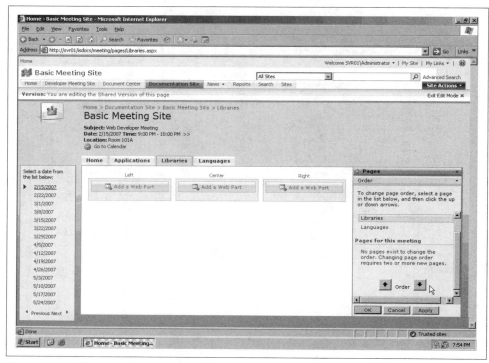

Figure 10-18. Changing the order of a web page

Adding a Tasks List

Before you can assign and track tasks, you need to create a basic task list to contain your content. While most Meeting Worksite templates include a Tasks List by default, this exercise will show you how to add a Tasks List Web Part. You can also follow these steps to add a Projects Tasks List Web Part to the Web Part page:

1. On the workspace site, click Site Actions and select Edit Page from the menu.
2. Click Tasks in the Add Web Parts task pane.
3. Scroll to the bottom of the Add Web Parts pane and in the "Add to" list, select a Web Part field on your Web Part page where you want to place the list.
4. Click Add to insert the Tasks List Web Part in the selected Web Part field.

Adding Tasks to a Tasks List

Now that you have a Tasks List on your site, it's time to start creating and assigning tasks:

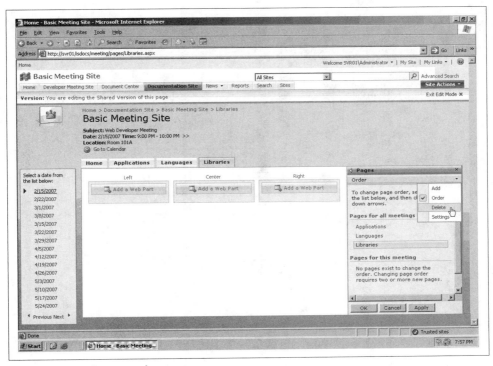

Figure 10-19. Deleting a web page

1. On your site at the Tasks List Web Part, under Tasks, click "Add new item."

2. When the Tasks page opens, add the following information:

    • The title of the task

    • Who you are assigning to the task

    • The priority of the task

    • A brief description of or instructions about the task

    • The start date

    • The due date

3. View this page in Figure 10-20, and then click OK to save your changes.

Updating Tasks in a Tasks List

As part of tracking tasks, you will probably want to update them as progress is made. Sometimes while working on a task, the team member will discover something that requires a change in the parameters of the work being done. This could include changing the due date, assigning additional users to the task, or changing the instructions on how to complete the task.

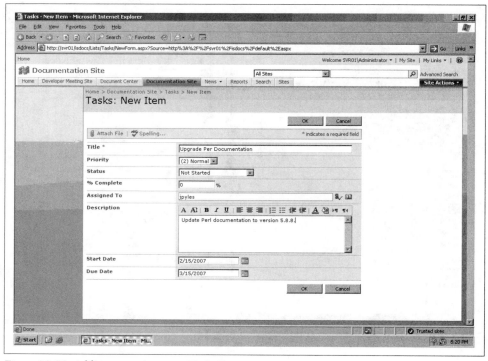

Figure 10-20. Adding a new item to a Tasks List

1. On the workspace site at the Tasks List, click the name of the task you want to modify, and then click on Edit Item.

2. Modify any of the information on the Task page, including:

    - Title
    - Task assignment
    - Task priority
    - The description or instructions relating to the task
    - Due date
    - Status
    - Progress toward completion

3. Click OK to save your changes.

Managing Attendees in a Meeting Workspace Site

The purpose of the Attendees List is to invite members to a meeting, record who was invited, and let people who have been invited submit notes, such as suggestions for the agenda. During or after the meeting, the Attendees List can be amended to reflect who actually attended.

When you create a Meeting Workspace site under a parent site, any user who has access permissions to the parent site will automatically be able to see the Meeting Workspace site. The administrator or site owner can manually change access rights as necessary.

All attendees are part of the workspace Members group, which gives them rights to view and submit contributions to the site. The Meeting Attendees List is another way to formally advertise and record information about business meetings. Attendees can be added to the list either through a meeting invitation sent from a SharePoint compatible email or calendar program or by directly adding them to the list.

If you use an email program such as Microsoft Office Outlook 2007, when you send a meeting invitation, anyone in the To field of the email will be added automatically to the Attendees List. Subsequently, if you modify the Attendees List on the site, you will have to modify your Outlook Calendar manually, since communication doesn't flow both ways.

You can add only valid SharePoint users to the Attendees list, and you must use either their username, domain name, or email address. Also, unlike Tasks Lists, you can only have one Attendees List on the site. If you add a second Attendees List to the site, the second list will simply be a duplicate view of the original. Any changes you make on the first list will be displayed on the second.

One interesting feature about the Attendees List is that it can't be deleted. You can remove all of the attendees if you are the meeting organizer or site owner or hide the list view, but the list part itself remains.

Adding to the Attendees List in the Meeting Workspace Site

Most of the Meeting Workspace templates include an Attendees List by default, so once the Meeting Workspace site is created, you can go right to work on the list.

 The exception is the Blank Meeting Workspace template.

1. Go to the bottom of the Attendees List and click Manage Attendees.

2. Click New on the toolbar.

3. Click Browse to navigate through the directory and locate the attendee's name; otherwise, type the name in the available field, as seen in Figure 10-21.

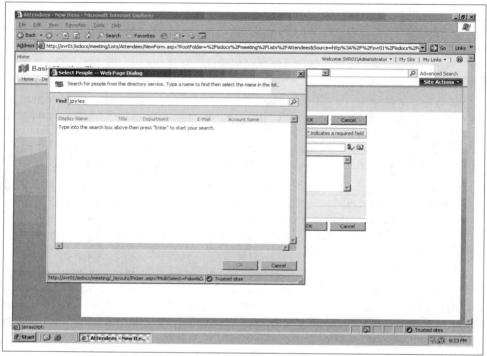

Figure 10-21. Adding a member to an Attendees List

4. Add any other information relevant to the attendee, such as whether attendance is optional.

5. When you are finished, click OK to add the attendee to the list.

Editing the Attendees List

One common reason for editing the Attendees List is if an attendee didn't show up. This keeps a record of people who were invited but didn't attend, so you can make sure they are brought up to speed on what they missed:

1. On the site, at the Attendees List, click the Edit button next to the name of the attendee you want to modify.

2. When the page containing the attendee's information appears, edit the fields and other elements as necessary, and then click OK to save your changes.

Deleting an Attendee from the List

Although it's possible to delete an attendee from the Attendees List, the rationale for such an action is questionable. On the surface, it seems to make sense to delete the names of people who were invited to the meeting but didn't attend. In that way, only the names of people who were at the meeting are present on the list. However, over the course of time, memories begin to fade and you might not recall whether a particular member was invited to a meeting. If you need to keep a record of not only who attended but also who was invited to a meeting, edit the Attendee's List to reflect that information instead of deleting the name from the list:

1. On the site at the Attendees List, go to the bottom of the list and click Manage Attendees.

2. Click on the attendee's name to display the menu, and then select Delete Item.

3. When the confirmation dialog box appears, click OK to send the item to the Recycle Bin.

Conclusion

If Web Parts and Web Part pages are the basic building blocks for determining how and where data is presented, then Meeting Workspaces are desktops and conference rooms that allow people to organize and present all these information elements pursuant to a goal or purpose. Regardless of the business-related activity, MOSS 2007 provides the specific arena to create, develop, and record everything necessary for the particular event. You will never again need to depend upon your hastily scribbled notes or memories of a staff meeting held six months ago to determine who was assigned responsibility for a critical project or task. Use SharePoint Meeting Workspaces to organize everything from your company's annual financial report to a coworker's birthday party. From planning to execution, this SharePoint feature will make all your group activities more efficient and productive.

CHAPTER 11

Creating and Managing Discussions

Introduction

MOSS 2007, like its predecessor, has the ability to create one or more discussion boards. A *discussion board* is a web venue where members can create content and respond to content created by someone else. Discussions are collected in "threads," usually by subject, and traditionally threads are organized by category. For example, let's say you manage a group of software developers and you want to create discussion groups for three broad areas: Applications, Languages, and Libraries (APIs). The easiest way would be to create three discussion groups, one for each category. Then, in the Languages discussion group, you could have threads regarding C++, C#, Perl, Python, Visual Studio, and so on.

The latest incarnation of discussion boards in SharePoint comes with a group created by default called Team Discussion. If you need only one board, you can change the name of the default board and use it. You can also create more boards to contain discussions either by category, by team, or by any other criteria that suits your needs. The most recent additions to the board are displayed on top, showing you which threads have had the most recent posts and which ones are the most popular.

If your email program supports it, you can submit content to the discussion board directly from your email client. It's just like sending any other email.

Discussion Group Views

Discussion groups are basically just lists and, like other SharePoint lists, you can filter the view depending on how you want the list to be presented. Additionally, there are three unique ways to filter the view of a discussion board:

Subject view

This view is available only for the top-level folder of the discussion group and presents discussions by their metadata, such as the titles of discussions.

Flat view

This is the default view for SharePoint discussion groups. The title of the discussion is at the top, and each reply is shown in a tree structure, similar to Usenet Newsgroups. This view is available only in content folders, not at the top level.

Threaded view

Like the Flat view, this view is available only in content folders. In this view, you can see whether a reply was made to the original posted message or to a subsequent message.

When you create or modify a view, there are a number of elements you can edit in the view:

Name

Gives the name of the discussion board view. You can also make this or any other view the default view for the discussion group.

Audience

Lets you determine whether this is a public or personal view. This option can be set only when you create the view.

 A public view can be seen by any user, but a personal view can be seen only by the person who configured it.

Columns

Lets you choose which columns of information appear in this view and in what order they appear.

 You can choose to display such column content as Attachments, Subject, Posted By, Modified By, and so on.

Sort

This option allows you to select a primary and secondary column and then sort the content, first by one column and then the other. Information in the columns can be sorted in either ascending or descending order.

Filter

Lets you either display all information from all columns or make visible only content from selected columns. You can filter only two columns by default, but clicking on Show More Columns lets you add more.

Group By

Allows you to group discussions by a particular column. For example, you can choose to group all discussions by Posted By so that each individual user's posts are collected together.

Totals

Contains the Count, Maximum, and Minimum options. You can either show the number of items present in a column by choosing Count or display the Maximum or Minimum values that can be contained by selecting those options in a drop-down box.

Folders

Lets you decide whether discussions should appear in folders.

Item Limit

Allows you to decide how many items will be visible in a view, regardless of how many items are actually present.

 See Chapter 14 and the "Customizing a List or Library View" section in Chapter 8 for more on understanding and modifying list properties.

Creating a SharePoint Discussion Board

The default discussion board called Team Discussion is created when you install MOSS 2007. If you need only a single discussion board, you can use the default board right away.

Using the Default Discussion Board

1. On your site, you can access the default discussion board by performing one of the following actions:

   • On Quick Launch, click Team Discussion, as shown in Figure 11-1.

   • Click View All Site Content and then click Team Discussion.

2. To change the default name for the board, click Settings and select Discussion Board Settings from the menu, as in Figure 11-2.

3. Under General Settings, click "Title, description and navigation," then modify the title and description fields with the desired content, as illustrated in Figure 11-3.

4. Click Save to exit the General Settings page, and then click the new name of the discussion board to return to the board.

When you return to your site's main page, you'll see links to both the default Team Discussion list and the new list in Quick Launch if you set them up to appear there.

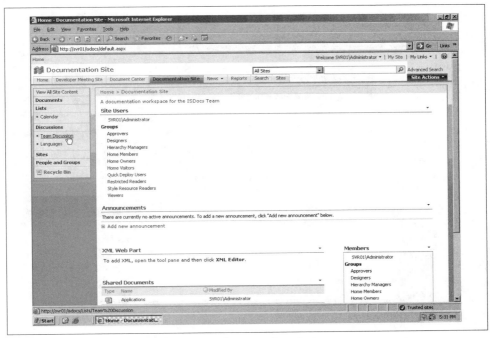

Figure 11-1. Using Quick Launch to open a discussion board

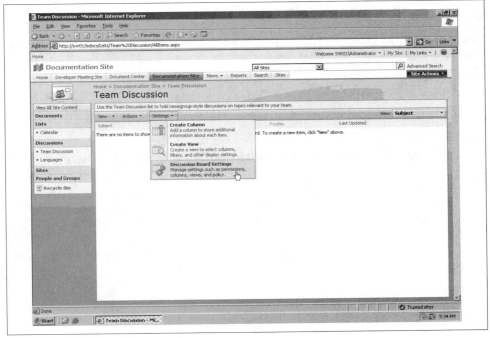

Figure 11-2. Selecting discussion board settings

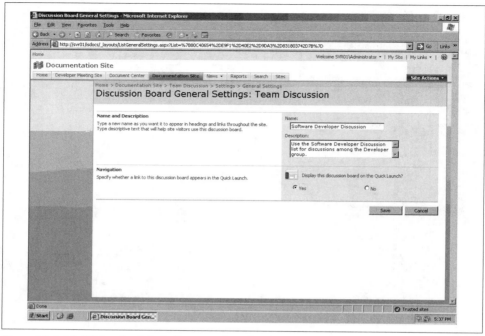

Figure 11-3. Modifying the default discussion board settings

Creating a New Discussion Board

You may want to create your own board from scratch or need to make additional boards in order to accommodate multiple groups or discussion types. Here's how you can create a new discussion board:

1. On your site, click Site Actions and then click Create.

2. In the Communications column, click on Discussion Board.

3. Type the name of your discussion board in the Name field.

4. Type a brief description of your board in the Description field.

 If you are going to enable the board to receive content via email, you can add the email address of the board to the Description Field so it is easy to find. You will create that email address later in this exercise.

5. Under Navigation, select whether or not you want a link to the board to appear in Quick Launch.

 This page is in the same format as the default Team Discussion page you modified in the previous exercise, as illustrated in Figure 11-4.

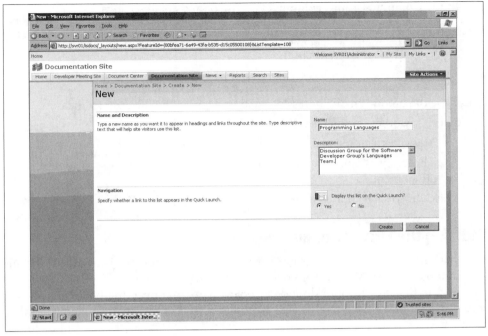

Figure 11-4. Creating a new discussion group

6. If you are going to enable the board to receive email content, under "Enable this list to receive email," click Yes.

> This option is available only if the server hosting SharePoint is enabled to receive email. Figure 11-4 shows that this server is not email-enabled.

7. Under Email Address, create a unique name for the email address of the board.

8. Click Create to save your actions and create the discussion board.

Configuring a Discussion Board to Receive Emails

If you created a discussion group without enabling the email option and you now want to have the board receive emails, you will need to follow the steps in this exercise. Once this task is finished, discussion board members can send board content directly from their email clients by specifying the board's address in the message's To: or Cc: fields:

1. Open the discussion board, either by using Quick Launch or from the View All Site Content page.

2. Click Settings, and then select Discussion Board Settings from the list.

3. In the Communications column, click "Incoming email settings."

 This option will not be available if the server hosting SharePoint is not enabled to receive email.

4. Type the unique email address of the board in the "Email address" field.

5. Select any other optional settings you want, such as:

   • Messages sent in email should keep their attachments.

   • The original email message should be saved in the discussion board as an attachment.

6. Click OK to save your changes.

Starting the First Discussion

Whereas a default discussion group is created when SharePoint is installed, default discussions are not. You will need to start the first discussion. Typically, the first post in the first thread on a discussion board is to announce the board's existence and welcome new members. It's also a good idea to post any rules or guidelines that board members are expected to follow. An example of such a message can be found in Figure 11-6 at the end of this exercise.

1. Open the discussion board, either by using Quick Launch or from the View All Site Content page.

2. Click New and select Discussion from the list, as in Figure 11-5.

3. Once the text window opens, type in whatever message you want.

 See the "Using the Discussion Board Rich Text Editor" section, later in this chapter, for formatting options.

4. When you are finished, click OK to save the content (Figure 11-6).

Your message is now accessible in the board.

Customizing a Discussion Board

Previously in this chapter, in "Discussion Group Views," you learned that three views can be set up for your board: Subject, Flat, and Threaded. You also read about the configuration options available for boards.

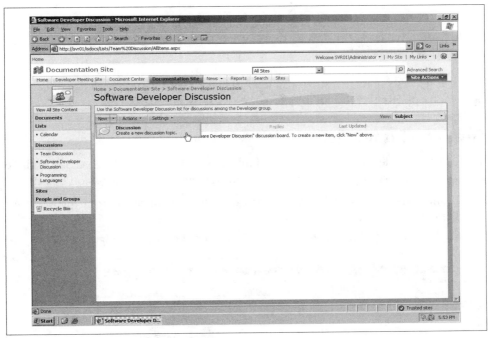

Figure 11-5. Starting a new discussion thread

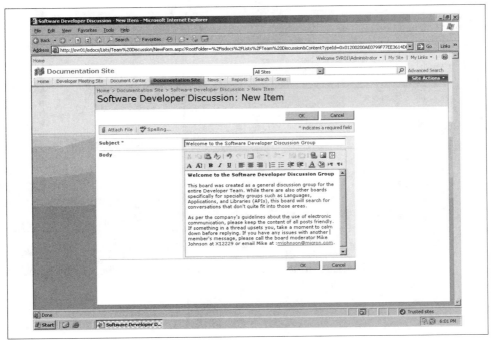

Figure 11-6. First post in the first discussion thread

The configuration options are available for all lists in SharePoint, but the Subject, Flat, and Threaded views are unique to SharePoint Discussion Boards.

The following sections will show you how to make use of your knowledge of list configuration options and configure different views for your board.

Creating a Custom View

You can either select one of the three default views for your board or use one of these defaults as the basis for creating a new customized view for the discussion board:

1. Launch the discussion board, either from Quick Launch or from the View All Site Content page.

2. Click Settings and then select Create View from the list, as in Figure 11-7.

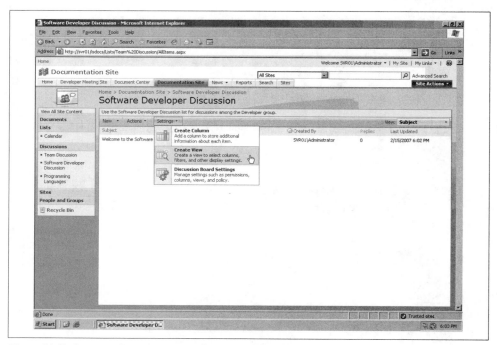

Figure 11-7. Opening Create View in a discussion group

3. On the Create View page under "Start from an existing view," click the name of the desired default view.

In addition to the Flat, Subject, and Threaded views discussed earlier in this chapter, you can also choose from two additional view format types:

- The Datasheet view allows you to view discussion group information in an editable spreadsheet format.
- The Gantt view allows you to view discussion list items in graphical Gantt Chart format, ideal for quickly tracking group member task progress. These options can be seen in Figure 11-8.

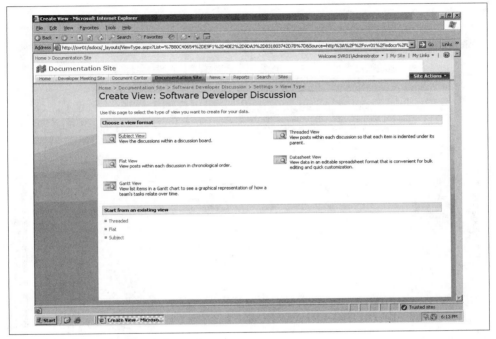

Figure 11-8. Discussion board view options

4. In the Name field, type a unique name for your custom view.

5. Select whether you want your new view to be the default for this board.

You can come back to this page at any time and change the default view of your board as you just did in Step 5.

6. In the Audience section, select whether this board will be visible in Public or Personal view.

See the "Changing Your Personal View of a Discussion Board" section, later in this chapter, for more information on personal views.

7. In the Columns section, click the checkboxes next to the columns you want to appear in the board.

8. Select the order the columns will appear from left to right on the board by using the drop-down arrows next to column names and choosing the appropriate values, as in Figure 11-9.

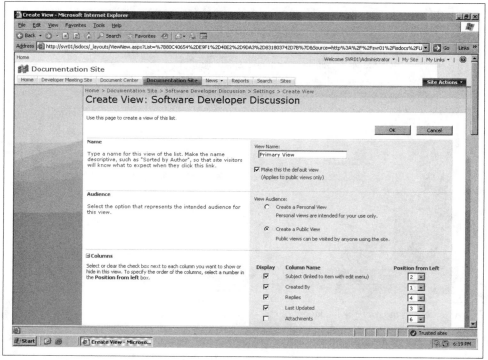

Figure 11-9. Configuring columns when modifying a discussion board view

9. In the Sort section, use the drop-down menus to determine which two columns will be used to sort the board view.

 For example, you can sort first by "Created by" and then by Subject (linked to item with edit menu). You can also choose None if you do not want to sort by columns. See sample sort options in Figure 11-10.

10. In the Filter section, select the filter options if you want to filter this view.

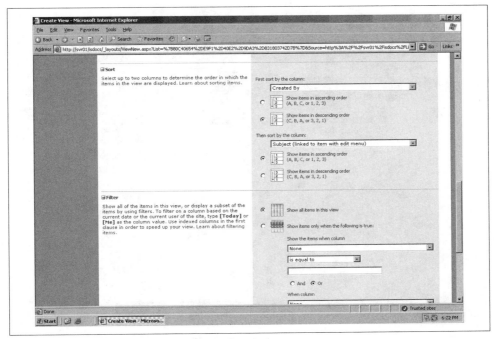

Figure 11-10. Sorting options in a discussion board view

11. In the Folders section, select whatever folder options you want to apply to your board.

12. Click OK to save your changes and finish creating your custom view.

As seen in Figure 11-11, if you made the customized view the default view, when you are returned to the discussion board, that view will be applied.

Editing a View

If you create a view and later want to change it, you can go back in and modify it. You actually can modify the folder-level view or the view of an individual discussion to have different views:

1. Launch the discussion board, either from Quick Launch or from the View All Site Content page.

2. With the discussion board open, perform one of the following operations:
   - If you want to modify the folder-level view, click the View menu and select the desired view, as in Figure 11-12.
   - If you want to modify the view of a specific discussion, click the discussion name to open it, click View, and then select the desired view, as seen in Figure 11-13.

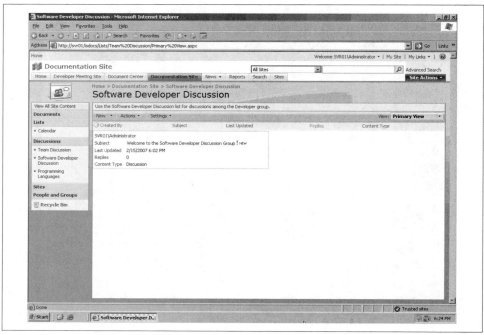

Figure 11-11. Customized view of a discussion board

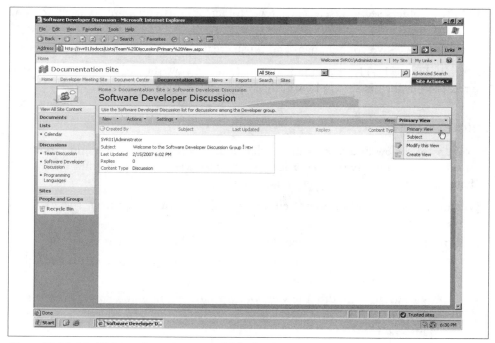

Figure 11-12. Modifying a discussion group folder-level view

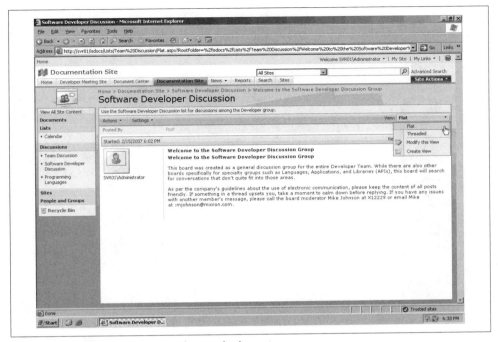

Figure 11-13. Modifying the view of a specific discussion

3. Click "Modify this View" on the View menu.

4. Make the desired modifications and click OK to save your changes.

Deleting a View

There are several reasons for deleting a view. You might create a custom view and later decide it doesn't meet your needs. You may create one or more custom views that reflect your organization's style and theme and then delete the original default views.

The one thing you can't do is delete all views. If you have only one view available and you try to delete it, you will receive an error message saying that you cannot delete the default view. If you have several views available and you try to delete the default view, you will receive a notice stating that you must select another view as the default prior to deleting the current view:

1. Launch the discussion board, either from Quick Launch or from the View All Site Content page.

2. Click Settings, and select Discussion Board Settings from the list.

3. On the "Customize *discussion board name* Discussion" page, scroll down to the Views section and click the name of the view you want to delete, as in Figure 11-14.

4. Click Delete and then OK to delete the view, as shown in Figure 11-15.

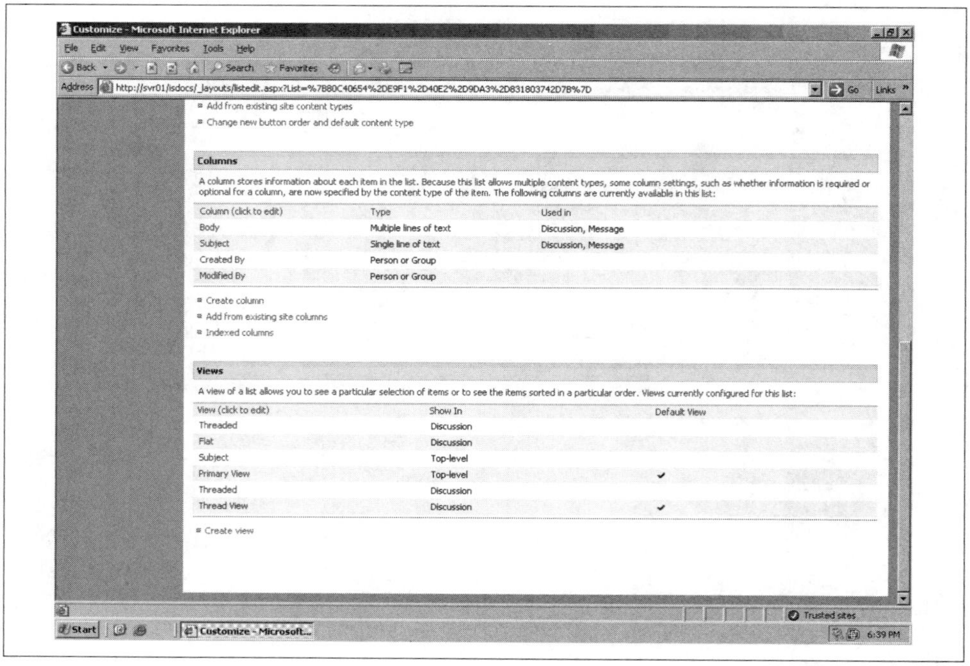

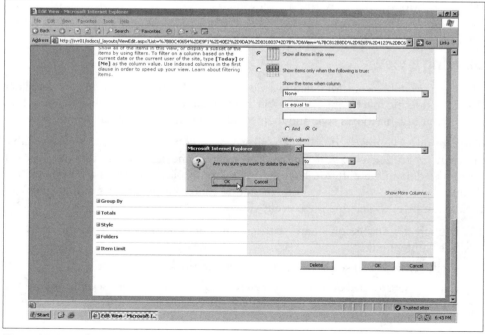

Figure 11-14. Selecting a view to delete

Figure 11-15. Deleting a view

Participating in a Discussion

Now that you've created your board, customized it, and added a welcome message, it's ready to host discussions. The following sections describe how board members can create a new discussion thread, post a reply in a thread, edit their submissions, and more.

Starting a Discussion Thread

In the "Introduction" section of this chapter, some examples of discussion boards were presented that would be appropriate for a team of software developers. The example groups were Applications, Languages, and Libraries (API). Let's say the three boards were created and one of the developers wants to start a discussion having to do with the Perl language in the Languages board. Here's how the developer would proceed:

1. Launch the discussion board, either from Quick Launch or from the View All Site Content page.
2. Click New and select Discussion from the list.
3. When the text editor opens, type a title for your discussion in the Subject field, such as "Core Perl Documentation Update."
4. Type whatever message you want in the text area.

 See the "Using the Discussion Board Rich Text Editor" section, later in this chapter, for formatting options.

5. Click OK to post your new discussion thread to the board, as shown in Figure 11-16.

Replying to a Discussion Thread

Naturally, the software developer who posted the announcement about the update to the Core Perl Documentation will be expecting responses or questions regarding the message. Here's how another developer would reply:

1. Launch the discussion board, either from Quick Launch or from the View All Site Content page.
2. Click the name of the discussion thread that you want to read and reply; in this case, the name is "Core Perl Documentation Update."
3. Click Reply in the bar above the message window, as in Figure 11-17.
4. Type and format your message as shown in Figure 11-18.
5. Click OK to post your reply to the discussion thread.

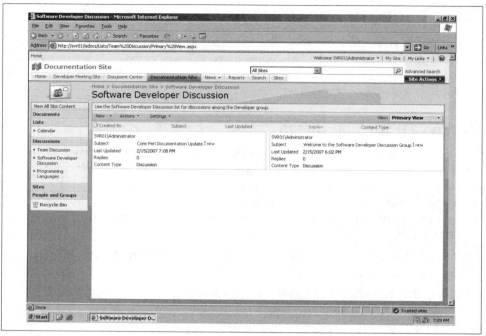

Figure 11-16. Posting a new discussion thread

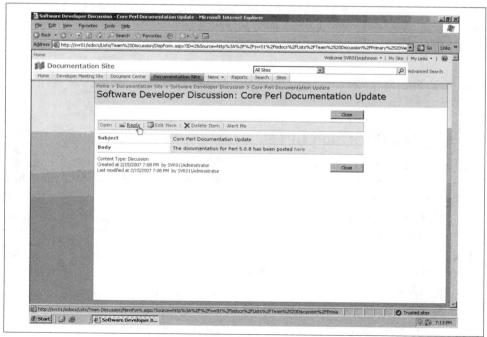

Figure 11-17. Starting a reply to a discussion thread

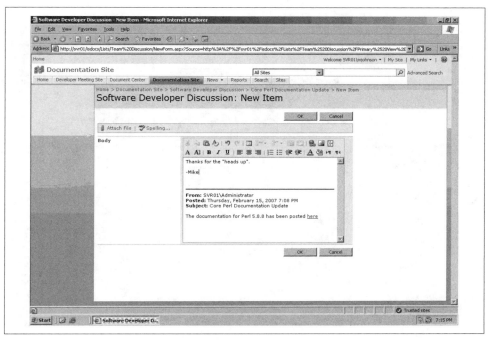

Figure 11-18. Typing and formatting a reply

Now the original message and this reply are accessible by the discussion board members. Although you cannot see the content of the reply because you are not in Threaded view, when you are returned to the main discussion group page, you can see that the value has been incremented by one under Replies, as in Figure 11-19.

Editing Discussion Thread Posts

After creating or replying to a discussion, you may realize that you made some sort of error—e.g., spelling, syntax, or factual—in your message. Unless you're the discussion board owner or an administrator, you can edit only the message you created. Although not required, discussion board etiquette suggests that whenever you edit one of your messages, you include a short sentence explaining the reason for the edit:

1. Launch the discussion board from Quick Launch or the View All Site Content page.

2. Depending on your specific situation, do one of the following:

   • If you are editing the original message, click to the right of the subject name for the thread to open the menu and then click Edit Item, as in Figure 11-20.

   • If you are editing a reply to a thread message, click the name of the discussion to open it, locate your reply, click View Properties next to your reply to open the menu, and then click Edit Item, as illustrated in Figure 11-21.

3. Edit the text of your message, and then click OK to save your changes.

Figure 11-19. Discussion thread reply as seen on the discussion group main page

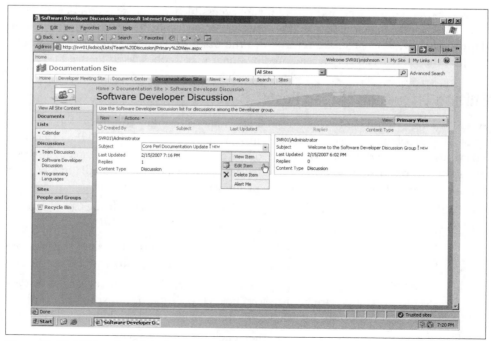

Figure 11-20. Editing the original post

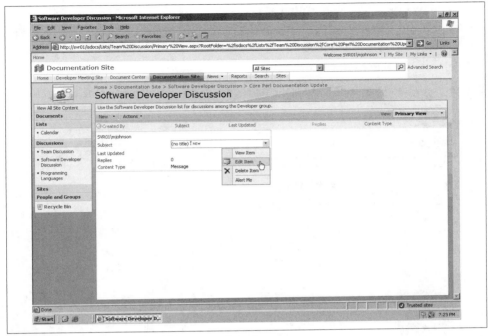

Figure 11-21. Editing a reply to a discussion thread

Using the Discussion Board Rich Text Editor

Besides entering plain text into the text editor, you can format your discussion message text to make it bold or italic, create bullet points, and access other word processing features. The toolbar above the text area gives you access to some of the more familiar formatting tools:

- Cutting and Copying text

 There's no Paste button; however, you can copy text from another source, click inside the text window to make it active, and then use the key combination Ctrl+P to paste the content from the clipboard to the text editor.

- Clipboard
- Undo and Redo buttons
- Insert Table
- Insert Hyperlink
- Select font size
- Select font color
- Bold, Italic, and Underline

- Align text by left, center, or right
- Bullets and Numbering
- Increase or Decrease indent
- Select text background color

Figure 11-22 shows a sample message with the toolbar visible above the text field.

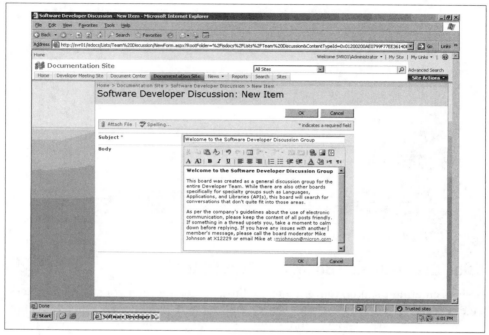

Figure 11-22. Discussion group Rich Text Editor format controls

Changing Your Personal View of a Discussion Board

Up to this point, we have been viewing the discussion board using the default public view. This is the view all members of the board see when they open it. However, you can choose to set up your own personal view of the board that only you can see. For example, you may prefer to view the discussion board entries as threaded rather than flat, or you may want to sort by Subject and "Created by" rather than Subject and the creation date.

Follow the steps presented in the "Creating a Custom View" section found earlier in this chapter to make those changes. To make the view your personal view, review step 6 in that exercise and select Personal instead of Public view. If you want to make this view your default personal view, select that option as presented in step 5 of that exercise.

You can also create a separate personal view of individual discussion threads. Go back to the "Editing a View" section in this chapter and follow the steps in that exercise. Make sure you are in your personal view of the board when you make these changes.

Conclusion

The art of discussion isn't dead; it's just gone "high-tech." In terms of MOSS 2007, discussions take advantage of the web format long used by Usenet groups and more recently seen in Internet discussion boards. Including discussion groups on your company's site collection allows various work groups or teams to interact with each other on common projects, regardless of where they are located. A team in Singapore developing an application in Perl can consult with the Perl Languages team in Boise, exchanging ideas and suggestions. This conversation is recorded so that these groups can refer back to what was said. Other departments or field offices can also glean any information from these threads as it applies to their projects. Once you've implemented this option in your site collection, you will never want to be without it.

CHAPTER 12

Creating and Managing SharePoint Groups and Users

Introduction

Traditionally, in any Windows Active Directory Domain, the responsibility for adding users and groups and assigning privileges to those groups has been in the hands of the server or domain administrator. User provisioning would include assigning access to all resources and objects in the domain, including intranet sites. MOSS 2007 allows the SharePoint Site owner to have control over the creation and administration of users and groups for Site Collections. This power gives local site administrators fine-grained control over who can and cannot interact with various parts of a portal. Rather than rely on a remote administrator, the local site administrator can grant, revoke, and modify permissions on a per-site, per-part, or sometimes even per-list element basis.

Permission Groups

There are three default SharePoint groups created when a site is created, and each group possesses default access permissions:

Owner
> The owner has full control of the site.

Members
> Members can contribute content and modify that content on the site.

Visitors
> Visitors to the site have read-only access.

It is unlikely that the default groups provided will meet all of your needs. However, you can create or modify SharePoint groups to satisfy any access or security needs required by your teams, departments, and overall organization in the following ways:

- Create a new SharePoint group and assign it unique permissions.
- Modify a default group by changing the default access permissions to suit your needs.
- Create custom permission levels and assign them to different SharePoint groups.

Site Owners and Site Collection Administrators have permissions both to modify default groups and permissions and to create unique groups and group permissions by default. They also can assign any other user or group Create Groups permissions to accomplish these tasks.

When a site owner or administrator creates a new group on a SharePoint site, the following additional access permission groups are created by default:

Approvers
> Assign users to this group if you want them to be able to approve or reject pending documents and list items. Items they approve become visible to both anonymous and restricted readers.

Designers
> This group is usually comprised of a limited number of administrators and web developers who are responsible for supporting the performance and look and feel of the site.

Hierarchy Managers
> This group can manage and modify the structure of the site and site collection. Members of this group can rename and move sites within the site collection hierarchy.

Home Members
> Use this group if you need to assign members Contribute permissions.

Home Owners
> Add only people to this group whom you want to have Full Control Rights on the site.

Home Visitors
> Like the Visitors group previously mentioned, members of this group have read permissions only.

Quick Deploy Users
> Members of this group are able to quickly update site content where the site uses separate levels for authoring content and deploying that content.

Restricted Readers
> Users in this group simply have read-only access to the site's content.

Style Resource Readers
> By default, all authenticated users are members of this group and have rights to read the Master Page Gallery and have Restricted Readers permissions to the Style Gallery.

To further secure your SharePoint site, it is recommended that you remove all authenticated users from this group, adding only those users who require these rights as part of their job function.

Viewers

Members of this group can only view lists, pages, and documents in the Server Rendering View.

See Figure 12-1 for an illustration of this list of groups.

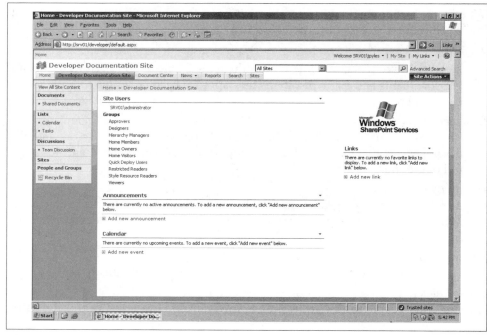

Figure 12-1. Permissions groups list

Security access can further be modified at the levels of a site, list, library, list item, library item, or document.

 See Chapter 22 for more information.

In order to add users to a group, they must belong to the authenticated users group on the local server or the domain. You can add authenticated users to the system with their usernames, domain usernames, or email addresses.

Adding and Configuring SharePoint Groups

Generally groups exist to control access rights to site or domain resources. SharePoint now gives site owners the ability to directly create and modify groups and to add or remove users from groups. Consequently, the server administrators can pay more attention to the server room and let you manage your own sites.

Adding Users to a Group

The default groups that come with SharePoint aren't particularly useful unless they contain users. Here's the process of adding users to a group:

1. On your SharePoint Site, click Site Actions and select Site Settings from the menu.
2. In the "Users and Permissions" column, click "People and groups."
3. On the "People and Groups" page, click Groups in Quick Launch.
4. On the All Groups page in the Groups column, click the desired group.
5. On the group's page, click New and select Add Users, as seen in Figure 12-2.

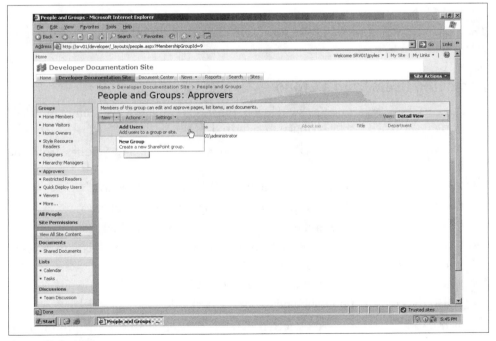

Figure 12-2. Adding a user to a group

6. Use one of the following methods to add users:
   - Type the names of the users you want to add in the available field, separating names with semicolons.
   - Click the Browse button to search for and select the desired usernames.

 Valid names to include in this field are usernames, Windows domain group names, or email addresses.

7. In the Give Permission section, make one of the following selections:
   - Choose a SharePoint group from the "Add users to a SharePoint group" list.
   - Choose "Give users permission directly," and then select the permission level you want to assign to this group.

 As you can see in Figure 12-3, you can also click the drop-down arrow to change the group and group permissions assignments for this user.

8. Click OK.

The users you added to the group now have the access permissions assigned to that group (Figure 12-3).

Removing Users from a Group

As users change departments, switch job functions, or leave the company, their access rights also need to be changed or removed.:

1. On your SharePoint Site, click Site Actions and select Site Settings from the menu.
2. In the "Users and Permissions" column, click "People and groups."
3. On the "People and Groups" page, click Groups in Quick Launch.
4. On the All Groups page in the Groups column, click the desired group.
5. Click the checkboxes next to the names of the users you want to remove, as seen in Figure 12-4.
6. Click the Actions menu, and then click Remove Users from Group.
7. When the confirmation dialog box appears, click OK.

When the screen refreshes, the selected users no longer appear in the group, as in Figure 12-5.

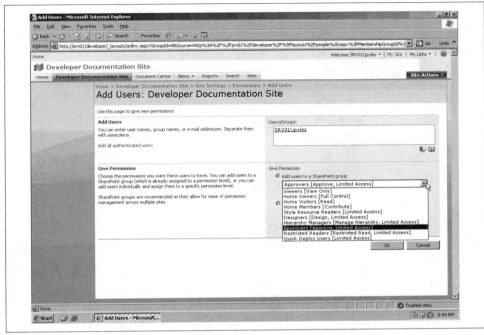

Figure 12-3. Assigning group rights while adding a user to a group

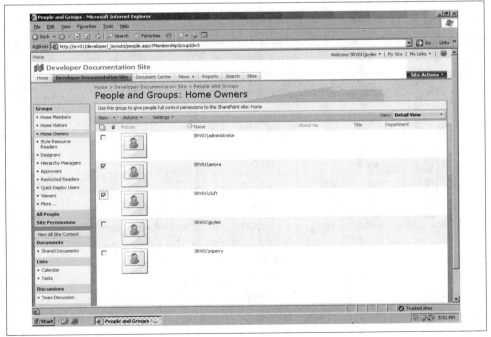

Figure 12-4. Selecting users to be removed from a group

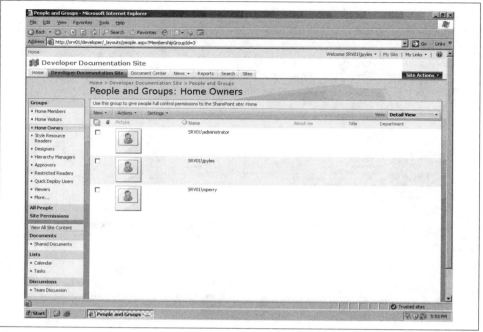

Figure 12-5. The selected users have been removed

Creating a New Group in SharePoint

As mentioned previously, it is unlikely that you will be able to make do with the default groups included in SharePoint. Fortunately, you can create and customize as many access groups as are necessary to construct the security model you need:

1. On your SharePoint Site, click on Site Actions and select Site Settings from the menu.

2. In the "Users and Permissions" column, click "People and groups."

3. On the "People and Groups" page, click New and then select New Group, as seen in Figure 12-6.

4. On the New Group page, in the Name and About Me Description section, type in a name and brief description for the group in the available fields.

5. In the Owner section, the person creating the group is automatically listed as the group owner. Only one person or group can be the owner, but you can change the name in this field to transfer ownership.

6. In the Group Settings section, select the users who should have the rights to view and edit the membership of this group. By default, group members can view the group and group owners can edit the group.

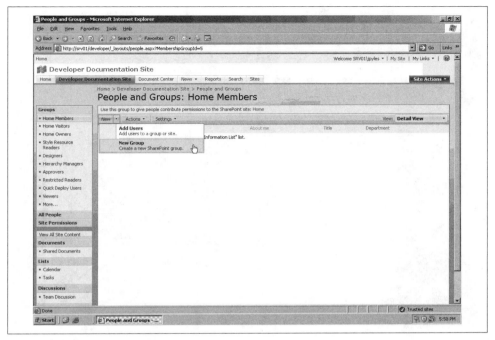

Figure 12-6. Creating a new group

7. In the Group Membership section, click Yes to allow people who request it to either join the group or leave the group, or click No to prevent it.

8. If you click Yes in step 7, you can click Yes right below to allow people to join automatically or click No to have the system send an email notification to the designated approver. In the available field, type in the email address of the approver.

> If email notification is not enabled, the email address field is grayed out, with a sample email address populating the field.

9. When you are done, click Create. See an example of this page in Figure 12-7.

> A warning may appear at the top of the page that states: "This site is using the same permissions as its parent site. The group you create will not automatically get permission to this site. To give a group permission to this site you need to give the group permission on the parent site."

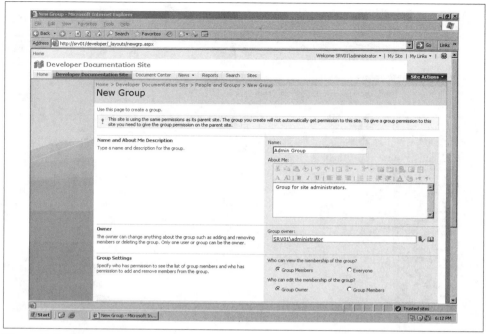

Figure 12-7. Configuring a new group

Editing Group Permission Settings

As seen in the prior exercise, "Creating a New Group in SharePoint," because the group was created at a subsite, it did not have permissions to that subsite. You will have to go to the All Groups list and edit the group's permissions. Those permissions options weren't previously available but will be in this exercise:

1. On your SharePoint Site, click Site Actions and select Site Settings from the menu.

2. In the "Users and Permissions" column, click "People and groups."

3. On the "People and Groups" page, click Groups in Quick Launch.

4. On the All Groups Page in the Groups column, locate and click the name of the desired group, as seen in Figure 12-8.

5. Click Settings, and then click Group Settings.

6. On the Change Group Settings page, scroll down until you see the Give Group Permission to this Site section and check at least one of the permission levels, as seen in Figure 12-9.

7. Click OK.

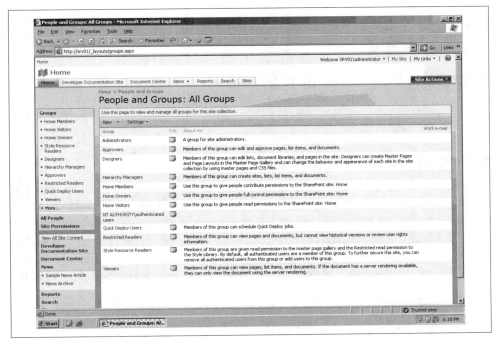

Figure 12-8. Selecting a group to edit

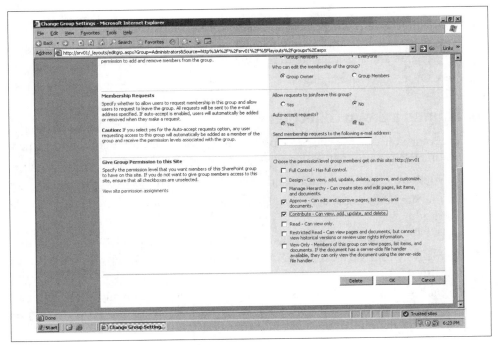

Figure 12-9. Editing the permissions of a group

If you do not add at least one permission level to the group, the group's users will not be able to access the site.

Maintaining SharePoint Groups

Once you have created and configured your groups, there are a number of ways you can maintain them on your site.

Editing a Group List in Quick Launch

Quick Launch makes it easy to find the names of groups and open them, but you might not always want every group you access to be available in Quick Launch. For example, you might want to have quick access to the readers and contributors group, but you might not want to provide easy access to the administrators or designers groups:

1. On your SharePoint Site, click Site Actions and select Site Settings from the menu.

2. In the "Users and Permissions" column, click "People and groups."

3. On the "People and Groups" page, click Groups in Quick Launch.

4. On the All Groups Page, click Settings and then click Edit Group Quick Launch, as in Figure 12-10.

5. On the Edit Group Quick Launch page, in the Groups field, add the groups you want to appear by either typing in their names or searching for them, or right-click a name and select Delete to remove it, as shown in Figure 12-11.

6. Click OK to save your changes.

Configuring a Group Collection

In SharePoint you can use the Set Up Groups option to create a collection of new and existing groups and then assign Owners, Members, and Visitors to those groups:

1. On your site, click Site Actions and then select Site Settings from the menu.

2. On the Site Settings page, in the "Users and Permissions" column, click "People and groups."

3. On the "People and Groups" page, click on Groups in Quick Launch.

4. On the All Groups page, click Settings and select Set Up Groups from the list, as in Figure 12-12.

5. On the "Set Up Groups for this Site" page, go to each section and either select an existing SharePoint group from the list or click "Create a new group" to do just that. See an example of this page in Figure 12-13.

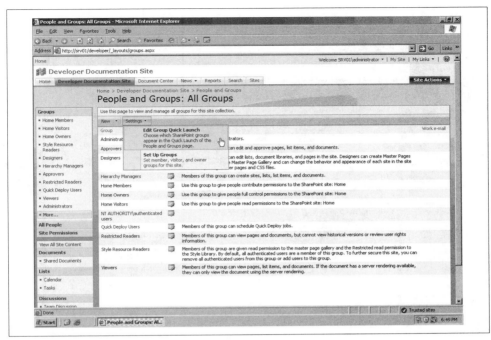

Figure 12-10. Editing the group Quick Launch menu

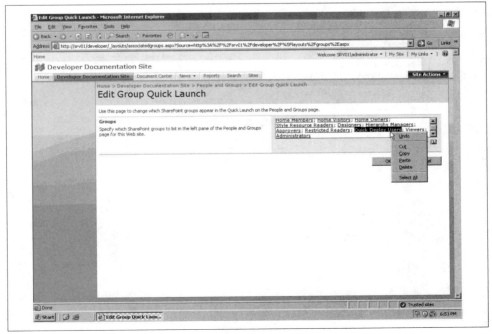

Figure 12-11. Deleting a group in the Quick Launch groups list

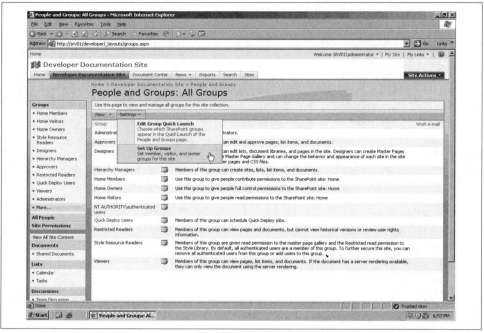

Figure 12-12. Accessing the Set Up Groups option

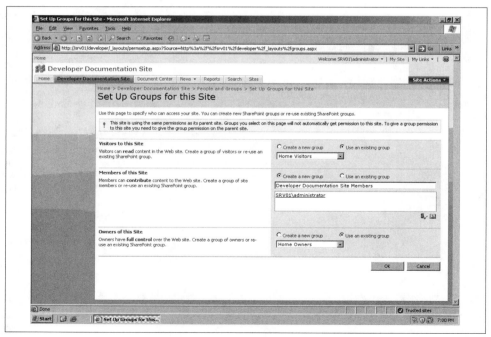

Figure 12-13. Configuring a collection of groups

If you choose "Create a new group," follow steps 4–8 in the exercise "Creating a New Group in SharePoint" to complete the creation process. Also, when you create a new group for a group collection, you can choose to either accept the group name automatically assigned by the system or manually give it a new name.

6. When you are finished, click OK.

 Notice that because you have used this option from a subsite, you are getting the same warning as you did in the earlier exercise "Creating a New Group in SharePoint." After this group collection is finished, you will have to repeat the exercise steps from Editing Group Settings for this collection.

Adding Groups to Summary Link Web Parts or Field Controls

You can use either a Summary Link Web Part or a Summary Link field control to add links to a web page in a site. This lets you organize groups by title or function, such as Programming Languages Groups or Network Engineers Groups. It takes only a few minutes to put these links together:

1. On the site, click Site Actions and select Edit Page from the menu.
2. In the Summary Link Web Part or field control, click New Group, as in Figure 12-14.
3. When the New Group Web Page dialog box appears, in the Group Header Name field, type a header name for your collection of group links and then click OK to finish.

Targeting Content Based on Group

There are multiple ways you can ensure that specific groups will receive or be able to view content relevant to their group. You can configure lists, libraries, links, and Web Parts to be viewed differently based on group membership.

 See Chapter 22 for more information about targeting content.

Enabling Audience-Based Targeting in a List or Library

In addition to creating multiple views to filter the content of a list or library, you can enable Audience-Based Content Targeting, which will allow people to see only specific items depending on their group membership:

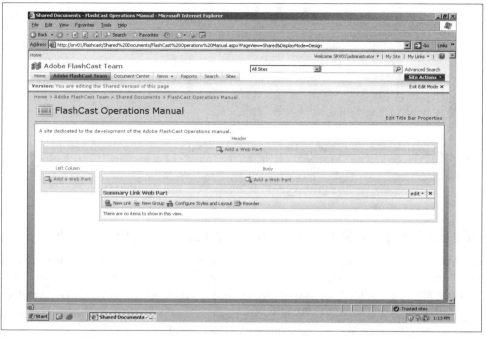

Figure 12-14. Adding a Group to a Summary Link Web Part

1. On your site, either click the list or library name in Quick Launch or click View All Site Content and then click on the list or library name.

2. On the toolbar, click Settings and then select the appropriate item, such as List Settings or Document Library Settings, as illustrated in Figure 12-15.

3. Under General Settings, click "Audience targeting settings."

4. Check the "Enable audience targeting" checkbox, as in Figure 12-16, and click OK.

5. Back on the Customize page near the top, click the name of the list or library to return there.

6. In the list or library, click the arrow next to the name of an item and select Edit Properties from the list, as in Figure 12-17.

7. In the Target Audiences list, select one or more groups that you want to be part of the targeted audience for this item.

8. Click OK. An example of this page can be seen in Figure 12-18.

Now when members of the designated group visit the list or library, any items targeted to the group will appear to its members. Items not targeted to that group will not be accessible.

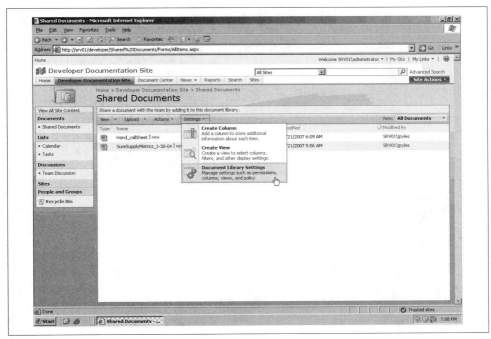

Figure 12-15. Selecting document library settings

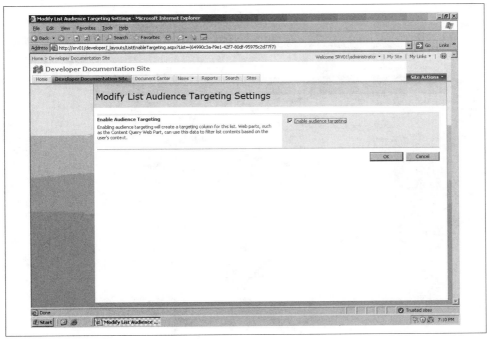

Figure 12-16. Enabling audience targeting

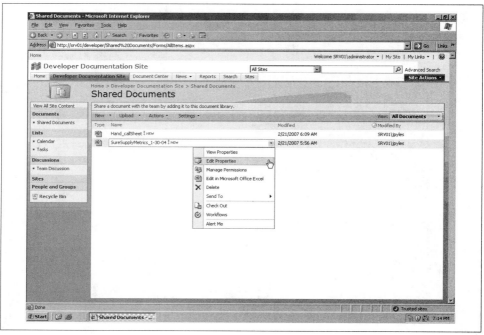

Figure 12-17. Editing the properties of a document

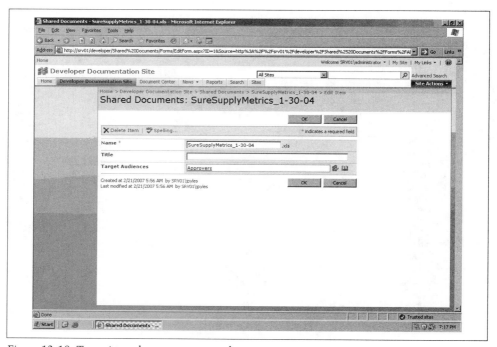

Figure 12-18. Targeting a document to an audience

Displaying Targeted Items in a Separate Web Part

Instead of waiting for members of various groups to visit a list or library to view the targeted content, you can display the content in a separate Web Part on their site so it will be readily available. For example, you might have a master list of work assignments as a list on an administrative page. You might want to create targeted lists for each team and display only the team's items on a Web Part on each team page.

First, add a Content Query Web Part to the appropriate Web Part page. This Web Part lets you build a query that can filter list and library items. After you have added the Web Part, do the following:

1. Click Edit on the Content Query Web Part to open the Web Part's tool pane.

2. In the tool pane in the Query section, click "Show items from the following list" and click the Browse button to open the Select a List or Library dialog box, as shown in Figure 12-19.

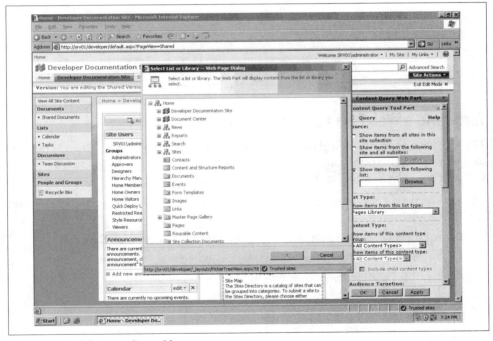

Figure 12-19. Selecting a list or library

 The default setting in this section is "Show items from all sites in this site collection," which sometimes presents an overabundance of information. After selecting "Show items from the following list" and clicking Browse, you may have to scroll through the dialog box to see all the choices. Also, some folders are expandable and contain more choices inside.

3. Select an option in the dialog box and click OK.

 The OK button will remain grayed out until you make a selection.

4. In the List Type section, select the type of list or library, such as Document Library.

5. In the Audience Targeting section, check the Apply Audience Filtering check-box to display these items to the group or groups you specified in the previous exercise, "Enabling Audience-Based Targeting in a List or Library" in step 6.

6. You can also check the "Include items that are not targeted" checkbox if you want the content to be displayed to nontargeted audiences.

7. Click OK to save your changes, and then click Exit Edit Mode.

 If you choose to paste a URL in the field available in the Query section in step 2 instead of browsing, make sure that the URL references a source in the current site collection. If you are performing this action in a site under the top-level site and you choose a list in the top-level site, the Web Part will not be able to display the information. Use the current site or any sites beneath it as library or list sources.

Targeting a Web Part to an Audience

The previous exercise, "Displaying Targeted Items in a Web Part," showed you how to specify which groups can view the contents of a Web Part. This exercise shows you how to make a Web Part itself available to a specific group:

1. On the page containing the desired Web Part, click Site Actions and then select Edit Page from the menu.

2. Click Edit on the Web Part and then click Modify Shared Web Part.

3. In the Web Part's tool pane in the Advanced section, add one or more group names to the Audiences List, as in Figure 12-20.

4. Click OK to finish.

 If you create a Web Part containing targeted list items for a particular group and then modify the Audiences List on that Web Part so that it does not include that group, group members will not be able to see the Web Part or any of the items it contains.

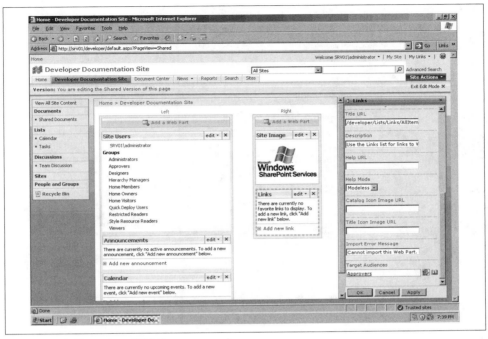

Figure 12-20. Targeting a Web Part to an audience

Targeting Navigation Links to an Audience

Like lists, libraries, and Web Parts, you can target navigation links to one or more groups. This allows those groups to visit parts of the site collection specifically relevant to them. Because it involves altering navigation in the site collection, you must have Designer permissions or higher to complete this exercise:

1. On the Portal Site, click Site Actions and select Site Settings from the menu.

2. Click Modify Navigation to open the Site Navigation Settings page.

3. Click Add Link, as in Figure 12-21.

4. On the Navigation Link dialog box, type the title of the link and then add the URL, either by typing or pasting in the link or by browsing to it.

5. If you want the link to open in a separate window, check the "Open link in new window" checkbox.

6. Type a brief description of the link in the Description field.

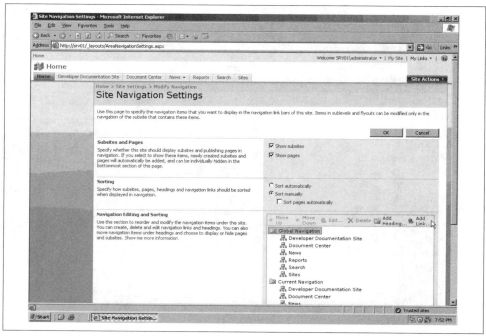

Figure 12-21. Clicking Add Link on the Site Navigation Settings page

7. Add one or more group names to the Audiences list and click OK to close the dialog box.

8. Click OK again to finish on the Site Navigation Setting page.

See an example of configuring this dialog box in Figure 12-22.

When the page with the navigation links is opened, only members of the specified group will be able to see the link.

Modifying Permissions to View Drafts by Group

When a document is first added to a library with an approval workflow, the document is in a draft or pending state until it is approved by a member of the Approvers group. Until then, only administrators, users with View Lists rights, and the author can see the draft. Document drafts are also created when an existing document is modified. The minor revision changes are not visible until published. You can change the default permissions and allow specific groups the ability to view draft documents:

1. In the desired list or library, click Settings and then click the appropriate selection, such as List Settings or Document Library Settings.

2. Under General Settings, click "Versioning settings."

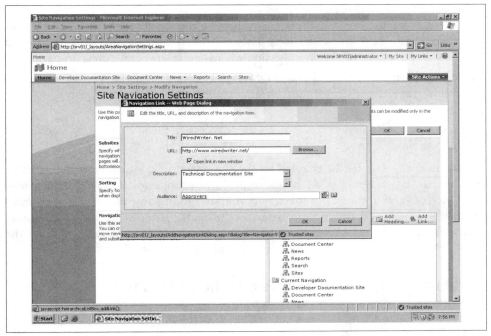

Figure 12-22. Targeting a navigational link to an audience

3. In the Draft Item Security section under "Who should see draft items," select the group name you want to be able to view drafts.

4. Click OK to finish.

In Step 3, the specific item could be called "Who should see draft items in this list" or "Who should see draft items in this document library," depending on whether you are working in a list or library.

Allowing Anonymous Users Access to SharePoint

Although this is not generally recommended, it is possible to allow anonymous users access to a SharePoint site and its lists and libraries. The preferred practice is to allow only authenticated users access, which means that anyone accessing the site collection is a member or your organization in some way.

If you allow anonymous users access, even with read-only privileges, they will still be able to view the information contained on the site, including email addresses, phone numbers, and other data you might not want available to the general public. You can allow or restrict anonymous user access in the following ways:

Allow Access to the Entire Site

> An anonymous user would be able to browse the top-level site and any subsites that inherit parent site permissions. They can open and read the contents of any list or library available in the site collection where parent site permissions propagate.

Allow Access only to Specific Lists and Libraries

> You can specify which lists and libraries can be accessed anonymously.

Nothing

> This completely denies anonymous users access to the site collection and any of its contents.

Anonymous access must be enabled by the site owner or administrator before these options can be accessed. One of the only justifications for allowing anonymous access to lists and libraries is if they contain information you want potential customers to view, such as content about your products and services. In that case, anonymous user access must be strictly limited to the specific content areas without the possibility of the user navigating to nonpublic areas of the site.

Enabling Anonymous User Access to the Entire Site

 To reiterate, enabling anonymous user access to the entire site is an extremely dangerous thing to do, since the general public would be able to browse the entire content of your site.

If you created a site within the site collection containing only publicly consumable information, allowed anonymous access to the site, and made sure that the subsite did not inherit permissions from the business parts of the site collection, you could create a show room of sorts, where you could display all of your products and services to customers and potential customers.

 It would probably be better to create a completely separate site for your web presence on the Internet.

1. On the site you want to enable anonymous user access, click Site Actions and select Site Settings from the list.

2. Under "Users and Permissions," click "Advanced permissions."

3. In the Settings menu, click on Anonymous Access.

 At this point in the process, you can select which parts of the site you will let anonymous users access, rather than the entire site itself.

Enabling Anonymous User Access to a List or Library

1. Open the list or library you want open to anonymous users.

2. Click Settings and select the appropriate item, such as List Settings or Document Library Settings.

3. In the Permissions and Management column, click the appropriate choice, such as "Permissions for this list" or "Permissions for this library."

4. To prevent the list or library from inheriting permissions from the site, click Actions, select Edit Permissions, and then click OK.

5. On the Permissions page, click Settings and then click Anonymous Access.

6. On the Change Anonymous Access Settings page, select the permissions that you want to grant to anonymous users for this list or library.

 If you select any permission level besides Read-only, anonymous users will be able to modify items in the list or library.

Anonymous access is not enabled by default. To allow anonymous access, the site administrator or owner must specifically enable the process.

CHAPTER 13

Creating and Managing Picture Libraries

Introduction

Picture libraries are similar in use and function to the document libraries you read about in Chapter 9. A picture library is basically a list of all of the graphics files you plan to store and display on your SharePoint site. In most cases, you will use the Picture Library as a collection point, and reference the content in other Web Parts and pages.

You can display any image in the Picture Library on any Web Part page using an Image Web Part. The Image Link property of the Image Web Part allows you to enter the URL of the desired graphic's location in the library. You can also use the Source Editor in the Content Editor Web Part to create a link to the graphic in HTML.

 See Chapter 8 for more details.

Once the graphic in the Picture Library is linked to a Web Part page, the image will be displayed in the part of the page containing the Image Web Part or, if linked with HTML, the image will appear where you have indicated in the link. If the image in the Picture Library is modified, the modifications will automatically appear on any page with a link to the Picture Library.

 If you do not know HTML well enough to control the size and location of an image link, use the Image Web Part.

Image libraries, like document libraries, can be accessed either by an individual site or by an entire site collection. Use the Image Library to restrict access to your graphics to just the site containing the library. Use the Site Collection Images Library to share your images with all the sites in the site collection.

MOSS 2007 includes page layouts that contain a Page Image field control and a Page Content field control. These field controls are used on site pages that are not Web Part pages, allowing you to add and edit content. An example of page field controls open in SharePoint Designer Toolbox is shown in Figure 13-1.

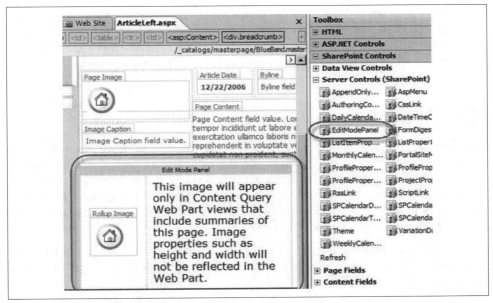

Figure 13-1. Page field controls

The Page Image field control is an element built into specific page layouts that allow you to add images to those pages. The specific page layouts containing Page Image field controls are:

- Article page with image on the left
- Article page with image on the right
- Intranet home page for internal access
- Welcome page with summary links
- Welcome page with a table of contents
- Welcome splash page

You can use a Page Image field control to add a graphic by linking to any picture or photo in the Picture Library.

Similar to the Page Image field control, specific page layouts in MOSS 2007 contain Page Content field controls. These controls enable you to add links to graphics using

HTML in a way similar to using the Source Editor in a Content Editor Web Part. By default, the page layouts containing Page Content field controls are:

- Intranet Home
- Welcome page with summary links
- Welcome page with table of contents

Your particular site may have other page layouts containing Page Image field controls and Page Content field controls. If you want to find out whether a page layout has either of these elements, you can edit the page by clicking Site Action → Edit Page. When the page is in Edit Mode, each element appears with a label. A Page Image field control is labeled Page Image, and a Page Content field control is labeled Page Content.

Slide Libraries

One variation on a picture library is a slide library. As the name implies, a slide library is used to contain all of your Office PowerPoint 2007 slides and slide shows. The Slide Library stores your slide shows as individual slides. However, each slide presentation is preserved and can be opened and presented using PowerPoint. You might want to use a slide library if your organization makes use of a large number of standard slides in custom presentations.

Just as with picture libraries, individual slides can be accessed and modified in the Slide Library. When the slide show is opened again, any modifications will appear in the presentation. The Library can be set up to share your slides with others, in the event that other people or teams need to use all of your presentation or just specific slides.

Creating Libraries

The process of creating image libraries is almost the same as creating any other library, with just some minor configuration changes. In fact, in SharePoint 2003, you could probably upload a Word document in a picture library and a GIF file in a document library, but trying to keep track of what was placed where would be chaotic. The reason for categorizing libraries by content type was primarily organizational rather than technical.

MOSS 2007 uses content types to specify what types of files must be stored in what kinds of lists or libraries. The properties of each content type—such as a graphic or document—are different, and a library set for a specific content type will have different options. For instance, the tools used to edit an image in a picture library are not the same as those available in a document library for editing a document.

Despite these differences, the actual library creation process is virtually the same from one library type to another.

Creating a Picture Library

1. On your site, click Site Actions and select Create from the menu.
2. Under Libraries, click Picture Library, as seen in Figure 13-2.

Figure 13-2. Starting to create a picture library

3. On the Create a Library Page, in the Name field, type the name of your library.

 You can have separate picture libraries if you want to organize your graphics by type. For instance, you can have a photograph library, a drawing library, a logo library, and so on.

4. Type a brief description of the library in the Description field.
5. If you want to add a link to this library in Quick Launch, click the Yes radio button under Navigation.
6. Under Picture Version History, if you want a different version of a picture to be created every time you edit a graphic, click the Yes radio button, as seen in Figure 13-3.

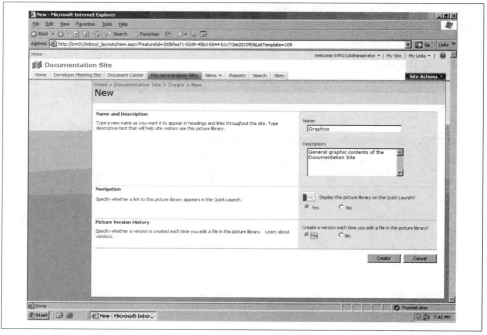

Figure 13-3. Configuring a new picture library

After the picture library is created, you are ready to add images to it.

Create a Slide Library

There is only one main difference between creating a slide library and creating a picture library:

1. On your site, click Site Actions and select Create from the menu.

2. Under Libraries, click Slide Library.

3. On the "Create a Library" page, in the Name field, type the name of your library.

4. Type a brief description of the library in the Description field.

5. If you want to add a link to this library in Quick Launch, click the Yes radio button under Navigation.

6. Configure the other available options, and then click Create.

The only difference between these two tasks is in step 2, where you choose the library content type (Figure 13-4).

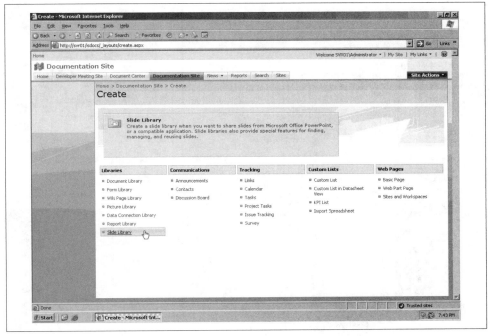

Figure 13-4. Creating a slide library

Add Content to a Picture Library

The instructions for adding image content to a picture library are also valid for adding PowerPoint .*ppt* files to a slide library:

1. Open the picture library, either from Quick Launch or by clicking View All Site Content and then clicking on the picture library name.

2. Click Upload and select Upload Picture from the menu, as in Figure 13-5.

3. Next to the Name field, click the Browse button.

4. Browse your computer's directory or the network to locate the desired graphic.

 It is usually best to store the graphic in the My Pictures directory on your local machine, so you can quickly and easily locate the desired picture.

5. If a prior version of this picture is already in the library and you want to overwrite it, verify that the "Overwrite existing file(s)" checkbox is checked.

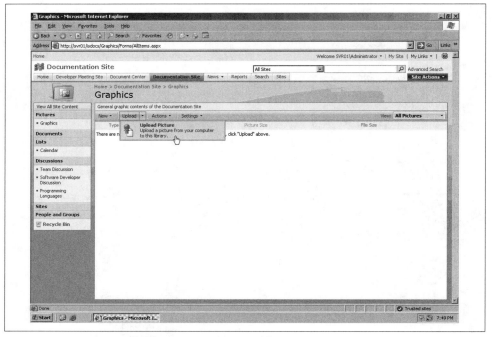

Figure 13-5. Starting to upload a picture to a picture library

In SharePoint 2003, if wanted to upload more than one picture file at the same time, you could click "Upload multiple files" and browse to the folder where the pictures were located. In that case, it would have been best to collect these files in the same folder on your hard drive. In this version of SharePoint, that option is not available from this page.

6. In the Version Comments field, you can add whatever note you would like about this version of the picture.

7. Click OK to upload the graphic or graphics into the picture library, as in Figure 13-6.

8. On the Edit Item page, you can configure the following properties of the graphic (see Figure 13-7; note that at the top of this figure, there is a notice that the picture was successfully uploaded):

Title

Add a name for the graphic in the Title field.

Date Picture Taken

You can include the date and time a photograph was taken or a graphic was created.

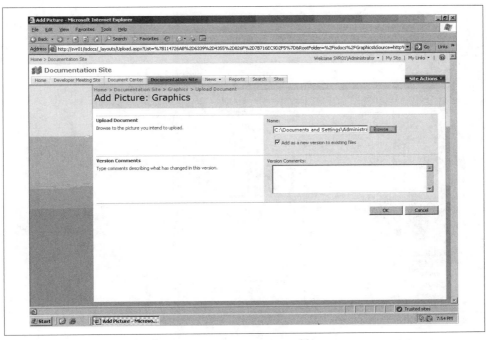

Figure 13-6. *Completed uploading a new picture to a picture library*

Description
> Add a brief description of the graphic in the Description field.

Keywords
> Add any descriptive keywords in the Keywords field.

 Adding keywords makes it easier to locate the graphic using a search engine.

9. Click OK to finish.

Editing and Managing Images in a Picture Library

A picture library is more than just a "holding cell" for your graphics. It is possible to edit graphics within the library itself and to control versioning of the picture library contents.

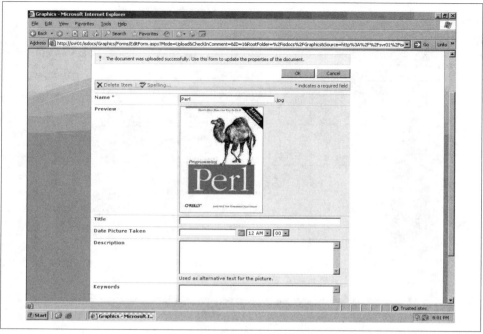

Figure 13-7. Editing an uploaded picture

Requiring Check Out in a Picture Library

The benefit of requiring that an image be checked out in order to be edited is that only one person can edit an image at a time. If the image is checked out and then another user attempts to check it out, the second user will receive a message indicating the image is unavailable. Once the first user has checked the image back into the library, any other user can access it and edit the graphic further. This procedure is more important for pictures than for documents, since it is almost impossible to "merge changes" on a picture:

1. Open the picture library, either by clicking its name in Quick Launch or by clicking View All Site Content and then clicking the library's name.

2. Click Settings and select Picture Library Settings from the menu.

3. Under General, click "Versioning settings," as seen in Figure 13-8.

4. Under Require Check Out, click the Yes radio button next to "Require documents to be checked out before they can be edited," as shown in Figure 13-9, and then click OK.

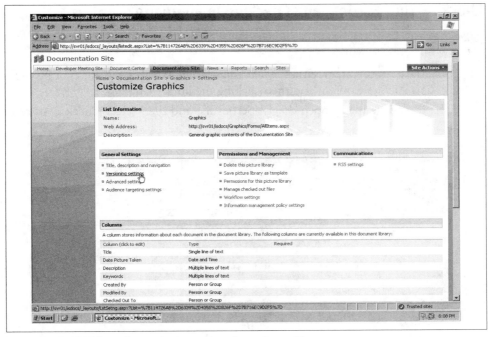

Figure 13-8. Modifying the versioning settings for a picture library

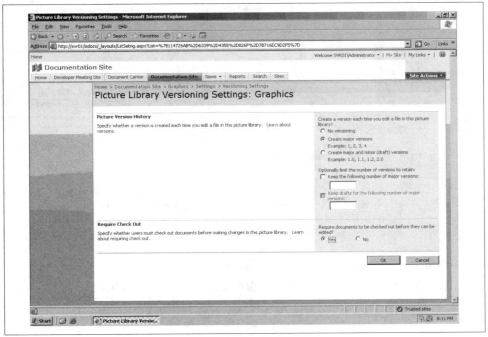

Figure 13-9. Configuring the Require Check Out option in a picture library

Checking Out, Editing, and Checking In an Image

Now that you have required that images must be checked out prior to editing, let's see how this process works:

1. Open the picture library, either by clicking its name in Quick Launch or by clicking View All Site Content and then clicking the library's name.

2. Click the image file to open the properties list and then select Check Out, as in Figure 13-10.

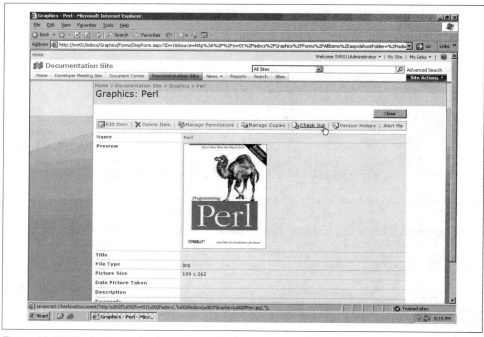

Figure 13-10. Beginning to check out a graphic from a picture library

3. Click on the graphic again to open it, and then click Edit Item.

 SharePoint does not have a built-in graphics editor. If you do not have any other editing program on your local computer, the picture will open in Edit Mode, as shown previously in Figure 13-7, but you will not be able to modify the graphic.

4. When you are finished changing the image, click OK.

5. Click the graphic again and then click Check In, as in Figure 13-11.

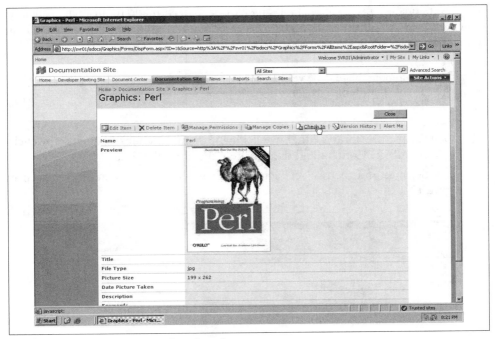

Figure 13-11. Checking in a graphic after editing

6. In the document Check In section, you can click Yes to keep the item checked out after checking in this version or No to check in the item.

 Versioning must be enabled in order to make these options available.

7. Click OK to check the graphic back into the picture library.

Enabling Versioning in a Picture Library

When you enable versioning, the Picture Library tracks each change made to an image by giving it a version number. This way, all the versions of an image can be saved and previous versions can be recovered. Versioning can be set up to track all versions of an image file or to retain only a limited number of versions.

Versioning can be set up to record both major and minor versions. Major versions are used when significant changes are made to an image, such as cropping, resizing, and modifying the color balance and contrast. The numbering system for major versions uses whole numbers: 1, 2, 3, and so on.

Minor versions are used when small changes have been made to an image, such as removing "red eye" from a photograph. Numbering for minor versions uses decimal numbering: 0.1, 0.2, 0.3, and so on.

 In other words, the versioning numbering system for libraries follows the same format as software versioning.

1. Open the picture library, either by clicking its name in Quick Launch or by clicking View All Site Content and then clicking the library's name.

2. Click Settings and then select Picture Library Settings from the list, as seen in Figure 13-12.

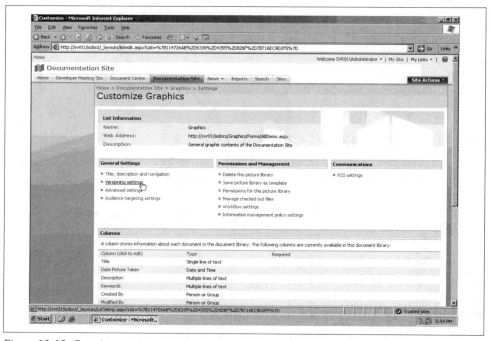

Figure 13-12. Opening versioning settings

3. Under General, select "Versioning settings."

4. Select one of the two following options in the Version History section:
   • Click "Create major versions."
   • Click "Create major and minor (draft) versions."

5. To control the number of versions of a file that will be retained, select from the following options, as in Figure 13-13:

- Click the "Keep the following number of versions" checkbox, and then enter the number of versions you want to retain.

- Click the "Keep the following number of major versions" checkbox, and then enter the number of major versions you want to retain.

- Click the "Keep drafts for the following number of major versions" checkbox, and then enter the number of major versions to retain in draft form.

6. Click OK to save the setup.

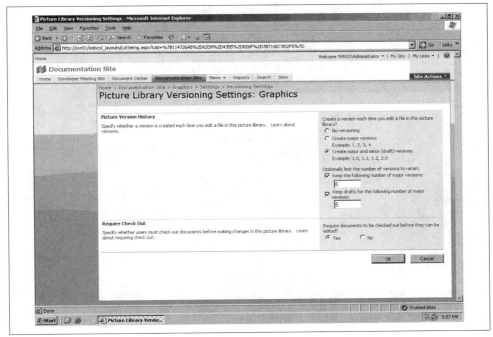

Figure 13-13. Configuring versioning in a picture library

Adding Images from a Picture Library to a Web Page

In Chapter 8, you learned how to add a Web Part to a Web Part page. Image Web Parts are added to Web Part pages using that process and then linked to images in the Picture Library. There are other methods of adding images, as described in the following section.

Adding an Image with the Page Image Field Control

If you are working on a page containing a Page Image field control, you can use it to add an image to that page.

1. On the page where you want to add the image, click Site Actions and select Edit Page to make the Page Image field control visible.

2. In the Page Image field control, click Edit Picture to open the Edit Image Properties Web Page dialog box, as in Figure 13-14.

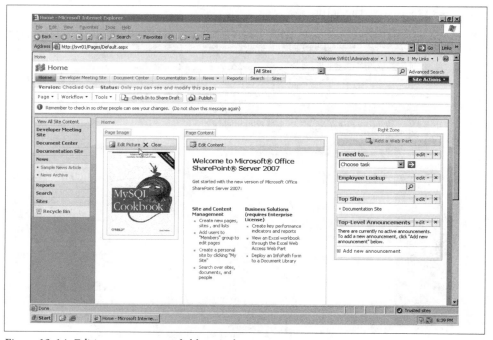

Figure 13-14. Editing a page image field control

3. In the General section, click the Browse button next to the Selected Image field.

4. After the Image Library opens in a separate window, select the desired image and click OK. This will cause the image library window to close and populate the Selected Image field with the URL of the chosen picture. (See Figure 13-15.)

5. Set the layout properties to what you want, and click OK to add the image.

6. If this is a top-level site, you may have to click Publish to exit Edit Mode.

As you can see in Figure 13-16, the new image is now present on the page.

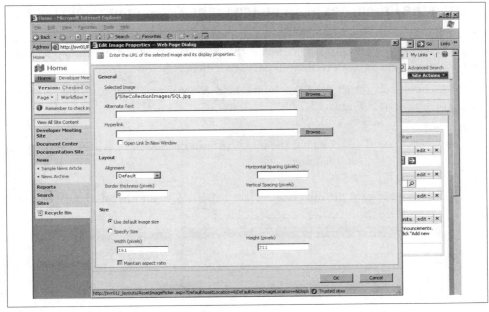

Figure 13-15. Adding the URL to a graphic

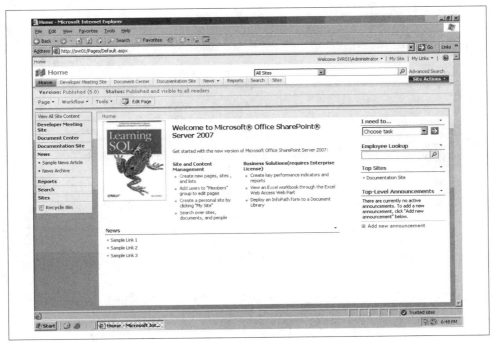

Figure 13-16. New figure has successfully been added to the Page Image field

Setting the Properties of an Image in the Page Image Field Control

In step 5 of the previous exercise, you were instructed to set the image layout properties. There are numerous image controls that you can use to affect the appearance and position of the image on the web page, specified as follows.

In the General section of the Page Image field control, you will find the following properties, as seen in Figure 13-17:

Alternate Text
> This is the text that appears if the image cannot be viewed or when you use your cursor to hover over the image.

Hyperlink
> Use this if you want the image to act as a hyperlink to another web page or site.

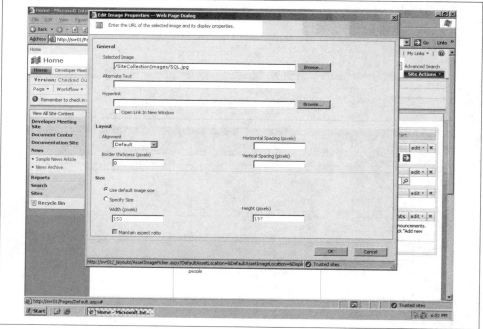

Figure 13-17. Page Image field control properties

In the Layout section, you will find the following:

Alignment
> This determines the position of the image within the Page Image field control.

 The Page Image field control is automatically sized to fit the selected image, so the alignment property is not meaningful.

Border thickness

Use this option if you want to create a border around the image and determine the thickness of the border in pixels.

Horizontal Spacing

Use this to create space to the left and right of the image, measured in pixels.

Vertical Spacing

Use this to create space at the top and bottom of the image, measured in pixels.

In the Size section, you will find the following:

Use default image size

Use this option if you want the size of the image to be determined by the image file's properties.

Specify Size

Select this option if you want to manually configure the width and height of the image in pixels.

Maintain aspect ratio

Use this option when you manually configure the image's size, to avoid distorting the image.

 If you do not maintain the aspect ratio of width and height, the image will appear distorted.

Adding an Image in the Page Content Field Control Using HTML

Whereas the Page Image field control is specifically designed to display images, the Page Content field control usually contains text data. You can, however, use the HTML Editor to add an image using standard HTML tags.

 Do not employ this option unless you have sufficient knowledge of HTML to design your own page. You will need to control all aspects of the image, including its size, border, alternate text, and so on.

1. On the page where you want to add the image, click Site Actions and select Edit Page to make the Page Content field control visible.

2. In the Page Content field control, click Edit Content to open the HTML Editor, and place the cursor in the place in the field control where you want to display the image, as in Figure 13-18.

3. Click Insert Image in the HTML Editor toolbar to open the Edit Image Properties – Web Page Dialog box.

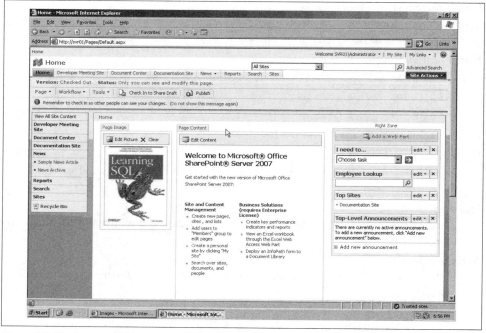

Figure 13-18. Opening Page Content field control for editing

You can also use the keyboard shortcut Ctrl-Shift-G.

4. In the General section, click the Browse button next to the Selected Image field to open the image library in a new window.

5. Select the desired image, and click OK to close the Image Library window and populate the Selected Image field with the URL of the selected image.

6. Set the layout properties to what you want, and click OK to add the image.

The layout properties for this field control are identical to the Page Image field control. See the "Setting the Properties of an Image in the Page Image Field Control" section, earlier in this chapter, for details.

Adding an Image in a Content Editor Web Part Using the Source Editor

Although not recommended, you can use the source editor in a Content Editor Web Part to insert an image with HTML. You must have a good knowledge of how this is done, since you will be manually linking, positioning, and aligning an image on the page using source code.

See Chapter 8 for details on working with a Content Editor Web Part.

The following exercise assumes that a Content Editor Web Part has already been added to a Web Part page and that you are at that specific page:

1. Click Site Actions and select Edit Page from the menu.

2. Click the arrow next to the Web Part title to open the menu and then click Source Editor, as in Figure 13-19.

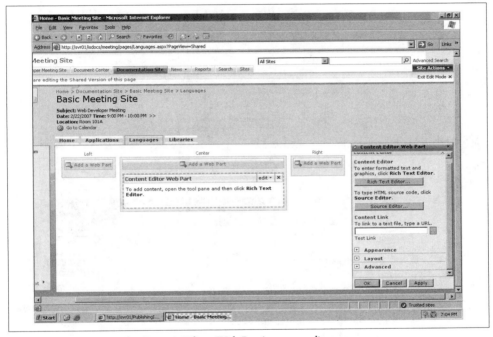

Figure 13-19. Opening the Content Editor Web Part's source editor

3. When the source editor opens, add your HTML, including the link to the image in the Picture Library, as shown in Figure 13-20.

4. When finished, click Save to close the source editor and then OK to close the pane.

The figure is added to the Content Editor Web Part according to the properties specified in HTML, as seen in Figure 13-21.

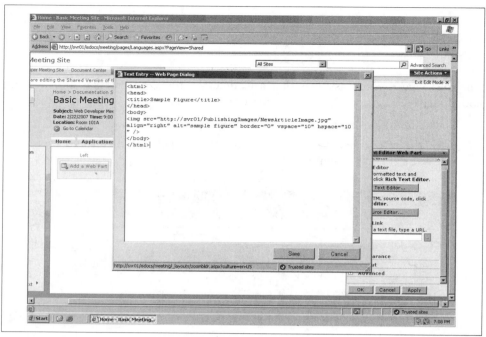

Figure 13-20. Adding HTML to the source editor

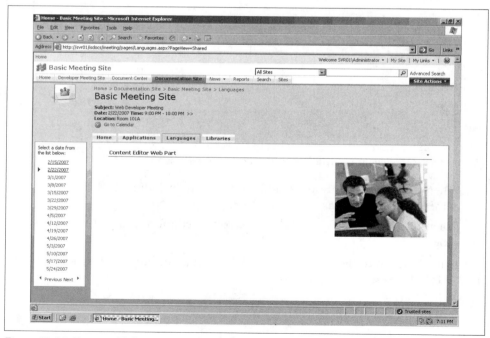

Figure 13-21. Figure added to Content Editor Web Part in HTML

The following is a very simple example of HTML source that places an image to the right of the page near the top:

```
<html>
<head>
<title>HTML Sample</title>
</head>
<body>
<IMG  src="http://svr01/graphics/logo-perl01.gif" align="right" vspace="1" alt=perl
hspace="10" border="0">
<BLOCKQUOTE>
<H2>Charter</H2>
<blockquote>
<P> Perl at our company is supported by the Developer Services Team. Our charter is
to provide quality support for Perl developers on all supported platforms,
with both language and distribution issues. </P>
</blockquote>
</BLOCKQUOTE>
</body>
</html>
```

CHAPTER 14

Creating and Managing Lists

Introduction

MOSS 2007 comes with a number of list templates. You will use different lists for different purposes on your site. You can access all of the lists by clicking on View All Site Contents and going to the Lists section of the page.

The list templates available in MOSS 2007 by default are:

Announcements

> These are used for sharing information with a group, including upcoming events, changes in staff, or other similar data. An Announcements List can contain images, hyperlinks, and formatted text.

Contacts

> These lists hold people, teams, and organizations you work with, your associates, and your customers. If you are using an email or contact management program such as Microsoft Office Outlook 2007, you can create and modify your Outlook contacts from inside of SharePoint.

Discussion Boards

> Discussions are presented as lists and are thus appropriate to mention in this context. See Chapter 11 to learn more.

Links

> These lists contain all of the hyperlinks commonly accessed by your company. You can create a single Links list, and then create different views appropriate for separate teams or departments.

Calendar

> These lists hold the date and time of specific events, such as meetings, presentations, training sessions, and holidays. MOSS 2007 lets you open both your SharePoint and Outlook 2007 Calendars side by side so you can compare and update them together.

Tasks

These lists are used to assign and track projects for individuals or groups.

Project Tasks

These lists are similar to Tasks lists, except they provide a visual or Gantt view with progress bars.

Issue Tracking

These lists are similar to Tasks lists but track the progression of events such as help desk issues instead of projects.

Survey

These lists allow you to query people or groups in your organization on a particular subject. For example, you can survey a group of software engineers on the feasibility of adding a new programming language to the list they support.

In addition to preconfigured list templates, you can create a customized list to suit specific needs. The Custom list is actually just another list template like those just mentioned, but its formatting is less complex. Additionally, any of the list templates can be modified to more closely satisfy your goals.

Creating Lists

In SharePoint, just about everything is either organized as or displayed in lists. In addition to the default lists, you can create your own customized lists to meet your requirements and even create lists based on Excel spreadsheet data. This section of the chapter shows you the different ways in which you can make and modify lists.

Creating a List Using a List Template

Creating a list from a template is a very similar process to creating a Site or Workspace from a template:

1. Either click Site Actions and select Create from the menu or click View All Site Content and click Create.
2. Start creating a list by doing one of the following:
   - Click a list type under Communications.
   - Click a list type under Tracking (see Figure 14-1).
3. Type the name of your list in the Name field.
4. Type a brief description of your list in the Description field.
5. If you want a link to your list placed in Quick Launch, click Yes under Navigation. Remember, you can click on View All Site Content to view all lists.

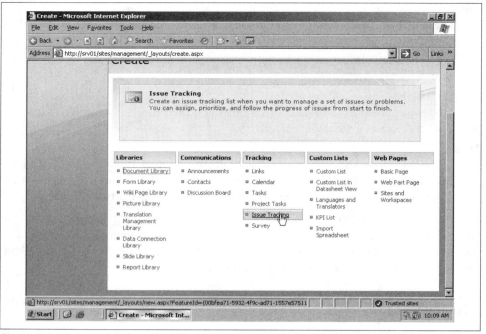

Figure 14-1. Opening a list template

> For some lists, an Email section will appear. If you want users to send content to the list from their email clients, click Yes under "Enable this list to receive email," and then add the email address to the list.
>
> For some lists, an Email notification section will appear. If you want to send email notifications from the list when list items are assigned to users, click Yes under "Send email when ownership is assigned?"

6. Click Create.

The list created from the template appears, ready to have content added (see Figure 14-2).

Creating a Custom List

When you create a Custom List, by default the list will contain fewer options than a ready-made list. After you create the list, you can configure it by adding different features, such as columns, so that the list functions just the way you want:

1. Either click Site Actions and select Create from the menu or click View All Site Content and click Create.

2. In the Custom List column, click Custom List, as illustrated in Figure 14-3.

3. Type the name of your list in the Name field.

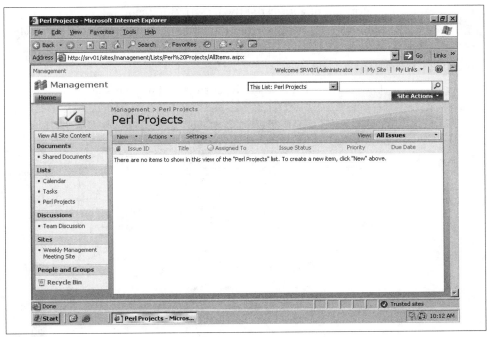

Figure 14-2. List created from a list template

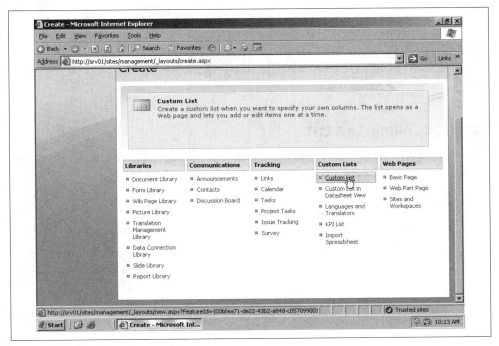

Figure 14-3. Creating a Custom List

4. Type a brief description of your list in the Description field.

5. If you want a link to your list placed in Quick Launch, click Yes under Navigation, as seen in Figure 14-4.

6. Click Create.

You now have a "bare bones" list, ready to be customized to your specifications.

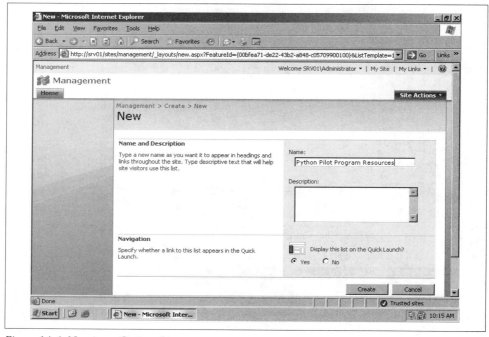

Figure 14-4. Naming a Custom List

Adding a Column to a List

Once the basic Custom List has been created, it's time to customize it. You can start by adding a column to the list:

1. Open the list, either by clicking the list's name in Quick Launch or clicking View All Site Content and then clicking the list's name.

2. Click Settings and select Create Column from the list, as in Figure 14-5.

3. Under Name and Type, type the name of the column in the Column name field.

4. Under "The type of information in this column is," select the property type for this column. Your choices are:

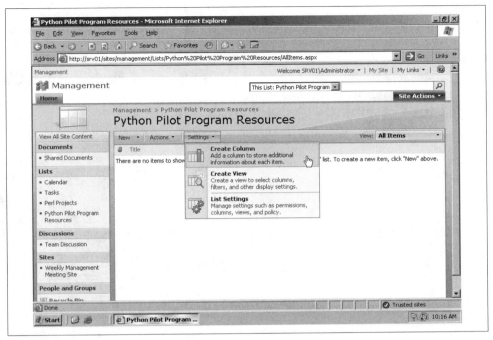

Figure 14-5. Adding a column to a list

Single line of text
Use this option when you want users to enter just a few words in a field.

Multiple lines of text
Use this option when you want to give users the ability to enter a sentence or two of text.

Number
This option allows users to enter in a number value.

Currency
This lets users enter in a monetary value.

Date and Time
This column type is used to contain calendaring information, such as date, day, and time.

Lookup
Use this option when you want to link the column to other data in the SharePoint site.

Choice
This property type allows or requires users to choose between two or more options in the list.

Yes/No

This option presents the user with an "either/or" selection, such as true/false or zero/one.

Hyperlink or Picture

This type lets the user either create a hyperlink to another web page or site or display an image through a link.

Calculated

Use this information type to display a column of calculated values.

You can see how these column choices appear in Figure 14-6.

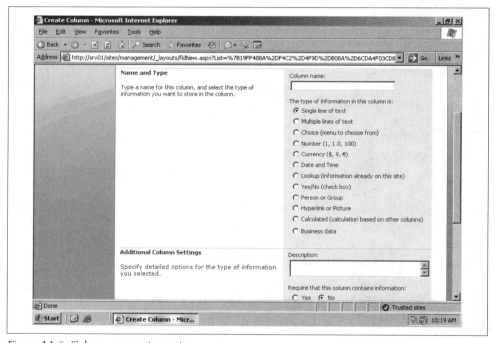

Figure 14-6. Column properties options

5. Under Additional Column Settings, type a description of the new column in the Description field.

Depending on the type of column option you chose in step 4, there may be additional selections available in this section. Figure 14-7 shows an example of how a column can be set up.

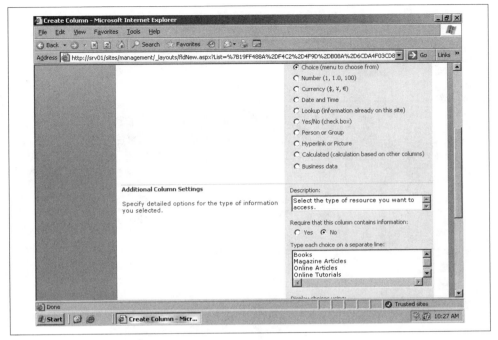

Figure 14-7. Creating a column

6. Click "Add to default view" if you want this column to appear in the default view of the list.

7. Click OK to add the column to the list. Figure 14-8 shows the result.

Notes on Creating a Lookup Column

The configuration of certain list columns can be more involved than others. A lookup column is designed to provide a filtered list of data already available on the site. You can retrieve information by looking it up from any part of the site using the "Get information" option from the drop-down menu, as shown in Figure 14-9. Use the "In this column" drop-down menu to select from the following options:

- ID
- Content Type
- Title
- Version
- Title (linked to item)

Check the "Add to default view" checkbox if you want this column to appear in the default view of this list.

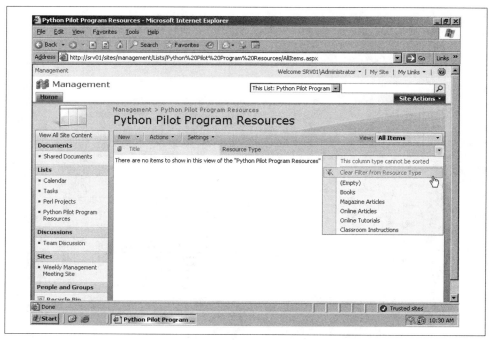

Figure 14-8. List with a customized column

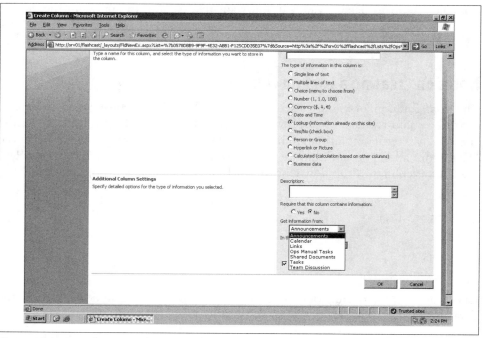

Figure 14-9. Get information from menu for creating a Lookup Column

Notes on Creating a Calculated Column

Another column that requires a closer look is the Calculated column. As you can see in Figure 14-9, the key to creating this column is what is input in the Formula field. You can write formulas to calculate a variety of items, from the age of a list item to a list of birthdays occurring this month. It's also possible to manipulate text using this column.

Writing complicated calculated formulas is beyond the scope of this chapter, but this section presents a simple example:

1. In the Name and Type area, click the "Calculated (calculation based on other columns)" radio button.

2. After the page refreshes, type a brief (optional) description of the column in the Description field.

3. In the Insert Column box, select Created.

4. In the formula field, type **=Created+180** to indicate that this column should provide a list of all list items created more than 180 days ago.

5. Click the Date and Time radio button.

6. When the page refreshes, under "Date and Time format," click the Date Only radio button.

7. If you want the column to be displayed in the default view of this list, check the "Add to default view" checkbox, and then click OK.

These settings are shown in Figure 14-10.

Creating a List Based on Spreadsheet Data

Sometimes the information you want to display in a SharePoint list already exists in spreadsheet format. Rather than reinventing the wheel, you can use the spreadsheet to create a new list. First, though, you need to make sure that all of the information in the spreadsheet is organized the way you want the list to be organized. For example, spreadsheet headings are converted to column names in the list.

Once the spreadsheet data is imported into the list, you can continue to modify the list and add more information. In order to perform this exercise, you must use a spreadsheet program compatible with SharePoint, such as Microsoft Office Excel 2007.

 See Chapter 18 for more information.

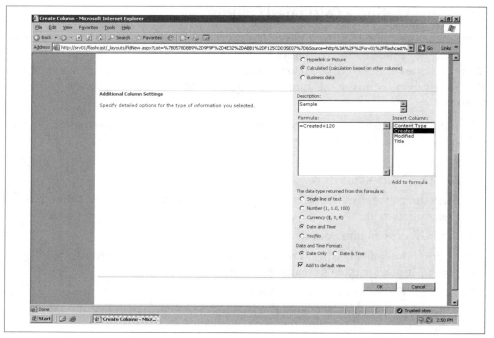

Figure 14-10. Creating a Calculated column

1. Either click Site Actions and select Create from the menu, or click View All Site Content and click Create.

2. In the Custom Lists column (Figure 14-11), click Import Spreadsheet.

3. Type the name of your list in the Name field.

4. Type a brief description of your list in the Description field.

5. Under "Import from Spreadsheet," click in the "File location" field, click the Browse button to navigate to the spreadsheet file, and then click Open.

In order for this option to be available, a spreadsheet application such as Microsoft Office Excel 2007 must be installed. If such a program is not available, you will still be able to create the list, but it will appear in Standard view rather than Datasheet view.

6. Click Import.

7. In the "Import to Windows SharePoint Services" list dialog box, type in the range of cells you want to import into your list from the spreadsheet, and then click Import to create the list.

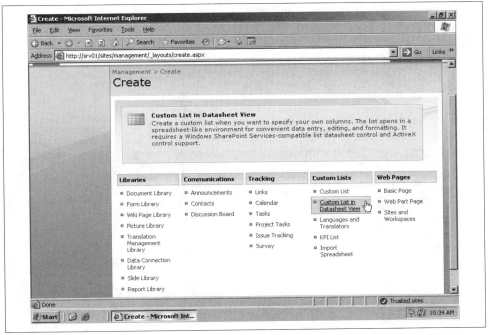

Figure 14-11. Creating a column from spreadsheet data

Creating a Project Task List

In Chapter 10, you learned how to create and manage a Task List. A Task List is used to keep track of which particular tasks have been assigned to which team members. You can also use the list to track the progress of the task.

A *Project Task List* is similar, but instead of keeping track of one task assigned to one person, this list manages a collection of tasks related to a particular project. For example, you may have a group of developers working on a project to create a new search application in Perl. You could have individual teams within the group, each managing a part of the project—for example, a Perl language team and a Perl modules team. Rather than scattering individual tasks in the project all over a Tasks List, you can organize them as a series of tasks under a single project:

1. Either click Site Actions and select Create from the menu, or click View All Site Content and click Create.

2. In the Tracking Column, click Project Tasks.

3. Type the srv name of your list in the Name field.

4. Type a brief description of your list in the Description field.

5. If you want a link to your list placed in Quick Launch, click Yes under Navigation. See what this page looks like in Figure 14-12.

 If an administrator has enabled email settings, you may see an E-Mail Notification section. Configure this setting to send email to a member or members when they are assigned a task.

6. Click Create.

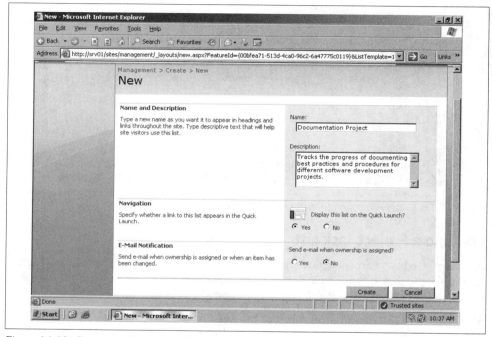

Figure 14-12. Creating a Projects Tasks List

Adding Tasks to a Project Task List

Now that the basic list is created, you can add project tasks.

1. Open the list, either by clicking the list's name in Quick Launch or clicking View All Site Content and then clicking the list's name.

2. Click New and select New Item from the list, as shown in Figure 14-13.

3. Type a name for the task in the Title field.

4. In the Priority section, click either the High, Medium, or Low radio button to assign a priority to the task.

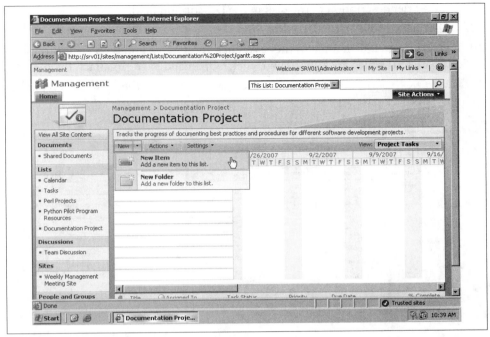

Figure 14-13. Adding a new task to a Project Task List

You will want to work with your team to establish criteria for task priorities.

5. In the "% Complete" section, type in the percentage value to indicate the task's progress toward completion.

Develop a method of determining task completion by percentage to avoid assigning arbitrary values.

6. In the Assigned To section, either type in the name or names of the members assigned to the tasks or search for them in the system.

7. Use Check Names to verify that the users you selected are in the system.

Members must be authenticated users in the system to be added to the list.

8. Type a brief description of the task in the Description field.

9. Click the calendar applets to add a Start Date and a Due Date for the task.

10. If you want to attach a file to the task, click Attach File and then click Browse to navigate to the file's location. Then, click "Open and Save" to attach the file.

11. Click OK to add the task to the Project Task List. View the new task configuration page in Figure 14-14.

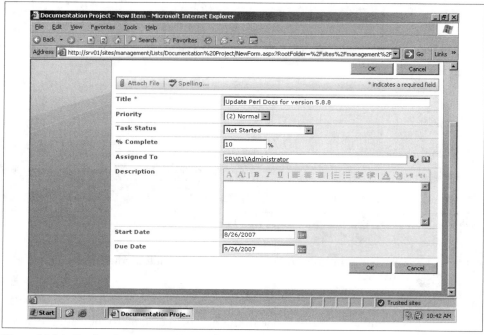

Figure 14-14. Configuring a new project task

Viewing a Project Task List

Depending on the kind of information you are looking for, you can choose from several different views when reviewing a Project Task List:

1. Open the list, either by clicking the list's name in Quick Launch or clicking View All Site Content and then clicking the list's name.

2. Click View, and then select one of the following options from the list:

Project Tasks

This is the default view for the Project Task List. It displays a bar chart with task names at the top. A list of all the tasks appears lower in the frame.

Active Tasks

This view shows only currently active tasks, and not those that have not been started or those that have already been completed.

By Assigned To
> Use this view if you want to view tasks grouped by the names of members assigned to those tasks.

Due Today
> Click this view if you only want to see those tasks that are due to be completed today.

My Tasks
> This view shows only the tasks that are assigned to you.

Editing and Deleting Tasks in a Project Tasks List

Sometimes task parameters will change, making it necessary to modify the task list. You will likely want to keep some sort of record of completed tasks, but not necessarily in this list. If you keep all historical tasks in the list, your list could end up being very crowded over time. Archive older completed tasks on a separate list, and delete them from your active projects list:

1. Open the list, either by clicking the list's name in Quick Launch or clicking View All Site Content and then clicking the list's name.

2. Click to the right of the task name and select one of the following:
   - Click Edit Item to edit the task.
   - Click Delete Item to delete the task.

3. Once you have made your selection, perform one of the following actions to finish the exercise:
   - If you are editing the task, make whatever changes are necessary and then click OK to save the changes.
   - If you are deleting the task, click OK in the confirmation dialog box.

Creating and Modifying RSS Support for Lists

If RSS feeds are enabled on your site, you can set and configure RSS for the following types of lists:

- Anouncements lists
- Blogs
- Calendar lists
- Discussion boards
- Document libraries
- Form libraries
- Picture libraries
- Surveys

RSS support must be enabled both in Central Administration and at the site collection level for this option to be available.

To modify the RSS settings:

1. Open the list, either by clicking the list's name in Quick Launch or clicking View All Site Content and then clicking on the list's name.

2. Click Settings and select List Settings from the list, as shown in Figure 14-15.

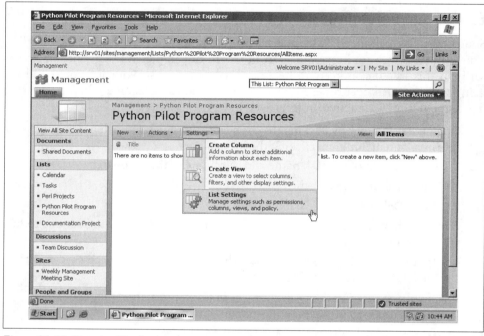

Figure 14-15. Opening List Settings

3. In the Communications column, click "RSS settings," as in Figure 14-16.

4. On the Modify List RSS Settings page in the List RSS area, click the Yes radio button under "Allow RSS for this list?"

5. In the RSS Channel Information area, configure the following properties:
   - Truncate multiline text fields to 256 characters?
   - Title
   - Description
   - Image URL

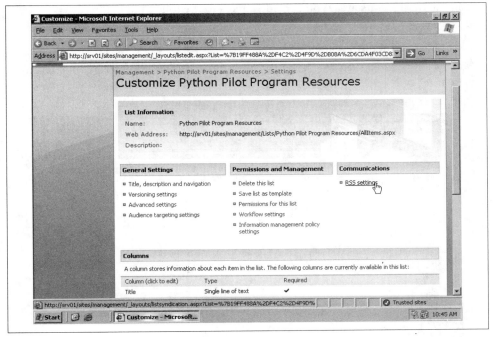

Figure 14-16. Creating an RSS feed in a list

6. In the Columns area, you can set the following columns to be displayed in the RSS description and also set their display order:

- Resource Type
- Content Type
- Created
- Created By
- Modified (*)
- Modified By (*)
- Title (*)
- Version

 The column types marked with an asterisk (*) are mapped to standard RSS tags.

7. In the Item Limits area, you can add values to the following fields:
   - Maximum items to include
   - Maximum days to include
8. Click OK to save your settings. See this configuration page displayed in Figure 14-17.

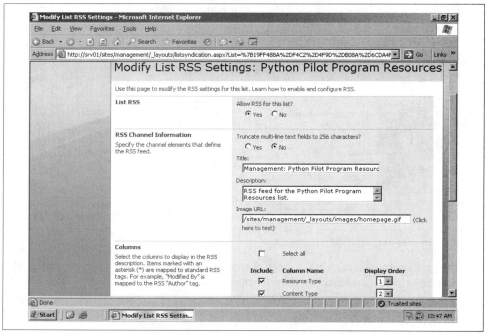

Figure 14-17. Configuring an RSS feed for a list

Managing List Templates

Earlier in this chapter, in the "Creating Lists" section, you read the exercise "Creating a List from a List Template." Building on that information, this section covers how to create and manage new list templates. Once you create one or more list templates, you can apply them on your site. You can also save a template on your local computer's hard drive and then upload it to a completely different SharePoint site or site collection.

Creating a List Template

1. Open the list you want to turn into a template, either by clicking the list's name in Quick Launch or clicking View All Site Content and then clicking the list's name.
2. Click Settings and select List Settings from the list.
3. In the "Permissions and Management" column, click "Save list as template."
4. On the "Save as Template" page, type a name for the list template in the File Name field.
5. Type a brief description of the list template in the Template Description field.
6. If you want to include the content of the list in the new list template, click the Include Content checkbox.

> This option is grayed out in Figure 14-18 because there is no content in the list.

7. Click OK to create the template. See the "Creating a List Template" page in Figure 14-18.
8. When the Operation Successfully Completed page appears, click OK.

> The original list's security settings are not saved to the template, so you will need to modify the template's settings immediately after creating it if you want to prevent unauthorized access. See Chapter 22, for more information.

Modifying List Template Properties

Modify the properties of any list template to better suit your needs:

1. On the site containing the list template, click Site Actions and select Site Settings from the menu.
2. In the Galleries column, click List Templates, as shown in Figure 14-19.

> If you cannot find a list templates entry in the Galleries column on a subsite, you may have to go to the top-level site before following the instructions in this exercise.

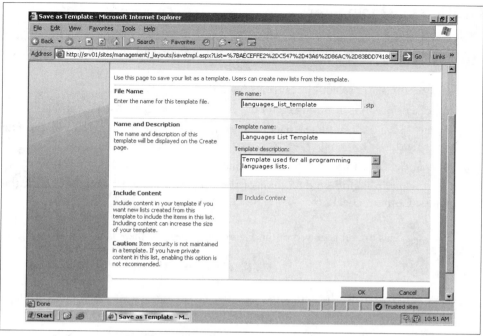

Figure 14-18. Saving a list as a list template

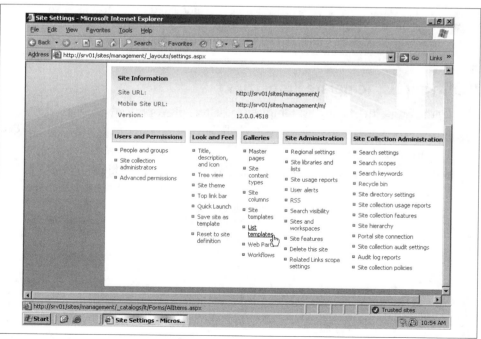

Figure 14-19. Editing the properties of a list template

3. On the List Template Gallery page in the Edit column, locate the desired template and click the Edit Document Properties applet, as in Figure 14-20.

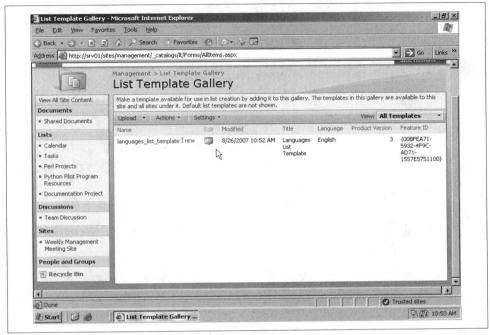

Figure 14-20. Edit Document Properties applet

4. After you complete your editing task, click OK to save your changes, as in Figure 14-21.

Downloading a List Template to Your Hard Drive

As mentioned earlier in this section, in addition to using list templates on your site, you also can share them with other SharePoint sites. The first step is to download a list template to the hard drive of your local computer:

1. On the site containing the list template, click Site Actions and select Site Settings from the menu.

2. In the Galleries column, click List Templates.

3. On the List Template Gallery page in the Name column, click the name of the list template you want to download.

4. In the File Download dialog box, click Save.

5. In the Save As dialog box, either type in the path to the folder where you want to save the template or browse to that folder by clicking the Browse button.

6. In the Download Complete dialog box, click Close to conclude the download.

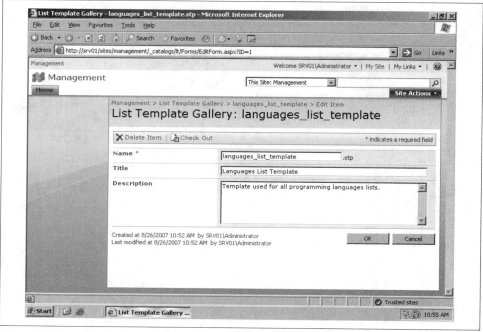

Figure 14-21. Saving changes to a list template's properties

Uploading a List Template to a SharePoint Site

Now that you've downloaded and saved a list template to your hard drive, you're ready to upload it to a separate site or site collection. You will need to have site owner or administrator rights to the site in order to perform the upload. This exercise assumes that you are on the site and ready to perform the upload:

1. On the site containing the list template, click Site Actions and select Site Settings from the menu.

2. In the Galleries column, click List Templates.

3. On the List Template Gallery page, click Upload.

4. On the Upload Template: List Template Gallery page, either type the path to the site template or click the Browse button and navigate to the folder holding the template.

5. If a different version of this template already exists in the gallery and you want to overwrite it when you upload the current version, click the "Overwrite existing file" checkbox.

6. Click OK to upload the template to the gallery.

Deleting a List Template from a List Template Gallery

If a list template becomes obsolete at some point, you can delete it from the gallery:

1. On the site containing the list template, click Site Actions and select Site Settings from the menu.
2. In the Galleries column, click List Templates.
3. On the List Template Gallery page in the Edit column, locate the desired template and click Edit Document Properties.
4. Click Delete Item.
5. When the confirmation dialog box appears, click OK.

Managing Large Lists

As you have seen so far, managing small lists is fairly easy. Over time, though, at least some of your lists will begin to grow and finally come to hold a large number of items. There are several ways to manage and organize very large lists in SharePoint.

These techniques are meant for lists that exceed 1,000 items. Once a list gets to be that size, the list or the site as a whole will suffer from a degradation of performance. This isn't caused by the existence of the list but by the volume of user activities on the list.

In theory, you can store millions of items in a list, but if you don't take steps to manage that volume, your list and site will slow to a crawl. The following are some methods for managing very large lists.

Indexing a List Column

Indexing a list column allows SharePoint to more quickly analyze data in that column, speeding up the process of accessing list items. Indexing goes hand in hand with filtering, but there are a few caveats. First of all, when you filter a view, the first filtered column must be a column that is indexed. Although you can index more than one column in a list, the more columns you index, the greater the performance hit on your database. Try to index only one column to receive the best results, or at least index only those columns that are frequently accessed:

1. Open the list, either by clicking the list's name in Quick Launch or clicking View All Site Content and then clicking on the list's name.
2. Click Settings and select List Settings from the list.
3. Under Columns, click "Indexed columns," as seen in Figure 14-22.
4. Click the checkbox next to the column you want to index and then click OK, as in Figure 14-23.

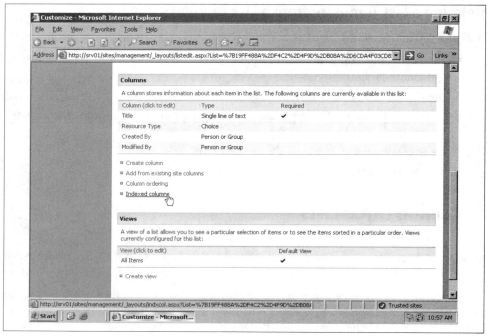

Figure 14-22. Choosing the "Indexed columns" option

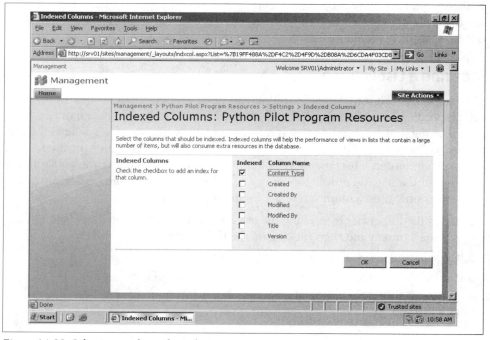

Figure 14-23. Selecting a column for indexing

Creating a Filtered View of an Indexed Column

Before applying a filter to an indexed column, make sure you have created all of the columns relevant to this list and have indexed the required columns:

1. Open the list, either by clicking the list's name in Quick Launch or clicking View All Site Content and then clicking the list's name.

2. Click the View arrow and select Create View from the menu.

3. Under "Choose a view format," select the view you want to create. The options are:
   - Standard
   - Calendar
   - Datasheet
   - Gantt Chart

4. Type the name of your view in the View Name field.

5. In the Filter section, click "Show items only when the following is true," and then use the drop-down list to select an indexed column.

 See the "Customizing a List or Library View" section in Chapter 8 and the "Discussion Group Views" section in Chapter 11 for a more detailed list of column filtering options.

6. After selecting the indexed column, in the subsequent field, type the property by which you want to filter.

7. Configure any other properties you want for this filtered view, and then click OK to save the view.

Adding an Indexed Column to an Existing Filtered View

You don't have to create a new view in order to use indexed columns. Here's how to add an index column to an existing view:

1. Open the list, either by clicking the list's name in Quick Launch or clicking View All Site Content and then clicking on the list's name.

2. Click the View arrow and select Modify this View from the menu.

3. Under Choose a view format, select the view you want to create.

4. Type the name of your view in the View Name field.

5. In the Filter section, click "Show items only when the following is true," and then use the drop-down list to select an indexed column.

6. After selecting the indexed column, in the subsequent field, type the property by which you want to filter.

7. Configure any other properties you want for this filtered view, and then click OK to save the view.

CHAPTER 15

Business Intelligence and SharePoint

Introduction

One of the many reasons to create an enterprise portal is to collect in one place all of the information necessary to make key decisions. Imagine if a product manager can see a sales report, a marketing analysis, the communication strategy, and the status of development on a new product line all on one page. The product manager can quickly look at all the relevant information and statistics to determine whether the product is on time, on budget, and still fits the target market. This concept is known as *business intelligence*, or having the right data at the right time in front of the right people to make the right decisions.

Microsoft Office SharePoint Server 2007 is a significant component in Microsoft's overall Business Intelligence solution. MOSS 2007 has a variety of tools to take large amounts of unstructured data and organize that information in a single, easy-to-use interface. This makes it relatively simple to have important documents, reports, and newsfeeds at your fingertips, assisting you in making corporate decisions.

The Business Intelligence (BI) features in SharePoint 2007 allow you to locate, manage, modify, and share data from many diverse sources, as well as store and present that data later in different presentations.

The new BI utilities in MOSS 2007 give everyone the tools to create meaningful analyses. No longer do developers or warehousing and data mining experts have to struggle with accessing vast amounts of unstructured data to provide useful reports.

SharePoint can connect to many data sources, including SAP, Siebel, and Microsoft SQL Server 2005. The resultant reports generated from acquired data can take the form of Excel workbooks, a SQL Server Reporting Services report, or a Microsoft Office Access report.

The key elements of MOSS 2007 Business Intelligence are:

- The Report Center
- Dashboards
- Excel Services
- External data sources
- Filter Web Parts
- Key Performance Indicators (KPIs)

These key elements can all be created as part of a Report Library on the Create page of your site, as shown in Figure 15-1.

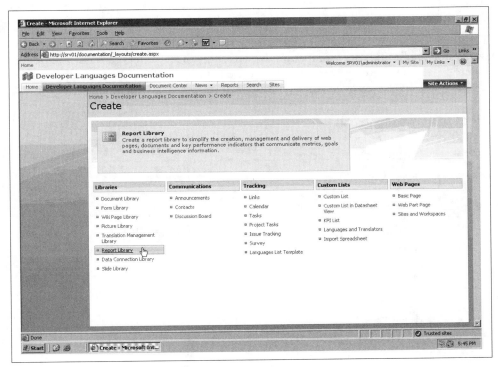

Figure 15-1. Creating Business Intelligence components

The Report Center

The Report Center is used to contain and organize Business Intelligence elements such as Dashboards, Key Performance Indicators (KPIs), document libraries, and connections to external data sources. The Report Center is one of many site templates in the Enterprise site template group. Other Enterprise site templates include the Document Center, Records Center, Site Directory, and more.

See Chapter 7 for more information on site templates.

The Report Center is completely customizable, providing access to page templates and Web Part pages, and allowing you to create and manage libraries, pages, and lists containing whatever business information you find necessary.

By default, one Report Center site is created when the Top-Level Portal site is created. However, a Report Center can be created for any group, department, or organization as needed. With appropriate permissions, information from the Report Center site can be accessed from any other site or site collection, allowing you to share your data with colleagues, customers, and associates.

The Report Center site template provides a single point of contact for anyone who wants the latest in your company's Business Intelligence reports. As you see in Figure 15-2, when a Report Center is first created, it is void of any content, allowing you to either add the default Web Parts yourself or to customize it with other selections.

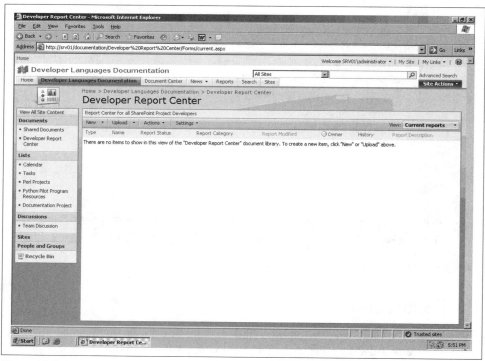

Figure 15-2. New Report Center

Creating and Customizing Dashboards

The MOSS 2007 Dashboard is a specialized web page template designed to collect and display information from many different sources. This can include charts, metrics, reports, and KPIs. The default Dashboard template contains the following Web Parts:

Excel Web Access Web Part
Adds an Excel workbook, worksheet, or worksheet range to the Dashboard.

The Apply Filter Web Part
Adds an Apply Filter button to the Dashboard.

The Related Information Web Part
Can be used to add a series of hyperlinks that connect to related web sites.

The Summary Web Part
Lets you add a text summary or description of the Dashboard.

The Contact Details Web Part
Lists the contact person responsible for the Dashboard.

(Optional) The KPI List Web Part
Adds visual KPIs to the Dashboard, showing how much progress a team member has made toward a goal.

You can also start with a generic Web Part page and add whatever Web Parts you want, creating a dashboard that will perform to your specifications. You can create a Dashboard from scratch, but it might be easier to start with the basic Dashboard template and modify it as needed.

 See Chapter 9 to learn more.

In Figure 15-3, you can see that information from several sources can be imported into a KPI, including manual input.

Once a key indicator has been created, the indicator's name and status are displayed, along with values signifying the goal and current value, as shown in Figure 15-4.

Excel Services Web Access

Rather than have partners and customers download copies of spreadsheet data from your server, the Excel Services Web Access (EWA) Web Part allows a single copy of an Excel Workbook to exist on a secure server. The EWA service publishes spreadsheet data in your BI Report Center, enabling any authorized person to access this information using only a web browser.

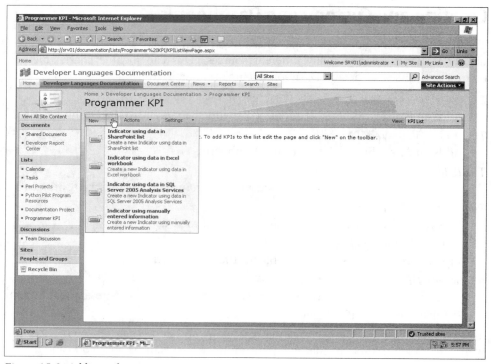

Figure 15-3. Adding information to a KPI

Using EWA enhances the security of your critical business data in the following ways:

- A single copy of the workbook is stored on a single secure server.
- Information can be published to the Report Center site as Read-Only.
- You can publish a snapshot of the workbook rather than the interactive version, preventing anyone from modifying data.
- All calculations are performed on the server, cloaking the business logic from people viewing the data via the Report Center.

EWA technology uses Dynamic HyperText Markup Language (DHTML) and Java-Script to provide web access to *.xslx-* and *.xslb-*formatted data without requiring that ActiveX controls be loaded in the observer's browser. The EWA Web Part can connect to other Web Parts, such as Dashboards, or to other Web Part pages.

Data in an Excel workbook either can be stored directly in the workbook that resides on your secure server or can come from an external data source, such as a database or an Online Analytical Processing (OLAP) cube.

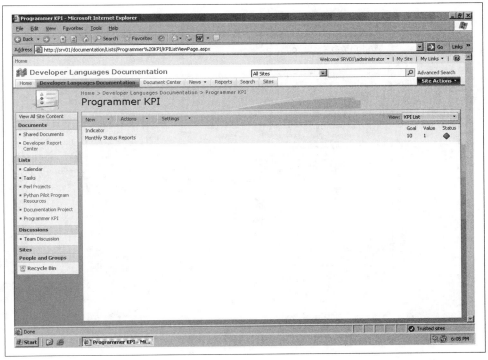

Figure 15-4. One key indicator in the KPI list

 Learn more about managing Excel within SharePoint in Chapter 18. Learn more about OLAP in the "Data Warehousing" section later in this chapter.

You can add an Excel Web Access Web Part to any Web Part page by selecting it in the Add Web Part page, as in Figure 15-5.

Touring Excel Services Web Access

An Excel Services Web Part is very similar to an actual Excel Workbook. Here's the breakdown of the different areas of the Web Part:

- The top of the Web Part holds the title and toolbar, which contains the commands, a drop-down list, and menus.
- The Web Part's primary pane displays one or more Excel workbooks in the worksheet view, one or more named items in the named items view, and an optional outline.

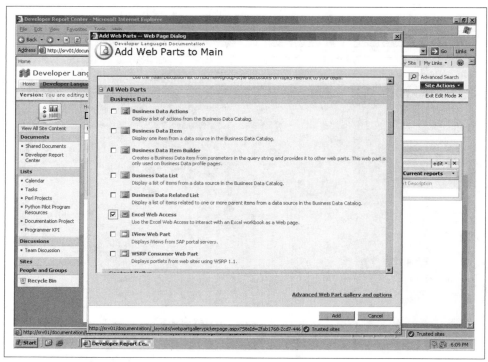

Figure 15-5. Adding an Excel Web Access Web Part

A named item can be an Excel element such as a table or chart.

- The Parameters Task pane contains data entry text fields, parameter labels, and tool tips.
- The field at the very bottom holds the refresh data messages.

Before the Web Part can contain meaningful information, you must first select an Excel workbook, as in Figure 15-6.

External Data Sources

Generally an external data source can be either external to the Report Center site but within SharePoint or completely external to SharePoint. External SharePoint sources can include Web Parts, Web Part pages, and Lists. Sources external to SharePoint can be SAP, Siebel, Microsoft Office Access 2007, and Microsoft SQL Server 2005. While it's outside the scope of this book, you can also write your own data sources.

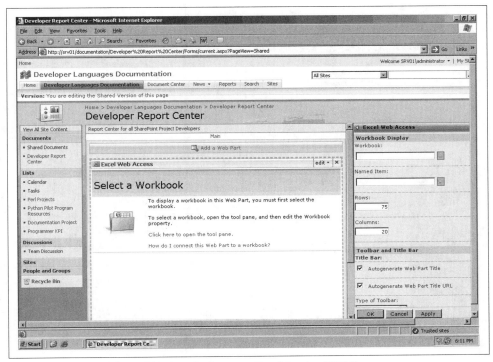

Figure 15-6. Selecting a workbook to display in an Excel Services Web Part

You can create connections to your external data sources and then store them in the Report Center's Data Connection Library (DCL). The DCL provides a single interface, allowing you to easily manage all of your external data connections. You can also create such connection libraries in any other part of your MOSS 2007 site as you see fit. Connections can be reused or shared as needed, and they allow anyone with access to view and interact with information from disparate data locations, all presented in SharePoint. As Figure 15-7 shows, creating a DCL is pretty much the same as creating any other list or library. One difference you may notice is that you have the option of versioning in this library. As your needs progress over time, you will likely find yourself either updating a data source you manage or finding that the owner of an external data source has modified that source. You can keep track of which version of the data source you have used at different points in time to identify the various data elements available in each version.

Imagine that in the original version of an external data source, you found regular access to a particular data element useful. As your needs changed, the data source was updated to not include that element. Then, suppose that a condition arises where you need to access that element. You can find it again by accessing the version of the data source that contains it.

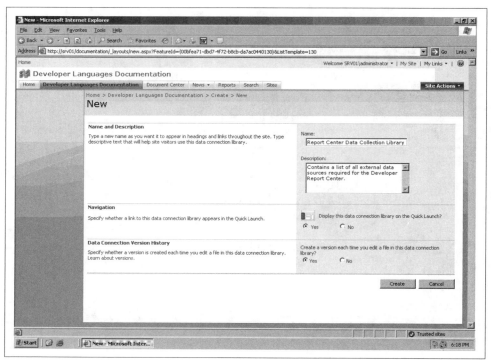

Figure 15-7. Creating a Data Connection Library (DCL)

The MOSS 2007 Business Data Catalog (BDC) part makes it easy to search your backend data sources. Use its search function to discover and integrate external data into SharePoint Web Parts. The search aspect of BDC transverses such sources as remote file shares, web sites, Microsoft Exchange Servers, Lotus Notes, and others, allowing you to locate the desired information and view or modify it from inside SharePoint.

Filter Web Part Information

Filtering information in libraries and lists lets colleagues and customers view and interact with only the most relevant data in a Web Part. For example, your department may provide support for Software Applications, Languages, and Libraries/APIs, but you may want to see only a list of supported applications. Filtering lets you select the Applications option on the supported software list, so that only applications such as COM+ and SQL Server appear. You can also store all of your sales data on a single list and filter it by region, year, or product.

MOSS 2007 provides 10 distinct Filter Web Parts. For example, the Current User Filter Web Part filters information based on the user's logon profile. This is a great asset to security and accessibility, presenting only data you want the user to see and hiding any data the user will not find useful.

 See Chapter 13 to learn more about filtering lists.

Using Key Performance Indicators (KPIs)

KPIs are visual indicators that show how much progress has been made in achieving one or more goals. Using KPIs to measure task metrics allows teams, managers, and organizations to quickly assess whether tasks are hitting their milestones and which parts of a task are ahead, behind, or on time.

For instance, if you are developing a new application for a customer, there may be different engineers working on the interface, libraries, and other project elements. KPIs can be used to measure the performance of each engineer on the project relative to the project goals (e.g., how many modules have been built, how many test cases have passed, etc.). This way, all of the stakeholders—including the engineers on the project—know to what degree the performance indicators align with the performance targets that were agreed upon before the project started.

You can use one of four KPI types:

- Use SharePoint Lists as a data source when they contain quantifiable information that contributes to the workflow. This can include metrics such as opening and closing dates of trouble tickets or percentages of sales within a month.
- Link an Excel Workbook to a KPI in MOSS 2007. As data in the workbook changes, it will be displayed in the KPI, indicating the level of progress. You can choose to display the workbook on the same SharePoint page using Excel Web Renderer (EWR).

 See Chapter 18 for more information.

- Set up a KPI to use Microsoft SQL Server 2005 Analysis Services to access database information. Usually a system administrator or database analyst will have to create the initial connection, but once it's in place, authorized users will be able to use the Analysis Services KPI.
- Manually configured KPIs are used when there is no formal, structured system of data collection, such as using emails or instant messaging.

Figure 15-8 shows several indicators on a KPI list, including goals and status.

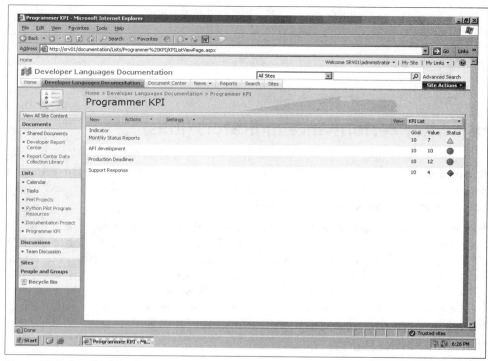

Figure 15-8. Standard KPI list

Performance Management

Performance Management is the process of creating and maintaining a high fidelity between employee performance and departmental or company goals. MOSS 2007 is only part of the Microsoft BI solution, and many other tools play vital roles in concert with SharePoint. Other applications and third-party tools that play a role in BI performance management include Business Scorecard Manager, ProClarity, and Microsoft Office PerformancePoint Server.

Business Scorecard Manager 2005

This application is included in the Microsoft Office PerformancePoint Server 2007 and utilizes the Microsoft Office Suite and SQL Server to provide specific performance indicators. Employees have access to a personalized scorecard of their work performance tracked by KPIs as compared to business goals. See Figure 15-9 for an example.

ProClarity

ProClarity is a third-party applications vendor and Microsoft partner. They provide Query and Analysis, Dashboard, Scorecard, and Reporting software solutions that interoperate with Microsoft SQL Server and Office products in order to enhance Microsoft's Business Intelligence application features.

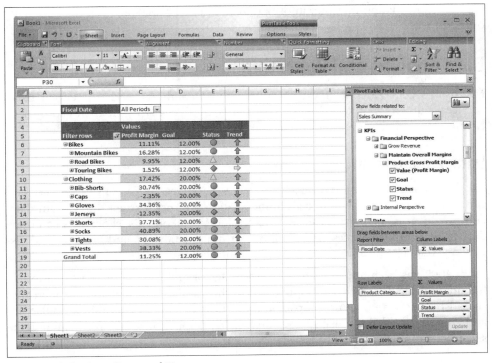

Figure 15-9. Business Scorecard Manager

Microsoft Office PerformancePoint Server 2007

This server-side application contains tools to let organizations plan, implement, and monitor their business processes and goals, specifically targeted at aligning manager and worker productivity and accountability to those goals.

As you can see, SharePoint 2007 includes some of the features required to implement successful performance management, including Dashboards and KPIs that gather data from SharePoint lists.

The Performance Management part of BI uses various integrated platforms to satisfy managing productivity, accountability, and goals. The following Microsoft and ProClarity technologies fully integrate to provide analysis and reporting on performance management data:

- Business Scorecard Manager
- ProClarity
- Microsoft Office SharePoint Server 2007
- Microsoft SQL Server 2005 Analysis Services

SharePoint does its part by providing multiple data views—in the form of Web Parts, Dashboards, and other display components—to offer secure, web-based displays of analyzed information that pull information from databases, spreadsheets, and many other sources.

Data Analysis and Reporting

Microsoft's Data Analysis and Reporting abilities combine Excel, SharePoint Excel Services, numerous other SharePoint elements, and ProClarity Analytics to provide cutting-edge collaborative performance analysis and reporting for the enterprise.

Data Management

Excel 2007 is fully supported for Microsoft SQL Server 2005 Analysis Services and can easily connect to the SQL central metadata repository, extract the relevant data, and present it in spreadsheet format. Excel and SharePoint Excel Services can draw data from multiple sources, including one or more databases, and organize and display raw data in a meaningful form using a single interface.

Excel 2007 has been improved to take advantage of multiprocessor server platforms, by running calculations on multiple CPUs at the same time. Excel also has increased spreadsheet row and column capacities, and now includes a resizable formulae bar and context-based Formulae AutoComplete. Additional new features include redesigned PivotTable views and a visualization engine.

 See Chapters 18 and 19 for more information on Excel and Excel Services.

A SharePoint Data Collection Library or DCL can organize multiple data sources in a single library so you can easily find a list of links to all of your data sources. Coupled with SharePoint's filtering and view capacities, you can present only those sources you desire for any meeting or group project. DCL provides safe and secure storage of database information in a single *.odc* file and can be used to access such data, even if the database is moved from one server to another.

 Go to the Office SharePoint Server Central Administration page for more information.

Document Management

SharePoint Document Libraries and Document Workspaces provide excellent tools for managing text-formatted data and presenting it in a web-accessible interface. Not only can you control the organization and presentation of documents, but you can also manage access rights so that only authorized users can view or modify a document. If you aren't sure which document contains the information you need, use SharePoint's search feature to quickly locate it. A SharePoint Document Center is shown in Figure 15-10.

See Chapters 9 and 17 for more information on document management.

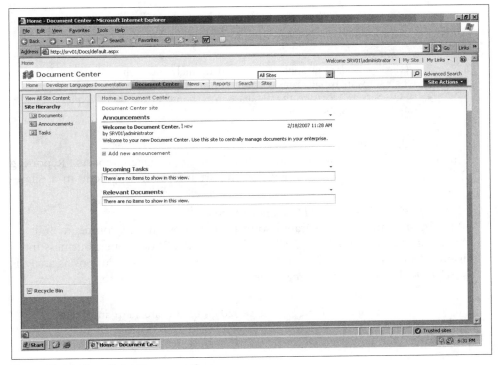

Figure 15-10. SharePoint Document Center

Data Analysis Publication

You can use SharePoint Web Part pages and sites to share your BI data analytics and reports within your organization or with business partners and customers. As mentioned earlier in the "Data Management" section, raw data from multiple sources can be organized contextually, allowing you to perform meaningful analysis of the information for meetings, reports, and collaboration. You can also provide granulated security so that only your selected audience can access and modify your data. Furthermore, the actual data remains in the database or other source so that server security as well as SharePoint security measures can be employed.

Data Warehousing

The Microsoft SQL Server 2005 data warehousing solution is the core source for BI information. SQL Server has a proven track record as a reliable, scalable, and productive database platform. Analysis and Reporting are at the heart of SQL Server's use as a BI tool:

Microsoft SQL Server 2005 Analysis Services (SSAS)
> Offers OLAP services and data mining, letting you specify particular dimensions in multidimensional data such as time and trend analysis views, and aiding you in the construction of complex analytical models. This technology is a completely new approach to administering, modeling, and querying data.

> OLAP is a class of applications used to analyze data in a database. This software usually runs on a server placed between the user and the SQL Server, accessing the database in response to the user's request and providing the required analytics.

SQL Server 2005 Reporting Services (SSRS)
> Microsoft's solution for creating and delivering managed reports. Reporting Web Parts allow SSRS to display SQL report information directly in a SharePoint site.

SQL Server Business Intelligence Development Studio
> Provides a completely integrated software development environment. Built on Visual Studio 2005 and specifically designed for the BI developer, Business Intelligence Development Studio can be used to develop such BI solutions as analysis services, database engines, integrations services, and reporting services.

> See *Learning SQL on SQL Server 2005*, by Richard Earp and Sikha Bagui (O'Reilly) for more information on SQL Server 2005.

See Figure 15-11 for an example of Business Intelligence Development Studio.

One of the other data sources you can use with SharePoint to provide BI data is Microsoft Office Access 2007. If you want to connect to and modify data stored in Access 2007, you can use a special web browser plug-in, and then use the Access Web Datasheet. This functions similarly to Excel Web Services in that you can view Access 2007 data in datasheet view from SharePoint. Office 2007 must be installed on the client computer to view either Excel or Access data. You can import or export data between SharePoint and Access and even move an entire Access database into SharePoint. You can also edit SharePoint data inside of Access. You can see an open Access file in Figure 15-12.

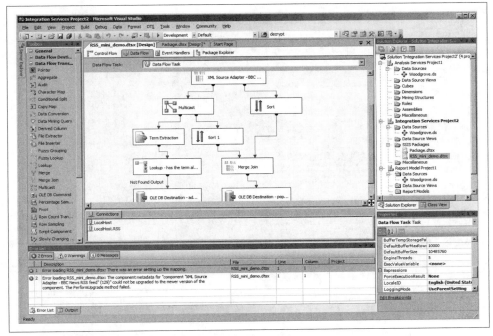

Figure 15-11. Business Intelligence Developer Studio

Exporting a Table from Access to SharePoint

One of the ways Access can add or transfer information into SharePoint is through an Access table that creates or modifies a SharePoint list.

 Access and SharePoint data types are not the same. When you export Access data to SharePoint, some Access elements are not transferred. Also, SharePoint does not support Access form and report types. Given this, exporting data from Access to SharePoint is most effective when you are adding information to an already existing list rather than creating one from scratch. Avoid exporting Access forms and reports to SharePoint, as SharePoint members will not be able to open them.

1. From Access, open the desired database file.
2. Select the table you want to export.

 Any child table you choose to export will take along any parent table it is linked to.

3. Click on External Data, click Export, and then select SharePoint List on the ribbon.

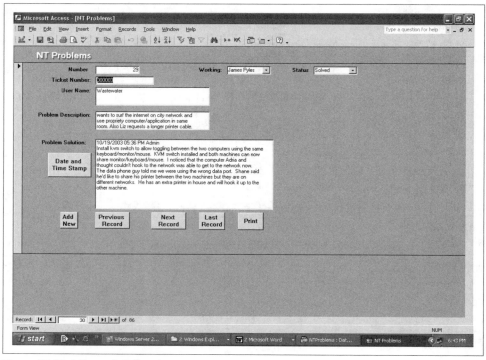

Figure 15-12. Microsoft Office Access

The ribbon has replaced many toolbars and menus in Microsoft Office 2007, organizing logical groups of commands under tabs. For example, in Word 2007's ribbon, clicking on the Home tab will reveal commands such as Copy, Cut, Paste, Bold, Spell check, and so on. Office 2007 applications that use the ribbon are Access, Excel, Outlook, PowerPoint, and Word.

4. In the Site Address field, type or paste in the URL to the SharePoint site where you want to export the table.

5. Type a brief explanation of table in the Description field.

6. To immediately see the SharePoint list after the table is exported, click the "Open the list when finished" checkbox.

7. Click OK.

8. If necessary, log in to the SharePoint site.

9. If you clicked the checkbox in step 6, the list will open the new or existing list when Access has finished the export.

10. If you want to be able to repeat this specific export again to update the list with new data from the same table, click "Save export steps" when prompted.

The actual data is only copied from Access to SharePoint, not transferred. As you change data in the database, you can repeat the export process to update the list. You can also specify that the data will not be exported but instead linked. When you link SharePoint to an Access table, any changes made on the linked table will display in the SharePoint list.

Exporting Data from SharePoint to Access

The door swings both ways: there is also a method of taking SharePoint list data and exporting it into an Access database. You can perform the following exercise only if Access 2007 is installed on your client computer:

1. At the SharePoint site, open the list, either by clicking the list's name in Quick Launch or by clicking View All Site Content and then clicking on the list's name.

2. Click Actions, and select Open with Microsoft Access from the list.

3. In the Name field, type in the name of an existing database, or if you want to create a brand new Access database, type in the new name.

4. Choose one of the following options:

   - "Import a copy of the list" will execute an import action similar to the previous exercise.

   - "Create a linked table" will link the table to the data in the SharePoint list.

Creating a linked table means that every time you change the data in the SharePoint list, the changes are automatically reflected in Access.

5. Click OK to open Access to the database you specified in step 3.

6. When Access opens on your local computer, you may be required to authenticate to the SharePoint site again. As you can see in Figure 15-13, you receive similar results when you export data from a SharePoint list into Excel.

7. When the database is created and modified, verify that the User Information List was also created.

SharePoint automatically copies the User Information Table to Access, listing the members of the SharePoint site. This is useful when you want to preserve list column information such as Created By and Modified By.

Once the process is completed, the list items will be displayed in Datasheet view in either Excel or Access, depending on the target application (Figure 15-14).

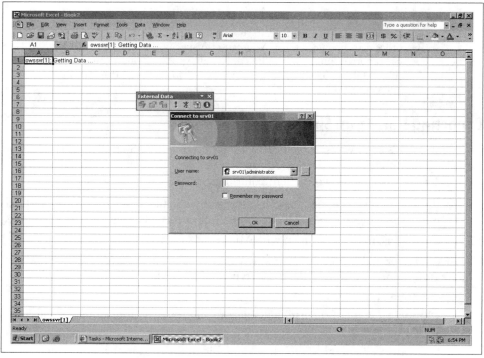

Figure 15-13. Importing list data into Excel

Editing Data Linked from Access to SharePoint

Editing database information linked to SharePoint allows you to dynamically modify the displayed data in the SharePoint list. If the list appears in a Web Part or Dashboard that is used for a BI purpose, that list will always present the most current data stored in Access.

One of the caveats is that you can't change the table's design in Access; you can change the design only from SharePoint. Another issue is that Access records are not checked out when you edit them, and it's possible for two people to modify the same record at the same time, causing inconsistent information to display in SharePoint.

Moving an Access Database to SharePoint

In order to view and modify an Access database, your client computer must have Microsoft Office Access installed. If this application isn't available, you will not be able to open Access files. You may want SharePoint users who do not have Access on their computers to be able to use your database information. Moving the database to SharePoint will allow a much larger audience to access it.

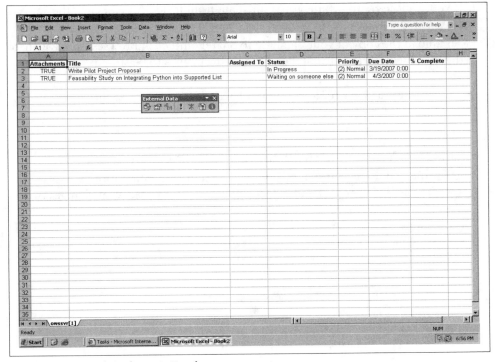

Figure 15-14. List data shown in Excel

Moving a database to SharePoint is a similar process to moving an Access database to SQL, and is done for the same reason: to "upsize" the database to a larger audience. However, upsizing a database to SharePoint creates a list for every table in the database.

Please keep this fact in mind when deciding to move a database to SharePoint. If the database contains an unusually large number of tables, you may have trouble managing such a large number of lists.

When the process is completed, the database tables are backed up in Access and the originals replaced with links to the SharePoint lists. From that point, all of the information in the database as viewed from Access resides only in SharePoint, although it is possible to restore the Access database from the backup:

1. In Access, open the desired database.

2. Click Choose External Data, click SharePoint Lists, and select "Move to SharePoint."

3. When the "Move to SharePoint" wizard launches, type or paste in the URL of the SharePoint site in the "What SharePoint site do you want to use?" field.

4. If you want users to be able to see the data from inside Access, click the "Save a copy of my database to the SharePoint site" checkbox.

5. To upload the copy of your database to SharePoint, click Browse and navigate to the document library in SharePoint where the copy is to be stored.

 If you didn't create a document library previously, choose the Shared Documents section.

6. Click Next. You may have to authenticate to the SharePoint site.

7. After the database transfer is completed, in the confirmation window that appears, click the Show Details checkbox if you want to see what changes Access made during the process.

8. Click Finish.

CHAPTER 16

Sharing Contacts and Meetings with Outlook

Introduction

One of the outstanding strengths of Microsoft Office SharePoint Server 2007 is the enhanced set of collaboration tools. Applications both within and outside of the Microsoft Office 2007 Suite can be used to share documents, create customized group and personal workspaces, and manage project lifecycles. Microsoft Office Outlook 2007 is a fully integrated collaborative component and can be used to provide alerts and notifications about content changes to a targeted group and to share scheduling calendars.

MOSS 2007 and Outlook work together in the following ways:

- Add content from emails—such as discussions, documents, and pictures—to a SharePoint site directly from Outlook.
- Synchronize events and meeting requests between the default calendar in Share-Point and your Outlook calendar.
- Create a Meeting Workplace site by adding an event in Outlook's calendar.
- Set up email support for SharePoint libraries, announcements, calendar lists, and discussion boards.
- Target emails to a specific SharePoint Group.

Using previous versions of SharePoint, if you wanted to add content from Outlook to SharePoint, you had to open Outlook and then launch SharePoint in a web browser. You would then have to manually add the information, usually through copy and paste. SharePoint 2007 makes it possible to directly email content to SharePoint the way you'd send an email to another person.

This feature is not enabled by default, so the site owner or administrator must go to the Central Administration page for your site and enable email support. Most Share-Point lists and libraries can be configured with their own email addresses so a site with incoming email support can receive emails and integrate their content directly into the list or library. Someone with Manage Lists rights or higher must configure an email address for the selected list or library. The following lists and libraries are able to receive content via email:

- Announcements lists
- Blogs
- Calendar lists
- Discussion boards
- Document libraries
- Form libraries
- Picture libraries

 If any of these lists is contained in a Meeting Workspace site, content cannot be added to the list via email, because this option is not available for meeting workspaces.

SharePoint, Outlook 2007, and Collaboration

Later portions of this chapter show hands-on exercises for getting things done, but first let's take a look at a small overview of how MOSS 2007 and MS Office Outlook 2007 work and play together.

Not only does SharePoint allow you to manage task lists much more aggressively, but so do all the other Office 2007 applications. Outlook 2007 comes with a To-Do List in the main interface that imports tasks from the rest of the Office Suite applications, including SharePoint, letting the user view tasks assigned from multiple applications and multiple workgroups and sites in a single interface. Calendar events and flagged messages also appear in the To-Do Bar. You can also subscribe to an RSS feed in a SharePoint site, so you can get up-to-the minute updates on the status of tasks assigned to you.

SharePoint, Outlook, and OneNote 2007

Another office appliance updated for Office 2007 bridges a certain gap between Outlook and SharePoint. OneNote 2007 is an electronic note-taking utility often used for meeting notes. Like pen and paper, you can use it to jot, scribble, doodle, and write down key ideas, questions, and tasks. What's different is what you can do with the information you create.

Within OneNote, the scribbles and drawings on the page are not static objects; you can add, move, and delete any of the content you create. For example, you can rearrange your notes and organize them by groups, subjects, and tasks. Here are some other examples of what you can do with OneNote:

- Insert documents and pictures into notes
- Record audio and video content into notes
- Send notes to other people and computers
- Take, organize, and format notes
- Use Search to find specific notes
- Use templates to customize notes

Like other Office 2007 products, OneNote can interact with SharePoint and share information. For instance, when you receive a meeting invitation in Outlook, that invitation data can be routed to both the calendars in Outlook and the calendar and announcements lists in SharePoint. The invitation data can be imported by OneNote and used to populate the notebook page. Action items in your meeting notes can be converted into tasks and exported both to Outlook's To-Do List and into a tasks list in SharePoint. OneNote notebooks can also be stored as documents in SharePoint site libraries. You can also create an email from inside of OneNote and send it to members of your distribution list, as well as to SharePoint libraries and lists.

Later in this chapter, you'll learn how to add information to lists, libraries, and groups from Outlook. To enable this functionality, your site owner or administrator must enable incoming email support in Central Administration.

Outlook 2007 and SharePoint My Site

As you will see in Chapter 21, each SharePoint user has access to a private, individualized web site within the site collection. There are default public areas of everyone's My Site that can be accessed if the owner gives you permission. The advantage of sharing information on your My Site is that it is a less formal arena than shared team sites, and you can organize information based on individual or small workgroup needs.

Traditionally, you consider putting people on a distribution list if you want to send a broadcast email message to a team or individuals with whom you are working. Then, if you are collaborating in some sort of web-based interface, you close our mail application, open a web browser, and get to work.

From Outlook 2007, this series of actions is unnecessary. While creating a mail message for someone you're working with, you can click to the right of the recipient's name to open a list and then select View My Site, as in Figure 16-1.

Once the other person's My Site web page is open, you can view whatever information he made public, including additional contact information, shared documents, their colleagues list, and a list of their site memberships, as in Figure 16-2.

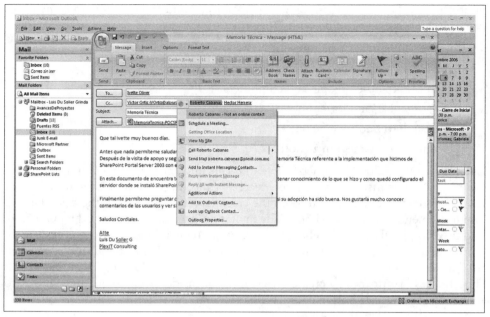

Figure 16-1. Connecting to an email recipient's My Site in Outlook

Your access to SharePoint sites depends on your access status. If you are not a member of a site, you will not be able to view it. SharePoint site administrators will usually add you to the Members group for a site if you need to access it.

Enabling Email Support in Central Administration

Before you can take advantage of the benefits of using Outlook with SharePoint, your administrator must enable email support in Central Administration. Figure 16-3 shows the Central Administration page.

To open the SharePoint Central Administration Web Application:

1. On the server hosting MOSS 2007, click Start and then click All Programs.

2. Click Microsoft Office Server and then click SharePoint 3.0 Central Administration.

3. If prompted, type your username and password in the dialog box and press Enter to open Central Administration.

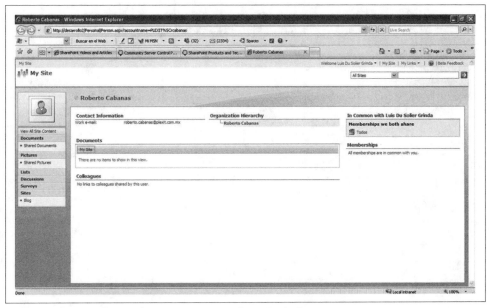

Figure 16-2. Opening a mail recipient's My Site from Outlook

Enabling Incoming Email Support

1. On the Central Administration page at the Home tab, click the Operations tab to open the page shown in Figure 16-4.

2. Under "Topology and Services," click "Incoming e-mail settings."

 When the Incoming E-Mail Settings page opens, if the SMTP service is not installed on your server, you will receive a message saying that it is a requirement before enabling incoming email support.

3. On the Configure Incoming E-Mail Settings Page under "Enable incoming e-mail," click the Yes radio button to enable email support.

4. Under Settings mode, click Automatic to automatically receive all your settings from the SMTP service, or click Advanced if you are using an email drop folder to receive mail.

5. In the Directory Management Service section under "Use the SharePoint Directory Management Service to create distribution groups and contacts?," click No, Yes, or Use Remote.

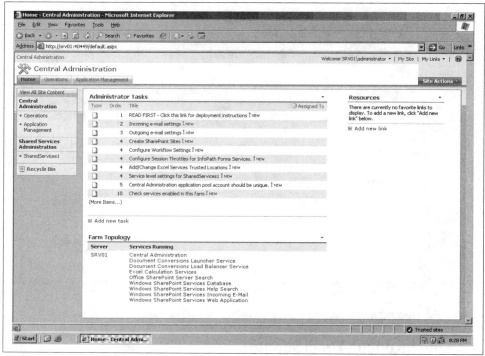

Figure 16-3. Central Administration

If you click Yes, you will need to configure the following:

- Specify a container where new distribution groups will be created (for example, OU=ContainerName, DC=domain, DC=com).

- Specify the location of the SMTP mail server (for example, *server.sharepoint. example.com*).

- Select Yes or No for "Accept messages from authenticated users only?"

- Select Yes or No for "Allow creation of distribution groups from SharePoint sites?"

- Select Distribution group request approval settings.

- If you click No, the Directory Management Service will not be able to connect SharePoint to your company's user directory, and you will not be able to create email distribution groups from within SharePoint.

If you select "Use remote" to indicate you want to use an alternate SMTP source, you will need to configure the following:

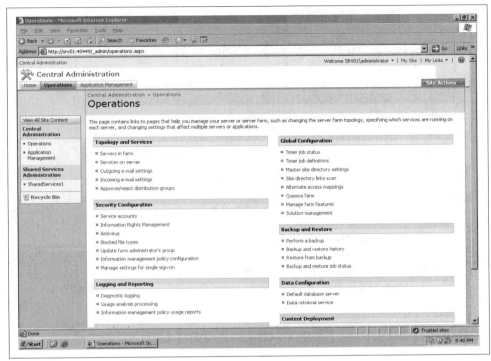

Figure 16-4. Central Administration Operations tab

- Specify the Directory Management Service URL (for example, *http://server: adminport/_vti_bin/SharepointEmailWS.asmx*).

- Specify the location of an SMTP service.

- Select Yes or No for "Accept messages from authenticated users only?" and for "Allow creation of distribution groups from SharePoint sites?"

6. Under Incoming E-Mail Server Display Address, enter a display address into the available field—for example, *mylist@example.com*.

7. If you are using an E-Mail Drop Folder instead of SMTP, specify the location of the folder—for example, *c:\inetpub\mailroot\drop*.

8. Click OK.

Configuring Email Support During Site Creation

Once email support is enabled in Central Administration at the top-level site, any subsites created under the portal site will inherit that support. To use Distribution Lists with SharePoint, enable the SharePoint Directory Management Service in

Central Administration as well. If these conditions are satisfied and you choose to create a new group when creating a new subsite, the following actions occur:

- You will be offered the option of creating an email distribution list and the opportunity to set an email address for that list.

- Any users you add to the group are automatically added to another group called Members and also added to the distribution list. Any changes made to either Members or the distribution list will synchronize.

- During the site creation process, both the teamsite discussion board and calendar will have email support enabled and be automatically assigned email addresses.

 The format for those two email addresses is:

- *GroupAddress.discussions@domain.com*
- *GroupAddress.calendar@domain.com*

These email addresses will be included in the distribution list, and whenever you receive an invitation to a meeting via Outlook that information will be sent to the calendar and archived in the discussion board.

Enabling Email Support for Lists and Libraries

Although the process for enabling incoming email support for the appropriate lists and libraries is similar, there are differences depending on the specific content container. See the "Introduction" section of this chapter for the names of the lists and libraries that support incoming email.

Enabling Email Support for an Announcements List

1. Click the name of the announcements list to open it, and then click Settings and select List Settings.

2. Under Communications, click "Incoming email settings."

3. In the Email section, click Yes to enable email support.

4. Type the email alias to be used to send email traffic to the list in the available field.

5. In the E-Mail Attachments section, click Yes to archive email attachments or No to discard email attachments.

6. In the E-Mail Message section, click Yes to save the original email as an attachment or No to discard the original email.

7. In the E-Mail Meeting Invitations section, click Yes to archive meeting invitations in the announcements list.

8. In the E-mail Security section, configure the available settings to determine whether to receive emails just from site members or from any email address.

 If you choose to let the announcements list receive traffic from any email address, unauthenticated users will be able to write content to the list by sending it an email.

9. Click OK to finish.

You can see an example of how this page is set up in Figure 16-5.

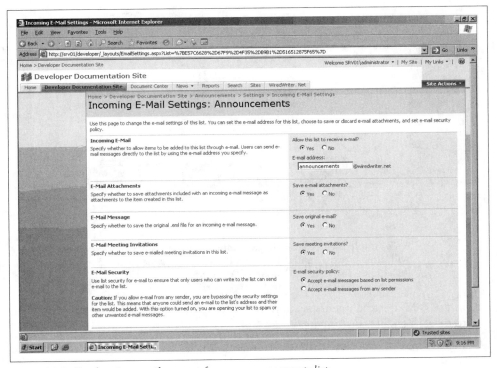

Figure 16-5. Configuring email support for an announcements list

Enabling Email Support for a Calendar List

1. Open the calendar list by clicking on its name, as in Figure 16-6, and then click Settings and select List Settings.
2. Under Communications, click "Incoming email settings."
3. In the E-Mail section, click Yes to enable email support.
4. Complete the email address to be used to send email traffic to the list in the available field.

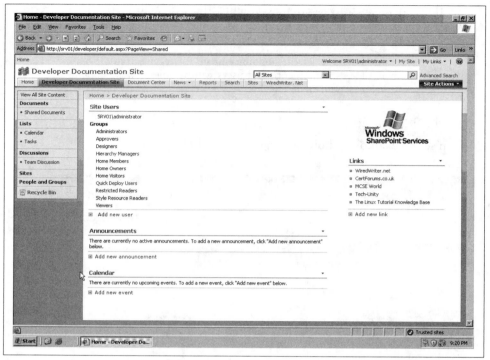

Figure 16-6. Opening a calendar list

An example is *calendar@domain_name.com*. The suffix of the address will already exist, and all you will need to provide is the prefix or "username," such as "calendar."

5. In the E-Mail Attachments section, click Yes to archive email attachments or No to discard email attachments.

6. In the E-Mail Meeting Invitations section, click Yes to archive meeting invitations in the calendar list.

Step 5 in this exercise is the same as step 7 in the previous exercise, "Enabling Email Support for an Announcements List." Because Share-Point email handlers are aware only of the individual email they manage, it's possible to send a meeting invitation to both an announcements list and a calendar list and have it archived in both locations. The same is true if the invitation is sent to a discussion board. See the subsequent exercise, "Enabling Email Support for a Discussion Board" for details.

7. In the E-Mail Security section, configure the available settings to determine whether to receive emails just from site members or from any email address.

8. Click OK to finish.

If you choose to let the calendar list receive traffic from any email address, unauthenticated users will be able to write content to the list by sending it an email.

Enabling Email Support for a Discussion Board

1. After opening the desired discussion board, click on Settings and select List Settings.

2. Under Communications, click "Incoming e-mail settings."

3. In the E-Mail section, click on Yes to enable email support.

4. Type the email alias to be used to send email traffic to the list in the available field.

5. In the E-Mail Attachments section, click Yes to archive email attachments or No to discard email attachments.

6. In the E-Mail Message section, click Yes to save the original email as an attachment or No to discard the original email.

7. In the E-Mail Meeting Invitations section, click Yes to archive meeting invitations in the discussion board.

8. In the E-Mail Security section, configure the available settings to determine whether to receive emails just from site members or from any email address.

If you choose to let the discussion board receive traffic from any email address, unauthenticated users will be able to write content to the list by sending it an email.

9. Click OK to finish.

See Chapter 11 for more information about discussion groups.

You can also enable email support for a discussion board when you are creating it, as shown in Figure 16-7.

Enabling Email Support for a Library

1. Open the library you want to configure for email support.

2. Click Settings, and then click Library Settings.

This will either be *Document* Library Settings, *Form* Library Settings, or *Picture* Library Settings.

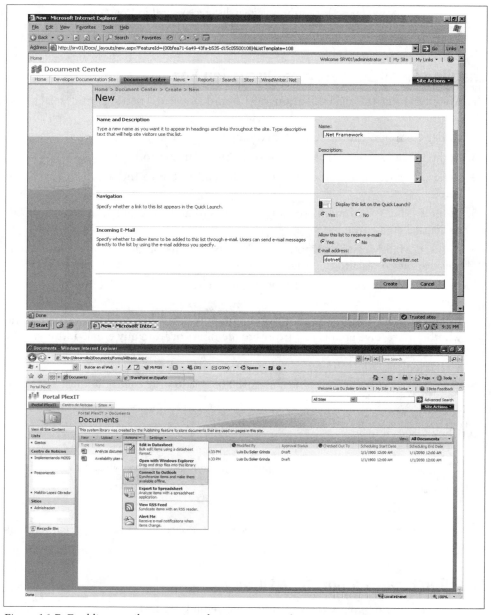

Figure 16-7. Enabling email support in a discussion group during creation

3. Under Communications, click "Incoming e-mail settings."

4. In the E-Mail section, click Yes to enable email support.

5. In the E-Mail Address field, type a unique name for the library's email address.

6. In the E-Mail Attachments section, under "Group attachments in folders," select Yes for one of the following:

- Save all attachments in root folder
- Save all attachments in folders grouped by email subject
- Save all attachments in folders grouped by email sender

7. To have the attachment overwrite existing files with the same name, click the Yes radio button, as shown in Figure 16-8.

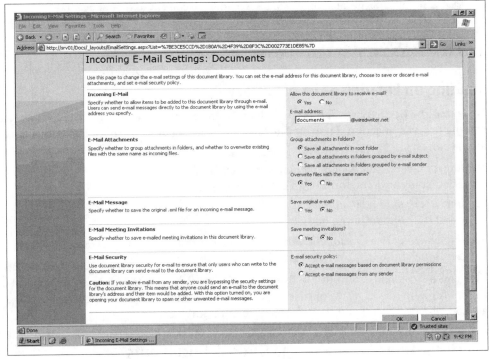

Figure 16-8. Configuring email support for a documents library

If you do not make this selection and then try to save an attachment with the same name as a library document, the following sequence of events will occur:

1. The system will add four randomly generated digits to the end of the attachment's name to create a unique name.

2. If action 1 fails, the system will add a globally unique identifier (GUID) to the end of the attachment's name to create a unique name.

3. If action 2 fails, the attachment is discarded.

8. In the E-Mail Message section, click Yes to save the original email as a separate document in the library or No to discard the original email.

9. In the E-Mail Meeting Invitations, select whether to save email invitation attachments as documents or to discard them.

10. In the E-Mail Security section, configure the available settings to determine whether to receive emails just from site members or from any email address.

 If you choose to let the library receive traffic from any email address, unauthenticated users will be able to write content to the list by sending it an email.

11. Click OK to finish.

Sending an Email to a List or Library

Now that the desired lists and libraries have been set up to receive emails, it's time to put the process in action. Here are the basics of sending email content to various lists and libraries:

Sending an email to an appointment list or calendar
  Send content in the form of an email meeting invitation.

Sending an email to a blog or discussion board
  Send the content in the body of the email.

Sending an email to a Document, Form, or Picture Library
  Send the content as an email attachment.

You can send emails to multiple lists, libraries, and distribution lists either by adding multiple names in the To: field separated by commas, or by using the To:, Cc:, and Bcc: fields to send your content to different addresses.

Synchronizing SharePoint and Outlook Documents

Once content is shared between a library and Outlook, it can be checked out for editing from either interface. If you need to work on any SharePoint documents offline, you can create a connection to Outlook directly from the library and save an offline copy there. This is useful for frequent travelers who don't always have access to a reliable Internet connection.

Once the offline document has been edited and a connection has been established between Outlook and SharePoint, the two versions of the document can be synchronized so the versions in Outlook and SharePoint are the same. Figure 16-9 shows you how to initiate the connection to Outlook from a document library.

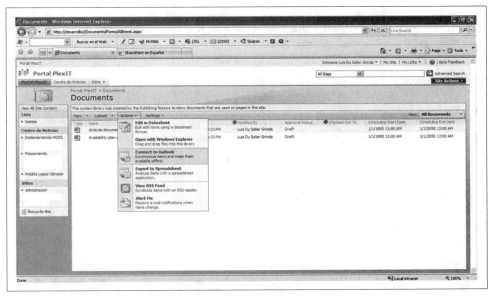

Figure 16-9. Connecting to Outlook from a Document Library

1. In the open document library, click Actions and select "Connect to Outlook" from the list.

2. When the confirmation dialog box opens, asking if you want to connect the library to Outlook (Figure 16-10), click Yes.

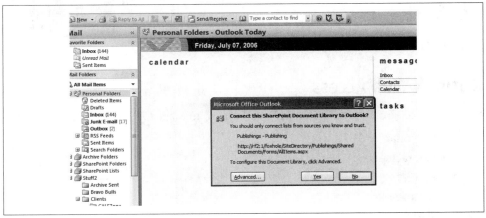

Figure 16-10. Confirming that you want to connect the Document Library to Outlook

The version of this document already in Outlook will be synchronized with the newer version in SharePoint. You can now edit it offline and when you are ready, synchronize the two documents again, updating the one in SharePoint with the changes you made. Figure 16-11 shows the offline SharePoint document in Outlook.

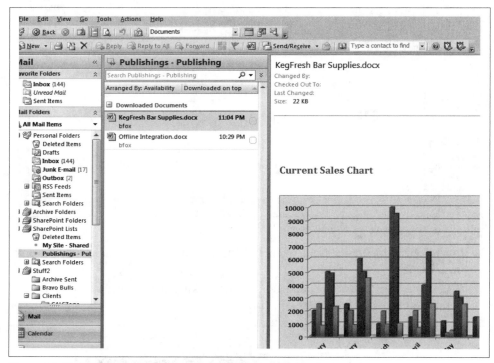

Figure 16-11. Offline document from SharePoint library in Outlook

Outlook Web Access

SharePoint 2007 offers five different Web Parts to manage Outlook Web Access:

- My Calendar
- My Contacts
- My Inbox
- My Mail Folder
- My Tasks

Outlook Web Access is really a function of Microsoft Exchange Server 2007 and Outlook 2007 together, since there are both server and client components. When the client software is installed on the user's computer and configured to use an Exchange 2007 server, the user will enjoy a wide variety of benefits in accessing email from a web browser interface.

SharePoint 2007 provides the previously mentioned Web Parts to integrate Outlook Web Access features within SharePoint sites and pages, so the user never has to leave the site in order to use the latest Outlook web features.

 Access to a mail account on an Exchange 2007 Server is necessary to use Outlook Web Access Web Parts.

A feature new to Web Access 2007 is the ability to configure SharePoint and Windows File Share Integration with Outlook Web Access. This allows Web Access users to access documents in SharePoint libraries. Unlike what you read about earlier in "Synchronizing SharePoint and Outlook Documents," Outlook Web Access users can only access a Read-Only copy of SharePoint documents. This means that Web Access users can't edit offline copies of documents stored either in SharePoint libraries or in Windows file shares.

Using Email Servers

Your email-enabled groups, libraries, and lists can receive emails routed through the server hosting the SharePoint site collection or via another server such as Microsoft Exchange Server. There are a few advantages to having mail routed through a separate server rather than being sent directly to SharePoint:

Authentication
    The SMTP service on the SharePoint server cannot require users sending email to authenticate to the system, but Exchange does have this ability. If you are using Exchange for your mail services, the site owner or administrator and go to Central Administration in SharePoint and select the option of accepting mail only from authenticated users.

Spam filtering
    Exchange has the capacity to filter unwanted mail traffic, preventing unsolicited mail from being received by SharePoint and perhaps subsequently posted to lists and libraries.

Regardless of the mail server option you select, if you are going to enable mail support for your site, take adequate security precautions to prevent your system from having viruses, adware, and spam introduced into SharePoint through mail traffic.

Conclusion

As you can see, SharePoint, Outlook, and all other Office 2007 products are fully integrated to provide seamless transfer of information between applications. You no longer have to think of the Outlook email and calendaring application as something separate from SharePoint. You can perform all of the familiar Outlook-related tasks from inside either Outlook or SharePoint. Regardless of whether you happen to be sitting in front of an open Outlook or SharePoint interface, you can quickly and simply schedule a meeting, send an email to a distribution group, or any other related task.

CHAPTER 17

Creating, Editing, and Managing Word Documents with SharePoint

Introduction

MOSS 2007 integrates with Microsoft Word 2007 and other Microsoft Office Suite applications in a variety of ways. The primary interface to Word documents in SharePoint is through Document Workspaces and libraries.

 See Chapter 9 for more details on those document management tools.

Typically, Word is used for writing reports, documenting best practices, recording procedures, and creating other text-based documents. Often a group or a team collaborates to create a single document. SharePoint allows workgroups to create, share, and modify a single Word document through a portal site. SharePoint and Microsoft Word 2007 work together by:

- Sharing Word documents with a specific team in a SharePoint Document Workspace.
- Storing Word documents in a document library, either placing all documents in one library or creating types of document libraries based on content, team, or team location.
- Controlling versioning of documents in document libraries.
- Assigning specific tasks on a document to team members.
- Creating email alerts for team members, and notifying them when a document has been created or modified.
- Creating and modifying a web page from a Word document using document-to-page converter tools.

The following list shows the main topics covered in this chapter:

- Content types and document libraries
- Manage document library workflow
- SharePoint, Word 2007, and collaboration

Content Types and Document Libraries

One of the benefits of managing documents in SharePoint is that you can organize them by content type. You may be used to thinking of documents in terms of their formatting, such as a Word document versus an Excel document and so on. Based on this perception, you would consider all Word documents to be the same. That's fine if you want to put all of your Word documents in one single repository and all Excel documents in a separate one, but what if the content in those differently formatted documents are related?

For example, let's say you are working on a proposal for a new software application. This proposal might include reports written in Word, spreadsheet information in Excel, and PowerPoint presentations. All these documents have different formats, but they contain content related to the same project. You might want to group all project-related documents under a content type of "Project Plans."

Conversely, a single document format, such as Word, may contain many different content types. You can create proposals, legal documents, organizational tables, hardware requirement lists, and newsletters. Each document serves a different purpose and may start from a different template, or require a different review process.

SharePoint lets you classify documents in terms of the following properties:

- Columns or metadata that you want to assign to a content type
- Document templates you create for this content type
- Customized forms you use with this content type
- Workflow options for this content type

Relative to document libraries and Word, this means that it is common for a document library to contain Word documents comprising several different content types.

Enabling Document Library Support for Multiple Content Types

Configuring a library to support multiple content types means that the library the documents occupy does not determine the nature of the documents; rather, the content type does:

1. Open the desired document library, either by clicking its name in Quick Launch or by clicking View All Site Content and then clicking the library's name.
2. Click Settings and then click Document Library Settings.

3. Under General Settings, click Advanced Settings.

4. In the Content Types section, click Yes to enable support for multiple content types.

5. Click OK to finish.

Adding a Content Type to a Document Library

Now that the document library is enabled for multiple content types, you can add a content type to the library:

1. Open the desired document library, either by clicking its name in Quick Launch or by clicking View All Site Content and then clicking the library's name.

2. Click Settings and then click Document Library Settings.

3. Under Content Types, click "Add from existing site content types."

4. In the Content Types section, on the Select Site content types from list, click the arrow and select the desired group of content types.

5. In that group in the Available Site Content Types list, select the desired content type and then click Add.

6. To add additional content types, repeat steps 4 and 5 as necessary.

7. When you are finished adding content types to the "Content types to add" list, click OK.

You can see this procedure at work in Figure 17-1.

Creating a Content Type

If the content type you need does not exist, you can create it:

1. On your site, click Site Actions and select Site Settings from the menu.

2. In the Galleries column, click "Site content types."

3. When the Site Content Type Gallery page opens, click Create.

4. On the New Site Content Type in the Name and Description section, type the name of the new content type and a brief description in the available fields.

5. In the "Select parent content type from" list, select the content group you will use as the basis for your new content type.

6. In the Parent Content Type list, select the parent content type you will use as the basis for your new content type.

7. In the Group section, choose to store the new content type in either an existing group or a new group.

8. Click OK to finish.

You can see an example of creating a content type in Figure 17-2.

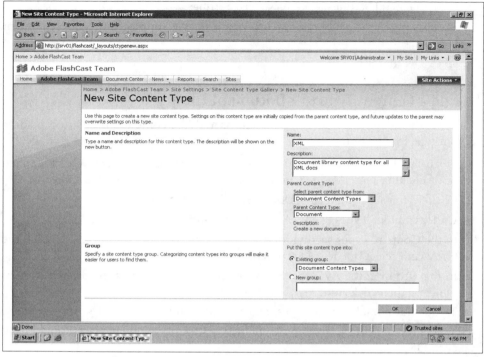

Figure 17-1. Adding a content type to a library

Changing the Order of Content Types

When you open a document library and click New, a list of existing content types will appear in the menu. For organizational purposes, you may want to change the order in which the content types appear. Also, by default, the first content type in the list is the default content type for your document library. You can move the name of the most commonly used content type in your library to the top and make it the default:

1. Open the desired document library, either by clicking its name in Quick Launch or by clicking View All Site Content and then clicking the library's name.

2. Click Settings and then click Document Library Settings.

3. Under Content Types, click "Change new button order and default content type."

4. In the Content Type Order section, if you want to remove the content type from the list, clear the checkbox next to the name of the item.

5. To change the position of the item in the new list, in the "Position from Top" column, click the drop-down arrow and select the number of positions you want to place the item from the top of the list.

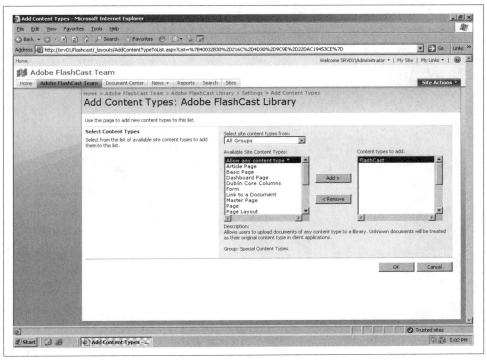

Figure 17-2. Creating a content type

For example, if you want the item to be at the top of the list, click the drop-down arrow and select 1.

You can see an example of how to accomplish this in Figure 17-3.

Associating a Document Template to a Content Type

Most organizations have standard formats for different kinds of documents, such as contracts, proposals, estimates, and so on. Rather than recreating that format every time you need such a document, create the content type in a document once and then save it as a template. That way whenever you need to create a contract, you can use the contract content type template. Once the template is created, you need to associate the template with the content type in your document library. Before you begin the following steps, have the URL to the template handy or the path to the template on your server:

1. Open the desired document library, either by clicking its name in Quick Launch or by clicking View All Site Content and then clicking the library's name.

2. Click Settings and then click Document Library Settings.

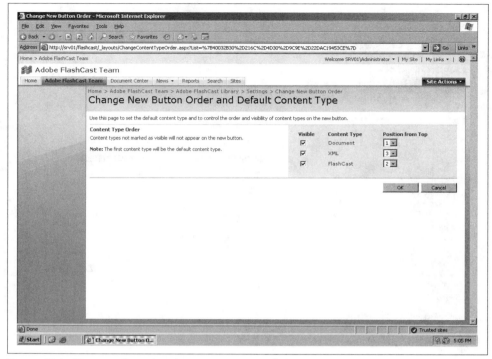

Figure 17-3. Changing the order of content types

3. Under Content Types, click the name of the content type that you want to change.

4. Under Settings, click Advanced.

5. In the Document Template section, click "Enter the URL of an existing document template" and then type or paste the URL to the document template in the available field.

There are four different URL types that are supported:

- Absolute: A URL example is *http://domain/templates/legal.doc*
- Site Relative: An example of this URL is *~/library_name/legal.doc*
- Server Relative: An example of this URL is *~/templates/legal.doc*
- Resource Folder Relative: This looks like *legal.doc*

6. If instead you want to upload the template, click "Upload a new document template" and then click Browse.

7. Browse to the template file using the Choose File dialog box, click the template's name, and then click Open.

8. When the template is uploaded, click OK.

As a general guideline, you should keep your templates in a separate document library from your actual documents, to protect against a user accidentally changing the template document. Your template library should be accessible only by the people responsible for the template definition, whereas the document library using those templates needs to be accessible by the group responsible for actually creating the final content.

Adding a Column to a Content Type

As you learned earlier in this chapter, two ways of defining a content type are creating columns or using metadata. Adding one or more columns lets you more specifically define the properties of the content type. Once you have more specifically defined the properties of content types, you can collect detailed data reports by tracking the specific metadata. Examples would be account number, sales region, product ID, and so on. You could create different content views for sales reports, divided by sales region, and a user in a particular region could access only those sales reports specifically assigned to her region:

1. Open the desired document library, either by clicking its name in Quick Launch or by clicking View All Site Content and then clicking the library's name.
2. Click Settings, and then click Document Library Settings.
3. Under Content Types, click the name of the content type where you plan to add a column, as in Figure 17-4.
4. In the Columns section, click "Add from existing site or list columns."
5. In the Select Columns section, click the "Select columns from" arrow and select the group you want to base the column on from the list.
6. Under "Available columns," click the column that you want to add, and then click Add to move the column to the "Columns to add" list.
7. Click OK to add the column or columns, as shown in Figure 17-5.

Managing Document Library Workflow

A document workflow involves the process of an author creating a document and sending it to one or more approvers before it is published. Usually documents that are not yet approved are in a pending state and can be viewed only by the author and site members with View Lists rights. Once the document is approved, it is visible to any authenticated user or to anonymous users if that feature is enabled.

See Chapter 12 for more information on anonymous user access to SharePoint.

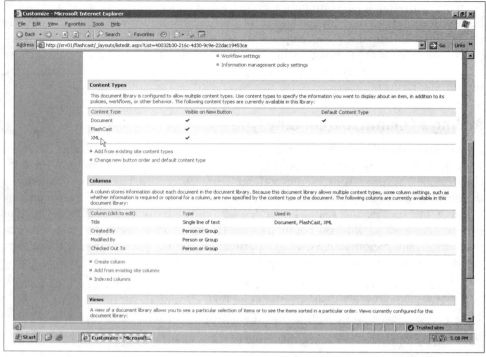

Figure 17-4. Under Columns, click "Add from existing site or list columns"

Before a Word document can enter an approval workflow, the document library must be enabled for this feature. Workflows operate differently depending on whether they are configured for a library, list, list content type, or site content type. This section focuses on adding workflows to document libraries.

Configuring Workflow in a Document Library

1. Open the desired document library, either by clicking its name in Quick Launch or by clicking View All Site Content and then clicking the library's name.

2. Click Settings, and then click Document Library Settings.

3. Under "Permissions and Management," click Workflow settings.

4. On the Change Workflow Settings page, click "Add a workflow."

5. On the "Add a Workflow" page, in the Workflow section, click the Approval workflow template.

6. On the "Add a Workflow" page, under Workflow in the "Select a workflow template" window, choose the type of workflow you want to add.

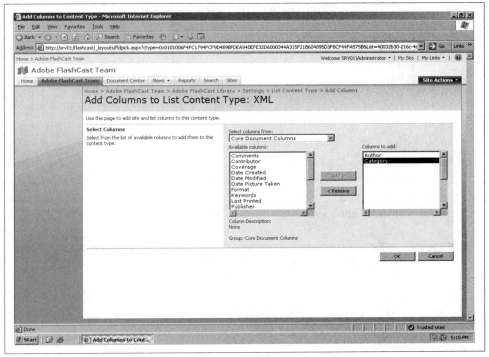

Figure 17-5. Adding columns to a content type

Options include:

- Approval
- Collect Feedback
- Collect Signatures
- Disposition Approval

7. In the Name section, type a unique name for the workflow.

8. In the Task List section, use the "Select a task" list and choose an option from the list. The default is Tasks.

9. In the Workflow History section, click the "Select a history" list and choose a history list to use with the workflow. The default is Workflow history.

10. In the Start Option section, specify how, when, or by whom a workflow can be started, and then click Next.

Using Workflow in a Document Library

It's one thing to configure a workflow, but to really get to know how this process operates, it's important to actually do a walkthrough. Once the workflow is created, you can see how it works by adding a document as a non-administrator:

1. Open the desired document library, either by clicking its name in Quick Launch or by clicking View All Site Content and then clicking the library's name.

2. When the library opens, click the Upload button and then click the Browse button to navigate to the desired document.

3. When you have located the document, click Open to populate the Name field with the path to the document, and then click OK.

4. When the document appears in the document library, in the Document Approval column click In Progress, as shown in Figure 17-6.

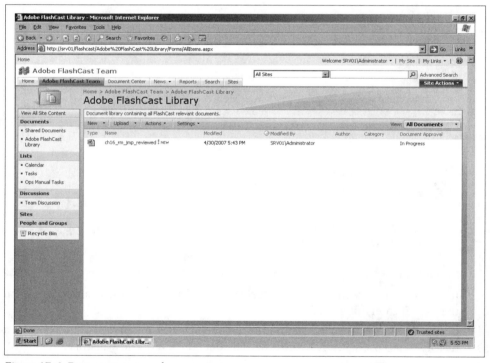

Figure 17-6. Document approval process

 Make sure you are logged in as Administrator or as another user who has approval rights in this library.

5. On the Workflow Status, Document Approval page under Tasks, in the Title column, click the "Please approve" link.

6. On the "Tasks: Please approve" page, you can type an optional comment in the "Type comments to include with your response" field, and then click either Approve or Reject.

   - Clicking Approve will allow the document to be added to the document library.
   - Clicking Reject will return the document to the author.

SharePoint, Word 2007, and Collaboration

There are quite a number of specific ways that SharePoint and Word work together. The key concept to remember is that you don't always have to open Word to work with Word, and you don't always have to open SharePoint to work with SharePoint. It's possible to get access from one to the other (or from any other Office 2007 application).

Though not exhaustive, the following section gives you an idea of how SharePoint and Word work together.

Comparing Document Versions

Often it is helpful to visually inspect different versions of a Word document in a document library. SharePoint and Word can make this possible:

1. Open the Word document stored in the document library, and click Review to open the Review ribbon.

2. Click the Compare arrow to open the list, and then click the specific type of comparison you want.

3. When the comparisons panes open, you will see the following:

   - The lefthand summary pane will show you a list of every version of the document in the library.
   - The righthand pane will show any to version that you want to compare.
   - The center pane holds a view of the document that is being compared to the original.

4. Close the view when you are finished.

Adding an Entry to Your SharePoint Blog from Word

Among the other sorts of lists you can use in SharePoint, you also can create a personal or professional blog. Blogs are an incredibly popular way to share your ideas and opinions in a linear fashion from one day to the next. Now you can choose to write entries in Word and then post them directly from your document.

Word 2007 is not enabled to publish to blogs by default, but you can configure this option manually:

1. In an open Word 2007 document, right-click in a blank area of the ribbon, and select Customize Quick Access Toolbar from the menu that appears.

2. When the Customize the Quick Access Toolbar and keyboard shortcuts window opens, under "Choose commands from," use the drop-down menu and select File.

3. In the pane directly below that menu, scroll down and select TBD from the list, and then click the Add button to move TBD to the Quick Access Toolbar.

4. When the button appears in the File Menu Options area, click it to configure your blog account.

5. When the "Register a Blog Account" dialog box appears, click Register Now.

6. When the New Blog Account dialog box appears, click the drop-down arrow and select SharePoint from the menu.

7. In the New Community Server Account dialog box under User Name, enter your username in the field.

8. Enter your password in the Password field.

9. In the Blog Post URL field, enter the URL to your blog.

10. Under "Automatically upload picture to my picture storage location," choose either "Don't upload pictures in my blog post" or "Post images to the following location."

    If you chose the second option, enter the path to the location in the available field.

11. Click OK, and when the confirmation dialog box appears, click OK again.

12. Type your blog entry on the Word page.

13. If it's not open on the ribbon, click the Blog Post tab, click the Publish button, and then click Publish from the list.

 You can also click on Publish as Draft if you aren't ready to make the post public.

14. You may have to authenticate to your blog account again. If so, enter your username and password in the available fields and click OK.

The post you created in Word now appears on your SharePoint blog.

CHAPTER 18

Creating, Editing, and Managing Excel Documents with SharePoint

Introduction

MOSS 2007 makes extensive use of Microsoft Excel 2007 in organizing and presenting information to teams, departments, and organizations. The primary methods of sharing data between Excel worksheets and workgroups and SharePoint are through Excel Services and Excel Web Access.

Excel Services is defined by three components:

- Excel Calculation Services (ECS) is the core of Excel Services, in some ways like the Report Center is the engine behind MOSS 2007 Business Intelligence. ECS loads worksheet and workbook data, calculates and refreshes internal and external data, and maintains connection sessions.
- Excel Web Access (EWA) is a specific Web Part that allows you to access and interact with an Excel workbook from a web browser using Dynamic Hypertext Tag Markup Language (DHTML) and JavaScript. EWA can be connected to other Web Parts or Web Part Pages.
- Excel Web Services (EWS) is a MOSS 2007 Web Service that offers numerous ways for a software engineer to use an Application Programming Interface (API) to develop applications based on data contained in an Excel workbook.

As a fully integrated component of MOSS 2007, you can take advantage of many SharePoint features to create, modify, and manage Excel workbooks directly from a SharePoint site.

The Excel Web Access Web Part displays spreadsheet information on a Web Part page in a format very similar to an Excel workbook. Features of the Web Part include:

- The title and toolbar in the top section, which displays menus, commands, and a drop-down list.
- The main window displays at least one worksheet in Worksheet view, a named item such as a chart or table in Named Item view, and an optional outline area.

- The Parameters Task Pane displays parameter labels, text boxes for data entry, and optional tool tips.
- The bottom section displays refresh data messages for external data sources.

Office Excel 2007 and Excel Services

The first step in utilizing Excel Services is to create an Excel worksheet or workbook. When you load your workbook into Excel Services, you allow that data to be accessible through SharePoint; however, Excel Services supports only a subset of Excel 2007 functionality. The following is a list of Excel features supported in Excel Services:

- Calculation
- Cells
- Charts
- Connections
- Consolidation data from ranges
- Data sources such as SQL Server 2000, Microsoft SQL Server 2005, OLEDB providers, and ODBC drivers
- Dates
- Excel tables
- Formatting
- Functions
- Names
- What-if analysis

There are a number of Excel 2007 features that are unsupported in Excel Services. If you attempt to access or use an unsupported feature, you will receive an alert saying so. The following is a list of the unsupported features:

- Attached toolbars
- Comments
- Consolidation data from PivotTable reports
- Controls for Form toolbars, Toolbox controls, and ActiveX controls
- Data sources for Microsoft Business Solutions, Windows SharePoint Services lists, SQL Server, and external data ranges and tables linked to Windows SharePoint Services lists
- Data validation
- Digital signatures
- Displayed formulas

- External references to linked workbooks
- Images and objects that are linked or embedded
- Ink features
- Legacy macro languages such as Microsoft Excel 4.0 Macro Functions and Microsoft 5.0 dialog sheets
- OLE and DDE links
- Queries, either text or web
- Security and Privacy
- Shared workbooks
- Visual Basic for Applications (VBA) code, macros, add-ins, and user-defined functions (UDFs)
- XML maps and embedded smart tags

Workbooks that contain unsupported features will not load or display in Excel Services properly. You will need to use the Excel Services command to save your workbook in Excel Services.

 The specifics of saving Excel Workbooks in Excel Services are described later in this chapter.

Another Excel Services feature allows you to expand or collapse data details in a Pivot-Table report. You can also choose different views of your workbook data. On the Excel Web Access Web Part, click the Open button to display the menu, click View, and then click either Worksheet view or Named Item view.

Publishing and Viewing an Excel Workbook in an Excel Web Access Web Part

One of the real strengths of SharePoint is the ability to view and manage information without having to leave SharePoint or open the document source directly. The Excel Web Access Web Part allows you to see and manipulate Excel Workbook data without actually opening Excel or even having Office Excel 2007 installed on your local computer. An example of a page showing Web Access Web Parts in a Web Part page can be seen in Figure 18-1.

 Verify that Excel Calculation Services is running by going to Central Administration. If the service is stopped, you will be unable to perform the following exercises.

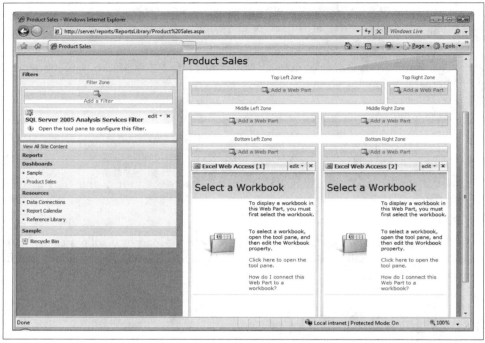

Figure 18-1. Excel Web Access Web Parts in a Web Part page

See Chapter 8 for more information on Web Parts and Web Part pages.

Enabling Trusted File Locations in Central Administration

Prior to publishing an Excel workbook in SharePoint, you (or your SharePoint administrator) must set up a trusted file location for your workbooks within the Shared Service Provider (SSP):

1. Open SharePoint Central Administration.

2. In the Quick Launch menu to the left, under Shared Services Administration, click the relevant SSP to open it.

3. Under Excel Services Settings, click Trusted File Locations, and select Add Trusted File Location from the list.

4. When the Excel Services Add Trusted File Location page opens, as in Figure 18-2, in the Location section under Address, type or paste the path or URL in the available field.

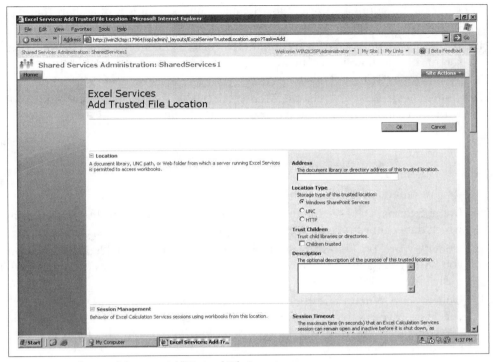

Figure 18-2. The Excel Services Add Trusted File Location page

5. Just beneath the address field, click either the UNC or HTTP radio button to select the link type.

6. Under Trust Children, if you want child libraries to the Excel document library to be trusted, click the Children Trusted checkbox.

7. Type a brief description of the function of the trusted location in the Description field.

8. In the Session Management section under Session Timeout, type the maximum time in seconds that an Excel Calculation Services session can remain open and inactive before it is shut down.

9. Under Short Session Timeout, type the maximum time in seconds that an Excel Web Access session can remain open and inactive, prior to any user interaction, before it is shut down.

10. Under Maximum Request Duration, type the maximum duration in seconds of a single request in a session.

11. In the Workbook Properties section under Maximum Workbook Size, type the maximum size in MB of a workbook that can be opened by Excel Calculation Services.

12. Under Maximum Chart Size, type the maximum size in MB of a chart that can be opened by Excel Calculation Services.

13. In the Calculation Behavior section under Volatile Function Cache Lifetime, type the maximum time in seconds that a computed value for a volatile function is cached for automatic recalculations.

14. Under Workbook Calculation Mode, select the calculation mode option of workbooks in Excel Calculation Services. The options are:
    - File
    - Manual
    - Automatic
    - Automatic except data tables

15. In the External Data section under Allow External Data, select the location from which data connections from external sources are made.

16. Under "Warn on Refresh," check the "Refresh warning enabled" checkbox if you wish to see a warning before refreshing external data for files from the previously indicated location.

17. Under "Stop When Refresh on Open Fails," click the "Stopping open enabled" checkbox if you want to stop the open operation on a file in this location if the file contains a "Refresh on Open" data connection and the file cannot be refreshed while it is opening.

18. Under External Data Cache Lifetime, type the maximum time in seconds that the system can use external data query results in both the Automatic refresh (periodic/on-open) and Manual refresh fields.

19. In the Maximum Concurrent Queries Per Session field, type in the maximum number of external data queries that can execute concurrently in a single session.

20. In the User-Defined Functions session under Allow User-Defined Functions, check the "User-defined functions allowed" checkbox if you want to allow user-defined functions to be called from workbooks in this trusted location.

21. Click OK to finish.

 The instruction in step 2 to click on "SharedServices1 (Default name)" assumes you are working with MOSS 2007 in a standalone server installation rather than on a server farm.

The Trusted File Location is created, as shown in Figure 18-3.

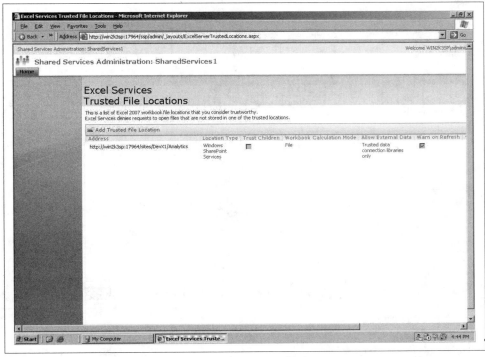

Figure 18-3. The Excel Services Trusted File Location is added

Publishing an Excel Workbook to a SharePoint Document Library

Before you can view an Excel workbook in an Excel Web Access Web Part, you must first publish the workbook to a SharePoint document library:

1. In the open Excel workbook, click the Microsoft Office button, as shown in the upper-lefthand corner of Figure 18-4.

2. From the list, click Publish, and then click Excel Services to send the workbook to the document library, as seen in Figure 18-5.

3. When the Save As dialog box appears, click the Excel Services Options button, and on the Show tab, select any item in the workbook you want to make available in the Web Access Web Part by clicking the desired checkboxes next to the item names.

4. Click the Parameters tab, and add any named ranges you want people viewing your workbook in Excel Services to be able to modify by clicking the Add button.

5. When you are finished with the dialog box, click OK.

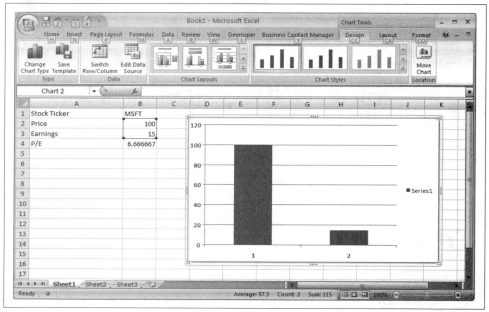

Figure 18-4. An open Office Excel 2007 workbook

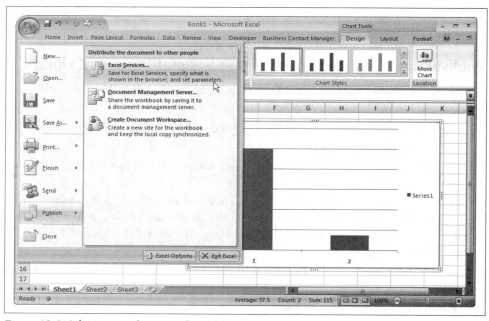

Figure 18-5. Selecting Excel Services from the Publish list

6. In the Save As dialog box, browse to the path of the document library.

 This is the location of the Trusted File Location you configured in the previous exercise.

7. Click the Save button to publish the Excel workbook to the trusted document library, as in Figure 18-6.

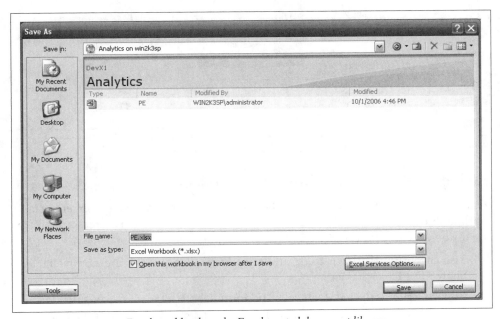

Figure 18-6. Saving an Excel workbook to the Excel trusted document library

Once an Excel Web Access Web Part is added to the appropriate Web Part page and the Web Part is linked to the Excel document, you can view the Excel workbook in the Web Access Web Part, as in Figure 18-7.

Working with Excel Web Access Data in Office Excel 2007

Despite the fact that you can work with spreadsheet data in SharePoint without using Office Excel 2007, there are times when you will want to save that information to your local computer. The following are methods and reasons for working with Excel Services data on your computer rather than inside SharePoint. The exercises in this section require Office Excel 2007 to be installed on your local computer.

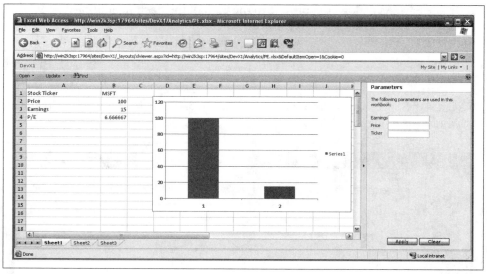

Figure 18-7. An Excel workbook open in an Excel Web Access Web Part

Saving Excel Workbooks from Excel Services

You can save Excel Services spreadsheet data to your local computer either as a workbook or a snapshot, depending on the features you need. The reasons for saving the data as a workbook are as follows:

- You can use the print features in Office Excel 2007, which are not available in SharePoint Excel Services.
- You can modify the values in cells and formulas to calculate new results.
- You can add or remove calculated columns in Excel tables and view different subtotals.
- You can add or update charts, including PivotTable and PivotChart reports, as you can see in Figure 18-8.
- You can use What-if analysis tools.

Figure 18-9 shows a Dashboard with Excel workbooks displayed using the Excel Web Access Web Parts.

Saving Excel Snapshots from SharePoint Excel Services

A *snapshot* is a restricted view of a workbook with only some of the spreadsheet information saved to your local computer. The rationale for using a snapshot over a workbook is that only the values within each cell are made available to end users; they are unable to see any of the formulas. Table 18-1 outlines what is and isn't saved to your hard drive when you use a snapshot.

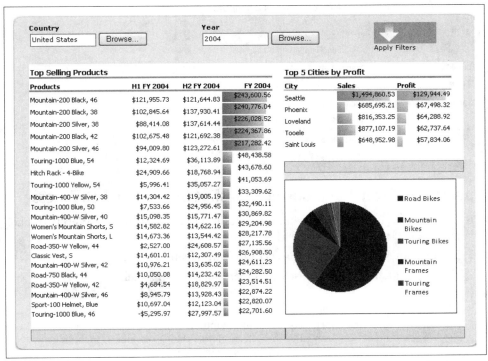

Figure 18-8. Excel 2007 PivotTable Tools

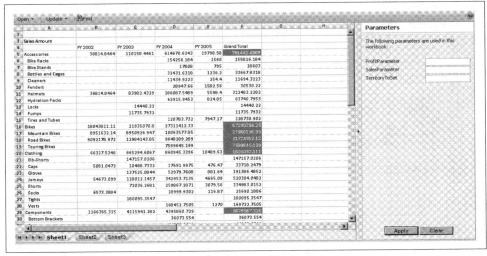

Figure 18-9. Excel workbooks displayed in an Excel Access Web Part on a Dashboard

Table 18-1. Saved and removed Excel data in a snapshot

Saved	Removed
Cell Values	Conditional Formatting
Formatting	Connections
Objects	Formulas
Visible Information	Hidden Data
	Interactive Features
	Private Information
	Web-Related Features

Opening an Excel Workbook or Snapshot from Excel Web Access

1. On the Web Part page containing the desired Excel Web Access Web Part, click the Open arrow to display the menu.

2. To open an Excel Workbook, select Open in Excel, as in Figure 18-10.

3. To open an Excel Snapshot, select "Open snapshot in Excel."

 If these options aren't available, you may not have appropriate rights to save this information on your computer. Also, the site owner or an administrator can hide the selections on the Open menu, including "Open in Excel" and "Open snapshot in Excel."

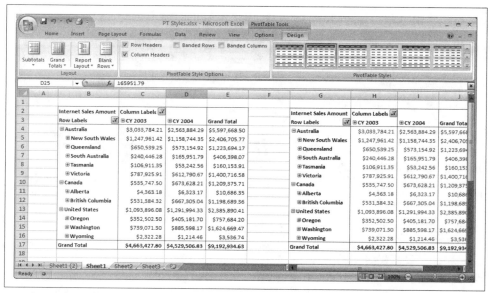

Figure 18-10. An Excel workbook opened in Excel

Printing from Excel Services

You can use different methods to print some or all of the spreadsheet data in a workbook.

Printing from Internet Explorer

This is a "quick and dirty" way to print information displayed in an Excel Web Access Web Part. The printed hard copy will include only the information currently displayed in your web browser. Any other information that you must scroll to view or that is on any other pages in the workbook will not be printed:

1. With the appropriate Web Part page open in your browser, go to the Web Access Web Part, and in the context menu that appears when you mouse over the workbook name, select "View in Web Browser."

2. When the workbook opens in the Web Part, navigate to the desired workbook page and area and then click File in the web browser's toolbar at the top.

3. To modify the page you want to print, select Page Setup in the File menu.

    You can also click on Page Layout on the ribbon in Excel, as in Figure 18-11.

4. To modify the page's orientation, click the Layout tab and select either Portrait or Landscape.

    This option is also available on the Page Layout ribbon, as in Figure 18-12.

5. To preview what this page will look like when printed, click Print Preview.

6. Click OK to close the dialog box, and then click File → Print to print the document.

If after viewing an Excel worksheet in Page Layout view you want to return to the Normal view, click the View tab on the ribbon and click Normal, as seen in Figure 18-13.

Printing a Saved Excel Workbook or Snapshot

Printing from a workbook versus a snapshot is a matter of which data is available in each format. The information in the "Working with Excel Web Access Data in Office Excel 2007" section earlier in this chapter outlines what is and isn't present in workbooks and snapshots. A saved snapshot or workbook can be printed in the same way you print an ordinary Excel workbook, as seen in Figure 18-14.

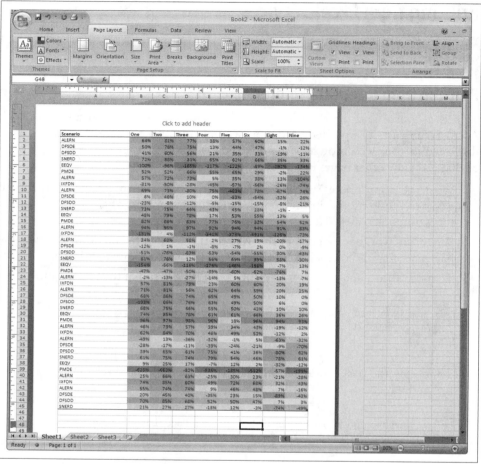

Figure 18-11. Page Layout option on the ribbon

Printing a Saved Excel Workbook or Snapshot Using Quick Printing

If you don't need to configure any of the options in the exercise "Printing a Saved Excel Workbook or Snapshot," you can print your document without using the Print dialog box. This method is quick and easy; however, be sure that the current print settings are what you want. If they aren't, you could end up with a printout you don't really want:

1. Open the saved workbook or snapshot in Excel 2007.
2. Click the Microsoft Office button, click Print, and then click Quick Print.

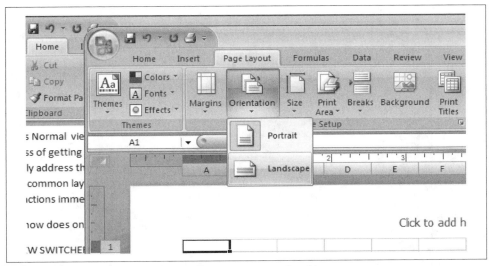

Figure 18-12. Orienting an Excel page for printing using the ribbon

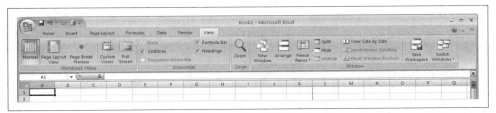

Figure 18-13. Returning to Normal view using the ribbon

 If you want to use this option with one click instead of going through the Print menu, follow steps 1 and 2 of this exercise, right-click on Quick Print, and select "Add to Quick Access Toolbar."

Connecting a List View Web Part to Excel Web Access Web Part

You can use this method to modify how Excel Web Access information is displayed. For instance, when you publish a workbook to Excel Services, you can select the specific Named Items you want to be seen in the Web Access Web Part. Once you've added that Web Part to a Web Part page and configured it to display your workbook, you can create a List View Web Part and add the Named Items to the list. When you add the List View Web Part to a Web Part page, it will display the Named Items as separate items in the list. Anyone clicking an item on the list will see only the information contained in the individual Named Item from the workbook.

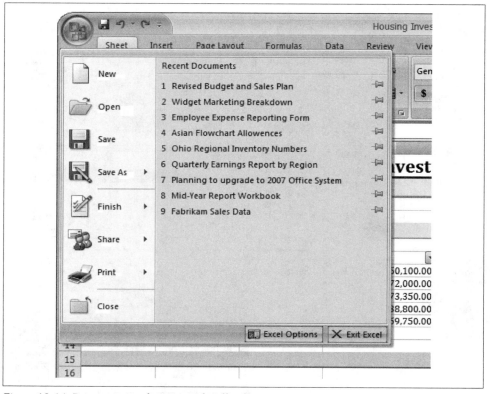

Figure 18-14. Printing using the Microsoft Office button

 See Chapter 14 for more information about lists and list Web Parts.

Connecting Web Parts Using an Excel Workbook URL

1. On the desired Web Part page, click Site Actions and select Edit Page from the menu.

2. At the Excel Web Access Web Part, click the Edit list button, click Connections, and then select Get Workbook URL From.

3. Browse to the desired List View Web Part and select it.

4. In the Configure Connection dialog box, select Document URL from the Field Name listbox, and then click Finish.

5. Click Exit Edit Mode to return to the standard view of the Web Part page.

Connecting Web Parts by Using an Excel Named Item

1. On the desired Web Part page, click Site Actions and select Edit Page from the menu.

2. At the opening screen of Excel Web Access Web Part, click the link "Click here" to open the tool pane.

3. In the tool pane, type or paste either the URL or UNC of the desired workbook in the Workbook text box, and then click OK.

4. At the Excel Web Access Web Part, click on the "Edit list" button, click Connections, and then select Get Named Item From on the list.

5. Browse to the desired List View Web Part and select it.

6. In the Configure Connection dialog box, select Title from the Field Name listbox, and then click Finish.

7. Click Exit Edit Mode to return to the standard view of the Web Part page.

Finding and Calculating in Excel Services

Microsoft Office Excel 2007 allows you to specify different calculation formulas in a workbook. Once you set up a formula in a workbook and publish it to SharePoint's Excel Services, your Excel calculation setting is supported and retained in the workbook. Table 18-2 presents the different calculation formula settings supported in both Office Excel 2007 and SharePoint Excel Services 2007.

Table 18-2. Calculation methods in Excel and Excel Services

Calculation method	Office Excel 2007 and SharePoint Excel Services 2007
Manual workbook calculation	You must manually initiate the calculation by issuing a toolbar or keyboard command.
Manual worksheet calculation	You must manually initiate the calculation by issuing a toolbar or keyboard command.
Automatic calculation	Your workbook is automatically recalculated whenever you change the formula or a cell referencing the formula.
Automatic except tables	Your workbook is automatically recalculated whenever you change the formula or a cell referencing the formula, except for any formulas and referenced cells that were created by an Excel Data Table as part of the What-if analysis suite of commands.
Recalculate Before Save	When you save the workbook, it is automatically recalculated and then saved.

 If you want to always be able to see when the workbook was last calculated, you can add the following in one of the cells contained in this formula:

```
="Last calculated at: "& TEXT(NOW( ),"m/d/yyyy h:mm")
```

An example of Excel's Formulas ribbon can be seen in Figure 18-15.

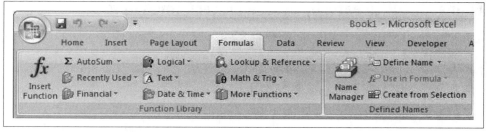

Figure 18-15. Excel 2007 Formulas ribbon

Calculating and Recalculating in Excel Services

The following exercise can be performed either with data in an Excel Web Access Web Part or when the workbook is being displayed in Web Browser view.

1. On the appropriate Web Part page, open the workbook in the Excel Web Access Web Part.
2. On the Web Part's toolbar, click the Update menu, and then click Calculate Workbook.
3. Repeat step 2 to perform a recalculation.

Finding Values with Excel Services

In addition to performing calculations, you can also find values in spreadsheet data, such as dates, numbers, and text. As in other Microsoft Office Find operations, the value you input is case-insensitive, so "find" is the same as "FIND." Also, cells may display a value such as (123) to indicate an underlying value of (–123). To find the cells, you must input the underlying value, not the value viewed in the cell. For example, in a column where the data has been formatted for accounting, negative numbers appear as positive numbers wrapped in parentheses. To find all cells with a deficit greater than 1,000, you would search for –1000 rather than (1000).

If the Find button is not on the Excel Web Access Web Part toolbar, the site owner or administrator may have configured Excel Services toolbar properties to not display Find.

1. On the appropriate Web Part page, open the workbook in the Excel Web Access Web Part.
2. On the Web Part's toolbar, click the Find button to launch the Find dialog box.
3. Click either Up or Down to set the direction Find progresses from the active cell.

4. Type or paste the value you want to find in the "Find what" field.

 The Excel Services Find function supports the use of wildcard characters such as "*" and "?". To find special characters such as asterisks, question marks, and tildes contained in workbook cells, you must first insert a tilde (~) character before adding the character you are trying to locate. For instance, if you want to find an asterisk in a workbook cell, you would type ~* in the "Find what" field.

5. Click Find Next to begin the find process, and click Find Next again to continue progressing through the workbook.

CHAPTER 19

Creating in SharePoint Designer 2007

Introduction

Those of you who have worked with Microsoft SharePoint Portal Server 2003 and Windows SharePoint Services v2 will definitely be familiar with Microsoft FrontPage 2003. FrontPage was Microsoft's recommended application for all SharePoint customizations. Well, Microsoft has changed the rules again. Say hello to the Microsoft Office SharePoint Designer 2007, a part of the Microsoft Office 2007 release.

With the new release, Microsoft has come up with a new set of tools for web site design:

- Microsoft Expressions Web Designer
- SharePoint Designer 2007
- Visual Studio 2005

The choice of which tool is best for you depends on your needs. Ideally:

- Use Expressions Web Designer if you are a professional web designer building dynamic standards-based web sites.
- Use SharePoint Designer 2007 if you are a solution creator, web designer, or content author using SharePoint Technologies.
- Use Visual Studio 2005 if you are professional web application developer.

Office SharePoint Designer 2007 is specifically designed to help you create and customize SharePoint web sites and workflows (for both Microsoft Windows SharePoint Services v3 and Office SharePoint Server 2007). Office SharePoint Designer 2007 allows you to:

- Customize SharePoint sites to meet your needs
- Build SharePoint applications quickly, without writing any server code
- Automate business processes with workflows
- Easily manage SharePoint sites

Office SharePoint Designer 2007 has a very intuitive interface, just like Microsoft FrontPage 2003, that enables you to create and refine SharePoint Sites and build workflow-enabled SharePoint applications and reporting tools quickly and easily. Using SharePoint Designer 2007, you can quickly become a solution creator, even if you are not a programmer or application developer.

With existing SharePoint Web Parts in Office SharePoint Server 2007 and ASP.NET controls, it is very easy to build SharePoint applications. You can use custom lists, forms, and data from external sources, and build custom workflows, all without having to write a single line of code. In this chapter, we will look at how to achieve each of these features in detail.

So what happened to FrontPage?

- Microsoft has discontinued FrontPage as of late 2006, but it will continue to support the application for the foreseeable future.
- There will be 100 percent compatibility between FrontPage and the new web authoring tools.

In this chapter, we will go through each through each of these scenarios: building a custom site, building applications, and automating business processes workflows.

Before we start our deep dive into utilizing Office SharePoint Designer 2007 to customize SharePoint sites, it is important to understand key concepts that affect the page customization.

Master Pages

A site home page's content and its formatting come from the default master page. Master pages are templates that are associated with pages. When a master page changes, all the pages associated to the master page also change. Hence, it is easy to update multiple pages simultaneously. Master pages make it easy to apply a common look and feel to your SharePoint site.

The default master page in Windows SharePoint Services 3.0 sites is named *default.master* and is located in the site's *_catalogs/masterpage* folder. This page controls the formatting of the home page and all the list item default pages. There are two ways to customize a site: start adding content to the regions of the home page or modify the site's default master page.

 Site home pages in Office SharePoint Server 2007 may be controlled by master pages other than the *default.master* page, depending on which master page was attached to the site definition when the site was created.

When you open the home page of a SharePoint site, you will see a screen similar to Figure 19-1. Note the placeholders that show up on selected areas. These placeholders define sections of the master page where you can add or edit content.

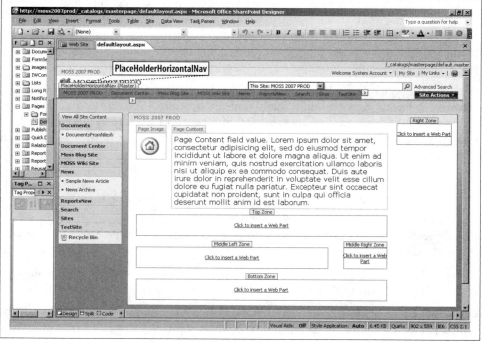

Figure 19-1. Page design view

Placeholders can also be used to reserve space for current functionality or future use. Master pages in Office SharePoint Server 2007 have more default required placeholders than do master pages in Windows SharePoint Services 3.0.

 On the region label, the placeholder name is followed by either (Master) or (Custom). Placeholders marked (Master) contain default content from a master page in the site, and placeholders marked (Custom) contain custom content that has been added to the current page.

In order to customize a placeholder, you need to first unlock the placeholder by selecting it and clicking on "Create custom content." You then can add custom content to the placeholder, as shown in Figure 19-2.

You can customize each placeholder independent of any other placeholder. However, you should remove content placeholders with great care. If you remove a content placeholder from your master page, every content page that supplies content for that region shows an error.

Just like the home page, you can customize each of the default pages in a SharePoint site. If there are changes that you cannot make to the placeholders, you can edit the master page that controls the page.

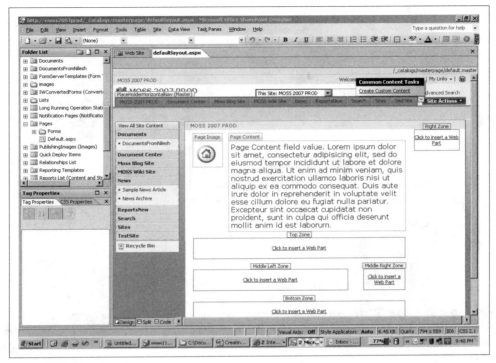

Figure 19-2. Creating custom content

Customizing SharePoint Sites

Ideally you will start with creating a site within Office SharePoint Server 2007 and then open it with SharePoint Designer 2007 to customize the site. We will start off with a basic team site on Office SharePoint Server 2007. When you open the site in SharePoint Designer 2007, you will see the screen as shown in Figure 19-3.

One of the most common tasks performed with customizing a site is branding the site to match a corporate site or intranet site. The most common changes include modifying the logo, changing style sheets, switching fonts, and realigning content to get the desired look and feel.

As you can see in Figure 19-4, SharePoint Designer 2007 provides many tools for performing these changes.

SharePoint Designer can be divided into five main zones:

Folder List
    Shows the list of files that are a part of this site.

Tag Properties
    Shows the properties.

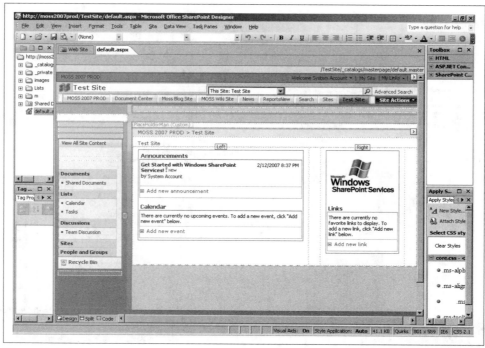

Figure 19-3. Basic team site

Toolbox

Shows the available components.

CSS Style Management

Allows you to easily adjust style attributes.

Main Content

Gives you an editor for viewing and changing a page.

You can add text or images to placeholders by selecting a placeholder and then making changes. For example, you can drag images that reside in your site from the folder list into the placeholder. Figure 19-5 shows how we can select a placeholder and edit it to create custom content.

Click on Create Custom Content. This allows us to edit this section. You can then change any property you want on the placeholder by using the different tools available from within SharePoint Designer 2007.

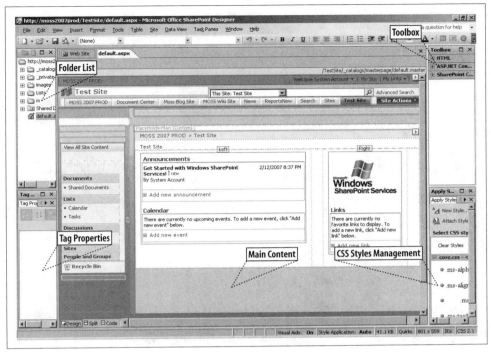

Figure 19-4. Available views

Building SharePoint Applications

One of the main uses of SharePoint Designer is to create and configure Data View Web Parts. You can use this part to easily bring in data from any one of the following data sources:

- SharePoint Lists
- SharePoint Libraries
- Database Connections
- XML Files
- Server-Side Scripts
- XML Web Services
- Business Data Catalog
- Linked sources

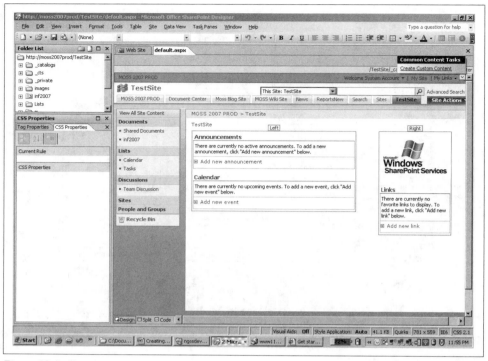

Figure 19-5. Creating custom content

For example, let's insert a Data View Web Part that connects to a database. Click Insert Data View from the Data View menu, as shown in Figure 19-6.

This will give you the option to select a data source from the resulting list. For our example, we will connect to a database. From the list of data sources, click "Connect to database," as shown in Figure 19-7.

This will pop up a dialog box that prompts for database connection information, as shown Figure 19-8.

Follow the default steps to configure a connection to a database. For our example, we will connect to the Northwind database on the SQL server, as shown in Figures 19-9 and 19-10.

Once the connection has been successfully established, you can insert the Data View Web Part by dragging it over to the desired section. You can then change the view property by selecting Data View Properties from the Actions menu on the Web Part, as shown in Figure 19-11.

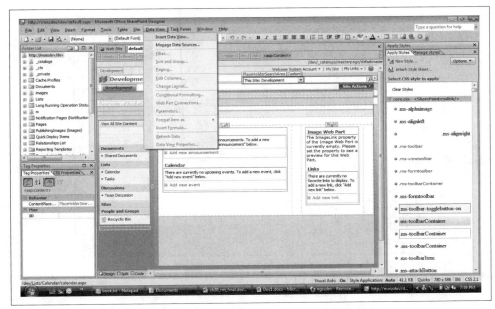

Figure 19-6. Insert Data View

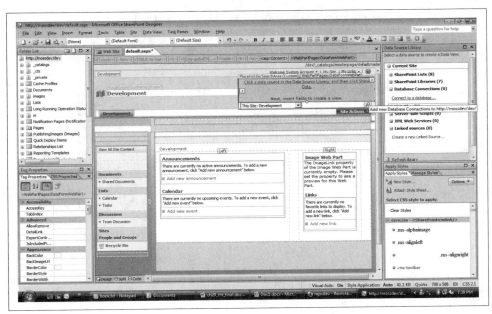

Figure 19-7. Connect to a database

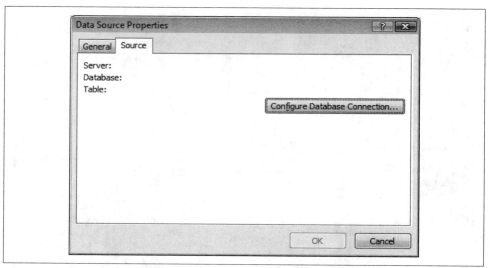

Figure 19-8. Database configuration screen

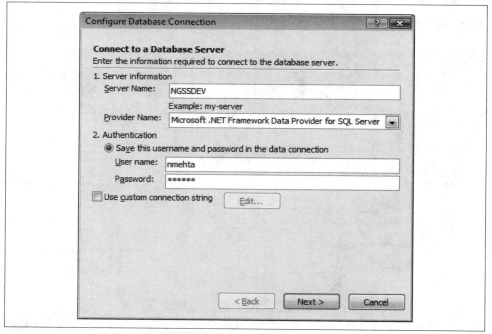

Figure 19-9. Set up the connection to the SQL Server

Figure 19-10. Select the Northwind database and its employee table

The Data View Properties dialog box (Figure 19-12) allows you to set properties on the Web Part, such as Toolbar options, header and footer styles, different HTML layouts, etc. Many of these properties are not available, or not as easily available, from the configuration screens inside the actual SharePoint site.

After you have made the necessary selections, save your settings. You can see the results by refreshing your site home page, as shown in Figure 19-13.

And that's it. The choices are vast. You can bring in data from any of your other corporate applications, as long as the application supports one of the data sources as mentioned earlier. You can also combine data from multiple sources to show a single view.

Creating Basic Workflows

SharePoint Designer 2007 allows you to create custom workflows for SharePoint sites without having to write a single line of code. In order to implement workflows, however, you must have the Windows Workflow Foundation part of .NET 3.0 installed on your computer. If you don't have Windows Workflow installed, you will be prompted to install it before you create a workflow (Figure 19-14).

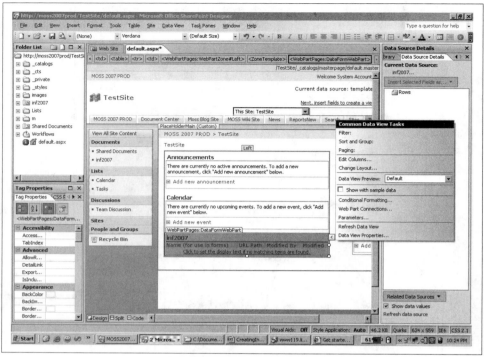

Figure 19-11. Setting properties on the Data View Web Part

Once you have the required Windows Workflow Foundation installed, click File → New → Workflow, as shown in Figure 19-15.

For the sake of simplicity, let's assume we will be implementing a really simple workflow of populating metadata field values for a document when it is uploaded to a SharePoint Document Library. Follow the simple steps for which you are prompted. In the first screen that shows up, as shown in Figure 19-16, enter a meaningful name for your workflow, such an "Item Added." Select startup options for the workflow from one of the following:

- Allow this workflow to be manually started from an item.
- Automatically start this workflow when a new item is created.
- Automatically start this workflow when an item is changed.

In this case, we will select the second option, "Automatically start this workflow when a new item is created."

On the next screen, enter a name for the step, such as "New Item Added." We can choose from any of the following conditions available out of the box to create a workflow. However, for the sake of simplicity, we will not select any criteria; instead,

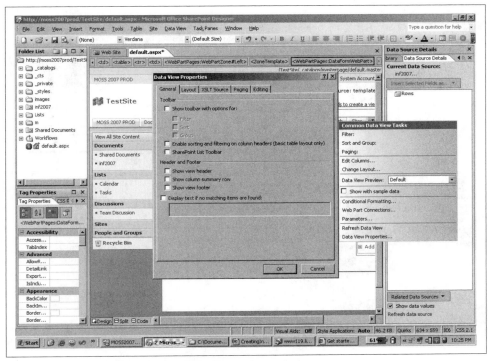

Figure 19-12. Data View Properties dialog box

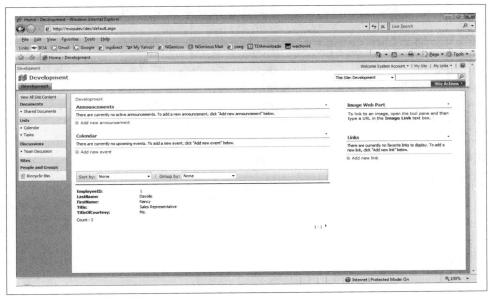

Figure 19-13. Data View Web Part sample results

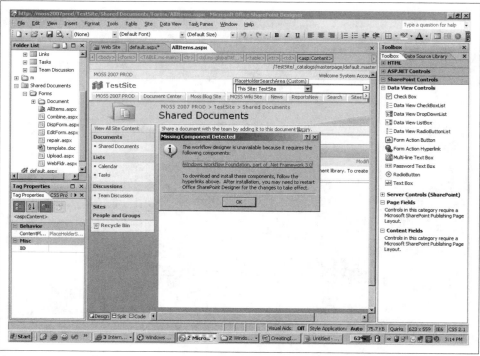

Figure 19-14. Installing the Windows Workflow Foundation part of .NET Framework 3.0

just set the action to populate the Department field value to IT whenever a document is uploaded to the library, as shown in Figure 19-17.

Click Finish to save and deploy the workflow, as in Figure 19-18.

Let's test the workflow now. Open the SharePoint site in a web browser. Upload a document to the SharePoint Document Library, and see whether it will populate the metadata field for Department. We will fill in the Title value, but the Department field is left empty, as in Figure 19-19.

Once the file has been uploaded properly, confirm that the Department field has been updated properly, as shown in Figure 19-20.

This is just an example of how you can create some basic workflows using SharePoint Designer without having to write even a single line of code.

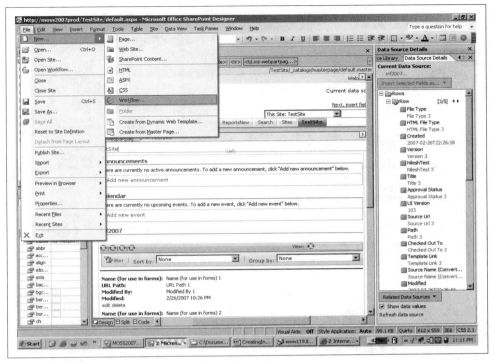

Figure 19-15. Creating a new workflow

Managing SharePoint Sites

SharePoint Designer 2007 also allows us to manage the SharePoint sites. The Site menu on the toolbar contains features that allow you to manage the SharePoint team site, as shown the Figure 19-21.

One of the most useful features available in SharePoint Designer 2007 for administering the SharePoint team sites is the ability to see the reports on the environment. Basic reports such as Site Summary, Files, Shared Content, Problems, and Usage are shown in Figure 19-22.

The site summary report gives us information about all the files in our site, as shown in Figure 19-23. This information is useful because it tells us about all the open issues related to our site.

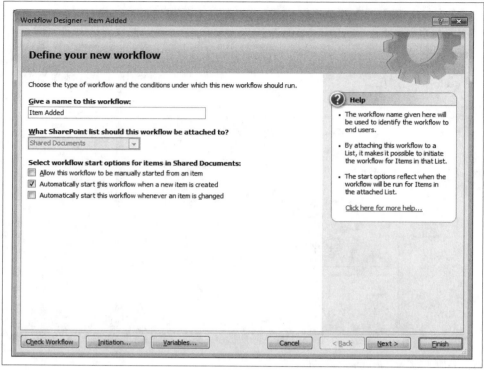

Figure 19-16. Defining the new workflow

With the navigation view, you can easily change the site's navigation by adding a new page or a custom link bar, as shown in Figure 19-24. In this figure, we are adding a link to the Microsoft site on the Quick Launch.

You can see on the home page that the Quick Launch now has an extra link that connects you to the Microsoft home page, as shown in Figure 19-25.

Another important setting that you can access from here is Contributor Settings. This allows setting permissions for each contributor on the SharePoint Team Site. There are three groups and three types of regions available for modification, as shown in Figure 19-26:

Groups
　　Content Authors (Default), Site Manager, and Web Designers

Region types
　　Text and Images; Text Only; and Text, Layout, and Images

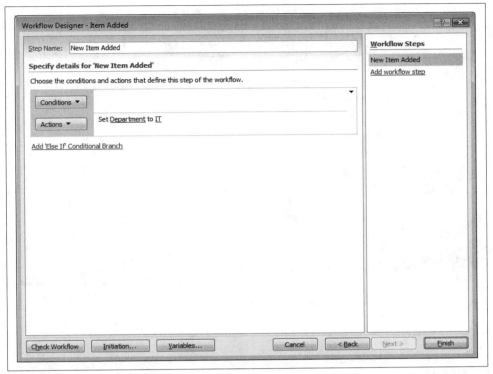

Figure 19-17. Defining conditions for the workflow

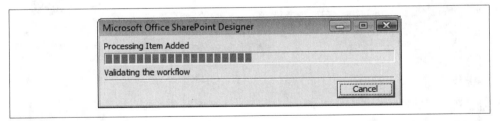

Figure 19-18. Saving the workflow

When you are modifying properties on the group, it allows you to set the following:

- Type of access to SharePoint Designer
- Allowing code view
- Allowing editing of pages in folders
- Creating new pages in the site

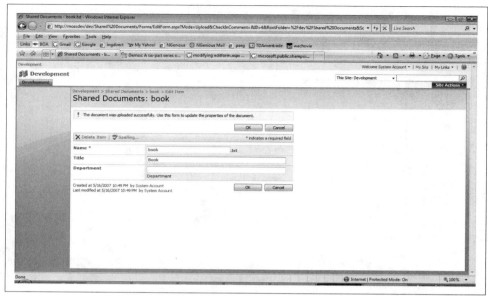

Figure 19-19. Uploading a file to the shared document library

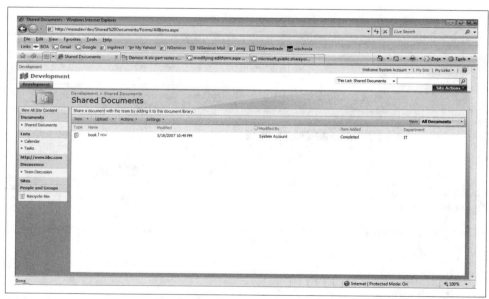

Figure 19-20. Document uploaded and field value updated

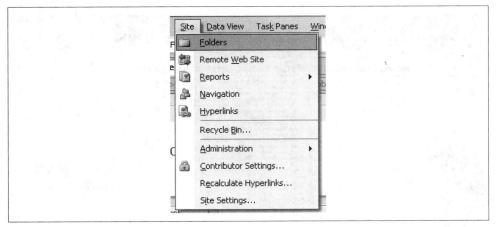

Figure 19-21. Site menu

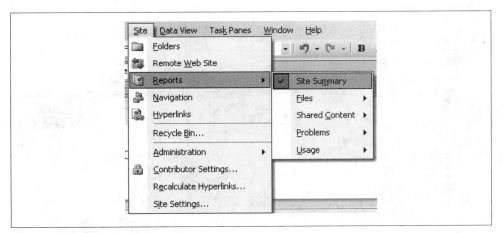

Figure 19-22. SharePoint site reports

- Allowing editing of text/images/tables and other control types
- Formatting of CSS styles
- Allowing addition/deletion of Web Parts

The other features are self-explanatory:

- You can change navigations and hyperlinks related to the current site.
- The Designer also allows you to directly connect to the Recycle Bin of the current site and retrieve documents/items that have been deleted.

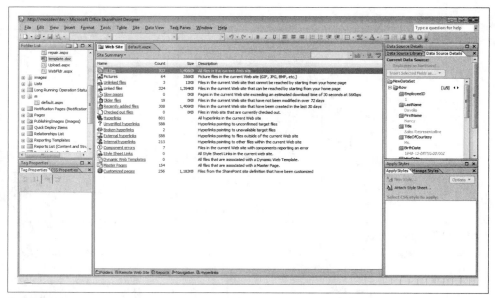

Figure 19-23. Site summary report

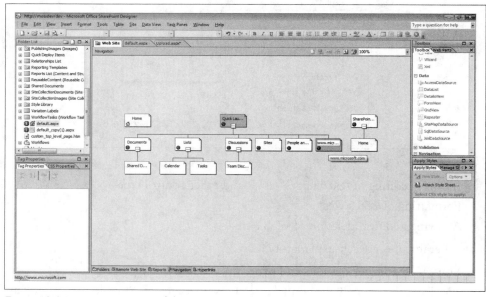

Figure 19-24. Navigation view of the site

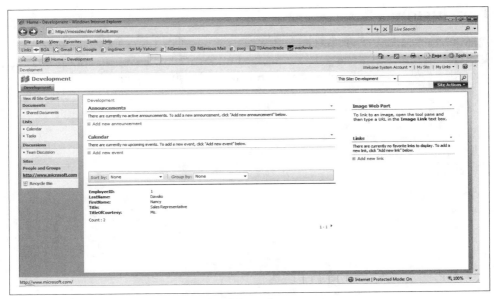

Figure 19-25. Customized navigation in Quick Launch

Figure 19-26. Contributor Settings

Conclusion

SharePoint Designer 2007 provides the powerful tools you need to deliver compelling and attractive SharePoint sites, quickly build workflow-enabled applications and reporting tools on the SharePoint platform, and tailor sites to your company's needs.

CHAPTER 20

InfoPath and SharePoint

Introduction

InfoPath is an XML-based electronic forms development product that Microsoft first released with its Office 2003 series. InfoPath was originally designed to be used as an effective data collection tool. The objective was to provide the end user with the ability to quickly build and deploy a form with an intuitive user interface. Since its introduction, the product has come a long way, with Microsoft enhancing both the built-in features and the development platform for building complex form solutions.

Prior to the introduction of the Office 2007 system, the InfoPath client application, like other Office products, had to be installed on every user's computer. In order to develop and use a form, the form had to be designed using InfoPath, and the resulting form template hosted in a network file share, or installed in individual users' machines, or uploaded into a form library in SharePoint, from where users could then fill up the forms. Filling up the form required InfoPath to be installed on the client machine.

With the advent of the Office 2007 system, Microsoft introduced a new server-side runtime to host InfoPath forms known as *InfoPath Forms Services*. InfoPath Forms Services is integrated into Office SharePoint 2007 as part of the Enterprise site collection Feature, and it is also available as a separate product called Forms Server 2007. Forms Server 2007/InfoPath Forms Services is built on top of WSS 3.0 as an ASP.NET 2.0 application, and its main purpose is to host InfoPath 2007 forms on the web browser, making it more widely accessible. The procedure to develop the form remains mostly the same, and is enhanced with the new features of InfoPath 2007, some of which are highlighted in the "Improvements in InfoPath 2007" section of this chapter. Once the form is hosted within InfoPath Forms Services, users can fill out the form using the browser and no longer need the InfoPath client application.

The main objective of this chapter is to explore the major configuration aspects of InfoPath Forms Services and some of the key integration features between Share-Point 2007 and InfoPath 2007. InfoPath 2007 introduces a lot of new data access, design, and deployment features. The new features discussed in this chapter are focused on the integration of InfoPath 2007 and SharePoint 2007.

In this chapter, you will learn to:

- Configure InfoPath Forms Services
- Deploy InfoPath Forms to SharePoint 2007 using the following options:
    - Deploy directly to the Form Library
    - Deploy the form template as a site content type
    - Administrator-approved form template deployment
- Configure Property Promotion and Property Demotion
- Develop and deploy Document Information Panels

 This chapter assumes that you are familiar with designing InfoPath forms. A detailed review of InfoPath forms design and all the new features associated with the design of the forms are beyond the scope of this chapter. For further information about the new features with Info-Path 2007, visit *http://office.microsoft.com/en-us/products/default.aspx*.

Improvements in InfoPath 2007

Previous releases of InfoPath had their own limitations, the first and foremost being that each client machine required InfoPath to be installed locally. Some other limitations include:

- Developing a connected InfoPath form raised some technical challenges and was complicated for end users.
- Developers did not have an integrated development platform.
- The product did not integrate tightly with other Office products, such as Word and Excel.

InfoPath 2007 extends the capabilities of its predecessor in different segments, such as added controls, deployment features, integration, and programmability. Some of the new capabilities of the product include:

- The ability to covert Word and Excel documents into InfoPath form templates.
- The ability to web-enable an InfoPath form using InfoPath Forms Services or Forms Server 2007.
- Embedding InfoPath forms into Office products such as Outlook.
- Design once—the ability that lets the form be built once and rendered in different modes and devices.

- Document Information Panel, an InfoPath form that is hosted inside Microsoft Word 2007, Excel 2007, or PowerPoint 2007, which can be used to edit document properties.
- Logic inspector, a component that provides a visual view of all rules embedded in the form.
- The ability to publish InfoPath form templates to a SharePoint form library or as a site collection content type.
- Reusable code sections called *Template Parts*.
- Integrated development environment inside Visual Studio 2005 using Visual Studio Tools for Office (VSTO).
- The ability to host InfoPath forms in custom applications.
- Information Rights Management—the ability to protect sensitive data in the forms.

One of the new integration features of InfoPath 2007 with other Office products (Word, Excel, and PowerPoint) is the Document Information Panel (discussed later in the "Forms Deployment" section of this chapter). This panel is an InfoPath 2007 form that allows users to edit metadata properties for documents within SharePoint. The Document Information Panel displays within the Office application (such as Word, Excel, and PowerPoint), and presents an intuitive user interface for collecting metadata. Since the panel is an InfoPath 2007 form, it can take advantage of the rich features of InfoPath 2007, such as built-in controls and rules to validate the data. Figure 20-1 depicts an InfoPath 2007 Document Information Panel within Word.

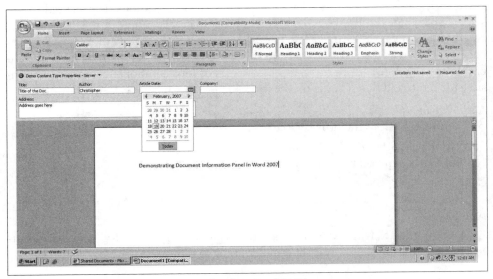

Figure 20-1. Document Information Panel within Word 2007

InfoPath Forms Architecture

Let's take a quick look at the main components of the InfoPath form and the Info-Path Forms Services architecture. The objective of this section is to provide an overall understanding of how the different components work.

An InfoPath form template (*.xsn*) file is actually a CAB file containing different components files. The following are some of the files contained inside the *.xsn*:

.xsf
> A manifest file that provides the basic definition of other form files

.xsl
> Defines the transformation for data into different views

.xsd
> Defines the data source schema

.dll
> Carries the custom logic built into .NET or COM

.htm and other resource files
> Custom HTML resource files and other resources for the form

When a form template is uploaded using administrative deployment (discussed later in this chapter), the template is stored in the content database of the site. Office Forms Services provide a server-side runtime environment for InfoPath Forms Services. While running on the browser, all rules, validation, and calculations are executed in the browser using a client-side script. All business logic is executed in the server. So, when the browser requests business logic execution, a postback is executed using low-cost XMLHTTP. *FormsServer.aspx* is an InfoPath Forms Services page that accesses the form's data from the content database and renders it to the client. Internally, InfoPath Forms Services consists of four components that are responsible for rendering this *.xsn* file on the browser:

ASP.NET modules
> Return HTML to the browser

InfoPath Forms Services HTTP Handler
> Forwards requests from IIS to Page Generator

Converter
> Responsible for converting the *.xsn* file into *.aspx* pages

Page generator
> Communicates with external data sources and is responsible for processing postback data from the browser and maintaining session state

Configuring InfoPath Forms Services

This section discusses some of the main configuration elements of InfoPath Forms Services.

The InfoPath Forms Services server-level configuration options are located in the SharePoint Central Administration → Application Management page. Figure 20-2 depicts the configuration section within the Application Management page.

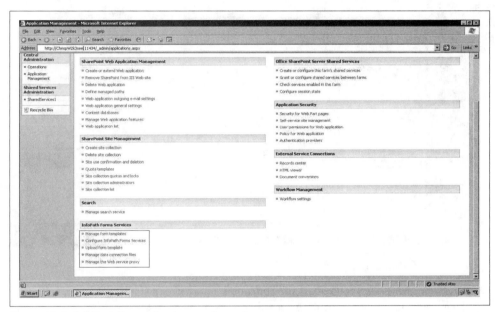

Figure 20-2. InfoPath Forms Services configuration

Let's discuss the "Manage form templates" and the "Configure InfoPath Forms Services" options of the Forms Services configuration page in a little more detail.

Manage Form Templates

This section allows administrators to perform the following actions:

Activate a form template to a site collection
> Administrators can use this option to make the form template available to users of a specific site collection. Activating the form template to a site collection activates a site collection feature and creates a form template in the form template library. Figure 20-3 depicts the feature that is activated by this process.

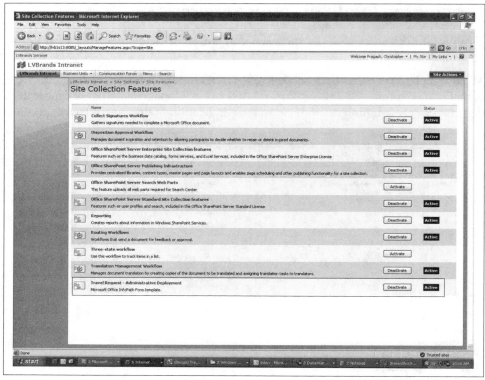

Figure 20-3. InfoPath Forms Services feature

Deactivate a form template from a site collection

Deactivating a form template terminates existing instances of the form, taking the form template offline immediately. This may result in data loss; therefore, careful consideration should be given before deactivating a form.

Quiesce a form template

Quiescing is a process that takes the form template offline gradually and prevents new sessions from being created. It allows existing sessions to be completed, thereby preventing data loss. When a form template is quiesced by the administrator, the form templates from all the site collections are taken offline.

Remove a form template

Removes the form template from the repository.

Configure InfoPath Forms Services

This page allows the administrator to configure some of the basic settings for the InfoPath Forms Services. There are different sections in this page; some of the more important sections are discussed here:

User Browser-enabled Form Templates

Administrators can choose to allow end users to browser-enable form templates, and also specify whether rendering the user-enabled form templates browser is allowed.

Data Connection Timeouts

Allows the administrators to specify a default timeout value and a maximum timeout value. Default timeout values can be overridden in form code but cannot exceed the maximum timeout limit specified by the administrator.

HTTP data connections

Choosing this setting will require SSL-encrypted connections for data connections that require Basic or Digest authentication types.

Embedded SQL Authentication

Form code that connects to a database may sometimes have usernames and passwords embedded in the connection string. This usually poses a security risk, as the connection string can be read in clear text in the solution manifest. This setting allows administrators to block forms that use embedded SQL authentication.

Authentication to data sources (user form templates)

Data connection files may have embedded authentication information in the UDC file or may store the application ID used for Single Sign On. Using this setting, administrators can allow or block forms that use such authentication.

Cross Domain Access for User Form Templates

Administrators can use this setting to control forms that access data from other domains.

Form Session State

This setting allows the administrator to configure the mode in which InfoPath forms will store session data. InfoPath Forms Services can maintain session data in two modes:

- SQL Server database (this approach is termed as using Session State Service)
- ASP.NET view state stored in the client side (termed *Form view*)

Using session state—i.e., storing the state data in the SQL Server database—increases the load on the database server, whereas storing the state in the browser (form view) increases the bandwidth usage between postbacks. One of the important aspects to remember about using Session State Service is that it requires the web application to be associated with a *Shared Services Provider* (SSP). SSP could be thought off as a layer that provides services such as searching user profiles, site search, Excel services, and audience. (A detailed discussion of SSP is beyond the scope of this chapter.) Session State Service mode is recommended for low-bandwidth users, whereas Form view is recommended in environments with smaller groups of users. Administrators can also enter a value for the session data size allowed for Form view state. InfoPath Forms Services will automatically revert to Session State Service when the session data size exceeds the value associated with the form view mode.

Figure 20-4 depicts the Configure InfoPath Forms Services screen.

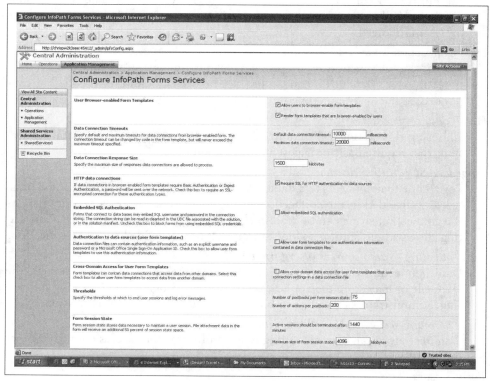

Figure 20-4. Configuring InfoPath Forms Services

InfoPath and SharePoint Integration Overview

In the previous section, we explored the server-side configuration of InfoPath Forms Services. In this and coming sections, we discuss how InfoPath forms can be integrated with SharePoint.

Prior to using InfoPath Forms Services within a site collection, the WSS 3.0 feature called Office SharePoint Server Enterprise Site Collection Features must be activated within the site collection. Depending on the Site Collection Template chosen for the site, this feature may already be active.

 To activate any WSS 3.0 feature, administrative privileges are required.

To activate the feature, follow the steps listed here:

1. Open the SharePoint site on which you wish to activate the feature.
2. Click Site Actions → Site Settings → Modify All Site Settings.
3. Under the Site Collection Administration column, choose "Site collection features."
4. Choose Activate for the "Office SharePoint Server Enterprise Site Collection features" option.

Before we delve into the how-tos of integrating InfoPath and SharePoint, let's take a minute to discuss the main integration areas and some of their uses.

InfoPath 2007 form templates can be published into a Windows SharePoint Services form library. If InfoPath Forms Services were not active within the site collection, filling up these form templates would require the InfoPath client application. With the help of the Office SharePoint Server Enterprise feature, these forms can be configured as browser-enabled. InfoPath forms that are used for a business processes such as timesheets, expense reports, travel requests, help desk requests, and so on are ideal candidates to be published to a form library.

InfoPath also provides tighter property integration with SharePoint forms libraries using Property Promotion and Property Demotion. Property Promotion allows a field in the InfoPath Form to be exposed as a column in the library, and Property Demotion allows editing of InfoPath form field values inside the Datasheet view or the property pages of the Form Library in SharePoint. Changing the value in the Datasheet view automatically changes the value in the corresponding field in the InfoPath Form. Let's consider the example of an expense form to better understand these capabilities. Two common fields within an expense form include a start date and an end date. When publishing an InfoPath form to the Form Library, if these fields were Promoted they would show up as columns within the Form Library, presenting a summary grid view with each expense form and its starting date and ending date in a single row within the grid. If these fields were then Demoted, the values of these fields could be changed from within the Form Library without opening the associated InfoPath form. Property Demotion applies only to properties that are Promoted; that is, in order to edit a field without opening the form, the field must first be exposed as a column.

InfoPath 2007 form templates can also be published as a SharePoint site content type, which creates a content type with the form fields as content type columns and allows the form to be used in multiple libraries and sites. Such forms serve the purpose of enriching the metadata collection process. Let's look at another example to understand the benefits of this capability. Assume that there exists a SharePoint content type for business contract documents and that this content type is used in different libraries and sites across the site collection. While uploading a contract document, users would be required to provide a vendor name and associate this with contract-specific information such as start date, end date, and payment methods. If an InfoPath form is associated with this kind of SharePoint content type, besides providing a rich user interface for the users, it can validate the data the users enter, allowing the user to choose from an existing list of vendors and automatically associating vendor-related information, thereby making the data more accurate. The form can also perform other functions, such as updating other corresponding data sources as required. New features of SharePoint 2007 and their integration with InfoPath 2007 provide better and more flexible approaches to developing simple yet powerful solutions.

 Content types are a new feature in SharePoint 2007. Content types are discussed in more detail in Chapters 1 and 2.

Another powerful integration point between InfoPath 2007 and SharePoint 2007 is a capability called the Document Information Panel. The objective of a document information panel is to use the rich UI features of InfoPath to capture metadata from within the office 2007 document being uploaded to the SharePoint library. To better understand this capability, let's look at another example. Assume that a user uploads a document using a SharePoint content type built for the purpose of proposal management. Some standard requests for proposal metadata columns may include project name, project stakeholders, and budget fields. When a document for this content type is being uploaded, the user is required to enter values for the metadata columns described above. InfoPath can be used to create a rich UI for these metadata fields, so the fields for stakeholders and other information can be validated and, if required, automatically populated. Additionally, this form can then be presented within the Office 2007 document that is being uploaded. This provides an easy and powerful way for the users to enter the required metadata.

Now that we have seen some of the uses of InfoPath and SharePoint integration, let's delve deeper into implementing these integrations. In this section, we will discuss the following main integration points between InfoPath 2007 and SharePoint 2007:

- Forms deployment
- Property Promotion and Demotion
- Document Information Panel development

Forms Deployment

InfoPath forms can be deployed in a number of ways: to a network location, embedded in an email, and published to SharePoint 2007. Within SharePoint 2007, InfoPath forms can be deployed three different ways:

- Deploy directly to the Form Library
- Deploy the form template as a site content type
- Administrator-approved form template deployment

The appropriate deployment option needs to be chosen based on the security restrictions and the data access requirements, among other things. Form templates that contain business logic require full trust. Form templates that do not use data connections managed by administrators or that do not contain business logic code can be deployed directly to a SharePoint site's form library by a user who has privileges.

Publishing to the Form Library

A user with appropriate privileges can publish an InfoPath form directly to the Form Library. Ideal candidates for such a deployment would be forms that do not use custom logic or data connections. To publish a form to the Form Library, follow these steps:

1. Select File → Publish, and click Next.
2. Specify the URL of the site where the form needs to be published, and click Next.
3. Ensure that Document Library is selected and that "Enable this form to be filled out by using a browser" is also checked. Click Next.
4. In the dialog box that appears, select "Create a new document library." If a document library for this form template already exists, select the "Update the form template in an existing document library" option.
5. If the "Create a new document library" option is selected, the next dialog box prompts you to enter a name for the form library. Specify a name for the form library and click Next.
6. In the next dialog box, choose the properties to be promoted and demoted, and click Next. Property promotion and demotion are discussed later in this chapter.
7. In the final dialog box, click "Publish" to finalize the publishing process.

To use the published form, navigate to the Form Library site and select New → New Document. By default, the form opens up in the InfoPath 2007 client program if the client machine has InfoPath 2007 installed. If the client machine does not have InfoPath 2007 installed, the form is rendered in the browser. Figure 20-5 depicts a form displayed in the browser.

For browser-enabled form templates, Form Library settings can be changed to make the browser the default display mode. To enforce browser-enabled forms to be displayed in the browser, follow these steps:

1. Navigate to the form library where the InfoPath form is deployed.
2. Choose Settings → Form Library Settings.

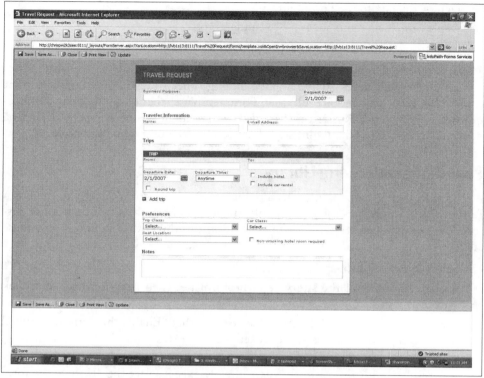

Figure 20-5. InfoPath form displayed in the browser

3. Select Advanced Settings.

4. Under Browser-enabled Documents, select "Display as a web page" and then click OK. Figure 20-6 displays this "Advanced Settings" page.

Publishing InfoPath Forms As a Site Content Type

As discussed in the overview section, this mode of publishing creates a site collection-specific content type that can be used in different libraries and sites across the site collection. To publish a form as a site content type, follow these steps:

1. Select File → Publish, and click Next.

2. Specify the URL of the site where the form needs to be published, and click Next.

3. Select Site Content Type, and ensure that the "Enable this form to be filled out by using a browser" is also checked.

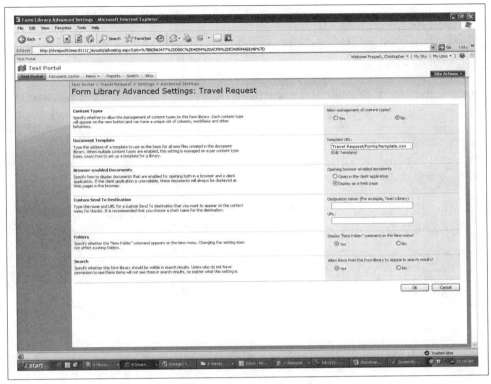

Figure 20-6. Form Library Advanced Settings

4. In the next dialog box, choose "Create a new content type" if you want to create a new content type, or choose "Update an existing site content type" if one already exists, and click Next. The latter option also updates all site content types that inherit from this content type.

5. In the next dialog box, browse to a location where the form template would be stored. This could be a form library on the site. Specify a name for the form template and click Next.

6. Specify the properties that need to be promoted or demoted and click Next.

7. Finally, click "Publish" to complete the process.

The site content type is now available for use throughout the site collection. In order to use the site content type, create a new document library, or modify the settings of an existing library, use these steps:

1. Click Settings → Document library settings.

2. In the next screen, choose "Advanced settings."

3. Select "Yes" for the "Allow management of content types" option under "Content Types," and click OK.

4. The settings page should now have a section called Content Types, as depicted in Figure 20-7.

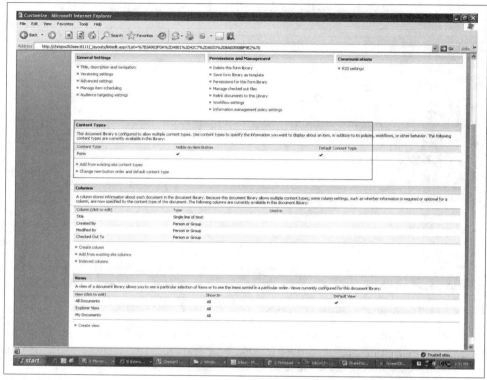

Figure 20-7. Configuring content types in the Document Library

5. To specify the content type published by the InfoPath form, click "Add from existing site content types."

6. Choose the content type name published by the InfoPath form from the list of available content types and click OK, as depicted in Figure 20-8.

7. To fill out a form for this content type, navigate to the document library page. The new content type should be available under the New option.

Administrative Deployment

Certain InfoPath forms require administrative approval before they can be hosted by Forms Services. Forms that contain custom code or forms that require "Full Trust" (i.e., the form can access local system resources or use a data connection managed by an

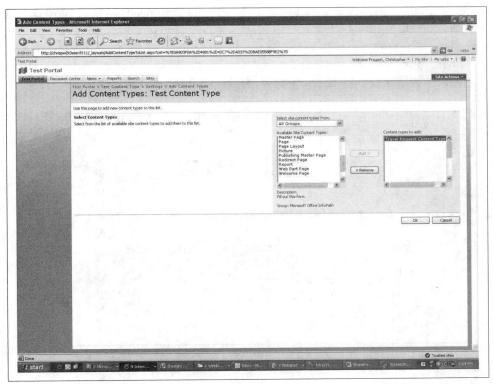

Figure 20-8. Adding a custom content type to the Document Library

administrator) all require a special deployment mode, known as *administrative deployment*. Administrative deployment allows forms to be uploaded to a central repository. The deployment is broken down into phases:

Phase 1
    The form needs to be published for administrative deployment.

Phase 2
    Upload the published form to the central repository.

Preparing the Form for Administrative Deployment

Before an InfoPath form can be deployed using administrative deployment in Info-Path Forms Services, it needs to be published. To publish a form for administrative deployment, follow these steps:

1. From the InfoPath 2007 File menu, choose Publish.

2. The dialog box that opens up specifies the options where the InfoPath Form template can be published. Make sure the option "To a SharePoint server with or without InfoPath Forms Services" is selected, and then click Next.

3. Specify the URL of the SharePoint site where the form needs to be deployed, and click Next. At this stage, InfoPath validates the SharePoint site.

4. The dialog box that follows provides different options for form deployment in SharePoint. For administrative deployment purposes, choose "Administrator-approved form template (advanced)" and click Next. Figure 20-9 depicts this.

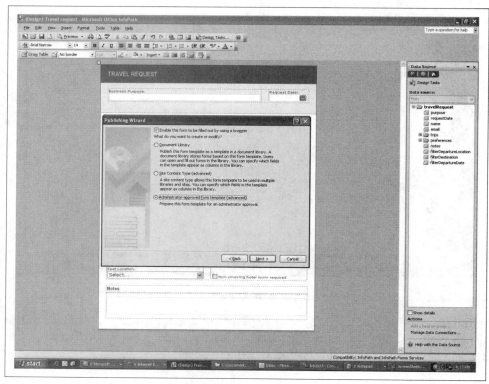

Figure 20-9. Preparing the InfoPath form for administrative deployment

5. In next dialog box, specify a location and template name for the form; click Next.

6. In the next dialog screen, specify the fields that need to be displayed as columns in the SharePoint site and click Next.

7. To add a field, click Add and select the field from the data source displayed. There is an option "Allow users to edit data in this field by using a datasheet or properties page" that appears in the Add dialog box. This option is used for "Property demotion" (discussed in the "Property Promotion and Property Demotion" section, later in this chapter).

8. In the final dialog box, choose Publish.

This form is now ready to be uploaded into the InfoPath Forms Services. To upload the form to InfoPath Forms Services, follow these steps:

1. From SharePoint's Central Administration page, choose Application Management.

2. Under the InfoPath Forms Services section, choose "Upload form template." The upload form screen also presents certain other options, such as the ability to upgrade existing form templates and the ability to control whether existing form instances should be allowed to complete or should be terminated. If the form template is being upgraded with significant changes, you can "quiesce" the form template (discussed under the "Manage Form Templates" section earlier in this chapter) before uploading the upgraded template. Figure 20-10 depicts the Upload Form Template screen.

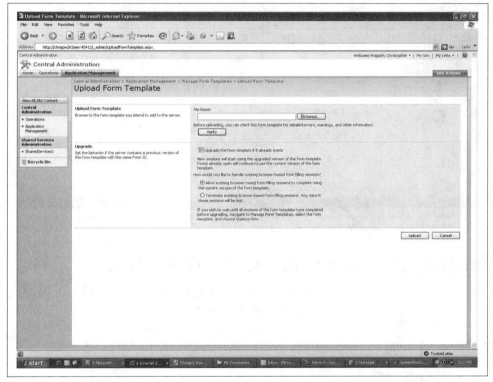

Figure 20-10. Uploading a form template in InfoPath Forms Services

3. In the page that opens up next, specify the location of the template that was published in the first phase.

4. In the upload page, there is a Verify button, which validates the compatibility of the form template with InfoPath Forms Services. If this form template is not compatible with InfoPath Forms Services, an error message is displayed. Figure 20-11 depicts a sample error.

5. Click OK to complete the upload process.

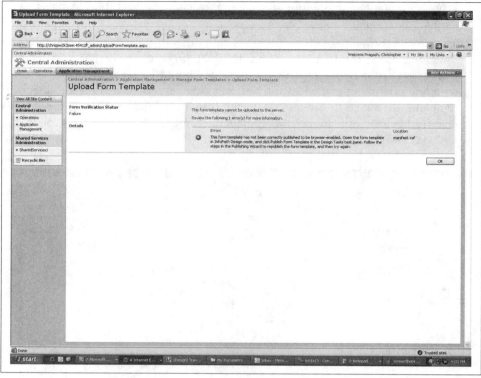

Figure 20-11. Form template compatibility error

Property Promotion and Property Demotion

Sometimes it is useful to view a data source field in InfoPath forms as a column in a SharePoint form library. This gives the user a quick view of certain properties of the specific form. Property Promotion involves promoting a field in the InfoPath form to appear as a column in the form library. Property Demotion, on the other hand, changes a promoted property so it can be edited in the Form Library Datasheet view or the property pages.

Configuring Property Promotion

Property promotion can be configured in two different ways: using the Tools menu or using the publishing wizard. There is really no difference between using the Tools menu or the publishing wizard with regard to outcome. To configure Property Promotion using the Tools menu, follow these steps:

1. Click Form Tools → Form Options.

2. Select Property Promotion.

3. Choose the fields that need to be promoted as columns in the Form Library, as shown in Figure 20-12.

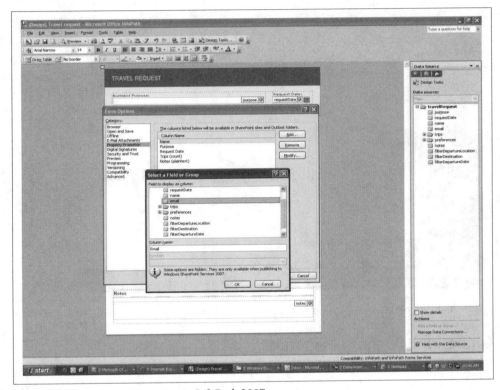

Figure 20-12. Property Promotion in InfoPath 2007

4. Repeat this process for all the fields that need to be promoted.

 Not all fields can be promoted as columns in the Form Library. In particular, certain fields that have recurring data cannot be promoted as columns in a SharePoint form library.

When the form is published to a SharePoint form library, the promoted columns will appear as columns in the form library. When a form is filled, the values of the promoted fields appear in the form library as column values. Figure 20-13 shows promoted properties in the SharePoint form library.

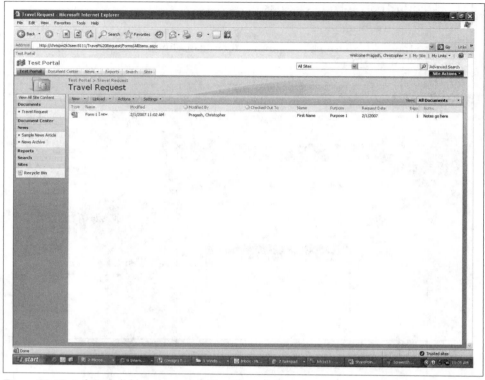

Figure 20-13. InfoPath fields promoted as SharePoint columns

Configuring Property Demotion

Property Demotion can be configured only on promoted properties. Additionally, it can be configured only while publishing a form template. To configure Property Demotion, follow the steps below:

1. Click File → Publish.

2. Select "To a SharePoint server with or without InfoPath Forms Services" and click Next.

3. Specify the URL of the SharePoint Site where the form needs to be published, and click Next.

4. Specify the deployment option (in this case, a document library), and select Next.

5. Choose "Create a new document library," and click Next.

6. Type the name of the new document library and click Next.

7. In the dialog box that appears:

- If there no properties available, click Add and select the properties to be promoted.

- If there are existing properties, select Modify.

8. In the dialog box that appears, select "Allow users to edit this field by using a datasheet or properties page" and click OK. One caveat of allowing properties to be edited in the Datasheet view is that the business logic is not executed. Info-Path 2007 displays a dialog box stating this when a property is selected for demotion. Figure 20-14 depicts the Property Demotion option in the publishing wizard.

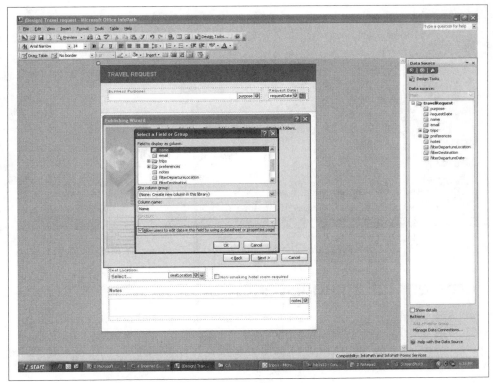

Figure 20-14. Configuring Property Demotion in InfoPath 2007

9. Finish the publishing process by clicking Publish.

Using Property Demotion

As discussed previously, Property Demotion allows the user to edit the form field value in the Datasheet view of the Form Library. To view the properties in a Datasheet

view, navigate to the form library in the SharePoint site, and then select Actions →
Edit in Datasheet. Figure 20-15 depicts the Datasheet view for the properties.

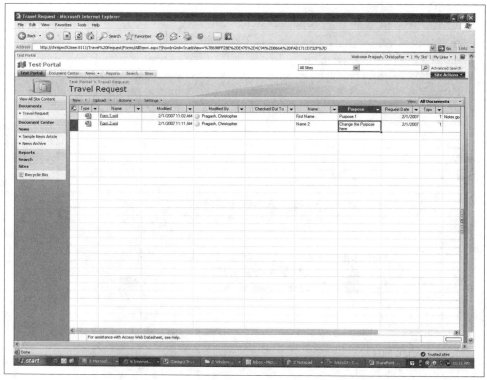

Figure 20-15. Using an InfoPath form's demoted properties in Datasheet view of the Form Library

Document Information Panel

The Document Information Panel is a new feature introduced in Office 2007. It provides users with a form that is displayed inside the client application, and it allows the user to enter metadata about the document. It is available in Microsoft Office Word 2007, Microsoft PowerPoint 2007, and Microsoft Office Excel 2007.

InfoPath 2007 can autogenerate the document information panel for a SharePoint content type. The fields in the panel are based on the columns of the associated content type. The panel can be customized with an InfoPath 2007 template for validating and customizing the look and feel of the form presented in the client application.

To demonstrate the development of a document information panel, we will begin with creating a sample content type.

Creating a Sample Content Type

To create a content type:

1. Navigate to the Site collection administration page.

2. Select "Site content types" under Galleries and click Create.

3. Enter a name for the content type; for this demo, let's call it "Demo Content Type."

4. Under the "Select parent content type from" category, choose Document Content Types.

5. Under Parent Content Type, choose Document.

6. Under "Put this site content type into," leave the default option selected and click OK.

7. To add custom columns to the sample content type, select "Demo content type" in the Site Content Type Gallery page.

8. To add columns to the sample content type, select "Add from existing site columns" under Columns. Figure 20-16 depicts the "Add Columns to Site Content Type" page.

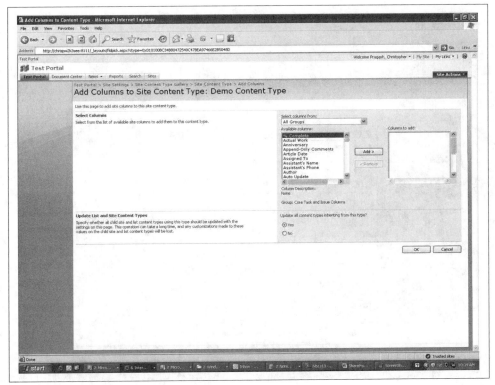

Figure 20-16. Creating a content type in SharePoint 2007

9. Select the following columns from the Available Columns list, and then click Add:

- Address
- City
- Company
- First Name
- Zip Code
- Fax Number

10. Click OK to complete creation of the content type.

Designing an InfoPath Form for the Demo Content Type

To design a form for the Demo Content Type, follow these steps:

1. Open InfoPath 2007 and select File → Design Form Template.

2. In the dialog box that opens up, choose "XML or Schema." Also, to make sure that InfoPath allows only browser-compatible controls, check the Enable Browser Compatible Features Only option and click OK. Figure 20-17 depicts this screen.

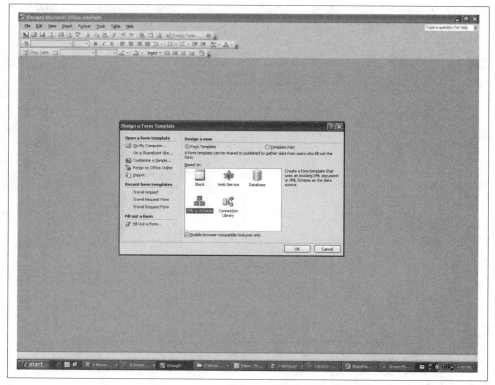

Figure 20-17. Creating a new Document Information Panel using SharePoint 2007

3. Enter the URL of the Site collection where the "Demo Content Type" was created and click Next. InfoPath 2007 queries the site collection and displays the list of content types available.

4. Choose Demo Content Type, and click Next and then Finish.

5. InfoPath automatically creates the form based on the columns in the site content type. To ensure the panel template is browser compatible, choose "Design checker" and then select Change compatibility settings, which displays the Form Options dialog box with the Compatibility option selected. Figure 20-18 depicts the Form Options dialog box that appears.

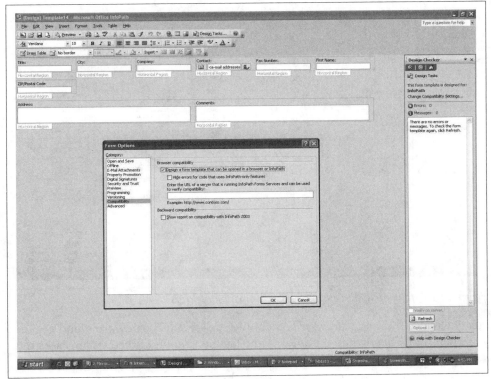

Figure 20-18. Configuring the Compatibility option in InfoPath Forms 2007

6. Document Information Panels appear inside the client application. Therefore, it is not mandatory to have the panel compatible with the browser, but you can choose to check the "Design a form template that can be opened in a browser or InfoPath" option if the template must be browser-compatible. Click OK.

7. The Design Checker reports compatibility and other binding problems and issues with the form. For the "Demo Content Type," the Design Checker should report compatibility issues with the Horizontal Region control. Some controls

in InfoPath are not supported in the browser. If a form template needs to be compatible with the browser, the Design Checker is a handy tool that can be used to create a fully functional browser-enabled form. Figure 20-19 depicts the errors reported by the Design Checker.

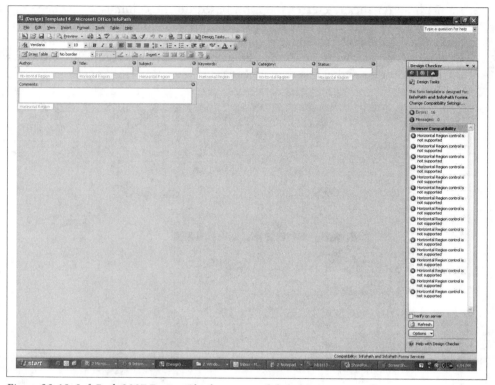

Figure 20-19. InfoPath 2007 Design Checker compatibility errors

8. To make the pane browser-compatible, delete existing controls and regions. Drag the "Three-column Table" in the layouts section of the Design Tasks toolbar to the form.

9. Drag the appropriate fields from the Data Source tab under Design Tasks toolbar into each column of the table. A sample panel is depicted in Figure 20-20.

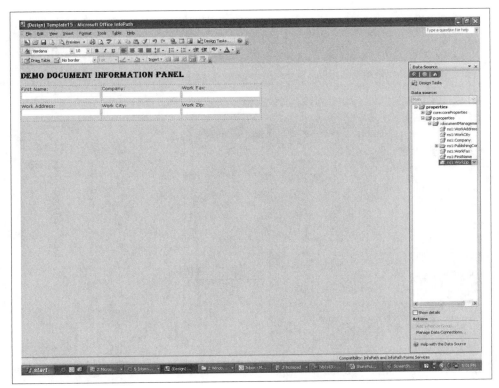

Figure 20-20. Sample Document Information Panel

10. Custom validations and rules can be added as required. With the finalized design, the template is now ready to be published as the document information panel of the demo content type.

11. To publish the template, choose Publish from the InfoPath 2007 menu.

12. InfoPath forces the template to be saved if this has not already been done. The Publish wizard is launched with the "As a document Information Panel template for a SharePoint site content type or list content type" option preselected. Figure 20-21 depicts the Publish wizard.

13. Choose Next, and a dialog box with the summary information about the site collection and the content type will appear. Choose Publish.

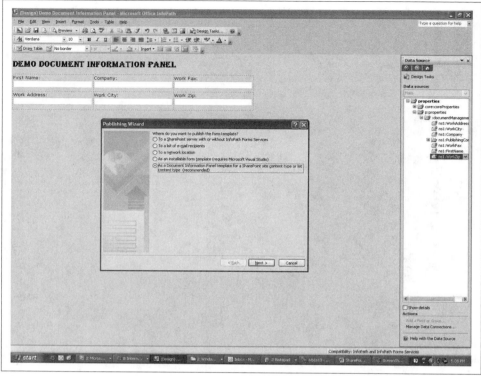

Figure 20-21. Deploying the Document Information Panel in SharePoint 2007

There is also an alternative approach to create the document information panel for a content type in SharePoint. The following steps describe this approach:

1. Navigate to the Site Content Type Gallery of the site collection.

2. Choose "Demo content type," and then choose Document Information Panel Settings. Figure 20-22 depicts a sample Document Information Panel Settings page.

3. Click "Create a new custom template," and InfoPath 2007 will open with the autogenerated form.

To use the document information panel, the content type needs to be associated with a document library. When the user saves a document to the library and selects the content type to save, the document information panel is presented within the application.

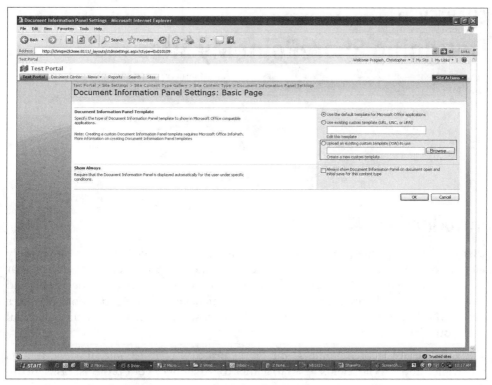

Figure 20-22. Document Information Panel Settings for a content type

Conclusion

In this chapter, we have discussed how the new InfoPath 2007 and InfoPath Forms Services in Office SharePoint Server 2007 can be used to deploy intuitive forms and make them available online. Combined with the power of workflow, security, and all the other list features built into Office SharePoint Server 2007, InfoPath Forms Services makes it easy to build and deploy powerful electronic forms based business process and to create UI-rich forms to capture metadata.

CHAPTER 21

Designing SharePoint My Sites

Introduction

Chapter 5 detailed the process of creating sites and site collections but only briefly mentioned My Sites. My Sites are created just like any SharePoint site except that they are intended to be accessed only by you and whomever else you decide should have access. SharePoint users can create and manage their own personal My Sites within the larger site collection structure and customize them for their individual use. Consider it a SharePoint site just for you.

The vast majority of SharePoint is built on the principle of collaboration between users and teams, and My Site can be used to gather together all of your projects, tasks, documents, and links. If you are involved in several teams or team projects, your SharePoint resources can be scattered across the site collection. Use your My Site to gather all of that information together and then organize it in a way that makes sense to you.

You can personalize My Site and then allow guests to access some of your information so they can learn more about your experience and qualifications or work with you on a project. You can also assign Privacy Groups to lists and libraries and control who has access to what on your My Site. This is like living by yourself in your house and inviting your neighbors over, but letting them see only the living room, kitchen, and bathroom.

Content Providers in SharePoint can use your My Site as a way to supply you with targeted information, depending on which groups you belong to. These providers are usually some form of management, such as your own supervisor, the managers of Human Resources, and other relevant departments.

When your My Site is created, it contains two parts by default: the private My Home site, which starts with a private home page, and the public My Profile site, which contains content that can be seen by others.

You do not have absolute control of your My Site. The main SharePoint site owner and administrators can determine the general look and feel of all My Sites, but you can add Web Parts and data. Management groups in your organization can create other sites called Personalization Sites within your My Site and fill them with specific information. Each Personalization Site appears as a tab on your My Site. For example, your company's public relations department may create a personalization site that displays all of the press releases and broadcast newsletters involving your projects.

That said, you are the administrator of your private My Home site and can tailor it to suit your personal needs and goals within SharePoint, as well as restrict access to some of the public information in My Profile.

 A site administrator must enable My Site functionality and create a My Site site collection before this option is available to site users.

Using Your My Site

Before getting into the nuts and bolts of My Sites, let's take a tour of the available features and how you can use them.

Tracking Members

You can use the Colleagues Web Part to keep track of team members, partners, and anyone else you regularly work with. When you use this Web Part, you can find out whether an individual has reported to work for the day and the activities she is involved in, such as a meeting or a phone call. You can be reminded of such details as when it's a team member's birthday or anniversary and be informed of major events, such as when she changes departments or are promoted.

Tracking Links

Your My Site has a separate My Links page, which you can use to add and organize links to any web site. You can collect links by project name or some other criteria and filter the links with Privacy Groups. Then only those groups you allow can see certain collections of links.

Tracking Document Approval

Configure a workflow for your documents so you can keep track of which have been submitted for approval, which were approved or rejected, the rationale for the decision, and tasks related to documents.

Storing and Sharing Documents

You can use the Documents Web Part on your My Site to link to any document you have ever created or modified on any SharePoint site in the site collection. You can also view any tasks assigned to you related to these documents. My Site is set up by default to show all the documents you are connected to on up to five sites in the site collection. You can add more sites if needed.

When you create a document in a Microsoft Office application, such as Word 2007, you can save that document to any of the document libraries on your My Site. By default, your My Site has four document libraries:

- My Pages
- My Pictures
- Private Documents
- Shared Documents

Any documents you save in the Shared Documents library automatically appear on the public page of your My Site; however, only you have access to documents saved in Private Documents. To save a document on your My Site from an Office 2007 program, click the My Site Places link in the application you used to create the document.

Storing and Sharing Information on My Site

In addition to documents, you can also use your My Site Public page to share other kinds of information. Anything you add to your public page becomes part of your profile, including any text and photos. You can post a list of your interests, projects, and a biography. Additionally, your manager can post information on your public page using Active Directory or LDAP and deploy database information such as your name, department, and work group.

You can filter information on your public page using Privacy Groups. This lets you provide your work phone number to everyone and allows you to show your mobile or home phone numbers only to certain groups. This is helpful in situations where only your work group is allowed to call or page you about a work situation.

The SharePoint search feature can be used to find people by the information included on their public site and profile. For example, let's say you have listed that you are proficient in the Perl and Python programming languages in either the Interests or Skills section on your public page. Another member of the site collection searching for someone knowledgeable in those languages could use the search feature to locate you.

You can also be located by your group affiliations, non-work interests, and who you work with, as long as that information has been listed on your My Site. For example, if you are a member of the *perlmonks.com* discussion group and someone else in the site collection was interested in learning about them, they could locate you using search and then email you some questions.

Creating Workspaces in My Site

In Chapters 9 and 10, you learned about creating and managing Document and Meeting Workspaces. You can create separate workspaces on your My Site as well, including a blog, a records repository, a team site, and a wiki site. You can use a Meeting Workspace to gather all of your materials in preparation for a meeting you are hosting. You can also create and use a Document Workspace to check out and work on a local copy of a document you are preparing, and then check the copy back into your team's document library.

A Document Workspace or library on your My Site also lets you track different versions of your documents.

 This option is available only if you have set up your library to track versions. See Chapters 9 and 13 for more information on setting up versioning.

Use this feature to track the history of a document, such as the number of major and minor versions that exist, who edited different versions of the document, and any comments made about the document by those who edited it.

 You can track both major and minor versions of a document in a library, but you can track only major versions in a list.

The first step in working with your My Site is to access it. While logged onto a Share-Point site, click on the My Site link in the top-right portion of the web page, as seen in Figure 21-1.

The first time you click the My Site link, SharePoint creates your new My Site on the fly. This might take a few moments. Once the creation process is completed, your default My Site opens, as shown in Figure 21-2.

Adding Basic Information to My Site

At this point, although your personal My Site is open, it doesn't contain any specific information about you, except your username in the title banner. You'll have to add whatever data you want your My Site to contain.

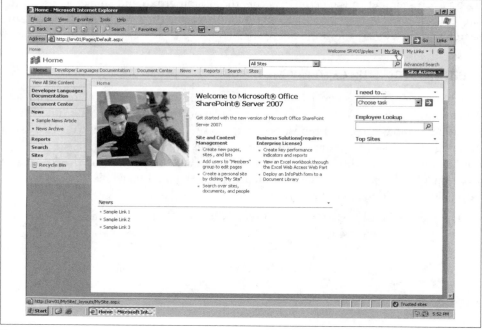

Figure 21-1. Opening My Site

Describing Yourself to My Site

You can add information to your My Site site that lets others know about your qualifications and interests:

1. On the My Site, click the "Describe yourself" link.

2. On the Edit Details page in the About Me field, type a brief description about yourself.

3. In the Picture section, click the Choose Picture button if you want to browse, locate, and upload a photo of yourself.

4. In the Responsibilities section, either type in or browse for a description of your job responsibilities and roles.

5. In the Skills section, type in any professional or personal skills you possess.

6. In the Past Projects section, type in the names of projects you've completed.

7. In the Interests section, type in any of your professional or personal areas of interest.

8. In the Schools section, enter any of the universities or other academic institutions you've attended.

9. In the Birthday section, add your birth date.

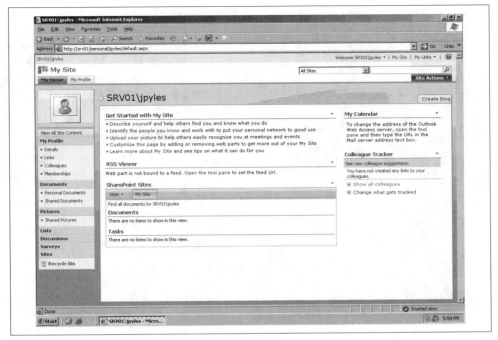

Figure 21-2. Default My Site site

10. If you have an assistant, add or browse to that person's name in the Assistant section.

11. In the Mobile Phone section, add your mobile phone number.

12. In the Fax section, add your fax number.

13. In the Home Phone section, add your home phone.

 Notice in the Show To column, the default values are Everyone. In the drop-down menus of some sections, you can change this value. You can set Privacy Groups on your personal information so that not everyone visiting your My Site can view your information. See the "Configuring Privacy Groups in My Site" section, later in this chapter, for details.

14. Scroll to the top, and click Save and Close.

A sample Edit Details page is shown in Figure 21-3.

 You've already seen how to upload a photo of yourself in the previous exercise, "Describing Yourself to My Site" and adding colleagues will be covered later in this chapter in the section "Managing My Colleagues in My Site."

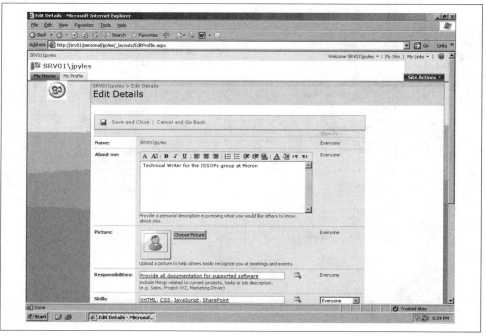

Figure 21-3. The Edit Details page in My Site

Adding a Web Part to My Site

You can add a Web Part to a My Site page just like on any other Web Part page in SharePoint:

1. On My Site, click "Customize this page" to open it in Edit Mode.
2. On the desired Web Part field, click the "Add a Web Part" link.
3. In the Add Web Parts box, click the checkbox by the Web Part you want to add (Figure 21-4), and then click Add.

The Web Part will be added to your My Site site.

Learning More About My Site

If you want to locate tips for managing your My Site, do the following:

1. On My Site, click "Learn more about My Site."
2. When the "Introduction to My Site" page opens, maximize it to see the entire contents, as in Figure 21-5.
3. When you are done reading, close the page.

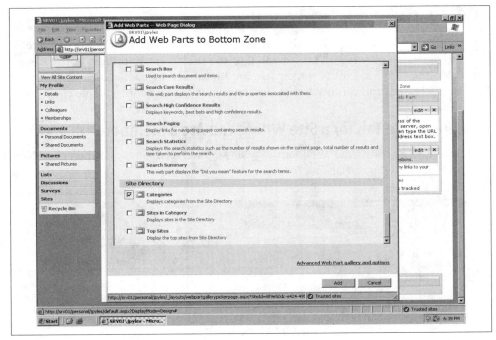

Figure 21-4. Adding a Web Part to My Site

Figure 21-5. Introduction to My Site page

Adding a Site Tab to My Site

You may want to create a site tab that links to another site from your My Site in order to view documents and tasks related to the site. You can do this both for sites you belong to and for sites of which you are not a member. Once the site and link have been created, you can reach that site from your My Site with a single click.

Creating a Site Tab for a Site Where You Are a Member

1. On the SharePoint Sites Web Part in your My Site, click Sites and then click New Site Tab, as in Figure 21-6.

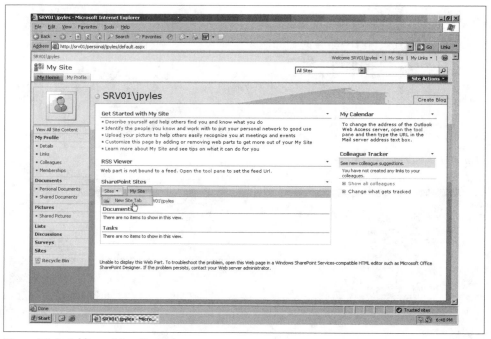

Figure 21-6. Adding a New Site Tab

2. In the "Create a new site tab" dialog box, click the "Select site from Memberships" list.
3. Select the site on the menu, and then click Create.

Creating a Site Tab for a Site Where You Are Not a Member

1. On the SharePoint Sites Web Part in your My Site, click Sites and then click New Site Tab.

2. In the "Create a new site tab" dialog box, click "Type SharePoint site URL and name."

3. Under Site URL, type or paste in the URL of the site that you want to add in the available field.

4. Under Site Name, type the name that you want to appear on the tab and then click Create, as in Figure 21-7.

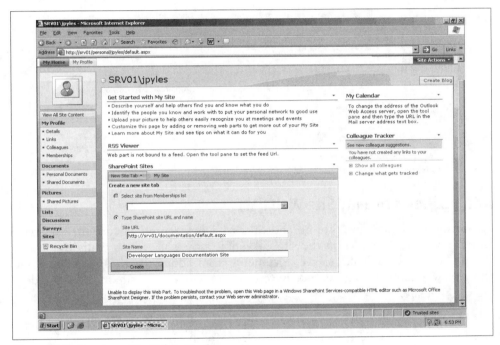

Figure 21-7. Creating a Site Tab in My Site

The new site tab will appear in the My Site Web Part bar, as in Figure 21-8.

Managing Your My Site

You can manage documents, tasks, and other information and material in your My Site, as you read earlier in the "Using Your My Site" section. The material in this section takes you through the steps involved in different aspects of My Site management.

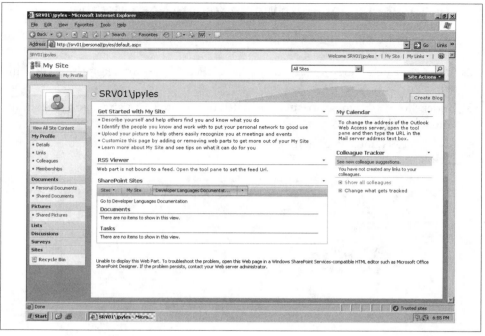

Figure 21-8. New site tab added to the My Site Web Part bar

Adding Views to a My Site Web Part

As mentioned earlier in "Storing and Sharing Documents," documents you have stored on up to five sites in the site collection are displayed on your My Site by default. If you would like to see documents from additional sites, you must add those views manually. You do not have to be a member of a site in order to add a view of that site:

1. On your My Site, click Site Actions and select Edit Page from the menu.

2. In the Sites Web Part, click Edit and select Modify Shared Web Part.

3. In the tool pane under View, in the "Number of tabs to show before More" field, replace the default value of 5 with the number of sites you want to display, as seen in Figure 21-9.

4. Click OK, and when you are back on the My Site page, click Exit Edit Mode.

Use this process to add as many site tabs to your SharePoint Sites Web Part bar as you need. If you add a large number of tabs, you may have to scroll left or right in order to see all of them, depending on your screen resolution.

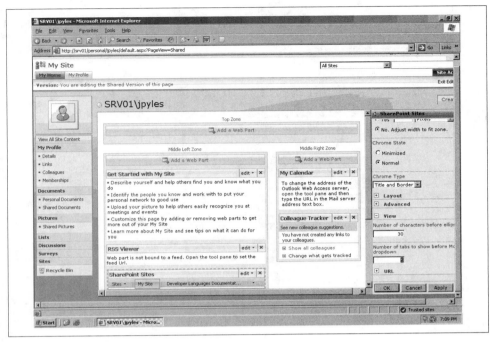

Figure 21-9. Editing a My Site view

Filtering Site Tabs on Your My Site Web Part Bar

As with any other list, you can filter what information is displayed to different groups. Here's how you show or hide a site on the SharePoint Sites Web Part bar:

1. On your My Site, click to the right of the site name you want to show or hide, and then click the Sites menu.

2. To hide the site tab, click Hide; to show a hidden site tab, click the site's name. See Figure 21-10 to locate the Hide option.

Deleting a Site Tab from Your My Site Web Part Bar

You can hide site tabs you do not want others to see, but you can also permanently delete a tab from your SharePoint Sites Web Part bar.

1. On your My Site, click to the right of the site name you want to delete, and then click the Sites menu.

2. Click Delete. (Refer to Figure 21-10 for the location of the Delete option.)

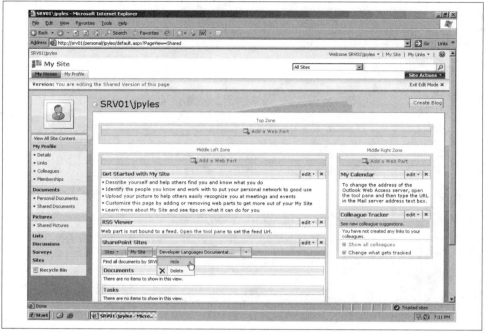

Figure 21-10. Hiding a site tab

If you are a member of the site you deleted, the site link will be moved to the Membership section of your My Site public page. If you are not a member of the site, it is permanently deleted from your My Site.

Viewing Tasks in My Site

1. To view tasks assigned to you on a particular site, either click that site's tab on the SharePoint Sites Web Part bar or click Sites and select the particular site from the list. See the result of this action in Figure 21-11.
2. When the site page opens, in the Tasks Web Part, click the name of a task or item link to open it.
3. Click Edit Item to open it in Edit Mode.
4. View and edit the task as necessary, as in Figure 21-12, and click OK to finish.
5. Click on the My Site link to return to your My Site.

Configuring Privacy Groups in My Site

You can allow or deny access to your My Site site by any member of the larger site or site collection. This does not mean that everyone you allow to see your My Site will have the same view of it as you do. You can assign privacy groups to different pieces of information on your My Site so that those groups have different views.

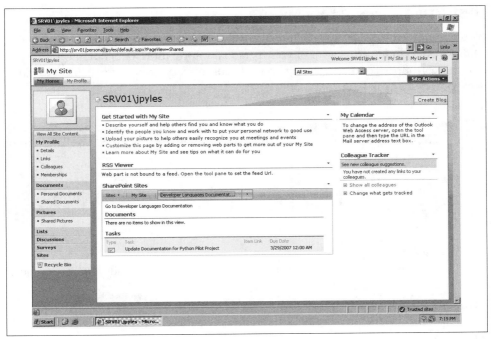

Figure 21-11. Viewing assigned tasks in My Site

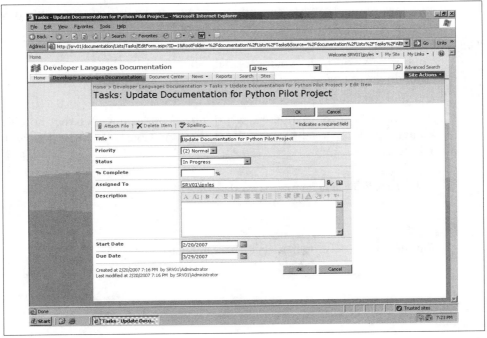

Figure 21-12. Viewing and editing an assigned task

Restricting Views of Your My Site

You can use Privacy Groups to filter the view of your site for different groups. This allows you to hide some or all of your personal information, depending on how you use those groups. There are five different default privacy groups you can set to either view or hide personal information:

Everyone

> The Everyone group contains only those names or groups you have given permissions to access your site, not the general members of the SharePoint site or site collection.

 Note that the following areas must be set to Everyone: Name, About me, Picture, Responsibilities, Assistant, and Account name.

My Colleagues

> This group contains your direct reports, your manager, and your peers; however, you can add anyone else to this group.

My Manager

> This contains the name of the person to which you directly report.

My Workgroup

> This group also contains your direct reports, your manager, and your peers by default; however, you can use the "Add Colleagues to My Workgroup" option to add anyone in your My Colleagues group to your My Workgroup group.

Only Me

> This option lets you make your personal information visible only to you. To enable it, do the following:

> 1. On your My Site in Quick Launch, click Details.
> 2. Next to the item you want to restrict (Interests, for example) in the Show To column, click one of the group names listed previously. See an example in Figure 21-13.

 To hide the item from everyone, click Only Me.

> 3. On the Edit Details toolbar, click "Save and Close."

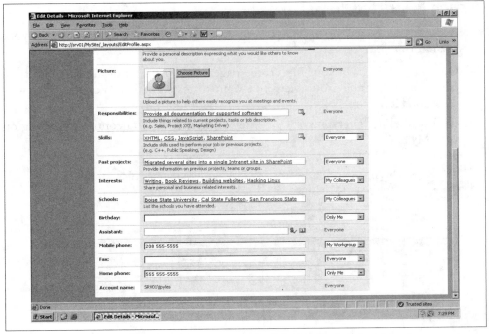

Figure 21-13. Applying privacy groups to items on the Edit Details page

Not only can you restrict views of your personal information on the public page—such as birthdays, interests, phone numbers, and skills—you also can restrict views to other information:

Colleagues
You can configure which groups can see individual members of your My Colleagues group.

Content Targeting
You can limit who can see the targeted content you receive from your manager.

Links and Lists
Limit views of links or lists, particularly if they are not directly work-related.

Search Results
Restricting views of your information to certain groups may result in an interest or membership not being linked to you in the search results. For example, if your membership to a non-work club is set to Only Me, it will not turn up in a search involving your name or memberships.

Testing Restricted Views

After you restrict a view by group, you can test it and see how that group sees your My Site information:

1. On your My Site, on your My Profile page, click "As seen by" at the top of the page, and select the group view you want to test. The My Workgroup view is illustrated in Figure 21-14.

2. Return to either Everyone or Only Me to end the test and continue working on your My Site.

 This option works by using Privacy Settings to filter views. It does not affect Security Settings.

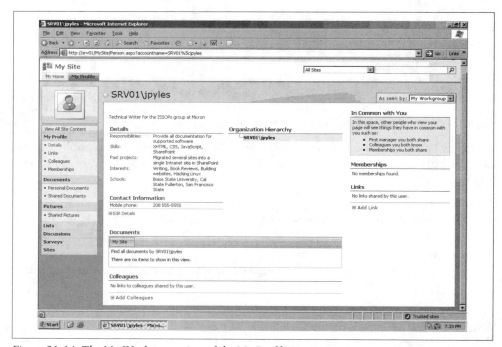

Figure 21-14. The My Workgroup view of the My Profile page

Managing My Colleagues in My Site

As previously mentioned in the section "Restricting Views of your My Site," the default members of your My Colleagues list are your direct reports, your manager, and your peers. You can add other members to this list and then restrict views of this list based on Privacy Groups. There are plenty of other options for managing your My Colleagues list.

Adding a Member to My Colleagues

1. On your My Site, click Colleagues in Quick Launch. Alternatively, if you are just getting started, under "Get Started with My Site," click "Identify the people you know."

2. On the My Colleagues list toolbar, click Add Colleagues.

3. On the Add Colleagues page, in the Identify Colleagues area, do one of the following:

   • To add the name of someone you know, type the user's name in the Type Names field, as in Figure 21-15, and click the "check names" icon.

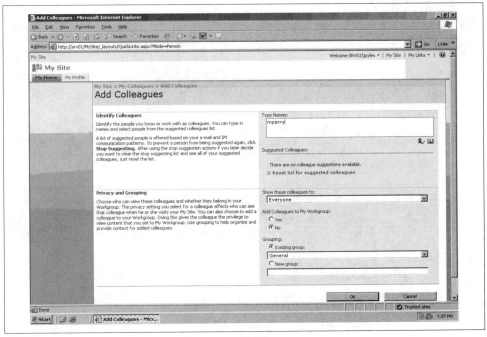

Figure 21-15. Adding a name in the Type Names field

   • To search for a user's name, click the Browse button next to Type Names. When the Select People dialog box appears, type some part of the user's name in the field, as in Figure 21-16. Click the magnifying glass to start the search. Look through the search results until you find the name of the desired user, and click Add.

4. After the names have been added, as in Figure 21-17, to filter who can see the new member's name in the My Colleagues list, type the name of one of the privacy groups in the "Show these colleagues to" field.

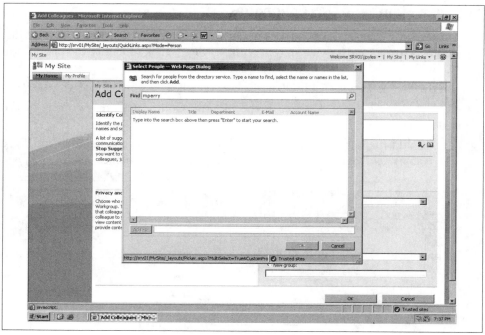

Figure 21-16. Adding a name by searching the system

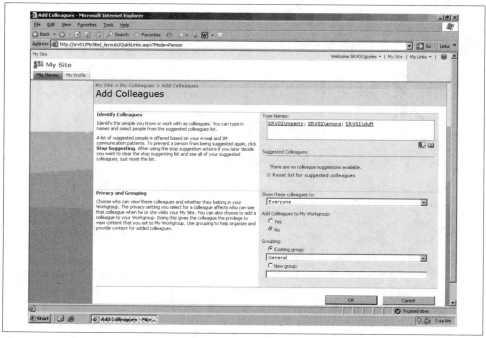

Figure 21-17. Validated names added to the Type Names field

See a list of Privacy Groups in the exercise "Restricting Views of Your My Site" earlier in this chapter.

5. If you want to add the new member to your My Workgroup list, click Yes under Add Colleagues to My Workgroup.

6. To add the new member to a group organized by project or role, under Grouping you can either click on "Existing group" and select a group from the list or choose "Create group" and type the name of the new group in the available field.

See the upcoming exercise "Organizing Colleagues Using Functional Groups" for more information.

Users must be present in the User Profile Store before performing this action. Normally, SharePoint 2007 and the earlier 2003 version automatically detects the nearest Domain Controller and imports the user's profile from Active Directory, an LDAP Server, or a Business Data Catalog. However, if SharePoint is unable to locate the appropriate source when you try to add users to your My Colleagues list, the action will fail.

Removing a Colleague from My Workgroup

1. On your My Site, click Colleagues in Quick Launch.

2. Select the colleague you want to remove from My Workgroup on the My Colleagues page.

3. In the My Colleagues toolbar, click Edit Colleagues.

4. Under Add Colleagues to My Work Group, click No to remove them.

In the exercise "Adding a Member to My Colleagues," you saw how to add a colleague to My Workgroup in step 5. If you want to add a colleague to My Workgroup sometime after he or she has been added to My Colleagues, in step 4 of the current exercise, click Yes instead of No.

Setting Alerts in My Colleagues

One of the handiest features in My Colleagues is the ability to keep track of specific events involving the people you work with. Here is a list of the alerts you can set up for anyone in your My Colleagues list:

Anniversaries
This is arguably the most important alert in the list. You can track any annual event using this alert. Set this alert and never again forget a birthday or anniversary.

Your manager or the site administrator can contribute to your Anniversaries alerts.

Blog Changes
Use this alert to track when a new post has been made to a colleague's blog.

Membership Changes
This alert lets you track when a person's membership in any SharePoint list changes. Examples are when a member either joins or leaves a workgroup or site.

New Documents
Receive an alert when a member adds a new document to SharePoint.

Out of Office
Use this option if you want to be notified when a colleague is out of the office. You will receive the alert whenever your colleague enables the Out of Office feature in Microsoft Exchange from their email client.

Profile Property Changes
This setting lets you receive an alert when some information in the member's My Profile changes, such as job title or direct report.

 If you are not in a privacy group on your colleague's My Site that is allowed to view some or all of these options, you will not receive alerts related to the hidden options.

1. On your My Site at the bottom of the Colleague Tracker Web Part, click "Change what gets tracked?"

2. Select one or more of the previously listed options to start receiving alerts.

 By default, you will receive any configured alerts on events that have occurred within the past 72 hours.

Organizing Colleagues Using Functional Groups

So far you've organized people as Colleagues and members of your Workgroup; however, you may find it useful to group colleagues by other criteria. For example, maybe you are working on a special project with just a few people in My Colleagues, or perhaps you are working with different combinations of people in My Colleagues on multiple projects. Grouping members by project would be more helpful then having to pick them out of your My Colleagues list every time you wanted to reference a particular team.

You can group people in any way you want, not just by project. Some examples are grouping by role, function, title, department, and so on. Here's the process of creating a group:

1. On your My Site, click Colleagues in Quick Launch.
2. Select the desired colleagues on your My Colleagues page.
3. Click Edit Colleagues on the toolbar.
4. Under Grouping, click on Select Group and either click the group you want or select New Group and type the name of the new group in the available field.

The selected colleagues will be added to the group. You can delete a group by reversing the process and removing all colleagues from a group. Once you empty the group, it will be automatically deleted.

 In your group list, you will see a group called Multiple Values if you have assigned colleagues to more than one group.

Deleting Members in My Colleagues

In any company with a fluid employee base, colleagues may be frequently added and deleted from your My Colleagues list. Here's how to perform the latter action:

1. On your My Site, click Colleagues in Quick Launch.
2. Select the desired colleague or colleagues on your My Colleagues page.
3. In the toolbar, click Delete.

Customizing My Site with Role-Based Templates

Out of the box, Microsoft Office SharePoint Server 2007 comes with the single, default template for all My Sites. Microsoft is developing several role-based My Sites templates so that, depending on your job function in your organization, you can customize your My Site to more effectively represent your role.

The specific construction of each role-based template is the result of the Microsoft Dynamics Customer Model, which identifies the various tasks of each job role in an organization. Thus, each template contains lists, libraries, and charts that are specific to the tasks that role performs.

As of this writing, there are two role-based templates available for download from Microsoft:

Controller-Financial Analyst

The general design of this template is based on this role's perceived tasks and goals, such as tracking corporate performance, budget projections, growth projections, and communicating with investors, management, and partners.

Sales Account Manager

The design of this role-based template is based on this role's perceived tasks and goals, such as tracking performance metrics, managing quarterly revenue, assessing customer satisfaction, and monitoring revenue augmentation.

Microsoft has announced that the following role-based templates will be released when available:

- Administrative Assistant
- Customer Service Manager
- HR Manager
- IT Manager
- Marketing Manager

CHAPTER 22

Applying Security to Your SharePoint Site

Microsoft Office SharePoint Server can be a great asset to your organization, but without the proper security considerations, it could cause problems within your organization or in extreme cases, become a devastating liability. This chapter covers the various mechanisms available for protecting your SharePoint site.

SharePoint security relies heavily on a breadth of topics outside the scope of this book, such as Windows Server 2003, Microsoft SQL Server, and network security, among others. Resources for additional information will be provided, however it is important to remember throughout the design, implementation, management, and administration of your SharePoint site that the security of your site does not exist in a vacuum. Numerous influences outside of SharePoint affect the security of your site collection and SharePoint.

As you go through the process of designing and implementing your SharePoint site, resist the "let's make it work and secure it later" mentality that's so common in many organizations. If you don't have time to properly implement security during implementation, you certainly won't have time to fix it all later. You will be in a position of either having to try to secure a system already in production or discovering that SharePoint has already been compromised from the outside or from internal users.

Topology Design Considerations

A secure implementation of Office SharePoint Server 2007 starts with a design conducive to security.

Environment-Specific Security Guidance

Microsoft's security guidance for Office SharePoint Server categorizes sites into four specific environments, and this chapter will use these as the basis for describing specific, security-oriented server deployments.

Internal team or department

This type of deployment generally consists of a small farm with two or three servers, and its users are restricted to one team or department in your organization. Microsoft states that this type of deployment is not hosted by the primary IT team in the organization; however, some organizations will have deployments of this type that are hosted by IT. This type of deployment has slightly lesser security requirements than other types of deployments because generally everyone who can access the site is authorized to access any of the information on the site. Many of the default security settings are intended for this type of environment, so securing this type of deployment usually requires less effort than the other types.

Internal IT-hosted

Microsoft refers to an internal IT-hosted deployment as one that provides services for multiple teams and departments within the organization. The security requirements for this type of deployment are typically more stringent because usually teams and departments are not authorized to access at least some information from other teams or departments due to the sensitive nature of the information.

External secure collaboration

An external secure collaboration environment is a server or farm accessible from the Internet to outside users. These users may be employees or contractors of your organization, or customers, resellers, suppliers, or business partners. These sites may also include some level of anonymous access in some circumstances—for instance, if your external secure site is an extension of your organization's public web site. In general, an external secure collaboration environment should not have any level of anonymous access enabled, to avoid disclosing sensitive information. However, in some environments, this may be desirable and an acceptable risk.

External anonymous access

An external anonymous access environment is one accessible from the Internet where outside users can access content on the site without authenticating. This is generally used as a public web site.

For details and checklists on specific security guidance for each environment, see the TechNet article "Choosing your security environment" at *http://technet2.microsoft.com/ Office/en-us/library/753fc3f6-e888-4bb6-ab67-288df065c2511033.mspx?mfr=true.*

Network Topology Design Considerations

Network topology design for your Office SharePoint Server farm is an important consideration. Usually this will be of most concern for sites accessible from the Internet, and occasionally for team or department sites.

Topology design for externally accessible sites

Sites that are accessible from the Internet have more stringent topology design requirements than internal sites. Frontend servers servicing requests from the Internet should be located in a Demilitarized Zone (DMZ). A DMZ is a dedicated network segment, usually located off of a third interface of your perimeter firewall, where servers providing services to Internet hosts are homed (Figure 22-1). The purpose of a DMZ is to protect these servers as much as possible, recognizing that these servers are at a higher risk of being compromised, and providing protection to the internal network in case a DMZ host is compromised.

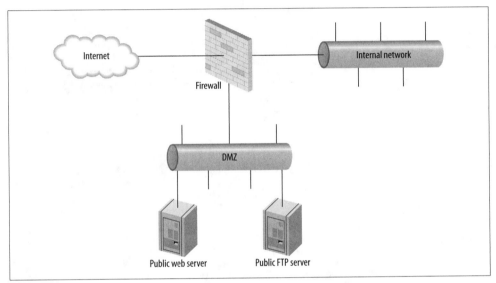

Figure 22-1. Typical DMZ layout

For Office SharePoint Server deployments, you may wish to implement a second DMZ to host the machines in your farm that are not directly accessible to outside users, such as your SQL Server and any application servers that potentially include search or indexing (Figure 22-2).

DMZ-less design. Every publicly accessible Office SharePoint Server environment should reside in a DMZ segment. However, in some small organizations with only a single server, like a Microsoft Small Business Server implementation, this may not be feasible for financial reasons. It may be desirable to make a site hosted on a multipurpose server on the internal network available externally. In these instances, if the risk and impact of an attacker compromising the entire internal network through this server is not a serious concern, the organization may choose to go without using a DMZ when considering the cost of a dedicated server deployment. This should be

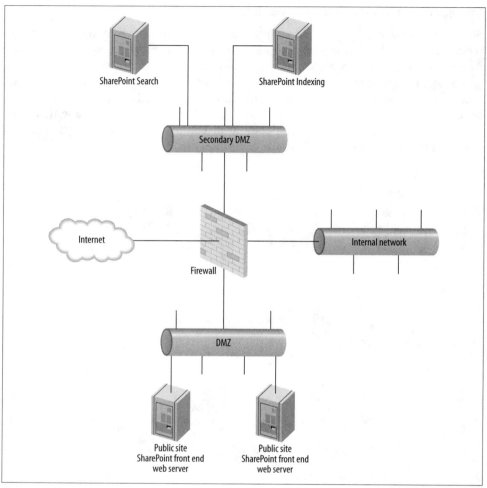

Figure 22-2. A two-DMZ SharePoint Server deployment

avoided in all but the smallest networks, and should never be used in a security-conscious environment.

Single or multiple DMZ design. Whether to implement one, two, or more DMZ segments depends on the security requirements of your environment. A single DMZ containing all servers in your Office SharePoint Server farm should be considered a minimum requirement. Segregating servers that are not directly accessible to users (such as your SQL Servers) and application servers (such as search and indexing) provides a greater level of protection for these servers, which need not be accessible directly to Internet users. If a web frontend server is compromised, additional DMZ segments may help limit the exposure to your database and application servers, and possibly prevent them from becoming compromised as well.

DMZ performance considerations. Putting a firewall between your servers will reduce the network performance between those servers. The level of performance impact depends mostly upon the performance capabilities of your firewall. For highly trafficked farms, a firewall has the potential to cause performance degradation for users of your site. This is not likely to affect most environments, but it is something to keep in mind when designing a high-traffic site. Always ensure the firewall is adequately sized to provide the required level of performance.

Topology design for team or department sites

For certain limited team or department sites, segregating the servers from other portions of the network may be desirable. Some departments in larger organizations that require a high degree of confidentiality and data protection have a dedicated network segment for that group and do not allow other parts of the network access to that segment. If the team or department using the site has its own dedicated segment, you should place the Office SharePoint Servers it will use in that protected segment as well.

Data Segregation Considerations

In designing your site and server topology, you will want to consider whether segregating data into multiple isolated servers or farms is the best approach for your deployment. This will mostly depend on the type of content and information your site will contain, and the users who will have any level of access to the site. Your security considerations for an external anonymous access site will differ considerably from an internal team or department site, for example.

The appropriate approach to determining your server design is to first perform at least a basic risk assessment. Outline what information will be stored on the site, its value, the likelihood of someone trying to gain unauthorized access, and the consequences of someone gaining unauthorized access. The results of this assessment will help you determine the appropriate level of effort and expense to put toward securing the assets on your site.

External secure collaboration and external anonymous access sites security considerations

If your SharePoint site will be accessible to users outside your organization—whether they are business partners, vendors, suppliers, customers, or anonymous users—you need to be extremely vigilant in designing and implementing security properly. If you have sensitive content that only internal users are authorized to access on the site, you should strongly consider deploying an internal server or farm with a separate site accessible only to internal users. This negates the potential of disclosing that information to outside users through human error in configuring security, or through newly discovered security vulnerabilities that may arise.

Internal team or department or IT-hosted site security considerations

Internal sites generally do not pose the same level of security risk as externally accessible sites. However, that's not to say they don't require consideration of potential security risks during site design. The same primary security risks also apply to internal sites—human error in security configuration, and the risk of newly discovered security vulnerabilities that may arise in the future. Generally, the latter is of less concern on an internal site, but the former is just as much of a potential issue, if not more so. If your site will contain highly sensitive information to which only some internal users require access, you should consider deploying a dedicated server or farm and a dedicated site for that sensitive information.

Secure Topology Design Checklists

Microsoft has secure topology design checklists available on TechNet, and you should follow these as closely as possible:

> *http://technet2.microsoft.com/Office/en-us/library/007ecb03-5808-495a-bb72-4f0641eaf8f21033.mspx?mfr=true*

They provide a condensed list of the topology design considerations covered at length in this chapter, as well as in some of the other referenced materials. Some of these considerations will not be feasible in all environments. For example, some require a farm with multiple servers, which probably will not be feasible in most small environments. Try to follow these checklists to the letter as much as possible, but understand that in certain environments the cost of some of these items will be prohibitive.

Server Hardening

Prior to installing Office SharePoint Server 2007 on any servers, you should first harden the servers per Microsoft's security hardening recommendations.

 When applying security to a server, especially if you aren't experienced with server hardening, there is a chance you will break something in the process. After applying each change, test to ensure the change functions as intended and that you haven't broken anything. If you continue securing other things and determine later that something is not functioning properly, it will be much more difficult to determine which step in the process caused the issue.

Windows Server Hardening

After installing Windows Server 2003, you should harden your Windows Server installation prior to installing any services or applications. Microsoft has made available the Windows Server 2003 Security Guide, a freely available 250-page document that provides detailed guidance on hardening your Windows Server 2003 systems. Some of the high points of this guide will be covered, but it will be left to you to download the document and review information specific to your deployment:

http://www.microsoft.com/downloads/details.aspx?familyid=8A2643C1-0685-4D89-B655-521EA6C7B4DB&displaylang=en

Use only NTFS filesystems

You should never use anything but NTFS on your server filesystems. There is no good reason to use FAT or FAT32 file systems on servers, and their use makes it difficult—and in some circumstances impossible—to maintain a secure server.

Update your server

Install all available service packs, roll ups, hot fixes, and other available updates from Microsoft Update. This ensures your system is protected from known vulnerabilities.

After addressing these two areas, the Security Configuration Wizard, as outlined in the next section, will assist you in numerous areas of the Windows Server 2003 Security Guide that are not covered in detail within this chapter.

Security Configuration Wizard

The Security Configuration Wizard (SCW) part of Windows Server 2003 can be installed by going to Add or Remove Programs in Control Panel and clicking Add/Remove Windows Components. You will see it available for installation in that list. After installation, you will find a link to the SCW help file on your desktop, and you can run the SCW from Administrative Tools.

The Security Configuration Wizard helps you reduce the attack surface of your server. The attack surface of a system can be defined as the number of potential ways for an attacker to compromise a server. By reducing the number of running services and applications, limiting network traffic to and from the server to the minimum required ports and protocols, and tightening the configuration of required applications and services, you limit your attack surface and reduce the likelihood of a successful compromise. This process can be done manually, but the Security Configuration Wizard will speed this process considerably.

The SCW includes numerous server role definitions to assist in applying the appropriate level of security to your server based upon its functions. Windows SharePoint Services 2.0 and SharePoint Portal Server are included, but at the time of this writing an extension for Office SharePoint Server 2007 was not yet available. By the time you read this, an update to SCW should be available to assist you in securing your Office SharePoint Server 2007 installation.

For more information on the SCW, refer to Microsoft's Security Configuration Wizard site:

http://www.microsoft.com/windowsserver2003/technologies/security/configwiz/default.mspx

Additional references

Windows Server 2003 Security Guide
   http://www.microsoft.com/technet/security/prodtech/windowsserver2003/w2003hg/sgch00.mspx

The Center for Internet Security Windows Server 2003 Benchmark
   http://cisecurity.org/bench_windows.html

Internet Information Services Hardening

Internet Information Services (IIS) 6.0 has come a long way, security-wise, from its predecessors. First, it is no longer installed in a default Windows Server installation. Windows 2000 Server installed IIS 5.0 by default, which helped in the proliferation of the Code Red and Nimda worms of 2001. The default configuration in IIS 6.0 is very restrictive, in contrast to IIS 5.0's default of enabling literally everything. Lastly, Microsoft devoted significant focus and resources to security throughout the development of IIS 6.0, in an effort to prevent it from becoming the security nightmare that IIS 5.0 became. This effort has proven to be quite successful; while IIS 5.0 had a long list of serious security vulnerabilities over the years, IIS 6.0 has a pretty solid track record to date.

If you are interested in a more in-depth review of the security changes in IIS 6.0, see this article from *SecurityFocus* on IIS 6.0 security:

http://www.securityfocus.com/infocus/1765

Since IIS 6.0 was developed with a significant focus on security and comes secure by default, you can move on to the next section, right? Not so fast! There are still a few quick, easy things you can do to ensure your IIS environment is as secure as possible.

Limit installed services

Do not install any subcomponents of IIS that are not required for your site to function. Every installed subcomponent is a potential attack vector for an intruder. The less you have installed, the less you need to secure and the fewer possibilities for your system to be compromised. Table 22-1 lists all the available IIS subcomponents and whether they are required for Office SharePoint Server 2007. Table 22-2 lists the subcomponents of the World Wide Web Service under IIS.

Table 22-1. IIS subcomponents

Component	Required?
Background Intelligent Transfer Service (BITS) Server Extensions	No
Common Files	Yes
File Transfer Protocol (FTP) Service	No
FrontPage 2002 Server Extensions	No
Internet Information Services Manager	Yes
Internet Printing	No
NNTP Service	No
SMTP Service	If site is mail-enabled, yes; otherwise, no
World Wide Web Service	Yes

Table 22-2. World Wide Web Service under IIS subcomponents

Component	Required?
Active Server Pages	Yes
Internet Data Connector	No
Remote Administration (HTML)	No
Remote Desktop Web Connection	No
Server Side Includes	No
WebDAV Publishing	No
World Wide Web Service	Yes

Inetpub directory placement

If possible, you should put your *inetpub* directory as well as your Office SharePoint Server installation on a dedicated partition rather than the system partition (generally the *C:* drive). IIS 5.0 suffered from numerous directory traversal vulnerabilities, as have many web applications. A directory traversal vulnerability allows a user to access files outside the intended web accessible folder (*inetpub*) by allowing them access to the entire partition where this folder is located. As a high-profile example, a directory traversal vulnerability in IIS 5.0 enabled the Nimda worm to infect IIS servers. A patch to fix this vulnerability was available prior to this worm breaking out and is the appropriate means of mitigating such a risk. However, locating the *inetpub* folder on a separate partition would have prevented this worm from infecting the server, because it required access to *cmd.exe* and *tftp.exe* on the system partition.

There are protections in IIS 6.0 and Windows Server 2003 to avoid directory traversal vulnerabilities and to limit the damage if one were discovered, but this is still a good precaution.

Limit anonymous access

If you need to permit anonymous access to your site, you should ensure the IUSR_*machinename* account does not have write access anywhere on your server's filesystem.

Additional references

IIS 6.0 Security Best Practices
http://technet2.microsoft.com/WindowsServer/en/Library/ACE052A0-A713-423E-8E8C-4BF198F597B81033.mspx

Security Guidance Center for IIS
http://www.microsoft.com/technet/security/prodtech/IIS.mspx

Security in IIS 6.0
http://technet2.microsoft.com/WindowsServer/en/Library/354F4539-982A-418C-BFE7-4D5155B83F4A1033.mspx

SQL Server Hardening

Hardening your SQL Server installation is another important aspect of Office Share-Point Server security, since all of your site content will be stored in your SQL database. The process of securing SQL Server is well documented by Microsoft and would require lengthy explanation. Rather than duplicating this available content, refer to the *Securing Your Database Server* chapter from MSDN:

http://msdn2.microsoft.com/en-us/library/aa302434.aspx

Additional SQL Server security references

SQL Server 2005 Security
http://www.microsoft.com/sql/technologies/security/default.mspx

10 Steps to Help Secure SQL Server 2000
https://www.microsoft.com/sql/prodinfo/previousversions/securingsqlserver.mspx

SQL Server 2000 Security Features and Best Practices
https://www.microsoft.com/technet/prodtechnol/sql/2000/maintain/sp3sec00.mspx

The Center for Internet Security SQL Server Benchmark
http://cisecurity.org/bench_sqlserver.html

SharePoint Authentication

Office SharePoint Server 2007 provides new authentication capabilities not found in past versions of SharePoint Portal Server. Previous SharePoint versions could authenticate only with Windows user accounts, either locally on the server or in an Active Directory domain. Although this is ideal for organizations that have already deployed

Active Directory and wish to use SharePoint as an intranet solution, it limited Share-Point's ability to be used as an extranet or public web site solution because organizations generally don't want to add accounts to their Active Directory for outside users. Office SharePoint Server 2007 offers a new authentication infrastructure that works inside of ASP.NET. This allows for a wide range of new authentication options.

The out-of-the-box supported authentication capabilities of Office SharePoint Server are LDAP, Microsoft SQL Server, and Active Directory (single domain only). Additional capabilities are available through ASP.NET authentication providers. For further information on ASP.NET authentication providers, refer to the following link:

http://msdn2.microsoft.com/en-us/library/eeyk640h.aspx

Windows Authentication Provider

The Windows authentication provider supports two methods of authenticating users, NTLM and Kerberos.

NT LAN Manager (NTLM)

The default method of Windows authentication in Office SharePoint Server 2007 is NT LAN Manager (NTLM). It offers the best compatibility, as it is compatible with pre-Windows 2000 versions of Windows and requires less configuration. However, it is not the recommended method of authentication because of the benefits of Kerberos.

Kerberos

Kerberos is the preferred method of Windows authentication for sites running all Windows 2000 and newer clients and servers. Kerberos is faster and more secure than NTLM, but requires some planning and configuration to utilize. For more information on implementing Kerberos as your Windows authentication provider, refer to the following site:

http://www.microsoft.com/windowsserver2003/technologies/security/kerberos/ default.mspx

Forms Authentication Provider

The forms authentication provider in Office SharePoint Server 2007 enables you to authenticate users to four authentication providers: Microsoft SQL Server, an LDAP server, Active Directory, and Web Single Sign On (SSO) with Active Directory Federation Services. Additional providers can be used, including other database servers such as Oracle, MySQL, and PostgreSQL, as well as files such as Microsoft Access and flat-text or XML files.

SQL Server authentication

SQL Server authentication is commonly used for users outside your organization who do not have accounts in your Active Directory domain. Using this authentication provider enables you to create accounts for outside users without giving them any rights to your Active Directory domain.

LDAP server authentication

The LDAP authentication provider enables you to authenticate users off of an LDAP server. You may use this for external users, or for internal users if your primary directory service is not Active Directory. This also can be used to authenticate your SharePoint users off of a directory hosted by a non-Windows server, including Unix, BSD, Linux, and any other operating system capable of running an LDAP server.

Active Directory

You may wish to utilize forms authentication even when Active Directory is your authentication provider. The most common use of Active Directory forms-based authentication is where internal users need access to a site from outside the organization's network. It may also be used in combination with other providers to provide Active Directory authentication for your internal users, and as another means of authentication for external users.

Web SSO with ADFS

Active Directory Federation Services (ADFS) is a new feature in Windows Server 2003 R2 that enables organizations to securely share a user's identity information across the boundaries of your organization's network. ADFS allows an organization to utilize its Active Directory infrastructure to provide controlled access to resources, without the security risk and operational challenges of configuring and maintaining trust between the separate Active Directory forests and separate networks.

ADFS can be a secure, convenient solution to allowing employees of business partners to authenticate to your network using their Active Directory credentials on their employer's network. Tables 22-3 and 22-4 list some resources.

Table 22-3. Active Directory Federation Services (ADFS) resources

Resource title	Resource link
Overview of Active Directory Federation Services (ADFS) in Windows Server 2003 R2	http://www.microsoft.com/WindowsServer2003/R2/ Identity_Management/ADFSwhitepaper.mspx
Windows Server TechCenter–Active Directory Federation Services	http://technet2.microsoft.com/WindowsServer/en/library/ 050392bc-c8f5-48b3-b30e-bf310399ff5d1033. mspx?mfr=true

Table 22-4. Resources with detailed instructions and information related to forms authentication

Resource title	Resource link
Forms Authentication Samples	http://technet2.microsoft.com/Office/en-us/library/ 23b837d1-15d9-4621-aa0b-9ce3f1c7153e1033. mspx?mfr=true
Forms Based Authentication in Office SharePoint Server	http://blogs.msdn.com/harsh/archive/2007/01/10/forms-based-authentication-in-moss.aspx#1464554
Plan authentication settings for web applications in Office SharePoint Server	http://technet2.microsoft.com/Office/en-us/library/d3e0e0fc-77b6-4109-87d6-53ad088db01d1033.mspx?mfr=true
SharePointSecurity.com—The Definitive Guide to MOSS Pluggable Authentication Providers	http://www.sharepointsecurity.com/content-99.html

Multiple Authentication Providers

It is possible to use multiple authentication providers on a single SharePoint site. There are numerous steps involved in this process, documented in detail in this post on the official blog of the Microsoft SharePoint Product Group:

http://blogs.msdn.com/sharepoint/archive/2006/08/16/702010.aspx

Use of Client Certificates

Client certificates can be used in combination with other authentication providers to provide a higher level of security for your site. The use of client certificates requires an individual certificate for every user, which can easily become an implementation headache on sites with more than a few users. You can think of requiring client certificates as a type of two-factor authentication: the user must have her certificate as well as her username and password to access the site.

For information on enabling the use of client certificates with your SharePoint sites, see the following portion of the IIS 6.0 documentation on use of client certificates:

http://www.microsoft.com/technet/prodtechnol/WindowsServer2003/Library/IIS/ 096519f4-3079-4571-9d28-8e5d286c5ab9.mspx?mfr=true

Single Sign On

Single Sign On (SSO) functionality in Windows Server enables you to authenticate users through your SharePoint site to content or data on other servers, without the user having to enter his credentials for each resource that is accessed. If your users will be accessing data from backend servers such as Enterprise Resource Planning (ERP) or Customer Relationship Management (CRM), you should implement SSO so they only have to authenticate once. Rather than duplicate information already available, see Microsoft TechNet's thorough, detailed guide to Configuring Single Sign On:

> *http://technet2.microsoft.com/Office/en-us/library/841080ca-3e3b-4dbc-a081-43c29c76b3551033.mspx?mfr=true*

Utilizing Encryption

Encryption is another important piece of your Office SharePoint Server security strategy that comes into consideration in three primary areas: site encryption, intra-server encryption, and storage encryption.

Site SSL Encryption

By default, Office SharePoint Server 2007 does not employ SSL encryption on its sites. Proper use of SSL on your SharePoint sites offers three benefits: confidentiality, integrity, and authentication:

Confidentiality
> You are likely aware of the fact that employing SSL on a site ensures that if the network traffic is intercepted in transit, it is not legible or open to decryption by an unauthorized party. This is important if you maintain sensitive data on your SharePoint site, especially if it is accessible over the Internet.

> There are two additional important benefits of using SSL that are less commonly known.

Integrity
> When using SSL, you and the server are both assured that the network traffic received was not modified in transit. Without the use of SSL, it is possible for traffic to be modified in transit, and there is no way for either party to detect the modification.

Authentication
> Authentication, in this sense of the word, does not refer to a username and password. In the case of SSL, authentication means you are assured of the identity of the remote server. The SSL certificate in use on the server identifies the name of the server to which you are connecting. This is important because an attacker could redirect your users to another server and intercept the user's authentication credentials, among other possibilities.

Proper use of SSL encryption

Employing SSL encryption on your site requires the use of an SSL certificate. An SSL certificate is generated by a Certificate Authority (CA). Web browsers come preinstalled with a list of trusted CAs, which is a list of companies known and trusted to follow specific stringent guidelines in issuing certificates. Two of the well-known CAs are VeriSign and Thawte, though there are more than 40 trusted organizations built into current versions of Mozilla Firefox and Internet Explorer. Large organizations commonly have an internal CA that is trusted by the web browsers on its internal network.

You can also generate your own SSL certificate. However, certificates that are not generated by a trusted CA will cause a certificate warning in the user's browser. Aside from the user confusion and support calls this is likely to generate, it also provides very little protection. It is possible to perform a man-in-the-middle attack on SSL connections, rendering the previously mentioned protections useless, and tools such as sslmitm are widely available to assist in accomplishing this. If someone is attempting a man-in-the-middle attack on one of your users, it will generate a certificate warning because the attacker will be using a self-generated certificate. If your users are accustomed to seeing certificate warnings when using your site, they will dismiss it as normal and your SSL will be worthless.

Always use a certificate that will not generate warnings in any of your users' browsers, and educate your users that if they ever see a certificate warning, they should stop what they are doing and call for help immediately. If users outside your organization will access the site, or you do not have a trusted internal CA, you need to purchase a certificate from a trusted CA. SSL certificates are not nearly as costly as they used to be, but some CAs still charge exorbitant prices. Make sure you compare prices between a few trusted CAs before purchasing. If your site is accessible only to internal users and you have an internal trusted CA, you can generate your SSL certificate from that CA.

Enabling SSL encryption

SSL encryption can be enabled on your site in the Internet Information Services Manager under Administrative Tools. First, you must prepare the certificate request from which a Certificate Authority will generate your certificate.

Preparing your certificate request. Under Web Sites, right-click on the site you wish to protect, and then click Properties. Click the Directory Security tab. Under "Secure communications," click the "Server Certificate" button. This will bring up the Web Server Certificate Wizard. At the Welcome screen, click Next.

At the next screen, select "Create a new certificate" (Figure 22-3) and click Next.

At the "Delayed or Immediate Request" screen, select "Prepare the request now, but send it later" (Figure 22-4) and click Next.

"Name and Security Settings" is the next screen (Figure 22-5). Fill in a name for the certificate (this is cosmetic only; you can leave it at the default), choose a bit length (the default of 1024 is fine), and click Next.

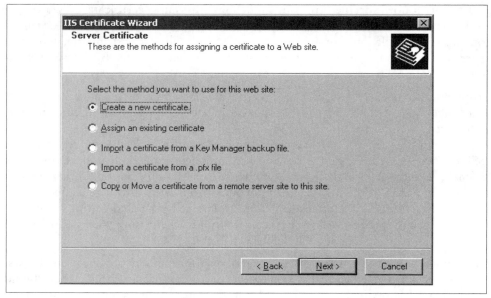

Figure 22-3. Create a new certificate

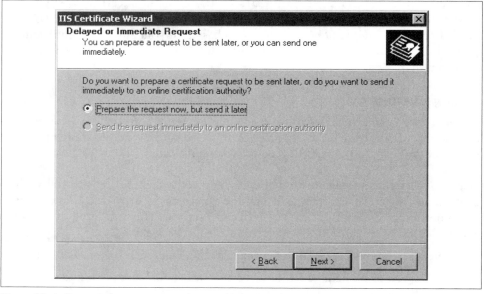

Figure 22-4. Prepare the request now, but send it later

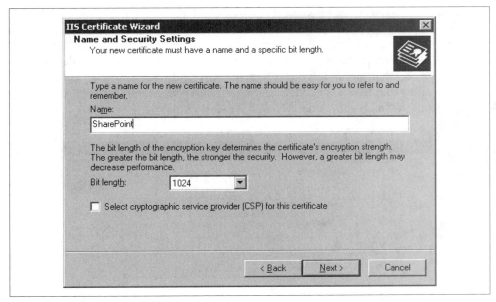

Figure 22-5. Name and Security Settings

At the Organization Information screen, fill in the name of your organization and your organizational unit (Figure 22-6).

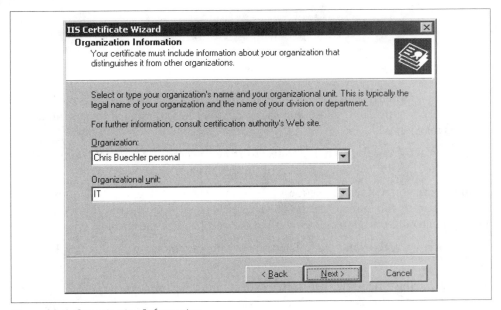

Figure 22-6. Organization Information

The Common Name screen is next (Figure 22-7). This is very important, because if you enter the wrong common name here, the certificate will always generate security warnings in your users' browsers. Enter the server name that your users use to connect to your server. If that's just the server's NetBIOS name (for example, SHARE-POINT), enter that here. If your users use the Fully Qualified Domain Name (FQDN), enter that here instead (for example, *sharepoint.example.com*). After filling in the Common Name appropriately, click Next.

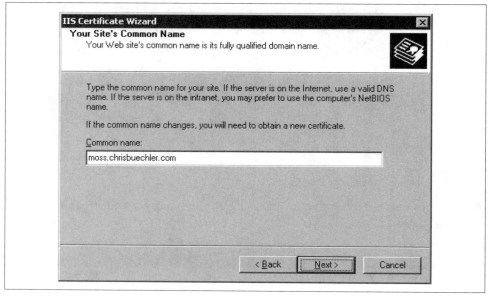

Figure 22-7. Common Name

At the Geographical Information screen, fill in your country, state/province, and city/locality (Figure 22-8). Note that these must be the full, official names; no abbreviations may be used.

Next, you will enter the filename to use to store the certificate request (Figure 22-9). Enter a path of your choosing, or accept the default and click Next.

At this point, you will see the Request File Summary screen (Figure 22-10). It will show the information you entered on the previous screens so you can confirm that it has all been entered correctly. After clicking Next, the certificate request will be created.

You have now successfully completed the certificate request wizard. Click Finish to exit it.

You now having a pending certificate request in the web site you selected. If there is a problem with the certificate request you created, you can delete the pending request by clicking the Server Certificate button on the Directory Security tab of the site's properties page, the same way you initiated the certificate request wizard.

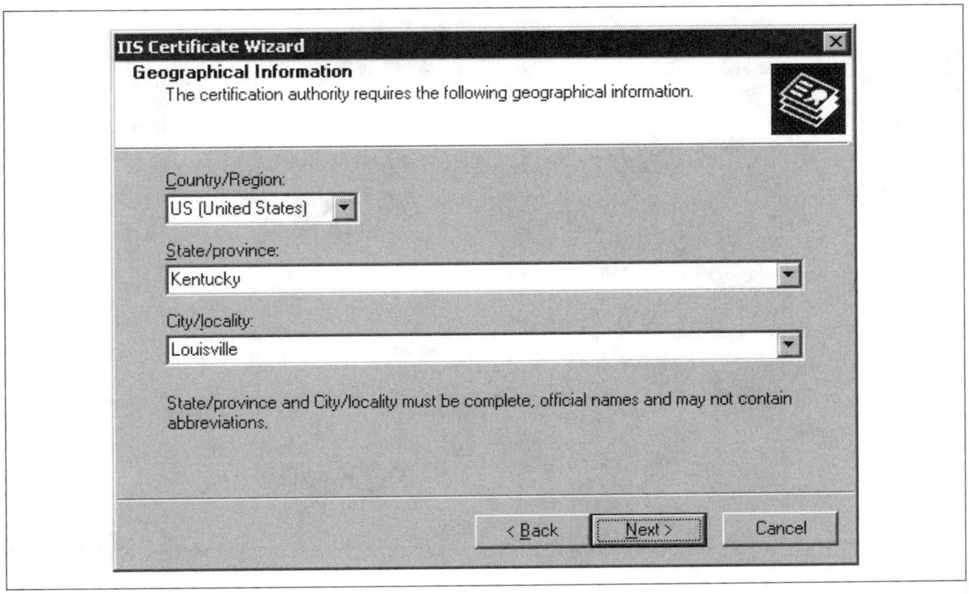

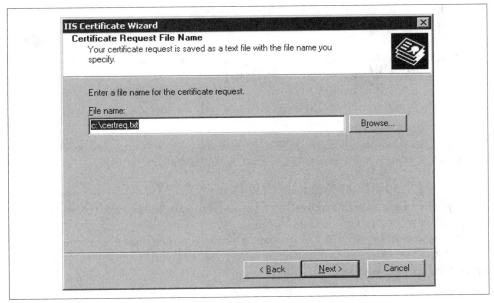

Figure 22-8. Geographical Information

Figure 22-9. Certificate Request File Name

After clicking Next on the initial page of the wizard, you will see the option of deleting the pending request.

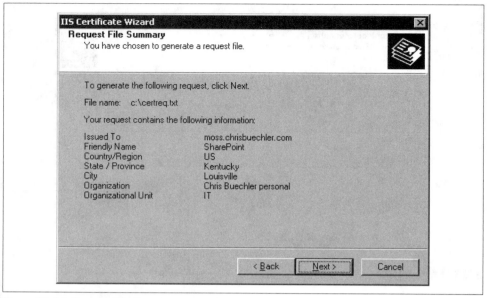

Figure 22-10. Request File Summary

Leave the web site properties screen up, as you will be coming back to it as soon as you have your certificate ready for installation.

Obtaining the SSL certificate. Now that you have the certificate request ready, you can obtain the SSL certificate. If you are going to purchase your certificate, I recommend first getting a test certificate from a trusted CA. Numerous CAs provide free test/trial certificates. If you search the Internet for "test SSL certificate," you will find numerous options.

You can also generate your own SSL certificate (for testing purposes only) with the Certificate Creation Tool available from Microsoft:

> *http://msdn2.microsoft.com/en-us/library/bfsktky3(VS.80).aspx*

Once you have your certificate ready for installation, continue to the next section.

Processing the certificate request. Now that you have your certificate, it is time to install it. Click the Server Certificate button again on the Directory Security tab of the properties page of your web site.

Click Next on the Welcome page of the wizard.

Select "Process the pending request and install the certificate" and click Next (Figure 22-11).

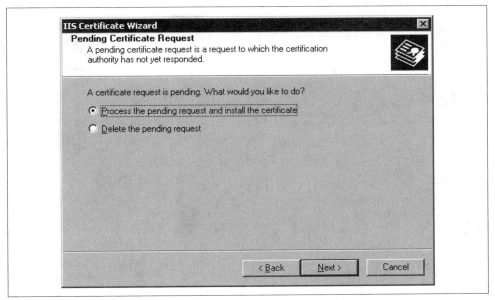

Figure 22-11. Pending Certificate Request

At the next screen, browse to or enter the path and filename of the certificate file you generated or received from the CA, and then click Next (Figure 22-12).

On the SSL Port screen, enter the port this web site should use. In most cases, you will want to accept the default of 443 (Figure 22-13).

The certificate summary screen will now be displayed, summarizing the details of the certificate about to be installed (Figure 22-14). Click Next.

You have now successfully installed the server certificate. Click Finish. Leave the Properties screen open with the Directory Security tab up.

You will now be able to access your site using SSL. By default, SSL is not required, and so you should configure your site to make the use of SSL mandatory. To do so, click the Edit button under "Secure communications" on the Directory Security tab. Check the top checkbox, "Require secure channel (SSL)," and click OK to force users to use SSL when accessing the site.

Intra-Server IPsec Encryption

IPsec is a suite of encryption protocols enabling secure access between hosts and networks. It is commonly used for Internet-based Virtual Private Network (VPN) connections, but it is equally capable of protecting network traffic between two hosts. In

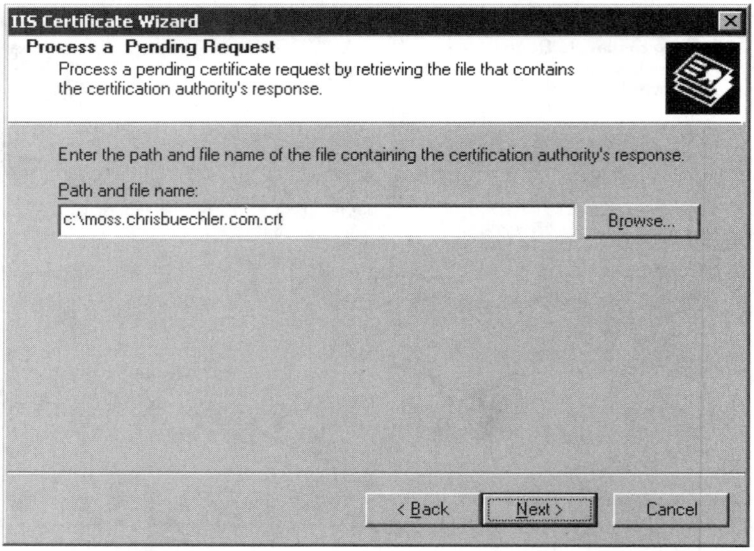

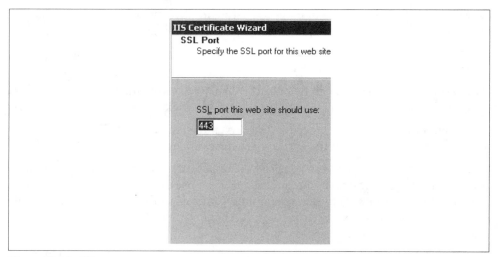

Figure 22-12. Path and filename

Figure 22-13. SSL port

environments where protecting intra-server communication is of concern, you will want to consider implementing IPsec between the servers in your farm. This somewhat involved process is documented in detail by Microsoft, so rather than duplicating this content, refer to the following URLs:

http://www.microsoft.com/technet/community/columns/secmgmt/sm121504.mspx
http://www.microsoft.com/technet/network/ipsec/default.mspx

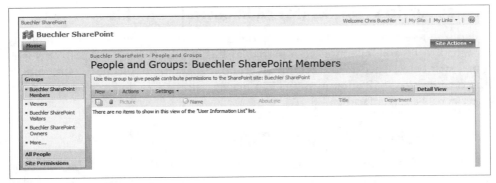

Figure 22-14. Certificate summary

Disk Encryption

If your servers are storing highly sensitive information, or are located in an environment lacking physical security, you may wish to implement disk encryption. This ensures that if someone physically takes your servers or disks, they cannot access the information they contain.

There are several commercial options for disk encryption, and Microsoft has built encryption functionality into Windows Server 2003 with the Encrypting File System (EFS) functionality. Implementing EFS is a lengthy process, and it is described in detail in the following TechNet article:

http://www.microsoft.com/technet/prodtechnol/winxppro/deploy/cryptfs.mspx

Levels of Administrative Rights

There are three levels of administrative rights in Office SharePoint Server 2007: farm/server, Shared Services Provider (SSP), and site. This granular approach is new to this version of the software. Depending on the segregation of administration responsibilities in your environment, you may wish to configure each of these independently.

Farm/Server Administrative Rights

Microsoft refers to this level of administrative rights as "tier 1." This level is usually assigned to your organization's IT system administrators. Those with this level of access rights perform tasks such as managing farm-wide settings and farm topology, creating site collections and new web sites, among other tasks.

Users and groups are assigned this level of access by being a member of the local Administrators group on the farm servers.

Shared Services Provider (SSP) Administrative Rights

Microsoft refers to SSP administrative rights as "tier 2." This level is commonly assigned to IT administrators in a particular business unit using the SSP, or sometimes will be assigned to the central IT group, depending upon the IT structure of the organization. SSP administrators can manage all the functionality of shared services across a server farm.

Site Collection Administrative Rights

Microsoft refers to this level of rights as "tier 3." Users defined as "site collection administrators" have full control over all web sites in the site collection. This level of access is not always restricted to IT staff. Technically savvy staff in other areas of the organization who will hold responsibilities for managing the site are commonly granted site collection administrative rights.

To configure Site collection administrators, click Site Actions anywhere on your site, then Site Settings. Under Users and Permissions, click "Site collection administrators." Users or groups can be added or removed on this page.

SharePoint Site Permissions and Groups

Before delving into details regarding how to assign permissions to your site and the objects within it, let's review the permissions available, as well as Office SharePoint Server's groups functionality.

When assigning permissions, it is important to always use groups. You should never assign any rights to an individual user, even when those rights are unique to that person's position. Using groups to assign rights—even if initially those groups contain only a single user—is beneficial because it enables you to easily change the person's level of access if he changes job functions. It also makes it easy to assign those same rights to another person if a similar position is added in the future, and makes it easier to transfer those rights to another user in the case of turnover.

Using groups may require a little more effort and planning up front in some circumstances, but it will almost always save you time and trouble down the road. It also makes it easier to maintain a secure environment.

SharePoint Site Permission Levels

There are eight levels of permissions available for users and groups in Office Share-Point Server:

- Full control
- Design

- Contribute
- Manage hierarchy
- Read
- Restricted read
- View only
- Limited access

These permissions are explained in the following sections. If you are familiar with NTFS filesystem permissions, the available SharePoint permissions are similar, but much more capable.

Full control

Full control means exactly what it implies: users with this level of permission can do everything granted by the other permission levels, as well as modify permissions.

Design

The design permission enables users to change the layout of a site, either via a web browser and through Office SharePoint Designer 2007.

Contribute

The contribute permission allows users to add and change an item or items, depending on the scope of the permission.

Manage hierarchy

The manage hierarchy permission gives users the ability to create sites, edit pages, and list items and documents.

Read

This permission enables users to read the site, page, or other item or items where this permission is granted. This also allows downloading of files available on the site, so they can be used and/or viewed in their native applications.

Restricted read

Restricted read allows users to view pages and documents, but not the rights assigned to those documents. It does not provide the ability to read any previous revisions to those items. This can be useful for things like organization-wide policies and procedures, where you want most users to be able to access only the current accepted version of these items.

View only

View only and read permissions may seem like the same thing, but there is one main difference between the two. If a user has only view-only rights to a file, and a server-side viewer for the file (such as Excel Services) is enabled, the user can only view the file using the server-side viewer and cannot work with the file in its native application. This functionality is not limited to Excel; Word, PowerPoint, and several other file types have server-side viewers.

Limited access

Limited access permissions are automatically assigned by Office SharePoint Server when you grant a user or group access to an object on your site that is contained in a higher-level object to which the user or group does not have access. This permission level cannot be directly assigned to a user or group.

Creating and Editing Permission Levels of Groups

If none of the built-in permission levels accommodate the rights you need to assign, you can create your own permission levels. These can be modified versions of an existing permission level, or they can be created from scratch.

Except for the full control and limited access permission levels, you can edit all of the other permission levels if the default configuration does not suit the security requirements for your environment. The following document, "Set permissions for publishing," from Microsoft Office Online, describes the specifics of permission levels, and the process of creating, editing, and deleting permission levels in step-by-step detail:

> *http://office.microsoft.com/en-us/sharepointserver/HA101577861033.aspx*

SharePoint Groups

There are four built-in groups in Office SharePoint Server sites: Members, Owners, Visitors, and Viewers. Their associated rights are shown in Table 22-5.

Table 22-5. Default SharePoint groups and their access levels

Group	Default access level
Members	Contribute
Owners	Full control
Visitors	Read
Viewers	View only

If these do not suit the requirements of your environment, you can modify the default permissions of these groups or create new groups to fit your needs. This is done from the Site Settings page, under the Site Actions menu. On the Site Settings page, click "People and Groups."

Object Security Functionality

There are six securable object types within SharePoint where you can assign rights to users and/or groups: sites, lists, libraries, folders, documents, and items. The following describes how rights can be assigned at each of these levels to achieve your desired level of security and control over the content of your site.

Site-Level Permissions

Site-level permissions provide the basis for access to every other object on your site. They determine who can access the front page of your site and what level of access they have to the site. By default, all content on your site inherits permissions from the site level.

Configuring site level permissions

To configure site level permissions, on the front page of your site, click Site Actions, and then Site Settings.

Under "Users and Permissions," you will see three items: "People and Groups," "Site collection administrators," and "Advanced permissions" (Figure 22-15).

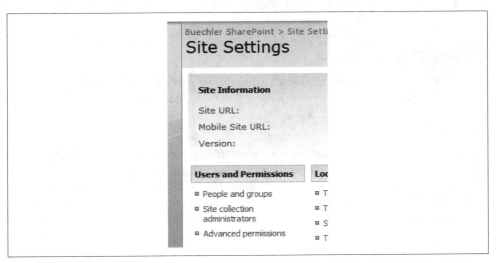

Figure 22-15. Users and Permissions

People and Groups. After clicking "People and Groups," you will see the Quick Launch list under Groups on the lefthand side of the page (Figure 22-16). The default items in this list are as follows, where *Sitename* is the name of your SharePoint site. These are the default built-in SharePoint groups, as discussed earlier in this chapter:

- *Sitename* Members
- Viewers
- *Sitename* Visitors
- *Sitename* Owners
- More…

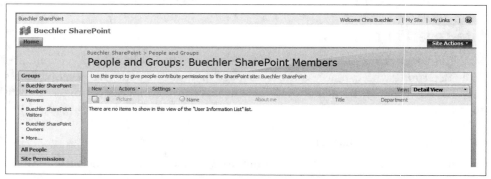

Figure 22-16. Groups screen

You can configure which items will appear in this Quick Launch list from any page under "People and Groups" by clicking Settings, and then Edit Quick Launch Groups (Figure 22-17).

At this screen you can add or remove groups from the Quick Launch list on the "People and Groups" page (Figure 22-18).

If you remove a group from the Quick Launch list, you can still access it through the "More…" link, which is always available on the Quick Launch list.

Advanced Permissions

Under "Users and Permissions" on the Site Settings page, you will see the Advanced Permissions link. This takes you to a page that lists in detail the users and groups that have been granted permissions on this site, along with the level of access they have been granted. You can add and remove users and groups from the site from this screen, as well as modify their levels of access rights.

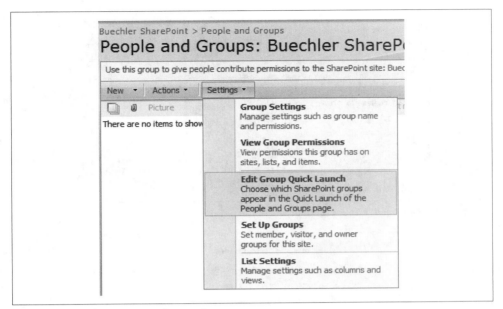

Figure 22-17. Edit Group Quick Launch

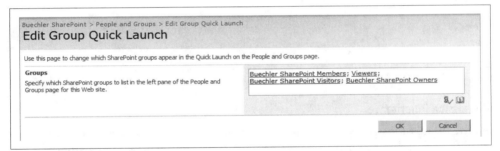

Figure 22-18. Quick Launch Groups edit screen

Library-Level Permissions

To view or edit the permissions of a library, while in the library click Settings, and then Document Library Settings (Figure 22-19).

At the next screen, under "Permissions and Management," click "Permissions for this library" (Figure 22-20).

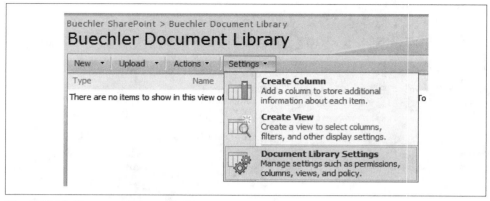

Figure 22-19. Document Library Settings

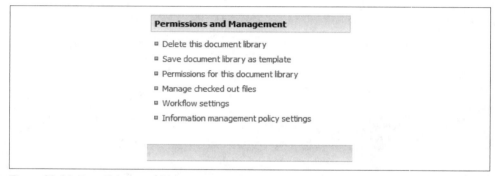

Figure 22-20. Permissions and Management

Permission inheritance

At the permissions page, unless the permissions of this library have been previously modified, you will see a message at the top explaining where the existing permissions are coming from: "This library inherits permissions from its parent Web site. To manage permissions directly, click Edit Permissions from the Actions menu."

For a library that requires differing permissions from its parent web site, click Actions, and then Edit Permissions. You can also manage the permissions of the parent object on the Actions menu.

When you click Edit Permissions on a library that is inheriting permissions from its parent site, you will receive a pop-up warning that you are about to create unique permissions for this library and that changes to the parent site's permissions will no longer affect this library. Click OK to continue.

Next, you will be looking at the same permissions list as before, except the list now can be edited at this level without affecting permissions at higher levels. If you decide later to revert to inheriting permissions from the parent site, you can do so by clicking Inherit Permissions on the Action menu.

Removal of permissions

To remove permissions from users or groups, check the user(s) and group(s) for which you want to remove permissions, click Actions, and then select Remove User Permissions (Figure 22-21).

Figure 22-21. Remove User Permissions

You will be prompted with a pop-up message confirming you want to remove these permissions. Click OK to do so.

Modification of permissions

You can modify the permissions of listed users or groups by checking the ones you wish to modify, clicking Actions, and then selecting Edit User Permissions (Figure 22-22).

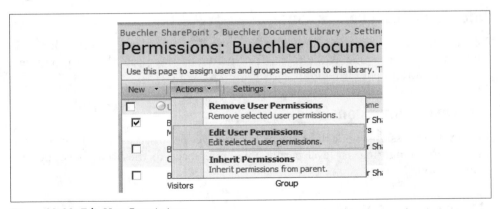

Figure 22-22. Edit User Permissions

You can check multiple users and groups, but only if you want to assign them all identical permissions.

Access requests

You can enable or disable access requests for a library by clicking Settings, and then selecting Access Requests on the Permissions page (Figure 22-23).

Figure 22-23. Access Requests

If the checkbox on the Manage Access Requests screen appears dimmed, access requests for this library are disabled.

Folder-Level Permissions

You can manage folder-level permissions within a library by clicking the drop-down box containing the folder name (without clicking the folder name itself), and then clicking Manage Permissions. By default, all folders inherit permissions from their parent folder or library. The permissions functionality and capabilities are the same as library-level permissions, just at a different scope. Refer back to the library-level permissions section for details on configuring permissions.

Document-Level Permissions

You can manage permissions individually at the document level as well. This functionality works the same as the folder-level permissions, so refer back to the previous section for more information.

List-Level Permissions

List-level permissions work the same as library-level permissions. For detailed information on configuring list-level permissions, refer back to the library-level permissions section.

Item-Level Permissions

Item-level permissions cover items in a list. By default, items inherit permissions from their parent folder or list. Item-level permissions function exactly the same as folder-level permissions.

Protecting SharePoint Sites with Microsoft ISA Server

If your SharePoint site is accessible from the Internet, a great way to provide another layer of security is to use a reverse web proxy. A reverse proxy accepts the HTTP or HTTPS traffic from the Internet, inspects it, and then forwards it on to the actual web server. It can even inspect HTTPS traffic because the SSL certificate resides on the proxy itself. It decrypts and inspects the traffic, and can then re-encrypt it and pass it onto the web server for end-to-end encryption, with application-layer inspection in between.

The ideal choice for reverse proxy with Office SharePoint Server is Microsoft Internet Security and Acceleration (ISA) Server. With ISA Server, users can first be forced to authenticate successfully to Active Directory via web form authentication, prior to any traffic passing through ISA Server to the Office SharePoint Server. This provides the benefit of not allowing traffic from the Internet to touch your SharePoint Server until after the user authenticates.

The following TechNet article describes this involved process in detail. Though it focuses on Windows SharePoint Services, it will work the same with Office SharePoint Server:

http://www.microsoft.com/technet/isa/2004/plan/isawss.mspx

Antivirus Usage

When discussing antivirus and SharePoint, there are two types of antivirus protection that come into consideration. First is the usual file-level server antivirus software. Second, because data in your SharePoint site is stored in a SQL Server database rather than in a typical filesystem hierarchy, file server antivirus does not protect you from infected content on your SharePoint site. Microsoft has built a virus scanning API (VSAPI) into SharePoint to allow for easy integration with various antivirus software packages that are specifically designed for Office SharePoint Server. Your preferred antivirus vendor likely has a solution specific to SharePoint that ties into the VSAPI. In order to scan files added to your SharePoint site for viruses, you must have a SharePoint VSAPI antivirus solution.

File-Level Antivirus

Whether or not to install file-level antivirus on any of your SharePoint servers typically comes down to corporate policy. Corporate policy usually requires antivirus software on all Windows systems, including all servers, desktop machines, and laptops. The conventional wisdom is to install file-level antivirus on every machine; however, depending on your environment, the conventional wisdom may not be so wise.

Antivirus software shouldn't be looked at as strictly a means of protection; vulnerabilities in antivirus software have been somewhat common as of late, and antivirus is becoming more routinely used as an attack vector. In November 2006, a worm exploiting a vulnerability in Symantec Corporate Edition antivirus products spread across the Internet to a limited number of machines. The flaw was patched six months prior, so up-to-date versions were not vulnerable. This is not the first such case and is not limited to Symantec. Almost every major antivirus and security software vendor has been affected by significant vulnerabilities. The Witty worm in March 2004 is the best-known case. It exploited an unpublished vulnerability in Internet Security Systems firewall software, and spread quickly. It was also highly destructive, overwriting random sectors of the hard drive on the infected systems.

Your Office SharePoint Servers should not have any need to access the Internet directly, even those that are accessible from the Internet, because servers can be Internet-accessible without being able to initiate connections out to the Internet. Updates should come from an internal update server, such as WSUS, and any other required downloads on servers should be downloaded on a workstation and then copied over the network. Updates should always be installed promptly. With no direct Internet access and promptly applied updates, it is extremely unlikely that your server will ever detect a virus, worm, or other malware in its lifetime. Based on past history, it's almost a certainty that your antivirus software will have some sort of significant security issue within the server's lifetime.

You will have to determine what is most appropriate in your environment, depending on your organization's security policy and other internal factors. Just keep in mind that antivirus all by itself doesn't guarantee secure systems.

SharePoint VSAPI Antivirus

The necessity of SharePoint VSAPI antivirus depends on the type of deployment you are planning. If you are planning an externally accessible site where users outside your organization can upload content, a SharePoint antivirus solution should be considered a must, since files coming from computers over which you have no control will be held on your servers and available to internal users and possibly other external users.

If you are hosting an internal-only site and are confident in your client antivirus protection, SharePoint antivirus may be viewed as either a desired additional layer of protection (with the potential for additional server vulnerabilities) or an unnecessary expense.

Antivirus Vulnerabilities

Given some of the preceding statements on antivirus, I don't want anyone to be under the impression that I am advocating abandoning the use of antivirus. That's far from the case. I just want you to realize that antivirus software is not a surefire means of protection, and in some situations has the potential to cause more harm than good.

Other Security Considerations

The following briefly reviews a few additional security-related items you should keep in mind while designing a security strategy for your Office SharePoint Server deployment.

Network Security

If the network of your SharePoint servers is not properly protected, all the security mechanisms you have in place on your servers and in Office SharePoint Server itself could potentially be subverted. When referring to "network security" in this section, the referenced topics are routers, switches, and firewalls.

Most Office SharePoint Server administrators probably have no control or influence over the network itself. General network security concerns need to be addressed, but are outside the scope of this book, and probably outside the job duties of most Office SharePoint Server administrators.

Your primary network security concern relevant to Office SharePoint Server is the network topology for publicly accessible and team or department sites, as covered earlier in this chapter.

The following MSDN chapter covers network security, including routers, switches, and firewalls, as it applies to protecting web applications:

http://msdn.microsoft.com/library/default.asp?url=/library/en-us/dnnetsec/html/ THCMCh15.asp

Physical Security

Physical security is another critical component of your overall Office SharePoint Server security strategy. Unless you properly employ strong encryption on all your disk drives, physical access to a server means it is relatively easy to gain administrative rights on that server and access all of the data on the server. This is even more the case when it is possible to physically remove the server from the premises, or even just remove the hard drives and leave the premises with them.

Admittance authentication and restrictions

The list of individuals authorized to enter any of your computer rooms should be as restricted as possible. If at all feasible, some sort of biometric authentication should be used for admission (such as a fingerprint scanner, palm scanner, etc.) in addition to a PIN code. Keys and combination locks are undesirable because they are much more difficult to control, and they do not maintain an audit log.

Facility considerations

Make sure the room itself is reasonably protected from unauthorized entry. If rooms adjacent to a raised-floor computer room also have raised floor, ensure the wall goes all the way down below the raised floor so people cannot crawl under the floor. If the facility has a drop ceiling, ensure the wall goes all the way up and doesn't stop at the ceiling tiles. An intruder could easily get above the raised ceiling in the insecure area, go over the wall, and drop into your computer room through the drop ceiling.

User Security Awareness Training

Your organization should require mandatory annual security awareness training for everyone with access to your network. You can do everything right from a technical perspective, but if your users are "vulnerable," all your efforts could be for naught.

The primary areas of focus for basic user awareness training follow. Your needs may differ, depending on your environment:

- Social engineering
- Creating strong passwords
- Proper password security (don't write them down or give them to anyone else, etc.)
- Phishing and related email security practices
- Safe web browsing

Host Intrusion Prevention Systems

To provide an additional layer of security on your servers, you may wish to consider a Host Intrusion Prevention System (HIPS) solution. There are several commercially available options with varying feature sets, but in general they do what their name implies—prevent your server from being compromised, at the host level. This can be better than a network-based Intrusion Prevention System (IPS) because the visibility of some things is better from the host's perspective. In particular, when utilizing encryption of network traffic, a network-based IPS is nearly useless because it cannot see what the network traffic actually contains. In that situation, a HIPS is important if you want effective intrusion prevention. As with antivirus, remember that security software shouldn't be looked at as only a helpful measure; this software could also contain vulnerabilities that allow the system to be compromised. Make sure you keep all your security software up to date.

Maintaining a Secure Environment

You have diligently hardened all your servers and applications and followed all of the security best practices in setting up your farm and sites—so now what? Without proper maintenance, your secure site will not stay that way for long. If someone asks, "Are we secure?" the correct answer is "Let me check" (unless you know you have security issues, in which case feel free to say "No"). Your site and network may be secure at this moment, but things in security change very rapidly and you could be vulnerable minutes or days after an update.

Patch Management

The foremost security concern of Windows Server and Office SharePoint Server administrators should be patch management. Ensuring that security patches for Windows Server, Office SharePoint Server, Microsoft SQL Server, etc. are applied to every server in a prompt fashion will go a long way toward keeping your Office SharePoint Server environment secure.

You should implement a patch management solution to ensure patching is done on a timely and consistent basis. Microsoft offers solutions such as Windows Server Update Services (WSUS) and Microsoft Systems Management Server (SMS), and there are other solutions that handle patch management (among other things) are also available from third-party vendors for a fee.

For further information on WSUS, visit the following URL:

http://www.microsoft.com/windowsserversystem/updateservices

Vulnerability Assessment

You should perform periodic basic vulnerability assessments against all servers that are a part of your farm. A vulnerability assessment can be defined as the process of identifying and quantifying vulnerabilities in a system. A more widely recognized term is "penetration testing." Though penetration testing and vulnerability assessment are not the same thing, when most people speak of penetration testing what they really want is a vulnerability assessment (see the link to "Penetration Testing versus Vulnerability Assessment" in Table 22-6 for further information).

A basic vulnerability assessment normally consists of running security scanning tools against your servers, which check for things such as vulnerable services or applications, missing patches, weak configurations, and other deviations from generally accepted security best practices. You can perform this basic level of assessment on your own, without a significant security background. Prior to initiating any security testing, it is critically important to have explicit permission in writing from your organization to do so. Attempting to bypass security measures on your network without appropriate prior consent could be grounds for termination of employment or, worse, could land you in jail on computer crime charges.

The Microsoft Baseline Security Analyzer (MBSA), offered by Microsoft as a free download, makes it easy to perform a limited vulnerability assessment without possessing much, if any, security knowledge. You can use MBSA to scan a single server, an IP address range, or an Active Directory domain. You need to run MBSA using an account with administrative privileges on all systems being scanned.

At the end of the scan, MBSA will provide a report on each system detailing the current security posture of the target. Specific actionable items are provided to help you remediate the issues discovered. After you fix the problems found the first time, you should run a second scan to check that everything was properly addressed. Repeat this process until the report comes back clean, or the issues discovered cannot be addressed in your environment for some reason and are deemed an acceptable risk by management.

Professional vulnerability assessment

There is much more to a true vulnerability assessment than what we just covered, and far more than can be covered in this book. If you do not employ security experts internally who are qualified to perform a complete vulnerability assessment, your organization should consider bringing in outside security experts to perform an assessment on an annual basis.

Be careful in selecting a company or individual to perform this work. Many security consultants will do nothing more than run a few tools (such as MBSA) and then simply hand you either a CD of the results or a huge binder with the results printed out, along with a big bill. A qualified security professional will analyze those results, compare results between multiple tools, and determine where to look closer for potential weaknesses that a scanning tool cannot find, along with other things that vary depending on the environment. Following the assessment, a report with specific verified findings you can actually use to improve your security posture should be provided.

Table 22-6 lists some relevant resources for further information on the topics covered in this section.

Table 22-6. Security tool resources

Resource title	Resource link
Microsoft Baseline Security Analyzer	*http://www.microsoft.com/technet/security/tools/ mbsahome.mspx*
Penetration Testing versus Vulnerability Assessment	*http://www.darknet.org.uk/2006/04/penetration-testing-vs-vulnerability-assessment/*
Open Source Security Testing Methodology Manual	*http://www.isecom.org/osstmm/*

Conclusion

This chapter covered a wide breadth of topics, much of which cannot be covered in detail in this book. Covering all the linked topics would require a chapter the length of this entire book, and so rather than duplicating existing content in areas not specific to Office SharePoint Server, numerous links have been provided because good step-by-step documentation already exists for these areas. For example, areas such as Windows Server and SQL Server security were not covered in great depth, so things specific to SharePoint security could be covered in more depth.

With the information and references provided in this chapter, you should have no problem implementing and maintaining a secure Office SharePoint Server environment. However, do not overlook the linked resources provided; an effective Office SharePoint Server security strategy and implementation depends on the knowledge provided in those links.

CHAPTER 23

SharePoint Administration

Introduction

As you might know by now, Office SharePoint Server 2007 includes a collection of components designed to serve specific functions, such as search, collaboration, business intelligence, business forms, content management, enterprise search, and so on. A web site that is built in SharePoint will use a combination of these components. For example, an intranet site will use the collaboration, search, business forms, and business intelligence components, whereas a site built for web content publishing will use the content management and search capabilities. Each of these different components has its own configuration requirements and other settings. Therefore, depending upon the different features being used in the site, the administrative tasks will vary.

The objective of this chapter is to discuss some of the most common administrative tasks performed at the different levels within the SharePoint 2007 environment. These tasks include the administration of server-level configurations, web applications, site collections, and site settings. A detailed review of every administrative option is beyond the scope of this chapter.

Please see Chapters 3 and 4 for in-depth coverage on administrative tasks related to server installation and server configuration.

SharePoint 2007 provides different utilities to perform the post installation configuration. These utilities can be divided into three main categories:

- SharePoint products and technologies configuration wizard
- Central Administration web site
- Command-line utilities

Certain administrative tasks can be performed using different tools. For example, tasks such as creating a site collection, backup, and restore can be performed using either the Central Administration options or the STSADM command-line utility.

Any web site built on SharePoint 2007 (intranet portal, publishing web site, etc.) will have a hierarchy of sites to organize the content. Building a web site in SharePoint starts with creating a web application. Then, one or more site collections, applied with a specific template, will be added to the web application. Each site collection will have one or more sites, and each site will have a collection of Web Parts and pages.

 For a detailed discussion on site hierarchy and designing sites, refer to Chapter 5.

Administration tasks at each level of the hierarchy vary. Tasks at the lower level of the hierarchy (site level) might include creating lists or configuring a user; these are the responsibility of the site owner. Tasks at the upper level of the hierarchy (site-collection or web-application level) might include activating or deactivating WSS features or configuring search; these would be the responsibility of SharePoint administrators. From a hierarchy perspective, the administration tasks can be broken down into the following different levels:

- Central Administration tasks, which mainly include options for administering the server farm. These tasks can be further subdivided into three main sections:
  — Operations
  — Application Management
  — Shared Services Administration
- Web application administration
- Top-level site administration
- Site administration

Office SharePoint 2007 presents a list of administrative tasks to be completed after the installation. Each of these tasks is a one-time configuration activity and is part of the configuration required to prepare an Office SharePoint Server 2007 farm for use. Not all the tasks in the administrative list need to be performed; the tasks required depend on the type of installation. Figure 23-1 depicts the list of administrative activities.

Common Central Administration Tasks

As mentioned earlier, Central Administration is divided into three main subdivisions based on functionality. The first one, operations, focuses on the configuration of servers and services, including server topology, overall SharePoint security, upgrade and migration, backup and restore, and content deployment. Content deployment is related to web content management and is required only if the portal requires automated content deployment. The second section, application management, deals with the tasks specific to application creation, site collection management, shared

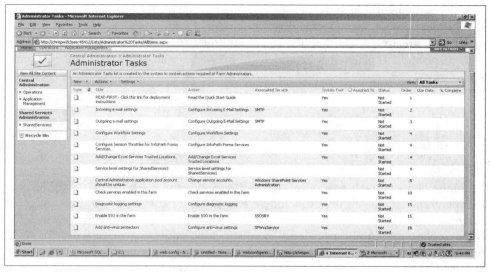

Figure 23-1. Administrative tasks list

services, InfoPath forms services, application-specific security, workflow, and data connections. The final section, Shared Services Provider (SSP), is used to configure the search, business data catalog settings, Excel services settings, SharePoint My Sites, and audiences.

Operations Page

This section explores some of the important and most common administrative tasks performed using the operations section.

Services on server

One of the first tasks in a server farm is to configure each server in the farm with appropriate services. This task is performed with the "Services on server" option under the "Topology and Services" section in the Operations page. SharePoint 2007 has five different roles that can be used to configure a server within the farm. Selecting a role enables the different services to perform that role's activities. Some of these services require further configuration. SharePoint Server 2007 provides a services indicator that displays the status of the service. Figure 23-2 depicts the different roles available to a given SharePoint server.

Outgoing Email Settings

In order to enable alerts and notifications, Office SharePoint server requires an outgoing email server. To configure an outgoing email server, select the Outgoing Email Settings option under the topology and services section of the operations page.

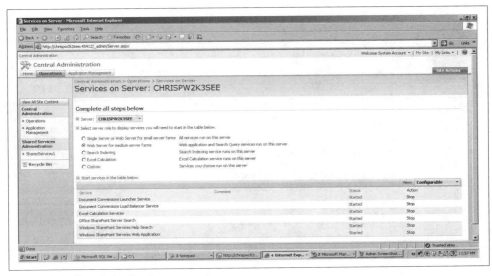

Figure 23-2. SharePoint Services on server

Incoming Email Settings

SharePoint 2007 contains a new feature that allows email messages to be stored directly in SharePoint lists. To make this feature work correctly, there are several components that need to be configured. If SMTP service is running on one of the farm servers, SharePoint configures the settings for incoming email automatically. Using the Operations → "Incoming email" settings, the server should be configured to accept incoming emails. The Advanced option can be used to explicitly specify the options, in case SMTP service is not running on the server. The directory management service in SharePoint 2007 can be used to integrate the list's email settings with the organization's active directory. When enabled, the directory management service creates an account for the list in the active directory, thereby allowing users to search for email-enabled SharePoint lists using the address book. The SPTimer service polls the mail drop folder and routes the emails to the appropriate lists. Figure 23-3 depicts the email configuration settings under the topology and services section in the operations page.

Once the email settings have been configured, the SharePoint list needs to be mail-enabled to accept incoming emails. The list settings page provides an option for configuring incoming emails for the list. This option is available only if the server has been configured to accept incoming emails. To set the list to receive emails, set the "Allow this document library to receive emails" option to Yes and provide an email address that users will use to send emails to this list. The configuration page also provides options for saving attachments, saving the original email files (*.eml*), saving meeting invitations, and specifying security (i.e., who can send emails to this list). Figure 23-4 depicts this page.

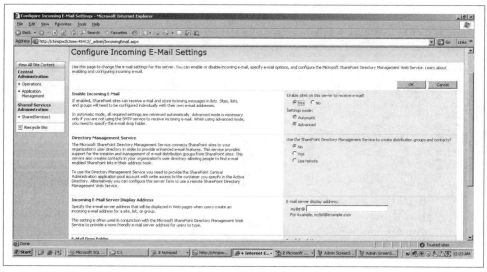

Figure 23-3. Configuring Incoming Email Settings

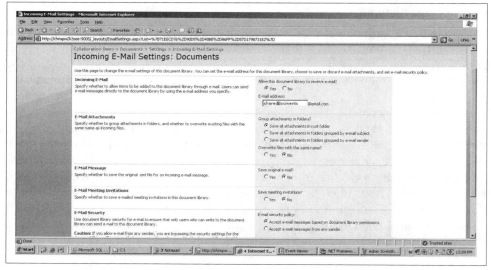

Figure 23-4. List incoming email settings page

Antivirus

The Operations → Antivirus option under the Security Configuration section allows administrators to apply antivirus settings, such as scanning documents on upload and download. Antivirus software is not included in Office SharePoint Server 2007, and so antivirus software specially built to support SharePoint must be installed on all frontend web servers. For example, Microsoft provides ForeFront Security for

SharePoint, a separate antivirus software specially designed to integrate tightly with SharePoint Server 2007. More information can be found at *http://www.microsoft.com/forefront/serversecurity/sharepoint/download.mspx*.

Blocked File Types

The Operations → Blocked File Types option under the Security Configuration section allows administrators to configure which file types need to be blocked from being uploaded into a SharePoint library. The list of blocked file types is maintained on a per–web application basis. To add new file types to the list, scroll to the bottom of the list and add each file type in a separate line.

Information Management Policy Configuration

SharePoint 2007 introduces a new policy-based system to manage documents. The idea is to create a policy based on certain features—such as barcodes, auditing, and labeling—and then associate a content type or library to a policy, thereby forcing the documents to follow the guidelines defined in the policy. The Operations → Information Management Policy Configuration page under the Security Configuration section allows the administrator to manage the features that could be used in a policy.

Office SharePoint Server 2007 comes with four different policy features:

Expiration
> The expiration feature is used to set the content expiration in a manner that can be tracked and managed.

Auditing
> The auditing policy feature can be used to log events such as viewing, editing, checking in, and deleting documents or list items.

Labeling
> The labeling feature allows users to attach document-specific notes that can be formatted, searched, and printed.

Barcode
> The barcode policy feature enables users to attach a barcode image to a document, thereby creating a unique identifier for the document.

There are three steps to implementing an information management policy:

Configure the policy features
> Select Operations → Information Management Policy to activate or deactivate the policy features.

Create a new Information Management Policy
> Use the site collection's Site Collection Policies page to create a new policy.

Apply the policy to the content type
> You can also apply it to the document library.

Information management policies are created at a site collection level. To create one, navigate to the Site Settings page of a site and choose the Site Collection Policies link under Site Collection Administration. Once a policy is created, it can be associated with a library or a list by navigating to the settings option of the library or list and then selecting the Information Management Policy Settings link under "Permissions and Management." Click New to create a new policy. Figure 23-5 shows a policy creation page..

Information Policy Usage Reports

The Operations → Information Management Policy Usage Reports option under the "Logging and Reporting" section in the operations page can be used to configure reporting on a site's information management policies. The reports are configured on a per–web application basis and can be scheduled. Figure 23-6 shows the Information Policy Usage Reports configuration page.

Usage analysis processing

The Operations → "Usage analysis processing" option allows the administrator to configure the SharePoint usage reporting service. Once configured, the service provides different categories of reports, such as summary, users, destination pages, search results and queries, and requests. This service allows administrators and users to monitor and query site usage statistics such as:

- Average number of requests per day
- Top pages used in the site
- Top users visiting the site
- Frequent search queries and results
- Overall usage of the site collection usage metrics

In order to configure the usage analysis reporting service, three different components need to be configured:

Windows SharePoint Services usage logging
> Using the Central Administration → Operations → "Usage analysis reporting" option, check the Enable Logging option and specify a time for processing the log. This will enable the logging at the WSS level.

Office SharePoint Server 2007 usage logging
> Navigate to the shared services provider home page and choose Usage Reporting under the Office SharePoint Usage Reporting section. Choose "Enable advanced usage analysis processing" and "Enable search query logging" and click OK. This configuration step needs to be performed on a per–shared services provider level. Figure 23-7 depicts the Office Server 2007 usage configuration page.

Activate the reporting feature for a portal
> Navigate to the Site Settings → Site Collection feature and activate the Reporting feature. This configuration step needs to be performed at a per-application level.

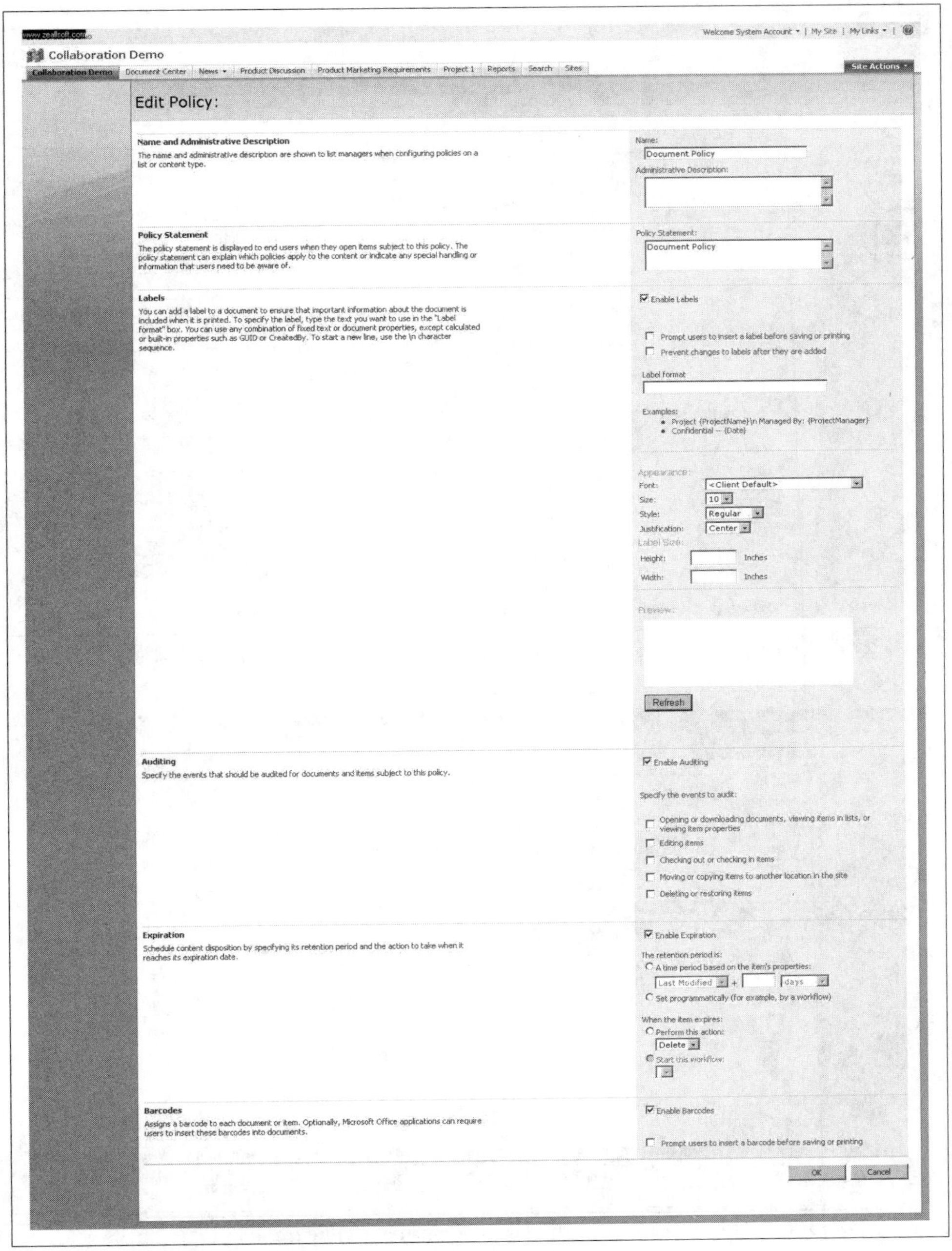

Figure 23-5. Information management policy creation page

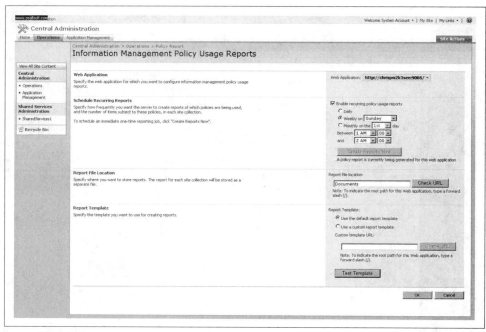

Figure 23-6. Information Management Policy Usage Reports configuration

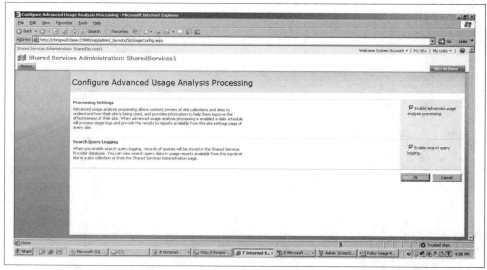

Figure 23-7. Office SharePoint Server 2007 Usage Reporting Configuration

Once configured and processed, the Site Settings → Site collection usage reports option can be used to view the reports. Figure 23-8 depicts the reporting page.

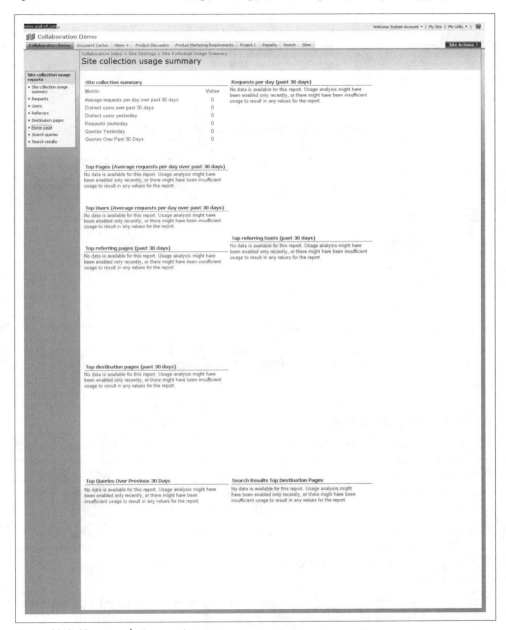

Figure 23-8. Usage analysis reporting page

Alternate access mapping

Using the Operations → Alternate access mappings option under the Global Configuration section, an administrator can configure multiple URLs for a given web application. Each web application can be configured with different URLs for the default, intranet, Internet, custom, and extranet public zones. To configure public URLs, choose the Edit Public URLs option from the Alternate Access Mapping page, and then select the web application to configure. Figure 23-9 depicts the Alternate Access Mapping page.

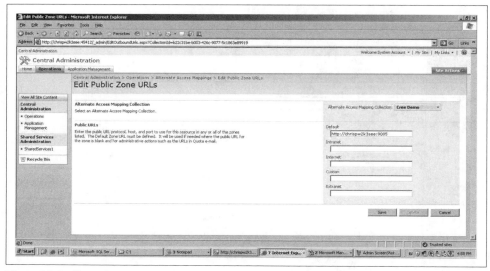

Figure 23-9. Alternate access mapping

SharePoint backup and restore

Office SharePoint 2007 provides different options and utilities for performing backup and restore. A backup and restore strategy should be planned, taking into consideration the different options, the strategy's pros and cons, and other environment settings. A new feature in SharePoint 2007 is a two-phase Recycle Bin, which users and administrators can use to restore deleted content from the Recycle Bin.

This section focuses on the different backup and restore options available in SharePoint 2007. To perform a successful backup and restore, Office SharePoint Server 2007 requires that the SQL server account have read and write privileges on the backup folders.

The Central Administration → Operations page provides a GUI-based mechanism to perform backup and restores at a web application or farm level. One drawback in using this interface is that the backup operation cannot be scheduled. To perform a scheduled backup operation, a command-line utility called STSADM (located in the "12 hive," which is *<install location>\Program Files\Common Files\Microsoft Shared\Web Server Extensions\12\bin*) can be used in a script, which can then be scheduled. In addition these two options (Central Administration and STSADM), third-party utilities also can be used to perform the backup and restore.

Backup and restore can be performed at different levels:

Farm-level backup
> This can be performed using the Central Administration → Operations → Perform a backup or with the –o backup operation with the -directory and -backupmethod full options with the *stsadm* utility. For example:
>
> ```
> stsadm –o backup –directory <location to store backup> -backupmethod full
> ```

Web application backup
> Use Central Administration or the –o backup operation with the –item "Farm\Windows SharePoint Web Application\webappname" option with the *stsadm* utility. For example, to back up:
>
> ```
> stsadm –o backup –directory <location to store backup> –item "Farm\Windows
> SharePoint Web Application\WebAppName" - backupmethod full
> ```
>
> To restore:
>
> ```
> stsadm –o restore –directory <location of backup> -item "Farm\Windows SharePoint
> Web Application\WebAppName" –restoremethod <new/overwrite>
> ```

Site collection backup
> Use the –o backup operation with the –url option in the *stsadm* utility. For example, to back up:
>
> ```
> stsadm –o backup –url <http://URL of site collection> -filename <location of
> backup filename .bak>
> ```
>
> To restore:
>
> ```
> stsadm –o restore –filename <location of the back file> -url <URL to restore the
> site collection>
> ```

Individual sites backup
> Use the –o export operation with the –url option. For example, to back up:
>
> ```
> stsadm –o export –url <http://URL of the site> -filename <location of the export
> file.bak>
> ```
>
> To restore:
>
> ```
> stsadm –o import –filename <location of the backup file.bak> -URL <URL to restore
> the exported site>
> ```

Database backup
> Configuration and content database can be backed up independently using the SQL server back utilities.

While performing backup and restores it is important to remember that custom Web Parts, custom component files, and settings are not backed up. To perform a successful restore, these components should be explicitly installed and configured.

As mentioned before, the Operations → "Perform a backup" option under the "Backup and Restore" section of Office SharePoint Server 2007 allows administrators to back up web applications, web application content databases, shared services content databases, and the configuration database. The page allows the administrator to choose either a specific web application or the entire farm for backup. To perform a backup of a web application, select the web application from the list presented; SharePoint 2007 automatically selects its content databases. In the next page, choose whether the backup performed should be full or differential, and provide a location for the backup file. Figure 23-10 shows step 1 of the backup operation.

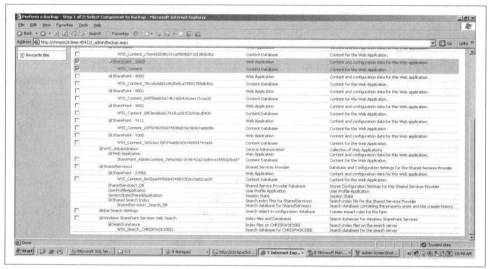

Figure 23-10. Backup step 1, selecting a component to back up

This procedure creates a set of files in the backup folder specified. To restore the portal from this backup, use the Operations → "Restore from backup" option. Specify the location of the backup file in step 1, and then step 2 will display the components available for restoration. Figure 23-11 displays this page.

Step 3 will display the available content database(s) for the web application to be restored. Step 4 provides the information to specify whether the restore should use the settings when the backup was performed (this will overwrite the web application) or restore the backup with a new configuration. Choosing the later requires a new web application name, URL, physical file location, and content database names. Figure 23-12 shows this page.

The Operations page also has sections for configuring the upgrade and migration of sites from WSS 2.0 and MCMS sites. Another available section is for configuring content deployment settings, which are required for publishing portals and sites.

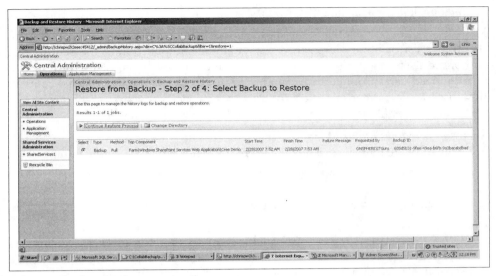

Figure 23-11. Step 2, select a component to restore

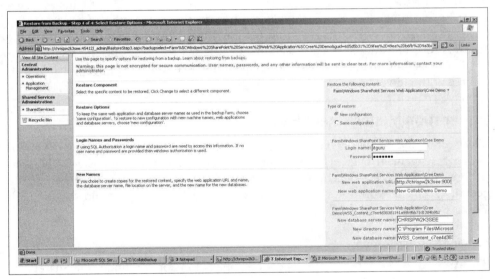

Figure 23-12. Specify component restore settings

In addition to these sections, there are certain other options that have not been discussed in this chapter, such as configuring single sign-on settings, diagnostic logging, and solution management, all of which are optional configuration elements. Information rights management, although not a required configuration, can be useful in protecting content. The following section briefly discusses this option.

Information Rights Management

Microsoft Office SharePoint Server 2007 supports Information Rights Management (IRM) at a list or library level. IRM allows administrators to limit the actions that authorized users can perform on specific document types. It can be used to prevent unauthorized users from copying, modifying, and printing the documents' content. IRM uses a file format–specific protector to manage the rights for files within a SharePoint list or library. IRM requires the following additional software:

Microsoft Windows Rights Management Services Client
This software must be installed on every frontend web server in the farm.

Microsoft Windows Rights Management Services for Window Server 2003 (SP 1 or later)
This server software must be available in the network.

File type protector
Office SharePoint Server 2007 includes protectors for InfoPath documents and Office documents. To use IRM on any other file type in a list or library, a separate protector must be installed on each frontend web server.

To configure the server with IRM, use the Operations → Information Rights Management option under the Security Configuration section. Once the server is configured, the List/library settings → Information Rights Management link under the "Permissions and Management" section can be used to apply specific security settings. For the Information Rights Management link to appear, IRM must be first configured at the server level.

Application Management Page

This section focuses on the common administrative tasks performed using the application management page. This page allows administrators to administer web applications, manage site collections, configure shared services for the farm, configure security, manage workflows, and administer external connections and the InfoPath Forms Services.

Creating web applications

The Application → "Create or extend web application" option under the SharePoint Web Application Management section is used to create and configure web applications. A web application by itself is essentially an empty container and needs to be provisioned with site collections or with a shared services provider.

To create a web application, use the "Application management" → "Create or extend web application" option. This page has options for creating a new IIS web site or using an existing one, creating a new application pool for the web site or using an existing one, options for a security provider for the web application, and specifying the database server and the content database name. It is a good practice to isolate each web application into its own application pools. To create a web application, follow these steps:

1. Specify a web site description. This will be used as the web site name in IIS.

2. Provide a port number. SharePoint 2007 provides an arbitrary port number.

3. Enter a host header if the URL of the web application is resolved by the DNS servers.

4. Specify a virtual directory location. By default, this is *Inetpub\WWWRoot\WSS\ VirtualDirectories\PortNumber*.

5. In the security configuration section, choose an authentication provider (Kerberos or NTLM), and specify whether the site allows anonymous access and whether the site uses SSL.

6. In the application pool section, specify an existing web application, or create a new application by choosing "Create a new application pool." Provide a name for the application pool and enter the credentials for the application pool.

7. Choose "Restart IIS automatically."

8. Specify the database server and specify the content database name.

9. Choose OK to create a web application.

Figure 23-13 displays the new web application page.

Web applications can also be created and mapped to other web applications. The extended web application exposes the content of the mapped web application. This way, a different authentication mechanism can be used for internal users and people from other domains or the Internet. To extend a web application, select "Create or extend a new web application" → "Extend a web application." Choose the web application to be mapped in the "Web application" section, and choose the application pool and security configuration as before. Since the extended web application exposes the content of the mapped web application, it does not have a content database of its own. Figure 23-14 depicts the page for extending a web application.

A web application hosting site collections needs to be associated to a SSP; therefore, SSP should be created prior to creating other web applications. A *Shared Services Provider* (SSP) provides services such as My Site, audiences, Office SharePoint usage reporting, search, Excel services, and the business data catalog. A web application hosting site collections is associated with one SSP, whereas a given SSP can serve multiple such web applications. To host the SSP, a web application is required. One special requirement for a web application hosting the SSP is that network services cannot be used as the application pool identity. SSP also requires another web application to host the MySite.

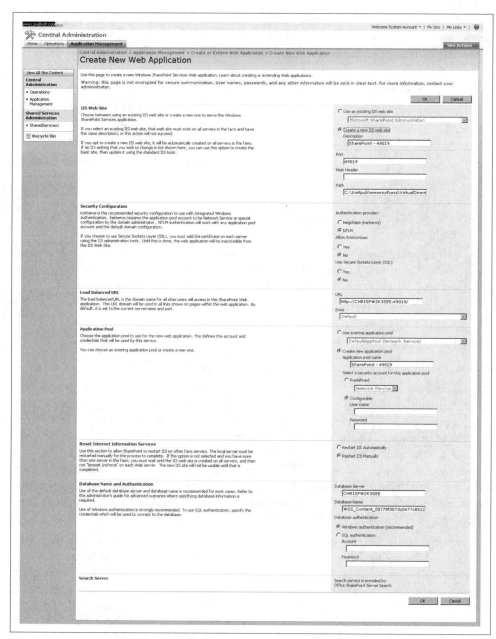

Figure 23-13. Creating a new web application

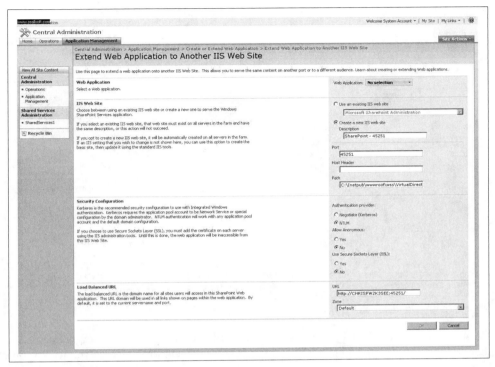

Figure 23-14. Extend a web application page

To create a shared services provider, choose Shared Services Administration → New SSP from the Central Administration page. Follow these steps to create a new SSP:

1. Specify a name for the SSP.

2. Specify a web application for the SSP. If a web application does not exist, choose "Create a new web application."

3. Choose a web application for the My Site. Again, choose "Create a new web application" if a web application does not exist.

4. Enter the credentials for the timer jobs run by the SSP.

5. Specify a database server name and content database name for SSP.

6. SSP uses a separate database for storing the search information. Specify a database server name and database name to be used as the search database.

7. Choose an index server in the farm. SharePoint Server will, by default, populate the available index servers from the farm.

8. Choose whether the web services for SSP will use SSL.

9. Click OK to create the SSP.

Figure 23-15 depicts the New Shared Services Provider page.

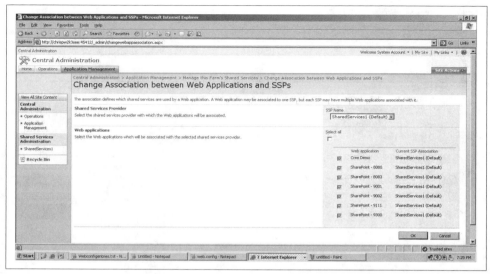

Figure 23-15. Changing SSP association

As mentioned before, each web application that hosts site collections requires an SSP. Each SSP can host multiple web applications. The association between the web application and the SSP can be changed using the Shared Services Administration → Change Association page. If there are multiple SSPs configured, you can choose the SSP in the drop-down list, choose the web application(s) that need to be associated with the SSP, and then click OK. Figure 23-16 depicts the change association page.

Define Managed Paths

The Application Management → Define Managed Paths option under the SharePoint Web Application Management section is used to define a managed path on a per web application basis. A managed path defines any custom paths in the URL that could be used by the site collections in the web application. A managed path can be either included (wildcard inclusion) or excluded (explicit exclusion). Wildcard inclusion is useful to create custom paths for site collections. Explicit exclusion could be used for custom web site applications under the SharePoint web application; in this case, the web application path is managed by SharePoint, but the custom web site path is not. To add a managed path, follow these steps:

1. Navigate to the Define Managed Path page from the application management page.

2. Under the web application section, choose the web application to define the managed path.

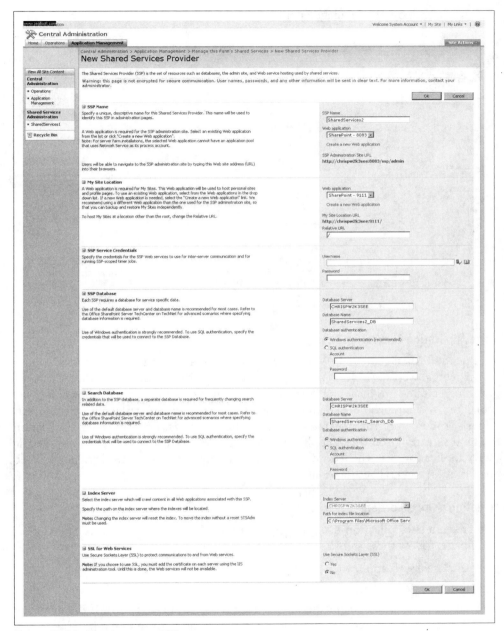

Figure 23-16. Creating a new SSP

3. Enter the path for inclusion or exclusion. Test the URL by clicking "Check URL."

4. Choose whether the path should be a "wildcard inclusion" or an "explicit exclusion," and then press OK.

Figure 23-17 shows the managed path page.

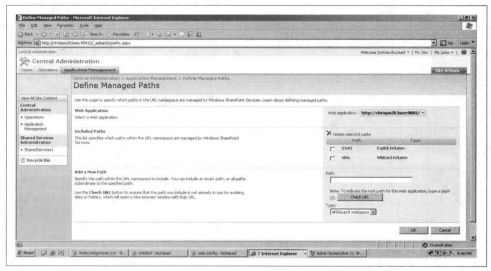

Figure 23-17. Managed path page

Web Application General Settings

Application Management → Web Application General Settings page can used to perform general web application settings such as setting the time zone for the web application, enabling or disabling RSS feeds and alerts, setting space quotas for site collections, defining the maximum upload size, and entering the Recycle Bin settings. To configure the general web application settings, choose "Web application general settings" from the "Application Management" page, and choose the specific web application for which to configure the settings. Figure 23-18 depicts the Web Application General Settings page.

Creating a site collection

To create a site collection using the Application Management → Create Site Collection page, follow these steps:

1. Choose a web application for which to create a site collection.

2. Enter a title for the web application.

3. Site collections can be created at the root or in a managed path. If the managed path is a custom managed path, choose one from the drop-down list if required. The managed path should already be created for the web application. Enter the URL name for the site collection.

4. Pick a template from the template categories (Collaboration, Meeting, Enterprise, or Publishing).

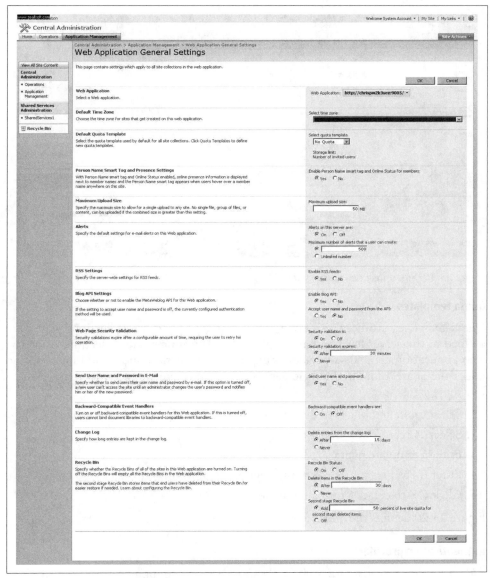

Figure 23-18. Web Application General Settings

5. Enter a primary site collection owner and an optional secondary owner.

6. Choose a quota for the site collection (discussed in the next section).

7. Click OK to create the site collection.

Figure 23-19 depicts the site collection creation page.

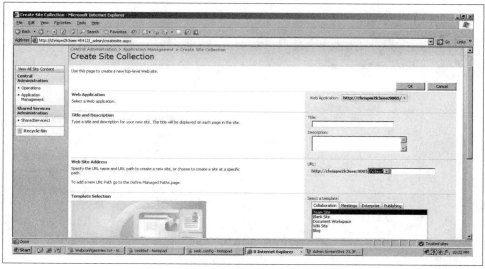

Figure 23-19. Site collection creation page

Quota templates

Quota templates are used to define space limitations for site collections. They are defined at the server level and are applied while creating a site collection, using the web application general settings or using the site collection quotas and locks option under the SharePoint Site Management section. To create a new quota template, follow these steps:

1. Select quota templates under the SharePoint Site Management section.
2. Select "Create a new quota template."
3. Enter a template name.
4. Enter the values for maximum storage and for warning emails.
5. Click OK to create a quota template.

Figure 23-20 depicts the quota template creation page.

Authentication providers

Authentication providers for web applications can be configured using the Application Management → Authentication Providers option under the application security section. This option can be used to configure or change the authentication type, enable/disable anonymous access, and change the IIS authentication settings to use NTLM or the Kerberos authentication protocol. Figure 23-21 shows the configuration of the authentication provider for the web application.

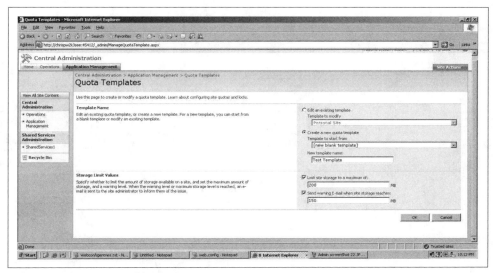

Figure 23-20. Quota template creation page

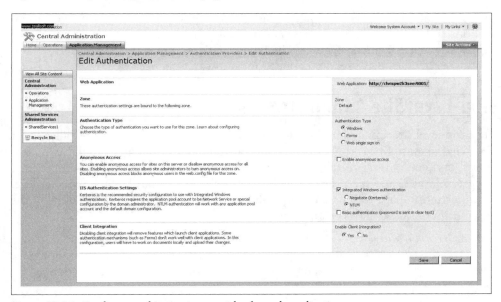

Figure 23-21. Configure authentication provider for web application

Workflow Settings

Using the Application Management → Workflow Settings page, configure the workflow settings, such as notifications for internal and external users and allowing user-defined workflow options for a given web application. Figure 23-22 shows the Workflow Settings page.

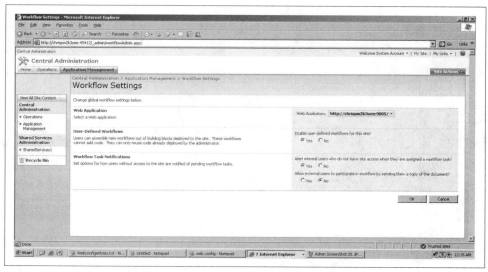

Figure 23-22. Workflow Settings page

The application management page includes other options for configuring web applications and for site collection management. Besides these administration options, the application management page also includes configuration settings for the InfoPath Forms services, external service connection, and search service.

Top-Level Site Administration

The top-level site administration page includes options for managing the galleries for Web Parts, master pages and layout pages, site templates, enabling and disabling features, and configuring search options for the site collection, auditing, and caching. The top-level site is the root of the site collection. Each site has its own site-level administration page (discussed later in this chapter). Discussed here are some of the options in the site collection administration:

Site collection features
> The site collection features option under the Site Collection Administration page can be used to activate and deactivate features for the entire site collection.

Site Collection Audit Settings
> These can be used to set the events that need to be audited. For a document library and list items, these events include:

> - Opening documents or document properties
> - Editing item
> - Check Out/Check In
> - Moving/Copying
> - Deleting or Restoring

Audit log reports

This option provides different types of reports that can be created using the auditing settings. Administrators can create custom reports by using "Run a custom report" under the Custom Reports section or by using another report from one of the following categories:

- Content activity reports
- Information Management Policy reports
- Security and Site Settings reports

Site collection policies

This lets administrators configure the information management policies for the site collection. Information management policies can be imported or created here.

Web Part Gallery

Using the Web Parts option under the Galleries page, administrators can configure new Web Parts for the site collection. Prior to this step, a Web Part needs to be installed in the server and marked as "safe" in the *web.config* file of the web application. Once the Web Part is installed, it can be made available to the sites in the site collection by populating the Web Part into the gallery. To populate a Web Part into a gallery, follow these steps:

a. Navigate to the Web Part Gallery (Site Settings → Web Parts)

b. Choose New in the Web Part Gallery page.

c. Choose the Web Part that needs to be populated in the gallery, and click Populate Gallery. Figure 23-23 shows the Populate Gallery page.

Site Template Gallery

The Site Template Gallery is used to upload site template (*.stp*) files.

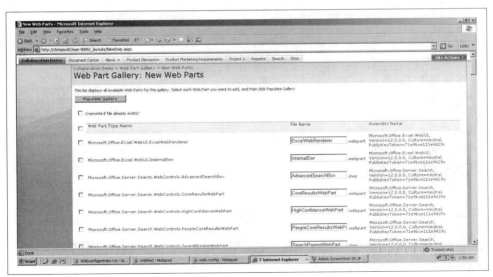

Figure 23-23. Populate Web Part Gallery

Site Administration

Site administration can be performed using the Site Settings link of the specific site. This section discusses some of the administrative tasks that can be performed at a site level.

Look and Feel—Master Page

Each site can be applied with its own master pages. Using the Site Settings → Master Page option under the "Look and feel" section, an administrator can change the site master page or system master page and provide an alternate CSS file. For a child site, either the master page can be inherited from the parent or it can apply one on its own. Figure 23-24 depicts the site master page settings page.

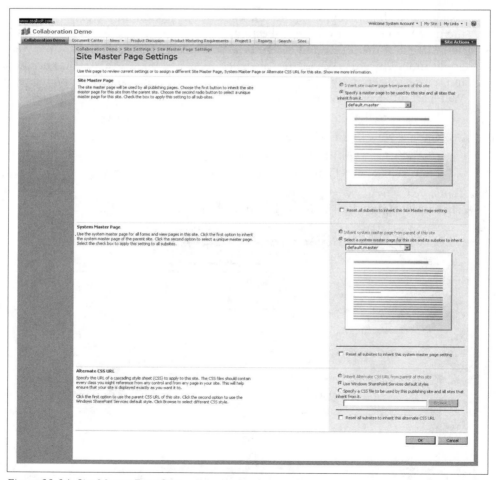

Figure 23-24. Site Master Page Settings

Look and Feel—Navigation

Using the Site Setting → Navigation option under the "Look and Feel" section, the site's global navigation (top menu) and the current navigation (left navigation) can be changed. SharePoint Server 2007 provides options to include/exclude subsites, hide/show specific items, manually add links to customize the navigation, and sort. The options available in the navigation page are different for a top-level site and for a child site. Figure 23-25 displays the navigation settings for a child site.

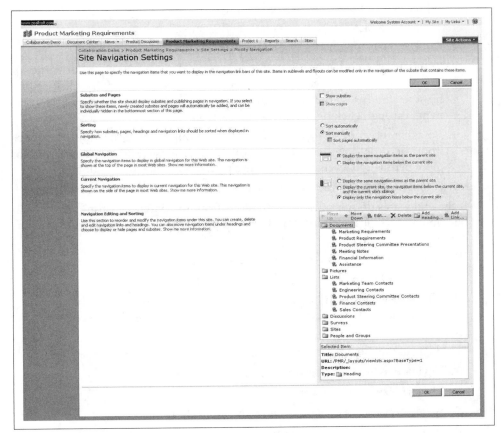

Figure 23-25. Navigation options for a child site

Look and Feel—Page layouts and site templates

This section allows administrators to specify the layouts and templates that subsites can use.

Look and Feel—Welcome Page

The administrator can set the welcome page for a specific site through this section.

Users and Permissions—People and groups

This section can be used to configure security for the site collection and the individual sites. SharePoint implements role-based (called a "group" in SharePoint terminology) security. A role itself is a collection of privileges/permissions. Roles are applied to SharePoint content objects such as sites, libraries, or lists. Users who belong to the role will have the permissions defined in the role on the applied content objects. A user or an AD group can be added to the role. SharePoint has predefined roles, such as approvers, hierarchy managers, designers, and visitors.

To add users or groups to a role, follow these steps:

1. Navigate to Site Settings → "People and groups."

2. Choose New → User.

3. Enter the users or AD groups by specifying the username, group name, or email. Alternatively, you can search for a user or group by clicking the browse icon below the Users/Groups text box. You can also check the username through clicking the check names icon.

4. To assign users to a predefined permission group, choose the available groups from the drop-down list. To give a user explicit permissions, choose one or more permission levels from the "Give permissions directly" section.

5. Choose OK to add the user to the group.

If the child sites do not inherit permissions from the parent, custom security can be implemented at the child sites. To break permission inheritance from the parent, follow these steps:

1. Navigate to Site Settings → People and Groups of a child site.

2. Select Site Permissions from the left navigation bar.

3. Choose Actions → Edit Permissions. This brings up a dialog box warning that security changes at the parent site will no longer be effective for this site. Click OK.

To add a custom SharePoint group, follow these steps:

1. Navigate to Site Settings → People and groups.

2. Choose New → New Group.

3. Specify a name for the group in the Name section.

4. Specify the owner of the group.

5. In the group setting section, specify whether members of the group will have rights to view or edit the group membership.

6. In the membership requests section, specify whether users should be allowed to request access to the group or request to leave the group.

7. Specify the permissions that the members of this group should have.

8. Click OK to create the group. Figure 23-26 depicts the New SharePoint Group creation page.

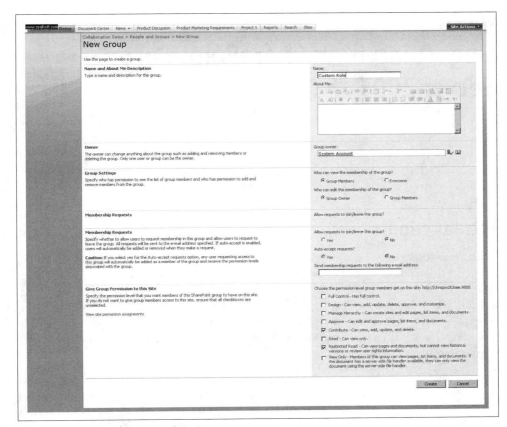

Figure 23-26. New SharePoint Group page

In addition to the administrative tasks discussed in this section, the site settings page for a site provides other options for configuring RSS feeds, creating new content objects (such as subsites, workspaces, lists, and libraries), and activating/deactivating features at the site level.

Conclusion

This chapter explored some of the common administrative tasks performed at the Central Administration level, site collection level, and site level. SharePoint administration varies according to the type of installation (single-server or farm), the set of features used (publishing, business data catalog, or Excel services), and other environment settings. Since administration tasks are performed at various levels, it is important from an organizational perspective to create a strategy for delegating administrative tasks among the system administrators, power users, and end users.

CHAPTER 24

Upgrading from SharePoint Portal Server 2003

Introduction

In the previous chapters, you have learned about all the different features of MOSS 2007. In this chapter, we show you how you can upgrade your current environment to MOSS 2007. As we all know, this seemingly simple process can be a real headache if we don't follow the right steps. This chapter will be completely directed toward system administrators, as they are the ones responsible for the upgrade. In this chapter, we discuss the various scenarios that might occur during an upgrade in your environment.

Depending on the size of your company, you will be coming in from a single server or a large server farm environment and will want to either stay the same in size or expand/reduce. There are three possible scenarios that are available for us to upgrade from SharePoint Portal Server 2003 to Office SharePoint Server 2007, as follows:

- In-place upgrade
- Gradual upgrade
- Database migration

An *in-place* upgrade is used to upgrade all SharePoint sites at one time, which is suitable for single-server or small deployments. A *gradual* upgrade allows finer control of the upgrade process by allowing one or more sites to be upgraded at a time. Both in-place and gradual upgrades take place on the same hardware on which your previous version is installed. A *database migration* allows you to move your content to a new farm or new hardware.

Before we start diving into the upgrade scenarios, we need to understand the road map that Microsoft has made available for us in terms of upgrades. Figure 24-1 shows the basic path for upgrade from a SharePoint Portal Server 2003 environment to an Office SharePoint Server 2007 environment.

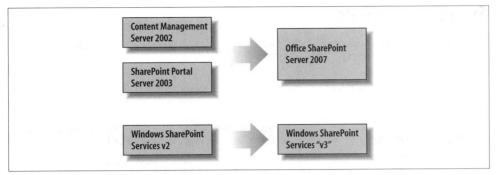

Figure 24-1. Supported upgrade paths for Office SharePoint Server 2007

 There is no direct upgrade path from SharePoint Portal Server 2001 to Office SharePoint Server 2007. However, we will discuss the scenario wherein you might have a backward-compatible SharePoint Portal Server 2003 environment and need to upgrade to Office SharePoint Server 2007. Also, we have shown the upgrade path from Windows SharePoint Services v2 to v3 in the diagram, but that will not be covered in this chapter. In Figure 24-1, we see the possible upgrade path from Content Management Server 2002 to Office SharePoint Server 2007. Although this is possible, discussion of that option is outside the scope of this book.

All the material on upgrading to Office SharePoint Server 2007 is available on Microsoft sites and documents; however, our goal here is to make it concise enough so that you don't have to go through hundreds of pages of documentation to find what you need. By the time you are done with this chapter, you should:

- Understand the upgrade options and advantages
- Understand options for handling customizations
- Support customizations for v2/2003
- Have a single, clear set of GUI and command-line options for the upgrade
- Understand how to prepare for an upgrade
- Perform the upgrade from SharePoint Portal Server 2003 to Office SharePoint Server 2007

 All the steps performed in this chapter have been implemented and tested with the Microsoft Office SharePoint Server 2007 RTM version.

Supported Topologies

Table 24-1 lists the supported and unsupported topologies when upgrading to Office SharePoint Server 2007.

Table 24-1. List of supported and unsupported topologies for an Office SharePoint Server 2007 upgrade

Existing Topology (SPS 2003)	Supported ending topology (Office SharePoint Server 2007)	Unsupported ending topology (Office SharePoint Server 2007)
Single server with MSDE	Single server with SQL Server 2005 express edition	Any farm
Single server with SQL server	Single server with SQL Server	Single server with SQL Server 2005 express edition, any farm
Small farm	Any farm	Single server with SQL Server 2005 express edition, any farm, single server with SQL Server
Medium farm	Any farm	Single server with SQL Server 2005 express edition, any farm, single server with SQL Server
Large farm	Any farm	Single server with SQL Server 2005 express edition, any farm, single server with SQL Server

 If you want to upgrade from a single server to a server farm configuration, you must first migrate from MSDE to SQL Server 2005 Express Edition to SQL Server, and then add additional servers to create a server farm. For information on migrating from MSDE to SQL Server, see "Migrating from MSDE to SQL Server" (*http://go.microsoft.com/fwlink/?LinkId=78008&clsid=0x409*).

Prerequisites for Upgrade

There are certain prerequisites to installing the Office SharePoint Server 2007 application on your server. If you launch the application setup, it will display a dialog box, as shown in Figure 24-2, stating that you do not have the prerequisites in place and need to install them before exiting.

The following are the steps that you want to implement in order to get ready for the installation:

1. The web server and application server computers must be running Microsoft Windows Server 2003 (Standard, Enterprise, Datacenter, or Web Edition) with Service Pack 1 (SP1) and must have Microsoft .NET Framework 3.0 and Microsoft ASP .NET 2.0.

2. Install Microsoft .NET Framework 3.0.

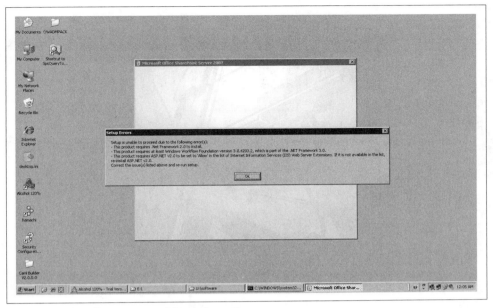

Figure 24-2. Installation prerequisites information message

3. Enable Microsoft ASP .NET 2.0:

   a. Click Start, point to All Programs, point to Administrative Tools, and then click on Internet Information Services (IIS) Manager.

   b. In the IIS manager tree, expand the tree and click the Web Services Extensions folder.

   c. In the details pane, as shown in Figure 24-3, click ASP.NET v2.0.50727, and then click Allow.

4. If you have not already applied Service Pack 2(SP2) for SharePoint Portal Server 2003, you must do so before upgrading. You must install Service Pack2 for both Windows SharePoint Services and SharePoint Portal Server 2003.

Perform Preupgrade Steps

Before we start upgrading our environment, we need to make sure that we have a rollback plan and that everything that we will need during the upgrade will be in place.

One of the first things that you should do is make sure that you have a complete backup of your current environment. In order to ensure that you can recover your existing environment, you must back up the databases that are used by Microsoft SharePoint Portal Server 2003, as listed in Table 24-2.

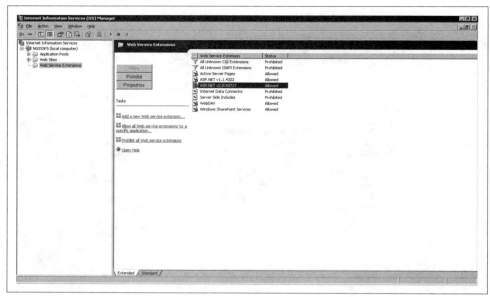

Figure 24-3. Enabling ASP.NET v2.0.50727

Table 24-2. SharePoint Portal Server 2003 database structure

Database type	Database name	Notes
Configurations Database	xxx_config_db	Required; one per farm
Site Database	xxx_SITE	Required; one per portal site
Profile Database	xxx_PROF	Required; one per portal site
Component Settings Database	xxx_SERV	Required; one per portal site
Single Sign-On Database	xxx_SSO	Optional; one per farm in case you have Single Sign-On implemented
Content Databases	STS_db_server_name_ID	Optional; there can be more than one, depending on the number of sites in your environment and their content

The database names in the previous table are samples of the default naming conventions. Your database names may vary depending on your implementation.

You can also use the SharePoint Portal Server 2003 backup and restore utility to generate a backup of your environment.

You should also back up any customizations (such as site definitions, Web Parts, and so on) and other necessary files in case you need to recreate your previous version environment.

Test your backups in a nonproduction environment and confirm that you can successfully restore the previous environment if necessary without any loss of data or customizations.

Next, you need to run the preupgrade scan utility provided by Microsoft as part of the Office SharePoint Server 2007 installation to determine any potential issues with the upgrade. If you have not successfully run this utility and you attempt to run the upgrade process, the wizard will exit and prompt you to run the tool.

 You must be a member of the Administrators group on the local computer to run this tool.

On the command line, change to the folder that contains the two files, and then run the following command to scan all servers in your server farm:

```
prescan.exe /c preupgradescanconfig.xml /all
```

You can use the preupgrade scan tool to scan all web sites in your environment (by using the /all parameter) or to scan a specific URL (by using the /v URL parameter). See Figure 24-4. If you do not supply a scoping parameter, all web sites will be scanned.

 Templates used by SharePoint Portal Server 2003 can be incorrectly identified during the preupgrade scan as custom templates unless you use the *preupgradescanconfig.xml* file when you perform the scan. This file contains additional logic to identify the portal site templates as standard templates used by SharePoint Portal Server 2003, rather than as custom templates based on Windows SharePoint Services 2.0.

You might need to run the upgrade utility more than once. After you resolve any issues from your first scan, you will need to run the utility again; otherwise, when you try to run the configuration wizard, you might see an error message that the prescan has not been run.

Unfortunately, as of now, the preupgrade scan utility is only a part of the Office SharePoint Server 2007 install and is not available as a standalone download. Therefore, you need to install Office SharePoint Server 2007 on a test environment and retrieve the *prescan.exe* file along with the *preupgradescanconfig.xml* file and copy them to the server running the existing version. These files are located in the *Drive:\ Program Files\Common Files\Microsoft Shared\Web Server Extensions\12\Bin* folder.

If you have modified your existing SharePoint Portal Server 2003 environment using Microsoft Office FrontPage 2003, you need to determine how you want to handle customized sites when you upgrade. You can choose to:

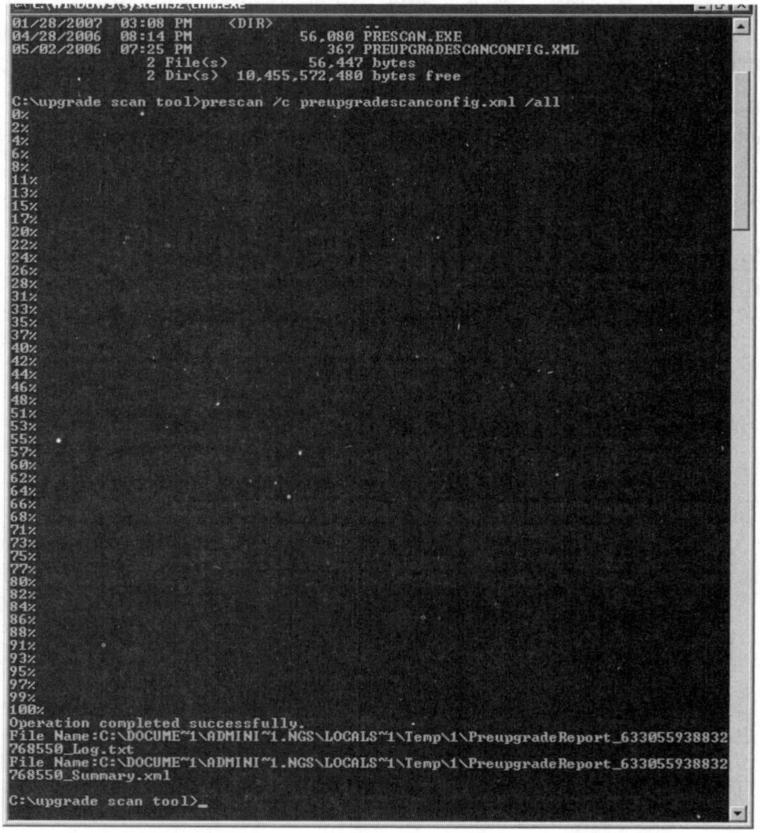

Figure 24-4. Upgrade scan tool

Keep the customizations

This approach will allow you to keep your existing customizations, in which case you really can't take advantage of the new capabilities of Office SharePoint Server 2007. There are three possible options for you:

- Do an in-place upgrade. By default, an in-place upgrade preserves customizations and does not reset to site definition. However, you may not be able to access certain controls, such as Site Actions.

- Do a gradual upgrade and keep the site in the previous version environment. This maintains the site exactly as it is, with the previous version functionality only.

- Do a gradual upgrade and upgrade the site, but do not reset any pages to the site definition. However, your site will be a mix of customized and uncustomized pages at this point.

Discard the customizations

If you are planning on completely redesigning your site, you can choose to reset all pages to use the default pages from site definition during the upgrade. For an in-place upgrade, after upgrading, use the Microsoft Office SharePoint Designer 2007 to reattach the default page layouts. For a gradual upgrade, use the upgrade option to reset the entire web site to use the site definition pages. This way, you can start with the new look and functionality, and then decide whether you want to customize the site again.

Redo the customizations

With this approach, you can take advantage of the new Master Pages model to apply your design, rather than customizing each individual page. After performing the in-place or gradual upgrade, modify the appropriate master pages and page layouts in the upgraded site to take on the previous version's look and feel, and then reattach the page layouts to all the customized pages. You can incorporate the new controls, such as the Site Actions menu, into your new page layouts as part of this work.

Additionally, during the in-place upgrade, you can also choose not to reset the pages to the site definition. This will preserve the customizations. After the upgrade, open the site and copy the customizations, and then reattach the page layouts and reapply your customizations to the master pages and page layouts as appropriate.

Possible Upgrade Options

At the beginning of the chapter, we mentioned that there are three possible options available for upgrading from SharePoint Portal Server 2003 to Office SharePoint Server 2007. Here we discuss these options in detail and define the steps that are involved in each of these processes.

In-Place Upgrade

As mentioned earlier, the in-place upgrade is most suitable for single-server or small deployments of SharePoint Portal Server 2003. In an in-place upgrade, you will be installing Office SharePoint Server 2007 on your existing environment. The previous version is overwritten with the new version, and the content databases are changed. Hence, this is not a reversible process—you cannot roll back to the previous version. When you run the in-place upgrade, the process upgrades your entire installation in a preset sequence. The following list shows the steps that need to be taken to implement an in-place upgrade. (For this in-place upgrade, I have an existing SharePoint Portal Server 2003 environment set up. It is a basic out-of-the-box setup with a couple of Windows SharePoint Services v2 sites and no customizations.)

1. Run *Setup.exe*.

2. This will bring up the Product Key dialog box (Figure 24-5). Enter the proper information to be able to move forward.

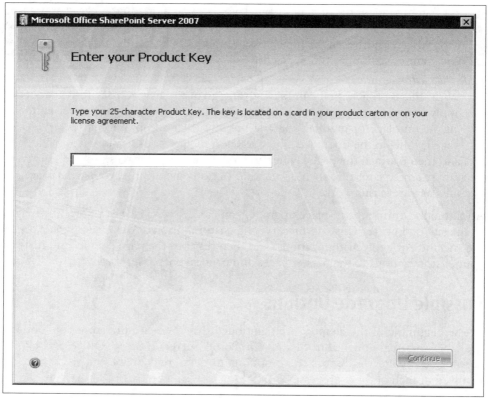

Figure 24-5. Office SharePoint Server 2007 Product Key installation page

3. On the Read the Microsoft Software License Terms page (Figure 24-6), review the terms, select the "I accept the terms of this agreement" checkbox, and then click Continue.

4. On the "Upgrade earlier versions" page (Figure 24-7), click "Yes, perform an automated in-place upgrade."

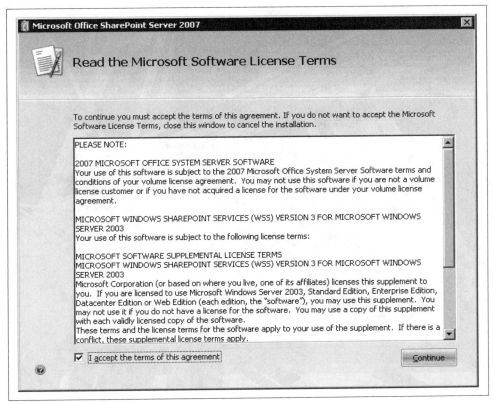

Figure 24-6. Office SharePoint Server 2007 install's License Terms page

5. On the Server Type tab (Figure 24-8), select your server type:

- Choose "Complete–Install all components. Can add servers to form a Share-Point farm" if this is the first server that you are upgrading in a server farm.

- Choose Web Front End if you are running an upgrade on an additional frontend web server in a server farm.

- Choose Stand-alone if this is a standalone server (not part of a server farm) and you want to use SQL Express for your database.

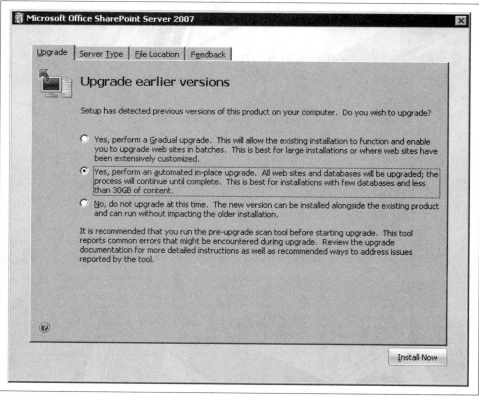

Figure 24-7. Office SharePoint Server 2007 install's upgrade type selection

6. On the File Location tab (Figure 24-9), select the locations where you want to install the applications.

7. Click Install Now to get the screen shown in Figure 24-10.

8. The setup runs and installs Office SharePoint Server 2007.

9. On the completion page (Figure 24-11), select the "Run the SharePoint Productions and Technologies Configuration Wizard now" if you have run the preupgrade scan tool previously. If you did not run the scan, you should run that first, before the configuration wizard.

10. In the SharePoint Products and Technologies Configuration Wizard on the Welcome page (Figure 24-12), click Next.

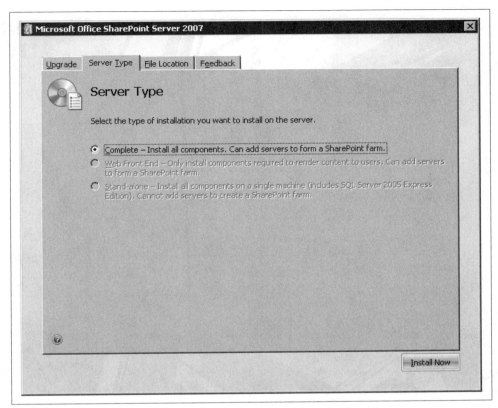

Figure 24-8. Complete install

11. A message appears, notifying you that Internet Information Services (IIS), the SharePoint Administration Service, and the SharePoint Times Service may need to be restarted or reset during the configuration. (See Figure 24-13.)

12. Click Yes to continue with the wizard. A message appears, notifying you that you should download and install new language template packs for the new version (Figure 24-14).

13. Click OK to confirm the message and continue with the wizard. Do not install the language template packs until you have completed running the configuration wizard.

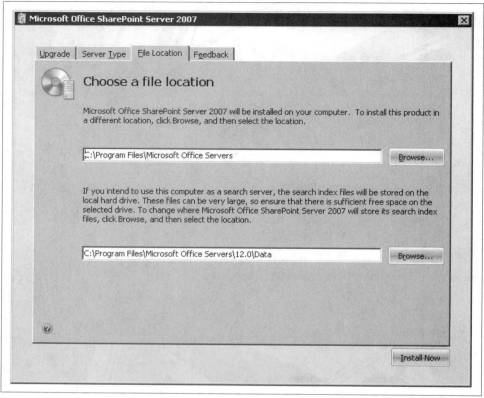

Figure 24-9. Location selection page

14. On the Configure SharePoint Central Administration Web Application page (Figure 24-15), if you want to use a specific port number for SharePoint Central Administration, select the "Specify port number" checkbox, and then type the port number you want to use. In the Configure Security Settings section, select either Negotiate (Kerberos) or NTLM, depending on your environment, and then click Next.

 To enable Kerberos authentication, you must perform additional configuration steps. For more information about authentication methods, see Plan authentication methods (Office SharePoint Server).

15. In the "Completing SharePoint Products and Technologies Configuration Wizard" page (Figure 24-16), verify the settings and click Next.

The configuration wizard runs and configures the configuration database and Central Administration Web application for Office SharePoint Server 2007 (Figure 24-17).

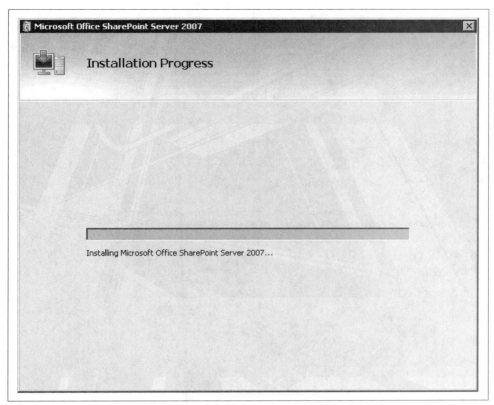

Figure 24-10. Install in progress

16. A message appears (Figure 24-18), notifying you that if you have a server farm with multiple servers, you must run the setup on each server to install new binary files before running the configuration wizard and starting the upgrade process.

   Depending on your server farm configuration, and where you are in the process of installing and configuring Office SharePoint Server 2007, you have three choices:

   • If this is the only server in your farm, no other actions are necessary. Click OK to continue with the wizard.

   • If you have other servers in your farm, and you have not yet run setup and the configuration wizard on the other servers, leave this message open on this server, and then run setup on the other servers in the farm. When all of the other servers are at this same stage, you can return to the frontend web server and click OK to continue with the SharePoint Products and Technologies Configuration Wizard.

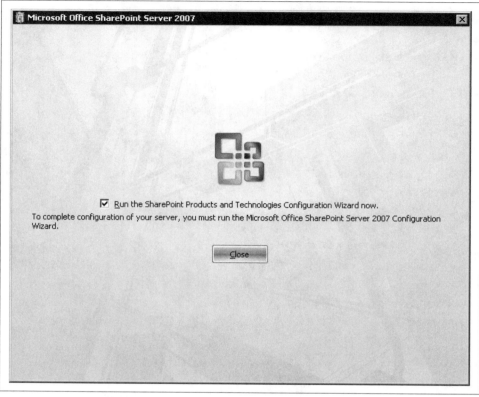

Figure 24-11. Install completed

- If you have already run setup on all the servers in your server farm and they are all at this stage, on a frontend web server, click OK to continue with the configuration wizard.

17. On the Configuration Successful page (Figure 24-19), review the settings that have been configured and then click Finish. The SharePoint Products and Technologies Configuration Wizard closes, and the Upgrade Running page opens. You may be prompted to enter your username and password before the Upgrade Running page will open. The upgrade process might take a while to complete. The Upgrade Running page refreshes every minute.

18. After the process has completed, click Continue. The Central Administration home page opens (Figure 24-20).

You will see at this point that some of the jobs that were started to configure SharePoint Products and Technologies might not have been completed. You can check the status of these jobs on the Timer Job Status page from the Central Administration page (Figure 24-21).

Figure 24-12. SharePoint Products and Technologies Configuration Wizard

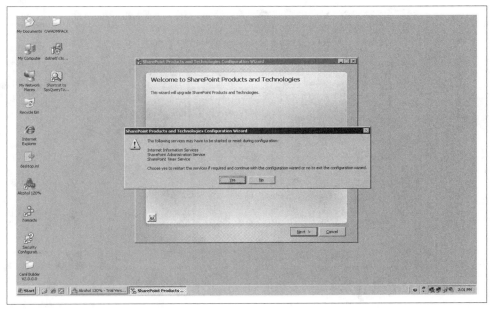

Figure 24-13. Restarting necessary services

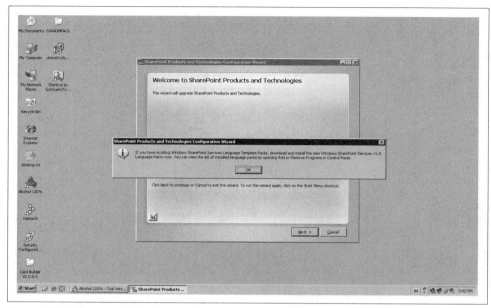

Figure 24-14. Language Template message

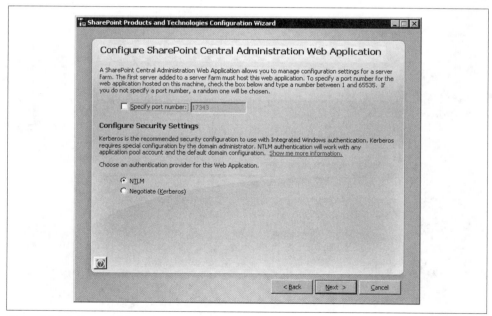

Figure 24-15. Central Administration Configuration

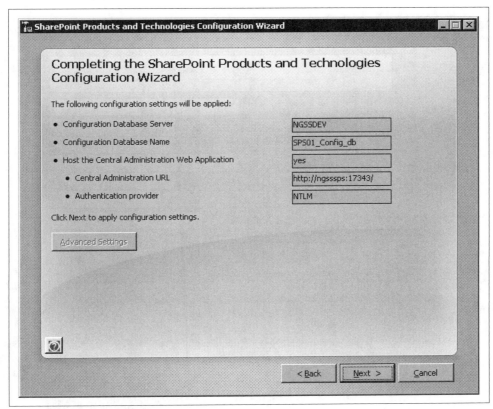

Figure 24-16. Completing configuration

It might be a few minutes before these jobs are completed. You can also go back to the Central Administration page and click Finalize Upgrade to complete the process. Once all the jobs have been successfully completed, you should be able to see the status (Figure 24-22).

Congratulations! At this point your upgrade has been successfully completed, and you can launch the home page of your portal (Figure 24-23).

If the upgrade fails or reports issues, you can refer to the logfiles for more information. The *Upgrade.logfile* is located at *%Windir%\Program Files\Common Files\ Microsoft Shared\Web Server Extensions\12\LOGS*.

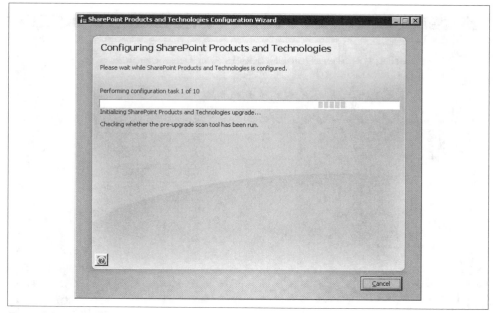

Figure 24-17. Configuration in process

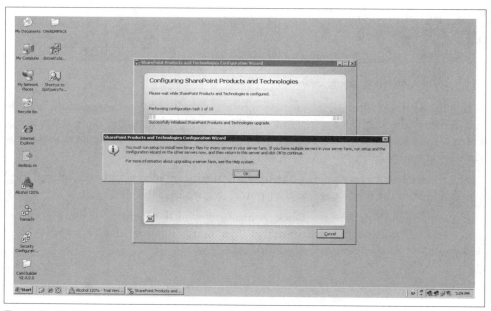

Figure 24-18. Message prompting to run install on every server in the farm

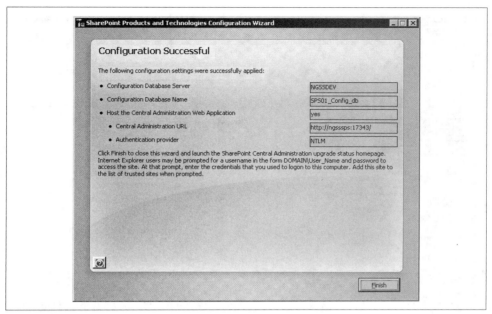

Figure 24-19. Configuration Successful page

Figure 24-20. SharePoint Central Administration page shows the status of the upgrade

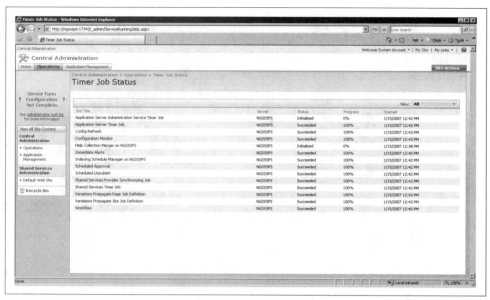

Figure 24-21. SharePoint Central Administration shows the status of pending jobs in the upgrade process

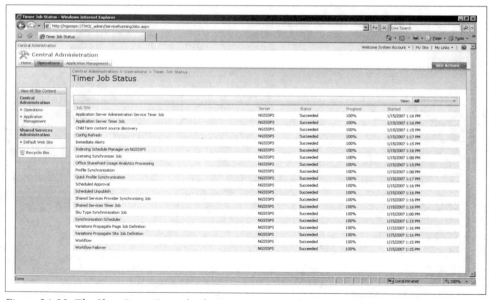

Figure 24-22. The SharePoint Central Administration page shows that all upgrade jobs have been successfully completed

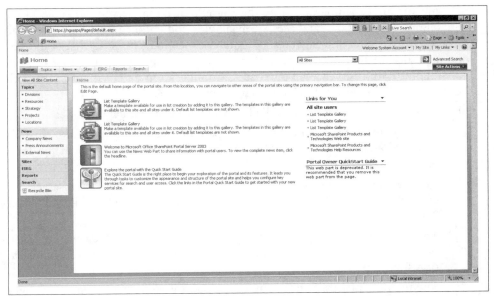

Figure 24-23. Site successfully upgraded to SharePoint Office Server 2007

Gradual Upgrade

Similar to an in-place upgrade, a gradual upgrade takes place on the same hardware that is used for your previous version. However, in a gradual upgrade, you can control which sites are upgraded at any point, and it allows you to run both versions of your portal at the same time. When you implement a gradual upgrade, the starting and ending topologies are exactly the same, except for the following differences:

- During and after the upgrade, the frontend web servers run both SharePoint Portal Server 2003 and Office SharePoint Server 2007. The site collections that were upgraded run under Office SharePoint Server 2007, whereas site collections that could not be upgraded or were not selected to be upgraded continue to run under SharePoint Portal Server 2003.

- During and after the upgrade, the application servers run both SharePoint Portal Server 2003 and Office SharePoint Server 2007 services. Upgraded portal sites consume Office SharePoint Portal Server 2007 shared services; portals that have not yet been upgraded or cannot be upgraded consume SharePoint Portal Server 2003 shared services. Additional services (such as Microsoft Excel Services) can be added after the upgrade.

- During and after the upgrade, both the SharePoint Portal Server 2003 and Office SharePoint Server 2007 databases are available. Content for upgraded sites exists in the Office SharePoint Server 2007 databases; content for sites that could not be upgraded or that need to remain as they were continue to be stored in the SharePoint Portal Server 2003 databases. Configuration databases exist for both Office SharePoint Server 2007 and SharePoint Portal Server 2003.

- Here's a description of what actually happens during a gradual upgrade:

  1. After performing all preupgrade steps, the server administrator installs Office SharePoint Server 2007 to the first frontend web server in the farm and then chooses Gradual Upgrade.

  2. The upgrade process runs and upgrades any data specific to each server (for example, search settings stored on the filesystem on SharePoint Portal Server 2003 servers).

  3. The upgrade process creates an *Office SharePoint Server 2007* web application to host SharePoint Central Administration, and the Central Administration site is created.

  4. The upgrade process creates a new configuration database to store configuration data for Office SharePoint Server 2007. Configuration data from the SharePoint Portal Server 2003 configuration data is copied into the new database. Single sign-on (SSO) is upgraded (it registers a new Office SharePoint Server 2007 service that talks to the previous version's SSO database).

  5. Once the Office SharePoint Server 2007 has been installed on the first frontend web server, the administrator needs to install this on the rest of the servers in the farm. If the environment uses shared services, the upgrade process will update all the user profiles and search data related to the portal that was selected for upgrade.

  6. The administrator selects the virtual server to be upgraded and specifies the target web application. The upgrade process will create the target web application and install any Web Parts deployed to the SharePoint Portal Server 2003 virtual server to the new web application.

  7. There will be a temporary content database created for each content database that existed in the previous version. The upgrade process will copy the site list from SharePoint Portal Server 2003 into the new environment. The process will first copy the site data to the temporary database and then upgrade the site in the temporary database. During this process, both the old and new sites are not available.

  8. After all the selected sites are upgraded, the content for these sites is moved to the Office SharePoint Server 2007 database, and then the temporary database is deleted.

9. After all upgrades have been completed, both the environments, SharePoint Portal Server 2003 and Office SharePoint Server 2007, are available. The administrator can uninstall the SharePoint Portal Server 2003 environment at this point if it is no longer needed.

One of the obvious things to note is what happens to site URLs during the upgrade process. Obviously, site URLs have to be unique; therefore, during the upgrade process we need to make sure that we have different domain URLs for each site: the old site and the new site (for example, *http://Portal_Old/sites/siteA* and *http://Portal_New/sites/SiteA*). Hence, before we start the upgrade process, we need to make sure that we have a temporary domain URL. The upgraded sites take over the existing URLs and user requests will be routed to their content, regardless of whether it has been upgraded. The redirection process happens as follows:

1. Before the upgrade process starts, you need to create a temporary domain URL.

2. During the upgrade process, you will be prompted to enter the temporary domain URL information from step 1. The process will move the previous version's site to the temporary domain URL, and the new version will take over the original URL.

3. A site redirect is automatically created for each site collection to send requests for the original URL to the previous version's site until the site is upgraded.

4. After the sites have been upgraded, the site redirections are deleted.

5. After all the sites have been upgraded, and you have deleted all of the previous version sites, you can manually remove the temporary domain URL from the Domain Naming System (DNS).

 During the upgrade process, browser access to the sites will work due to the redirects; however, certain applications, such as the Microsoft Office clients, will not be able to access sites via redirects. Be aware that this URL redirection can cause hardcoded links within sites or documents to break.

So, let's begin the installation and configuration of Office SharePoint Server 2007 for a gradual upgrade. This will install the new version alongside the previous version. After the installation is completed and you have configured Office SharePoint Server 2007, you can then determine which site collections to upgrade and when to upgrade them.

When upgrading a server farm, be sure to upgrade all of the servers in the server farm in the following order:

1. Run setup to install the new version on all servers in the server farm.

2. Run the SharePoint Products and Technologies Configuration Wizard on the frontend web server that contains SharePoint Central Administration.

3. Run the SharePoint Products and Technologies Configuration Wizard on the Index Job Server.

4. Run the SharePoint Products and Technologies Configuration Wizard on all other frontend web servers or search servers in the farm in any order.

At this point, we need to make sure that all the prerequisite software for installing Office SharePoint Server 2007 is in place.

If your medium or large server farm contains one or more servers that are not frontend web servers, and you have used the Default Web Site in Internet Information Services to host a SharePoint site, your upgrade may fail with a message that the Default Web Site cannot be upgraded. To work around this issue, before running the upgrade, create a web site on a different port on all nonfrontend web servers, and then restore the name to Default Web Site. You do not need to rename the web site on any frontend web servers in the server farm.

Next, let's start the installation of Office SharePoint Server 2007 in a gradual upgrade. Make sure that you have performed all the preupgrade steps mentioned earlier the in-place upgrade instructions. Once again, I am going to start with the following environment: two SharePoint Portal Server 2003 Portals, with each of these having a few sites based on the old Windows SharePoint Services templates.

Most of the screenshots are the same as the in-place upgrade, so only the different screenshots are shown here:

1. Run *setup.exe*.

2. On the "Enter your Product Key" page, type the product key, and then click Continue.

3. On the "Read the Microsoft Software License Terms" page, review the terms, select "I accept the terms of this agreement" checkbox, and then click Continue.

4. On the "Upgrade earlier versions" page, click "Yes, perform a Gradual upgrade" (Figure 24-24).

5. On the Server Type tab (Figure 24-25), select your server type:

   • Choose Complete if this is the first server that you are upgrading in a server farm.

   • Choose Web Front End if you are running the upgrade on an additional frontend web server in a server farm.

6. Click Install Now.

7. The setup wizard runs and installs Office SharePoint Server 2007.

8. On the completion page (Figure 24-26), clear the "Run the SharePoint Products and Technologies Configuration Wizard now" checkbox, and then click Close.

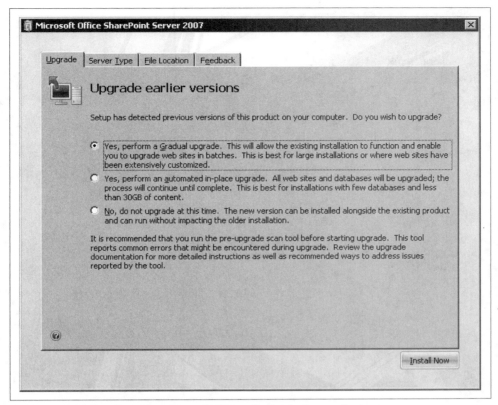

Figure 24-24. Office SharePoint Server 2007 install, Gradual type selection

Before you start the SharePoint Products and Technologies Wizard, make sure you have performed the following steps:

- Run the preupgrade scan tool as provided with Office SharePoint Server 2007 installed and be sure to address any issues identified.

- Deploy any upgrade definition files.

- Install any language template packs for Office SharePoint Server 2007. Alternatively, you can install them after you complete the upgrade process, and then use the command line to upgrade any sites that depend on the language template packs.

- If you have a server farm, follow the earlier instructions for installing Office SharePoint Server 2007 on each index server and frontend web server in your server farm. After install is completed on all the servers, you can start the configuration wizard.

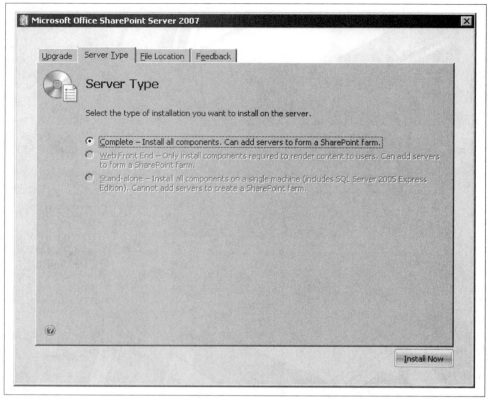

Figure 24-25. Office SharePoint Server 2007 install, Complete type selection

 Do not add any servers to your server farm after this point in the process. Running the SharePoint Products and Technologies Wizard upgrades the configuration database. This database contains the list of servers in the farm, and any servers added to the farm after the Configuration Wizard has been run will not be included in the database, and therefore will not appear in the v3 topology. If you need to add servers to your farm, do so either before the upgrade or after you have completed the upgrade process.

Next, run the SharePoint Products and Technologies Configuration Wizard:

1. Click Start, point to All Programs, point to Administrative Tools, and then click SharePoint Products and Technologies Configuration Wizard.

2. In the SharePoint Products and Technologies Configuration Wizard, on the "Welcome to SharePoint Products and Technologies" page, click Next. A message appears, notifying you that Internet Information Services (IIS), the SharePoint administration Service, and the SharePoint Timer Service may need to be restarted or reset during configuration.

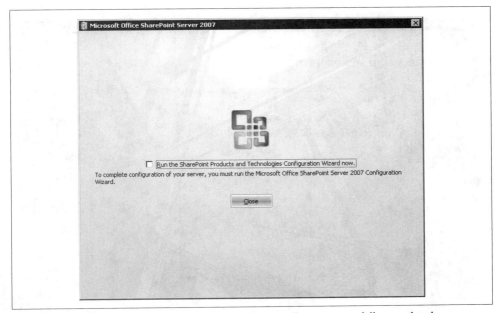

Figure 24-26. Office SharePoint Server 2007 install, installation successfully completed

3. Click Yes to continue with the wizard.

4. On the "Connect to a server farm" page (Figure 24-27), select "No, I want to create a new server farm" and click Next.

5. On the Specify Configuration Database Settings page (Figure 24-28), in the "Database server" text box, type the name of the server running Microsoft SQL Server 2000 or Microsoft SQL Server 2005.

6. In the "Database name" box, either leave the default (SharePoint_config) or type a new database name.

7. In the Specify Database Access Account section, type the username and password for connecting to the SQL Server, and then click Next.

 This account must have rights to create databases. If SQL Server is running on a separate server from your web frontend server, then this account must also be a domain account. This user account must be a member of the following SQL Server security roles: Database Creator and Security Administrator.

8. On the Configure SharePoint Central Administration Web Application page (Figure 24-29), if you want to use a specific port number for SharePoint Central Administration, select the "Specify port number" checkbox, and then type the port number to use.

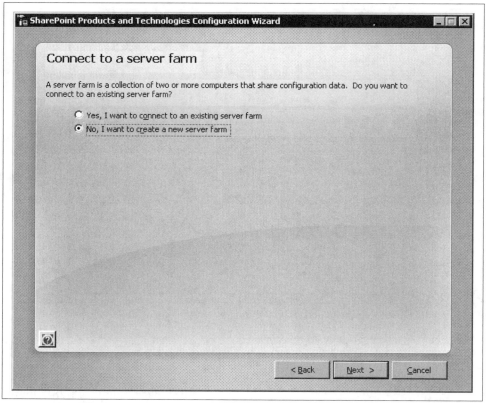

Figure 24-27. SharePoint Products and Technologies Configuration Wizard—creating a new server farm

9. In the Configure Security Settings section, select either Negotiate (Kerberos) or NTLM, depending on your environment, and then click Next.

 To enable Kerberos authentication, you must perform additional configuration. For more information about authentication methods, see "Plan authentication methods (Office SharePoint Server)."

10. In the "Completing the SharePoint Products and Technologies Configuration Wizard" page (Figure 24-30), verify the settings and click Next. Then, finalize the configuration settings (Figure 24-31).

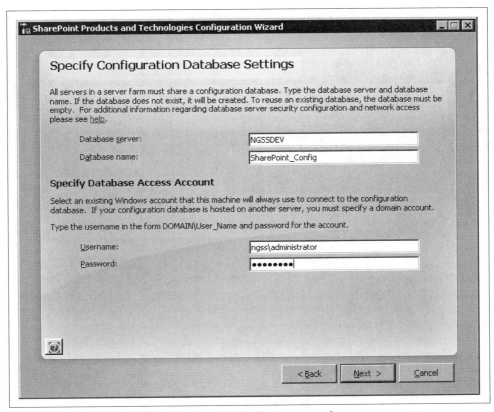

Figure 24-28. Configuration Database settings for the new server farm

11. If you have a server farm in multiple servers, a message appears, notifying you that you must run setup on each server to install new binary files before running the configuration wizard and starting the upgrade process. Depending on your server farm configuration, and where you are in the process of installing and configuring Office SharePoint Server 2007, you have these choices:

   • If this is the only server in your farm, and you have not yet run setup and the configuration wizard on the servers, leave this message open on this server, and then run setup on the other servers in the farm. When all of the other servers are at this same stage, you can return to the frontend web server and click OK to continue with the SharePoint Products and Technologies Configuration Wizard.

   • If you have already run setup on all servers in your server farm and they are all at this stage, on a frontend web server, click OK to continue with the configuration wizard.

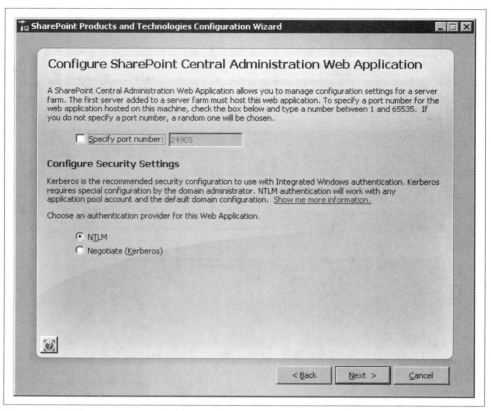

Figure 24-29. SharePoint Central Administration configurations

12. On the Configuration Successful page, review the settings that have been configured, and then click Finish (Figure 24-32).

   • After you click on Finish in the Configuration Successful page, the SharePoint Central Administration page opens and allows you to see the status of pending jobs that will allow the upgrade process to finish successfully.

Upgrade sites

After you have performed a gradual upgrade, you can determine which sites to upgrade and when. Site upgrade can be implemented using either the upgrade pages in the SharePoint Central Administration Web Site or the upgrade operation on the command line. The command-line utility is more useful for large batches of sites at different times or if you have installed a language template packs upgrading other sites in your environment.

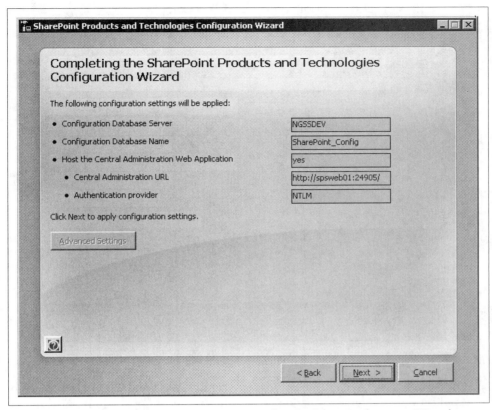

Figure 24-30. Completing the SharePoint Products and Technologies Configuration Wizard

Upgrade sites with Central Administration Pages. There are two phases in the process for upgrading sites from the Central Administration pages. First, create a new web application to host the upgraded versions of sites. Then, upgrade one or more site collections.

 You must upgrade the root site collection before you can upgrade any other site collections in the web application.

Create a new web application to host upgraded sites

1. In Central Administration, on the Operations tab, under "Upgrade and Migration," click "Site content upgrade status," as shown in Figure 24-33.

2. On the Site Content Upgrade Status page (Figure 24-34), next to the URL you want to upgrade, click "Begin upgrade."

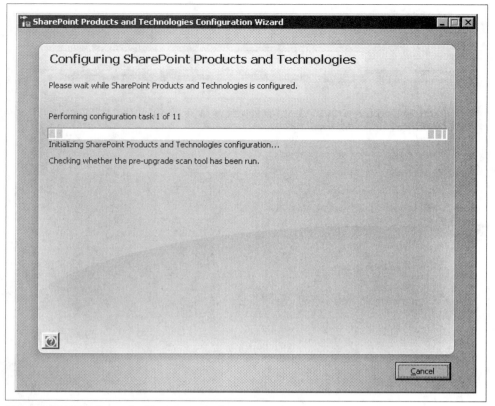

Figure 24-31. Finalizing the SharePoint configuration settings

3. On the Set Target Web Application page (Figures 24-35 and 24-36), in the "Web Application to Upgrade" section, verify that the web application you want to upgrade appears, as shown in Figure 24-35.

4. In the "New URL for Original Content" section, type a port number in the Port box, and then in the Host Header box, type the host header to use (if needed), as shown in Figure 24-35.

5. In the Application pool for New Web Application section, select "Create new application pool." In the "Application pool name" box, type a name, and then select either Predefined or Configurable.

   • If you selected Predefined, select which account to use.

   • If you selected Configurable, type the account name to use, and then type the password for that account.

 You cannot use the same application pool that you used for the previous version. You can use the same user account, but you must create a new application pool or use an application pool that you already crated for your upgraded sites.

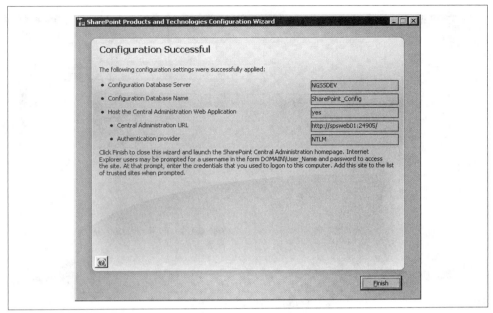

Figure 24-32. Configuration Successful page

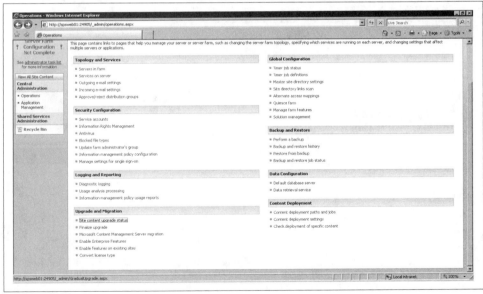

Figure 24-33. Upgrade and Migration Status in Central Administration

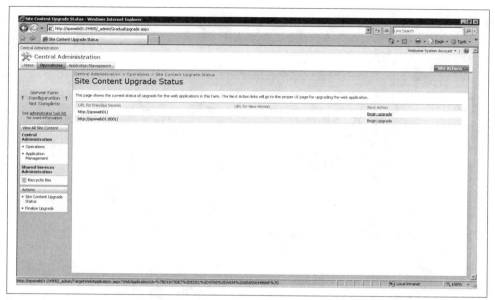

Figure 24-34. Site Content Upgrade Status page

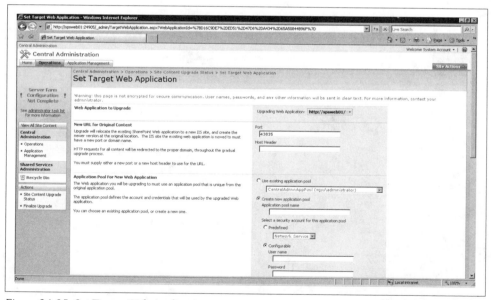

Figure 24-35. Set Target Web Application page

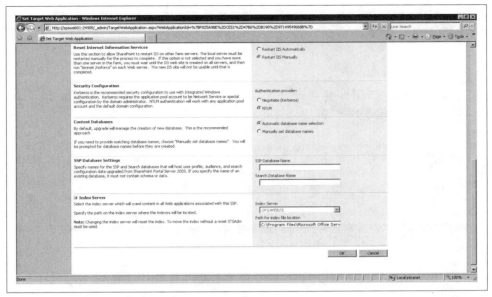

Figure 24-36. Set Target Web Application page (lower half)

6. In the Reset Internet Information Services section, select either Restart IIS Automatically or Restart IIS Manually. If you choose Restart IIS Manually, you will need to restart IIS after the web application is created in the final step in this procedure.

7. In the "Security configuration" section, under Authentication Provider, select either Negotiate (Kerberos) or NTLM depending on your environment. If you select Kerberos, you will have to perform additional steps as defined in the Office SharePoint Server 2007 Installation guide.

8. In the Content Databases section, select either "Automatic database name selection" or "Manually set database names."

9. In the SSP Database Settings section, in the SSP Database Name box, type the name for the Shared Services Provider database.

10. In the Search Database Settings section, type the name for the Search database.

11. In the Index Server section, in the Index Server box, select the Index Server to use.

12. Click OK:

- If you choose to manually set the database names, the Database Names page opens. Type the names to use for the temporary content databases and the new version content databases for this web application, and then click Save.

- An Operation In Progress page appears while the new web application is created. Once the web application has been created successfully, you will see the Site Collection Upgrade page, as shown in Figure 24-37.

If you choose to restart IIS manually, you must now run *iisreset/ noforce* on each frontend web server in your server farm.

Upgrade Site Collections.

1. On the "Site Collection Upgrade" page (Figure 24-37), select the checkboxes next to the sites you want to upgrade, and then click Upgrade Sites.

 You must upgrade the root site collection before you can upgrade any other site collections in the web application. If you are upgrading multiple site collections at one time, the root site collection must be included in the first set of sites that you upgrade.

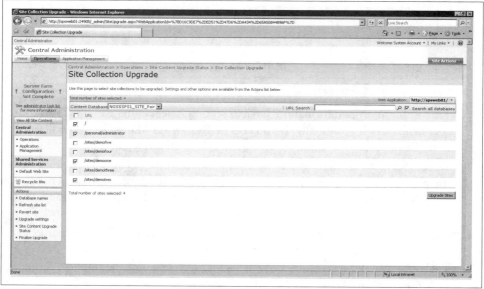

Figure 24-37. Site Collection Upgrade page

2. On the Sites Selected for Upgrade page (Figure 24-38), verify the number of site collections, the storage used, the originating database, and the target database, and then click Continue.

3. The Upgrade Running page (Figure 24-39) opens, and the upgrade runs for the selected site collections. This may take few minutes or a few hours, depending on how many site collections you have selected and how large the site collections are. If the upgrade fails or reports issues, you can refer to the logfile generated at the following location: *%windir%\Program Files\Common Files\Microsoft Shared\Web Server Extensions\12\Logs*. The trace log is named in the following format: *Machine-name-YYYYMMDD-HHMM.log*.

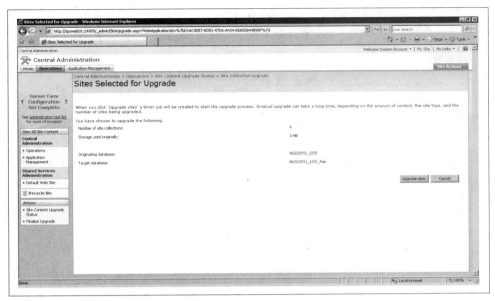

Figure 24-38. Sites Selected for Upgrade page

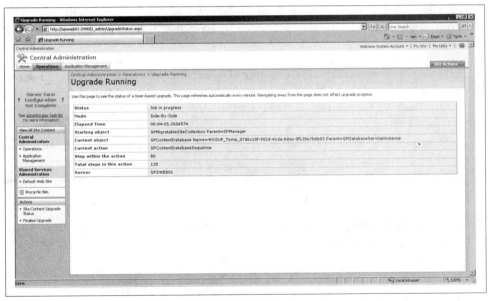

Figure 24-39. Upgrade Running page

4. After the upgrade process is completed successfully (Figure 24-40), click Home to return to the Central Administration home page.

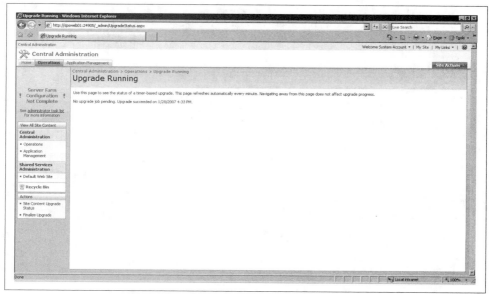

Figure 24-40. Site Collection Upgrade completed successfully

At this point, if you access your site URL, you will see that the site collection root (Figure 24-41) has been upgraded to an Office SharePoint Server 2007 site (as shown in Figure 24-42), and the corresponding subsites that you selected have also been upgraded. On the other hand, the sites that you did not select for upgrade (Figure 24-43)—for example, Demo site five—still have the previous version template associated to the site. You can upgrade this site at any point by going back to the Central Administration step and performing the same steps again.

The target URL that you had set up—in our case, *http://spsweb01:9000*—still has the portal from the previous version and the related subsites (Figure 24-44). This shows how you can have both versions of the portal side by side (Figure 24-45).

Perform a gradual upgrade with shared services (upgrading the parent portal first). Upgrading SharePoint Portal Server 2003 in a Shared Services requires that you perform the upgrade actions in the following specific sequence:

1. Upgrade the parent portal.
2. Upgrade the personal site host.
3. Upgrade My Sites.
4. Upgrade Team Sites.
5. Upgrade Child Portals.

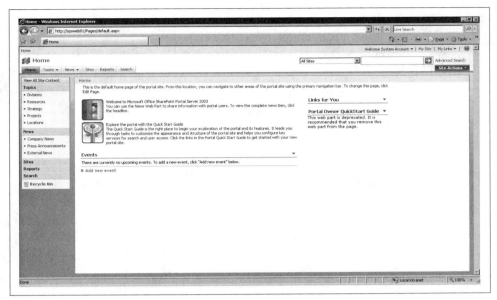

Figure 24-41. Upgrade Site Collection page

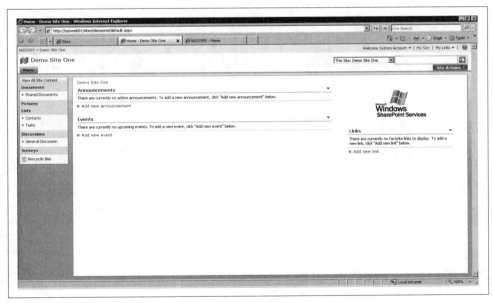

Figure 24-42. Upgraded Site page

Upgrades of My Sites, team sites, and child portals can be done in any sequence; however, it is advisable to upgrade all My Sites at the same time, for consistent user experience.

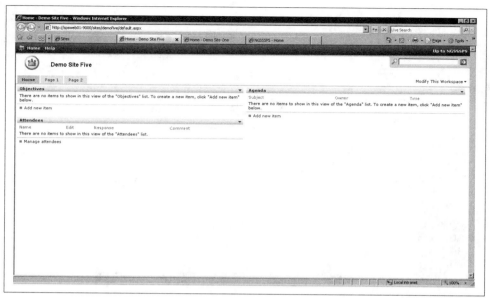

Figure 24-43. *Unselected sites not upgraded still utilize the template from the previous version*

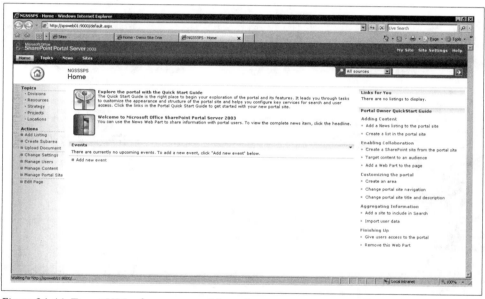

Figure 24-44. *Target URL where our portal from the previous version is still available*

Upgrade the parent portal. During a gradual upgrade in shared services, create a SQL Server backup file for the profile (PROF) and Component Settings (SERV) databases. This backup is stored in the default data directory for SQL Server, usually

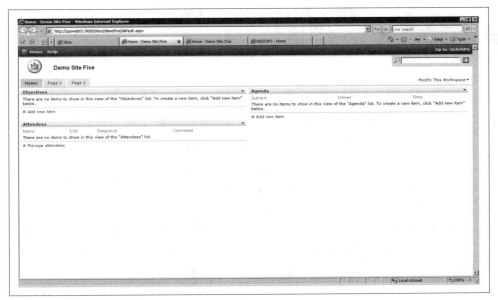

Figure 24-45. Both versions of the portal

%PROGRAM FILES%\mssql\data. Make there is enough disk space available to generate these backup files:

1. Install and configure Office SharePoint Server 2007 for a gradual upgrade. Be sure to run setup on all servers in the farm.

2. Install language templates if necessary.

3. Check the logfiles for any open issues.

4. Configure the web application through the Central Administration pages.

5. Copy any Web Parts from the bin to the Office SharePoint Server 2007 web application. Copy all Web Parts marked as "safe control" in the *web.config* file. Install any upgraded Web Parts using their corresponding installers.

6. Prepare to upgrade the site collections:

    • Run the preupgrade scan tool again, review the reports, and troubleshoot issues.

    • You can use the command-line tool instead of Central Administration if you want to schedule the upgrade process or want to upgrade large numbers of site collections (more than 100 or so).

7. Upgrade the site collections, making sure to upgrade the root site web site first.

8. Review the Shared Services Settings. You will have to:

    • Recreate any search scopes.

    • Review upgraded content source definitions, crawl rules, etc.

- Configure profiles and audiences to be synchronized between and Office SharePoint Server 2007.
- Review the Manager properties of user profiles in Office SharePoint Server 2007.
- Run a full crawl on the new portal site.

Upgrade the personal site host. Generally, the personal site and team sites hosts are the same as the parent portal. Perform the following steps only if you configured the Personal Sites or Team Sites to be on their own server farm:

1. Install and configure Office SharePoint Server 2007 for a gradual upgrade. Be sure to run setup on all servers in the farm.
2. Install language templates if necessary.
3. Configure the web application through the Central Administration pages.
4. Upgrade site collections, making sure to upgrade the root site web site first.
5. Review the upgraded sites.

Upgrading the Portal Using Database Migration

During the upgrade process, if you are planning to utilize new hardware or just redesign your portal layout, you can choose to use the database migration method rather than using in-place or gradual upgrade. During the database migration, you perform an in-place upgrade on the database, but you do not upgrade your server farm configuration data. Even though this option is probably more complicated and tedious, it might be your best option if you have numerous customized sites.

In order to perform a database migration, first implement the following steps:

1. Create the new Office SharePoint Server 2007 environment.
2. Migrate data to the new environment using backed-up databases from the previous versions.

Preparing the New Office SharePoint Server 2007 Environment

Before you can start the database migration, you need to set up the new Office SharePoint Server 2007 environment, which includes recreating the web applications, reapplying the configuration settings, and copying any customizations over from the old environment. After you deploy Office SharePoint Server 2007, you need to:

1. Run the preupgrade scan tool and address any issues that are logged by the application.
2. Create a web application for each virtual server that was in the old environment.

3. Manually reapply farm configuration settings, such as the email server, farm-level security, alternate access settings, included paths, and Shared Service settings, including search settings.

 Because search settings from SharePoint Portal Server 2003 were stored both in the registry on the server and in a database, you must recreate your search database and reconfigure your search settings when you perform a database migration.

4. Manually copy all customizations into your new farm. Make sure to install any of the following that you might need:
   - Custom Site Definitions
   - Custom Style Sheets
   - Custom Web Parts
   - Custom Web Services
   - Language packs

And so on. After you have finished all of these steps, you can proceed and migrate the databases. When you perform a restore of a database and add it to the farm, the upgrade process runs and upgrades the entire database. Before you start the process, you also want to stop all users from adding any new data so that your backups contain the most current data. You can do this by setting your databases to read-only; this will allow them to see data but not add anything new.

Backing up SQL databases is a pretty normal procedure, so I will not go into those details here. After you have configured your new Office SharePoint Server 2007 environment, restore the backup copies of the databases. Restore one database at a time, and verify that it has worked before you restore the next database.

Adding Databases to the Web Application

When you add the content databases, be sure that the root site for the web application is included in the fist content database you add. After you have added this content database, you can add all the others in any sequence.

 If you are using My Sites, you need to upgrade the site content database first. When restoring of the Shared Service Providers (SSP), select the checkbox to configure the My Site Web application, choose the web application for the portal, and then type /My Site as the relative path.

You must use the command-line utility to add a content database to a web application.

You cannot add the same content database more than once to a farm, even on different web applications. Each site collection in a content database (including each portal site) has a globally unique identifier (GUID) associated with it, registered in the configuration database. Therefore, it is not possible to add the same site collection twice to the farm, even in separate web applications. If you need a duplicate copy of a site collection in the same farm, first attach the database that contains the site collection to a separate farm, and then use the *stsadm.exe* backup and restore operations to copy the site collection over to the desired farm. The backup and restore process creates a new GUID for the site collection.

Add a content database to a web application with the command-line utility. On the command line, run the following command:

```
Stsadm.exe -o addcontentdb -url URL [-databaseserver servername] -databasename
databasename [-DatabaseUser username -DatabasePassword password] [-SiteWarning
number] [-SiteMaximum number] [-SearchServer servername]
```

That's it! Repeat the restore and add database procedures for the remaining steps. Review the upgrade logfiles and make sure there were no issues logged. As mentioned before, the logfiles are located at *%Program Files%\Common Files\Microsoft Shared\Web Server Extensions\12\Logs*.

Perform Post-Upgrade Steps

In order to finalize upgrade process, we need to perform the following post-upgrade steps:

1. Review upgraded sites. After the upgrade has been completed using the gradual upgrade method, you should keep the original sites available for some time and review the upgrade sites to make sure that all features and functionality have been upgraded successfully.

 The URLs of the old sites will change during the gradual upgrade process. Make sure that site owners are notified of the old and new URLs for the site so they can access them properly, compare differences, and verify that everything is functioning smoothly.

2. Copy missing components, if any, from the old site to the new site by using a SharePoint-compatible web page editor, such as Office SharePoint Designer.
3. Update or redeploy any Web Parts that no longer function properly.
4. Determine whether any pages need to be reset to the site definition version. If you have any pages that have been customized and do not show the new version's

functionality, you should consider resetting the pages to the site definition to apply the new version's look and functionality, and then reapplying your customizations. You can perform this step from the site settings page in your site, and you can reset either individual pages or the entire site.

Revert to a Previous Version Site (Office SharePoint Server)

If you want to discard the results of a gradual upgrade for a particular site and need to revert to the previous version site, you can do so by using the following procedure.

 Reverting back to the previous sites deletes the upgraded sites. Be sure to copy any elements you might need from the upgraded site (by using a web page editor that is compatible with Microsoft Office SharePoint Server 2007, such as Microsoft Office SharePoint Designer 2007).

After you have made any necessary changes in the previous version site, you can try upgrading the site again:

1. In the Central Administration page, on the Operations tab under Upgrade and Migration, click "Site content upgrade status."

2. On the Site Content Upgrade Status page, next to the URL that contains the site you want to revert, click Continue Upgrade.

3. On the Site Collection Upgrade page, on the Actions menu, click "Revert site."

4. On the "Revert to Non-Upgraded Site" page, in the Select Upgrade Site Collection section, find the Site Collection box, click the down arrow, and then click Change Site Collection.

5. On the Select Site Collection page, click the URL for the site collection you want to revert, and then click OK.

6. On the "Revert to Non-Upgraded Site" page, click Continue.

Checklist for Reviewing Upgraded Sites

Use the following checklists to walk through your site and identify any issues you need to address.

Web Parts

1. Do all the Web Parts from your original site show up in your upgraded site?

2. Are the Web Parts displayed correctly in the correct Web Part Zone and in the correct size?

3. Are there any extra or missing Web Parts?

Styles and Appearance

1. Do all the images used on your pages display correctly?
2. Are the appropriate cascading style sheet colors and styles used in the appropriate places?
3. Does the theme you applied to your site still look the same?
4. Do you have any JavaScript controls that are not working?

Areas

Areas and subareas undergo many conversions during upgrade; ultimately, they are converted into subsites within the portal site collection. The home pages for your areas and subareas have been moved into the Pages library for each subsite, and URLs for sites and subsites in Office SharePoint Server 2007 now follow the logical navigation structure. So, instead of the URL *http://portal_name/c2/*, you will see *http://portal_name* or *http://portal_name/sites/*.

1. Do all of your previous areas and subareas now show up as subsites in the upgraded site collection and appear in the correct order in navigation? Are there any extra subsites?
2. If an area in your original site was hidden from navigation, is the subsite still hidden in the upgraded site?
3. Are the names of the subsites showing up correctly in the navigation?

Customized (unghosted) pages

A page that has been customized using a SharePoint-compatible Web Page editor such as Office FrontPage 2003 is called an *unghosted page* because it is no longer simply a view of the default version of that page.

1. Are your customizations still in place?
2. Can you still get to the editing controls on the page?
3. Are your customizations still appropriate in the new environment, or do you want to update to the new functionality or look?

Common Issues

This section reviews some of the common issues that come up while upgrading.

Known Issues for Preupgrade Scanning

We'll start with the known issues for preupgrade scanning.

Upgrade is blocked if you use "localhost" as your server name

Using "localhost" as your server name can cause many issues in your environment and is not recommended. If you are using "localhost" as your server name, when you run the preupgrade scan tool, this issue is logged and the upgrade cannot proceed. You must rename the server computer and then run an operation in prescan before you continue with the upgrade. Follow these steps to rename your server and fix the issue for the preupgrade scan tool:

1. Back up the configuration database.

2. From the command line, change to the following path: *%windir%\Program Files\Common Files\Microsoft Shared\Web Server Extensions\12\bin*. Then run the following command to change the server name in the configuration database:

   ```
   stsadm.exe -o setconfigdb -databaseserver <Server Name> -connect
   ```

 If you are using the database migration path to upgrade, this operation will not resolve the issue, because you are upgrading to a different configuration database. Instead, you must use a script to fix this issue in the content databases directly.

From the command line, change to the following path: *%windir%\Program Files\Common Files\Microsoft Shared\Web Server Extensions\12\bin*. Then run the following command to clear the issue for the preupgrade scan tool:

```
Prescan /fixlocalhost
```

On the command line, run the following command to rerun the preupgrade scan process:

```
prescan /all
```

- If it is successful, proceed with the upgrade.

- If it still fails, then there is still a service using the localhost server name. At this point, upgrade is not blocked, but some services may not upgrade successfully.

Known Issues for In-Place Upgrade

- You must use a domain account, not Network Service, for server farm upgrades, even if you used a Network Service account for the previous version. For either in-place or gradual upgrades in a server-farm environment, you should use the same credentials that you used in the previous version environment. Be sure that the domain account has the appropriate rights on the SQL Server.

- If your medium or large server farm contains one or more servers that are not frontend web servers, and you have used the default web site in Internet Information Services (IIS) to host a SharePoint site, upgrade may fail with a message that the Default Web Site cannot be upgraded. To work around this issue, before running the upgrade, rename the Default Web Site in IIS to something else on all non-frontend Web Servers (such as the Index server), and then run the upgrade. Finally, restore the name to Default Web Site.

- In-place upgrade may fail if there are multiple portal sites with the same URL in your environment with the following error: "An item with the same key has already been added." This error results if you have any orphaned portal sites— sites that exist in IIS or on the filesystem but not in the configuration database. Your environment may have gotten into this state by any of the following ways:

  — You accidentally deleted and then recreated the IIS web site that hosts a portal site.

  — You unextended an existing virtual server and then re-extended the same virtual sever to host a new portal site.

  — You have more than one IIS Web Site for the same port number.

  You can always look at the list and manage portal sites page in SharePoint Central Administration and see whether there are any portals with the same URL. Determine which site is in use and which is the orphaned site, and then delete the orphaned site before running the upgrade.

- In-place upgrade might display the wrong URLs for sites in Central Administration if you create the Central Administration site on a non-frontend web server, such as the Index server. This can make Central Administration display incorrect host names for the URLs of the web sites being upgraded on the Site Content Upgrade Status page. To work around this issue, you can add an alternate access mapping for the Central Administration site to point to the correct URL for the frontend web server:

  1. In the Internet Information Services Manager on the frontend web server, locate the hostname and port number for Central Administration.

  2. Open Central Administration on the Index Server, and on the Operations tab, find the Global Configuration section and click Alternate Access Mapping.

  3. On the Edit Public Zone URLs page, click the Alternate Access Mapping Collection down arrow and select Change Alternate Access Mapping Collection.

  4. In the "Select an Alternate Access Mapping Collection" box, click Central Administration.

  5. In the Public URLs section, in the Intranet box, type the correct URL for Central Administration on the frontend web server, and then click Save.

  6. On the frontend web server, open Central Administration. On the Operations tab, find the Upgrade and Migration section and click "Site content upgrade status." The URLs should display correctly.

- If you have an unusual start address, such as *http://server_name/server_name.com*, as a start address for indexing, the search upgrade might fail to upgrade the start addresses and file types, and you must enter these configuration settings manually in your Office SharePoint Server 2007 environment.

Known Issues for Gradual Upgrade

- You must use a domain account, not Network Service, for server farm upgrades, even if you used a Network Service account for the previous version. For either in-place or gradual upgrade in a server-farm environment, you should use the same credentials that you used in the previous version environment. Be sure that the domain account has the appropriate rights on the SQL Server.

- If you have upgraded a child portal that consumed shared services from a parent portal, you must update the alternate portal site URL mappings to point to the upgraded URL. Otherwise, when users search from the child portal, they may not see content added to the child portal.

 These steps must be performed in the SharePoint Portal Server 2003 environment.

Update the alternate portal site URL mappings:

1. Open SharePoint Central Administration for SharePoint Portal Server 2003.

2. Under the Portal Site and Virtual Server Configuration, click "Configure alternate portal site URLs for intranet, extranet, and custom access."

3. On the drop-down menu for the upgraded site on the child portal, click Edit.

4. On the Change Alternate Access settings page, in the intranet URL box, enter the original site's URL, and then click OK. You should now have a default URL pointing to the upgraded site and an intranet URL pointing to the original site.

5. Perform a crawl for the SharePoint Portal Server 2003 environment.

- If you have an unusual start address, such as *http://server_name/server_name.com*, as a start address for indexing, the search upgrade might fail to upgrade the start addresses and file types, and you must enter these configuration settings manually in your Office SharePoint Server 2007 environment.

- No crawl is performed on a parent portal if the following conditions are met:
  — You are using Shared Services
  — You have a large server farm with more than one index server
  — There is an exclusion rule for the parent portal on one of those index servers.

  To generate the indexes, you can either delete the rule or change the rule from exclude to include, and then perform the crawl again.

- If you are using index propagation between farms, it takes a while to initialize the query servers. On each of your query servers, run the following command to be sure they are initialized:

```
stsadm.exe -o osearch -propagationlocation <application directory>
```

where `<application directory>` is the location above the index data for all SSPs, such as:

```
applications
SSP1 (as a GUID)
SSP2 (as a GUID)
SSP3 (as a GUID)
```

- After a gradual upgrade, the parent portal site might not have only the original start addresses, not the correct temporary URLs listed for start addresses. To work around this issue, use the following process:

    1. In the Search administration pages, add an exclusion rule to delete any content now stored in the Office SharePoint Server 2007 environment.

    2. Add a content source to crawl the new URL for sites still in the environment.

    3. Perform a crawl in the environment.

Known Issues for Database Migration

- You cannot add the same content database more than once to a farm, even on different web applications. Each site collection in a content database (including each portal site) has a globally unique identifier (GUID) associated with it, registered in the configuration database. Therefore, it is not possible to add the same site collection twice to the farm, even in separate web applications. If you need a duplicate copy of a site collection in the same farm, first attach the database that contains the site collection to a separate farm, and then use the *stsadm.exe* backup and restore operations to copy the site collection over to the desired farm. The backup and restore process creates a new GUID for the site collection.

- When you perform a database migration, you do not need to migrate and attach the SharePoint Portal Server 2003 component settings database (the search database, usually named "*ID*_SERV," where *ID* is an ID such as your server name). Rather, you must recreate the search database and reconfigure your search settings when you perform a database migration, because Search settings from SharePoint Portal Server 2003 were stored both in the registry on the server and in the database, and a database migration does not contain all settings. If you attach the component settings (search) database during database migration, the upgrade process will fail when upgrading the shared services, and you may see the following message: "Could not find stored procedure 'dbo.proc_MSS_PropagationGetQueryServers'." Perform the database migration again, and do not attach the component settings (*ID*_SERV) database.

Known Issues for Customized Sites

Certain customizations are not allowed in the *web.config* files for subfolders within a virtual server. For example, the AUTHENTICATION and SESSIONSTATE nodes are not allowed within the *web.config* file at this level. Modifying the *web.config* file in ways that are not recommended can result in unexpected upgrade results. Be sure to follow the recommended practices for customizations, including customizations to *web.config*.

CHAPTER 25

Using Server-Side and Client-Side Web Parts

Introduction

Previous chapters introduced different types of SharePoint creations, including webs and web templates, Web Parts, lists, and basic customization of Web Part pages. This chapter develops the wonderful ecosystem of Web Parts. There are essentially two distinct reasons for the initial popularity of SharePoint Team Services (STS), the original precursor of Windows SharePoint Services (WSS). The first is the concept of lists and the second is Web Parts. Both features enabled power users to quickly assemble simple web-based applications without the need to engage expensive developer services.

Web Parts offer reuse on a scale that goes beyond traditional components and, as such, carry the promise of good return on investment for companies. Web Parts have grown up since the early days, to the point that they have fully influenced the ASP.NET platform. They are a major reason why the SharePoint platform continues to grow at such an incredible pace. Not only is the third-party Web Part market growing strong due to the enormous popularity of WSS 2.0 but, now that Web Parts are a part of ASP.NET 2.0, availability of third-party products and solutions will undoubtedly explode. A number of Web Parts have already been introduced in Chapter 8. In this chapter, we address Web Parts in a slightly different way. In addition to introducing the remaining Web Parts, we will look at the details of a Web Part and how to manage, create, package, and deploy custom Web Parts.

What exactly is a Web Part? It is a web component (similar to a "Portlet") that exposes functionality and enables users to interact with the data, look-and-feel, and behavior of the site. Essentially it is a specialized ASP.NET Server Control (a type of component) that can be added to a page, typically to a specialized container called a Web Part zone that is exposed on an ASP.NET page hosted within WSS or Microsoft Office SharePoint Server 2007 (MOSS). These ASP.NET pages are called Web Part Pages. Although most Web Parts have some kind of user interface (UI) that exposes data or functionality to an end user, there could be Web Parts that are totally hidden from visual interaction with the users. Web Parts offer the following benefits:

- Reusability and improved productivity
- Increased ROI
- Standardization and simplification of applications
- Integration, where Web Parts can exchange information
- Customization and personalization
- Page Design

The entire Web Part ecosystem may seem complex to a beginner, but can be broken down into manageable chunks of knowledge that are easier to understand. There are several aspects of the Web Part ecosystem that are useful to know:

- The Power User and Business User approach, which focuses on the existing Web Parts and means of utilizing them to the fullest
- The Administrators and Operators approach, which focuses on architecture, maintenance, deployment, and troubleshooting of Web Parts
- The Web Master and Web Developer approach, which focuses on advanced configuration and development of Web Parts

At the end of this chapter, you will be able to:

- List and understand Web Parts that ship with WSS and MOSS
- Place and configure Web Parts on pages
- Understand the relationship between Web Parts and different elements of MOSS
- Install Web Parts, including Windows SharePoint Services 2003 Web Parts, and make them available to users
- Configure connected Web Parts with a browser and SharePoint Designer
- Develop simple Web Parts with Visual Studio 2005
- Use Visual Studio 2005 Extensions for WSS
- Develop complex Web Parts with Visual Studio 2005

Web Parts for Power Users and Business Users

Although it may seem odd to mention a power/business user in a technology book, we have to realize that it is actually the business users that, in most circumstances, sponsor and approve the acquisition of MOSS. The business users also look at how effectively the technology can be applied to solve business problems. An in-depth knowledge of Web Parts can impact the decision between using MOSS or a competitive solution.

There are other forms of MOSS extensibility beyond the Web Services sitetTemplates and Web Parts discussed in this book. Some of the other extensibility elements include:

- Controls
- Custom actions and action groups
- List instances and templates
- Site definitions
- Documents
- Fields
- Content types
- Modules
- Workflows

Web Parts and MOSS

Instead of drilling down into all of the Web Parts, we'll describe the relationship between Web Parts and lists, which seems to be a common point of confusion. Most people, having played with WSS or MOSS for some time, have a tendency to ask why the number of Web Parts keeps changing.

When opening the Add Web Parts dialog, as in Figure 25-1, on an ordinary Web Part page, we will typically see the Lists and Libraries grouping. This grouping represents every single list and library that exists within the site and is currently visible to users (besides permissions, there is also a Hidden property for each list).

Lists are the major data storage element within MOSS. Every item that is created from within the Create page—Libraries, Communications, Tracking, and Custom Lists—inherits, in object-oriented speak, its functionality and behavior from the basic list. Also, the majority of lists and libraries implement some custom functionality to achieve its business purpose. The beauty of inheritance allows you to standardize a majority of the metadata programming against every single list style and template.

The list of Web Parts within the lists and libraries expands and contracts when new lists and libraries are added to or deleted from the site. Simply speaking, whenever a new list is added, a new ListViewWebPart Web Part is added with the same name as the added list, with a predetermined view, depending on the type of list created. In other words, each list view you create in SharePoint is actually an instance of a fundamental Web Part that is built into the MOSS framework—namely, the ListViewWebPart.

When someone wonders why there is no Issues Web Part on a particular site, it's because there is no corresponding Issues list. This pretty much explains why some people can see more Web Parts than others within their sites—it's just that there are more lists on some sites.

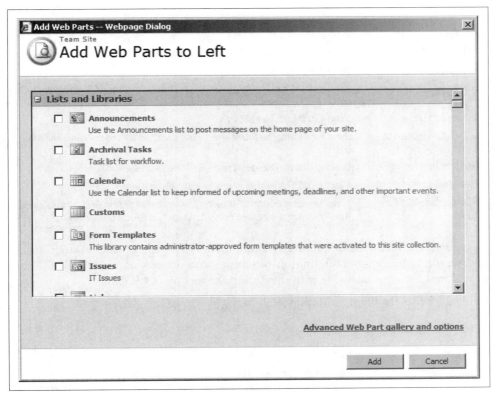

Figure 25-1. Add Web Parts dialog

Built-in Web Parts

Building on the core Web Parts that were described in Chapter 8, we will add all of the remaining Web Parts that belong both in the WSS code base and in MOSS. For more details on the use of some of these Web Parts, consult their associated chapters. To maintain consistency, the Web Parts are listed in the same sections as they are organized in the catalog.

Additionally, the majority of the Web Parts listed in the following tables are available only with MOSS, and not with WSS. Web Parts for lists and libraries, as well as Web Parts in the Default and Miscellaneous sections, are provided with WSS. There are also other Microsoft Web Parts that integrate the SharePoint platform with other products (such as Project Server or Reporting Services Integration), and they either ship directly with the product or are available for download from the Microsoft Download site. Table 25-1 lists the Business Data Web Parts.

Table 25-1. Business Data Web Parts

Web Part	Description
Business Data Actions	Shows actions associated with BDC, tied to a Type and an Item
Business Data Item	Shows a single item from BDC
Business Data Item Builder	Allows for filtering and building parameters to be reused by other BDC Web Parts on profile pages
Business Data List	Shows a list of items from BDC
Business Data Related List	Shows items that are configured as related entities within BDC and configured within the Web Part
Excel Web Access	Shows an Excel workbook based on the Excel Server and Excel Web Access
IView Web Part	Allows use of SAP iViews and integration with SAP portal servers
WSRP Consumer Web Part	Allows for reuse of external WSRP portlet providers that implement WSRP 1.1 specification, typically equivalent to backend Web Part technology in the Java portal world

Business Data Web Parts are utilized in conjunction with the Business Data Catalog, and require additional configuration of entities and actions within the BDC. Business Data Catalog is available with the Enterprise version of MOSS.

Table 25-2 lists the Content Rollup Web Part.

Table 25-2. Content Rollup Web Part

Web Part	Description
Site Aggregator	Allows for display of content from multiple sites via a simple tab-like interface, displaying Documents and Tasks assigned/owned by the user on the sites. Sites have to be added manually.

Site Aggregator, as seen in Figure 25-2, is typically used on a My Site to show a particular user bits and pieces of other sites that are specifically relevant to the user. Other forms of aggregators can be achieved via RSS aggregators, custom queries, and a number of third-party Web Parts.

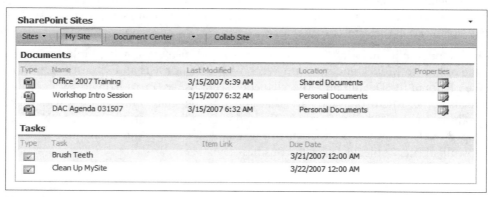

Figure 25-2. Site Aggregator

Table 25-3 lists the Dashboard Web Parts.

Table 25-3. Dashboard Web Parts

Web Part	Description
Key Performance Indicators (KPIs)	Displays contents of a KPI-enabled list. You must create a KPI list and use an existing list as one of the KPIs in order to utilize an existing list. Additionally, this allows direct interaction with the KPI list, and a tie-in of KPIs from Excel Services, Microsoft SQL Server Analysis services, and manually entered values.
KPI Details	Displays details of a single KPI defined in a KPI list, along with a graphical version of the indicator (that can be different than the default).

Dashboard Web Parts, as seen in Figure 25-3, should be used instead of the default List View Web Parts whenever KPI lists are involved. These Web Parts provide rich interaction with KPI data sources and data as well as a very slick display. They are always a great hit during a demo, and are relatively easy to configure. KPI Web Parts and KPI lists are available only with a MOSS Enterprise license.

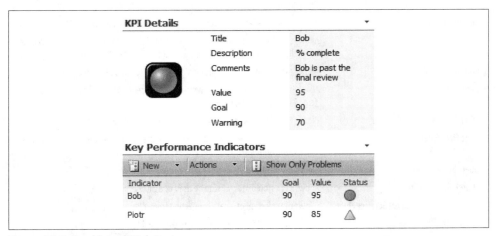

Figure 25-3. Dashboard Web Parts

Default Web Parts are used on a typical collaboration portal and help organize some simple content that is not available via other parts (Table 25-4). These Web Parts, along with some of the Miscellaneous Web Parts, allow for creation of complex portal content and navigation without the need for any other tools.

Table 25-4. Default Web Parts

Web Part	Description
I need to...	Displays a drop-down list of tasks, typically shown on the Collaboration site
RSS Viewer	Displays data from an RSS feed
This Week in Pictures	Displays an image and ties in to a slide show based on an Image Library

Table 25-4. Default Web Parts (continued)

Web Part	Description
Content Query Web Part	Shows a set of results based on a configured query, almost like a Data View that is capable of spanning multiple lists and libraries across the site collection
Summary Link Web Part	Allows the display and organization of a set of links
Table of Contents Web Part	Displays the navigation hierarchy of the site

Filter Web Parts are a staple of interactive Web Part pages, allowing the designer to relate one piece of data to another (Table 25-5). With a growing number of Web Parts supporting Web Part connections, the filters provide a very simple way of producing a variety of relationships on the pages. There are three types of Filter Connections: Automatic, User, and List-based, which support a variety of Data Types, from simple Text all the way to multiple values in a list.

Table 25-5. Filter Web Parts

Web Part	Description
Business Data Catalog Filter	Allows use of BDC as a basis for filtering data in other Web Parts
Choice Filter	Allows the designer to enter a selection of entries for use as a filter (entries cannot be modified as long as the filter is connected to another Web Part)
Current User Filter	Allows use one of the user's profile fields to be used as a filter, or user NT ID
Date Filter	Allows use of the date as a filter, which can be current, specific, or an offset day (e.g., 7 days after today)
Filter Actions	Button that allows for users to apply a set of filters and save the connection settings
Page Field Filter	Allows one of the page metadata fields to be used as a filter (this is useful for pages that exist in libraries)
Query String Filter	Allows use of one of the parts of query string as a filter
SharePoint List Filter	Allows data stored in any list to be used as a filter
SQL Server 2005 Analysis Services Filter	Allows the selection of a data connection from a library
Text Filter	Allows the use of user-entered data to create a filter

Whereas the List View and Filter Web Parts provide designers the ability to display and glue content that is available on the site, the Miscellaneous Web Parts (Table 25-6) provide the ability to fill in the gaps with some interstitial content as well as external XML or web-based content.

Table 25-6. Miscellaneous Web Parts

Web Part	Description
Contact Details	Information about the contact person for a page or site
Content Editor Web Part	Allows designers to edit simple HTML content within the page
Form Web Part	Allows HTML form controls to be used on a page and to connect to other Web Parts
Image Web Part	Displays a single image on the page

Table 25-6. Miscellaneous Web Parts (continued)

Web Part	Description
Page Viewer Web Part	An IFrame control that can display external content, linked by file or HTTP protocol
Relevant Documents	Displays documents that are relevant to the current user based on some query that is defined in the Tool pane
Site Users	Displays a list of user members and their presence indicators
User Tasks	List of tasks for the user for all tasks within the site collection
User Display	Displays the username for currently logged on user
XML Web Part	Allows use of XML (including remote XML) and XSLT to display content

There are also some legacy Office Web Parts that were available with SharePoint Server 2003: Office Datasheet, Office PivotChart, PivotTable, PivotView, and Office Spreadsheet. Additionally, there is a free advanced Content Editor Web Part available from Telerik called r.a.d. editor; see *http://www.telerik.com/products/sharepoint/overview.aspx*.

Outlook Web Parts allow the use of Outlook Web Access (OWA) elements directly within the SharePoint portal, usually within My Site pages (Table 25-7). When the Outlook Web Access URL is populated in the profile, the user sees the My OWA button.

Table 25-7. Outlook Web Parts

Web Part	Description
My Calendar	Displays the user's default calendar
My Contacts	Displays the user's default contacts
My Inbox	Displays the contents of a user's inbox folder
My Mail Folder	Displays an arbitrary Outlook folder for an end user
My Tasks	Displays the user's tasks

Search Web Parts (Table 25-8) make up their own ecosystem, tailored specifically to serving search results, as seen in Figure 25-4. Overall, they are very flexible and provide a great degree of customization. There are more Web Parts available when the Knowledge NETwork components of SharePoint are installed. For more information, follow the KN blog at *http://blogs.msdn.com/kn*.

Table 25-8. Search Web Parts

Web Part	Description
Advanced Search Box	Used for searches on the Advanced Search page (an example of customization of this Web Part is provided later in the "Adding Custom Column to Search" section)
People Search Box	Used for people-specific searches
People Search Core Results	Displays core results for people-related searches
Search Action Links	Search action links, including RSS, Alert, and sorting links

Table 25-8. Search Web Parts (continued)

Web Part	Description
Search Best Bets	Displays related Keyword, Best Bet, and High Relevancy items
Search Box	Standard Search Box that shows up on every page
Search Core Results	Displays results of most common searches (the most frequently customized Search Web Part)
Search High Confidence Results	Shows Keywords, Best Bets, and other high confidence results
Search Paging	Displays links for navigation between pages
Search Statistics	Displays basic search statistics, number of results, time
Search Summary	Web Part that shows auto-correction suggestions in a "Did you mean" format

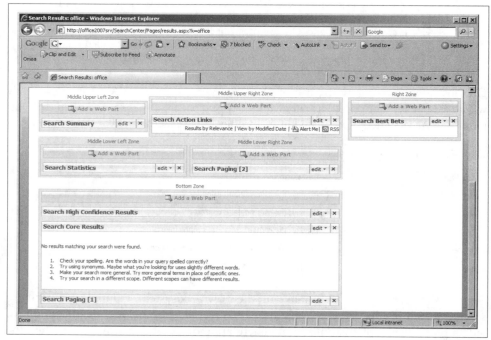

Figure 25-4. Search Web Parts on a Search Results page

Site Directory Web Parts provide an enhanced way of navigating through sites without the use of tabs or the lefthand-side tree structure (Table 25-9).

Table 25-9. Site Directory Web Parts

Web Part	Description
Categories	Displays categories stored in Site Directory in several flexible styles
Sites in Category	Displays sites in a specific category
Top Sites	Displays top level sites based on a fixed query but with a flexible location

Web Part Architecture

Web Part architecture is a nebulous domain of knowledge, depending on both administrative and developer skills. Knowledge of the Web Part architecture is useful to an administrator, who has to manage some custom Web Parts, and useful to the developer, who has to design custom Web Parts and package them for later deployment.

A Web Part can be as simple as a single configuration file, or a *.webpart* or *.dwp* file, or an installable package, which may include a number of assets. Understanding different elements of a Web Part is the key to best development practices and effective troubleshooting.

Although ASP.NET Web Parts work slightly differently, all SharePoint Web Parts must derive from one of two base classes, and they cannot utilize User Controls or Custom Controls directly as Web Parts:

- `System.Web.UI.WebControls.WebParts.WebPart`
- `Microsoft.SharePoint.WebPartPages.WebPart`

Although `Microsoft.SharePoint.WebPartPages.WebPart`-based Web Parts may be considered legacy, they do offer several features that are not possible to achieve with ASP.NET Web Parts, including:

- Cross Page Connections
- Connections to Web Parts placed on pages outside of Web Part zones
- Client Side Connections
- Data Caching infrastructure

Architecturally, Web Parts are most similar to .NET Custom Controls, but offer several important benefits and work with the underlying SharePoint Web Part infrastructure.

In order to use SharePoint Web Parts, you must have a web page that contains a `WebPartManager` object and one or more `WebPartZone` objects. Fortunately, in SharePoint, these objects are already present on every Web Part page. In other words, as a SharePoint developer, all you really need to worry about is creating Web Parts. The rest of the framework, although relevant for ASP.NET developers, is automatically provided by SharePoint.

There is a user community around a "Son of Smart Part" Web Part (created by Jan Tielens) that allows developers to utilize simple User Controls within WSS and MOSS. To find out more about this Web Part, go to *http://www.smartpart.info/default.aspx*.

User Controls are one of the easiest elements to build in ASP.NET that combine an intuitive UI and business logic.

Since WebPartManager is already built into the pages, the designer or developer does not have to worry about any plumbing associated with the implementation of the Web Part management pages, personalization, or storage.

Physical Resources

There can be a number of files associated with Web Parts, including a Web Part configuration file, an assembly, a registration for the *web.config* file, and occasionally additional resource files or policy settings.

Web Part XML configuration files are either *.dwp* files, representing the SharePoint 2003–style Web Parts, or *.webpart* files, representing the ASP.NET 2.0–style Web Parts. These files would typically be used as part of a site definition, as part of a Web Part Catalog (this is a *wpcatalog* folder underneath your web application root directory), uploaded to a Web Part library, or simply imported onto a page.

Next, the Web Part assemblies are the code compiled into a *.dll* file. Web Part assemblies may have some additional files associated with them, depending on the type of development performed. The *.dll* files will typically be installed into the web site's */bin* directory (e.g., *C:\Inetpub\wwwroot\wss\VirtualDirectories\81\bin* for a web application installed on port 81), or to the global assembly cache (GAC), which is located in the *C:\WINDOWS\assembly* directory, as seen in Figure 25-5. Assemblies that are deployed to the GAC are available to all applications running on the server, and require execution with full trust privileges. Deployment of assemblies into a bin directory typically allows for easier manual deployments than into GAC, and requires only partial trust security. Commonly, assemblies deployed into GAC may be locked by the application server, and may require an artificial stop of the application in order for these assemblies to be released.

 The best overall .NET utility, *Reflector for .NET*, also has its use with Web Part deployments and reverse engineering of existing code. After an assembly is loaded into Reflector, you should be able to see the exact string required for the Assembly attribute below. Otherwise, you may have to jump through hoops to find the appropriate information. Reflector can be downloaded from *http://www.aisto.com/roeder/dotnet/*.

Each Web Part assembly also needs to be properly registered within the *web.config* file, and, if necessary, a Code Access Security (CAS) policy must be created. The *web.config* file holds Web Part registrations in the *SafeControls* section, with each Web Part or assembly registered as a *SafeControl* entry. Each element has the following attributes:

- Assembly, which holds the exact assembly registration string as it would be deployed in the GAC, consisting of assembly name, version, culture, and a public Key Token

- Namespace, which represents the exact namespace of our Web Part

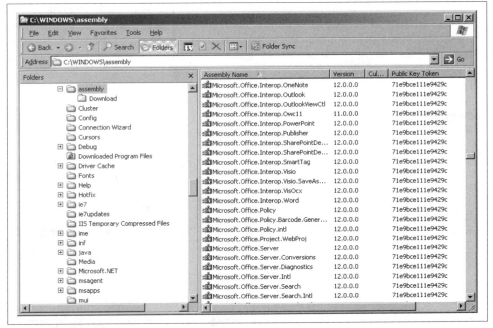

Figure 25-5. Global assembly cache

- TypeName, which represents the type within the Web Part (typically set to '*')
- Safe (optional)
- AllowRemoteDesigner (optional)

Without the SafeControl entry, an assembly used by the Web Part simply cannot be used within MOSS. Here is a sample entry that is actually used later in this chapter:

```
<SafeControl Assembly="HelloMOSS, Version=1.0.0.0, Culture=neutral,
PublicKeyToken=9f4da00116c38ec5" Namespace="HelloMOSS" TypeName="HelloMOSS"
Safe="True" />
```

The security policy is defined in the *web.config* file as well. There are two entries, one where it is declared *SecurityPolicy* and another where it is actually used, called *trust*.

 Custom CAS Policies are beyond the scope of this book. By default, a Web Part can only access resources within its own boundaries, and a few basic assemblies, but not external assemblies that, for instance, would allow the Web Part to access databases or files.

For the sake of being able to run and test any code, you can set the trust element to "Full":

```
<trust level="Full" originUrl="" />
```

This setting allows every Web Part to use any assembly, and thus a rogue piece of code could potentially do some damage with this setting.

Last, there are external resource files associated with the Web Parts (resources can also be embedded inside the assemblies). These are resources such as JavaScript files, images, and some other common elements that can be utilized at the client side. There are two potential locations where the extra resource files can be placed (Table 25-10); one of them is highlighted in Figure 25-6.

Table 25-10. Placement of resource files

Deployment style	Location and description
GAC	Resources deployed to the virtual _wpresources directory in the format of wpresources/assemblyName_publicKey/
bin	Resources deployed to the physical wpresources folder underneath the web server root folder

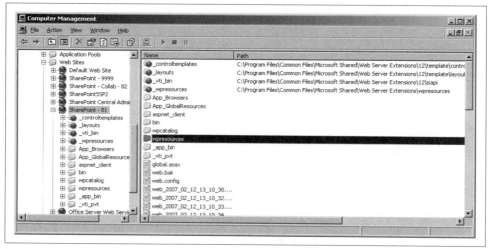

Figure 25-6. Web Part resources

Additionally, a Web Part may rely on some other piece of MOSS infrastructure and contain references to some modules, lists, or controls. These other elements would be placed in some other appropriate directory dedicated to site definitions, modules, or user controls. Web Parts that carry dependencies on other parts of MOSS are typically bundled in *.wsp* files that define a full solution. In other words, if you are packaging a Web Part that acts as the center point of a particular page layout, you will package the full page definition with the Web Part. When the package is deployed and activated, users will see the custom Web Part and any of the additionally packaged assets.

Web Parts for Administrators

There are only a couple of activities related to the lifecycle of a Web Part performed by the operator or administrator of a site. Depending on how a Web Part is created and packaged and what technologies it utilizes, there are different tasks associated with each.

As explained in the previous section, Web Parts are comprised of different files and resources. These can sometimes come in "zipped" by the developer with some light instructions, or they can come in a specialized deployment package.

Installing Web Parts

There are a number of techniques and tools that can be used to install Web Parts in WSS and MOSS, listed in Table 25-11, ranging from a number of manual steps to full-blown MSI installers. Most of these approaches take pretty good care of the work behind the scenes, and typically deploy files into correct locations and update the *web.config* for the correct web application.

Table 25-11. Web Part installation options

Web Part package	Description
MSI installer	An MSI installation file will probably come with some additional installation instructions. On one hand, it may be the easiest way to deploy Web Parts; on the other hand, you will have the least amount of control over what you do.
CAB file	This is an older style of deployment that was available with WSS 2.0 and SPS 2003 platform. CAB files have to be installed on frontend servers by running the *stsadm –o addwpppack –filename filename. cab* command from the command prompt: *C:\Program Files\Common Files\Microsoft Shared\web server extensions\12\bin\stsadm* There are a number of additional switches for this command: • lcid • url • globalinstall • force • nodeploy
WSP file	This is the new solution package file that can be used to deploy Web Parts and other solution elements. Behind the scenes, it is also a CAB file format, but contains different files. It is automatically created by Visual Studio, based on the Visual Studio extensions for WSS. The WSP packages are also installed with the *stsadm* utility mentioned earlier. Most WSP files typically also ship with a batch file that will automate all of the installation steps. If there is no batch file, you will use *stsadm* to add the solution, deploy the solution, and activate the feature contained in the solution: ``` stsadm -o addsolution -filename filename.wsp stsadm -o deploysolution -name packagename" -local - allowGacDeployment -url urlname stsadm -o activatefeature -id featureid -url urlname ```
Just files, aka *xcopy* deployment	In some cases, you may simply be handed a bunch of assemblies and, potentially, some *.webpart* or *.dwp* files, which you will have to copy to the appropriate location. The Web Part assembly will either go to the */bin* directory or the GAC (*c:\Windows\assembly*), and the *.webpart* will go inside the */wpcatalog* directory. You will also be responsible for modification of the *web.config* file and for adding the Web Part information into the <SafeControls/> section. This is fully explained later in the "Developing Web Parts from Scratch" section.

Troubleshooting Web Parts for Administrators

There are a few things that an administrator has to be prepared for to support MOSS. Unfortunately, babysitting Web Parts may be one of the necessary duties. There can be many potential problems associated with the execution of Web Parts:

- Improperly registered Web Parts will show an error: "The type could not be found or it is not registered as safe." In order to fix this, you must fix the *web.config* file for the web application in question. Also, validate whether the SafeEntry is correct for this Web Part.

- Web Parts might have improper security policies.

- Slow-running Web Parts. If a majority of the pages run significantly faster than others, those pages may have problems with one or more of their Web Parts. There can be a number of reasons for the speed of execution, starting with business logic, volume of data to process, speed of data connections, and external dependencies on web services or external sites.

- Slow Web Parts can be removed from the site either with the help of SharePoint Designer or directly from the page. You can enter append "*?contents=1*" to the end of the URL to open the Web Part Page Maintenance page, as seen in Figure 25-7.

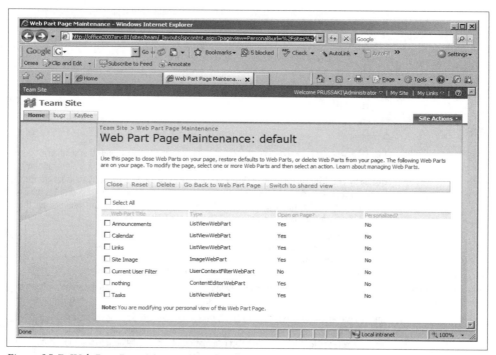

Figure 25-7. Web Part Page Maintenance page

The top toolbar shows whether you are using a personal or shared view, and the grid below displays all of the Web Parts, along with their type and status on the page. By selecting the checkbox and clicking Reset or Delete, you can easily control a misbehaving Web Part:

- If the page will not open at all, or your Web Part or control may be outside of a Web Part zone, your next option is to modify the page, either using SharePoint Designer or by resetting the page or site to its original site definition, as seen in Figure 25-8. Before resetting to a site definition, you should always make a backup of the site. The Reset Page to Site Definition Version maintenance page is available directly from the Site Settings page in the Look and Feel column; you will have to enter the full address of the page. After you reset the page, all of the customizations outside of Web Part zones on the page will be removed.

 Web Parts can exist outside of Web Parts zones, just because they are standard Server Controls. They can be placed on any part of the page as part of a Site Definition, or when editing a page outside of the web browser, as with Notepad or SharePoint Designer.

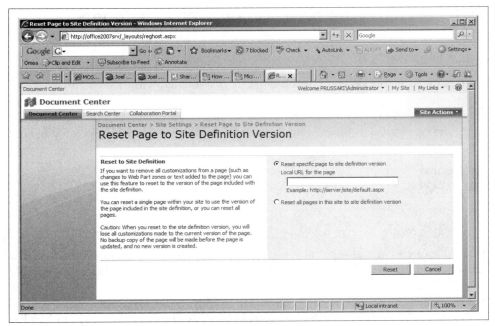

Figure 25-8. Reset Page to Site Definition Version

- Certain Web Parts, such as the List View or the Data View Web Part, may be dependent on existing lists. This dependency is usually through a link to the target part's GUIDs. When a list is moved, deleted and recreated, or moved with the use of the object model, the GUID may change without properly being reflected in the connected Web Part. The best way to solve the problem is to recreate the connections, or to use SharePoint Designer to locate GUID elements and fix them to the appropriate list or view GUID. Typically, the GUID element would be an element such as <ListName> that would be visible in the code pane of the window. You could find out the proper GUID by placing a similar Web Part tied to the same list.

- Finally, you should really profile and stress test any custom developed Web Parts, and talk to the vendor who developed them (if it is a third-party Web Part) in case you see any problems. There are going to be many factors that impact the performance of a Web Part, starting with caching and personalization options, and ending with slow-running code, exception handling, and memory usage.

 The Online Gallery, when enabled, pulls Web Parts out of MSNBC. This gallery acts just like one of the poorly behaving Web Parts, and adds 10–20 seconds to the call. If necessary, just import the Web Parts locally, and serve it by creating your custom gallery.

Web Parts for Web Masters and Web Developers

Using Web Parts on Pages

As mentioned before, Web Parts are typically instantiated within Web Part zones on a page, such as in Figure 25-4 earlier in the chapter, where six pages were seen within the screenshot. There are a number of ways in which Web Parts can be placed on the page, and there are a number of modes that Web Parts exhibit while interacting with the page:

- Normal Mode
- Edit Mode
- Design Mode
- Catalog Mode

Naturally, Web Parts are typically managed directly on the page, imported from the catalog, or uploaded. Web Parts can interact with a page in a number of modes and display different results. Once a Web Part exists on a page and a page is in Edit Mode, you can simply move the Web Part around with drag-and-drop or use properties to place Web Part in a different zone. MOSS's standard master page handles zones that cover the Editor and Catalog zone automatically.

Zones can control whether users are allowed to add, delete, move, or resize the Web Parts, whether users can personalize Web Parts, and whether users can modify settings for all users. Once these properties are set, they can be changed only by the administrator or a designer using a tool such as SharePoint Designer.

There are many settings that can impact the ability to use and configure a Web Part on a page. Some portals may disallow editing of pages via policy, but this and other settings can also be set on a page or even a Web Part zone level. Common properties that can be set are the ability to personalize a Web Part, Web Part orientation, or some common Chrome properties, such as a Web Part frame or a title.

Web Part Configuration

Web Parts expose a number of properties that allow their simple configuration (Table 25-12). Although each Web Part can expose a number of custom properties directly in the configuration pane, as well as custom configuration sections, the built-in infrastructure provides three configuration panels for Appearance, Layout, and Advanced properties.

Table 25-12. Web Part configuration options

Web Part property page	Description
Appearance	Appearance controls Title, Height and Width, Chrome State, and Chrome Type. These settings basically allow you to override the way that your Web Part box area is displayed.
Layout	Layout controls where the Web Part is displayed on the page, and contains properties such as Visible On Page, Direction, Zone, and Zone Index.
Advanced	Advanced properties also control appearance and some additional behaviors. Its properties are: Allow Minimize, Allow Close, Allow Hide, Allow Zone Change, Allow Connections, Allow Editing in Personal View, Export Mode, Title URL, Description, Help URL, Help Mode, Catalog Icon Image URL, Import Error Message, and Target Audiences.
Default	Typically, the core of the configuration will be shown on the default property page. Most of the core MOSS Web Parts display their properties here.
Custom	There can be other property pages created for a Web Part, and the default order can be modified. If the Web Part requires complex configuration, it will expose this functionality either via some custom page or directly on the surface of the Web Part, when the Web Part is in the Edit or Design Mode.

Configuring Connected Web Parts

A more specialized element of configuration is the ability for Web Parts to connect with one another. Unlike other properties set within the Web Part property pages, connectivity is configured via an action tied to the title menu. Using Web Part connectivity is a great way to create dynamic web-based applications without necessarily using any development tools. Sample Web Part Connectivity is shown in Figure 25-9.

After a page or a Web Part is taken into an Edit Mode, you can click the Edit button, and expand the Connections submenu. Depending on the type of connectivity exposed by the Web Part, and on the availability of other Web Parts on the page, typically you will be able to see some choices from which to select. For instance, the

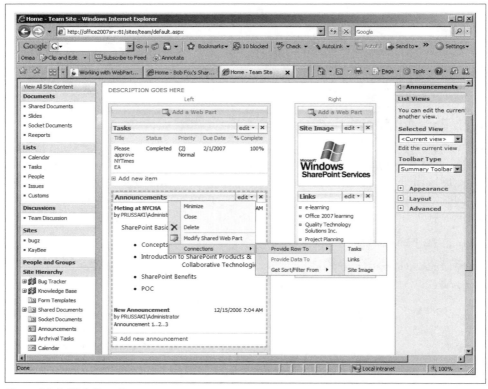

Figure 25-9. Web Part Connection

Data View Web Part, as seen in the example, allows the use of Provide Row data, Provide Data, and Get Sort/Filter. After selecting one of the active items, you will see a choice of Web Parts that are capable of accepting a connection. If the choices are grayed out or inactive, there are no Web Parts on the page capable of accepting a connection. Different Web Parts will provide different connections and accept different data. Not all data types can be passed in a connection.

Additionally, Web Part connections can be configured in SharePoint Designer. Although use of SharePoint Designer "unghosts" the Web Part pages, it also allows greater flexibility in terms of Web Part connectivity. Whereas autogenerated connectivity between Web Parts created with the browser UI typically creates ugly radio buttons, SharePoint Designer allow you to create connections based on images, links, or other HTML elements.

Web Part connectivity also depends on the interface implemented by the Web Part, as well as availability of Web Parts that implement a complimentary interface. For the older style Web Parts, not only do you need a provider and a receiver, but you also need compatible interfaces. For the new WSS 3.0 Web Parts, communication is performed via a shared interface, and registration of this interface in two Web Parts is via ASP.NET attributes. Specific interfaces used to cover Web Part connectivity are covered later in the "Advance Web Part Development" section.

Development Environment for MOSS

Thus far, we have mainly dealt with existing Web Parts; for the remainder of this chapter, we will deal with creation of new Web Parts. Developing Web Parts requires a development environment.

Perhaps one of the weakest experiences with MOSS is that of the casual developer. Many user group meetings and conferences are filled with water cooler talk focused on configuration of the development environment (Table 25-13). Simply speaking, for the very best environment you will need to develop directly on the server. If you install all elements in a standalone environment (MOSS, SQL 2005, or Visual Studio 2005), you will get simplified deployment and debugging that you would not be able to achieve otherwise. Once you have built and tested your Web Part, you can package it and deploy it on your multiserver farm as part of a scheduled production release.

Table 25-13. Different development environments

Environment	Benefits and problems
Simple Windows XP or Vista	Although development is possible, you will not be able to debug a majority of the code, and you will have to go through a number of manual steps to configure and deploy code. MOSS 2007 and SQL 2007 are hosted on another machine, while you use Visual Studio 2005 to code and compile.
Virtual Machine	Probably the most common environment. Recommended configurations for host OS require at least 2 GB of RAM and a fast disk (possibly external). This is also very easy to fix if something breaks. You can install all elements on the Virtual Machine, or break it apart and reuse some existing infrastructure. Since SQL Server tends to eat up a lot of resources, it should be externalized if possible.
Windows 2003 Server	Similar to the Virtual Machine, but less resource-intensive. You will still need high-end hardware to run the server and desktop applications at the same time; at worst, you should be running MOSS 2007 and Visual Studio 2005 on the same machine.

There are also some external components in a typical environment, such as email and the domain server. They are definitely not required, but still nice to have from an infrastructure perspective. Visual Studio 2005 is certainly not a requirement for Web Part or SharePoint development, but it does make a few things easier. You would need some kind of an editor (Notepad) and .NET SDK to compile the code.

You will also have to create a reference to the SharePoint assemblies. These are stored on frontend servers at: *[windows volume]\Program Files\Common Files\Microsoft Shared\web server extensions\12\ISAPI* (or *60\ISAPI* for SPS 2003 assemblies). You will have to make a share on a server in order to access it from your development workstation (if working remotely), or just map it locally.

Developing Web Parts with Visual Studio 2005

Web Parts in MOSS 2007 have 2 distinct flavors, depending on whether the older or newer API is used. The older API is derived from legacy SharePoint 2003 technology (aka the Microsoft.SharePoint namespace), and since the Web Part technology has now been included directly in Windows, the new API is based on Microsoft ASP.NET 2.0. The new Web Parts are now a part of the `System.Web.UI.WebControls.WebParts` namespace.

 Unless you have a specific reason for using SharePoint 2003–style Web Parts, stick to the new API, as it will make them compatible with other ASP.NET-based apps. The old API had an additional interpage and client-side connectivity capability, whereas the new API performs connections on the server side.

A typical approach to Web Part development and deployment is similar, regardless of whether the developer starts with a simple class project or with Visual Studio 2005 Extensions for WSS. The main difference would potentially lie in the deployment approach, where the developer can choose the *xcopy* deployment instead of the *msp* package automatically built by the Visual Studio. Actually, a majority of the Web Part's inner workings are identical to that of an ASP.NET Server Control. For a simple Web Part, the process looks as follows:

1. Create a project (class or Web Part).
2. Create a class file that will inherit from base *WebPart*.
3. Override the Render method if you want your Web Part to display something.
4. Override other methods as needed to use other controls, handle events, create properties, and edit screens.
5. Create an *snk* key file and enter it in the *AssemblyInfo.cs* file to sign the assembly.
6. Build your Web Part.
7. Deploy your Web Part using the *xcopy* approach, or create a secondary project that creates an *MSP* deployment project (Visual Studio 2005 Extensions for WSS handle it for you).
8. Place the Web Part on the page.
9. The next sections cover this process in more detail.

Visual Studio 2005 Extensions for WSS

Visual Studio 2005 Extensions for WSS provide a collection of tools and project templates that create simple starting point for development of Web Part–style projects. Literally, the Web Part template provides sufficient code for the simplest Web Part and for its deployment with a simple F5 click. This code, as well as some additional plumbing steps, would work as a standard "Hello World" sample.

```
using System.Runtime.InteropServices;
using System.Web.UI;
using System.Web.UI.WebControls.WebParts;

namespace SimpleWebPart
{
    [Guid("25ed441d-9c4a-4892-8a71-99edc1f2a1d2")]
    public class SimpleWebPart : WebPart
    {
        protected override void Render(HtmlTextWriter writer)
        {
            writer.Write("Hello to Bob from Piotr");
        }
    }
}
```

Visual Studio 2005 Extensions package is available to download from:

*http://www.microsoft.com/downloads/detailsaspx?familyid=
19F21E5EB715-4F0C-B9598C6DCBDC1057&displaylang=en*

These Extensions provide a number of useful project templates.

There is also an older version of the toolkit for SharePoint Server 2003, which provides a SharePoint Web Part template. It may make sense to keep Visual Studio 2003 handy to support older Web Parts, or at least to copy the project template.

The following steps create a simple "Hello MOSS" Web Part in Visual Studio 2005, with Visual Studio 2005 Extensions for WSS on a development machine with MOSS 2007 installed on the default port 80:

1. With Visual Studio 2005 opened, click File → New → Project (Figure 25-10).

2. From the New Project dialog box, select Visual C# and Web Part, fill in the Name and Location, and click OK (Figure 25-11).

3. Navigate the *HelloMOSS.cs* code file, and edit the *Render* method (Figure 25-12) so that the body is:

```
protected override void Render(HtmlTextWriter writer)
{
    writer.Write("Hello MOSS");
}
```

4. Study the contents of the Solutions Explorer window. When you expand the Properties section you will notice *AssemblyInfo.cs* and *Temporary.snk*. *Temporary.snk* is a Strong-Name-Key file, which allows .NET to sign an assembly so that it can be checked for tampering, and the *AssemblyInfo.cs* file allows the developer to embed some additional metadata about the assembly and associate the *.snk* file to the project. The References section does not contain anything extraordinary other than the addition of the *Microsoft.SharePoint* assembly as a reference. You will need this reference if you use the SharePoint WSS API, which would refer to something within the site.

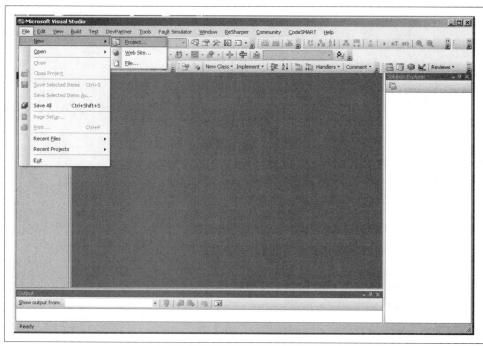

Figure 25-10. Open a new project

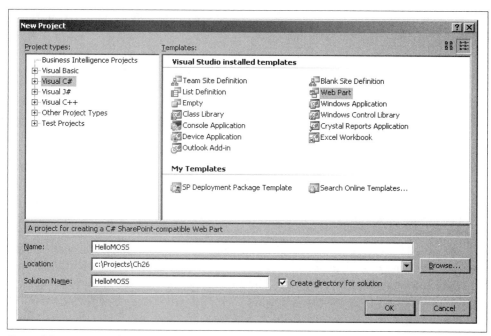

Figure 25-11. New Web Part project

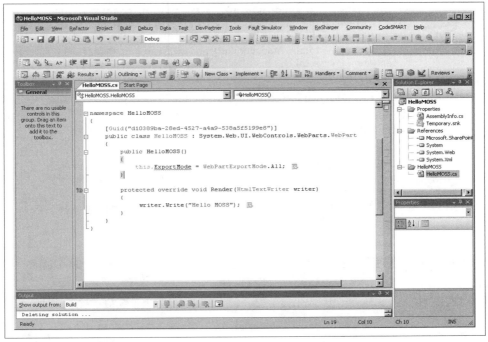

Figure 25-12. Render method

5. Expand the Output window on the bottom of Visual Studio screen, and hit F5 to watch the progress of building the project and its deployment. Depending on the speed of your development server and whether your machine has been warmed up, this process can take from 30 seconds to 5 minutes. We will go through the details of each step taken later on, and identify exactly what changes have taken place behind the scenes.

Looking at the detailed steps in the output window, you can observe the following, which save a lot of time:

a. Compilation is completed.

b. Deployment project is created.

c. Solution is created.

d. Batch file for management of the solution is created.

e. Solution is added.

f. Solution is deployed.

g. Features are activated.

h. IIS is restarted.

During subsequent build-and-deploy sessions with the project, your Web Part will additionally be Deactivated, Uninstalled, Retracted, and Deleted, but it will still remain on the page. This is because a *.webpart* or a *.dwp* file is totally independent from the Web Part that exists in the form of an assembly.

6. Next, you need to add your Web Part to the page. Open your portal or site, go to the page where you want to add the Web Part, open it in Edit Mode, and click "Add a Web Part" (see Figure 25-13).

By default, the Web Part built with this method is created as a solution containing features. This solution is tied at a Site Collection scope. As a result, going to a different site collection or a different Web Application will not show the Web Part as available in the catalog, unless it is added, deployed, and activated.

Figure 25-13. Edit Mode and Add a Web Part

7. The Web Part you create with the F5 button will automatically register for the default portal, and will be inside the Miscellaneous Web Parts catalog section. It will also have the same name as the project you have created. In this case it is the HelloMOSS Web Part (Figure 25-14). Select the checkbox and click Add. Exit the Edit Mode if necessary.

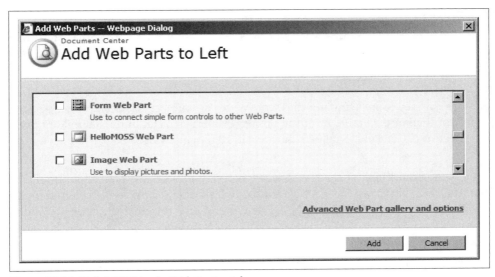

Figure 25-14. HelloMOSS in the Web Part catalog

8. Finally, the fruit of your labors, the HelloMOSS Web Part, appears near the top of the page (Figure 25-15).

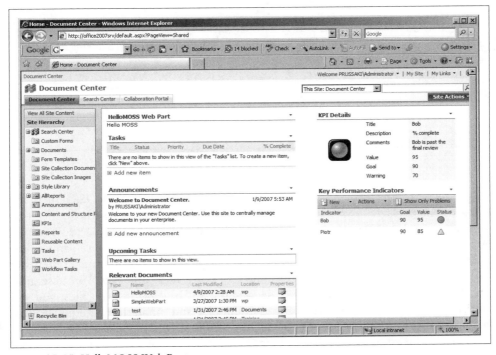

Figure 25-15. HelloMOSS Web Part on a page

Behind the scenes

The magic of hitting F5 in Visual Studio takes care of a number of other steps that you would otherwise have to handle manually. Later on, we'll develop a simple Web Part without using any tools, but it is equally important to know what the tools have done.

Besides the necessary template files, the Web Part project has some other settings (some of them are editable from the Project Properties page, in the SharePoint Solution section). Basically, it allows automated deployment of Web Parts into a local server.

First, you should look at the directories where the project was created and built. In our example, this was the *C:\Projects\Ch25\HelloMOSS* directory, which contains the Visual Studio solution file. The DEBUG build directory and the code are underneath in the *C:\Projects\Ch25\HelloMOSS\HelloMOSS\bin\Debug* directory, as seen in Figure 25-16. There are several files that are of significant interest to us:

- *HelloMOSS.wsp*
- *Setup.bat*
- Solution directory

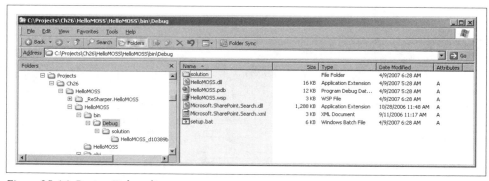

Figure 25-16. Project Debug directory

These files are created by the Web Part project template. *HelloMOSS.wsp* is the deployment package, and the *setup.bat* is the command prompt setup utility that interacts with MOSS via the *stsadm* utility and takes care of Adding, Deploying, and Activating the solution (as well as subsequent uninstallation steps). You can also see that there is a solution directory, which actually represents the internal contents of the *HelloMOSS.wsp* file. There are a couple of XML files, our Web Part assembly, and the *.webpart* file. If you look at the *manifest.xml* and *feature.xml* files, you will notice that they represent a unique solution file, and similarly a unique feature, where the feature ID is tied to the GUID attribute of the HelloMOSS class, as declared in the project (also visible in Figure 25-16).

The next element that may be of interest is the *setup.bat* file, which manages the registration of the assembly within the server. Using the command prompt, as seen in Figure 25-17, we open the location of the *setup.bat* file and execute *setup -?* to look at the available options. Using this tool, you can control solution installation and uninstallation as well as the activation and deployment of the solution to a particular site collection of your choice. This provides a decent level of flexibility, as it may be tedious to open so many sites to activate a feature.

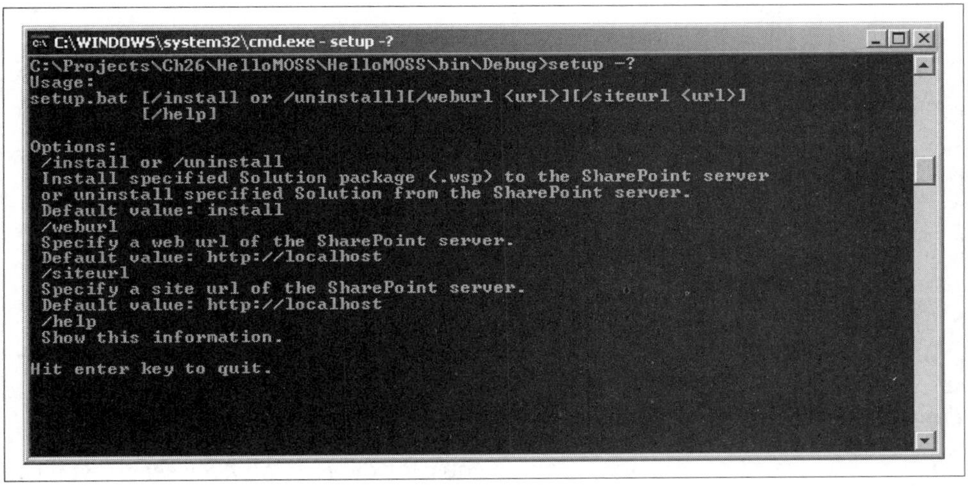

Figure 25-17. Command prompt options of setup.bat

Since the *setup.bat* tool was used, next we can look at how and where the files included in the solution were deployed. Based on previous experience, we know these can be deployed to the GAC or to the *bin* directory, and additionally, we know that these are deployed as full-blown features.

First, we can look at the Site Collection's set of features. I used the *setup.bat* tool to activate the feature in another site collection (e.g., *http://localhost/sites/collab*). Now, to open the site:

1. Click the Site Actions drop-down list.

2. Click Site Settings (and optionally All Site Settings, depending on the template).

3. In the Site Collection Administration section, click Site Collection Features. (Note that there is also a Site Features button, which is tied into a web and not into a site collection.)

4. The Site Collection Features page (as seen in Figure 25-18) shows a HelloMOSS feature that is already activated.

5. Going back to the Site Settings page, click the Web Parts link in the Galleries section.

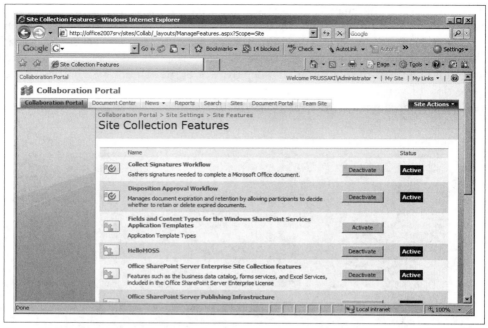

Figure 25-18. Site Collection Features

6. The Web Part Gallery page shows an entry for the *HelloMOSS.webpart*; you can click the name of the Web Part to see its preview. You can also click the Edit icon to modify the Web Part Properties, as seen in Figure 25-19.

Next, we can verify that the Web Part has been deployed to the GAC (which implies it was deployed globally) and check its registration in the *web.config* file. To navigate to the GAC, simply open Windows Explorer and open *c:\WINDOWS\assembly*, where *c:\WINDOWS* represents the place where your OS has been installed by default, as seen in Figure 25-20.

Finally, we validate the SafeControls section inside the *web.config* file (Figure 25-21), which, by default, exists in the *c:\inetpub\wwwroot* directory. Our Web Part's registration is shown in the following line:

```
<SafeControl Assembly="HelloMOSS, Version=1.0.0.0, Culture=neutral,
PublicKeyToken=9f4da00116c38ec5" Namespace="HelloMOSS" TypeName="HelloMOSS"
Safe="True" />
```

Building Web Parts from Scratch

Obviously, if you are not working with the Visual Studio 2005 Extensions, you will have to complete all of the behind-the-scenes work yourself. Typically, there are a few more steps before the code shown earlier becomes a real Hello World–style Web

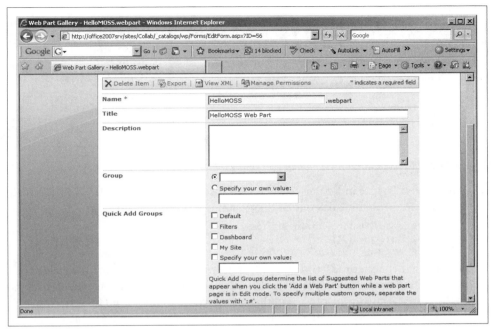

Figure 25-19. Web Part Gallery displaying properties of a Web Part

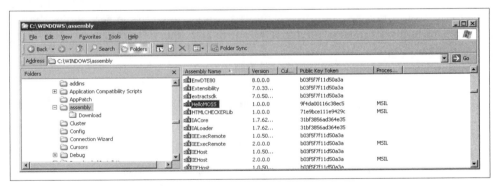

Figure 25-20. HelloMOSS inside GAC

Part on a page. To develop a simple Web Part from scratch, you will most likely follow these steps:

1. Select a class project template to create your Web Part.

2. Add references to necessary assemblies in your project, and declare the namespaces in the Using section of your Web Part. Instead of the typical `System.Data`, you will typically add `Microsoft.SharePoint` and `System.Web`. Similarly, you can add references to other assemblies, and then declare the namespaces in the Using section.

Figure 25-21. The SafeControls section in web.config

Since Web Parts can be derived from `Microsoft.SharePoint` or from `System.Web`, you should probably alias one of these namespaces to make it clear:

```
using System.Runtime.InteropServices;
using System.Web.UI;
using System.Web.UI.WebControls.WebParts;
```

3. Implement the methods and properties necessary for a Web Part lifecycle. First, you will inherit from a `WebPart` (make a choice between a `System.Web WebPart` and a `Microsoft.SharePoint` one), and then standard methods would be very similar to the Server Control implementation, you should override `CreateChildControl` and `RenderWebPart` or `Render` methods. If you want to use ASP.NET controls in your code, first you have to declare them, and then use `CreateChildControl` to add them to the Controls collection used by the Web Part. The example here shows the use of a label, but a similar approach is used with any other control:

```
private Label lblMessage;
protected override void CreateChildControls ()
{
        lblMessage = new Label ();
        lblMessage.Width = Unit.Percentage (100);
        lblMessage.Font.Name = "arial";
        lblMessage.Text = "";
        Controls.Add (lblMessage);
}
protected override void RenderWebPart (HtmlTextWriter output)
{
        lblMessage.RenderControl(output);
}
```

4. Create a key file to sign your assembly and compile the code. This can easily be achieved in Visual Studio, as you can create *.snk* files in the Signing section of your project properties (or manually with the *snk.exe* utility). You have to sign your assemblies if you deploy them to the GAC, but it is not necessary if it is deployed to the *bin* directory.

5. Deploy the assembly. Here you can simply copy the *.dll* file to the *GAC* or *bin* directories. Note that if your assembly is in both locations, by default it should be retrieved from the *bin* directory first.

6. Set security (if necessary); for simple development, you can set the trust level to "Full." For more complex development, you will have to create a Code Access Security (CAS) configuration:

```
<trust level="Full" originUrl="" />
```

7. Modify *web.config* as shown before, by adding your Web Part information to the SafeControls section.

8. Create a *.webpart* or *.dwp* file. You can either create this file by hand or have it be generated automatically for you. From the Web Part Gallery page, click New, and then click the Populate Gallery button. This Web Part is obviously not installed as a feature and does not have to be activated. A sample structure of a *.dwp* file is shown here:

```
<?xml version="1.0" encoding="utf-8"?>
<WebPart xmlns="http://schemas.microsoft.com/WebPart/v2" >
    <Title>title</Title>
    <Description>description</Description>
    <Assembly>assemblyname</Assembly>
    <TypeName>typeName</TypeName>
    <!-- Specify initial values for any additional base class or custom
properties here. -->
</WebPart>
```

9. Add the Web Part to the page—this is the same as for any other Web Part.

10. Configure any settings for the Web Part.

Developing Complex Web Parts

Examples in the previous sections have shown all of the necessary steps to develop a Web Part. For hardcore ASP.NET developers, this is probably very familiar, as it is similar to the development of Server Controls.

 When looking at the API and the documentation, carefully observe any new members that have been inherited versus any older members that are marked as obsolete. Members marked as obsolete will typically suggest a new member or interface that should be used instead.

Even if you use a tool such as Reflector to study the Object model, you will be able to read the developer's comments about most types and even link within the reverse-engineered members.

Table 25-14 lists common Web Part samples and tricks.

Table 25-14. Common Web Part samples and tricks

How To	Sample and description
Access external resources	The following snippet allows you to access resources that are deployed in the *wpresources* or *_wpresources* folders: ``` SPWeb cWeb = SPControl.GetContextWeb(Context); Type cType = BaseWebPart.GetType(); string classPath = SPWebPartManager. GetClassResourcePath(ccWeb, ccType); ```
Access embedded resources	The following allows you to retrieve files that have been embedded inside the assembly itself: ``` string filePath = Page.ClientScript.GetWebResourceUrl(this. GetType(), "AssemblyName.folder.filenname.gif"); ```
Develop with a user control	Some people find it easier to develop with a designer pane. As such, you can easily add user controls. In your project, click Add New Item. Then, from the C# section, select User Control. Once your user control is created, simply add it to the page, just like any other server control.
Provide ASP.NET-style Web Part communication	ASP.NET-style communication is done in two distinct ways, depending on whether you want to support existing interfaces or just develop something custom that is specific to your solution. As you can see from the SDK, all of the SharePoint-style communication methods are marked as obsolete. New styles of communication are: • Filters: `System.Web.UI.WebControls.WebParts.IWebPartParameters` • Cells: `System.Web.UI.WebControls.WebParts.IWebPartField` • Lists: `System.Web.UI.WebControls.WebParts.IWebPartTable` These interfaces obviously are implemented by other elements of MOSS and provide on-page communication. To create a custom Web Part communication, you can simply create a custom interface used for exchange of data, and then mark two methods (one in a receiver Web Part, one in a sender Web Part) as ConnectionConsumer and ConnectionProvider, where the provider returns the shared interface and the consumer accepts it as a parameter.

Conclusion

Web Parts are clearly the technology that makes the SharePoint platform so useful and easy to operate. Whether you develop your own Web Parts or reuse existing Web Parts, you should be aware of where the Web Parts come from, how they interact with the rest of the application, and which Web Parts ship with MOSS. There is no sense in developing new functionality if it already exists!

Also, solid knowledge of what happens behind the scenes is key for administrators as well as developers. You need to know how to troubleshoot your Web Parts, how to deploy them, and, for developers, all of the different pieces and development methods.

CHAPTER 26

Using SharePoint Web Services

Introduction

As one of its extensibility mechanisms, Microsoft Office SharePoint Server 2007 (MOSS) offers a number of Web Services. Web Services are a critical part of a service-oriented architecture, enabling remote and heterogeneous systems to interact effectively. The Web Services that come with MOSS provide an easy way to access and manipulate data within SharePoint while maintaining security and supportability of the system. They are fairly simple to use and understand, but due to their simplicity, they may not be as optimized as a custom set of Web Services, which can provide different sets of operations.

 There may be a temptation to manipulate data stored in content or configuration databases, just because it seems doable. However, this is an unsupported scenario that could lead to corruption of data and destruction of your portal. Use the provided APIs or Web Services for integration instead of directly manipulating the database.

So, what are *Web Services*? In short, Web Services are a set of standards and protocols that enable software systems to exchange information via XML. Web Services have been "in the works" since 1998 under a variety of names—for example, XML RPC and SOAP. The main reason for the tremendous growth of Web Services is how easy it is to understand the protocols and formats involved. Interoperability is also a major selling point. Web Services, unlike many previous attempts at distributed computing, made it possible for mainframes to talk to Unix-based applications or for Unix to talk to Windows applications. As a result, Web Services became a de-facto standard for exposing connectivity to an application. Each Web Service will typically expose its interface description, via the Web Service Definition Language (WSDL), and then implement a Simple Object Access Protocol (SOAP)–based endpoint capable of interpreting incoming messages in XML format (the request) and returning XML data back (the result).

That said, you might ask the following: when and why would anyone choose to use Web Services to interact with MOSS? The standard MOSS and WSS sets of APIs that are typically used to build Web Parts and ASP.NET applications can only run on a machine where WSS or MOSS is actually installed. Hence, Web Services are practically the only way that someone can access MOSS data from a remote machine. Whenever MOSS is the definitive source of data, or even just metadata, web services should be utilized as the integration mechanism of choice. MOSS Web Services are typically used for integration with desktop applications that connect to the collaborative workspaces, as integration to some line-of-business applications that may track a status of a workflow, or just for looking up data in a list.

What about the reverse? What are the technologies that allow consumption of external data within MOSS? There are several, including the following that are associated with Web Services:

The Business Data Catalog (BDC)
> The BDC provides a specification for connectivity into databases or Web Services.

XML and Web Services for Remote Portlets (WSRP) Web Parts
> These Web Parts allow consumption of the data purely on the UI site, coming either in a generic XML format or in a more specific WSRP specification that is supported by many portal and line-of-business application vendors.

With the foundation of Web Services firmly set, now we'll focus on the detailed capabilities and usage of the Web Services within MOSS. At the end of this chapter you will be able to:

- Describe major Web Services associated with MOSS and WSS
- Locate and invoke these Web Services through some standardized tools
- Utilize any of these Web Services in code
- Utilize other APIs, such as FrontPage RPC
- Create your own Web Service that utilizes MOSS APIs

Services Associated with MOSS and WSS

As platforms, WSS and MOSS are built on a staggering amount of reusable elements and features, which translate into a fairly large number of Web Services. Overall, there are more than 26 documented Web Service definitions, plus various Web Services for additional Application Services (e.g., for SlideLibrary functionality), and the endpoints are typically dynamically structured. That is, the access to the endpoint provides an implicit context to the location within the MOSS portal or web site. It is probably impractical to go into the detail of every single Web Service. Instead, after a brief introduction, we'll focus on the commonalities between the Web Services and how to harness them.

This chapter assumes that you are already familiar with the Web Service technology as a core concept, and know how to utilize or create a simple ASP.NET Web Service on your own. Also, this chapter does not delve into the Web Services Extensions (WSE).

There are 20 core Web Services that are associated with WSS (see Table 26-1, later in this chapter). As WSS is the heart and soul of MOSS, these Web Services provide the first level of data access. The majority of the Web Services are located at the *_vti_bin* absolute directory, as seen in Figure 26-1. However, the services are also accessible from a relative directory as well. For instance, if there is a site in a location *\sites\HR*, there would be access to the web services via *\sites\HR_vti_bin*. These directories, as seen in IIS in the figure, are essentially virtual directories that map to a directory within the WSS 12 hive on the physical filesystem: *C:\Program Files\Common Files\Microsoft Shared\web server extensions\12\ISAPI*. It is worth noting that these services run under the same application pool as the portal, but they have their own *web.config* file.

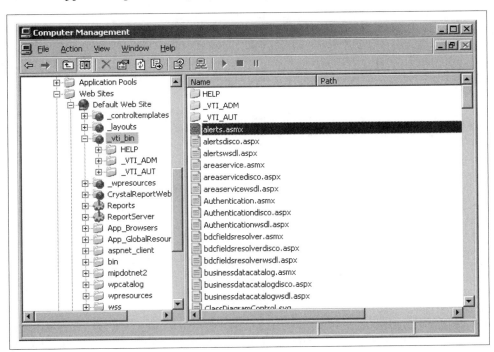

Figure 26-1. Web Services in IIS

The main exception to this rule is the Administration Web Service, which is installed within the administration site. The Administrative Web Service exists within the *_vti_adm* virtual directory that corresponds to the *C:\Program Files*

Common Files\Microsoft Shared\web server extensions\12\ADMISAPI physical directory. When browsing for the Web Services within IIS, the browser starts from the
root directory, and you can only use the web browser to study the structure of the
Web Service endpoint, as seen in Figure 26-2. Based on the standard configuration,
these Web Services cannot be called with HTTP Post or HTTP Get commands, and
you must use real SOAP commands even to test the service—not a very friendly
approach for a developer.

 In the next section, we will work with a free tool that allows us to
access these Web Services. Additionally, we'll look at different ways to
reconfigure IIS in order to make access easier and make it possible to
access the services from other systems.

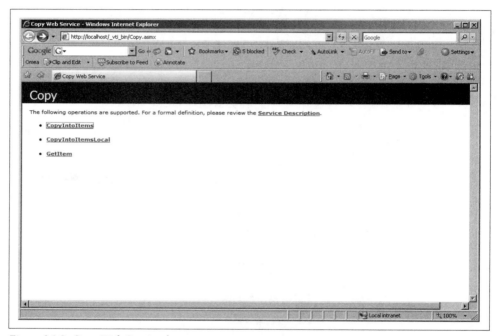

Figure 26-2. Copy Web Service documentation

Looking at the files inside IIS, you can see that for each Web Service—for example,
alerts.asmx—there are two additional files: *alertsdisco.aspx* and *alertswsdl.aspx*.
These are two additional ASP.NET pages that would be used for integration with development applications. The first simulates the older *.disco* files, and the second simulates
the dynamically generated WSDL definition, which, in the case of MOSS Web Services,
is static. There are also some other Web Services that are not documented.

A brief study of the MOSS Web Services shows that they partially mimic the standard object model of WSS and MOSS, and as such, enable drill-down into data by successive calls to the site, web, and list Web Services if necessary. In order to use them, the programmer should be familiar with the SharePoint object hierarchy as well as any nuances of navigating the structure. Unlike in a pure object-oriented (OO) model, where one object or collection can instantiate another, in the Web Services world, you have to instantiate and create each object explicitly and then request it. Due to the granular nature of the Web Services, the developer sometimes has to make several invocations before being able to get the data or a method, which is somewhat tedious compared to standard OO practices.

Table 26-1 provides an overview of the available web services.

Table 26-1. Available WSS 3.0 Web Services

Web Service	File	Description
Administration Web Service	Admin.asmx	Allows for simple management of the site, such as deleting and adding sites
Alerts Web Service	Alerts.asmx	Allows for control of Alerts within the site
Authentication Web Service	Authentication.asmx	Allows for simple authentication into the MOSS or WSS applications, especially if the Authentication mode is Forms
Copy Web Service	Copy.asmx	Allows for copy of items between different locations
Document Workspace Web Service	DWS.asmx	Allows for means of managing Document Workspace sites; primarily used by the Document Management pane
Forms Web Service	Forms.asmx	Allows for control of forms used in the UI
Imaging Web Service	Imaging.asmx	Allows for control of picture libraries
List Data Retrieval Web Service	DspSts.asmx	The workhorse of data access that allows users to perform queries against data in lists
Lists Web Service	Lists.asmx	Allows retrieval of list metadata and performance of simple operations against list data
Meetings Web Service	Meetings.asmx	Allows for creation and management of Meeting Workspace sites
People Web Service	People.asmx	Allows for control of security groups
Permissions Web Service	Permissions.asmx	Allows for control of permissions within a container
Site Data Web Service	SiteData.asmx	Another workhorse that can provide site metadata, list metadata, and list data
Sites Web Service	Sites.asmx	Allows for management of site templates
Search Web Service	SPSearch.asmx	Allows for access to Windows SharePoint Services search functionality; in MOSS scenarios, the MOSS search Web Service should be utilized (*search.asmx*)
Users Web Service	UserGroup.asmx	Allows for control of users, user groups, and cross-site groups

Table 26-1. Available WSS 3.0 Web Services (continued)

Web Service	File	Description
Versions Web Service	*Versions.asmx*	Allows for control of file versions
Views Web Service	*Views.asmx*	Allows for controls of different views for each list
Web Part Pages Web Service	*WebPartPages.asmx*	Allows for control of content on the Web Part Pages
Webs Web Service	*Webs.asmx*	Allows for control of Webs, which represents subsites within a site and provides more granular control

The most commonly used Web Services are List Data Retrieval Web Service, Site Data Web Service, and Lists Web Service. For instance, the index server uses Site Data Web Service internally while performing a server crawl. Each Web Service represents a unique aspect of WSS, and in most cases, different services will be used for specialized tasks.

 You should be aware of the fact that there is a "soft" limit of 2,000 items per view. Performance will fall whenever more than 2,000 items are retrieved within a single operation. In such cases, you may opt to limit your queries, or use Views to access data. Guidelines are published on TechNet in a "Plan for software boundaries" article:

*http://technet2.microsoft.com/windowsserver/WSS/en/library/
2aa12954-2ea7-475c-9dce-663f543820811033.mspx?mfr=true*

The Web Services that are associated purely with MOSS are defined in Table 26-2.

Table 26-2. MOSS-only Web Services

Web Service	File	Description
Area Web Service	*Areaservice.asmx*	Now obsolete
Official File Web Service	*OfficialFile.asmx*	Allows for sending files into Records Repository
Published Links Web Service	*PublishedLinksService.asmx*	Allows for access of published links that point to WSS sites targeting a current user
Search Web Service	*Search.asmx*	Allows access to the enterprise search
User Profile Change Web Service	*UserProfileChangeService.asmx*	Allows changes to be made to the user profile
User Profile Web Service	*UserProfileService.asmx*	Allows access to many elements of the users' profiles, as in My Site
Workflow Web Service	*Workflow.asmx*	Allows manipulation of the workflow and workflow-related tasks

Key Elements and Data Structures

Full discussion of all different classes and members would be overly repetitive, and would not add value to the already available WSS SDK. Just looking at some of the more popular Web Services, such as Lists in Figure 26-3, and a sample operation,

Get Lists, as in Figure 26-4, shows the volume of information that each developer would have to process to learn all the details.

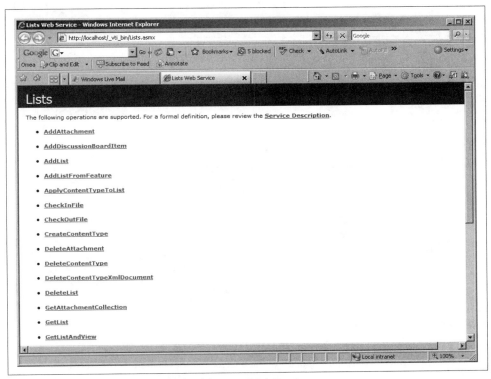

Figure 26-3. Operations and methods of the Lists Web Service

Thus, the question is how to simplify and distill this information in order for it to be useful in the long run. First, you need to familiarize yourself with the basic descriptions of these Web Services, and then mentally map them to the features and elements of WSS and MOSS. Once you are comfortable with this notion, you can further group and divide these based on their functionality and the type of operation they perform: do they represent an object within WSS, or are they a specialized class for data retrieval?

Once you look at the Web Service descriptions and peek at their operations, either online or via the SDK, the intent of their use becomes transparent. For instance, many people associate the People, Permissions, and Users Web Services with common user and security administrative activities, whereas Site Data, Webs, and Lists are typically used for management of sites and their metadata, as well as manipulation of list data. The next commonly used Web Services are Search (or *SPSearch. asmx*) and List Data Web Services, which are used to retrieve data. Clearly, the choice of a Web Service depends on your end goal.

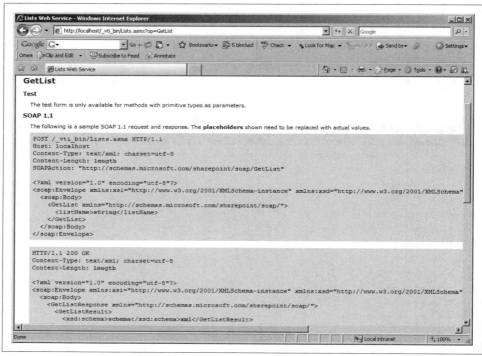

Figure 26-4. The GetList operation of the Lists Web Service

But what about file operations? Where are they? There is the Versions Web Service's AddAttachment operation, but nothing really specific to file upload and download. Unfortunately, Web Services as a technology is not an ideal choice for transporting large binary chunks of data. Instead, there is a different API, FrontPage RPC, discussed later in the chapter.

After looking at each Web Service, you can further explore each operation by clicking on it (as in Figure 26-4). Here you will be able to see typical Request and Response SOAP envelopes. Additionally, you can see placeholder information and its type within each operation, which gives a fairly good hint about the information that is expected. The Response part of the operation unfortunately needs a bit more explanation. The majority of the Responses contain fairly complex data, and the on-screen text, as seen here, simply does not provide detailed information:

```
<GetListResult><xsd:schema>schema</xsd:schema></GetListResult>
```

Fortunately, the WSS and MOSS SDKs contain significant amounts of documentation on Web Service Request and Result details, including great code samples and sample complex schema structures that may be required of or returned from each

---

Web Service. For operations that are not documented, use of the right tool or perhaps some light coding will typically help you understand the underlying data. There is simply no substitute to the way MOSS Web Services are treated in Visual Studio 2005.

Do leverage the WSS SDK on its own, as it is not included in the MOSS SDK. Throughout this chapter, the Web Services that are listed as WSS Web Services are found in the WSS SDK only, and you will not find them in MOSS documentation.

Invoking Web Services

Calling a Web Service method is one of the best ways to learn about its behavior and data. Although some of the operations may require a fairly complex request envelope, there are plenty of tools that can make this easy. With some of the Web Services, it is also possible to invoke a Web Service directly from InfoPath, or even create an application where the user can enter data that is passed on as a request to the Web Service. The magic of InfoPath lies in its ability to work with WSDL, and its ability to automatically create and lay out form elements based on an XML schema contained in simple WSDL.

Additional Web Service tools are available for other Office applications, such as Excel and Visio. As a developer you can use Visual Studio Tools for Office, and there is also a Web Services Toolkit for Office XP and Office 2003 applications, available from Microsoft's download center.

In cases where WSDL uses more complex schemas to describe the Request and Response formats, programmers move up to more advanced tools, and eventually work with Visual Studio. Some of the Web Services, such as the Query Web Service or Site Data Web Service, utilize a lot of dynamic XML to specify parameters and then return dynamic XML based on the requested parameters.

Most of the XML structures, unless defined directly in a Web Service schema (e.g., Site Data Web Service) are documented in the WSS SDK in the Collaborative Application Markup Language Core Schemas. While making Web Services very flexible, they also make it harder to use. It is almost impossible to work only with Visual Studio due to the dependencies in CAML and complex elements that are declared as XmlNode or String.

Let us approach this by looking at some sample structures and same common data elements that are often used by different Web Services to retrieve data. Other elements tend to reflect the .NET object model in terms of their structure (Table 26-3).

Table 26-3. Common data elements

Element	Description and sample
listName viewName	GUID representing an internal name of a List: {231D4FDD-0333-4FF5-9E0F-26FA85076362} In some cases, this is just the text representing the name of the list.

query	A CAML query can be used by Web Services as well as the .NET APIs. It is simply an XML-based stack notation of a query representing a condition, a field, and a value, used in GetListItems or Query operations:
	<pre><Query>
	 <Where>
	  <Or>
	   <Eq>
	     <FieldRef Name="Author" />
	       <Value Type="Text">Piotr</Value>
	   </Eq>
	   <IsNull>
	     <FieldRef Name="Published"></FieldRef>
	   </IsNull>
	  <Or>
	 </Where>
	</Query></pre>Even if this format looks odd at the beginning, it is quite understandable. Since this is XML, you must be careful about proper capitalization of every element, which is unusual since it follows PascalCase and not the typical XML camelCase. AND is an <And> element, and OR is <Or>. The comparison operators are similar (for example, = becomes <Eq>), and other operators are <Neq>, <Gt>, and <Lt>.

viewFields	This field can restrict or allow return of certain fields within the result set. Oddly enough, when this element is declared as string, the outside element </ViewFields> is not required:
	<pre><ViewFields>
	<FieldRef Name="ID" />
	<FieldRef Name="Title" />
	<FieldRef Name="Author" />
	<FieldRef Name="FileLeafRef" />
	</ViewFields></pre>

queryOptions	This element controls a variety of query related subelements within:
	<pre><QueryOptions>
	<IncludeMandatoryColumns>TRUE</IncludeMandatoryColumns>
	   <DateInUtc>TRUE</DateInUtc>
	</QueryOptions></pre>

The resulting response for most of the data queries also follows the familiar CAML format, which is actually very similar to the XML results provided in the .NET API from the SPListItemCollection (Table 26-4).

Table 26-4. XML results provided in the .NET API from the SPListItemCollection

Property	Description
Xml	All of the data is represented by properties within a <row> element wrapped in a <data>. All of the properties are either default or requested by the viewFields element. Its data types are described within the XmlDataSchema.
XmlDataSchema	This schema describes the elements and properties of the XML data set.

Using Microsoft Office to Call Web Services

Our first application will require a Web Service with a relatively simple signature, as mentioned previously; a lot of Web Services use GUIDs when referring to lists. Our application will connect to the Lists Web Service and retrieve some of the basic information about each list, including its Internal Name in the form of a GUID.

To retrieve data from InfoPath for our application, follow these steps:

1. Open InfoPath.
2. Select Design Form Template.
3. Select Web Service.
4. Select Receive Data.
5. Enter the location of your Lists service. In this case, with a portal installed directly on the root of my server, we enter *http://localhost/_vti_bin/Lists.asmx* and click Next.
6. In the next screen, select GetListCollection as an operation we are going to execute.
7. Enter the name for the data connection as Get List Collection Connection.

   At this point, we simply need to drag and drop the necessary elements on the screen.
8. Expand the dataFields section in the Data Source until the List group is visible.
9. Drag the element onto the Drag Data Fields Here section and choose a Repeating Section control to represent the results, as seen in Figure 26-5.

   There are no Query Fields for this operation, so we can just run the form in the preview mode.
10. From File Menu, select "Preview and Form."
11. Click Run Query, and answer Yes to any warnings.
12. Every List at the site level is returned with some metadata.

This exercise can be repeated and enhanced with additional functionality for several other Web Services. However, retrieval of list data may be not be a simple drag-and-drop wizard exercise. In many cases, Web Services will simply return a big XML blob.

Using WebService Studio

Without a generic Web Service desktop application capable of speaking SOAP, it would be hard to inspect the functionality and inner workings of Web Services, especially in light of the big XML blobs just mentioned. Also, very few people are capable of reading the documentation and using everything as-is. Luckily, there are many tools that are capable of dynamically reading the WSDL definition. For example, WebServiceStudio 2.0 is provided by the GotDotNet web site. When used to execute the same GetListCollection operation, you can see the request/response parameters in a friendlier format (Figure 26-6).

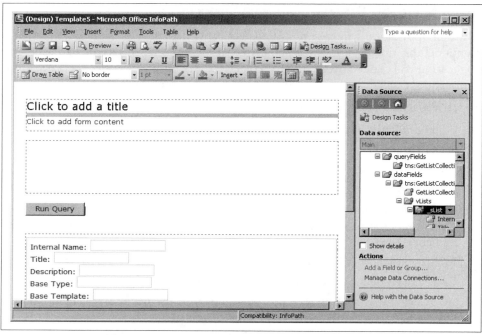

Figure 26-5. InfoPath designer as client to Web Services

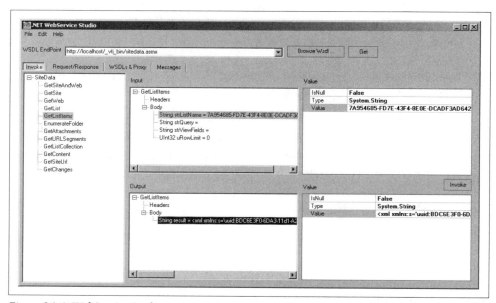

Figure 26-6. WebService Studio

GotDotNet will be phased out by July 2007, but currently the direct access to the WebService Studio is:

http://www.gotdotnet.com/Community/UserSamples/Details.aspx?SampleGuid=65a1d4ea-0f7a-41bd-8494-e916ebc4159c

WebService Studio has several screens allowing the operator to utilize and look into different features while working with a Web Service (see Table 26-5).

Table 26-5. WebService Studio screens

Screen/Tab	Description
Invoke	Displays all operations of a web service, and allows the user to enter values to execute any of the operations, as well as to explore results in a tree-like structure.
Request/Response	Displays details of a SOAP request and a SOAP response, including any errors. If a Web Service calls, and the application shows an Error message; clicking Continue will allow you to inspect the nature of the error on this screen.
WSDL & Proxy	Displays all details of a WSDL definition, breaking it down into operations, elements, and endpoints.
Messages	Displays any messages that are executed during the execution. Essentially, this is nothing more than an application log.

WebService Studio, as well as other commercial tools, such as XMLSpy or Stylus Studio, allow for a quick inspection of a Web Service's internals. Some of the tools work better than others, but generally they are worth their weight in gold. Instead of spending 5–20 minutes writing code to figure something out with Visual Studio, the tools let you know what each Web Service is capable of delivering in a very short time. These tools are also useful when you're not necessarily interested in writing a full .NET application. You can use these tools if you already have an application that can handle XML and Web Services, and you're simply interested in figuring out sample data and an XSLT transformation.

Suppose you're looking to retrieve some Contacts data to use with a Web Part on another server, or perhaps another application simply requires information stored in a typical Contacts list (I'm assuming you have only some of the data, such as the GUID):

1. Open WebService Studio, or your favorite application.
2. Point to the WSDL file, and enter *http://servername/sitepath/_vti_bin/sitedata.asmx?WSDL*.
3. Retrieve the WSDL by clicking the Get button.
4. Select the GetListItems operation.
5. Select the strListName element, and enter a GUID of a list as its value.

You can retrieve a GUID of a list by executing the GetListCollection method. By clicking Invoke, the results are populated with all lists. Next, you can find the Contacts list by looking at list Title elements, and retrieve the list's GUID, or its InternalName:

1. Press Invoke.

2. The Output section shows a single Results string, as the data inside represents the dynamic XML.

3. Selecting the Request/Response page, you can see the detailed response within the GetItemsResult element, similar to the XML results shown here and in Figure 26-7:

```
<xml xmlns:s='uuid:BDC6E3F0-6DA3-11d1-A2A3-00AA00C14882'
     xmlns:dt='uuid:C2F41010-65B3-11d1-A29F-00AA00C14882'
     xmlns:rs='urn:schemas-microsoft-com:rowset'
     xmlns:z='#RowsetSchema'>
<s:Schema id='RowsetSchema'>
   <s:ElementType name='row' content='eltOnly' rs:CommandTimeout='30'>
      <s:AttributeType name='ows_ID' rs:name='ID' rs:number='1'>
         <s:datatype dt:type='i4' dt:maxLength='4' />
      </s:AttributeType>
...
   </s:ElementType>
</s:Schema>
<rs:data ItemCount="60">
   <z:row ows_ID='3' ows_ContentTypeId='0x010100424AAB20493AB5479311D949BB3EFCFF'
...
ows_RepairDocument='0' />
</rs:data>
</xml>
```

WebService Studio and related tools allow you to monitor low-level communication between the client and the server and may help you troubleshoot and understand the resulting XML.

Changing a Web Service Configuration with MOSS and IIS

The default configuration of Web Services within WSS and MOSS is quite different from a standard ASP.NET Web Service, which typically allows greater leeway in terms of using different protocols and also uses the default authentication.

Since Web Services primarily represent external connectivity as well as interoperability, you should be aware of their capabilities:

- They only support SOAP and SOAP12, and there are no HTTP POST or HTTP GET endpoints.

- Their authentication is configured to follow MOSS, which is typically NTLM or Kerberos and may not work well with other SOAP stacks.

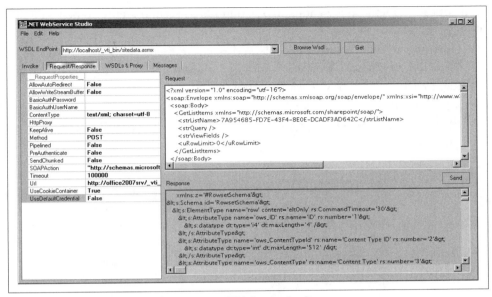

Figure 26-7. SOAP Request and Response in WebService Studio

There is no real supported way to use HTTP POST and HTTP GET because of the *web.config* settings and the static definition of the WSDL. In *web.config*:

```
<protocols>
  <remove name="HttpGet" />
  <remove name="HttpPost" />
  <remove name="HttpPostLocalhost" />
  <add name="Documentation" />
</protocols>
```

And finally, within the WSDL we have only two ports declared that support SOAP and SOAP12 bindings. Here is a snippet from *alertswsdl.aspx*:

```
<wsdl:service name="Alerts">
  <wsdl:port name="AlertsSoap" binding="tns:AlertsSoap">
    <soap:address location=<% SPHttpUtility.AddQuote(SPHttpUtility.
HtmlEncode(SPWeb.OriginalBaseUrl(Request)),Response.Output); %> />
  </wsdl:port>
  <wsdl:port name="AlertsSoap12" binding="tns:AlertsSoap12">
    <soap12:address location=<% SPHttpUtility.AddQuote(SPHttpUtility.
HtmlEncode(SPWeb.OriginalBaseUrl(Request)),Response.Output); %> />
  </wsdl:port>
</wsdl:service>
```

Next is the matter of providing good access to clients. As long as the Web Service clients are within the MS Windows and Active Directory sphere of influence, there is probably nothing to worry about. However, providing proper access to other platforms brings forth the questions of authentication and security.

Authentication methods are configured within IIS, as seen in Figure 26-8. To modify authentication settings:

1. Open the IIS management console and navigate to the web site you'd like to configure, or a virtual directory.

2. Right-click the node and select Properties from pop-up menu.

3. Select the Directory Security tab.

4. Click the Edit button of the "Authentication and Access Control" section.

5. Change the Authentication Methods here.

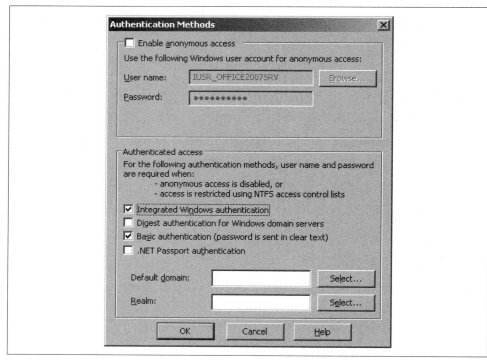

Figure 26-8. IIS Authentication configuration

The optimal method for configuring a dual type of access typically requires using two virtual servers pointing to the same database, each configured with a different setting:

- Virtual server 1 should use Integrated Windows Authentication.

- Virtual server 2 should use Basic Authentication and be configured for SSL if the access needs to be secure.

Don't change the authentication settings for the _vti_bin_ virtual directory to Basic Authentication, as the Search element of MOSS uses Web Services. Changing the settings at a directory level may break Search.

Also, when exposing your server to the Internet, configure SSL to ensure that the communications and passwords are not exposed.

The last common problem with use of Web Services is proper authorization. Whereas a site administrator would readily configure access for individual user accounts, Web Services tend to access it behind the scenes, and occasionally they may not have access to data, purely due to a simple omission. In this case, the Web Service access should be granted the same way that a MOSS search account (a non-expiring service account) is configured, via Policy for Web Applications:

1. Open Central Administration.
2. Click Application Management.
3. Navigate to Policy For Web Application.
4. Ensure that the appropriate application is selected from the drop-down list.
5. Click Add Users.
6. Select the appropriate Zone and then click Next.
7. Add the user account in the Choose Users Box (Figure 26-9).
8. Select Full Read, or select Full Control if the Web Service will interact with the data.
9. Optionally select Account Operates As System (for accounts that have Full Control) if you don't want this access to be logged individually, but rather as System.

Utilizing Web Services with Visual Studio

Consumption of Web Services is one of the strong points of Visual Studio. A typical Web Service consumer will be a command application, a desktop application, or a service. Other applications may require some additional security configuration in the code, so for the sake of simplicity, we'll focus on a standard desktop application calling Web Services.

Here, in just few lines of code, we'll be able to recreate the same functionality as in InfoPath and WebService Studio combined. As shown in Figure 26-10, we will use two Web Services to retrieve lists from the server, and then, once we obtain the GUID of each list, we will be able to retrieve data from the list.

1. First, create a new Windows Application Project.
2. Next, add references to the Web Services:
   a. Right-click the root node of the project in Solutions Explorer.
   b. Select Add Web Reference.

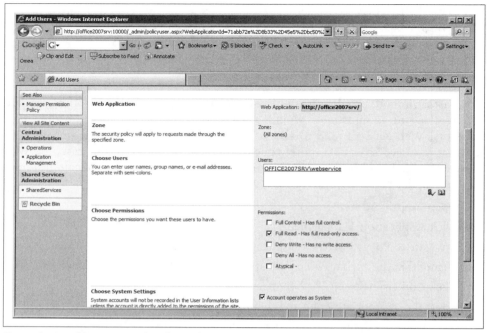

Figure 26-9. Add Users in Policy for Web Application

   c. In the Add Web Reference dialog box (Figure 26-11), you have to navigate to the Web Service you will utilize. If working with a local server, you can select the "Web Services on the Local Machine" link and navigate to the Lists Web Service; if working with another server, enter the URL of the Web Service. If you intend on binding to a specific web site within your portal, enter its full path, such as:

```
http://servername/sitepath/_vti_vin/Lists.asmx
```

   d. Next, when the documentation is displayed, validate that this is a correct web service and provide a proper name for the local reference, such as ListsWS.

   e. You can study the Object Model of the newly referenced Web Service by right-clicking the reference and choosing View in Object Browser.

3. Next, we add few controls to the form:

   a. Two buttons: Retrieve Lists and Get Data

   b. Combo box to display the lists in the site

   c. Label

   d. Text box to display stored information

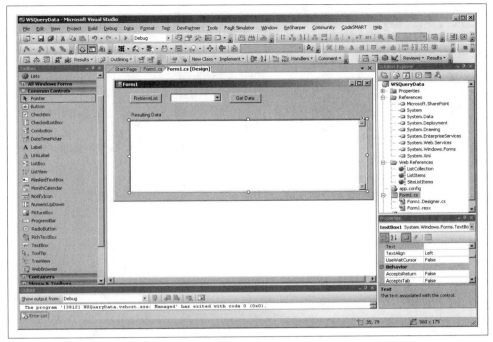

Figure 26-10. Visual Studio and WSS Web Services

4. Finally, we add code:

    a. To bind to a web service:

    ```
    ListItems.Lists _listItems = new ListItems.Lists();
    /*Authenticate the current user */
    _listItems.Credentials =
    System.NET.CredentialCache.DefaultCredentials;
    /*Set the Url property of the service for the path to a subsite.*/
    _listItems.Url = "http://localhost/_vti_bin/Lists.asmx";
    ```

    b. To retrieve data from the web service:

    ```
    System.Xml.XmlNode nodeListItems =
    _listItems.GetListItems(listName, "", query, viewFields, rowLimit,
    queryOptions, "");
    ```

    c. To display the data in a crude way:

    ```
    /*Loop through each node in the XML response and display each item.*/
    foreach (System.Xml.XmlNode listItem in nodeListItems)
    {
        textBox1.Text += listItem.OuterXml;
    }
    ```

5. Compile and run the code.

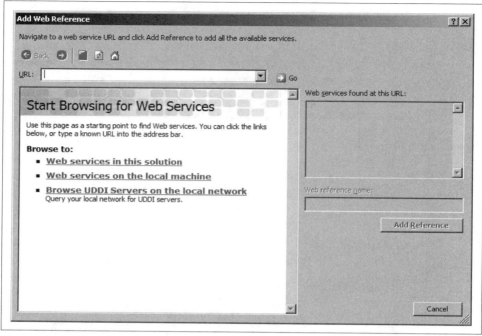

Figure 26-11. Add Web Reference

6. Click the button to populate the list combo box.

7. Select a list from a combo box and click the button to get list data.

Consuming Web Services is very easy in Visual Studio 2005, as the Intellisense quickly allows you to select a proper method, and allows you to see its signature and its type.

 Remember that the path of the Web Service reference may affect the context of the web site with which you're working. After your Web Service proxy is instantiated in your code, you can change the URL endpoint by using the URL property.

Related APIs

As mentioned earlier, there are two related APIs that can be utilized with WSS and MOSS for remote operations. As such, they are closely related to Web Services that effectively perform similar activities.

The key difference between these APIs is that they perform very specialized activities, namely file upload and download operations. The main reasons why these are important are:

- Web Services simply do not perform as well as these protocols, requiring larger-than-file XML messages (due to encoding) as well as larger memory requirements, due to chunking and serialization. Although some of these problems could be alleviated with use of Dime and WSE 3.0 extensions, they would still not match the performance of the APIs covered in this section.

- Industry-wide support for these web services allows other document management and line of business applications to easily integrate with WSS and MOSS.

FrontPage RPC

FrontPage RPC generally refers to a set of FrontPage Remote Procedure Calls that provide the functionality to create, upload, download, change, and move documents in a SharePoint server, typically via HTTP POST commands.

FrontPage RPC interacts with the server via a single specialized DLL (*owssvr.dll*), provides over 40 different method calls, and allows batching of commands via CAML Batch element, which reduces the number of round-trips required to complete an activity:

> *http://servername/[subpath/]_vti_bin/owssvrdll?Cmd=MethodName[&Param1=Value1*

Some of the document management-related activities (among many others) are:

- Check in document
- Check out document
- Get Docs MetaInfo
- Get document
- Get documents
- Move document
- Put document
- Put documents
- Uncheckout document

This API is well documented within the WSS SDK, and there are also a large number of applications and code samples in the community sites that utilize FrontPage RPC as a means of working with files within WSS and MOSS.

 A sample document upload application is available through GotDotNet.

The following contains an example of how to upload a file to a SharePoint library via the FrontPage RPC protocol:

> *http://www.gotdotnet.com/Community/UserSamples/Details.*
> *aspx?SampleGuid=5451793d-288c-4fed-8e79-6c44ab0550e2*

WebDAV

WebDAV, which stands for Web-based Distributed Authoring and Versioning, is an extension to the standard HTTP protocol that allows creating, changing, and moving documents over an HTTP protocol. Unfortunately, contrary to what its name suggests, it lacks good support for versioning of the documents. Consequently, this API is typically used more for interoperability rather than for building full-blown remote document management applications.

Within Microsoft's developer section is part of an old Exchange server documentation:

http://msdn2.microsoft.com/en-us/library/ms985516.aspx

You can download a sample DavCopy application from the SharePoint Products and Technologies directory:

http://www.microsoft.com/sharepoint/downloads/components/results.
asp?s=A&c=davcopy

Programming Custom Web Services

Custom Web Services can be developed the same way as a typical Web Application, or, with few additional steps, your Web Service can be placed side-by-side with other Web Services installed with WSS and MOSS.

Assuming that you are familiar in developing a Web Application for the WSS platform within the *_layouts* directory, you can follow the same steps in developing all of the business functionality for your Web Service.

 WSS directories are part of a "12 hive": *C:\Program Files\Common Files\ Microsoft Shared\web server extensions\12* where *_vti_bin/* corresponds to the *\ISAPI* directory, and *_layouts* corresponds to *\TEMPLATE\ LAYOUTS*.

Your Web Service utilizes the WSS and MOSS APIs the same way as a standard Web Part or Web Application would:

1. Add the `Microsoft.SharePoint` assembly reference to your project.

2. Add appropriate using directives, such as:
   ```
   using Microsoft.SharePoint;
   using Microsoft.SharePoint.Utilities;
   ```

3. Obtain the context for the Web Service:
   ```
   SPWeb _web = SPContext.Current.Web;
   ```

4. Utilize the WSS API.

5. Modify the trust level policy if needed.

6. Utilize the `AllowUnsafeUpdates` web property if your Web Service modifies any WSS data.

Additional steps required to deploy Web Services to the *_vti_bin* directory include:

1. Generation of a static discovery and WSDL files

2. Deployment of Web Service files to the *_vti_bin* directory

3. Deployment of assemblies to GAC

Only the first step is nontrivial, and uses *disco.exe*, which is a part of the .NET 2.0 SDK, typically located at *C:\Program Files\Microsoft Visual Studio 8\SDK\v2.0\Bin*:

1. Open the command prompt and navigate to the location where *disco.exe* is installed.

2. When running *disco.exe*, enter the location of your *.asmx* file, such as *http://servername/_layouts/appname/webservicename.asmx*.

3. Replace the opening XML declaration with SharePoint references:

```
<%@ Page Language="C#" Inherits="System.Web.UI.Page"%>
<%@ Assembly Name="Microsoft.SharePoint, Version=12.0.0.0, Culture=neutral,
PublicKeyToken=71e9bce111e9429c" %>
<%@ Import Namespace="Microsoft.SharePoint.Utilities" %>
<%@ Import Namespace="Microsoft.SharePoint" %>
<% Response.ContentType = "text/xml"; %>
```

4. In the *.disco* file, replace the method name and binding, and rename the file as *WebServiceNamedisco.aspx*:

```
<contractRef ref=<% SPEncode.WriteHtmlEncodeWithQuote(Response, SPWeb.
OriginalBaseUrl(Request) + "?wsdl", '"'); %>  docRef=<% SPEncode.
WriteHtmlEncodeWithQuote(Response, SPWeb.OriginalBaseUrl(Request), '"'); %>
xmlns="http://schemas.xmlsoap.org/disco/scl/" />
<soap address=<% SPEncode.WriteHtmlEncodeWithQuote(Response, SPWeb.
OriginalBaseUrl(Request), '"'); %>  xmlns:q1="http://tempuri.org/" binding="q1:
HelloWorld" xmlns="http://schemas.xmlsoap.org/disco/soap/" />
```

5. In the *.wsdl* file, change the binding of the SOAP address near the bottom of the file, and rename the file to be *WebServiceNamewsdl.aspx*:

```
<soap:address location=<% SPEncode.WriteHtmlEncodeWithQuote(Response, SPWeb.
OriginalBaseUrl(Request), '"'); %> />
```

Conclusion

If you need to utilize Microsoft Office SharePoint Server 2007 data or functionality from a non-MOSS machine, most likely you will use Web Services or FrontPage Remote Procedure Call APIs. In some scenarios, you will find out that the Web Services provided are too generic or too chatty, and instead you will build your own set of Web Services.

Either way, this chapter has provided information on how and when you should access MOSS data from an external system that does not have MOSS APIs installed, as well as a simplified way to understand the nuances of each Web Service provided.

Use of Web Services is similar to the use of MOSS and WSS APIs: you must bind to a specific location, and then walk through the object model hierarchy to access the data.

CHAPTER 27

Using SharePoint Server for Search

Introduction

In previous chapters, we went through installation of the Microsoft Office Share-Point Server 2007 (MOSS) multiserver farm, as well as basic usage scenarios of a majority of the MOSS features. Installation and configuration of Search, even for simple use of out-of-the-box features, is very important to the overall health of your MOSS farm, as well as the health of your end users' search results.

Search in MOSS 2007 offers many significant improvements over SharePoint Portal 2003, and starting with the Office 2007 release, it is also available as a standalone product. Simply speaking, Search is an increasingly important tool for the end users as more and more data is stored in repositories that are indexed by the MOSS Search. But why is it important to an end user? Consider, for instance, as an end user, a task of finding a document stored either on a local computer or somewhere on a corporate file share. Finding the document in the first scenario may take up some time, depending on the user's personal folder organization or use of some desktop search, but the second scenario may literally take hours. This is where the Search part of MOSS steps in. MOSS Search is one of the tools that will allow you to do such a search, and not only will it index data in MOSS sites, but, among other data sources, it will also index web sites, file shares, Microsoft Exchange, and with additional work, many other line of business applications via its Business Data Catalog. A well-tuned Search literally can save hours of productivity per person.

Whether you are migrating from the Microsoft SharePoint Server 2003 or just starting out, overall Search components require a bit of planning and configuration—just installing Search will not yield any results. Hence, working with Search will be one of the key tasks for an administrator while configuring all of the elements of the MOSS farm. For medium and large companies, implementing and tuning Search will become a significant project task. Many different options should be researched before the implementation, including the number of servers involved, use of dedicated servers, scheduled crawls, and use of content access accounts.

More significantly, there will be day-to-day operational tasks associated with Search, ranging from service monitoring and dedicated backup, to usage reporting monitoring and inclusion of content owners in tuning of best bets and relevancy results.

Finally, developers can work with Search in many different ways, as many aspects of the technology are meant to be extensible. It is important to think of Search as yet another potential development platform. Not only can the developers write indexing add-ons, such as IFilters, but the developers can also write custom search applications or even customize existing elements of Search. A nice example of such a Search customization is the People search, a distinct tab that offers different options from a standard Search tab. The People search offers unique Web Parts and improved display of the results specifically for finding other people.

At the end of this chapter, you will be able to:

- Understand Search from the end user's perspective
- Understand different features of Search
- Understand the architecture of Indexing and Search
- Understand the basic administration elements of Search services
- Understand advanced configuration options
- Understand the extensibility options associated with Search

Search from the End User's Perspective

Search is one of the few applications that have become somewhat commoditized in the eyes of the end users. With Internet growth being fueled by many search services—such as Yahoo, Google, and MSN—everyone has an opinion and decent knowledge of what "search" is, what it should do, and how fast it should work. Search applications that deviate from common characteristics can be misunderstood by users and their adoption can fail. Fortunately, Search services in MOSS follow the majority of these characteristics, and therefore should be very familiar to most users.

Basic use of search is intuitive enough that almost no training is necessary, but it may be worthwhile to educate users on advanced searches, and eventually on enhanced application searches. MOSS is capable of searching through almost all of the data stored on the server, and it is capable of searching lists, content stored on different pages, document properties (metadata), and document contents (full-text search).

 There are some small differences in Search when moving from Windows SharePoint Services 2.0 or SharePoint Portal Server 2003 to Windows SharePoint Services 3.0 or MOSS 2007. Although we will not dwell on the details, it is worth mentioning that WSS-style site searches now automatically include subsites, and automatically use Portal features (if available). Additionally, use of multiple search words automatically uses AND, not OR as in the past, which significantly improves the search results.

We'll start off by discussing the common elements of Search that will be utilized by the end users, and then move onto the common tasks that power users or web designers can undertake to customize the search experience under MOSS.

Search Elements Across Pages

Search as an application includes a number of different elements that are visible to the end user (Table 27-1). Figure 27-1 shows a modified tab in a Search center application, with custom Web Parts from a Knowledge Network application. Conceptually, the tab is similar to Google but provides some improvements, such as the Refine Your Search Web Part, which allows for interactive filtering of search results.

Table 27-1. Search elements

Element	Purpose/Placement
Search Box	• All Portal Pages, except settings and property pages
Search Scopes (Figure 27-2)	• Link to advanced search page
	• Search scopes drop-down (context-sensitive up to a list or site)
	• Specialized use of search box with certain property keywords or symbols (implicit AND between search words)
Search Center (Figure 27-1)	• Search-specific part of a portal enabled via use of features; also available as template
	• Customizable by site owners, in terms of location, appearance, new types of searches, or utilization of certain properties
	• Typically contains a search box and links to advanced search
	• Can contain specialized tabs for unique searches, e.g., people, external people, etc.
Search Results (Figure 27-3)	• Same as Search center, plus results Web Parts
	• Any restrictions (language, number of results) can trigger advanced search
Advanced Search (Figure 27-4)	• Ability to use complex logic
	• Additional filters available: language, content type, property
	• Search multiple scopes

As seen in Figure 27-1, a customized MOSS-based Search application, such as the Knowledge Network enhancement, can provide tremendous value to an organization. A collection of Web Parts provides a web-friendly way to:

- Locate exact matches
- Locate relevant matches (organized in an easily understood way)
- View other relevant information (such as web advertisements)
- Work with search refinement options
- Leverage additional help

 Knowledge Network will be a freely downloadable add-on to MOSS as a Technical Preview in the first half of 2007. Watch the KN blog at *http://blogs.msdn.com/kn/*.

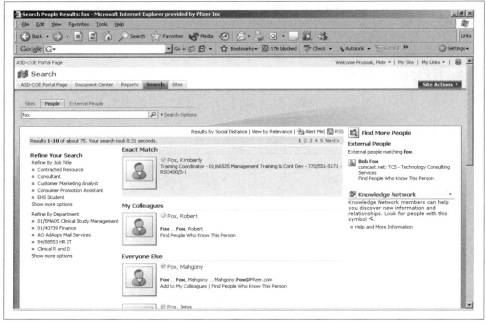

Figure 27-1. Search Web Parts in action for Knowledge Network

In this sample, many different parts of Search have been utilized, but in most circumstances, the basics of Search will suffice. Next, we will go through the very simple scenarios of searching basic content embedded directly within a MOSS site.

Using Search

A user's first direct experience with Search will be via the Search Box, available in the top-right corner of the page (Figure 27-2). The search box allows the user to select a scope of the search, which is either context-sensitive (this site) or preconfigured by the administrator. Next, the user can enter search text, and either click on the magnifying glass to proceed with the search or select Advanced Search.

The search text itself can contain keywords, special characters, and property filters. If multiple search terms are used, MOSS assumes that an implicit AND has been used. Hence, when a user types in "quick brown fox," the search is interpreted as "quick AND brown AND fox." In the previous versions, SharePoint Search used OR, which led to too many results. Next, Search server can utilize different styles of keywords. Keywords can be classified as *words* (one or more characters with no spaces of punctuation), *phrases* (multiple words enclosed in quotation marks), or a *prefix* (part of a word). Further, keywords can be combined with special characters, which may signify inclusion or exclusion from search results. The default behavior of using multiple words without special characters is a simple AND, but without the guarantee of inclusion.

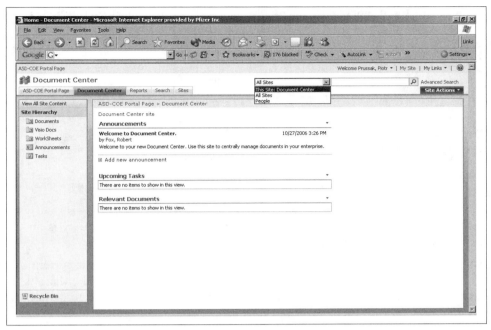

Figure 27-2. Use of Search Scopes

Table 27-2 lists these special characters.

Table 27-2. Special characters

Character	Action
+	Must contain content followed by "+"
-	Must not contain content followed by "-"

The next major enhancement to MOSS Search is the ability to use Property Filters without using the Advanced Search option. This is a popular extension to the major search engines, and users should be educated about this feature in order to utilize it successfully. Table 27-3 lists some of the popular properties.

Table 27-3. Properties

Name	Description
site	The URL property that must be specified in full. It can be a property from a SharePoint site or an external site, if such was indexed. This should not contain a trailing "/" symbol.
author	Author's name. It must be enclosed in quotes if it contains a space, or a network ID can be used.
title	Title property. It should be enclosed in quotes if it contains spaces.
duplicate	Allows the search to identify duplicate results (which are typically collapsed).
scope	Specifies the friendly name for the scope, as in the Scope drop-down box.

Armed with these different elements of search syntax, we can take a look at some examples and interpret what they would represent in Table 27-4.

Table 27-4. Queries and interpretation

Query	Interpretation
Author:"Piotr Prussak" site:http://portal/sites/training	Find documents authored by Piotr Prussak in a training site.
Title:sharepoint −author:"bob fox"	Find anything with a title "sharepoint" AND where Bob Fox is not the author.
Department:HR department:IT	Find anything where the custom column "department" is set to HR OR IT.
Site:http://portal1 site:http://portal2	Find results from either of the portals.

One key difference between use of standard keywords and properties is that when two Property Filters for the same property are used, the resulting query is an OR query and not an AND query.

What about security? The Enterprise Search will hide all results that the current user of the web site is not entitled to view at query time. In other words, there is no chance that the user can see the result, unless they would have access to it via other means.

The results screen, in its simplest form (Figure 27-3), has a number of interesting elements. First, there is a repeat of the search query in the query box. Next, near the top, there are links allowing the user to change the ordering of the results, as well as to set up alerts or an RSS feed for the underlying search (which is processed once a day). The following line represents an approximate number of results, the processing time, and a simple paging mechanism.

Finally, the results are broken down into High Confidence Results, or Exact Matches (if there are any), and partial matches. The results display an icon, signifying the type of the result, title of the result, and partial text with hit highlights. Underneath each result, the URL as well as some additional metadata are shown.

For those who would prefer to change any of the elements of MOSS search, the layouts and the contents of the Search and results pages are quite customizable. Indeed, many things can be easily modified or reconfigured. Latter parts of the chapter are dedicated to the possible modifications of the Search features.

 There are also several third-party products that further enhance the MOSS search capability. You can find a number of them at the Microsoft Partner Site: *http://directory.partners.extranet.microsoft.com/*.

Finally, the advanced search screen (Figure 27-4) offers clear options to users who would like a very targeted and specific search, but who may not be familiar with all

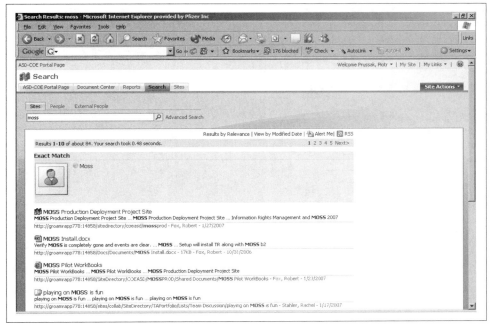

Figure 27-3. *Standard search results*

of the keywords and property filters that could be entered in the search box otherwise. Advanced search allows users to specify the search terms in a text entry box, to disambiguate a potential use of AND and OR, and select the use of + and – symbols.

Additionally, the screen allows additional specification of the language, type of the target documents, and entry of any of the additional properties that would mimic the use of a property filter in the earlier examples. In order for a property to be listed in the Pick Property drop-down, the property value must be both crawled and managed. Both of these settings are covered in the "Administering Search Services" section.

 For the truly hardcore users who like to tinker with different tools and APIs, there are two more ways to utilize Search services without dragging out Visual Studio 2005 and using the .NET APIs. One of them is the simple URL access, and the second is the Search web service.

Search Web Parts and Search Center

The next natural step is customization of the Search features visible to the end user. Although there are many administrator-type and developer-type options available, there are also many things that can be done by information workers and power users of the portal. Search Center, after all, works on the same infrastructure as all other pages, and is based on the Web Part architecture. MOSS's Search Center ships with

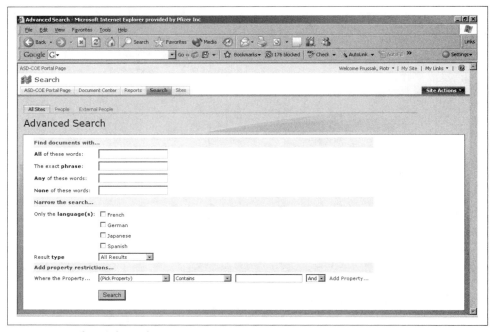

Figure 27-4. Advanced search screen

five pages and 11 Web Parts. Although information workers should also be involved in fine-tuning configuration of Search services, knowledge of the Search Center pages is important, as it introduces concepts such as Keywords, Best Bets, Search Statistics, and content targeting.

 You can't really edit pages behind the simple WSS Search. WSS Search is typically employed when the This Site scope is used in the text box.

Before you start with Search Center, you have to make sure that your site has Search deployed, or that your site is linked to a portal with a Search Center. If there is no Search Center deployed, it can simply be created as a subsite.

To create a Search Center subsite from the Site Actions menu:

1. Select Create.

2. Select Sites and Workspaces.

3. Fill in typical site details (name, URL).

4. Select either Search Center With Tabs or Search Center from the Enterprise templates box.

5. Click Create.

The Search Center with Tabs template includes an in-page tab-like interface (which does not interfere with top navigation) and provides an additional People search tab. This template is a preferred interface when different Search screens might be developed for more specialized end user searches.

 There may be a temptation to allow for a lot of personalization, but Search is one of the areas where this can lead to unnecessary confusion. With out-of-the-box settings, a Contributor can edit a search page only if she created it. As an administrator, you can always prevent people from creating pages by modifying permissions in the Pages library.

The Results page features seven Web Part zones, which allow you to add any Web Part from the Web Part catalog (the default query page has only two zones, and the Advanced Search has four zones). You can switch to the Edit Mode (Figure 27-5) by clicking on the Site Actions menu. In order to edit the page, it will need to be checked out, and in order for everyone to see the changes, the page will have to follow the standard process associated with editing Web Part pages: it must be checked in, published, and approved.

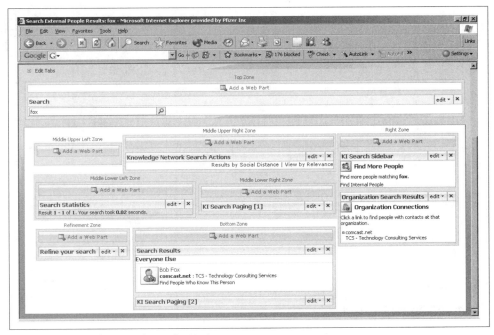

Figure 27-5. Search page tab in Edit Mode

With the page in Edit Mode, you can now move, add, delete, or configure any of the Web Parts. Typically, the Results page is of most interest, as most of the prebuilt Web Parts are available. All of the Web Parts on this page work very well with each other, and they plug into the same result set available on the page. When adding new Web Parts within the Search Center, the Add Web Parts pop-up groups all Search-related Web Parts in one logical unit (Figure 27-6).

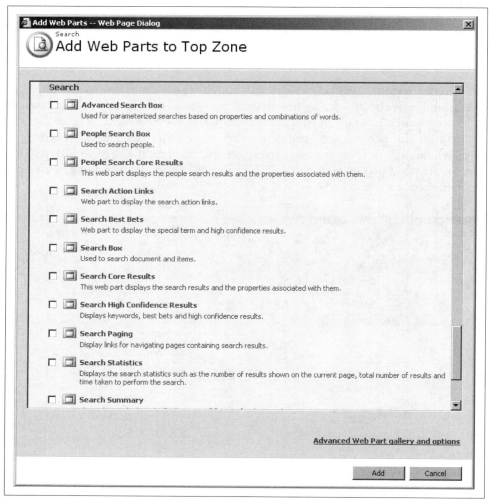

Figure 27-6. Search Web Parts

Table 27-5 shows the Web Parts that are directly related to Search. The majority of them are customizable even further, and some can provide data to other Web Parts.

Table 27-5. Web Part names and purposes

Web Part name	Purpose
Advanced Search Box	Used for advanced searches on the Advanced Search page (an example of customization of this Web Part is provided in the "Adding Custom Column to Search" section).
People Search Box	Used for people-specific searches.
People Search Core Results	Displays core results for People-related searches.
Search Action Links	Search action links include RSS, Alert, and sorting links.
Search Best Bets	Displays related Keyword, Best Bet, and High Relevancy items. These are covered in more detail in "Advanced Configuration Options," later in this chapter.
Search Box	The standard search box.
Search Core Results	Displays the results of most common searches. This is the most frequently customized Web Part.
Search High Confidence Results	Shows Keywords, Best Bets, and other high-confidence results.
Search Paging	Displays links for navigation between pages.
Search Statistics	Displays basic search statistics.
Search Summary	Shows autocorrection suggestions in a "Did you mean" format.

For instance, the Search Core Results Web Part can be easily configured to show different results, including the internal contents of the resulting text. The display is controlled by a selection of columns and a configurable XSLT. This is a very flexible Web Part and should be the first element of customization of any of the result pages.

In order to configure the Core Results Web Part, the page needs to be in Edit Mode, and the user needs to click the Edit button next to the Web Part. Unfortunately, due to the unusual size of the Web Part zone, the property editor may have to be minimized and the browser maximized in order to see the properties. Some of the most useful properties are listed in Table 27-6.

Table 27-6. Useful properties

Property	Purpose
Results Per Page	Number of hits to show per page
Sentences In Summary	Length of the text under the title of the result
Highest Result Page	Maximum number of results that the user can reach
Default Results View	Ordering of the results
Remove Duplicate Results	Check if duplicate results should be collapsed
Enable Search Term Stemming	Check if keywords and results can be approximated using word stem (e.g., running versus run)
Permit Noise Word Queries	Check if previously defined noise words can be utilized in search
Selected Columns	XML definition of the columns to be retrieved
XSL Editor	XSLT style sheet that can be used to transform the results

Working with existing pages and Web Parts may not necessarily be sufficient in every single case where some deeper level of customization is desired. For instance, there may be some fixed queries, or potentially a brand-new application developed with new Web Parts (similar to the Knowledge Network mentioned earlier). In such cases, new pages and new tabs can be added to the Search Center site, as seen in Figure 27-7.

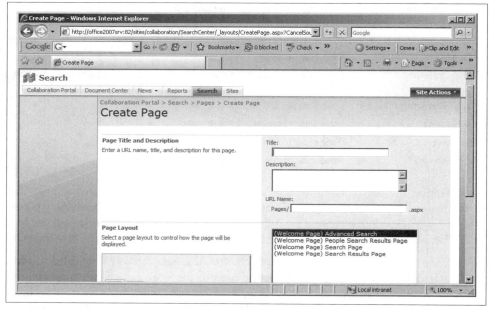

Figure 27-7. Create Page in Search Center

The process is very familiar:

1. From the Search Center, click on Site Actions.
2. Select Create Page.

 In order for the Search to work, you should add two or three separate pages to the site, a Search page and a Results page. Once a Search page is added, you will need to configure Web Parts and edit Target Search options.

3. On a newly created Search Page, select the Search Box Web Part and click Edit.
4. In the Miscellaneous section (Figure 27-8), edit the Target Search Results Page URL to point to the newly created Results page.
5. Optionally, you may also edit the Advanced Search Page if you have created one.

Figure 27-8. Configuration of Search Box

6. Modify any other Web Part settings on both pages.

7. Click Add New Tab to complete navigation.

8. Typically, you will also want to add a custom search Scope and content type via SSP to target search results.

Different Features of Search

So far we have taken a look at Search functionality from the end user's (and perhaps a power user/developer's) perspective. Now, switching to the IT professional or a business decision maker, we need to look at the features that make Search happen behind the scenes. From the overall feature perspective, there are some major features of Search that ship specifically with MOSS, and some that ship directly with Windows SharePoint Services. Following the direct comparison of the most important features, there are also some secondary and nontrivial features that are worth mentioning.

 True wildcard search is not readily available within the basic User Interface, but it is supported via the APIs. Additionally, it is supported by some third-party tools, such as Ontolica.

Unlike the previous version, where WSS team sites were not capable of using the SharePoint 2003 Search, once a WSS site functions under the Office Server itself, it is capable of inheriting all of its features. Without the Office Server, the features are slightly limited (Table 27-7).

Table 27-7. WSS and MOSS Features

Common Features	WSS	MOSS
Index SharePoint Content	X	X
Index Web sites, Exchange, file shares, Notes, LOB		X
Rich Results	X	X
Alerts	X	X
RSS	X	X
Remove Duplicates	X	X
Scopes, Managed Properties		X
Best Bets, Results Removal, Query		X
Tabs		X
People Search, Knowledge Network		X
Business Data Catalog		X
Query API, Web Service	X	X
Admin API		X

 Results Removal is a new feature that allows quick removal of a URL from the results. As it occasionally happens, a popular document can be deleted. Instead of allowing the users to find the document in the search results and meet with disappointment (at least until the index is refreshed), the document can be manually removed from search results.

Clearly, the differences between the two products are quite significant in terms of Search technology, starting from the advanced indexing capabilities of MOSS down to the superior Web Parts. What about other esoteric features and improvements over other products and versions?

Word stemming

This is the ability to properly trim endings of words at index and query time so that proper matches can be made. This also means users don't have to create wild-card searches to find words that are closely related to one another; for example, "bathing" and "bather" will both use the stem "bath." To use this feature you have to turn on Enable Search Term Stemming in the Search Core Results Web Part.

Security trimming

The ability to properly filter results and display only the results to which the user has appropriate access.

Improved relevancy

New logic within the indexes map the distance between terms as well as relevancy within a document. For example, if a term is in a headline, it is more important than in the body of the document.

Query reporting

A great improvement for the server operator and the person who is responsible for managing overall quality of the data and search results within an organization. For example, people often look for particular HR documents, such as company vacations, but since every person may use a different search term, the administrator can set up keywords, best bets, and a thesaurus to point users to the document.

Shared engine

The search engine is now shared among all of the other Microsoft applications. This means that all of the bug fixes and improvements will ideally trickle in faster than if there were multiple engines to maintain.

Performance improvements (continuous propagation, security change crawl, change log crawl)

A lot of improvement went into the new indexing and gathering elements of the search, and they work significantly better and faster than in the past.

 If the existing security trimmings are not sufficient, as may be the case with scans of external catalogs, a custom security trimming may be developed through the ISecurityTrimmer interface.

Architecture of Indexing and Search

Because the Search component is actually the only element of the MOSS infrastructure that tends to span just about any physical piece of the environment, it is also the most challenging to set up and to configure. A simple introduction to its architecture and to the inner workings of the system will potentially avoid future setup nightmares and configuration pitfalls.

To start off, see Figure 27-9 for a graphical representation of communication paths between some of the core features and elements of Search. In the middle, we have the core elements, the Index engine, and the query engine behind Microsoft Search. The index engine retrieves search configuration data from the database and is responsible for crawling the data sources and compiling the index. Query Engine, on the other hand, only works with the built index (as well as some additional configuration data) to serve the Search results.

 Contrary to popular opinion, MOSS Search does not perform a full-text search directly against the data in the database. The gatherer part of the Index engine actually walks through every known piece of content against a Web Front End (WFE) server using standard HTTP protocol, discovering the content before deciding whether it fits the criteria of being indexed.

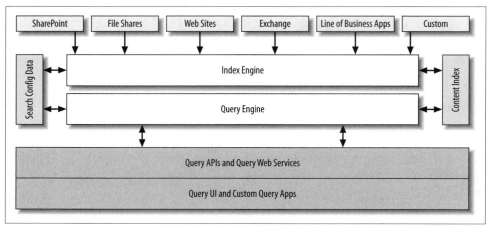

Figure 27-9. Core elements of Search technology

Data flow across processes

Perhaps the best illustration is the actual flow of data within the Search, from the time a document is uploaded to the portal to the moment that the document is found via search by another end user:

1. Document is uploaded to the portal by the end user.
2. Index engine starts its gatherer to collate content.
3. Index server retrieves data from the configuration database and retrieves rules, crawler rules, and impact rules.
4. Index server selects the appropriate protocol handler to work with the MOSS data source.
5. Index engine starts looking at the Web Front End server.
6. Index engine finds a new document via the change log and retrieves its metadata.
7. Index engine checks the rules to see whether the document should be included in the index.
8. Index engine retrieves the document itself.
9. Index engine opens an appropriate handler (IFilter) to do a full-text index of the document.
10. Index engine processes the document, and places the appropriate information in the content index database.
11. Database is propagated to the search engine.
12. Document can be found via search.

Because the index propagation is done via NetBIOS, your propagation may run into trouble if there is a firewall between the Index and the Search servers.

Backup of indexes

Although the data in the portal can be backed up with an off-the-shelf SQL backup tool, the backup of the index is slightly more complicated because the index includes database tables as well as the resulting index files. As such, you must use the built-in backup utilities to achieve a full fidelity index backup. With a basic SQL backup, you will back up the database part of the index, which means that upon a restore, index propagation will commence, and the end users will not be able to search immediately. Thus, as part of your disaster recovery plan, you should include the time to propagate the indexes.

Server architecture

Depending on the needs and characteristics of the deployment, you may choose a variety of configurations. The typical choices will be influenced by server geography, volume of data, and volume of searches. Table 27-8 describes these factors and their solutions. There are several important rules to observe:

- There can be multiple Search servers that will answer the queries made by the end users or via the API.
- There can be only one Index server per SSP.
- You can have a dedicated frontend server to be used for crawling content.

Table 27-8. Factor and solution

Factor	Solution
Multiple geographic sites	Consider using multiple SSPs if the volume of data is significant in each site.
Large volume of content	Index daily, and use incremental updates combined with continuous propagation. If index times spill over to business hours, consider use of a dedicated server for crawling data.
High frequency of updates	Index more frequently, and observe closely the speed of updates as well as performance of the frontend servers.
Large volume of search queries	Monitor search performance and add new Search servers as necessary.
High impact of indexing on frontend servers	Utilize a dedicated frontend server if the impact of the performance is noticeable to the end users.

 When using a dedicated Web Front End Server, the underlying mechanism adds entries in the HOSTS file on the Index server, which may not work if multiple NIC cards are used and host headers are not used. Since the entries are automatically added by SharePoint, this may not work and might be hard to troubleshoot.

Administering Search Services

Administration of Search services can be a daunting task. The larger the server deployment, and the more content stored, the harder things become. Ideally, administration and configuration should be a task for a broad team, and could potentially include application architects, server and network operators, SharePoint administrators, and analysts and information workers. The majority of the administrative elements begin at the SharePoint Operations Center during the initial configuration of the portal and the Shared Services Provider (SSP), and then move onto the individual Web Applications and Site Collections. Options that are configured during the initial setup of the farm are accessible from the Manage Search Service page within the Application Management section, which is covered later in "Advanced Configuration Options."

 When initially installed, MOSS does not automatically crawl any content; crawls have to be initiated manually, or scheduled via the Content Sources and Crawl Schedules page.

Assuming that an SSP has already been configured in a farm, the bulk of the Search configuration lies in the Configure Search Settings Page, as seen in Figure 27-10.

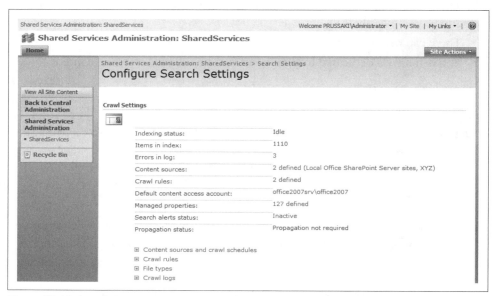

Figure 27-10. Search Settings page

Key Search Crawl Settings properties and action pages that can be managed are listed in Table 27-9.

Table 27-9. Search Crawl settings

Crawl setting	Description and use
Content Sources and Crawl Schedules	This page allows immediate management of crawls, as well as configuration of various sources of data and their schedules, that can be Full or Incremental. This is covered in detail in the upcoming "MOSS Content Source configuration" section.
Crawl Rules	Administration of crawling rules that decides whether a given page or site will be crawled (typically at least one per Web Application). Rules are specified via wildcards, and additionally, different content access accounts can be configured here.
File Types	Lists and manages extensions of files that will be indexed. Note that Access, ZIP, or PDF documents are not included here. If you add a new file extension to be indexed, ensure that the appropriate IFilter is also installed on the Index server. For instance, to index Acrobat files, you need to download and install the Adobe Acrobat IFilter.
Crawl Logs	Report pages that indicate actual results of each log, which are useful in troubleshooting crawl problems. Results are broken down by hostname (or URL) and status of each crawl attempt. Further, you can filter on specific warning or error messages that are causing problems. Generally, if you start seeing a lot of errors in the crawl logs, it may mean that either data is changing quite often or the frontend server may not be able to cope with the load induced by the indexer.
Default Content Access Account	This page allows you to configure an account that would be used for crawling. It should not be an administrator or a well-known account. This account will also be added to the Policy for Web Application with Full Read permission.
Metadata Property Mappings	Administer the ability to search site columns and map them to some meaningful names for use with Search and Advanced Search. Use of this feature is described in the upcoming "Adding Custom Column to Search" section.
Server Name Mappings	This page is used to provide translations between the addresses used in the crawl and addresses being returned in the results. This is similar to the Alternate Access Mappings page, but typically is used with other content sources.
Search Based Alerts	Use these settings to activate or deactivate subscriptions to alerts for search results (compiled daily).
Search Result Removal	Lists any URLs that should be removed from Search Results. This is useful for any deleted or embarrassing search results.
Reset All Crawled Content	Erases the content index.

 If you use an administrative account to crawl site content, and hide unpublished drafts from ordinary readers, the search results may show some undesirable parts of the document in the document summary, as the crawl account will have access to the unpublished document.

Additionally, Shared Services are also responsible for the Scope Administration pages and the Authoritative Pages (covered in the "Advanced Configuration Options" section later in this chapter).

In the Scope Administration pages, you can manage farm-wide scopes that are visible within the search boxes. Scopes can be configured as either shared per farm or applicable to a specific site. Additionally, scopes can target specific Search Pages as well as specific content. Scope rules can be made out of the following:

- Web addresses
- Properties (based on `Author`, `contentclass`, `Site`, or `SiteName`)
- Content sources
- All content

Further, each rule can be `Included`, `Required`, or `Excluded`. As you add new scopes to the system, it is important to keep mental track of their exclusivity. If you want to have separate and independent scopes for certain document types or web sites, make sure that one scope includes a rule (or requires it) and another one excludes that particular rule. In fact, the All Sites scope excludes the `SPSPeople` content class (shown in Figure 27-11), and as a result, would never display people on the main search results page.

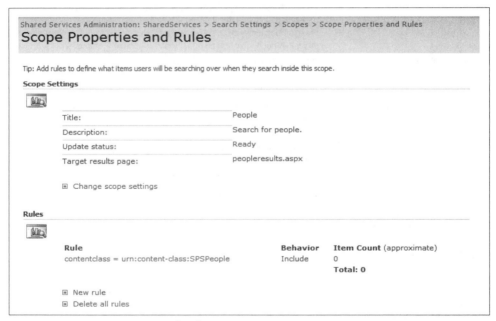

Figure 27-11. Scope Properties and Rules

If, for instance, your portal depends on a particular document type, you can create a scope rule where a `contentclass` property restriction is equal to the document type in question. Similarly, a scope rule can be based on a subsite or a custom content source, such as your Exchange public folders.

Advanced Configuration Options

The next few options are typically used with bigger farms, or when there is a need to gather data from external sources or to fine-tune the querying or search results.

Application Management: Manage Search Service

One of the Search administration pages actually lies within the Application Management page, within the Manage Search Service section (Figure 27-12). It is a mishmash of farm-wide and application-specific settings, which generally ties the integration between the application, the farm, and the SSP on a single page. The Shared Services section simply indicates and links to the Shared Services Provider associated with a given Web Application, as well as the management pages we've worked with throughout this chapter.

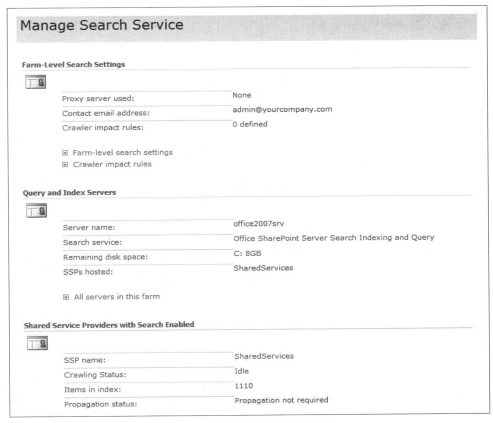

Figure 27-12. Manage Search Service

The Manage Search Service page is the place where you can change the options that were originally set during the configuration of the farm, either on the Farm-Level Search Settings page or via the Office SharePoint Server Search Indexing and Query link.

The Managing Farm-Level Search Settings deals with configuration for external searches, and allows you to configure information such as:

- An email address associated with the crawler
- Proxy settings to be used when crawling other servers
- Connection and request acknowledgement timeouts
- SSL certificate name warnings settings

Next, in Figure 27-13, you can see the Configure Office SharePoint Server Search Service Settings On Server *servername* administration page. This page mixes server and farm settings for configuration of service-related properties. Table 27-10 lists the search configuration elements.

Table 27-10. Search configuration elements

Configuration element	Description
Query and Indexing	Indicates the role for which the server will be used. Note that the Office SharePoint Server Search must be started for this to be available.
Contact E-mail Address	This is the email address associated with the crawling account.
Farm Search Service Account	This is an account that is used by the Windows service, not the account that is used to gather data. It must have privileges to use the search databases and to run as a service.
Index Server Default File Location	This is the location where index files are stored, but in order for it to be edited, you must use STSADM, utility in the BIN folder. You should monitor disk activity and place this on a fast, dedicated disk if necessary.
Indexer Performance	This allows the administrator to set the impact of indexing on SQL and internal server resources.
Web Front End and Crawling	This setting allows you to select a dedicated WFE as a target for crawling. Note that there are some situations in which a dedicated WFE does not work (described previously in the "Architecture of Indexing and Search" section).

The last element of the farm-level management is the Impact Rules management page, which allows us to edit Crawler Impact Rules, as in Figure 27-14.

Crawler Impact Rules are used to throttle the retrieval of requests that are made against the Web Front End (WFE) server. In many cases, the WFE simply is not capable of serving as many pages as the crawler can request. This results in poor performance at the WFE, along with crawl errors associated with the data source. Most likely this type of problem indicates an underpowered server, combined with heavy ASP.NET processing, which results in longer processing of the pages. This can be fixed in two ways: by disallowing the crawl of the ASPX pages within the site (this is configured within the Site administration settings) or by changing the Request Frequency within an Impact Rule.

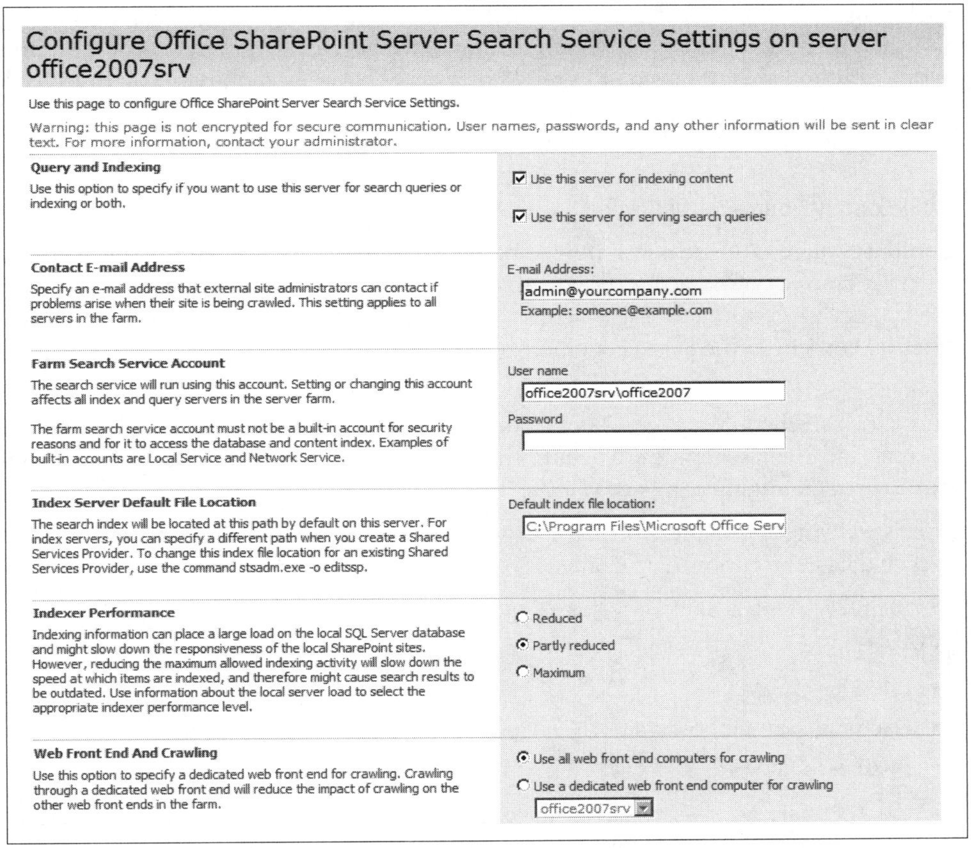

Configure Office SharePoint Server Search Service Settings on server office2007srv

Use this page to configure Office SharePoint Server Search Service Settings.

Warning: this page is not encrypted for secure communication. User names, passwords, and any other information will be sent in clear text. For more information, contact your administrator.

Query and Indexing

Use this option to specify if you want to use this server for search queries or indexing or both.

☑ Use this server for indexing content

☑ Use this server for serving search queries

Contact E-mail Address

Specify an e-mail address that external site administrators can contact if problems arise when their site is being crawled. This setting applies to all servers in the farm.

E-mail Address:

admin@yourcompany.com

Example: someone@example.com

Farm Search Service Account

The search service will run using this account. Setting or changing this account affects all index and query servers in the server farm.

The farm search service account must not be a built-in account for security reasons and for it to access the database and content index. Examples of built-in accounts are Local Service and Network Service.

User name

office2007srv\office2007

Password

Index Server Default File Location

The search index will be located at this path by default on this server. For index servers, you can specify a different path when you create a Shared Services Provider. To change this index file location for an existing Shared Services Provider, use the command stsadm.exe -o editssp.

Default index file location:

C:\Program Files\Microsoft Office Serv

Indexer Performance

Indexing information can place a large load on the local SQL Server database and might slow down the responsiveness of the local SharePoint sites. However, reducing the maximum allowed indexing activity will slow down the speed at which items are indexed, and therefore might cause search results to be outdated. Use information about the local server load to select the appropriate indexer performance level.

○ Reduced

● Partly reduced

○ Maximum

Web Front End And Crawling

Use this option to specify a dedicated web front end for crawling. Crawling through a dedicated web front end will reduce the impact of crawling on the other web front ends in the farm.

● Use all web front end computers for crawling

○ Use a dedicated web front end computer for crawling

office2007srv ▾

Figure 27-13. Office SharePoint Server Search Service Settings

Add Crawler Impact Rule

* Indicates a required field

Site

Type the name of a site. Do not include the protocol (for example 'http://').

Site: *

myportal

Request Frequency

Indicate how the crawler will request documents from this site.

For minimal impact, request fewer documents simultaneously or set a delay between requests.

● Request up to the specified number of documents at a time and do not wait between requests
Simultaneous requests:

4 ▾

○ Request one document at a time and wait the specified time between requests
Time to wait (in seconds)

| OK | Cancel |

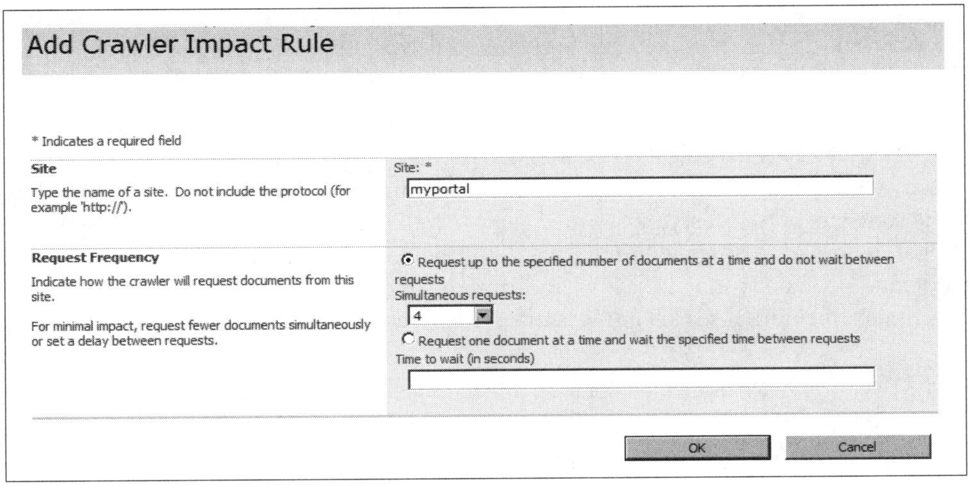

Figure 27-14. Add Crawler Impact Rule

Each Impact rule is associated with a URL that is used for crawling a SharePoint site, and then a request frequency, which can be represented either in terms of the number of simultaneous requests or in terms of a delay between requests. You must look at the performance of the WFE server to determine the optimal request frequency, while also balancing out the need for a short indexing time.

MOSS Content Source configuration

Content Source configuration allows for indexing and management of schedules of different sources of data that flow through the index. Most commonly, this will be used to set up a schedule for a default data source, but also it will be used to add external content to the Search engine, such as external web sites or file shares.

Content Source configuration is available from the SSP, from the Content Sources And Crawl Schedules page. There you can see the listing of available Content Sources and their schedules. Clicking the New Content Source link opens the Content Source Configuration Page (Figure 27-15).

After specifying the name, you have to specify the desired indexing handler or effectively indicate the appropriate Content Source Type, which can be one of the following:

- SharePoint Sites
- Web Sites
- File Shares
- Exchange Public Folders
- Business Data

Next is the start address, which will typically be *http://servername* or *\\servername\ share* for a folder share. Unlike previous versions of Index server, you can associate a single content source with multiple addresses. In order for the Business Data crawl to take place, the Business Data Catalog must first be configured within the Shared Services Provider. For the Exchange Server, you'll typically configure the search of public folders via the HTTP protocol.

The Crawl Settings section adjusts dynamically and is context-sensitive to the Content Source Type (Table 27-11). Crawl Settings displays several options, ranging from single page crawls to unlimited crawl within the content source. It is unadvisable to use very broad settings, especially for web sites (e.g., unlimited page or server hops), as broad settings will potentially kill the content source and may never finish indexing. In fact, it may be easier and more economical in the long run to integrate results from external search engines into MOSS rather than index big sites.

 When adding a People source to an existing SharePoint Sites index, you have to use an *sps3://* moniker instead of the usual *http://* in order to leverage it.

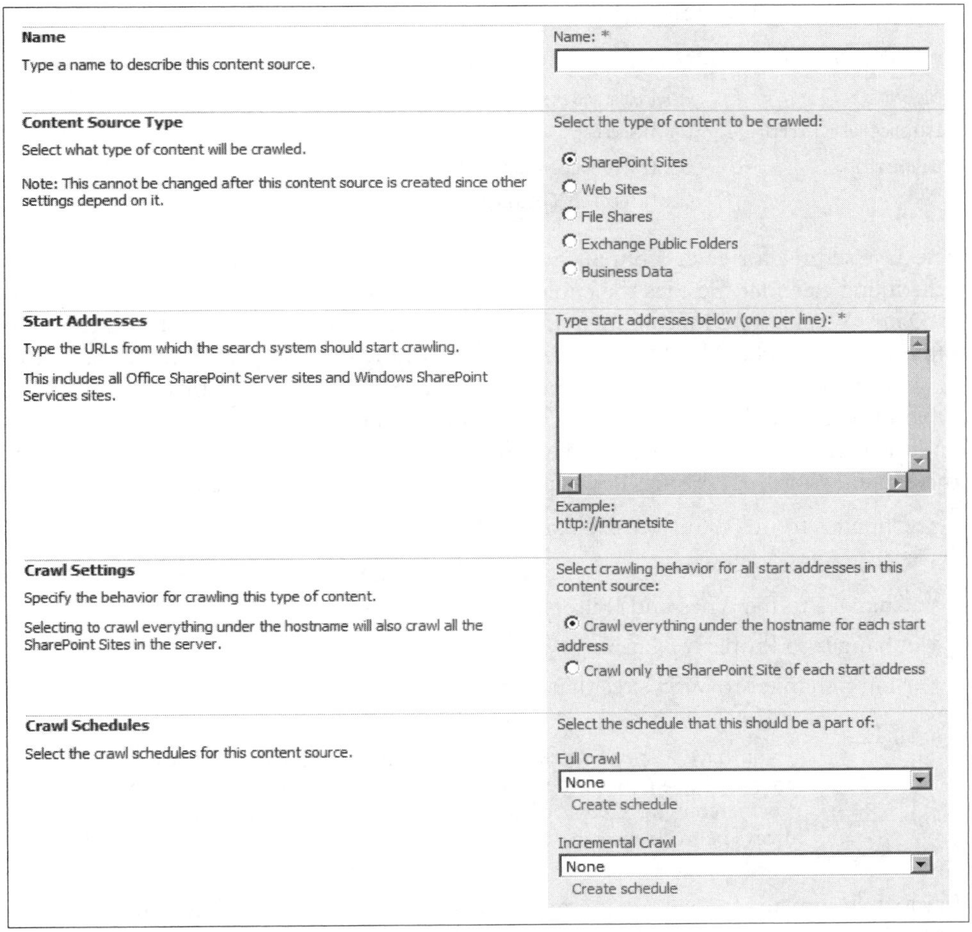

Figure 27-15. Content Source Configuration page

Table 27-11. MOSS Crawl Settings

Content Source Type	Crawl Settings
SharePoint Sites	Crawl everything
	Crawl only the top level site
Web Sites	Crawl all pages within the server
	Crawl single page
	Custom
	Allow *x* page hops
	Allow *x* server hops

Table 27-11. MOSS Crawl Settings (continued)

Content Source Type	Crawl Settings
File Shares	Crawl folder and all subfolders
Exchange Public Folders	Crawl folder only
Business Data	Crawl entire Business Data Catalog
	Crawl a specific BDC application

The last setting for each Content Source is the schedule, which resembles a typical scheduling calendar. Besides the choice of Crawl Schedule frequency, which can be set at Daily, Weekly or Monthly intervals, there are additional settings that indicate how often the given schedule should be repeated and how long the crawl should last. Each Content Source can have two different types of crawls, Full Crawl or Incremental Crawl. Obviously, to build an index from scratch, you will need to start off with a Full Crawl, and the Incremental Crawl will intelligently pick up additions, deletions, and changes to the content source. There are, however, other times when the Full Crawl must be run:

- Changes to the inclusion/exclusion rules
- Changes to a crawl account
- Changes to file types and IFilters
- Changes to Property Mappings
- Major changes to WSS sites that delete the Change Log

 If you have a specific site that requires high-frequency updates, consider adding a new Content Source specific to that site and fine-tuning the Incremental Crawl schedule to a point where the index would always be fresh enough.

In most circumstances, a daily Incremental Crawl schedule should be sufficient.

Authoritative pages

Generally, the Authoritative pages make sense only in the context of using multiple Content Sources, and the concept of Result Relevance may not be applicable to single portal sites. Essentially, the Authoritative pages increase the relevancy of a page by decreasing the click distance to the source of truth. Administration is very simple, as there are four entry boxes, allowing for entry of the following:

- Most Authoritative Pages
- Second-Level Authoritative Pages
- Third-Level Authoritative Pages
- Sites to Demote

As such, when indexing a number of content sources and observing the quality of the search results (as described in the next section), there is a possibility that a page with better information could be presented further down the results listing than a page with the best match. Thus, in order to increase the rank position, the administrator should add the site that hosts the more relevant data as the Most Authoritative Page, and perhaps add the useless site as the Site to Demote.

This feature is useful when indexing many content sources that potentially have similar data—for instance, your intranet site versus your public Internet site. Most likely, your intranet would have the most relevant information.

Search Query/Results Monitoring

One of SharePoint's most desirable features for information officers is the ability to monitor query and results statistics via the Query Reporting Tool (Figure 27-16). The tool creates graphs as well as different types of reports that can be exported to Excel or PDF formats. These are available for each SSP within the Search Usage Reports section, and the Search Results page is available via the menu on the lefthand side of the page. Based on this information, you may want to fine-tune best bets, scopes, authoritative sites, and plan capacity of your Search services. This page displays the following reports:

- Queries Over Previous 27 Days (bar chart)
- Queries Over Previous 12 Months (bar chart)
- Top Query Origin Site Collections Over Previous 30 Days (pie chart)
- Queries Per Scope Over Previous 30 days (pie chart)
- Top Queries Over Previous 30 Days (text summary)

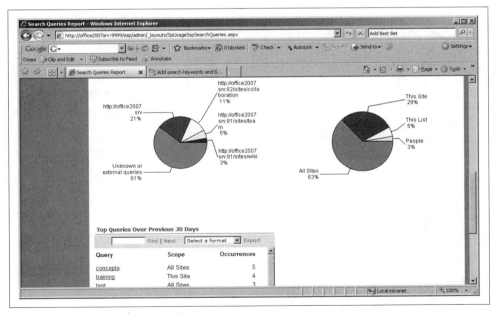

Figure 27-16. SSP Search Queries Reports

Similarly, the Search Results Report has the following reports available:

- Search Results Top Destination Pages (text summary)
- Queries With Zero Results (text summary)
- Most Clicked Best Bets (text summary)
- Queries With Zero Best Bets (text summary)
- Queries With Low Clickthrough (text summary)

The Search Results Reports page is very useful because it highlights the problem areas, or at least the areas where addition of Best Bets or Authoritative sites may increase the end users' ability to find relevant information using Search.

Unfortunately, these pages are buried within the administrative features, and may not find an appropriate audience. The typical consumer of these reports should be the site collection administrator who is managing the Best Bets.

Search Configuration in Sites and Site Collections

Looking away from the SSP, and at individual sites and portals, there are many advanced search settings that are configurable only from the Site Collection or Site level. In order to open these settings, you have to select Site Settings (or Modify All Site Settings) from the Site Actions drop-down menu. Depending on the site template and privileges, your Site Settings page may be hidden under a particular submenu. Figure 27-17 displays the Site Settings page at the Site Collection level, and highlights management pages that are relevant to Search.

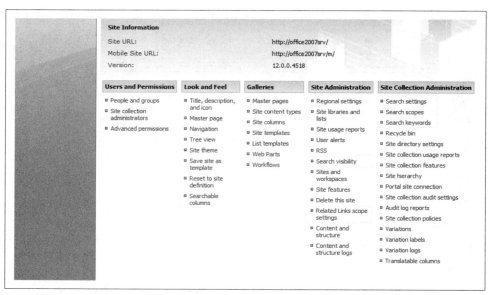

Figure 27-17. Site Settings page at Site Collection level

Depending on the context of the Site Settings page, some of the management options that are listed in Table 27-12 and visible in Figure 27-18 may not be available; however, if they are available, their meaning and management screens will be identical.

Table 27-12. Search Configuration options

Page	Description and use
Searchable Columns	This page allows you to view all of the columns used on the site and to select the columns that should be excluded from crawling. For columns that are not relevant or are frequently updated (via some automated means), this could be a way of exclusion from repetitive crawls.
Search Visibility	This page sets web-level availability of the results within Search. Additionally, the page allows fine-grained control over indexing of the ASPX pages on the site.
Related Links Scope Settings	Use these to manage local site scopes that will be visible only when using a Search Box within the site.
Search Settings	Set the ability to use a specific Search Center and advanced scopes for a Site Collection.
Search Scopes	Manage local Site Collection scopes against the scopes that are provided by the SSP
Search Keywords	Ability to manage keywords, best bets, and any associated approvals. This is a place where a site collection administrator can easily influence the contents of the search results screen.
Expired Keywords	
Keywords Requiring Review	

Finally, the Add/Edit Keyword page, as seen in Figure 27-18, can be launched at a site collection level from the Manage Keywords page. It provides a quick way for an information officer to enhance the search experience. Based on the Query and Search Result data, you can easily steer the users in a proper direction by providing additional synonyms, a definition, or even best bets to increase the value of the Search Results page (this is where the contents will eventually show up).

Similar to the result advertisements in Google, the targeted results show up on the righthand side of the page (refer back to Figure 27-1). Typically this feature is used when a large number of queries target a particular search term—for instance, "vacation" on an HR site, with no proper exit pages. In such a case, the administrator can associate the term "vacation" with a couple of synonyms, such as "holidays" or "days off," and provide a link to the company policy on vacations.

A Keyword or a Keyword Phrase consists of the following elements: synonyms, best bets, definition, contact, and various dates associated with publishing and visibility. Synonyms are important because they allow association of various elements with a best bet or a definition. Best bets are important because they allow the site administrator to advertise a particular link or a location as a good result for a particular query. Similarly, a definition, as well as a contact, can provide additional clues to the end user about the applicability of the suggested result.

Add Keyword

* Indicates a required field

Keyword Information

The Keyword Phrase is what search queries will match to return a keyword result.

Synonyms are words that users might type when searching for the keyword. Separate them using semicolons.

Keyword Phrase: *

Synonyms:

Best Bets

Best Bets are the recommended results for this keyword.

Best Bets will appear in search results in the order listed.

Add Best Bet

Keyword Definition

Definition is the optional editorial text that will appear in the keyword result.

A A¹ | B I U | ≡ ≡ ≡ | ⅛ ⅜ | ⅜ ⅜ 🖼 | A 🖉 | ᵗ ᵗ

Contact

The contact is the person to inform when the keyword is past its review date.

Contact:

Publishing

In the Start Date box, type the date you want this keyword to appear in search results.

In the End Date box, type the date you want this keyword to no longer appear in search results.

The Review Date box, type the date you want this keyword to be reviewed by the contact.

Start Date
2/13/2007

End Date (Leave blank for no expiry)

Review Date

Figure 27-18. Add Keyword

 When managing a list, one of the options on the Customize List page is the Indexed Columns page. This indexing is not directly related to Search, but rather to CAML queries, similar to the way that SQL Server columns are indexed. If none of the Web Parts or custom code utilizes CAML, there is no need to add any columns for indexing.

Adding Custom Column to Search

Besides enhancing the search with a keyword or a best bet, the second typical scenario is the ability to add a site column that shows up in a custom list to the Advanced Search screen. For the sake of the exercise, we're assuming that this column already exists and is called "CompanyName":

1. Open SSP and navigate to the Search Settings Page.
2. Open the Metadata Property Mappings page.

3. Click New Managed Property:

    a. Provide a name for the new property, "CompanyName" (making sure it is unique).

    b. Select the proper type; in our case, it is Text.

    c. Click Add Mappings and find the CompanyName (Text) Property in the New Managed Property screen by searching "Company" and clicking Find.

    d. Click OK.

4. Perform a Full Crawl.

5. The content is now available to be searched via standard search.

6. Modify the Advanced Search Box Web Part on the Advanced Search page:

    a. Expand the Properties section and open the Properties dialog box to add new properties that should be shown.

 Open the contents in an XML editor, and do not edit this in the default entry box.

    b. Add the following to the <PropertyDefs> node:

```
<PropertyDef Name="CompanyName" DataType="text" DisplayName="Company" />
```

    c. Add the following to the <ResultType> node:

```
<PropertyRef Name="CompanyName" />
```

    d. Click OK twice and exit the page Edit Mode.

7. Results should be visible on the screen.

Extensibility Options Associated with Search

Although Web Part and application development areas are covered in different chapters, Search has its own set of APIs available for consumption. The basic APIs are fully covered in the Object Model chapter, and the Search Web Service in the chapter on Web Services, but there are some additional technologies of interest:

- WSS .Net APIs
  - `Microsoft.SharePoint.Search.Administration` namespace
  - `Microsoft.SharePoint.Search.Query` namespace
- MOSS .Net APIs
  - `Microsoft.Office.Server.Search.Administration` namespace
  - `Microsoft.Office.Server.Search.Administration.Security` namespace
  - `Microsoft.Office.Server.Search.Query` namespace
  - `Microsoft.Office.Server.Search.WebControls` namespace

- Search Web Service
- Specialized SQL Syntax
- URL syntax for executing queries
- IFilter technology

 There are also several obsolete legacy Portal APIs that should not be used. They are in the `Microsoft.SharePoint.Portal` namespace, and have all been replaced by the `Microsoft.Office.Server` namespace.

The preceding list gives a good account of all extensibility options that are available to Search developers. The key APIs specific to execution and access to SharePoint are obviously the .NET APIs, but all of the work underneath is actually carried out via specialized SQL-like search queries. Also of some interest is the URL syntax for executing queries, as it essentially allows the developer to reuse the existing search infrastructure to quickly provide some customized searches.

Specialized SQL syntax

The Enterprise Search extends the SQL-92 and SQL-99 standards to provide additional functionality in the area of search. For those who already know standard SQL, the query format is very familiar:

```
SELECT <columns>
FROM SCOPE()
WHERE <conditions>
ORDER BY <columns>
```

The following table describes these standard clauses.

Clause	Description
SELECT	Specifies columns to be returned
FROM SCOPE()	Somewhat deprecated; has to be FROM SCOPE(), and actual scope is selected within the WHERE clause
WHERE	Specifies Search conditions that indicate a match
ORDER BY	Specifies sort order for the results

Although the basic clauses are the same as in standard SQL, some other features and keywords may be unavailable, and there are two specialized predicates: CONTAINS and FREETEXT. Additionally, the main areas where Search queries extend SQL Search include the ability to use 127-character column names, accent insensitivity, use of a thesaurus, and a looser interpretation of the NULL predicate. A typical query to display a title, path, and author is:

```
SELECT title, path, author FROM Scope() WHERE CONTAINS('author:Piotr Prussak') AND
"scope"='Books' AND FREETEXT(DEFAULTPROPERTIES, 'MOSS') ORDER BY Path ASC
```

There are some deprecated elements from SharePoint Portal 2003 Search: COALESCE_TABLE, RANK BY, UNION ALL, MATCHES, FROM <scope> (now part of the WHERE clause), and CAST, as well as column weighting.

Unlike SQL Server queries, where columns are defined in tables or views, the columns that are available for Searching are only defined in SSP's Search Settings on the Metadata Property Mappings page. What makes the metadata search work well is the ability to map multiple site columns into a single search column, where, for instance, a Contact Name column and an Employee Name column could both be mapped to the same property LastName. Two additional common results columns are Rank and LastModifedTime, which are often used to sort the results.

URL syntax

Another possible way of utilizing MOSS Search is via the URL syntax. The decision to have either a piece of code that submits HTTP GET queries or screen-scrapes pages is up to you. The syntax is very simple, but it is somewhat more limited as compared to the other forms of Search. Typically, the URL queries are submitted to a specialized search page, such as *results.aspx* within the Search Center. In most circumstances, all parameters are combined, but be careful when submitting only a partial URL syntax, as the results page may fail to render results. The parameters are outlined in the following table.

Parameter	Example	Description
k	Results.aspx?k=MOSS	Specifies keyword to be searched
s	Results.aspx?s=Piotr%20Site	Specifies the scope
v	Results.aspx?v=date	Specifies order, where v can be either *date* or *relevance*
start	Results.aspx?start=2	Specifies a page to display

A full URL query may look like this:

```
Results.aspx?k=moss%20books&s=people&v=relevance&start=3
```

That URL query would look for the following:

- Keyword = moss books
- Scope = people
- Order view = relevance
- Start page = 3

 IFilter development is outside of the scope of this book. There is more information to be found on various Microsoft and third-party web sites specializing in this technology, such as the blog *http://blogs.msdn.com/ifilter/* or MSDN's *http://msdn2.microsoft.com/en-us/library/ms691105.aspx* and *http://www.ifilter.org/*.

Conclusion

Search Services are a very significant feature of MOSS. Because of Search's complexity, it may take a diverse team some time to master all of its configurable elements. It will also be one area of your portal deployment that will typically require regular care and feeding. Not only should you be on the lookout for general performance of indexing and search in terms of numbers of errors, accuracy, or speed, but also study the search patterns of end users and tweak keywords, as along with best bets.

Last, for a happy Search Environment, here are some best practices:

- Know the environment:
    - Utilize dedicated frontend servers for large or busy sites.
    - Schedule for off-hours, especially full updates.
    - Schedule wisely, when speed of updates is critical.
    - Use Crawler Impact Rules if crawling against a live frontend.
- Use Automated Crawl Lists for each Web Application with a host header.
- For global or multisite deployments, consider dedicated crawlers and SSPs for each site.
- Use the same account for crawling, but use a non-administrator account.
- Use MOSS Backup and Restore to back up indexes.
- Pause indexes if needed, and do not stop them, as this triggers a full update.
- Monitor performance and results.
- Utilize Query and Results Reports to study user behavior.
- Utilize Keywords, Best Bets, and Authoritative Sites to improve user experience.

CHAPTER 28

Using the SharePoint Object Model

Windows SharePoint Services 3.0 is basically an extension of the ASP.NET 2.0 framework, a platform to build collaborative solutions. Just like ASP.NET, where you have all kinds of starter kits, WSS 3.0 offers something similar with a number of starter templates, such as team sites, wikis, blogs, etc. Just as WSS 3.0 is built on ASP.NET, Microsoft Office SharePoint Server (MOSS) 2007 is an extension of WSS and provides additional features, such as enhanced portal capabilities, improved search, and the business data catalog. Because both WSS and MOSS are based on ASP.NET, you can tweak, tune, customize, enhance, and extend the core SharePoint platform to meet your organization's needs. In this chapter, you will learn about the SharePoint Object Model, which defines how SharePoint works and provides you with the core API for modifying SharePoint for your needs.

 Although the content of this chapter is important for administrators to understand in a general sense, some knowledge of programming and ASP.NET is required to completely understand this material.

In a sense, everything is possible, but you will need a solid understanding of both ASP.NET 2.0 and the SharePoint object model in order to create customized solutions for your business needs. There are a number of ways to leverage the power of the SharePoint object model, including:

- Building custom Web Parts
- Building application pages, located in the _layouts_ virtual directory, that are compiled into a single DLL and can contain code
- Building feature activation event handlers
- Accessing SharePoint from ASP.NET web applications and web services
- Building Windows Forms applications to provide rich user interfaces for SharePoint
- Creating console applications for performing batch operations against SharePoint

- Creating event handlers for lists, libraries, sites, and content types
- Creating SharePoint workflow applications

This chapter provides an overview of the object model, focusing on the ways you can use the object model to enhance and extend SharePoint. The chapter also includes information and instructions on how to package and deploy your custom components.

Exploring the Microsoft.SharePoint Namespace

Basically, all SharePoint development starts with the *Microsoft.SharePoint.dll*, which you can find in the *C:\Program Files\Common Files\Microsoft Shared\web server extensions\12\ISAPI* directory. This assembly is the core of the Windows SharePoint Services object model. It contains the `Microsoft.SharePoint` namespace, which is an obvious starting point for exploring the SharePoint object model.

Accessing a Site Collection with SPSite

In the `Microsoft.SharePoint` namespace, you will find two of the core objects from which you start when developing against SharePoint: `SPSite` and `SPWeb`. The `SPSite` object represents a SharePoint site collection, consisting of a top-level site and all of its subsites. Conversely, *SPWeb* represents a specific site within a collection. You need to start with a reference to `SPSite` and then find your particular `SPWeb` site of interest.

One common way to leverage SharePoint is to connect to a SharePoint site from an external program, such as a desktop application or independent ASP.NET web site. In order to get a reference to a SharePoint site, you must create an instance of `SPSite`. To get a reference to an `SPSite` object for a specific site collection from within an application external to SharePoint (e.g., a console application or an ASP.NET web site), you can use the `SPSite` constructor by passing in either an absolute URL or the site collection GUID. The URL can be a SharePoint Portal Server site, a Windows SharePoint Services site, or a Windows SharePoint Services site collection. I have used the absolute URL to instantiate the `SPSite` object in this code sample:

```
//Dispose must be called when creating objects with the new operator
SPSite sitecollection = new SPSite("http://moss");
Console.WriteLine(sitecollection.ContentDatabase.ToString());
SPSite.Dispose();
Console.ReadLine();

//using construct
using (SPSite sitecollection = new SPSite("http://moss");)
{
  Console.WriteLine(sitecollection.ContentDatabase.ToString())
}
```

Note that the SharePoint object model contains a number of managed objects—most important in this instance are SPWeb and SPSite—which use unmanaged code to do the heavy lifting. If you create one of these objects yourself with the constructor method, you should make sure that you add in the necessary code to explicitly dispose of the object when you have finished using it. You can do this by explicitly calling the Dispose method or through the use of the C# using construct (as shown in the previous code listing). Failure to dispose of the object can result in unusual behavior, such as high memory usage or frequent recycling of the SharePoint application pool. It is recommended to use the Dispose method instead of simply calling the object's Close method. For more information about this subject, take a look at the MSDN white paper "Best Practices: Using Disposable Windows SharePoint Services Objects."

Accessing a Site Collection from Within a Web Part

If you are already working within the SharePoint context, perhaps building a custom Web Part, you need to use a different technique to access the site collection. The static SPControl class, which is a member of the Micrsoft.SharePoint.WebControls namespace, provides the methods necessary to access the Web Part's container. You will need to call the GetContextSite method and pass in the current HttpContext. This method will return the site collection where the Web Part is currently running:

```
public class SiteInspector : WebPart
    {
        protected override void RenderContents(System.Web.UI.HtmlTextWriter writer)
        {
            SPSite sitecollection = SPControl.GetContextSite(this.Context);
            writer.Write(sitecollection.ContentDatabase.ToString( ));
        }
    }
```

When you are using the SPControl object to get access to the SharePoint object model, you should not dispose the object yourself, since the SharePoint application will handle this for you. Calling the Dispose or Close method when using the SPControl will give a violation error.

Remember that SharePoint Web Parts run by default in a partially trusted environment, which means that they have limited access to certain resources. Windows SharePoint Services is, by default, configured with *WSS_Minimal* trust—meaning that the previous code will give a Microsoft.SharePoint.Security.SharePointPermission when deployed to the *bin* folder. You should create a custom policy file or deploy your Web Part to the Global Assembly Cache (GAC). Assemblies installed in the GAC run with full trust.

Accessing a Specific Site with SPWeb

In order to access a particular site within the site collection, you will need a reference to an SPWeb object, which represents a single SharePoint site. There are different methods to access an SPWeb object. You can use the AllWebs property of the SPSite class to return all sites within the site collection, or one of the GetSubwebsForCurrentUser methods to return all the subsites for the current user. Within a Web Part it is even easier, since you can use the GetContextWeb method of the SPControl class to return an SPWeb object that represents the current web site, as follows:

```
SPWeb site = SPControl.GetContextWeb(this.Context);
```

After constructing the SPWeb object, the developer can access the information of the site using the public properties of the SPWeb object, as displayed in Table 28-1.

Table 28-1. Public properties for the SPWeb object

Name	Description
AllowAnonymousAccess	Specifies whether anonymous access is allowed for the site
Author	Returns the user who has created the site
Files	Gets the SPFileCollection with all files in the site
HasUniquePerm	Boolean value that specifies whether a site has unique permissions
Language	The Locale ID (LCID) for the language used on the site
Lists	Gets the SPListCollection with all lists in the site
ParentWeb	Gets the parent web site for the site
Properties	Gets a reference to an SPPropertyBag for the properties of the site
RegionalSettings	Gets the regional settings (SPRegionalSettings) currently implemented on the site
Theme	The name of the theme applied to the site
Title	Title for the web site
URL	Gets the absolute URL for the site
WebTemplate	Gets the name of the site definition used to create the site

The Properties property is of type Microsoft.SharePoint.Utilities.SPPropertyBag, which is an extension of the System.Collections.Specialized.StringDictionary class. The property bag is a hash table with the key strongly typed to string. In this property bag, you can store any object by name. This way you can add your own properties to SharePoint sites. If you take a look at the Properties of a SharePoint site, you will notice that it already contains a number of key-value pairs, as demonstrated by the code in this listing:

```csharp
using System;
using System.Collections.Generic;
using System.Text;
using System.Web.UI.WebControls.WebParts;
using Microsoft.SharePoint;
using Microsoft.SharePoint.WebControls;
using Microsoft.SharePoint.Utilities;

namespace DolmenWebParts
{
    public class SiteInspector : WebPart
    {
        protected override void RenderContents(System.Web.UI.HtmlTextWriter writer)
        {
            SPWeb site = SPControl.GetContextWeb(this.Context);
            StringBuilder sb = new StringBuilder();
            sb.Append("<b>Title:</b> ");
            sb.Append(site.Title.ToString());
            sb.Append("<br><b>Created by:</b> ");
            sb.Append(site.Author.LoginName.ToString());
            sb.Append("<br><b>Total number of files:</b> ");
            sb.Append(site.Files.Count.ToString());
            sb.Append("<br><b>Regional settings:</b> ");
            sb.Append(site.RegionalSettings.ServerLanguage.DisplayName.ToString());
            sb.Append("<br><b>Theme:</b> ");
            sb.Append(site.Theme.ToString());
            sb.Append("<br><b>Site definition:</b> ");
            sb.Append(site.WebTemplate);
            sb.Append("<br><u><b>Properties:</b></u><br>");
            SPPropertyBag props = site.Properties;
            foreach (string key in props.Keys)
            {
                sb.Append("<b>");
                sb.Append(key.ToString());
                sb.Append("</b>: ");
                sb.Append(props[key].ToString());
                sb.Append("<br>");
            }
            writer.Write(sb.ToString());

        }
    }
}
```

In SharePoint 2007, you gain a number of new features with regard to the sites and site collections. For example, you can now move and "re-parent" web sites within an SPSite. There are also fewer barriers across sites (SPWeb) in SharePoint 2007. In WSS 2.0 and SPS 2003, sites were silos: it was hard to share data across them. Through a variety of new features—such as cross-web lookups and cross-site queries—it is now a lot easier to access data across webs.

Handling Files and Folders in SharePoint

A site consists of a hierarchy of files and folders. The files are represented through SPFile objects and folders through SPFolder objects. A file can be a SharePoint Web Part page, an item in a document library, or a file in a folder. The next code sample creates a Web Part, which shows the total size of all files in a certain SharePoint site. To display the total size, add a call to the GetTotalSize method in the Render method.

```
private long GetTotalSize(SPWeb site)
{
  long lTotalsize = 0;

  foreach (SPFolder folder in site.Folders)
  {
     lTotalsize += GetFolderSize(folder);
  }
  return lTotalsize;
}

private long GetFolderSize(SPFolder folder)
{
  long lFolderSize = 0;
  foreach (SPFile file in folder.Files)
  {
    //Gets the size of the file in bytes,
    //excluding the size of any webparts used in the file
    lFolderSize += file.Length;
  }
  foreach (SPFolder subfolder in folder.SubFolders)
  {
    GetFolderSize(subfolder);
  }
  return lFolderSize;
}
```

The SPFile object has a Properties property—similar to SPWeb.Properties, which contains certain document metadata. These property bags are exposed on the SPWeb, SPFile, SPFolder, and SPListItem classes.

There is one other method of the SPFile that deserves special attention: RevertToContentStream. This method will return a file to its original uncustomized state so that its logic becomes cached in memory (also known as ghosted or uncustomized) rather than stored in the database. Once a Web Part page gets modified with SharePoint Designer 2007, it will become a *customized page*. This means that instead of being based upon a site definition residing on the local filesystem of the web server, the page is retrieved from the SharePoint content database. This provides for additional overhead in the databases and causes pages to load more slowly, although the impact is not as grave as with SharePoint 2003. The SPFile class also has a property named `CustomizedPageStatus` that will return an `SPCustomizedPageStatus` enumeration, as shown in the next code snippet:

```
SPFile homePage = site.GetFile("default.aspx");
if (file.CustomizedPageStatus == SPCustomizedPageStatus.Uncustomized)
{
   // home page is ghosted/uncustomized
}
else
{
   // home page has been unghosted/customized
}
```

Working with Web Parts and Web Part Pages

One of the changes in the new object model has to do with how you manage Web Parts on a Web Part page in SharePoint. The `GetWebPartCollection` method from previous SharePoint versions has been marked obsolete and should be replaced by the `GetLimitedWebPartManager` class, which returns the Web Part manager (`Microsoft.SharePoint.WebPartPages.SPLimitedWebPartManager`) associated with a Web Part page. The next code sample will add a task Web Part in the left zone and an image Web Part to the right zone of the home page of a SharePoint team site. Notice that the `GetLimitedWebPartManager` class uses the `PersonalizationScope.Shared` parameter; this means that the properties for the Web Parts you are manipulating can be customized, but not personalized. In other words, the content will be the same for every user, but each user can decide to relocate the part or minimize or maximize it:

1. Create a new console project in Visual Studio 2005.

2. Add a reference to both the `System.Web` and the Windows SharePoint Services assemblies.

3. Add the following code:

```
SPSite sitecollection = new SPSite("http://moss");
          SPWeb site = sitecollection.OpenWeb();
          SPFile page = site.GetFile("default.aspx");
          SPLimitedWebPartManager mgr = page.
GetLimitedWebPartManager(PersonalizationScope.Shared);
          //Add task listview Web Part to left zone
          SPList list = site.Lists["Tasks"];
          ListViewWebPart listViewWebPart = new ListViewWebPart();
          listViewWebPart.ListName = list.ID.ToString("B").ToUpper();
          //Set the guid using binary (base2) string representation
          listViewWebPart.ViewGuid = list.DefaultView.ID.ToString("B").
ToUpper();
          mgr.AddWebPart(listViewWebPart, "Left", 1);
          //Add image webpart to right zone
          ImageWebPart wp2 = new ImageWebPart();
          wp2.ChromeType = PartChromeType.None;
          wp2.ImageLink = @"/_layouts/images/ipvw.gif";
          mgr.AddWebPart(wp2, "Right", 0);
```

The image you are using in the image Web Part can be found under *C:\Program Files\Common Files\Microsoft Shared\web server extensions\12\TEMPLATE\IMAGES*. Once you've compiled and run your code, the result should look like Figure 28-1.

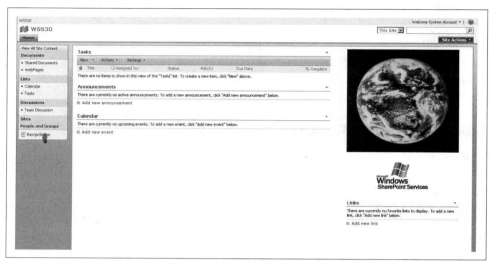

Figure 28-1. Web Part page with Web Parts added with SPLimitedWebPartManager

In a similar fashion, you can modify existing Web Parts on pages or remove Web Parts from a Web Part page. Other related classes are the SPUserStorage class, which maintains information about the user of a Web Part page and the amount of space the user is consuming in bytes, and the SPUserStorageCollection class, which represents a collection of SPUserStorage objects used to maintain storage information for all users of a Web Part page.

Accessing SharePoint Lists and Libraries Through Code

A SharePoint list is represented by the SPList class. To access all the items in a list, you will need to use the Items property. If you want to have access to the different fields in your list, you will need to use the Fields property. When you start from the SPWeb class, you can use the SPWeb.Lists property to return a SPListCollection object. This collection contains an SPList object for every list on the web site. Almost everything in SharePoint is based on a list from the standard lists, such as the task list or calendar list, document libraries, and a number of base catalogs.

There are a couple of enhancements to the SharePoint data storage capabilities of lists and libraries:

- Use of folders in both lists and document libraries
- Better versioning mechanisms, with support for minor and major versioning as well as version pruning

- A two-phase Recycle Bin
- Security at document and item level
- An enhanced events framework
- Indexed fields to support large lists
- Content types
- Email integration, which allows you to assign an email address to a list or library

One of the main reasons to use folders within document libraries is to overcome a limitation of SharePoint document libraries. According to capacity white papers, you will need to use folders once your number of documents exceeds 2,000. There is also a difference in how you add an item to a folder in a list or a document library. The next code sample shows how you can add a document to a folder in a document library. It retrieves a file from the local filesystem of the SharePoint server and adds it into the directory called *Test* within the document library Shared Documents:

```
using System;
using System.Collections.Generic;
using System.Text;
using Microsoft.SharePoint;
using System.IO;

namespace FolderOM
{
    class Program
    {
        static void Main(string[] args)
        {
            //Open sitecollection
            using (SPSite sitecollection = new SPSite("http://moss"))
            {
                // Get web
                using (SPWeb site = sitecollection.OpenWeb())
                {
                    SPFolder doclibfolder = site.GetFolder("/Shared Documents/Test");

                    // upload document
                    FileStream fStream = File.OpenRead(@"c:\demo.docx");
                    Byte[] contents = new byte[Convert.ToInt32(fStream.Length)];
                    fStream.Read(contents, 0, Convert.ToInt32(fStream.Length));
                    SPFile uploadedFile = doclibfolder.Files.Add("demo.docx", fStream);
                    SPListItem listitem = uploadedFile.Item;
                    listitem["Title"] = "Demo document";
                    listitem.Update();
                }
            }
        }
    }
}
```

Adding items to a folder in a list works a little differently, as shown by the next code sample, in which we add a new task item into a folder within a list:

```
using System;
using System.Collections.Generic;
using System.Text;
using Microsoft.SharePoint;
using System.IO;

namespace FolderOM
{
  class Program
  {
    static void Main(string[] args)
    {
      using (SPSite sitecollection = new SPSite("http://moss"))
      {
        using (SPWeb site = sitecollection.OpenWeb())
        {
          //Add a task to the Demo folder within the Tasks list
          SPList list = site.Lists["Tasks"];
          SPFolder folder = site.GetFolder("/Lists/Tasks/Demo");
          if (folder.Exists)
          {
            SPListItemCollection items = list.Items;
            SPListItem item = items.Add(folder.ServerRelativeUrl,
SPFileSystemObjectType.File, null);
            item["Title"] = "Task added from code";
            item.Update();
          }

        }
      }
    }

  }
}
```

The user interface to create a folder within a SharePoint list is not visible by default. If you want to work with folders, you need to activate the interface by performing the next steps:

1. Open your SharePoint list in your browser.

2. Go to Settings → List Settings.

3. Select Advanced Settings underneath the General Settings category on the List Settings page.

4. Change the radio button for the Display New Folder command on the new menu to Yes.

Using the Enhanced Events Framework to Back Up SharePoint Sites Upon Deletion

One of the major improvements in both WSS 3.0 and Microsoft Office SharePoint Server 2007 is the enhanced event handler framework. An event handler is a .NET assembly that is created to handle events triggered by user actions within SharePoint. In SharePoint Portal Server 2003, only asynchronous event handlers were supported on document libraries.

Enhancements to the event handler architecture include:

- New events supported for lists, document libraries, and content types
- Support for events firing at site level, such as adding users, creating lists, etc.
- Support for events related to changes in list schema, such as adding a column or a content type
- Support for synchronous and asynchronous events
- Feature activation events

An example of a synchronous event is the ItemDeleting event. If you add your own event handler code, the code will be executed synchronously on the same worker thread as SharePoint itself. This means that SharePoint will wait until your code is finished and make sure that you haven't canceled the event before proceeding with its own deletion code. Your code will execute before a change is committed to the database. After the change has been made to the database, another event, ItemDeleted, will occur where you can execute extra code. This code is loaded on a new worker thread and executed asynchronously. The base class for all event handling in SharePoint 2007 is the Microsoft.SharePoint.SPEventReceiverBase class. We will implement an event handler to catch the ItemDeleting event; therefore, we will need to inherit from SPWebEventReceiver. Next we will be using the new Content Migration framework in SharePoint to back up a SharePoint site before the delete is committed to the database.

The main classes we are going to use are SPExport, SPExportObject, and SPExportSettings for performing the backup. These classes in the Microsoft.SharePoint.Deployment namespaces support importing and exporting SharePoint content as well as content dependencies such as security settings, workflow, and other metadata. First, we are going to construct an SPExportObject object, where we can specify what we want to export—a file, folder, site, or site collection—by setting the appropriate SPExportObject.Type.

Next we will need to initialize an instance of the SPExportSettings class with the required export settings and then pass the SPExportSettings object to the SPExport class.

Set the FileCompression property to true to make sure that you will package all exported files into a single CAB file. Both of these steps are shown in the following code sample:

1. In order to create and deploy an event handler, we need to write a class library, sign it with a strong name, deploy our assembly to the GAC on the SharePoint server, and then register the assembly with SharePoint. These steps are explained later Create a new class library project in Visual Studio 2005.

2. Add a reference to the Windows SharePoint Services assembly to get access to the SPWebEventReceiver class from which you will need to inherit.

3. Add the necessary *using* statements and override the WebDeleting virtual method in SPWebEventReceiver base class by adding in the following lines of code:

```
using System;
using System.Collections.Generic;
using System.Text;
using Microsoft.SharePoint;
using Microsoft.SharePoint.Deployment;

namespace EventhandlerSample
{
    public class HandlerDemo : SPWebEventReceiver
    {
        public override void WebDeleting(SPWebEventProperties properties)
        {
            SPExportObject exportsite = new SPExportObject();
            exportsite.Type = SPDeploymentObjectType.Web;
            exportsite.ExcludeChildren = true;
            exportsite.Id = properties.Web.ID;

            //Specify export setting
            SPExportSettings settings = new SPExportSettings();
            settings.ExportObjects.Add(exportsite);
            settings.FileLocation = @"c:\exportdata\";
            settings.BaseFileName = "exportdata" +
              properties.WebId.ToString() + ".cmp";
            settings.FileCompression = true;
            settings.LogFilePath = @"c:\exportdata\logs\sitebackup"
              + properties.WebId.ToString() + ".log";
            settings.ExportMethod = SPExportMethodType.ExportAll;
            settings.SiteUrl = properties.FullUrl;

            //Run export job
            SPExport export = new SPExport(settings);
            export.Run();

        }
    }
}
```

4. Give your assembly a strong name.

5. Deploy the assembly to the Global Assembly Cache (GAC) on the SharePoint server(s).

6. Register your event handler with the SharePoint server. In SharePoint 2003, you could use the user interface to register an event handler, but this is no longer possible. However, there are two other options. The first option is to use the new Features framework, which provides a way to package, deploy, and activate your own customizations on top of SharePoint. The second option is using the SharePoint object model to register the event handler. I will show you the second method.

7. Add a second project with type Console Application to your solution.

8. Again, add a reference to the Windows SharePoint Services assembly.

9. You will need the exact strong name for the class (assembly name, version, culture, and public key token):

   a. To find the exact class and assembly name, you can use .NET Reflector.

   b. Open .NET Reflector and click File → Open.

   c. Select your event handler assembly and click OK.

   d. Next, select the node for your assembly and look at the details in the bottom of the .NET Reflector screen.

10. Add the following lines of code to register the event handler. Change the last few lines to match the strong name for your assembly.

```
private static void RegisterForWeb(string siteurl,string webname,string assembly,
string classname)
        {
            using (SPSite site = new SPSite(siteurl))
            {
                using (SPWeb web = site.OpenWeb(webname))
                {
                    web.EventReceivers.Add(SPEventReceiverType.WebDeleting,
assembly, classname);
                }
            }
        }

        static void Main(string[] args)
        {
            RegisterForWeb("http://moss",
                "demosite",
                "EventhandlerSample, Version=1.0.0.0, Culture=neutral,
PublicKeyToken=03490ab303ed89ea",
                "EventhandlerSample.HandlerDemo");
        }
```

You can also use the .NET Reflector to take a look at how the Share-Point assemblies are implemented. Most of the assemblies are not obfuscated.

Once the event handler is registered, any user who deletes a site will have an extra safety net. Before the delete completes, your handler will create an offline export. If you need to restore the site, you have three choices:

- Writing custom code using the `SPImport` and `SPImportSettings` classes in the Content Migration Object Model.

- Using the import operation of the `stsadm.exe` command-line utility. For more information, use `stsadm.exe -help import` or `stsadm.exe -help export`. With SharePoint 2003, you could do something similar with the *smigrate.exe* command-line utility. This utility is no longer available, but is replaced with these new options, which provide full-fidelity (including security) site collection and subsite backups.

- Using the `importweb webservice` method for the *http://<Site>/_vti_bin/Sites.asmx* web service.

Implementing a Security Rollup Web Part

SharePoint's security rights are managed through permission levels, where a permission level consists of a set of rights corresponding to the values of the `Microsoft.SharePoint.SPBasePermissions` enumeration. These permissions are assigned to people and groups through a role assignment. Access control to the content itself can be configured at multiple levels:

- Web application: `SPWebApplication`
- Site collection: `SPSite`
- Site: `SPWeb`
- List or document library: `SPList`
- Item or document: `SPListItem`

If you need to get access to the defined permission levels, you can use the methods and properties defined by the `ISecurableObject` interface (see the next section). If you need an overview of the security rights defined for a specific site, you can use the `RoleAssigments` property, which will return an `SPRoleAssignmentsCollection`. This collection shows the combination of the users or groups (`SPPrincipal`) and their associated security rights (`SPRoleDefinition`), as shown in this code sample:

```
using System;
using System.Collections.Generic;
using System.Text;
```

```
using System.Web.UI.WebControls.WebParts;
using Microsoft.SharePoint;
using Microsoft.SharePoint.WebControls;

namespace DolmenWebParts
{
    public class SecurityRollUp : WebPart
    {

        protected override void RenderContents(System.Web.UI.HtmlTextWriter writer)
        {
            SPWeb site = SPControl.GetContextWeb(this.Context);
            writer.Write("Site has unique permissions:" + site.
HasUniqueRoleAssignments.ToString() + "<br>");
            SPRoleAssignmentCollection roleassigcoll = site.RoleAssignments;
            foreach (SPRoleAssignment roleassig in roleassigcoll)
            {
                SPPrincipal principal = roleassig.Member;
                writer.Write(principal.Name + ":");
                try
                {
                    SPGroup group = (SPGroup)principal;
                    foreach (SPUser user in group.Users)
                    {
                        writer.Write(user.Name + ",");
                    }
                }
                catch (Exception ex)
                {
                }

                SPRoleDefinitionBindingCollection roledefcoll = roleassig.
RoleDefinitionBindings;
                foreach (SPRoleDefinition roledef in roledefcoll)
                {
                    writer.Write(" - "+ roledef.Description+"<br>");

                }
            }
        }
    }
}
```

Handling Authorization Information: The ISecurableObject Interface

One of the core concepts in working with security in SharePoint 2007 is the
ISecurableObject interface, which exposes the role assignments and permissions for
an object. The SPWeb, SPList, and SPListItem all implement this ISecurableObject
interface. This interface exposes the properties and methods described in Table 28-2.

Table 28-2. ISecurableObject interface properties and methods

ISecurableObject properties/methods	Description
`AllRolesForCurrentUser` property	Gets all role definitions for the current user and returns an `SPRoleDefinitionBindingCollection`.
`EffectiveBasePermissions` property	Gets the current user's effective base permissions on the object, including group membership and policies. Returns the `SPBasePermissions` value.
`FirstUniqueAncestor` property	Returns an `ISecurableObject` interface that represents the first unique ancestor.
`HasUniqueRoleAssignments` property	Returns `true` if the object has unique security; otherwise, returns `false`.
`ReusableACL` property	Returns an `SPReusableAcl` object that represents the raw access control list (ACL) information.
`RoleAssignments` property	Returns an `SPRoleAssignmentCollection` object that represents the role assignments for a uniquely securable object type.
`BreakRoleInheritance` method	Creates unique role assignments for the object. Supply a Boolean parameter to specify whether you want to copy the parent's permissions (`true`) or not (`false`).
`CheckPermissions` method	Checks the permission for a given set of rights (using the `SPBasePermissions` parameter) and returns an access denied message when it fails.
`DoesUserHavePermissions` method	Returns true if the current user has the right to perform a certain action.
`ResetRoleInheritance` method	Removes the local role assignments and reverts to role assignments from the parent object.

You should use the `CheckPermissions` method within code for verifying that a user does indeed have permission to execute that part of the code. If the user does not have sufficient permissions, an `UnAuthorizedAccessException` is thrown.

The `DoesUserHavePermissions` method should be used to check whether the user has proper access to do something—for example, adding links to the user interface. To use the `DoesUserHavePermissions` method, you will need to pass in the `SPBasePermissionsEnum` flagged for the permissions you want to verify. It is, however, also possible to pass in an `SPPermissionsGroup` enumeration, which groups the different base permissions into the predefined SharePoint permission groups (contributor, administrator, reader, guest, etc.). In other words, with `SPPermissionsGroup`, you can assert that a user belongs to the contributor group rather than using `DoesUserHavePermissions` to check that the user has both read and write access.

The next code sample shows how you can check whether a user has access to the built-in usage statistics before displaying the link:

```
if (SPControl.GetContextWeb(this.Context).DoesUserHavePermissions(
    SPBasePermissions.ViewUsageData))
  {
    writer.AddAttribute(HtmlTextWriterAttribute.Href,
      "_layouts/usagedetails.aspx");
    writer.RenderBeginTag(HtmlTextWriterTag.A);
```

```
    writer.Write("Usage statistics");
    writer.RenderEndTag( );
}
```

Running Code with Elevated Privileges

The default security context for SharePoint code is the authenticated user at that moment. This means that when a user opens a page that has a Web Part on it and accesses a resource that requires extra permissions, he will get an access denied error. Sometimes it is necessary to override this default behavior. In SharePoint 2003, this was done using impersonation, but SharePoint 2007 provides another mechanism with the Microsoft.SharePoint.SPSecurity.RunWithElevatedPrivileges method.

It's important that you don't use the SPContext.Current.Site, SPContext.Current.Web, SPControl.GetContextWeb, or SPControl.GetContextSite methods, as these security contexts are the same as the default. Your code will still run in the context of the user.

The Microsoft.SharePoint.SPSecurity.RunWithElevatedPrivileges method enables you to supply a delegate method that runs a subset of code in the context of the system account:

```
using System;
using System.Collections.Generic;
using System.Text;
using System.Web.UI.WebControls.WebParts;
using Microsoft.SharePoint;
using Microsoft.SharePoint.WebControls;

namespace DolmenWebParts
{
  public class ElevatedPrivileges : WebPart
  {
    protected override void RenderContents(System.Web.UI.HtmlTextWriter writer)
    {
      SPSite sitecollection = SPContext.Current.Site;
      SPWeb site = SPContext.Current.Web;

      SPSecurity.RunWithElevatedPrivileges(delegate( )
      {
        //do things assuming the identity of the SharePoint system account
        using (SPSite elevatedsitecoll = new SPSite(sitecollection.ID))
        {
            using (SPWeb elevatedsite = elevatedsitecoll.OpenWeb(site.ID))
            {
                writer.Write("Storage:"+elevatedsitecoll.Usage.Hits.ToString( ));
            }
        }
      });

    }
  }
}
```

When your code uses `Microsoft.SharePoint.SPSecurity.RunWithElevatedPrivileges` and accesses resources outside of SharePoint—such as accessing a file on the web server or creating a separate connection to a SQL Server database—your code will use the SharePoint application pool account. However, when your elevated privileges code performs operations within SharePoint, such as deleting a document or creating a SharePoint list, it uses the built-in *SHAREPOINT\system* account. You should use this technique with care because it can open potential security holes within your SharePoint solution.

Implementing an Auditing Solution in WSS 3.0

Both Microsoft Office SharePoint Server 2007 and Windows SharePoint Services 3.0 provide support for auditing. The auditing policy feature in Microsoft Office SharePoint Server logs events and operations performed on documents and list items. You can configure auditing to log events such as when a person modifies a document, views a document, performs a checkin or checkout, changes the permissions for documents, or deletes a document. This auditing policy feature is not activated for Windows SharePoint Services, and there is no user interface available to work with these audit logs. Microsoft Office SharePoint Server 2007, on the other hand, provides extensive support for auditing using the built-in policies framework. However, the base framework is available through the `Microsoft.SharePoint.SPAudit` class. When you activate auditing, WSS will write audit entries within the `AuditData` table of the SharePoint content database.

You can enable auditing in WSS 3.0 at the site collection level or for an individual list by updating the `Audit` property of the `SPSite` or `SPList` objects, as shown in the next code sample. This is done by setting the `AuditFlags` property, which is based on the `SPAuditMaskType` enumeration. These enumeration values are bitwise flags that can be combined to configure a specific set of auditing events:

```
sitecollection = new SPSite("http://moss");
            sitecollection.Audit.AuditFlags = SPAuditMaskType.All;
            sitecollection.Audit.Update();

            site = sitecollection.OpenWeb();
            SPList list = site.Lists["Shared Documents"];
            list.Audit.AuditFlags = SPAuditMaskType.Delete | SPAuditMaskType.
CheckIn;
            list.Audit.Update();
```

Once you have enabled audit logging, you can query the audit log by creating a new instance of the `SPAuditQuery` class. You can create a query that uses the following properties to limit the results returned:

- Use `SPAuditQuery.AddEventRestriction(eventid as SPAuditEventType)` to limit results returned to a specific event.

- Use `SPAuditQuery.RestrictToList` and `SPAuditQueryRestrictToListItem` to filter out audit logs for specific lists or specific list items.

- Use `SPAuditQuery.SetRangeStart` and `SPAuditQuery.SetRangeEnd` to specify date ranges.
- Use `SPAuditQuery.RestrictToUser` to return audit logs for a specific user.

After you've defined your query, you need to call the `SPSite.Audit.GetAuditEntries` method using the `SPAuditQuery` instance as an input parameter. This method will return a `SPAuditEntryCollection` class, which contains a collection of audit events that you loop over:

```
using System;
using System.Collections.Generic;
using System.Text;
using Microsoft.SharePoint;
using Microsoft.SharePoint.WebControls;
using System.Web.UI.WebControls;
using System.Web.UI.WebControls.WebParts;
using System.Data;

namespace DolmenWebParts
{
    public class AuditPart : WebPart
    {
        GridView gridview;

        protected override void OnInit(EventArgs e)
        {
            gridview = new SPGridView();
            gridview.AutoGenerateColumns = false;
        }

        protected override void CreateChildControls()
        {
            this.Controls.Clear();

            SPSite sitecollection = SPControl.GetContextSite(this.Context);
            SPWeb site = sitecollection.OpenWeb();
            SPList list = site.Lists["Shared Documents"];


            SPAuditQuery query = new SPAuditQuery(sitecollection);
            query.RestrictToList(list);
            query.SetRangeStart(DateTime.Now.AddDays(-7));
            query.SetRangeEnd(DateTime.Now);

            DataTable dtAudit = new DataTable();
            dtAudit.Columns.Add("User",typeof(string));
            dtAudit.Columns.Add("Eventtype", typeof(string));
            dtAudit.Columns.Add("DocLocation", typeof(string));
            dtAudit.Columns.Add("Occurred",typeof(DateTime));

            DataRow drRow;

            SPAuditEntryCollection auditcollection = sitecollection.Audit.
GetEntries(query);
```

```
                    foreach (SPAuditEntry entry in auditcollection)
                    {
                        drRow = dtAudit.NewRow( );
                        //Convert UserId to Name
                        drRow["User"] = site.SiteUsers.GetByID(entry.UserId).Name.ToString( );
                        //Convert audit time from GreenWich Mean Time to time zone of the web
        server
                        drRow["Occurred"] = entry.Occurred.ToLocalTime( );
                        drRow["Eventtype"] = entry.Event.ToString( );
                        drRow["DocLocation"] = SPControl.GetContextWeb(this.Context).Url + "/
        " + entry.DocLocation.ToString( );
                        dtAudit.Rows.Add(drRow);
                    }


                    BoundField boundField = new BoundField( );
                    boundField.HeaderText = "User";
                    boundField.DataField = "User";
                    gridview.Columns.Add(boundField);


                    boundField = new BoundField( );
                    boundField.HeaderText = "Occurred";
                    boundField.DataField = "Occurred";
                    gridview.Columns.Add(boundField);

                    boundField = new BoundField( );
                    boundField.HeaderText = "Event";
                    boundField.DataField = "Eventtype";
                    gridview.Columns.Add(boundField);

                    HyperLinkField urlfield = new HyperLinkField( );
                    urlfield.HeaderText = "Document";
                    urlfield.DataTextField = "DocLocation";
                    urlfield.DataNavigateUrlFields = new string[] { "Doclocation" };
                    gridview.Columns.Add(urlfield);

                    gridview.DataSource = dtAudit;
                    this.Controls.Add(gridview);

                    gridview.DataBind( );
                }
            }
        }
```

You need administrator privileges to call the GetEntries method, so if you want your
Web Part to also work for other users, you must add in the SPSecurity.
RunWithElevatedPrivileges method, as shown in the previous section. For an overview
of the auditing extensibility options for both Windows SharePoint Services and Office
SharePoint Server, see the SharePoint Server 2007 code sample "Item-level auditing."*

---

* *http://www.microsoft.com/downloads/details.aspx?FamilyId=0E4DD1E7-4B1D-4CB1-B906-*
  6D5D272C8E9D&displaylang=en

Performing Cross Site Queries with Microsoft.SharePoint.SPSiteDataQuery

The SPSiteDataQuery class extends the possibilities of the Query class, which was already present in WSS 2.0. Unlike the Query class, which would only work within one site, the new SPSiteDataQuery class in combination with the GetSiteData method allows you to perform queries against all types of lists across sites by passing in a Collaborative Application Markup Language (CAML) query. The next example Web Part returns all tasks within a site collection that are overdue:

```
using System;
using System.Collections.Generic;
using System.Text;
using System.Web;
using System.Web.UI.WebControls;
using System.Web.UI.WebControls.WebParts;
using Microsoft.SharePoint;
using Microsoft.SharePoint.WebControls;
using System.Data;

namespace DolmenWebParts
{
    public class TaskRollUpPart : WebPart
    {
        protected override void RenderContents(System.Web.UI.HtmlTextWriter writer)
        {
            GridView gridview = new GridView() ;
            DataTable dtGrid;

            string sQuery="";
            try
            {
                SPSite sitecollection = SPControl.GetContextSite(this.Context);
                SPWeb site = sitecollection.OpenWeb();

                SPSiteDataQuery qry = new SPSiteDataQuery();
                sQuery = "<Where><And><Lt><FieldRef Name='DueDate' />"
                    + "<Value Type='DateTime'><Today /></Value></Lt><Neq>"
                    + "<FieldRef Name='Status' /><Value Type='Text'>Completed</Value>
</Neq></And></Where>";
                qry.Query = sQuery;
                qry.Lists = "<Lists ServerTemplate='107' />";
                qry.ViewFields = "<FieldRef Name='Title' /><FieldRef Name='DueDate'/>
<ProjectProperty Name='Title' />";
                qry.Webs = "<Webs Scope='SiteCollection' />";

                DataTable dtQuery = site.GetSiteData(qry);
                dtGrid = new DataTable();
                dtGrid.Columns.Add("SiteTitle", typeof(string));
                dtGrid.Columns.Add("Title",typeof(string));
                dtGrid.Columns.Add("Duedate", typeof(DateTime));

                DataRow drNewRow;
```

```
            foreach (DataRow drRow in dtQuery.Rows)
            {
                drNewRow = dtGrid.NewRow( );
                drNewRow["SiteTitle"] = drRow["ProjectProperty.Title"];
                drNewRow["Title"] = drRow["Title"];
                drNewRow["DueDate"] = drRow["DueDate"];
                dtGrid.Rows.Add(drNewRow);
            }
            gridview.AutoGenerateColumns = true;
            gridview.DataSource = dtGrid;
            gridview.DataBind( );
          gridview.RenderControl(writer);
        }
        catch (Exception ex)
        {
            writer.Write("<font color='red'>"+ ex.ToString( )+ "</font>");
        }
      }
    }
  }
```

You will need to set a couple of properties for the `SPSiteDataQuery` class, as shown in the previous example:

Lists property
> A CAML string that specifies the different lists to return. The example shows how to return all lists using a specific server template. You can also pass the identifiers for specific lists to return or a `BaseType`.

ViewFields property
> A CAML string that defines the fields to return. Each field is represented by a `FieldRef` tag. A field is identified by its `ID` or `Name` attribute. You can also retrieve certain properties for the containing list or site through the `ListProperty` or `ProjectProperty` tags.

Webs property
> A CAML string that defines the web sites to include in the query. This is specified by the `Scope` attribute, which has two possible values: `SiteCollection` (for all web sites in the same site collection) and `Recursive` (for all subsites of the current `SPWeb` object).

 Fortunately there are some tools to help you construct the CAML query, since this isn't always intuitive. My personal favorite is the Stramit SharePoint CAML Viewer 2007, written by Renaud Comte. You can download it from CodePlex at *http://www.codeplex.com/Wiki/View.aspx?ProjectName=SPCamlViewer*.

Microsoft Office SharePoint Server 2007 contains some out-of-the-box Web Parts that use this cross-site query ability, such as the Documents and Tasks Roll-up Web Part on the My Site, the Data View Web Part, and the Content By Query Web Part.

To improve the performance of a large list or library, you can add an index to a column. This index can be used by the SPSiteDataQuery class to speed up the retrieval of items. For more information on how to set up an index, see "Indexing a List Column" in Chapter 14.

The Features Framework

The Features framework enables you to package SharePoint functionality (be it a SharePoint list definition, a site definition, some Web Parts, UI components, or a combination of the previously mentioned) and to deploy it in a flexible way on SharePoint 2007. The framework provides a more granular approach for adding functionality since you don't need to wrap your new functionality in a completely new site definition.

SharePoint 2007 has been built upon this same feature framework; all the standard built-in list types are created as separate features. You will find them under *C:\Program Files\Common Files\Microsoft Shared\web server extensions\12\Templates\Features*.

The next sample shows the feature that defines the Announcements list:

```
<?xml version="1.0" encoding="utf-8"?>
<Feature
Id="00BFEA71-D1CE-42de-9C63-A44004CE0104"    Title="$Resources:
core,announcementslistFeatureTitle;"    Description="$Resources:
core,announcementslistFeatureDesc;"
Version="1.0.0.0"
Scope="Web"
Hidden="TRUE"
DefaultResourceFile="core"
 xmlns="http://schemas.microsoft.com/sharepoint/">
<ElementManifests>
    <ElementManifest Location="ListTemplates\Announcements.xml"/>    </
ElementManifests>
</Feature>
```

The Feature element can have a number of attributes, as seen in the previous example:

Id (required)
> A GUID to identify the feature.

Title (optional; limited to 255 characters)
> The previous example references a resource file that can be found in *C:\Program Files\Common Files\Microsoft Shared\web server extensions\12\Resources*. The *$Resources:core* notation specifies that the core resource file is used.

Version (optional)
> A System.Version-compliant representation of the version of a Feature.

Scope (required)
> Possible values are Farm (farm), WebApplication (web application), Site (site collection), or Web (web site).

Hidden (optional; default value is FALSE)
This setting specifies whether the feature is visible in the list of features on the Site Features page.

DefaultResourceFile (optional)
Name of the resource file used.

There also is an `ElementManifests` element, which points to the location of another XML file that contains the different Elements that the feature implements. The next sample shows the *Announcements.xml* file, which is found in the *ListTemplates* sub-folder of the Announcements feature:

```
<?xml version="1.0" encoding="utf-8"?>
<Elements xmlns="http://schemas.microsoft.com/sharepoint/">
    <ListTemplate
        Name="announce"
        Type="104"
        BaseType="0"
        OnQuickLaunch="TRUE"
        SecurityBits="11"
        Sequence="320"
        DisplayName="$Resources:core,announceList;"
        Description="$Resources:core,announceList_Desc;"
        Image="/_layouts/images/itann.gif"/>
</Elements>
```

The `ListTemplate` element defines a list that can be provisioned in a SharePoint site. Those who have worked with SharePoint 2003 site definitions will notice that this looks similar to the *ListTemplate* section of the ONET.XML.

The `xmlns` attribute is required—if you do not add it, your feature will not install. There is, however, also another advantage: you can enable XML Intellisense in Visual Studio 2005. The XML editor in VS2005 provides a schema cache underneath *%installdir%\xml\schemas*. This schema cache is used to include standard XML schemas that are used for Intellisense and XML document validation. To add a new schema, you can easily copy the existing one, *catalog.xml*, rename it to *customcatalog.xml*, and replace the existing content with your own association declaration:

```
<SchemaCatalog xmlns="http://schemas.microsoft.com/xsd/
catalog">

<Schema href="file://C:/Program Files/Common Files/Microsoft
Shared/web server extensions/12/TEMPLATE/XML/wss.xsd"
targetNamespace="http://schemas.microsoft.com/sharepoint/"/>

</SchemaCatalog>
```

So, every time you edit one of the SharePoint XML files, you should change the `xmlns` attribute to *http://schemas.microsoft.com/sharepoint/*, and VS2005 will automatically give you Intellisense support.

Table 28-3 shows a number of different Element types that you can use.

Table 28-3. Overview of Element types

Element type	Description and example
Module	Allows you to add files into SharePoint sites, either inside a document library or as a normal file. The Module element contains a File element that defines the file to provision. If you want to add it inside a document library, you will need to add the `Type="GhostableInLibrary"` attribute: ``` <Elements xmlns="http://schemas. microsoft.com/sharepoint/"> <Module Name="MPages" List="116" Url="_catalogs/masterpage"> <File Url="Minimal.master" Type="GhostableInLibrary" /> <File Url="ContosoRed.master" Type="GhostableInLibrary" /> </Module> </Elements> ```

List instance	Creates a list at feature activation; you can also use a Data element to add default data to the list:
	
	``
	<?xml version="1.0" encoding="utf-8" ?>
	<Elements xmlns="http://schemas.
	microsoft.com/sharepoint/">
	  <ListInstance
	      Id="DemoDocLib" Title="Demo"
	      Description=""
	      TemplateType="101"
	Url="DemoDocLib">
	  </ListInstance>
	</Elements>
	``

Custom Action	Allows you to add custom UI elements in the form toolbar, content type settings page, context drop-downs, and the site setting drop-down (see the next example).
Content type	Allows you to create a schema definition that you can reuse and apply to multiple list definitions.
Field	Allows you to create a custom field.
Workflow	Contains the definition for a workflow.
Event	``` <Elements xmlns="http://schemas.microsoft. com/sharepoint/"> <Receivers ListTemplateId="104"> <Receiver> <Name>ItemDeletingEventHandler</Name> <Type>ItemDeleting</Type> <SequenceNumber>10000</SequenceNumber> <Assembly>Assemblyname</Assembly> <Class>ClassName</Class> <Data></Data> <Filter></Filter> </Receiver> </Receivers> </Elements> ```
Delegate control	Allows you to replace existing controls, such as the WSS search control, with another control.

The following steps show how you can use a feature to add some custom actions to the form toolbar. This example adds a custom search action that leverages Windows Live Search:

1. Create a new folder called *LiveSearch* underneath *C:\Program Files\Common Files\Microsoft Shared\web server extensions\12\TEMPLATE\FEATURES*.

2. Create a new *feature.xml* file within the *LiveSearch* folder containing the following XML snippet:

```xml
<Feature Title="Live Search"
  Scope="Web"
  Id="39F4FE5B-B770-416c-B4AF-3EE710D4DA1B"
  xmlns="http://schemas.microsoft.com/sharepoint/">
  <ElementManifests>
    <ElementManifest Location="Elements.xml" />
  </ElementManifests>
</Feature>
```

3. Create a corresponding *Elements.xml* file as specified in the Location attribute of the ElementManifest node. If you go over the different attributes, you will notice the RegistrationId attribute, which specifies the associated list or item content type. The Sequence attribute specifies the ordering priority for the action, and the Location specifies where the UI element should be added:

```xml
<Elements xmlns="http://schemas.microsoft.com/sharepoint/">
  <CustomAction
    Id="LiveSearch1"
    RegistrationType="List"
    RegistrationId="101"
    Location="EditFormToolbar"
    Sequence="106"
    Title="Live Search">
    <UrlAction Url="{SiteUrl}/_layouts/LiveSearch.
Aspx?ListId={ListId}&amp;ItemId={ItemId}"/>
  </CustomAction>
  <CustomAction
    Id="LiveSearch2"
    RegistrationType="List"
    RegistrationId="101"
    Location="DisplayFormToolbar"
    Sequence="106"
    Title="Live Search">
    <UrlAction Url="{SiteUrl}/_layouts}/LiveSearch.
Aspx?ListId={ListId}&amp;ItemId={ItemId}" />
  </CustomAction>
  <CustomAction Title="Live Search"
      Sequence="10"
      RegistrationType="List"
      RegistrationId="101"
      Location="EditControlBlock"
      Id="LiveSearch">
```

```
            <UrlAction Url="{SiteUrl}/_layouts/LiveSearch.
    Aspx?ListId={ListId}&amp;ItemId={ItemId}" />
        </CustomAction>
    </Elements>
```

4. Create a new ASP.NET page called *LiveSearch.aspx* underneath *C:\Program Files\ Common Files\Microsoft Shared\web server extensions\12\TEMPLATE\LAYOUTS*, and add the following lines of code to this page:

```
<%@ Page language="C#" AutoEventWireup="true" %>

<%@ Import Namespace="Microsoft.SharePoint" %>


<script runat="server" >

protected override void OnLoad(EventArgs e)
{
    Guid listId = new Guid(Request["ListId"].ToString( ));
    int itemId = Convert.ToInt32(Request["ItemId"].ToString( ));

    SPWeb web = SPContext.GetContext(this.Context).Web;
    SPList customList = web.Lists.GetList(listId, false);

    SPListItem item = customList.GetItemById(itemId);
    string url = "http://search.live.com/results.aspx?q=" + Server.
UrlEncode(item.Title);
    Response.Redirect(url);

}

</script>
```

After you have deployed all of the files that make up your complete feature, you will need to perform two additional steps:

1. Install the feature using the *stsadm.exe* command:

```
stsadm.exe -o installfeature -filename livesearch\feature.xml
```

2. Activate the feature by using either the features administration page in the browser or the *stsadm.exe* command

```
stsadm.exe -o activatefeature -filename livesearch\feature.xml -url http://moss
```

Deploying Customizations with SharePoint Solutions

In the previous section, I talked about how you can use the Features framework to extend SharePoint. But at a certain point, you will still need to deploy these features to your SharePoint servers (be it on a single server or for a complete web farm). This is where SharePoint solution packages are used. Solution packages are cabinet (*.cab*) files with a *.wsp* filename extension and a manifest file. This package can contain .NET assemblies, feature definitions, site definitions, etc. Building these SharePoint solution packages is a tedious and error-prone process; for a detailed description, take a look at *http://msdn2.microsoft.com/en-gb/library/aa543741.aspx.* Fortunately, there is an alternative that uses Visual Studio 2005 extensions for WSS.

Visual Studio 2005 Extensions for WSS

Visual Studio 2005 Extensions for WSS 3.0 (the November CTP version is available from *http://www.microsoft.com/downloads/details.aspx?FamilyID=19f21e5e-b715-4f0c-b959-8c6dcbdc1057&DisplayLang=en*) contains a number of tools for developing custom SharePoint applications: Visual Studio project templates for Web Parts (the successor to the Web Part project templates for WSS 2.0/SPS 2003), site definitions, list definitions, and, last but not least, a standalone utility program, the SharePoint Solution Generator. After you have installed Visual Studio 2005 Extensions for WSS 3.0 (VSEWSS), you will get the additional Visual Studio 2005 Project Templates, as shown in Figure 28-2.

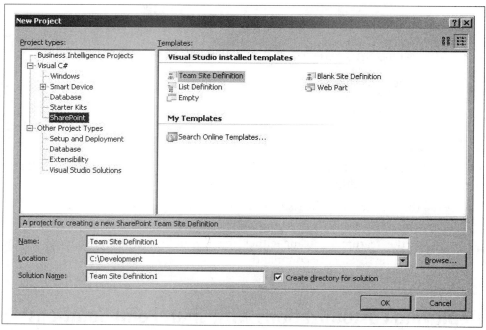

Figure 28-2. Additional Visual Studio 2005 Project Templates for VS2005 Extensions for WSS 3.0

An interesting feature of VSEWSS is the F5 run/debug option for the different types of projects. You can create a project and hit F5, and everything will be built and deployed to SharePoint for you (behind the scenes, it's using all the magic from the post-build steps in VS2005). It even creates a SharePoint Solution Package (WSP file) for you.

Another great thing in VSEWSS is the SharePoint Solution Generator, which will allow you to extract all of the modifications you made, either within a browser or with SharePoint Designer 2007, and add it to a Site Definition project. In this project, you will get your modified style sheet, all the necessary XML files (ONET.XML, SCHEMA.XML, and so on), and the ASPX pages (for all of the list forms and the default one). Starting from here, you can work with it further and add extra list definitions, Web Parts, and so on.

Working with the Microsoft Office SharePoint Server 2007 Class Libraries

Microsoft Office SharePoint Server 2007's object model covers a whole lot of new areas that were not available in the previous version. The first place that developers encounter this huge increase in available functionality is when you take a look at the assemblies available for use in the Add Reference dialog box from Visual Studio 2005, which will list the next SharePoint-related references.

Excel Services UDF Framework (Microsoft.Office.Excel.Server.UDF.dll)
This assembly provides access to the User Defined Functions within Excel Services documents.

Excel Web Services (Microsoft.Office.Excel.Server.WebServices.dll)
This assembly provides access to the web service support built into Excel Services.

Microsoft Content Publishing and Management (Microsoft.SharePoint.Publishing.dll)
This is the assembly that contains the enhanced publishing functionality, previously available in Microsoft Content Management Server 2002.

Microsoft Office Server component (Microsoft.Office.Server.dll)
The main assembly for all Office SharePoint Server–specific functionality, such as the Business Data Catalog, audience and user profiles, etc.

Microsoft Office Server DLC components (Microsoft.Office.Policy.dll and Microsoft.Office.Workflow.Tasks.dll)
Used to provide Document Life Cycle functionality in Office SharePoint Server 2007.

Microsoft Office SharePoint Server components (Microsoft.SharePoint.Portal.dll, Microsoft.SharePoint.Portal.SingleSignOn.dll, and so on)
These are the core server features for WSS and MOSS.

Microsoft Office SharePoint Server Search (Microsoft.Office.Server.Search.dll)
This is the new, enhanced search engine functionality, available only for Office SharePoint Server 2007, which provides a scalable search model to crawl content both within SharePoint and in external content sources.

Windows SharePoint Services (Microsoft.SharePoint.dll)
   The top-level DLL contains the core object model.

Windows SharePoint Services Search (Microsoft.SharePoint.Search.dll)
   This provides access to the SharePoint search components.

Windows SharePoint Services Security (Microsoft.SharePoint.Security.dll)
   This DLL contains the security model for SharePoint.

Windows SharePoint Services Workflow Actions (Microsoft.SharePoint.
WorkflowActions.dll)
   This assembly stores the workflow components and gives you programmatic
   access to creating and managing workflows.

The next sections take a look at some of these new namespaces.

Developing Against the Business Data Catalog

The Business Data Catalog (BDC), a new technology within Office SharePoint Server
2007, provides access to line of business applications through metadata. Developers
will define business data through metadata in XML format, and a number of out-of-
the-box Web Parts provide end users with access to the data in these backend systems. Besides using these out-of-the box BDC Web Parts, you can also integrate this
data within the user profiles, as a field type within SharePoint lists or libraries and
within SharePoint search.

 Whenever you want to connect a backend line of business system, you
will need to create an XML metadata file for it, which is called the
application definition file. This application definition file needs to com-
ply with the *BdcMeta.XSD* XML schema, which you can typically find
at *\Program Files\Microsoft Office Server\12.0\Bin*. There are, however,
some tools available to create these application definition files automatically. For an example, take a look at the Metadata Manager for Office
SharePoint Server at *http://www.bdcmetaman.com/default.aspx*.

Besides these out-of-the-box features of Office SharePoint Server 2007, it is also possible to develop custom code against the BDC. The main advantage for programming against the BDC is that the BDC provides a single approach for integrating
backend systems, without developers needing to know multiple APIs. When you
want to build a custom BDC application, there are two different object models to
work with:

Runtime object model
   For use by BDC client applications, this model provides a standard API for
   reading and querying the Business Data Catalog. This object model is available through *Microsoft.Portal.dll* and uses the following namespaces:
   `Microsoft.Office.Server.ApplicationRegistry.Runtime` and `Microsoft.Office.`
   `Server.ApplicationRegistry.MetaData`.

Administrative object model

This can be used to create, read, update, and delete metadata within the BDC. It is available in the following namespace: `Microsoft.Office.Server.ApplicationRegistry.Administration`.

When you take a look at the object model, you will notice that the XML schema and the metadata object models map closely to one another. There are 13 metadata objects, as shown in Figure 28-3. The key objects to know are:

LobSystem

A data source such as a database, SAP, Siebel, and so on. Within the application definition file, it is the root node.

LobSystemInstance

A LobSystem will have exactly one connected LobSystem, which is used to define connection and authentication information.

Entity

Defines the business objects in the backend system, such as customers and products. Entities contain Identifiers, Methods, and Actions.

Method

Defines an operation related to an Entity, such as "Get Products." A Method has a `MethodInstance` coupled to it that defines how to use the Method.

FilterDescriptor

Allows you to retrieve specific Entity instances by supplying Parameters.

Actions

These provide a link-back mechanism through links.

Association

A relationship between entities.

The next example shows how you can create your own Web Part that displays the different entities for a specific system. The Web Part uses the application definition based on the Adventure Works BDC example in MSDN and lists all the fields for the product entities. When you create the Web Part, you will first need to add references to the Windows SharePoint Services assembly, the `Office.Server` assembly, and the `Microsoft.SharePoint.Portal` assembly. You also see that the entry point for doing BDC development is the `ApplicationRegistry` object, which allows you to access all the different BDC objects, such as `LobSystem`, `Entity`, and the associated methods:

```
using System;
using System.Collections.Generic;
using System.Text;
using System.Web;
using System.Web.UI.WebControls;
using System.Web.UI.WebControls.WebParts;
using Microsoft.SharePoint;
using Microsoft.Office.Server;
using Microsoft.Office.Server.ApplicationRegistry;
using Microsoft.Office.Server.ApplicationRegistry.Runtime;
```

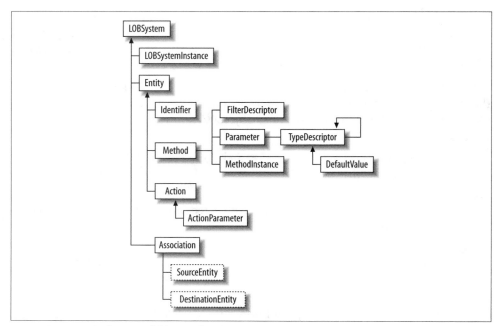

Figure 28-3. BDC object model hierarchy

```
using Microsoft.Office.Server.ApplicationRegistry.MetadataModel;
using System.Data;


namespace DolmenWebParts
{
    public class BDCWebPart  : WebPart
    {


        private static DataTable GetTableFromFields(FieldCollection fieldcollection)
        {
            DataTable dt = new DataTable();
            foreach (Field f in fieldcollection)
            {
                dt.Columns.Add(f.Name,Type.GetType(f.TypeDescriptor.TypeName));
            }
            return dt;
        }

        protected override void RenderContents(System.Web.UI.HtmlTextWriter writer)
        {

            NamedLobSystemInstanceDictionary lobSystems = ApplicationRegistry.
GetLobSystemInstances();
```

```
            LobSystemInstance lobSystem = lobSystems["AdventureWorksDWInstance"];
            Entity product = lobSystem.GetEntities()["Product"];

            FilterCollection filtercollection = product.GetFinderFilters();

            IEntityInstanceEnumerator productInstanceEnum = product.
     FindFiltered(filtercollection, lobSystem);

            DataTable dtProducts = GetTableFromFields(product.GetFinderView().
     Fields);

            while (productInstanceEnum.MoveNext())
            {
                IEntityInstance productinstance = productInstanceEnum.Current;
                DataRow drNew = dtProducts.NewRow();
                foreach (Field f in product.GetFinderView().Fields)
                {
                    if (productinstance[f] != null)
                    {
                        drNew[f.Name] = productinstance[f];
                    }
                }
                dtProducts.Rows.Add(drNew);
            }
            productInstanceEnum.Close();

            GridView gvProducts = new GridView();
             gvProducts.AutoGenerateColumns = true;
             gvProducts.DataSource = dtProducts;
             gvProducts.DataBind();

             gvProducts.RenderControl(writer);

        }
    }
}
```

Building Custom Search Applications with Microsoft.Office.Server.Search.Query

If you want to start building your own custom search solutions on top of Microsoft Office SharePoint Server 2007, you can use the new Microsoft.Office.Server. Search.Query object model. In your code, you should use either the FullTextSQLQuery or the KeyWordQuery class. Common properties and methods for these two classes are defined in the Query base class; you should, however, never directly use this class. The decision to choose between FullTextSQLQuery and KeyWordQuery depends on the complexity of the search queries you want to implement. With the KeyWordQuery class, you can directly pass a keyword or a SharePoint property filter to the search service without having to construct a full SQL query.

There is not only a new Query object model, but also a new Search Administration object model, which you can use to manipulate search settings. The Enterprise Search Administration object model is implemented in the `Microsoft.Office.Server.Search.Administration` namespace, found in the *Microsoft.Office.Server.Search.dll*. The main classes in the Administration object model are listed in Table 28-4.

Table 28-4. Main classes in the Search Administration object model

Class	Purpose
Content	Allows you to specify which content to crawl, specifying crawl settings and schedules.
Schema	Allows you to extend the metadata property schema information by adding managed properties, mapping crawled properties to managed properties, etc.
Scopes	This class searches scopes.
Keywords	Allows you to manage keywords and best bets in Office SharePoint Server 2007.
Ranking	Allows you to access the ranking algorithms used for computing search relevance.
Propagation	Manages propagation.
LogViewer	Crawls logs.

The next Web Part shows how you can construct your own search Web Part that uses the `FullTextSQLQuery` object. Within the `GridView`, which displays the search results, you will see a column that allows you to tag a certain search result as a best bet for the search term (you should also implement an extra check for controlling whether a keyword already exists, but I left this out for simplicity's sake):

```
using System;
using System.Collections.Generic;
using System.Text;
using System.Web;
using System.Web.UI;
using System.Web.UI.WebControls;
using System.Web.UI.WebControls.WebParts;
using Microsoft.Office.Server.Search.Query;
using Microsoft.SharePoint;
using Microsoft.SharePoint.WebControls;
using Microsoft.Office.Server;
using System.Data;
using Microsoft.Office.Server.Search.Administration;

namespace DolmenWebParts
{
    public class DemoSearchWebPart : WebPart
    {
        private ImageButton btnSearch;
        private TextBox txtQueryText;
        private Label lblWarning;
        private GridView gvResults;
        private DataSet ds;


        protected override void OnInit(EventArgs e)
```

```csharp
        {
            gvResults = new GridView( );
            gvResults.RowCommand += new GridViewCommandEventHandler(gvResults_
RowCommand);
            gvResults.AutoGenerateColumns = false;

            HyperLinkField colTitle = new HyperLinkField( );
            colTitle.DataTextField = "Title";
            colTitle.HeaderText = "Title";
            colTitle.DataNavigateUrlFields = new string[] { "Path" };
            gvResults.Columns.Add(colTitle);

            BoundField colAuthor = new BoundField( );
            colAuthor.DataField = "Author";
            colAuthor.HeaderText = "Author";
            gvResults.Columns.Add(colAuthor);

            ButtonField colBestBet = new ButtonField( );
            colBestBet.Text = "Add as best bet";
            colBestBet.CommandName = "BestBet";
            colBestBet.HeaderText = "";
            gvResults.Columns.Add(colBestBet);

        }

        protected override void CreateChildControls( )
        {
            this.Controls.Clear( );
            txtQueryText = new TextBox( );
            txtQueryText.Width = 300;
            this.Controls.Add(txtQueryText);
            btnSearch = new ImageButton( );
            btnSearch.ImageUrl = "/_layouts/images/gosearch.gif";
            btnSearch.Click += new System.Web.UI.ImageClickEventHandler(btnSearch_
Click);
            this.Controls.Add(btnSearch);
            lblWarning = new Label( );
            this.Controls.Add(new LiteralControl("<br>"));
            this.Controls.Add(new LiteralControl("<hr>"));
            this.Controls.Add(lblWarning);
            this.Controls.Add(gvResults);
        }

        void btnSearch_Click(object sender, System.Web.UI.ImageClickEventArgs e)
        {
            if (txtQueryText.Text != string.Empty)
            {
                this.PerformQuery(txtQueryText.Text);
            }
            else
            {
                lblWarning.Text = "Please enter a keyword";
            }
        }
```

```csharp
void gvResults_RowCommand(object sender, GridViewCommandEventArgs e)
{

    int index = Convert.ToInt32(e.CommandArgument);
    GridViewRow row = gvResults.Rows[index];
    HyperLink link = (HyperLink)row.Cells[0].Controls[0];
    CreateBestBet(txtQueryText.Text, link.NavigateUrl.ToString(), link.Text);

}

private void CreateBestBet(string term, string url, string title)
{
    Keywords keywordmgr = new Keywords(SearchContext.GetContext(SPContext.
Current.Site), new Uri("http://moss"));
    KeywordCollection keywordcoll = keywordmgr.AllKeywords;
    Keyword keyword = keywordcoll.Create(term, DateTime.Now);
    keyword.BestBets.Create(title,"",new Uri(url));
}


private void PerformQuery(string keyword)
{
    string querytext = string.Empty;

    querytext = "Select title, path, author from SCOPE() where FREETEXT(*,'"
+ keyword + "')";


    FullTextSqlQuery query = new FullTextSqlQuery(ServerContext.Current);
    query.QueryText = querytext;

    query.ResultTypes |= ResultType.RelevantResults;
    query.TrimDuplicates = true;
    query.IgnoreAllNoiseQuery = true;
    query.EnableStemming = false;

    ResultTableCollection resultColl = null;
    ResultTable resultTable = null;

    resultColl = query.Execute();
    resultTable = resultColl[ResultType.RelevantResults];
    if (resultTable.TotalRows != 0)
    {
        lblWarning.Text = "Number of results found " + resultTable.TotalRows.
ToString();

        ReadResultTable(resultTable);
    }
    else
    {
        lblWarning.Text = "No results found";
    }
}

private void ReadResultTable(ResultTable results)
```

```
    {
        DataTable relResultsTbl = new DataTable( );
        relResultsTbl.TableName = "Relevant Results";
        ds = new DataSet("resultsset");
        ds.Tables.Add(relResultsTbl);
        ds.Load(results, LoadOption.OverwriteChanges, relResultsTbl);

        FillResultsGrid(ds);
    }

    private void FillResultsGrid(DataSet ds)
    {
        //Bind the data to the DataGrid
        gvResults.DataSource = ds;
        gvResults.DataBind( );
    }
  }
}
```

When you create a custom application that needs to access the search object model, you will first need to add a reference to Microsoft.Office.Server as well as to the Microsoft Office SharePoint Server Component (*Microsoft.SharePoint.portal.dll*) and to Microsoft Office SharePoint Server Search (*Microsoft.Office.Server.Search.dll*). You might notice that the query syntax is similar to standard SQL queries. In this example, the FREETEXT full-text predicate was used, but it is also possible to use the CONTAINS predicate.

The CONTAINS full-text predicate also supports wildcard characters, whereas the FREETEXT does not.

When you execute a query, a ResultTableCollection object is returned, which contains a number of ResultTable objects that are easily read—as shown in the ReadResultsTable method in the example—since they implement the IDataReader interface. The search results returned in these ResultTables are grouped in four categories, as defined in the Microsoft.Office.Server.Search.Query.ResultType enumeration; in the example, we return the main result set (ResultType.RelevantResults).

The standard search Web Parts used on both the search page and the search results page are easy to customize without using any code, by modifying the Web Part properties or applying a custom style sheet to them. However, it is not possible to extend the search solution by adding your own Web Parts on the page and integrating them with the standard Web Parts through Web Part connections. The standard Web Parts communicate through hidden objects using a proprietary protocol. This means that if you want to extend the functionality, you must code the standard search functionality in your Web Part set as well.

User Profiles and the My Site

A user profile holds information about the site users in a number of properties. This information can be used to describe users or to target information to specific groups of people (an audience). The My Profile page on the My Site is the main location where this user information is visible. The Index server also crawls this information so that it can be searched as well. Audience targeting allows content contributors to push certain content to a specific group of users, which is called an audience. An audience is defined by rules that include or exclude users. Microsoft Office Share-Point Server 2007 maintains these user profiles in SQL Server, but the information can be imported from other data sources, such as:

- Active Directory
- Lightweight Directory Access Protocol directories (which is not Active Directory)
- Databases and enterprise applications (such as SAP or PeopleSoft), by defining a Business Data Catalog connection

The main classes are found in the `Microsoft.Office.Server.UserProfiles` namespaces.

There are three main objects to handle information within the User Profile store:

`UserProfile`
Allows you to access profile properties, the My Site, personalization links, and so on.

`UserProfileManager`
Gives access to a collection of `UserProfile` objects and allows you to create, edit, and retrieve user profile objects and properties from the user profile store.

`UserProfileConfigManager`
Manages the user profile configuration.

The main classes are found in the `Microsoft.Office.Server.UserProfiles` namespace. Although `Microsoft.SharePoint.Portal.UserProfiles` is still present for backward compatibility, it is better to use the new namespace. Another important change is the support for multivalue profile properties. The `IsMultivalued` parameter indicates whether the property supports multiple values. The object model returns these values of a multivalue property as an `ArrayList` object of type `UserProfileValueCollection`. SharePoint Server 2007 also allows you to set privacy policies on user profile properties, to restrict who can view the property. This is done by setting the `Microsoft.Office.Server.UserProfiles.Property.DefaultPrivacy` property to a specific `Privacy` enumeration. The next sample code shows how you can enumerate for existing user profiles, check whether they have already created a My Site and then create the My Site in code, and, last but not least, modify one of the multivalue properties (`Skills`):

```
using System;
using System.Collections.Generic;
using System.Text;
```

```csharp
using Microsoft.SharePoint;
using Microsoft.Office.Server;
using Microsoft.Office.Server.UserProfiles;

namespace UserProfileDemo
{
    class Program
    {
        static void Main(string[] args)
        {
            using (SPSite sitecollection = new SPSite("http://moss"))
            {

                ServerContext context = ServerContext.GetContext(sitecollection);
                UserProfileManager profileManager = new UserProfileManager(context);

                foreach (UserProfile u in profileManager)
                {
                    //Display name and loging
                    Console.WriteLine(u["PreferredName"].Value.ToString());
                    Console.WriteLine(u["AccountName"].Value.ToString());
                    if (u.PersonalSite == null)
                    {
                        Console.WriteLine("Personal site does not exist for " +
u["PreferredName"].Value.ToString());
                        u.CreatePersonalSite();
                    }
                    //Add entry to the My Links listing of the My Site
                    QuickLinkManager qMgr = u.QuickLinks;
                    qMgr.Create("Dolmen", "http://www.dolmen.be", QuickLinkGroupType.
General, "", Privacy.Public);

                    //Retrieve the multiple-value property skills
                    UserProfileValueCollection valuecollection = u["SPS-Skills"];

                    //Add a new value to a multiple-value property
                    valuecollection.Add((object)"Communication skills");

                    //Set privacy control to My Colleagues
                    valuecollection.Privacy = Privacy.Contacts;
                    u.Commit();


                }
            }
            Console.WriteLine("Hit any key to continue");
            Console.ReadLine();
        }
    }
}
```

InfoPath Forms Services: Using the XMLFormView Control

Office SharePoint Server also embeds InfoPath Forms Services, which allows you to create browser-enabled InfoPath forms. This means that you no longer need to have InfoPath installed on the client to fill in InfoPath forms. InfoPath Forms Services is built as a feature on top of Windows SharePoint Services 3.0 and is available in Office SharePoint Server 2007 or by installing Forms Server 2007 (separate SKU) on top of Windows SharePoint Services.

Forms Services can act as a runtime host for the InfoPath forms that you deploy to SharePoint. Forms Services can convert InfoPath forms into ASP.NET pages so that the form can be filled in within the browser, similar to how it is filled in with a full client InfoPath installation.

To extend or automate your InfoPath solutions, you will need to take a look at the two main namespaces for InfoPath Forms Services, which are:

Microsoft.Office.InfoPath.Server.Administration

> Allows you to automate template administration on the server. The most important objects are the FormsService class, FormTemplateCollection, and the FormTemplate class. The FormsService class, the root object for InfoPath Forms Services, allows you to perform the same actions that are available on the Configure InfoPath Forms Services page in SharePoint Central Administration. The FormTemplate class represents an InfoPath form that has been deployed to InfoPath Forms Services.

Microsoft.Office.InfoPath.Server.Controls

> Contains the XmlFormView control used for rendering a form template in a custom Web Page on the server.

The next code snippet shows how you can access the administrator-approved form templates for the current SharePoint server. To use the next code snippet, you will need to add a reference to the *Microsoft.Office.InfoPath.Server.dll*, which is located in *Program Files\Microsoft Office Servers\12.0\Bin*:

```
protected override void RenderContents(System.Web.UI.HtmlTextWriter writer)
    {

        SPFarm farm  = SPFarm.Local;

        FormsService formssvc = farm.Services.GetValue<FormsService>();
        FormTemplateCollection formscoll = formssvc.FormTemplates;
        foreach (FormTemplate formstemplate in formscoll)
        {
            writer.Write("<li>"+formstemplate.DisplayName+ " (Workflow enabled:"
 + formstemplate.WorkflowEnabled.ToString()  + ")</li>");
        }
    }
```

The samples on MSDN (see "Hosting the InfoPath 2007 Form Editing Environment in a Custom Web Form") show how you can embed the XmlFormView control within your own ASP.NET pages. It is also possible to use this control within your own custom Web Parts, as shown in the next example.

First, you need to add a reference to the *Microsoft.Office.InfoPath.Server.dll*. If you take a look at the CreateChildControls method, you will notice that I added two event handlers. These events allow communication between the hosting control (a web page or a Web Part in this case). The event handler for the Close event is used to redirect the user to another page when the InfoPath form is closed. The event handler for the Initialize event allows you to modify or read values within the InfoPath form during the initialization phase:

```csharp
using System;
using System.Collections.Generic;
using System.Text;
using System.Web;
using System.Web.UI.WebControls.WebParts;
using Microsoft.Office.InfoPath;
using Microsoft.Office.InfoPath.Server.Controls;

namespace DCAWebParts
{
    public class IFPWebPart : WebPart
    {
        private XmlFormView viewform;
        private string _xsnlocation = string.Empty;
        private string _closeredirect = string.Empty;

        [Personalizable(),WebBrowsable(),
        WebDisplayName("Location InfoPath Template"),
        WebDescription("URL of the web-enabled InfoPath form to display")]
        public string XSNLocation
        {
            get { return _xsnlocation; }
            set { _xsnlocation = value; }
        }

        [Personalizable(),WebBrowsable(),
        WebDisplayName("Redirect URL"),
        WebDescription("Redirect naar het sluiten van een InfoPath")]
        public string CloseRedirect
        {
            get { return _closeredirect; }
            set { _closeredirect = value; }
        }

        protected override void CreateChildControls()
        {
```

```
        base.CreateChildControls();

        viewform = new XmlFormView();
        if (_xsnlocation != string.Empty)
        {
            viewform.XsnLocation = _xsnlocation;
            viewform.Initialize += new EventHandler<InitializeEventArgs>
(viewform_Initialize);
            viewform.Close += new EventHandler(viewform_Close);
            this.Controls.Add(viewform);
        }
    }

    void viewform_Close(object sender, EventArgs e)
    {
        //Implement redirect or some other close action
    }

    void viewform_Initialize(object sender, InitializeEventArgs e)
    {
        //Read or modify values
    }
```

Conclusion

This chapter offered an overview of the Microsoft.SharePoint namespace, which embeds the base classes you need in everyday SharePoint development. After that, we took a look at some of the Office SharePoint Server class libraries.

However, this chapter has uncovered only the tip of the iceberg. There are many more development opportunities for Windows SharePoint Services and Office Share-Point Server 2007. The object model is used to create applications that support business intelligence, workflow, document lifecycle management, and content management. Remember that the Windows SharePoint Services Developer Center* and the Office SharePoint Server Developer Portal† provide you with access to a number of invaluable resources.

---

* http://msdn2.microsoft.com/en-us/library/ms778813.aspx
† http://msdn2.microsoft.com/en-us/office/aa905503.aspx

CHAPTER 29

Web Content Management

Introduction

Web Content Management (WCM) is a set of features integrated into SharePoint 2007 that allows users to create and manage content-centric web sites, providing the ability to author, review, and publish content over the Web. These features were part of *Microsoft Content Management Server 2002* (MCMS), which has been incorporated into Office SharePoint Server 2007. Combined with other built-in capabilities such as workflow and enterprise search, Office SharePoint 2007 offers a rich set of features for web-based content management.

Web Content Management in Office SharePoint 2007 integrates tightly with Microsoft Office 2007 products, such as Word 2007 and InfoPath 2007. Content can be authored using these Microsoft Office products, and the resulting documents can then be converted on the server side to pages using the document converters built into SharePoint (discussed in the "Smart Client Authoring" section, later in this chapter). Custom document converter components can also be created for file types that are not built into SharePoint.

WCM in Office SharePoint Server 2007 could be the subject of an entire book. This chapter provides an overview of working with publishing features, such as configuring, customizing, and using the WCM features. The chapter is divided into five main sections:

- Architecture
- Configuring the publishing features
- Customizing a publishing site
- Content management
- Smart client authoring

Architecture

Web content management is built as a WSS 3.0 Feature. The Office SharePoint Server Publishing Infrastructure Feature first needs to be activated within the site. If the site is applied with any of the publishing templates, this feature is activated automatically. WCM uses the lists infrastructure of WSS 3.0 to store templates, resources, and pages. Therefore, WCM components can take advantage of the list capabilities (covered in detail in Chapter 14), such as versioning, auditing, security, and workflow.

In Office SharePoint 2007, the publishing infrastructure consists of the following two main templates:

Master pages

> These pages contain placeholder controls for content and navigation controls. Master pages also contain the overall site branding elements, such as banners, logos, search, login controls, and the page editing toolbar (used by content authors and approvers). Master pages are stored in the Master Pages and Layout Pages gallery of the site collection and are represented by a *.master* extension.

Layout pages

> Layout pages are built for specific SharePoint content types. Content types define the structure—in other words, the fields—of the data collected from the content authors. Layout pages contain content controls, also called field controls, which are associated with specific fields of the content type. Layout pages can also be created with zones for Web Parts, thereby allowing authors to add Web Parts. Layout pages are created with an *.aspx* extension and are also stored in the master pages and layout gallery of the site collection.

Combined, the master page and the layout page dictate the final page, resulting in its overall look, as depicted in the block diagram shown in Figure 29-1.

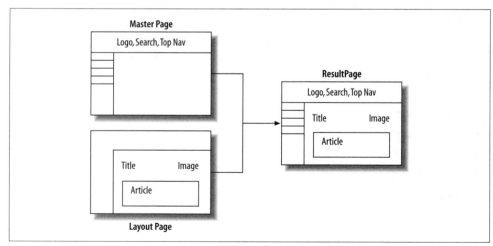

Figure 29-1. Master page and layout page architecture for a WCM site

In Office SharePoint Server 2007, content storage and presentation are separated. Content types define the storage structure, and layout pages are used to present the content. Multiple layout pages can be created for a given content type, thus allowing multiple views of the same type of content. This is accomplished using the following:

Master pages
> Defines the overall look and feel of the web site.

Content Types
> This collection of settings defines the information that is published.

Page Layouts
> Defines the display layout for the content. A layout page is built for a specific content type, whereas a content type can have multiple layout pages associated with it.

Page Libraries
> Collection of web pages created for a specific publishing site.

Let's take an example of a news web site to understand the purpose of the master page and layout pages. The web site's overall look and feel, such as its banners and navigation, is governed by the master page. Any change in the master page will reflect on all the sites that inherit that master page. From a content perspective, let us assume that the web site uses different SharePoint content types defined for different news types, such as breaking news, sports news, business news, international news, and so on. Each content type will have its own set of columns and other related settings, such as workflows. Layout pages, as the name suggests, consist of content controls, such as text boxes, rich text controls, or image placeholders, which are mapped to the columns of a content type. To create a news article page, an author would choose an appropriate layout page. When the news page is approved and published, the resulting page will have the look and feel designed in the master page and the content of the layout page. We will explore more on the master page and layout pages in the "Creating and Configuring a SharePoint WCM-Enabled Site" section of this chapter.

A typical page rendering in a publishing web site follows a three-step process:

1. When the request for a web page comes in, SharePoint retrieves the layout page associated with the page.

2. The master page is then retrieved.

3. Content associated with the layout's field controls are retrieved and presented in the final web page.

WCM-enabled sites have two master pages:

Site Master Page
> Defines the look and feel of the published pages in the site.

System Master Page
> Defines the look and feel of the system pages, such as the home page for the Master Page Gallery and the settings pages.

In most cases, you will want to modify the Site Master Page rather than the System Master Page. The Site Master defines the content that most users will see, whereas the System Master defines only the internal content visible to SharePoint administrators and site designers.

Master page settings for a WCM-enabled web site can be changed using the "Master page" option under the "Look & Feel" section of the Site Settings page. Figure 29-2 depicts this page.

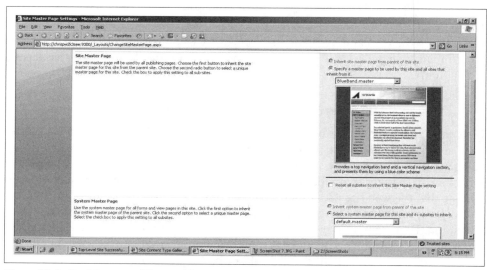

Figure 29-2. Site Master and System Master setting page

Creating and Configuring a SharePoint WCM-Enabled Site

As discussed earlier, WCM is deployed as a standard SharePoint Feature. This feature is pre-enabled when a site collection is created with publishing templates (discussed later in this chapter). Sites created with other templates can take advantage of the publishing capabilities by activating the "Office SharePoint Server Publishing Infrastructure Feature." Figure 29-3 depicts the activated SharePoint 2007 publishing feature.

Create a WCM-Enabled Site

Office SharePoint Server 2007 comes with two publishing site templates:

Collaboration Portal
    This template could be used for small to medium size intranet portals.

Publishing Portal
    This template could be used for creating Internet-facing web sites and intranet sites for large corporations.

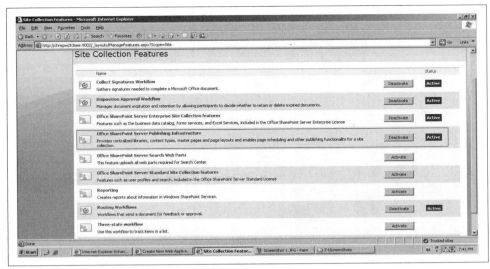

Figure 29-3. Site Collection Features with Publishing Feature enabled

To create a site with the publishing portal, follow these steps:

1. Create a web application:

   a. Open the SharePoint 3.0 Central Administration and select Application Management.

   b. Under SharePoint Web Application Management, select "Create or extend a web application."

   c. In the "Create or extend a web application" page, choose "Create a new web application."

   d. Specify the host header port number, application pool account, and other information, and click OK. A new web application is created at the specified port number.

2. Create a site collection and apply the publishing site template:

   a. Click the Create Site Collection link in the page that appears after a new web application has been created. Alternatively, you can also go to the "Application management" page in Central Administration and choose "Create a Site Collection." Make sure the "Select a web application" link points to the new web application created in the previous step.

   b. Fill in a Title and choose the Publishing tab under "Select a template," and then choose Publishing Portal. Figure 29-4 depicts this screen.

3. Click OK to create a site collection with the publishing feature.

Site collections created or activated with the publishing template are preconfigured with the following two categories of content types:

Figure 29-4. Site collection creation page

Page layout content types

This category contains content types related to pages that would be used by content authors and editors for publishing, for example, articles and welcome pages.

Publishing content types

This category includes system content types for master pages (applied to all master pages) and page layouts (applied to all pages libraries). Publishing content types define the base columns for all publishing content types.

 Content types are discussed in more detail in Chapters 1 and 2.

Customizing a WCM-Enabled Site

In this section, we will take a look at the following actions involved in creating and customizing a WCM-enabled site:

- Creating a custom master page and setting the default site master
- Creating a custom layout page and creating a page using the layout
- Creating a welcome page and setting the default welcome page
- Creating an article page and approving the page
- Configuring anonymous access to the web site

Creating a Custom Master Page

The best approach to creating a custom master page is by copying an existing master page and then customizing the layout as necessary. To create a custom master page, follow these steps:

1. Open the Office SharePoint 2007 Designer and select File → Open Site. Enter the URL of the WCM-enabled web site created in the previous steps. Click OK to open the site in the SharePoint Designer.

2. Select "_catalogs" under the site name, and select "MasterPage (Master page gallery)."

3. Right-click BlueBand.Master, one of the built-in master pages that comes with the SharePoint 2007 publishing feature, and select Copy.

4. Paste the file inside the "_catalogs" → MasterPage library, and rename the file as CustomSite.Master.

5. Double-click CustomSite.Master to open the page in the SharePoint Designer. Figure 29-5 depicts this screen.

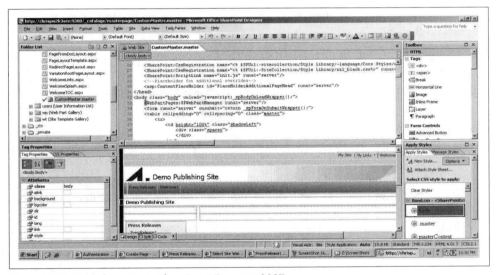

Figure 29-5. Publishing site in SharePoint Designer 2007

Customize the master page as required using the Designer.

Office 2007 SharePoint Designer is an intuitive tool used to customize SharePoint 2007 sites and pages. The Designer contains areas for presenting the preview and the code-behind for the page, sections to edit the CSS styles that apply to the page or selected control, a toolbar with the list of controls that can be used in the page, and the Properties window to configure the control properties. The Designer consists of three main views:

Code view
> The code view presents a full view of the ASP.NET code-behind.

Design view
> The design view displays the full view of the page as it would look in the browser.

Split view
> Displays the code and the preview in the same page. In the split view, the Designer allows you to choose a specific control in the preview window or code window, and it automatically highlights the control in the other window.

 If you aren't familiar with SharePoint Designer, see Chapter 19.

Once the changes are complete, the master page needs to be published before it can be used on the site:

1. To publish the master page, right-click the CustomSite.Master page in the folder list window and select Check In.

2. Choose "Publish a major version" in the "Check in" dialog box that appears and click OK.

3. The Master Page Gallery is configured with an approval workflow by default. When a new document is checkedinto the library through the Designer, a dialog box with the text to modify the status of the page appears. Click Yes in the dialog box.

4. The Master Page Gallery page opens up, and the new CustomSite.Master page appears in the Pending category. To approve the status of this page, click the drop-down button for the page and click Approve. Figure 29-6 depicts the screen.

This master page now needs to be set as the default site master page for the layout pages. To set the default master page, follow these steps:

1. Navigate to the web site and select Site Actions → Site Settings → Modify All Site Settings.

2. Choose Master Page under the "Look & Feel" option

3. Select CustomSite.Master in the drop-down listbox under Site Master Page and click OK. This page can also be used to set an alternate CSS file and the system master page.

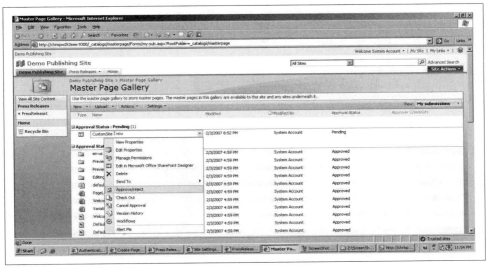

Figure 29-6. Master Page Gallery. approving a customized master page

Creating a Custom Layout Page

This example creates a layout page that contains an authoring container and field controls for the columns in the article content type. To create a custom layout page, follow these steps:

1. In the SharePoint Designer, click File → New.

2. Choose the SharePoint Content tab and select SharePoint Publishing.

3. In Content Type Group, select Page Layout Content Types.

4. In Content Type Name, choose Article.

5. Provide a URL and a Title for the Layout and click OK. Figure 29-7 depicts this screen.

6. The toolbox in the SharePoint Designer displays the page fields and the content fields associated with the content type. The Edit Mode panel control under the Server Controls category in the toolbar is used as the authoring container control. Controls placed inside this control will not be published in the pages.

7. The content fields and the field controls can be dragged into the layout pages and organized into HTML tables, as in the sample custom layout page depicted in Figure 29-8.

8. To publish the custom layout page, right-click on the page in the "Folder list" window of the Designer and click Check In.

9. In the dialog box that follows, click "Publish a major version."

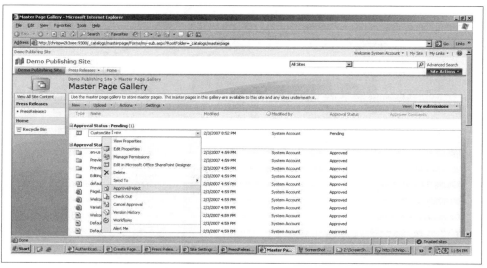

Figure 29-7. Creating a new layout page in SharePoint Designer 2007

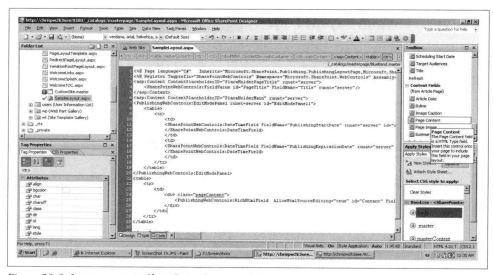

Figure 29-8. Layout page in SharePoint Designer 2007

10. As with the master pages, the layout pages need to be approved through the workflow.

11. To create a new page using the newly created layout page, navigate to the Website Site Actions → Create Page and choose the title of the layout created earlier. Figure 29-9 displays the page created with the sample layout.

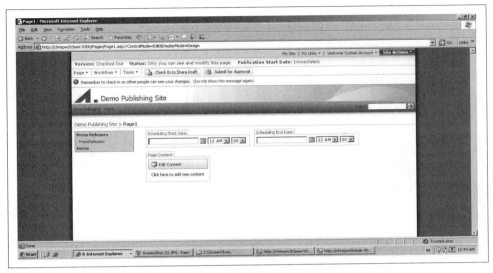

Figure 29-9. Sample layout page

The Schedule Start Date and Schedule End Date field controls can be used to schedule the publishing of the page. This is discussed a little later in the "Content Scheduling" section of this chapter.

Customizing the Navigation

The left navigation and top navigation in a SharePoint site can be customized using the Site Navigation Settings page. Custom navigation controls can also be plugged into the master pages. To customize the built-in navigation, choose Modify Navigation under Site Actions of the root site. Some of the customization options are as follows:

- The "Show subsites" and "Show pages" options, when checked, display the subsites and pages as navigation elements in the top navigation (also considered the global navigation) and the left navigation.
- Custom Links can be added to the navigation using the Add Link option.
- Hide menu options by selecting the title in the navigation and clicking Hide.
- Control the navigation item hierarchy by selecting the specific navigation element and choosing Move Up or Move Down.

Figure 29-10 depicts the Site Navigation Settings page.

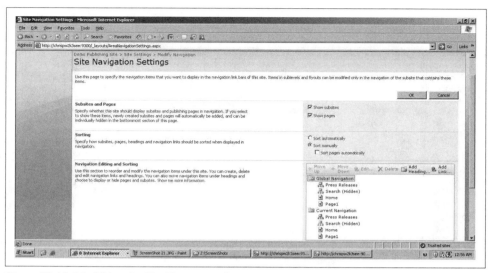

Figure 29-10. Modifying the Site Navigation Settings page

Creating a Welcome Page

To create a custom welcome page for the WCM-enabled web site, follow these steps:

1. Navigate to the web site and click Create Page from the Site Actions menu.

2. The next page presents the default set of page layouts available out-of-the-box with the Publishing Portal template. Enter a title and URL for the welcome page, choose the "Welcome Page with Table of Contents" option, and click OK.

3. A page is created with the page editing toolbar at the top. The page editing toolbar contains a set of options that the authors can use to perform different actions, such as publish the page, submit the page for approval, start a workflow, set the page publishing settings, and check unpublished items. Enter text for the welcome page and select Save from the Page option in the page editing toolbar.

4. Submit the page for approval by clicking on "Submit for Approval." This starts the workflow process. If the author has "Quick deploy" privileges (discussed later in this chapter), the author can directly publish the page by choosing the "Publish from the Workflow" option on the page editing toolbar.

5. Authors with appropriate privileges can approve the page by clicking on Site Actions → "Manage Content and Structure."

6. Click on the Page library in the left navigation.

7. Click the drop-down option on the custom welcome page and select "Approve." Figure 29-11 depicts this screen.

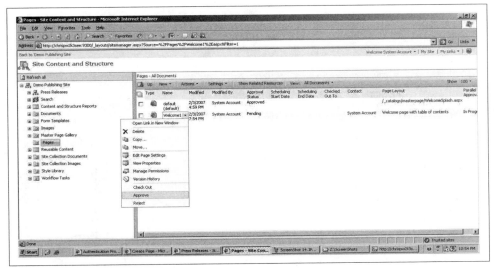

Figure 29-11. Site Pages library—approving a new welcome page

The newly created welcome page needs to be set as the default welcome page before visitors can see it. To set the new welcome page, follow these steps:

1. Navigate to the web site and select Site Actions → Site Settings → Modify All Site Settings.

2. Select Welcome Page under the "Look and Feel" section; this opens the Site Welcome page.

3. Select Browse, choose the created custom welcome page, and select OK. Figure 29-12 depicts this screen.

Creating an Article Page

The default publishing template creates a subsite called Press Releases. To create a new press release page, follow these steps:

1. Navigate to the Press Releases site.

2. Choose Create Page from the Site Actions menu.

3. Choose any of the article page layouts—for example, "Article Page with body only."

4. Provide a title and URL and click Create. A page with the page editing toolbar at the top and controls to enter article content is created. Figure 29-13 depicts the newly created page.

5. SharePoint includes an HTML editor control to insert and format text or HTML. Authors can use this tool to copy and paste formatted HTML. For the news article sample page, enter some sample text in the Page Content area.

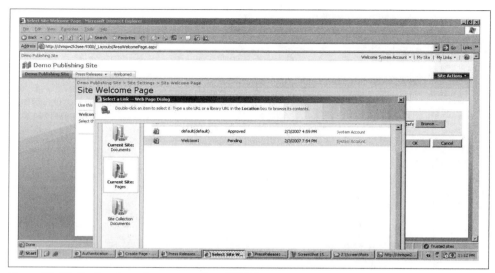

Figure 29-12. *Setting the welcome page for a WCM site*

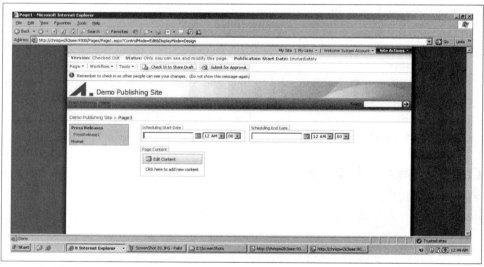

Figure 29-13. *Creating an article page in a WCM-enabled site*

6. To save the page, choose Page → Save from the page editing toolbar.

7. To publish a page, choose "Submit for approval" from the page editing toolbar, and the workflow drives the approval process for the page.

Configuring Anonymous Access

Internet-facing web sites need to be configured with anonymous access to allow visitors to view the pages without being challenged for authorization. Configuring anonymous access for a WCM-enabled site is a two-step process: configuring the authentication provider with anonymous access, and then configuring the web site to allow anonymous access.

To configure the authentication provider for anonymous access, follow these steps:

1. Navigate to the Central Administration page for SharePoint.

2. Select Authentication Providers under Application Security.

3. Select Default from the available authentication providers; this opens up the Edit Authentication page. The default authentication provider is the Windows authentication provider. SharePoint builds on ASP.NET 2.0 and hence can take advantage of the pluggable authentication provider model of ASP.NET 2.0. You can also configure a database-based forms authentication provider or other custom providers for authentication in SharePoint. A detailed analysis of this configuration is beyond the scope of this chapter.

4. In the Edit Authentication page, check the Enable Anonymous Access checkbox under the Anonymous Access section and click OK. Figure 29-14 depicts the Edit Authentication page for default provider.

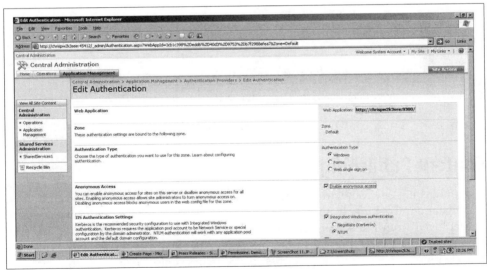

Figure 29-14. Configuring anonymous access for a WCM site authentication provider

Once the authentication provider has been configured for anonymous access, the web site can now be enabled for anonymous access. To configure the web site, follow these steps:

1. Navigate to the publishing web site and select Site Actions → Site Settings → Modify All Site Settings.

2. Choose Advanced Permissions under "Users and Permissions."

3. From the Permissions page, choose Site Settings → Anonymous Access.

4. Choose Entire Web Site from the Anonymous Access setting page and click OK. Figure 29-15 depicts this screen.

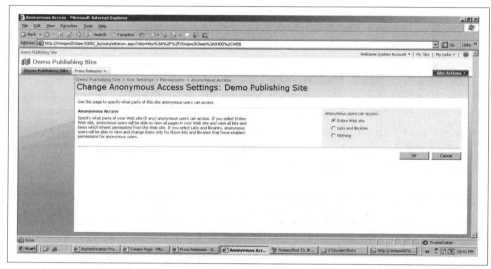

Figure 29-15. Enabling anonymous access to a WCM site

The web site is now configured for anonymous access.

Content Publishing

In a publishing environment, different servers would be used for content authoring, staging, and publishing. In such a scenario, content approved for publishing needs to be deployed from the staging area to the production server. To facilitate this process, SharePoint 2007 provides built-in content deployment capabilities. This section explores the main components of content deployment and the different configuration aspects involved in setting it up.

Content Deployment

One of the many features of WCM is the built-in content scheduling and content deployment capabilities. This section explores the content deployment features in more detail.

Content deployment in configured in two phases:

Path

> A path represents the connection between the source and the destination web applications. When a path is created, a quick-deploy feature associated with the path is also created. Quick deploy is a special job that can be configured to run at frequent intervals and allows authors to publish content immediately without waiting for the scheduled content deployment job to run. Authors need to belong to the Quick Deploy Users group in order to publish content through this special job.

Job

> A job is associated with the path and represents the deployment of a specific site collection or site under the source web application. A job can be scheduled to run at a specific time, and can also be configured to deploy all or incremental changes.

To configure content deployment, follow these steps:

1. Navigate to the SharePoint 2007 Central Administration and select Operations.
2. Select "Content Deployment Paths and Jobs" under Content Deployment. Figure 29-16 depicts this screen.

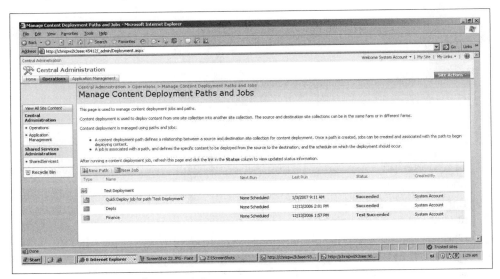

Figure 29-16. Content Deployment settings page

3. The first step is to set up a path. Click New Path, and in the page that opens, enter a title and description for this path.

4. Choose the source web application from the drop-down list, and then choose the site collection from the "Choose site collection" option. "/" represents the root.

5. Enter the URL of the Central Administration of the destination server, enter the connection information, and choose the Connect option.

6. From the drop-down for the destination web application, add the site collection on the destination server.

7. The content deployment feature can move content with all the security intact or without any security. This can be configured in the Security Information section of the page. Press OK when all information is complete. Figure 29-17 depicts the screen.

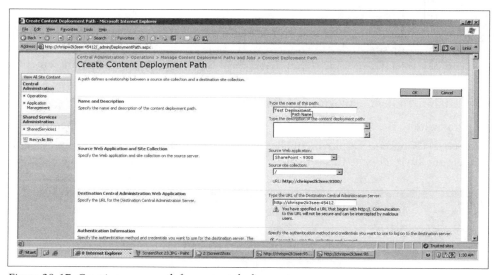

Figure 29-17. Creating a new path for content deployment

8. Once the path is configured, the next step is to configure the job. To create a job associated with a path, in the "Manage content deployment paths and jobs" page under the Operations section, select the Path created in the previous step and choose Create Job.

9. Enter a name and description for the job, and choose the deployment path created in the previous step.

10. Choose "Entire site collection" if you want to deploy the entire site, or choose specific sites by selecting "Specific sites within the site collection." You can choose an individual site or the branch of the site.

11. Some other options for the job include:
   - Setting a schedule for the job to execute
   - Option to deploy new or all content
   - Option to configure email alerts based on successful or failed jobs.

   Figure 29-18 depicts the screen.

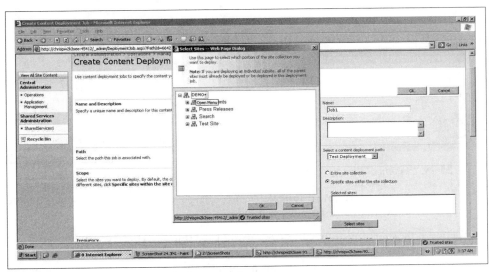

Figure 29-18. Creating a content deployment job

12. Click OK to create the job. To test the job, click on the job in the "Manage content deployment Path and Jobs" page and choose Test.

Content deployment deploys the pages and any dependent objects associated with the page collection. Content deployment will take the most recent major (published) version and the most recent minor (draft) version of a page. If the page contains any custom assemblies or Web Parts, these need to be explicitly configured on the destination site. Another important aspect to remember is that deployment assumes that the source site is being replicated in the destination web application. In other words, what you have in the source site is what you'll get on the target site.

Content Scheduling

Content scheduling lets authors publish pages during a specified time period. For content scheduling to work correctly, the library containing the pages must have versioning and moderation enabled. There is no other explicit configuration that needs to be done for scheduling to work. To check for the versioning setting of a page, go to the settings page of the library and select Versioning. The document version setting should be set to "Create major and minor versions." Figure 29-19 depicts this screen.

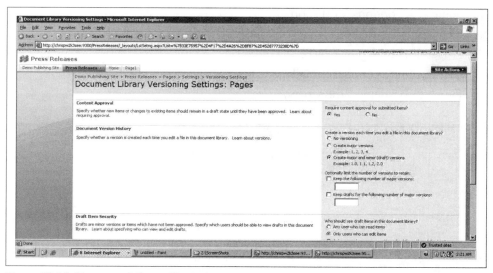

Figure 29-19. Document Library Versioning settings page

When a page is edited, a new minor version of the page is created, and when a page is approved, a new major version is created.

The scheduling date and time can be set using the content types Schedule Start Date and Schedule End Date. Using the page versioning and moderation built into the SharePoint lists, the scheduling system automatically brings the page online at the specified start date and takes the page offline at the specified end date.

Site Variations

Site Variations is a publishing feature that allows maintenance of parallel structures of the web site. A real-world example of this feature would be a multilingual website. For example, when a press release is published, the page could be published in all language web sites at the same time. Using variations, when a page is created in the "source" web site, it is automatically replicated to the "target" sites of other language. The replicated page still needs to be published separately through the workflow. A couple of things to notice about the variations are that they do not translate pages across different languages and that the replication of change is one-way—from the source (master site) to the target site (variation site)—and not both ways.

To set up the variations, follow these steps:

1. Navigate to the WCM-enabled site and navigate to Site Actions → Variations under the Site Collections Administration section.

2. Choose the site where the variation sites would be created under the web site.

3. Some of the other options you can specify while configuring variations are as follows:

- Specify whether the feature should automatically create variation sites and pages.
- Specify whether the target page needs to be republished when a source page is deleted and republished.

4. Once you have all the necessary options, click OK. Figure 29-20 depicts the variation page.

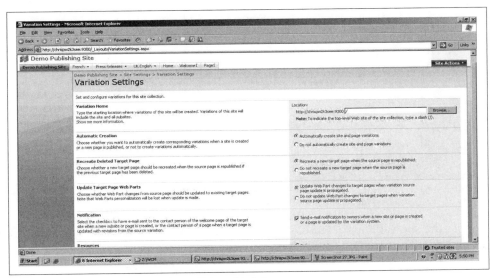

Figure 29-20. Variation settings for WCM-enabled site

Once the variation root has been configured, the next step is to configure the variation labels. Variation labels represent the different sites that will be maintained in parallel by the feature. To create a variation label, follow these steps:

1. Navigate to the site settings page of the site and select Variation Labels from the Site Collection Administration section.

2. Provide a name, description, and display name for the label, and also specify the locale for this site variation. One of the variation labels needs to be set as the source from which the features will replicate. To set the source label, choose "Set this variation to be the source variation" checkbox under the "Source variation" section of the page. Also choose a template for this site.

3. Repeat the label creation (step 2) to set up target site variations. The "Source variation" section will now be disabled, as only one site can be set up as the source.

4. Once all the variation sites have been set up, click Create Hierarchies in the Variation Labels page under the site settings. This creates subsites for each label and replicates the site hierarchies from the source to the target sites. Figure 29-21 depicts a sample Variation Labels page after the site hierarchies have been created.

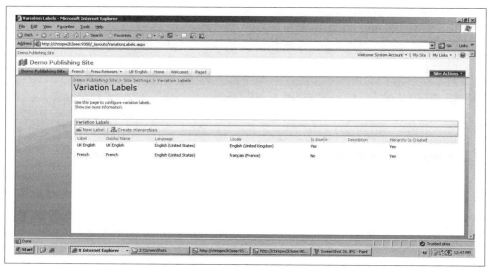

Figure 29-21. Variation labels for a WCM site

To test the site variation feature, navigate to the source site and create a subsite or article page. The variation feature automatically creates the same page in all the other target sites.

Smart Client Authoring

Office SharePoint Server 2007 allows content authors to create content using Office products such as Word 2007 and then convert the document into a web page using the built-in document converters. Office SharePoint Server 2007 ships with document converters for Word 2007 and InfoPath 2007. For other document types, custom converters can be developed using the SharePoint API. This section explores the overall configuration of the document converters and then uses Word 2007 to create a sample article page.

Configuring document converters for SharePoint 2007

The document conversion process in SharePoint uses the following services:

Conversion Load Balancer Service
 The balancer service is responsible for activating the appropriate document conversion launcher service in a server farm.

Conversion Launcher Service
 This service is responsible for launching the appropriate document converter.

Document converters are configured at a web application level. Once activated for a web application, document conversion cannot be disabled for specific sites or libraries within the web application.

Configuring document conversion is a two-step process. The first step is to configure the load balancer and launcher services; the second is enabling the document conversion for the web application. The following steps can be used to configure the document conversion:

1. To configure the Load Balancer Service:

   a. Navigate to the SharePoint Central Administration Operations page.

   b. Choose "Services on Server" under the "Topology and Services" section.

   c. Select Document Conversions Load Balancer Service. Enter the port number on which to run this service and choose OK. If the service is not already started, choose the Start link under Action.

2. To configure the Document Conversions Launcher Service:

   a. From the "Services on Server" page, choose "Document conversions launcher service."

   b. Select the server that runs the Load Balancer service, enter a port number to run this service, and choose OK. On the "Services on Server" page, click the Start link under Action if the service is not already started.

3. To enable document conversion in the web application:

   a. Navigate to the SharePoint 2007 Central Administration page and choose "Document conversions" under the External Service Connections section.

   b. Select the web application to be configured with the document conversion services. Choose Yes for the "Enable document conversions for this site" option and click OK. This page can also be used to customize the different converter settings and to specify a schedule for block processing. Figure 29-22 depicts the document conversion settings page for a web application.

Using document conversion

Once the document conversion settings have been applied to a site, a Convert Document menu appears for documents within the document libraries. Figure 29-23 depicts this menu option for a Word 2007 document within a document library.

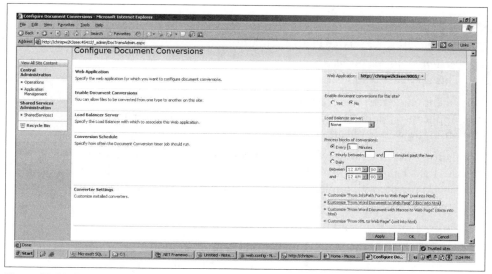

Figure 29-22. Document Conversions Settings page

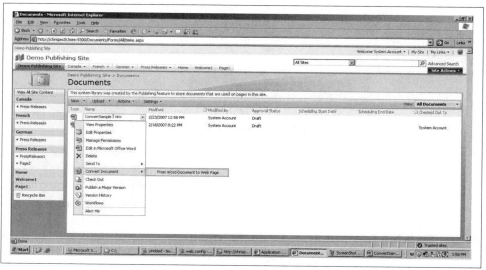

Figure 29-23. Convert Document Menu option

To demonstrate the document conversion process, Figure 29-24 shows a simple Word document.

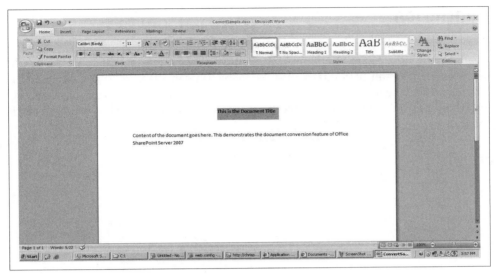

Figure 29-24. Sample Word 2007 document

Once the document is uploaded to the document library and converted using the Convert Document option, the converted page should look like the one in Figure 29-25.

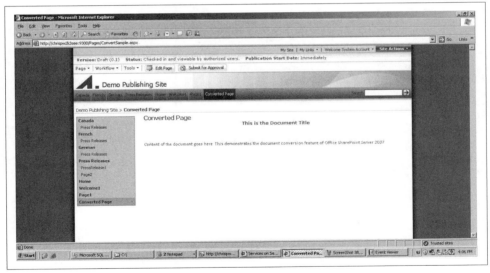

Figure 29-25. Sample converted page

Conclusion

In this chapter, we have explored the basic web content management functionalities available in Office SharePoint Server 2007. We discussed how to configure the WCM features, created and customized a WCM-enabled site in SharePoint, and explored the content deployment features built into the product. SharePoint's extendable and pluggable architecture creates a flexible platform for building complex content-centric sites.

Index

Symbols

- (minus sign), in Search syntax, 667
+ (plus sign), in Search syntax, 667

A

Access
    data linked to SharePoint, editing, 360
    data source for SharePoint BI data, 356
    exporting SharePoint data to, 359
    exporting table to SharePoint, 357
    moving database to SharePoint, 360
    two-way integration in SharePoint
        2007, 126
access requests for a library, 516
Actions menu options, differences in
        SharePoint 2007, 123
Actions object, 727
Actions Web Part (Business Data), 28
Active Directory authentication, 496
    ISA Server and, 517
    in WSS 2.0, 37
Active Directory Federation Services
        (ADFS), 496
ActiveX controls, browser support required
        for Datasheet view, 109
Add/Edit Keyword page, 691
administration, 524–553
    common tasks, Central
        Administration, 525–538
    application management
        page, 538–548
    operations, 526–538

configuration utilities,
        post-installation, 524
    Search services, 680–682
        Configure Search Settings Page, 680
        Scope Administration pages, 681
        Search Crawl Settings, 681
    site, 550–553
    tasks at different levels of the
        hierarchy, 525
    top-level site, 548
        site collection administration, 548
    Web Parts for administrators, 618–622
        installing Web Parts, 619
        troubleshooting Web Parts, 620
Administration Web Service, 641
administrative deployment, 447
Administrative object model (BDC), 727
administrative rights, levels of, 507
administrative tasks list, 525
Administrator Tasks area (Central
        Administration), 57
Advanced Permissions, 512
advanced search screen, 668
AJAX-type controls (in ASP.NET 2.0), 34
All Site Content page, 82
Alternate access mappings option, 534
Alternate Data Views connection type, 173
Analysis Services (see SQL Server 2005
        Analysis Services)
AND (search queries), 666
    disambiguation in Advanced search, 669
Announcements list
    enabling email support, 370
    feature that defines, 719

We'd like to hear your suggestions for improving our indexes. Send email to *index@oreilly.com*.

Property Promotion and Property Demotion (InfoPath), 441, 450
  configuring property demotion, 452
  configuring property promotion, 450
Protocol Handlers, 21
Public page (My Site), 464
  Social Networking Web Part, 4
publishing and deployment features (ECM), 23
publishing content types, 744
Publishing Portal template, 142, 742
Publishing Site, 141
Publishing site template, 141
  choices in sites, 141
Publishing Site with Workflow template, 141

Q

Query class, 716, 729
Query Engine (Search), 677
Query list with Excel option (Office Links), 129
query reporting (Search), 677
Query Reporting Tool, 689
query role
  application server failures and, 64
  redundant deployment, 63
query servers, order of installation, 69
Query Web Service, use of dynamic XML, 647
Quick Print, 406
quiescing a form template, 438
quota templates, 546

R

read permissions, 509
Really Simple Syndication feeds (see RSS feeds)
real-time data validation (forms), 26
Records Center site template, 140
Records Management feature (ECM), 25
redundancy recommendation, application server roles, 65
references, Web Service, 656
Refine Your Search Web Part, 665
region types, modifying with SharePoint Designer 2007, 426
rejecting sites, 97
Related List Web Part (Business Data), 28
relevance feature (Enterprise Search), 18

relevance of search results, Authoritative pages and, 688
relevancy improvements (Search), 676
Remote Procedure Calls (RPCs), FrontPage RPC, 659
Report Center, 28, 45, 84, 343
  Data Connection Library (DCL), storing external data connections, 349
Report Center site template, 140, 344
Report with Access option (Office Links), 128
reporting feature for a portal, activating, 530
Reporting Services, SQL Server 2005 (SSRS), 356
reports
  audit log reports, 549
  generated from business intelligence data sources, 342
  SharePoint site reports, 425
Request and Response SOAP envelopes, 646
Resources area (Central Administration), 57
response for data queries (Web Services), 648
restricted read permissions, 509
result relevance, Authoritative pages and, 688
Results page (Search), 689
ResultTable objects, 733
ResultTableCollection object, 733
ResultType enumeration, 733
reverse proxy, ISA Server, 517
Rich Text Editor, 162
  formatting discussion board posts, 267
rich web forms, 26
RoleAssigments property, 710
role-based security, 552
role-based templates, 483
roles, exposing with ISecurableObject, 711
routing documents, 217
rows
  menu options in Datasheet view, 116–118
  Provide Row To command, 176
RPCs (Remote Procedure Calls), FrontPage RPC, 659
RSS (Really Simple Syndication) feeds
  automatic, in WSS 3.0, 40
  support for lists, creating and modifying, 331
  use in MOSS 2007, 13
Runtime object model (BDC), 726

X

Colophon

The animals on the cover of *SharePoint 2007: The Definitive Guide* are various types of buntings, the common name for small, plump birds of the family *Emberizidae* (the sparrow family). Among the buntings pictured are the snow bunting (*Plectrophenax nivalis*), a North American type noted for its white plumage; the corn bunting (*Miliaria calandra*), a European type and the largest of the buntings; and finally, the yellowhammer (*Emberiza citrinella*), a Eurasian type with a yellowish head and breast.

Buntings are similar in habits to finches, and as such, in the past they were often grouped with the finch family *Fringillidae*. Buntings are distinguished by their stubby, cone-shaped bills, which are perfect for cracking seeds. Fruit and insects round out their diet. A bunting's coloring can vary widely depending on its sex and type—for instance, the male indigo bunting's plumage is a rich, metallic blue while its female counterpart is dull brown.

One particularly interesting member of the bunting family is the ortolan (*Emberiza hortulana*), which is considered a delicacy in French country cuisine. In the past, ortolans were netted, kept in darkened rooms to disrupt their normal feeding schedule, and then fattened with a diet of oats and millet. They were then roasted whole and sucked up in one bite—including the bones—through the rectum. Traditionally, the diner covered his head and his dish with a napkin to enhance the aroma as he ate. Due to their dwindling numbers, capturing and serving ortolans is now restricted by French law.

The cover image is from *Dover Animals*. The cover font is Adobe ITC Garamond. The text font is Linotype Birka; the heading font is Adobe Myriad Condensed; and the code font is LucasFont's TheSans Mono Condensed.

Try the online edition free for 45 days

Get the information you need when you need it, with Safari Books Online. Safari Books Online contains the complete version of the print book in your hands plus thousands of titles from the best technical publishers, with sample code ready to cut and paste into your applications.

Safari is designed for people in a hurry to get the answers they need so they can get the job done. You can find what you need in the morning, and put it to work in the afternoon. As simple as cut, paste, and program.

To try out Safari and the online edition of the above title FREE for 45 days, go to www.oreilly.com/go/safarienabled and enter the coupon code IYZVGCB.

To see the complete Safari Library visit:
safari.oreilly.com

Related Titles from O'Reilly

Windows Administration

Active Directory Cookbook, *2nd Edition*

Active Directory, *3rd Edition*

DNS on Windows Server 2003, *3rd Edition*

Essential Microsoft Operations Manager

Essential SharePoint

Exchange Server Cookbook

Learning Windows Server 2003, *2nd Edition*

MCSE Core Elective Exams in a Nutshell

MCSE Core Required Exams in a Nutshell, *3rd Edition*

Monad (AKA PowerShell)

Securing Windows Server 2003

SharePoint Office Pocket Guide

SharePoint User's Guide

Windows Server 2003 in a Nutshell

Windows Server 2003 Network Administration

Windows Server 2003 Security Cookbook

Windows Server Cookbook

Windows Server Hacks

Windows XP Cookbook